LABOR RELATIONS

LABOR RELATIONS

TENTH EDITION

Arthur A. Sloane
University of Delaware

Fred Witney

Prentice
Hall

Prentice Hall, Upper Saddle River, New Jersey 07458

Library of Congress Cataloging-in-Publication Data

Sloane, Arthur A.
    Labor relations / Arthur A. Sloane, Fred Witney.—10th ed.
        p. cm.
    Includes bibliographical references and index.
    ISBN 0-13-032424-8
    1. Industrial relations—United States.   2. Collective bargaining—United States.
    I. Witney, Fred–   II. Title.
HD8072.S6185 2001
331.8—dc21

                                                                    00-056663

Executive Editor: David Shafer
Managing Editor (Editorial): Jennifer Glennon
Assistant Editor: Michele Foresta
Editorial Assistant: Kim Marsden
Marketing Manager: Michael Campbell
Marketing Assistant: Katie Mulligan
Managing Editor (Production): Judy Leale
Production Editor: Keri Jean
Permissions Coordinator: Suzanne Grappi
Associate Director, Manufacturing: Vincent Scelta
Production Manager: Arnold Vila
Manufacturing Buyer: Diane Peirano
Design Manager: Patricia Smythe
Designer: Steve Frim
Interior Design: Lee Goldstein
Cover Design: Steve Frim
Cover Photo: Oli Tennent/Stone
Manager, Print Production: Christy Mahon
Composition: UG / GSS Information Services, Inc.
Printer/Binder: Courier Westford/Lehigh

Credits and acknowledgments borrowed from other sources and reproduced, with permission, in this textbook appear on appropriate pages within text.

10 9 8 7 6 5 4 3 2
ISBN 0-13-032424-8

Dedicated to the Memory of
FRED WITNEY,
A Giant in the Field of
Labor Relations and a
Superb Colleague and Friend

Brief Contents

Contents

Preface

$\mathcal{T}$here are no prerequisites to this book beyond an interest in labor–management relations. It has been designed to serve as an aid to all readers who desire a basic understanding of unionism in its natural habitat. With such a thrust, however, the volume focuses on certain areas, necessarily minimizing the treatment of others.

Labor Relations brings in, for example, sufficient economic material to allow a fundamental appreciation of the union–management process and stops at that point. Throughout, it has tried to make the various topic treatments short enough to be interesting while at the same time long enough to do justice to the subject. On the other hand, it in no way restricts itself to what is commonly described as collective bargaining. Its focus is on the negotiation and administration of labor agreements, with emphasis on the more significant bargaining issues as they now appear between the covers of the contracts. And these topics cannot profitably be studied in isolation. Labor relations can best be viewed as an interaction between two organizations—management and the labor union—and the parties to this interaction are always subject to various, often complex, environmental influences. Only after the reader gains an understanding of the evolving management and labor institutions, and only after the environment surrounding their interactional process has been appreciated, can he or she attempt to understand bargaining itself in any satisfactory way.

The book consequently begins with a broad overview of the general nature of the labor–management relationship as it currently exists in the United States (Part I). It then moves to a survey of the historical, legal, and structural environments that so greatly influence contractual contents and labor relations behavior (Part II). Finally, it presents a close examination of the negotiation, administration, and major contents of the labor agreement itself (Part III).

Through description, analysis, discussion questions, minicases (many of them with ethical dimensions) and selected arbitration cases drawn from the authors' own experiences, understanding of all these aspects of labor relations will, hopefully, be imparted.

This tenth edition, the first one written since Fred Witney's 1999 death, is marked by many changes—mainly additions, although all of the chapters have been given some streamlining and the new volume is essentially the same in size as its predecessors. Even in the four years since the ninth edition, developments in the field have warranted the inclusion of new material on card checks, labor's recent turn to different and more aggressive leadership, fast-track presidential authority and unions, major developments in public policy in the past few years, and the dues rebate controversy. I have also enlarged upon the prior treatment that Fred and I gave managerial health care cost containment, arbitration, the GM-UAW-Saturn relationship, and miscalculations in bargaining. Tax-deferred retirement savings plans are additionally now dealt with, as is the topic of the AFL-CIO and cyberspace. And the discussion of a host of other topics has, of course, been given a significant updating.

Many new visual aids are included also, as are an extensively revised bibliography, an amended mock negotiation problem, and a glossary.

Nonetheless, I have exercised self-restraint in the rewriting. Only changes that can be defended on the grounds of general improvement of *Labor Relations* have been incorporated. I have always firmly believed in the old Puritan dictum that "nothing should ever be said that doesn't improve upon silence," and also share with the late Calvin Coolidge the conviction that "if you don't say anything, no one will ever call upon you to repeat it."

ACKNOWLEDGMENTS

When a book has reached the stage of a tenth edition, it stands indebted to so many people that individual acknowledgment is futile. As in the case of the prior editions, students, friends from the ranks of both management and labor, and colleagues at other educational institutions have offered constructive suggestions and many of these have been implemented. Rita M. Beasley, who cheerfully and competently provided many helpful services on behalf of this volume, does deserve a special citation, however. And so, for the same reasons, do the University of Delaware's Myrt Werkheiser and Nancy Sanderson.

Nor can the contributions of five outstanding Prentice Hall staffers—Managing Editor Jennifer Glennon, Production Editor Keri Jean, Managing Editor Judy Leale, Editorial Assistant Kim Marsden, and Acquisitions Editor David Shafer—go unrecognized. Most of all, I appreciate the support that Louise P. Sloane, my wife, gave me throughout the process: Everyone else will have to be satisfied with the acknowledgments; she alone may also share in the royalties.

ARTHUR A. SLOANE

PART I Setting the Stage

CHAPTER

1

Organized Labor

and the Management

Community: An Overview

1

*O*ur society has historically placed a high premium on property rights. Because of this, and perhaps also because the American soil has nurtured a breed of highly individualistic and aggressive managers, employers in this country have accepted unionism through the years approximately as well as nature tolerates a vacuum.

Symbolic of management sentiments in the mid-nineteenth century, for example, were the comments of the editors of the *New York Journal of Commerce* relating to current demands of the printers in that locality:

> Who but a miserable craven-hearted man, would permit himself to be subjected to such rules, extending even to the number of apprentices he may employ, and the manner in which they shall be bound to him, to the kind of work which shall be performed in his own office at particular hours of the day, and to the sex of the persons employed, however separated into different apartments or buildings? . . . It is marvelous to us how any employer, having the soul of a man within him, can submit to such degradation.[1]

Five decades later, George F. Baer, president of the Philadelphia and Reading Railroad, relied on God rather than ridicule in setting forth views that were no less representative of many employers of *his* time. In a 1903 letter, Baer replied to a citizen who had requested him "as a Christian gentleman" to make concessions to the striking workers on his railroad, as follows:

> I see you are evidently biased in your religious views in favor of the right of the working man to control a business in which he has no other interest than to secure fair wages for the work he does. I beg of you not to be discouraged. The rights and interests of the laboring man will be protected and cared for, not by the labor agitators, but by the Christian men to whom God in His infinite wisdom has given control of the property interests of the country.[2]

Sinclair Lewis used fictional satire to make his points, but real-life counterparts of his small-town businessman George F. Babbitt were sufficiently in supply to make *Babbitt* an instant success when it was published in 1922. Babbitt's opinions on the subject of organized labor were forthright, if not entirely consistent:

> A good labor union is of value because it keeps out radical unions, which would destroy property. No one ought to be forced to belong to a union, however. All labor agitators who try to force men to join a union should be hanged. In fact, just between ourselves, there oughtn't to be any unions allowed at all; and as it's the best way of fighting the unions, every businessman ought to belong to an employer's association and to the Chamber of Commerce. In union there is strength. So any selfish hog who doesn't join the Chamber of Commerce ought to be forced to.[3]

In our own day, management views on the subject are considerably more sophisticated and far less emotion-laden. Major changes have affected the employment relationship and contributed to the lessening of overt antiunionism. The findings of industrial sociology and applied psychology have led to an employee-centered management approach that was unknown earlier. Far greater worker expectations have been fostered by a new social climate derived from the ending of mass immigration, growing levels of education, and the spread of the world's most ambitious communications network. The old-time owner-manager, holding a major or exclusive proprietary interest in his business, has now been substantially displaced. He has been succeeded by the hired administrator, oriented toward management as a profession, as much an employee as the people far below in the organizational hierarchy, and increasingly aware that profitability is not the only test of performance today (and that community responsibilities are also prime considerations). Finally, the right of workers to organize and bargain collectively, free of employer restraint or coercion, has been protected by statute since the mid-1930s.

In this new setting, progress in union–management relations has undeniably been made. Violence in labor disputes has all but disappeared. The incidence of strikes has been almost steadily decreasing, and strikes now consume a minuscule portion of total working time—in the neighborhood of one-tenth of 1 percent in most recent years. A greater willingness by both parties to resort to facts rather than to power or emotion as a basis for bargaining is in evidence. And, indeed, unions have now been completely accepted by some managers, with outspoken attacks on organized labor in general being relatively rare from *any* employer quarter.

For all these developments, however, unions are still far from welcome in the eyes of the employer community. If the attacks are more muted and less belligerent than they were, they nonetheless exist on a wide scale. Some time ago, one observer summed up what he saw as the modal situation then. With word enlargement to explicitly incorporate women into the description, these words are wholly appropriate even now:

> Even if the manager does not view the union as a gang, he often still feels that (unions) strike a discordant note in the happy home. Once there, unrest develops. A peer group outside the home becomes more important to the children than the parents; the father's powers are challenged; the child begins to think his goals are not synonymous with those of the parents (he may even want his allowance raised); and, perhaps worst of all, he wants to have his voice heard in how the home should be run.[4]

THE STAYING POWER OF UNIONS

In the face of this management enmity, on the other hand, unionism has shown absolutely no tendency to retreat. Owing primarily to the inroads of changing technology and the resulting employment decline, as well as to changing market demands affecting manufacturing, organized labor has, it is true, lost some of its membership in recent years, both in absolute and in relative terms. And, despite some claims that the fast-growing white-collar sector will soon become more hospitable to collective bargaining, it is equally true that union penetration in this area thus far has fallen considerably short of its potential. But it is no less a matter of record that over five times as many workers are union members today as was the case in 1932, and it is quite apparent that the 16.2 million employees who currently constitute the labor movement in this country exhibit no notable signs of disenchantment with it.

As the nature of our labor force changes, whatever one's speculation about the problems awaiting unionism is (and, as will be shown, the speculation is both optimistic and pessimistic from the union viewpoint), **collective bargaining** and **labor unions** are here to stay. (Exhibit 1-1 shows members of the Air Line Pilots Association demonstrating their support for their labor organization in a recent Labor Day parade.)

EXHIBIT 1-1

SOURCE: *Air Line Pilot*, October 1998, front cover.

In this introductory chapter, then, we must examine why workers, apparently in complete disregard of their employers' wishes, join and remain in unions; and why, beyond the extremely general reasons suggested by the preceding paragraphs, employers so steadfastly continue to oppose the concept of unionism. Before we discuss these questions, however, we must assess the current status and strategic power of the American labor movement itself.

THE STATE OF THE UNIONS TODAY

❖ The Broad Statistics

Completely reliable statistics relating to union membership in this country have never been available. Some unions in reporting their figures have traditionally exaggerated to gain respect and influence for the union itself within the total labor movement, to make the union officers look better by showing a rise in enrollments during their term of office, or merely to hide a loss of membership. Other unions have been known to report fewer members than they actually have for financial reasons (for example, to avoid paying per capita taxes to labor federations to which they may belong, particularly the **American Federation of Labor—Congress of Industrial Organizations [AFL-CIO]**) or because of bookkeeping practices that exclude workers currently on strike (or those on layoff from work) from the list of present members.

The figure of 16.2 million employees is commonly accepted as an appropriate one, however. According to the best current estimates of the **U.S. Bureau of Labor Statistics (BLS)**, this total includes some 9 million union members in private industry and 7.2 million government workers. It excludes approximately 1.5 million Canadians who belong to international unions with headquarters in the United States. It also excludes almost 2 million U.S. wage and salary employees, over half of whom are employed in the government sector, who are represented at their workplaces by a union but who are not union members. Not being required to join a union as a condition of continued employment, these employees have for a variety of reasons chosen not to do so. Nor do the BLS estimates include union members who are currently unemployed.

As the United States entered the twenty-first century, the 16.2 million people in its unionized workforce represented about 13.9 percent of all U.S. workers. Although this statistic was down appreciably from the 35 percent of the nation's labor force that unions represented four decades earlier, it still allowed organized labor significant influence in at least some sectors.

❖ The Concentration of Unionism

Close to 40 percent of all employees in federal, state, and local government are now in the ranks of unions. And in the vitally important private-sector worlds of transportation and public utilities the union proportion is a reasonably impressive 26 percent. Other major private industries with above-average union membership percentages are construction and manufacturing, with almost 20 percent in each case.[5]

More specifically, about 35 percent of the nation's **blue-collar workers**, those whose job duties are primarily manual in nature, continue to be represented by unions. And in some blue-collar bastions the nonunionist is a relative rarity. The great majority of manual workers in such smokestack industries as automobiles and steel, for example, carry union cards, and the same can be said for their counterparts in aerospace, rubber, agricultural implements, the needle trades, paper, and brewing. Organization also covers a substantial, if somewhat lesser, percentage of the blue-collar employees in the printing, oil, chemical, electrical, electronic, pharmaceutical, and shoe industries and in the increasingly vital world of communications.

States and cities with a high percentage of their workers in all of these industries show, not surprisingly, a high proportion of unionized employees. Seven states—California, New York, Illinois, Michigan, Ohio, Pennsylvania, and New Jersey—account for over half of all union members. There are, in fact, more union members in California alone than there are in 10 southern states combined. Washington, Wisconsin, Minnesota, Nevada, Indiana, Oregon, Hawaii, Connecticut, Rhode Island, and Alaska also have ratios of union membership to total labor force population that place them well above the national average. Several major cities, too, that are comparatively dependent on the industries cited—Pittsburgh, Detroit, and

Seattle, among others—currently have at least 90 percent of their manufacturing-plant workers covered by union contract. On the other hand, states and cities without large representation from these industries tend to show considerably lower figures: In both North Carolina and South Carolina, less than 6 percent of the nonagricultural labor force belongs to a union, and anyone who wagers that a random work group in Charlotte or Charleston (or Jacksonville or New Orleans, for that matter) is a nonunion one is very likely going to win.[6]

Union strength, then, is highly concentrated in areas that are strategic to our economy. If organized labor has thus far been notably unsuccessful in its attempt to organize such white-collar (and fast-growing) sectors as trade, services, and finance and such remaining pockets of nonunionism in manufacturing as the textile industry, unions have been cordially greeted by the workers in much of large-scale industry. Indeed, the labor movement today bargains with many of the most influential managements in the country, those that regularly take the lead in price and wage movements. From trucking, whose importance to the nation is such that its major employer association has for years boasted as its motto "If you got it, a truck brought it," to the focal points of any advanced industrialized nation in durable goods production, unions are important. They have power, accordingly, where the possession of power is particularly significant.

❖ The Importance of Blue-Collar Workers to Unions

Titles do not always accurately portray the kind of worker represented by a union. For example, Mickey and Minnie Mouse, Donald Duck, and Goofy—in fact, most of the employees at both Disneyland and Disney World—are Teamsters. So are some state troopers in Michigan, college professors at the U.S. Merchant Marine Academy, tree surgeons, egg farmers, and race car drivers, in addition to thousands of truck drivers and warehousemen—the traditional Teamster base. Teachers in Oklahoma City belong to the Laborers Union, and taxicab drivers in Chicago are members of the Seafarers' International Union. The United Automobile Workers currently represents secretaries at Columbia University, teaching assistants at the University of California, lawyers in Detroit, writers at New York's *The Village Voice*, and several hundred other white-collar groups. But official names are at least generally indicative, and a reading of the names of the nine largest internationals in the year 2000, as offered in the following table, gives further evidence of the importance of blue-collar workers to labor.

Union	Number of Members
International Brotherhood of Teamsters	1,400,000
American Federation of State, County, and Municipal Employees	1,200,000
Service Employees International Union	1,100,000
United Food and Commercial Workers	1,000,000
United Automobile Workers	800,000
American Federation of Teachers	700,000
International Brotherhood of Electrical Workers	660,000
Communications Workers of America	500,000
United Steelworkers of America	500,000

Source: Based on estimates published by the U.S. Department of Labor.

Of these nine largest unions (which collectively today account for over half of all union members), only four appear even from their names to be outside of labor's main blue-collar mold, and in three of these four cases that appearance is somewhat misleading. Many members of the American Federation of State, County, and Municipal Employees perform such definitely blue-collar assignments as stock handling and pothole patching. The United Food and Commercial Workers represents mainly manual workers. And there are more janitors and custodial employees in the Service Employees International Union than there are anything else. Most members of the American Federation of Teachers do, on the other hand, teach.

WHITE-COLLAR EMPLOYEES

If the labor movement is predominantly a blue-collar one, however, this is no longer true of the U.S. labor force itself. In 1956, the number of **white-collar workers** exceeded that of blue-collar workers in this country for the first time in our nation's history. And the gap has been steadily widening ever since. The service sectors—including trade, finance, and government—have continued to expand, while the blue-collar sectors—particularly manufacturing, mining, and transportation—have actually, in the face of improved technologies and changing consumer demands, shown employment declines.

Less than 15 percent of workers in U.S. industry are now employed in manufacturing and construction, as compared with 23 percent two decades ago. Meanwhile that graphic symbol of the nation's service sector, the McDonald's hamburger empire, has expanded to the point where it employs more than nine times as many workers as does USX (formerly United States Steel). In fact, employment in the iron and steel industry, which peaked at 952,000 in 1957, had fallen to not much more than half that total by the end of the 1990s, and jobs in automobiles, chemicals, apparel, and other older industries had demonstrated similar decline by then. Whether or not "smokestack America" was actually in its decline at the time of this writing, most experts *believed* that it was and that all the grim employment trends would only continue.

Certainly, the AFL-CIO has had no reason to think otherwise. At its 1999 convention, it announced the discouraging findings of an ambitious study that it had just completed: Job growth in the United States had, for some time, been most rapid in the white-collar industries where unions had been weakest, whereas job losses had been largest in the more heavily unionized blue-collar sectors. From 1984 to 1997, for example, the study found that the nation's 30 fastest-growing industries (including hotels, finance, retail trade, and child care) had created 26 million new jobs but that only 5 percent of the workers in these sectors had joined unions. On the other hand, in the eight industries—all of them heavily blue-collar ones, including automobiles and steel—that had lost the most jobs (some 2.1 million of these collectively), a staggering 80 percent of the terminated jobs had belonged to union members. "In overall terms," the federation's primary researcher for the study declared, in something of an understatement, "the economy is moving against us." Pointing out that the jobs had often been lost because employers had moved operations overseas to capitalize on lower-cost workers there, he added, "We're somewhat a victim of our own success. Heavily organized industries have high wages and benefits."[7]

❖ Labor's Primary Cause for Concern

More than any other factor, this changing complexion of the labor force has given organized labor cause for concern. Its inability to recruit white-collar workers on any significant scale has been primarily responsible for its slippage from representing 35 percent of the labor force in 1959, and 20 percent of U.S. workers in 1983, to its afore-mentioned position of representing just about 14 percent. Unless it can do far better than it has to date in organizing the nation's millions of clerical, sales, professional-technical, and other employees, organized labor will, by simple mathematical logic, see the percentage drop even more—perhaps to the 10 or 11 percent level.

This is not to say, of course, that unions do not exert a major collective bargaining influence on behalf of some groups of white-collar workers. Such white-collar types as musicians and actors have, for years, been willing joiners of labor organizations. For instance, the Screen Actors Guild (SAG) not only represents most of Hollywood's actors and actresses, but isn't doing badly peddling a host of products adorned with the SAG name and logo in an effort to capitalize directly on membership pride. (Exhibit 1-2 illustrates this side activity, the kind of thing to which many other unions have also started to turn in an effort to increase their treasuries.) In recent years, white-collar governmental employees have joined unions by the hundreds of thousands and the American Federation of Teachers has grown from 60,000 members in the 1960s to almost 12 times that number now.

Also exhibiting no small amount of organizational success have been the Postal Workers and the Letter Carriers (each with current memberships around 300,000). The Letter Carriers offer, among other selling points for membership, a particularly attractive insurance plan and, as Exhibit 1-3 illustrates, they haven't been at all bashful in touting its existence.

Some 40 percent of all college faculty members, 45,000 physicians, almost 50,000 engineers, and several thousand lawyers are in the ranks of unions at the present time. Nurses on the East and West Coasts are also far more often bargained for collectively than they are not. In addition, as even the most casual follower of the news must be aware, professional athletes in all major league sports are not only collectively bargained for, as essentially none of them were a relatively few years ago, but they also have engaged in notable work stoppages.

In their fourth bargaining impasse since 1981, the 800 members of the Major League Baseball Players Association concluded a mammoth 234-day strike that had wiped out the 1994 League Playoffs and World Series, three weeks after the 1995 season was to have started (at that, they returned to their jobs a week ahead of baseball's regular umpires, who had been locked out by the owners for 120 days). Earlier in 1995, a lockout involving the 700 members of the National Hockey League Players Association was resolved after three and a half months, less than three years after this same union had struck for 10 days.

The 1,500 National Football League players, perhaps humbled by their experience in 1987, when scores of their football-playing union colleagues crossed the picket line and joined replacement players on the football field to bring an end to a 24-day strike, have not participated in a work stoppage since. But to make up for this last stillness on the labor scene, the National Basketball Association briefly locked out its 400 players in mid-1995 and the first major league work stoppage in that sport's history became a reality. And the last scenario was repeated for a much longer period of time three and one-half years later: A lockout was terminated in early 1999 only after six months had elapsed and the entire 82-game season had given every promise of going down the drain. As it was, only a 50-game schedule was able to be played.

For all of this, there has been no particularly impressive change in total union penetration of the white-collar field in recent years. In 1956, some 2.42 million white-collar workers were in unions; a decade later, the figure had risen only to approximately 2.7 million, despite the growth of this sector by several million more jobs, to over 26 million by the late 1960s. And by the year 2000, with an even more rapid growth in total white-collar employment in the intervening years, the union rolls had advanced only to about the 5 million mark, a point clearly far short of the saturation level. Nor had even these modest gains of organized labor been evenly spread throughout the white-collar world. Most of them had been gained strictly from the public-service sector, where, as we shall see, in many cases favorable legislation had made the enrollment of new members both comparatively easy and comparatively meaningless: In Texas, for example, public-sector unions can neither bargain collectively for wages nor—even in the case of teachers' unions—strike, and any resemblance between these labor organizations and, say, the Teamsters in Michigan is strictly coincidental.

SOME PROBABLE EXPLANATIONS

Why has the white-collar world been so relatively unreceptive to the union organizer when its blue-collar counterpart has been so hospitable? Among the many explanations for labor's general failure to date in penetrating the white-collar frontier, the following may well be the most accurate. Taken collectively, they also constitute some rather formidable grounds for union pessimism in the years ahead.

❖ Unions and the Media

The public has in recent years been inundated with news of seemingly irresponsible union strikes and commensurately unstatesmanlike settlements, union leaders' criminality, and **featherbedding** situations. The resulting poor image of the labor movement, as conveyed by the media, may well have alienated hundreds of thousands—and, conceivably, even millions—of potential white-collar union joiners. In an age when even the occupant of the White House can be determined by public image, this factor—although it is not only unquantifiable but even basically unprovable—cannot be overlooked.

This topic should in any event receive far more attention than it has heretofore been given. Certainly, as has long been observed by thoughtful students of labor relations, unions most often get into the headlines for activities that cover them with discredit. A union leader's criminality will invariably do the trick. And so, too, will news of any seemingly irresponsible union strike, or almost any charge, if made with sufficient vigor, that unionized employees are receiving pay for work that is not performed (or "featherbedding").

Thus, there may well be significant numbers in the general population who believe that "Construction Strike Threat Looms" is a regular, if somewhat repetitious, column appearing in their local newspaper. (*Looms*, from all available evidence, is the only verb utilized in such situations, a phenomenon similar to that pertaining to "Prison Riots," which can only be "Quelled"—or for that matter "Last Minute Settlements," which can do only one thing to strikes, namely, "Avert" them.) And one can only guess at how many Americans think that "Featherbedding" is part of the official job designation of the "Railroad Firemen." It is also true, as the late A. J. Liebling once commented, that the public is regularly informed that "Labor *Demands*" but that "Management *Offers*"; and few can argue with a further observation of that famous journalist that when General

EXHIBIT 1-2

SOURCE: *Call Sheet*,
October/November
1996.

HOW TO ORDER FROM
THE SAG STORE:

• Orders can be mailed, faxed or phoned in.
• We accept checks, American Express, Visa and MasterCard. (Sorry, no C.O.D.'s.) PLEASE DO NOT SEND CASH.
• Please make checks payable to: INCENTIVE INNOVATIONS, INC.
• Please indicate sizes where applicable.
• Please allow 3-4 weeks for delivery via standard UPS Ground. If you would like your SAG merchandise sent Federal Express and you have a Federal Express account, please indicate your account number on the order form.

NOTE: Minimum merchandise order is $10.00 (excluding freight).

FAX, CALL OR MAIL ORDER TO:
Phone: (800) 850-3301   Fax: (818) 325-2518

c/o INCENTIVE INNOVATIONS
14242 VENTURA BLVD., 3RD FLOOR
SHERMAN OAKS, CA. 91423

IMPORTANT INFORMATION: ALL MERCHANDISE IS SUBJECT TO CHANGE, MAY BE WITHDRAWN OR MAY UNDERGO DESIGN CHANGE WITHOUT PRIOR NOTICE. ALL SALES ARE FINAL. IF YOU HAVE ANY QUESTIONS, PLEASE CALL THE SAG STORE at (800) 850-3301.

ALL MERCHANDISE IS UNION-MADE IN THE U.S.A.

SCREEN
ACTORS
GUILD

MOUSE PAD
An ideal gift for your computer. Plastic-coated mouse pad with drop shadow logo.

CERAMIC COFFEE MUG
Early call? Oversized 11-ounce ceramic coffee mug in rich cobalt blue with logo etched in white.

HIGHLIGHTER SET
Make your role stand out with this set of highlighters in a clear plastic pouch.

COMMUTER MUG
On the run? 12-ounce plastic mug with white accents and drop shadow logo.

SAG CARDS
Got your SAG card? Here's a whole deck of standard-sized playing cards.

LEATHER LUGGAGE TAG
On location? Embossed leather luggage tag holds a standard-size business card concealed by a fold-over flap.

KEY TAG
Elegant round antique bronze 12-gauge tag.

CLASSIC CLOISONNE PIN
Wear your membership proudly with this beautiful lapel pin with military clutch back.

PLACE YOUR
HOLIDAY ORDER
TODAY!

★ THE SAG STORE ★
ORDER FORM

ORDERS RECEIVED
BY DEC. 2ND WILL
BE SHIPPED BY
DEC. 16

ITEM #	DESCRIPTION	S	M	L	XL	PRICES	QUANTITY	TOTAL
SAG-101	CERAMIC COFFEE MUG					$ 7.50 EA.		
SAG-102	COMMUTER MUG					$ 3.50 EA.		
SAG-103	DENIM JACKET					$ 48.50 EA.		
SAG-103	DENIM JACKET (XXL)					$ 53.00 EA.		
SAG-103	DENIM JACKET (XXXL)					$ 55.00 EA.		
SAG-104	DENIM SHIRT (BLUE)					$ 32.50 EA.		
SAG-104	DENIM SHIRT (BLUE) (XXL)					$ 37.00 EA.		
SAG-104	DENIM SHIRT (BLUE) (XXXL)					$ 39.00 EA.		
SAG-105	BASEBALL SHIRT					$ 27.50 EA.		
SAG-106	CLOISSONE LAPEL PIN					$ 3.00 EA.		
SAG-107	FLEECE JACKET					$ 65.00 EA.		
SAG-107	FLEECE JACKET (XXL)					$ 69.50 EA.		
SAG-107	FLEECE JACKET (XXXL)					$ 71.50 EA.		
SAG-108	CANVAS ATTACHE					$ 32.00 EA.		
SAG-109	LEATHER & WOOL JACKET					$165.00 EA.		
SAG-109	LEATHER & WOOL JACKET (XXL)					$185.00 EA.		
SAG-110	SAG PLAYING CARDS					$ 4.00 EA.		
SAG-111	MOUSE PAD					$ 4.00 EA.		
SAG-112	KEY TAG					$ 4.00 EA.		
SAG-113	LEATHER LUGGAGE TAG					$ 4.50 EA.		
SAG-114	MEGA LEATHER ORGANIZER					$ 75.00 EA.		
SAG-115	COMPACT LEATHER ORGANIZER					$ 35.00 EA.		
SAG-116	LEATHER SCRIPT BINDER					$ 45.00 EA.		
SAG-117	T-SHIRT					$ 7.50 EA.		
SAG-118	SWEATSHIRT					$ 23.00 EA.		
SAG-119	HIGHLIGHTER SET WITH CLEAR POUCH					$ 6.50 EA.		
SAG-120	BASEBALL CAP					$ 10.00 EA.		

Please include postage charges using this chart:

FOR ORDERS BETWEEN:	PLEASE ADD POSTAGE OF:
$10.00 - 15.00	$3.95
$15.01 - 25.00	4.95
$25.01 - 35.00	5.95
$35.01 - 50.00	6.95
$50.01 or more	7.95

SUB-TOTAL:	$
CA. residents add appropriate sales tax:	$
POSTAGE:	$
HANDLING:	$ **4.25**
GRAND TOTAL:	$

SHIP TO: _____

_____

_____

_____

PHONE: _____

AMEX/VISA/MC. _____

EXP. DATE _____

SIGNATURE _____

FED. EX. A/C#: _____

FAX, CALL OR MAIL ORDERS TO:
Phone: (800) 850-3301   Fax: (818) 325-2518
C/O INCENTIVE INNOVATIONS, 14242 VENTURA BLVD., 3RD FLOOR, SHERMAN OAKS, CA., 91423

HOW TO ORDER FROM THE SAG STORE:
* Orders can be mailed, faxed or phoned in. *NOTE: Minimum merchandise order is $10.00 (excluding freight).*
* We accept checks, American Express, Visa and MasterCard (sorry, no C.O.D.'s). PLEASE DO NOT SEND CASH.
* Please make checks payable to INCENTIVE INNOVATIONS, INC.
* Please indicate sizes where applicable.
* Please allow 3-4 weeks for delivery via standard UPS Ground. If you would like your SAG merchandise sent Federal Express and you have a Federal Express account, please indicate your account number on the order form.

All merchandise is subject to change, may be withdrawn or may undergo design change without prior notice. All sales are final. If you have any questions, call the SAG Store at (800) 850-3301.

ALL MERCHANDISE IS UNION-MADE IN THE U.S.A.

Why Are These People Smiling?

The U.S. Letter Carriers Mutual Benefit Association is *your* insurance company, owned and operated by letter carriers. No money is spent on commissioned salesmen. And those savings are passed on to you in the form of benefits, lower premiums and dividends—making MBA programs a sound investment for you and your family. Put a smile on your face with the affordable options that best meet your insurance requirements. **Call or write MBA today for more information.**

National Association of Letter Carriers
U.S. Letter Carriers Mutual Benefit Association
100 Indiana Avenue, N.W., Suite 510, Washington, D.C. 20001-2144

1-800-424-5184 (Tuesdays & Thursdays, 8:00 a.m.-3:30 p.m. ET)
202-638-4318 (Monday-Friday, 8:00 a.m.-3:30 p.m. ET)

Vincent R. Sombrotto, *President*   Michael J. O'Connor, *Director*
Board of Trustees: James G. Souza, Jr., Chairman • Lawrence D. Brown, Jr. • John W. DiTollo

MBA. INSURANCE FOR LETTER CARRIERS.

Motors workers go out on strike for more wages, this is major news, whereas the president of General Motors takes his considerably larger income home quietly.

From labor's point of view there is, of course, an intrinsic unfairness in such a factor. It is conflict, as more than one media member has observed, that makes the headlines. The large majority of union agreements that are peacefully renegotiated year after year go virtually unnoticed by the reporters of the news, but the few strikes of any dimensions are treated with the journalistic zeal of a Bernstein or Woodward. The overwhelming proportion of union officials continue to lead their lives in full compliance with the laws of the land, but this seems insignificant to the news compilers in the face of the conviction of a single general president of the International Brotherhood of Teamsters (IBT): Five of the last seven holders of that position have been indicted, and three—including James R. Hoffa, arguably the best-known labor leader of all time—went to jail. It is understandable, if ironic, that these developments received substantial media coverage. It is no less ironic that at least Hoffa continues to be a household word even today, albeit most often through the vehicle of generally tasteless jokes that appear to circulate as widely now as they did in the immediate aftermath of his 1975 disappearance (e.g., "Question: Who was the last person ever to see Jimmy Hoffa? Answer: Jacques Cousteau"). Meanwhile most people could not name the current IBT president if their lives depended on it (it's Hoffa's son, James P. Hoffa, a career labor lawyer until he was elected). And charges that unions demand pay for work that is not performed totally dwarf the large body of evidence that featherbedding is engaged in by only a small segment of unionized employees.

Yet what editor can justify headlines proclaiming that "Local 109 of the American Federation of Musicians Is a Very Statesmanlike Local," that "Business Agent Duffy Gabrilowitz of the Plumbers Union Is One Hundred Percent Honest," or that "Management Says That Flight Attendants Are Giving a Fair Day's Work for a Fair Day's Pay"? Only, we suspect, a journalist with a strongly developed suicidal urge. Accordingly, the large segment of the population that allows its opinions of unionism to be molded only by those labor activities receiving wide publicity is understandably—if, for organized labor, unfortunately—less than enthusiastic about the institution. An incalculable but undoubtedly formidable number of white-collar workers—unlike their blue-collar counterparts, who are generally in a better position by virtue of proximity to perceive strengths as well as weaknesses in unionism—fall into this population category.

❖ Union Leadership

The labor movement has, at least until recently, been distinguished by uninspiring bureaucratic leadership that has seemed to be only dimly aware of the white-collar problem and totally unimaginative about discovering any solutions. The complaint of labor scholar J. B. S. Hardman that "superannuated leaders, who have outlived their usefulness, are probably met more frequently in the labor movement than in any other militant social movement," although it was made many years ago and intended to apply exclusively to the late 1920s, could fit into any typical outsider's critique of labor's current performance between the 1970s and the late 1990s.[8]

Until a significant change was made in AFL-CIO leadership in 1995, something that will be considered in some detail in the next chapter, and commensurate alterations were soon made thereafter in the high commands of many of the AFL-CIO constituent unions, there was much validity to a charge made some years earlier by the United Automobile Workers that labor's top policy makers had become isolated from the mainstream and too frequently acted like a comfortable, complacent custodian of the status quo. Those at the apex of union hierarchies themselves had in these years become surrounded with the trappings of success. As a respected labor journalist could accurately point out, "The hair-shirt has given way to white-on-white broadcloth, imported fabrics, and custom tailoring" and the expense account prequisites of labor's major officials had become totally indistinguishable in their lavishness from those of leaders in the business community.[9] However, somewhere in the transformation from crusader for the underdog to accepted member of the establishment, both the sense of mission and the creative spark to implement it seemed to have been dampened by affluence. The bulk of labor leadership appeared to be resting comfortably on its laurels, lacking motivation to reenter the organizational arena and expend the energy, money, and, above all, imagination that were required by such an elusive potential constituency as the white-collar sector.

Nor was organized labor exactly in the hands of youthful crusaders. Those at the top of the union hierarchy were frequently septuagenarians and octogenarians, prompting a remark by one unhappy observer that "some of the board members of some of the unions, when they have a board meeting, look like a collection of a wax museum," and a comment by essayist Wilfrid Sheed that "the widespread impression that Labor consists of aging white men guarding their gains may be an exaggeration verging on libel; but it is widespread."[10]

That things are at long last now changing detracts not a bit from the validity of including past labor leadership as a major explanation for the labor movement's past failures in organizing white-collar workers.

❖ Unique General Properties of White-Collar Workers

White-collar workers possess certain unique general properties that may tend to work against unionization in any event.

White-collar employees have long felt superior to their blue-collar counterparts and have tended to believe that joining a union (an institution traditionally associated with manual workers) would decrease their occupational prestige. A certain autonomy at work, however little it may be in many cases, is imparted to the holder of the white-collar job as it is not to the factory or construction worker. Prior educational achievements, modes of dress and language, relative cleanliness of work situations, and even job locations within the enterprise also typically give the white-collar jobholder much more in common with management than with the blue-collar employee. Income based on salary rather than wages further weakens the potential bonds between the two submanagerial classes. Nor, clearly, can the sheer fact that society generally looks down on manual work and places its premium on mentally challenging employment be disregarded in explaining the superiority complex of the white-collarite.

In an economy such as ours—where for most people the more basic needs have now been relatively well satisfied—the role of such status considerations can be considerable. To ask the white-collar worker to identify by unionization with the steel worker, truck driver, and hod carrier—and to follow in the traditions of Samuel Gompers or John L. Lewis (to say nothing of the leadership of the Teamsters or of former Mine Worker president Tony Boyle, of whom it was once said that he could immeasurably increase the moral level in a room simply by leaving it)—is consequently, by its very nature, no small undertaking.

However tenuous it may be, white-collar workers can also at least perceive some opportunity to advance into managerial ranks, whereas blue-collar employees are typically limited in their most optimistic advancement goal to the "gray area" of the foremanship. Unlike the wearers of the white-collar, the blue-collar workers sense (usually quite accurately) that educational and social deficiencies have combined to limit their promotional avenues within the industrial world, and they can adjust to the fact that they are permanently destined to be apart from and directed by the managerial class. Because such a fate is often not nearly as clear to white-collar workers (partially for the reasons cited in the previous paragraphs), they are understandably more reluctant to join the ranks of unionism and thus support what is potentially a major constraint on employer freedom of action.

The considerably higher proportion of women in white-collar work than in blue-collar work has served as a further dampening force for organization. By and large, women have historically been notoriously poor candidates for unionism. In many cases until now (although the situation has changed radically in recent years), the job has been thought of as temporary—either premarital or to supplement the family breadwinner's paycheck (often on a sporadic basis)—and, consequently, the union's argument of long-run job security has had little appeal. In other cases—perhaps as high as 25 percent at the time of this writing—the job is a part-time one, also to the detriment of the union organizer. Nor can the labor movement's traditional aura of militant masculinity be eliminated as a possible causal factor in explaining the female response to organizational attempts. ("There's no way we're going to attract them," one concerned union leader has said, "with the tank-top, tattoo, tough guy image.")

Finally, many white-collar workers with professional identifications—engineers, college professors, and institutionally employed doctors, for example—continue to believe that for them there is still much more to be gained from individual bargaining with their employer than from any form of collective bargaining. Viewing the latter as an automatic opponent of individual merit rewards, they tend to perceive the unionists within their professions either as mediocrities in need of such group support or as masochists.

SOME GROUNDS FOR UNION OPTIMISM

If it is thus tempting to begin sounding the death knell for the labor movement on the grounds that its failure to penetrate the critical white-collar frontier can be explained by a combination of factors that seem to be at least collectively insurmountable, realism dictates that several other factors also be pondered. And these additional considerations can lead one to an entirely different conclusion regarding the future of organized labor in the white-collar area.

❖ Union Economic Gains

The same newsprint, television, and radio announcements that have brought news of union misdoings to the white-collar population have also informed this primarily nonunion audience of highly impressive income improvements in the unionized sector. For example, few nonunionists are entirely unaware of the gains in the heavily organized construction sector that by 1999 were adding $5.50 per hour and more to the wages of skilled craft workers over the next three years, or in many cases more than half as much as the monies received as *total* hourly wages by workers in wholesale and retail trade, finance, insurance, real estate, and many other parts of the white-collar world. The imminence of a situation in which the lowest income for even a common laborer in the construction industry would soon be some $35,000 or more could only have been received with considerable envy by the unrepresented bank employee whose current earnings, despite a college degree, placed him or her at not much more than two-thirds of this figure. And knowledge of the fact that substantial overtime opportunities at hefty premiums were also available to such unionists—as they were most frequently not to white-collar workers—could only increase the latter's flow of adrenalin.

In fairness, it must be recognized that the historically overtight labor markets and fractionalized bargaining structure of construction have made it a labor union extreme from the viewpoint of wage aggrandizement. It is also true that workers in this sector were sometimes paying a significant penalty in recent years for the munificence of their earlier settlements: They were not always employed, their labor costs having made their employers noncompetitive with nonunion contractors. But the kind of invidious comparisons engendered by the construction totals clearly extends to other situations.

At the time of this writing, for example, the median weekly earnings of unionized workers across all industries according to the U.S. Department of Labor were $659 as against $499 for nonunion members nationwide. These figures reflected the simple fact that unionists were in well-paying blue-collar jobs, of course, but they at least hinted at the possibility that these jobs could have been well paying because they were in fact so often bargained for collectively. For unionists, too, fringe benefits are typically much more lavish than they are for nonunionists: 85 percent of all union members have health insurance compared with 57 percent of nonunion employees.[11] By the estimates of some economists, the benefits of union members are typically worth about three times as much as the benefits of unorganized workers.

Nor can the white-collar population indefinitely be expected to be indifferent to truck driver incomes (symbolically, the *International Teamster* magazine could report some years ago that "recently a professor at ivy-covered Williams College in New England returned to the Teamsters as an over-the-road driver because he could double his salary at Williams")[12] and to various other highly remunerated (and overwhelmingly unionized) workers such as longshoremen, tool and die makers, and airline mechanics. For that matter, San Francisco sanitation workers were receiving more than $37,000 in annual base wages alone in the late 1990s, and this figure, even though far from the poverty level, paled by comparison with the $99,016 (including overtime) that was then averaged by full-time dock workers on the West Coast, to say nothing of the more than $200,000 earned by most senior pilots at the nation's major airlines.

The 400,000 employees of General Motors, Ford, and DaimlerChrysler represented by the United Automobile Workers didn't, with rare exceptions, earn any eye-catching kind of money, but the $45,000 that they typically received as gross pay in 1999 (without overtime) gave them almost exactly twice what the average U.S. worker got paid in the same year.

The responsibility for the relatively high standards of living involved here certainly does not rest completely with unionism. Clearly, one must also examine such a variety of other factors as skill levels, industrial ability to pay, imperfections in the product market, and industrial productivity (among others) in explaining these wage levels. And one can readily cite such unionized areas as the boot and shoe industry and the meatpacking industry, where the overall situation often allows no real wage improvement at all and, consequently, none is received by organized labor.

But the hazards of accepting the more impressive union bargaining totals at their face value are not particularly relevant in this context. Misleadingly or not, such dollar amounts often symbolize in a highly visible fashion the ability of unionism to effect dramatic wage gains. And, as the gap between the incomes of the blue-collar and white-collar worlds continues to widen, a greater willingness to consider union membership may conceivably be the result. Indeed, appreciation of the fact that snobbishness neither purchases groceries nor pays the rent seems already to have accounted for some of the increased willingness of at least teachers and nurses to undertake such a consideration.

❖ New Types of Union Members

The definite upsurge in unionism among government employees—although probably attributable far more to enabling legislation than to any pronounced rank-and-file militancy—is combining with the (lesser) emergence of collective bargaining in other white-collar areas to gradually weaken the nonmember's traditional association of organized labor with manual work. As previously implied, the process is still an excruciatingly slow one from labor's viewpoint. But the growing presence of these higher-status, better-educated federal civil servants and state employees (to say nothing of the previously mentioned college faculty members, physicians, lawyers, and nurses) in union ranks can be expected only to erode the older images in time. Whether this psychological change will be sufficient in itself to win over more than a fraction of the untapped white-collar market for the labor movement is another question. But, certainly, one of the grounds for labor's failure until now will have been dissipated.

❖ New Leadership

The new slate of AFL-CIO leaders, headed by John J. Sweeney, seems to be far more committed to organizing white-collar workers than its predecessors were. The primarily blue-collared Service Employees International Union had nearly doubled in size in the 15 years prior to 1995 when Sweeney headed it. As AFL-CIO president, Sweeney immediately promised to spend more than $20 million annually on organizing efforts (up from a puny $2 million a year under the previous regime), and he has steadily honored this pledge. He has also made good on a commitment to encourage the AFL-CIO constituent international unions, which have traditionally footed almost all of the bills for organizing, to spend much more than they ever did for this purpose. The lion's share by far of this spending has been earmarked for the white-collar world.

❖ Changing White-Collar Employee Working Conditions

Finally, the working conditions of white-collar employment are now changing in a direction that may weaken both the superiority complex and promanagement sentiments of the white-collar wearer.

The very individuality of white-collar work is now disappearing from much of the industrial scene. An accelerating trend toward organizational bigness has already combined with the demands of technological efficiency to make cogs in vast interdependent machines of many clerks, computer operators, technicians, and even engineers, rather than allowing them to remain as individuals working alone or in comfortably small groups in these categories. White-collar workers, no less than blue-collar ones, are increasingly becoming bureaucratized. More and more, as a general statement, they are the victims of routine. Ever larger numbers of their jobs have become less desirable. Blue-collar workers by no means covet white-collar positions as they once did.

In the years ahead, all of this should only accelerate. The advance of technology, in various forms from word-processing equipment to elaborate computerized design systems, is now proceeding at a faster rate in offices than in factory atmospheres, and many of the analytical and decision-making challenges once allowed the white collarite are slowly disappearing as it does so. The enormous productivity gains that such new developments have brought about have also caused, quite justifiably, considerable job uncertainty and can of course also generate a definite decrease in the economic value of job skills. (Indeed, the Bureau of Labor Statistics has estimated that between 1980 and 1997 almost 2 million white-collar workers—many of them, of course, in the smokestack industries—did lose their jobs because of plant shutdowns and changing economics.) Awareness that remote computer terminals can remove the work from the office altogether and assign it to such away-from-the-office subcontractors as mothers of small children and the physically handicapped is hardly cause for celebration among currently employed white-collar workers. Nor is the fact that the computer (since it constitutes an indefensible luxury if allowed to be idle) is starting to force many white-collar employees into one of the thus far most distinguishing features of factory work, shift work. It does not seem overly rash to assume that these changes could radically alter the complacent self-image of the white-collar wearers by blurring the traditional perceived differences between the nature of their work and that of their blue-collar counterparts.

And, in such an atmosphere, it may well be that the white-collar workers' long-standing feeling of affinity with management as well as their sense of self-actualization on the job will also evaporate, to the point of rendering the white-collarites far more susceptible than they have been in the past to the overtures of the union organizer.

Thus, a case can be made for either position. It is difficult to deny that future white-collar unionization does face great obstacles. But it is probably no less advisable to hedge one's bets before writing off organized labor as an institution doomed to an ultimate slow death because, having long ago captured the now-shrinking blue-collar market, it has realized its only natural potential. If the grounds for union optimism must necessarily remain speculative, nonetheless there are enough of them and there is sufficient logic to each of them to justify at least some amount of hopefulness on the part of the labor movement.

LABOR'S PRESENT STRATEGIC POWER

Until 1997, it would probably have been accurate to say that the last major strike in which unions received any meaningful amount of public support took place when Richard Nixon was in his first term as president: the nationwide stoppage of the postal workers in 1970. In such headline-catching situations over the next 27 years as, for example, the 1981 air traffic controllers' strike, the 1987 football players' walkout, and the 1994 baseball players' strike, the U.S. citizenry definitely sided with the managements. But when 185,000 Teamsters struck United Parcel Service (UPS) in August 1997, 55 percent of all U.S. citizens supported the union whereas only 27 percent backed UPS, with 18 percent of respondents undecided.[13]

And if a Gallup poll conducted in 1985 revealed that the public ranked labor leaders next to last—just above car salesmen—among a variety of occupational choices offered in terms of ethics and honesty,[14] in 1999 one major poll found that 56.1 percent of "likely voters"[15] believed that unions have a positive effect on the nation and another revealed that 54 percent of young workers if given the opportunity would either "definitely" or "probably" vote for a union.[16] In 1998, another respected research project had shown that 49 percent of women would like to be in a union, marking a graphic change from past female attitudes, as would 40 percent of men.[17] As the labor specialist of *Business Week* could assert in 1999 after examining these and similar studies, "If even half of the employees who say they favor union representation had been allowed to vote for unions, organized labor would represent as much as 35% of the American workforce today—the same share it held at the peak of its power . . ."[18]

That workers have not been allowed to so vote is to at least some extent due to federal and state legislation that in some ways can be construed as antilabor (see Chapter 3). And this is not the only formidable obstacle, beyond the white-collar challenges cited previously, that labor now faces. Unions have been handicapped, too, by such current factors as the national trend to smaller, decentralized facilities, resulting in more personalized worker treatment; industry's present tendency to locate new facilities in smaller, semirural, and often southern communities, climates not conducive to a hearty reception for the union; and the growing levels of income across the nation, stripping some of the effect of union promises of a "living wage." Nor can the stiff competition from foreign companies with their markedly lower labor costs that U.S. employers now face be ignored by unions.

Yet, for all these adverse factors, it is still of some relevance for anyone who attempts to predict the labor movement's future that in the unions' two centuries on the American scene they have faced even greater obstacles than these and have ultimately surmounted them. As Chapter 2 relates, the history of U.S. labor is in many ways a study of triumph over economic, social, and political adversity. Perhaps the recent shift in public opinion regarding the labor movement may be signaling the start of a great new growth period for unions.

But, however one views organized labor's future, its present strategic power cannot be denied. The labor movement's concentration of membership in the economy's most vital sectors has meant that the less than one-sixth of the labor force that bargains collectively has been an extremely influential minority. One may not agree with the newspaper headlines that a particular strike has "paralyzed the economy," but it appears to be an acceptable generalization that the wages or salaries and other conditions of employment for much of the remaining portion of the labor force are regularly affected to some degree by the unionized segment.

Thus, if the exact future dimensions and membership totals of organized labor are today in some doubt, the importance of collective bargaining is not. Nor can one dispute labor's staying power, given the labor movement's deep penetration into virtually all the traditional parts of our economy and its continuing hold upon these areas. And if modern managers are unhappy with unionism, realism dictates not that they wait for it to vanish from the scene, but that they apply their efforts toward improving the collective bargaining process by which they—and all of us—are so likely to be directly affected.

WHY WORKERS JOIN UNIONS

Questions concerning human behavior do not lend themselves to simple answers, for the subject itself is a highly complex one. "Why do workers join unions?" clearly falls within this category.

In his widely accepted theory of motivation, however, the late psychologist A. H. Maslow has provided us with helpful hints, although the theory itself relates to the whole population of human beings rather than merely to those who have seen fit to take out union membership.[19]

Maslow portrays man (a category that presumably also encompasses "woman") as a "perpetually wanting animal," driven to put forth effort (in other words, to work) by his desire to satisfy certain of his needs. To Maslow, these needs or wants can logically be thought of in terms of a hierarchy, for only one type of need is active at any given time. Only when the lowest and most basic of the needs in this hierarchy has been relatively well satisfied will each higher need become, in turn, operative. Thus, it is the *unsatisfied* need that actively motivates man's behavior. Once a need is more or less gratified, man's conduct is determined by new, higher needs, which up until then have failed to motivate simply because man's attention has been devoted to satisfying his more pressing, lower needs. And the process is for most mortals unending, since few people can ever expect to satisfy, even minimally, all their needs.

At the lowest level in this Need Hierarchy, but paramount in importance until they are satisfied, are the *physiological* needs, particularly those for food, water, clothing, and shelter. "Man lives by bread alone, when there is no bread"; in other words, any higher needs are inoperative when a person is suffering from extreme hunger, for one's full attention must then necessarily be focused on this single need. But when the need for food and the other physiological essentials is fairly well satisfied, less basic, or higher, needs in the hierarchy start to dominate behavior, or to motivate people.

Thus, needs for *safety*—for protection against arbitrary deprivation, danger, and threat—take over as prime human motivators once man is eating regularly and sufficiently and is adequately clothed and sheltered. This is true because (1) a satisfied need is no longer a motivator of behavior, yet (2) man continues to be driven by needs, and (3) the safety needs are the next most logical candidates, beyond the physiological ones, to do this driving.

What happens when the safety needs have also been relatively satisfied, so that both of the lowest need levels no longer require man's attention? In Maslow's scheme of things, the *social* needs—for belonging, association, and acceptance by one's fellows—now are dominant, and man puts forth effort to satisfy this newly activated type of want.

Still higher needs that ultimately emerge to dominate man's consciousness, always assuming that the needs below them have been gratified, are in turn *self-esteem* needs, especially for self-respect and self-confidence; *status* needs, for recognition, approval, and prestige; and finally, *self-fulfillment* needs, for realization of one's own potential and for being as creative as possible.

All this constitutes an oversimplification of Maslow's Need Hierarchy. Maslow himself qualified his concept in several ways, although only one of his reservations is important enough for our purposes to warrant inclusion here: He recognized that not all people follow the pattern depicted and that both desires and satisfactions vary with the individual.

Even in the capsule form presented here, however, Maslow's contribution is of aid in explaining why workers join unions. The many research findings that now exist on this latter topic basically agree that all employees endeavor to gratify needs and wants that are important to them because of dissatisfaction with the extent to which these needs and desires have been met.[20] They also agree that, although what is important among these needs and wants varies with the individual employee, much of the answer depends on what has already been satisfied either within the working environment or outside it. Many of these studies also support Maslow's hierarchy for the majority of workers in approximately the order of needs indicated by Maslow.

❖ Physiological Needs

It should not be surprising that dissatisfaction with the extent of physiological need gratification is no longer a dominant reason for joining unions in this country. In our relatively affluent economy, few people who are working have any great difficulty in satisfying at least the most basic of these needs. In an earlier day, before the advent of minimum wage laws and other forms of legal protection, this was not as true, and, as has already been suggested, union promises of a living wage were of great appeal to many workers. However, those members of the labor force who today are frustrated in trying to satisfy their minimal needs for food, clothing, and shelter are those who are *unemployed*, not the most logical candidates for union membership. The research substantiates the downplaying of the role of physiological needs rather conclusively. Significantly, one of the most thorough of the studies found that not one employee out of 114 workers in a large industrial local union became a union member primarily for this purpose.[21] (This is hardly to say that union members have lost interest in higher wages and other economic improvements. As will be shown later, the desire for these benefits persists as strongly as ever. The point is, however, that this desire now stems from higher need activation. Money can satisfy more than just the physiological needs.)

On the other hand, research suggests that dissatisfaction with the extent of gratification of (1) safety, (2) social, and (3) self-esteem needs—in approximately that order—has motivated many workers to join unions. To a lesser extent, status and self-fulfillment needs have also led to union membership.

❖ Safety Needs

Unions are uniquely equipped, in the eyes of thousands of workers, to gratify safety needs. If very few of the 200,000 labor–management contracts currently in force in the United States are identical, at least this much can be said for virtually all of them: They are generally arrived at through *compromise*, and they define in writing the "rules of the game" that have been *mutually agreed upon* to cover the terms and conditions of employment of *all* represented workers for a specific future period of time. The union thus acts as an equal partner in the bilateral establishment of what has been called a "system of industrial jurisprudence." And in the interests of minimizing conflict among the workers it represents, it strives to inject uniformity of treatment—particularly in the area of job protection—into the contract.

Union membership can consequently provide workers with some assurance against arbitrary management actions. The union can be expected to push for curbs against what it calls "management discrimination and favoritism" in, for example, job assignment, promotional opportunity, and even continued employment. However well-meaning are a management's intentions, the employer cannot guarantee that it will not at times act arbitrarily, for in the absence of such checks as the union places on its actions, it is always acting unilaterally. Satisfaction of the safety needs—in the form of considerable protection against arbitrary deprivation, danger, and threat—is thus offered by the union in its stress on uniformity of treatment for all workers. Many employees, particularly after they have perceived arbitrary action by management representatives, have found the appeal irresistible.

❖ Social Needs

The social needs are also known to be important, if secondary, motivators of union membership. Especially where the work itself must be performed in geographically scattered locations (as in many forms of railroad employment, truck driving, or letter carrying) or where the technology of the work minimizes on-the-job social interaction (as on the automobile assembly line), the local union can serve the function of a club, allowing the formation of close friendships built around a common purpose. But even when the work is not so structured, local unions foster a feeling of identification with those of like interests, often in pronounced contrast to the impersonality of the large organization in which the worker may be employed. Increasingly, unions have capitalized on their ability to help satisfy social needs. As the latter have become more important to members of the labor force (not only because of the declining frustration of the lower needs but also because general leisure time has increased), unions have become increasingly ambitious in sponsoring such activities as vacation retreats, athletic facilities, and adult education programs for members only. But unions have never been reluctant to publicize the social bonds they allow: It is not by accident that internal union correspondence has traditionally been closed by the greeting "Fraternally yours," that the official titles of many unions have always included the word "Brotherhood," and that several labor organizations continue to refer to their local unions as "lodges."

Exhibit 1-4, drawn from the major publications of three different unions, shows some of this potential togetherness. National Association of Letter Carriers members can retire to a large union-administered Florida retirement village; members of Local 1199 Health and Human Service Employees members can apply to send their children to a members-only summer camp; and although Mine Workers—such as those shown here with their families wearing anti–global warming treaty shirts—hardly hold a monopoly on union-sponsored picnics, they can typically count on attending several such events every year if they are so inclined.

Social pressure has also been instrumental in causing workers to join unions. Employees often admit that the disapproval of their colleagues would result from their not signing union application cards. Normally, the disapproval is only implied. One study, for example, unearthed such explanations from workers who had joined unions as "I can't think of a good reason, except everybody else was in it," and "I suppose I joined in order to jump in line with the majority." On occasion, however, the pressure has been considerably more visible, as evident in this quotation from the same study: "They approached you, kept after you, hounded you. To get them off my neck, I joined."[22]

❖ Higher Needs

Other workers, at higher levels, have explained their union membership as being attributable mainly to their desire to ensure that they will have a direct voice, through union election procedures, in decisions that affect them in their working environment. Such employees tend to participate actively in union affairs and to

EXHIBIT 1-4

Above: Mary Lou and Bob Huber (r.) and Jane and John Burbrish give their food orders to Lisa at Nalcrest's restaurant, which provides residents with an easy and tasty alternative to cooking.

Below: Retirees look forward to the weekly visits of the produce truck. A small market is also located in Nalcrest.

NALCREST
SNAPSHOTS

- Located in Central Florida on Route 60, midway between Tampa on the Gulf Coast and Vero Beach on the Atlantic Coast.

- 500 garden-style apartments arranged in clusters of four to 10 apartments, all on ground level.

- Monthly rents are $256 for efficiencies, $271 for one-bedrooms and $287 for two bedrooms (no two-bedroom apartments are expected to be available in the foreseeable future). Apartments are leased unfurnished on a yearly basis.

- Rental fee includes water, sewage, trash removal, basic cable TV, interior and exterior maintenance, and use of all recreational facilities.

- Residents must be retired and healthy enough to take care of normal housekeeping chores. No pets allowed.

- For information and an application, contact the Nalcrest office at P.O. Box 6359, Nalcrest, FL 33856-6359 or call 941-696-1121.

Above: Residents check their mailbox daily in the Nalcrest Post Office, home of the 33856 zip code.

Nalcrest, Florida

Photo: H.R. Oakman

Above: Nalcrest General Manager Jerry Kane (r.) stops to chat with Bob Richmond in Nalcrest's fitness center, which sports the motto, "Don't quit—keep fit."

Left: Aerial view of the Central Florida community, which is surrounded by 150 acres of undeveloped land.

SOURCE: *Postal Record*, March 1999, p. 20.

EXHIBIT 1-4

(continued)

SOURCE: *1199 News*, November 1999, p. 23.

Apply Now For Summer Camp Programs

Get ready for next summer!

This year the 1199 Benefit Fund's Anne Shore Camp program sent some 600 1199 kids on three to four-week stays at sleepaway camps throughout New York, New Jersey and New England. The program, open to kids aged six to 15, is free of charge. If you want your child to attend camp next summer, fill out the 1199 Benefit Fund Summer Camp coupon below. Mail it back no later than Jan. 28, 2000.

In a separate program, 1199's Home Care Benefit Fund sent over 125 eligible members' kids to camp. Home care members should fill out the 1199 Home Care Summer Camp Program coupon below and return it no later than Feb. 28, 2000.

1199 CAMP APPLICATION FORM 2000
THIS IS A THREE AND FOUR WEEK SLEEPAWAY CAMP.
Member's
Name_____
SS#_____
Address_____
City_____ State_____ Zip_____
Home phone_____ Work Phone_____
Employed at_____ Job title_____
Shift Worked_____
Child's Name_____
Age as of 7/1/2000_____
School_____ Div (Check one): Drug__ Hosp__ Guild__ RN__
Camper (check one): New__ Repeat__ What Years?__
Please print all information and return separate coupon for each child, postmarked no later than Jan. 28, 2000 to: 1199 National Benefit Fund, Anne Shore Camp Program, P.O. Box 955, N.Y., N.Y. 10108-0955.

1199 HOME CARE SUMMER CAMP PROGRAM
Only Home Care Members Should Use this Coupon
Member's
Name_____
SS#_____
Address_____
City_____ State_____ Zip_____
Home phone_____ Work Phone_____
Employed at_____ Job title_____
Shift Worked_____
Child's Name_____
Age as of 7/1/2000_____
Camper: New_____ Repeat (If yes, which years?)_____
Please print all answers and return to 1199 Home Care Benefit Fund Camp Program, 330 West 42nd St., 8th floor, N.Y., N.Y. 10036. Only one child per family is eligible. Postmark must be no later than Feb. 28, 2000.

EXHIBIT 1-4

(continued)

SOURCE: *United Mine Workers Journal,* November–December 1998. Credit: Greg Young, United Mine Workers of America.

use rather freely such phrases as "I wanted to have a voice in the system." The underlying rationale of this behavior is a clear one: Managements do not normally put questions relating to employment conditions to worker vote; unions, however imperfectly, purport to be democratic institutions. To these workers, representation by a labor organization has appeared to offer the best hope in our complex, interdependent, and ever-larger-unit industrial society that their human dignity will not be completely crushed. On this basis, self-esteem needs can, at least to some extent, be appeased.

Finally, a relatively few other employees have found in the union an opportunity for realization of their highest needs—for status and self-fulfillment. They have joined with the hope of gaining and retaining positions of authority within the union officer hierarchy. For the employee with leadership ambitions, but with educational or other deficiencies that would otherwise condemn that employee to a life of prestige-lacking and unchallenging work, opportunities for further need satisfaction are provided.

Unionization, then, results from a broad network of worker needs. The needs for safety, social affiliation, and, to a lesser extent, self-esteem appear to be of primary importance to employees in the contemporary United States. And it would appear that these needs are being relatively well met by unions, or workers would have exercised their legally granted option of voting out unions in far greater measure than they have done.

This in no way minimizes the role of money and other economic benefits, for these—which unions have not been reluctant to seek, even with their members' incomes at today's high levels—are, as noted earlier, clearly related to needs beyond the physiological. Health insurance and pensions lend protection against deprivation, for example, and wages themselves can increase not only safety but status. But it does emphasize the role of protection against arbitrary treatment, formal group affiliation beyond the framework of the employing organization, and—for some workers—an opportunity for participation in the system. By definition, management can never itself satisfy either of the first two worker needs. Thus far, in unionized establishments, it has failed to satisfy employees on the last ground.

WHY MANAGERS RESIST UNIONS

Some time ago, after years of successfully withstanding union organization attempts, a small-scale New York City dress manufacturer discovered that a majority of his workers had finally become union members. Immediately thereafter, these employees struck for increased job security and improved pension benefits. On the very first morning of the strike, the manufacturer's wife—who was also the firm's bookkeeper—reported to work at her customary hour of 8 A.M. She was amazed to see her husband out on the picket line, addressing the strikers as follows: "Sam, you stand over there; Harry, you stand eight yards in back of Sam; and Leo, you come over here, eight yards behind Harry." The puzzled woman posed the natural question, "Jack, what on earth are you doing?" And the manufacturer replied, "I want they should right away know who's boss!"

The outcome of this particular labor–management struggle is unknown. But the episode nonetheless furnishes a clue as to one reason why managers are considerably less than enthusiastic about unions. As we have already seen, collective bargaining necessarily decreases the area of management discretion. Every contractual concession to the union subtracts from the scope that the management has for taking action on its own. As E. Wight Bakke observed many years ago, "A union is an employer-regulating device. It seeks to regulate the discretion of employers . . . at every point where their action affects the welfare of the men."[23] Yet it is the manager, not the union, who tends to be held ultimately responsible for the success or failure of the business. Hence, employers feel it essential that they reserve for themselves the authority to make all major decisions, including those the union might construe to be affecting "the welfare of the men." In short, they feel that they must still be allowed to remain, on all counts, "the boss."

Behind such a sentiment is a managerial awareness, continuously reinforced for all administrators of profit-making institutions by day-to-day realities, that management hardly owes its exclusive allegiance to its employees. Clearly, employee needs are important and, for that matter, can be ignored for any length of time only with complete disregard for the continued solvency of the enterprise. But exactly the same can be said of the pressures exerted on management by the firm's customers, stockholders, competitors, and suppliers. Were these pressures not opposing ones, management's job would be far easier than it is. But because there are so many points of conflict, an aggressive union can make the managerial role a highly difficult one.

The desire to retain decision-making authority is by no means, however, strictly attributable to a managerial desire for peace of mind. Unions undoubtedly do add to the personal unhappiness and consequent morale problems of managers, but the resistance to unionism is often based also on a genuine and deep concern for the welfare of society. Countless managers believe that only if management remains free to operate without union-imposed restrictions can U.S. business continue to advance. And only through such progress, they believe, can it provide employment for our rapidly growing labor force, let this nation compete successfully in world markets, and increase general living standards. By decreasing managerial flexibility (in the form of work-method controls, decreased workloads, increased stress on the seniority criterion in the allocation of labor, and various other ways), it is argued, unions endanger the efficiency upon which continued industrial progress depends.

Admittedly, even in the absence of unionism, management's ability to make decisions in the employee-relations area is not an unlimited one. A widespread network of federal, state, and community legislation now governs minimum wages, hours of work, discrimination, safety and health, and a host of other aspects of employee life with complete impartiality as to whether the regulated firms are organized or nonunion. Moreover, where employers encounter tight labor markets (those in which new employees are difficult to recruit), they tend to accommodate at least their more visible personnel practices—wages and other economic benefits, in particular—to what the market demands. Finally, the prevalent values of our times must always be considered. It is a hallmark of our ever more sophisticated society that workers expect to be governed by progressive personnel policies that are based on objective standards whenever possible. Most nonunion firms have attempted to conform to these values no less actively than have most unionized enterprises.

The fact remains, however, that managers who are not bound by the restrictions of labor agreements, and who do not have to anticipate the possibility of their every action in the employee relations sphere being challenged by worker representatives through the grievance procedure have considerably more latitude for decision making than do their counterparts at unionized places.

If the previous paragraphs help to explain the major reasons for management's jaundiced view of the labor union, they do not acknowledge other reasons that frequently bolster this view. There are, undoubtedly, several such reasons.

In the first place, many employers tend to look upon the union as an *outsider*, with no justifiable basis for interfering in the relationship between the management and its employees. The local union, with which the management is most apt to engage in direct dealings, typically represents workers of many competitive enterprises, and hence by definition it cannot have the best interests of any particular management at heart. Worse yet, runs this charge, the local is often part of a large, geographically distant international or national union, by which it is closely controlled, and thus is not allowed to give adequate consideration to unique problems within its locality.[24] Beyond this, the union (whether local, international, or some intermediate body) has objectives and aspirations that are very different from those of the particular employer: Where the latter seeks to maximize profits within certain limits, the union seeks such goals as the maximization of its own membership and of its general bargaining power.

Second, the manager may look upon the union as a *troublemaker*, bent upon building cleavages between management and workers where none would otherwise exist. Even aside from the previously noted fact that the union grievance procedure allows all management actions affecting areas delineated in the labor contract to be challenged and therefore regularly provides an opportunity for controversy that is normally absent in nonunion situations, there is some truth in this charge. Particularly where the union occupies an insecure status (in the absence, for example, of the **union shop**), its leaders may find it essential to solicit grievances in order to keep the employees willing to pay union dues. But even where the labor organization does have such security, grievances may still be encouraged by union officials, and for several logical reasons: Ongoing grievances can later be dropped in return for management concessions; individual union leaders can point to a record of effective grievance handling as they seek to rise within the union hierarchy; and unpopular managers can be displaced if *their* superiors are sufficiently uneasy about high grievance rates within their units. And, of course, union representatives may simply prefer to have management—or, if need be, an arbitrator—deny the grievance rather than do it themselves: Managers and arbitrators do not have to stand for reelection and can more easily afford to incur worker wrath.

Third, many managers view unions as *underminers of employee loyalty*. In order to understand this point of view, one does not have to fully embrace the philosophy that high worker motivation levels depend on appreciative employees who view the employer as a benefactor and work for him or her to a great extent out of gratitude. It is sufficient to imagine the reactions of employers who have prided themselves on providing good wages and working conditions and showing a personal concern for the individual problems of their employees upon learning that a majority of their workforce has suddenly decided to "go union." These employers may use such epithets as "ingrates" in speaking of their own employees, but it is more likely that the union itself will bear the brunt of the censure. It is human nature to attribute one's defeats to forces beyond one's own control (an irresponsible union misleading our employees and turning them against management) rather than to factors looked upon as controllable (employee attitudes). The previously cited fact that management can *never* itself provide either full protection against arbitrary treatment or formal group affiliation independent of the employer is overlooked by managers at such moments. So, too, is a silver lining in the situation-namely, that it is entirely possible for workers to have dual loyalties, to the union *and* to the employer.[25]

A fourth root of tension may arise simply because the previously discussed *reputation* of the labor movement has preceded the arrival of unionism in the place. This has been a particularly influential factor in the resistance of some managers to collective bargaining in the recent past. Not being forced to deal with a union until now and, primarily because of this freedom, knowing little more about labor unions than they have been told by the media, such relatively unsophisticated employers have been alarmed by the widely publicized reports of irresponsible union strikes, union-leader criminality, and featherbedding charges that have found their way onto newspaper front pages and television screens over the past decades. These managers have asked, in effect, "How can you expect us to welcome an institution whose representatives engage in such activities?" To them, the old joke, "'How many Teamsters does it take to screw in a light bulb?' 'Ten. You got a problem with that?'" is anchored to a solid foundation of fact.

Fifth, and rounding out the list of major causes of the executive's opposition to organized labor, are the *major values of the labor movement* as these are perceived by management. Some of these values—a stress on seniority, work-method controls, and decreased workloads—have already been mentioned in the context of threats to decision making. There are, however, many other such shared union values that bother management at least as much.

Security, for example, has far more favorable connotations to unionists than it does to employer representatives. Higher managers by definition have a history of successful achievement behind them and hence are willing to take chances because they are relatively optimistic as to the outcome. The average union member, feeling that the probabilities of success in risk taking are low, and, indeed, often believing that he or she is running in a race that is fixed, presses the union leadership to obtain even greater protection in the current job.

Democracy is a hallmark of the union value structure, and union representatives who bargain with managements are usually elected, as indicated, through a process that at least claims to be democratic. Managers whose hierarchy is based on merit and experience are thus forced to bargain, often on issues with major ramifications for the organization, with unionists who may have no better credentials for their role than the possession of a plurality of votes in a popularity poll.

And where the management representative speaks glowingly of individualism and declares that America's economic triumphs have been based on it, the union sees itself as part of a social movement and places a premium on group consciousness.

As for efficiency, which scores high on the management scale of values, to the union it smacks of a callous disregard for worker dignity and even worker health. Accordingly, it is something to be regarded with deep suspicion by employee representatives and to be resisted whenever resistance is practicable.

LABOR RELATIONS CONSULTANTS

Increasingly, in recent years, employers have succumbed to an urge to use labor relations consultants, who are usually either lawyers or psychologists, to prevent a union from gaining bargaining rights or to get rid of an established union through a decertification election (about which more will be said in Chapter 3).

Informed estimates place the number of such consulting firms at an absolute minimum of 1,000, with at least five times that number of individuals directly involved in what unions bitterly call "union busting" and many employers contend is merely the providing of assistance to employees who genuinely want a nonunion environment. The AFL-CIO itself believes that a staggering 75 percent of all managements now turn to these consultants expressly to gain help in thwarting unionization and that they pay them over $100 million each year. Others would place these latter figures at lower, although still significant, levels.

Some members of this new growth industry at times advise their employer clients to engage in activities that are quite illegal under national labor policy, such as placing agents in the workplace to spy on employees; harassing and discharging union members; avoiding the hiring of blacks (who are—in the opinion of at least one practitioner in this line of work—"more prone to unionization than whites"); and initiating decertification elections. Others guide managements in engaging in bad-faith, uncompromising bargaining so as to provoke a strike in which the employer can replace unionized employees with a nonunion workforce.

Some labor relations consultants are also adept at helping their management clients thwart union organizing drives by the blunt device of firing workers who seem to be particularly active in such drives. Even if the union takes such cases to court, time is definitely on the employer's side here. The cases can, with appeals, take up to five years for resolution, and even with an ultimate union victory the dismissed workers may no longer be available to return to their jobs. One-on-one meetings with workers and arguments that a union is an unnecessary third party will also often frustrate a union-organizing drive.

Consultants also have been known to suggest to relevant clients that a company that purchases another company can legally get around recognizing the seller's union simply by hiring less than a majority of the seller's employees. And their expertise is also at times provided to employers who wish to legally move their unionized work to their nonunion facilities (some of which have been newly created for just this purpose). Given the current state of labor relations law, as Chapter 3 will explain in much more detail, consultants have a wide area of lawful tactics and strategies to place at their clients' disposal and by no means need move beyond what public policy allows in order to be effective.

In addition to providing such personalized services, some consultants hold seminars open to all comers for a fee. Favored topics here are "Making Unions Unnecessary," "Avoiding Unions," and "Putting the Union Organizer on the Defensive." Members of the profession also produce a wide variety of articles, books, and cassettes that find a lucrative market among antiunion managements. For at least some of the consultants, it's nice work if you can get it: Six-figure annual incomes are not at all uncommon in this specialized, controversial field. Seven-figure incomes have been attained.

Exhibit 1-5 summarizes the far-from-subtle thoughts of one union—the Federation of Nurses and Health Professionals, a division of the American Federation of Teachers—regarding the recent experiences of some of its members with "union-busters."

LABOR RELATIONS IN THE PUBLIC SECTOR

If the unionized percentage of the total civilian labor force has registered some definite slippage in recent years, and if the figures from the overall white-collar frontier in the recent past can be described as essentially unchanged, organized labor can point with satisfaction to its organizational successes in the fastest-growing employment sector of all, that of the public employee.

In 1940, according to the official figures of the U.S. Department of Labor, the nation's governmental workforce at all levels (federal, state, and local) numbered 4.2 million, or 9.6 percent of total payroll employment. By 1960, the figure had exactly doubled, to 8.4 million. And, rising even more dramatically when compared with overall labor force figures, it reached the 12.5 million mark by the end of the 1960s. By 1976, it had climbed to almost 15 million (and over 18 percent of total payroll employment in the country), although this was to be its high-water mark for many years. After the late 1970s, negative reaction from the taxpayers to the rapid growth caused the figures to hit a plateau for a while, albeit in no way to decrease. By 1999, there were about 18 million such workers.

No reliable figures for union membership among government employees are available for the period before 1956, when civil servants in the Bureau of Labor Statistics (BLS) began collecting this kind of data. But where the BLS's information reveals 915,000 governmental unionists in 1956 (heavily concentrated in the federal service, and particularly among its postal, shipyard, and arsenal employees), the same agency reported almost 1.5 million organized workers only eight years later, and by 1999 was estimating that about 7.2 million public employees—widely distributed throughout all levels of government and embracing a spectrum that included such disparate types as engineers, zookeepers, firefighters, jail guards, teachers, sewage workers, and common laborers—were in union ranks.

Thus, it should come as no surprise that the greatest rate of growth in the entire labor movement has occurred among unions that represent, either exclusively or primarily, public employees. The American Federation of State, County, and Municipal Employees (AFSCME), gaining 1,000 new members a week in recent

EXHIBIT 1-5

Jersey nurses win fight to organize

Cooper Hospital hired some of the most skillful union-busters in the country but they could not intimidate these nurses.

■ THE COMPUTERS SAID, "NO" BUT the people said, "Yes." That's how the union organizing drive at Cooper Hospital in Camden, N.J., ended last summer as nurses voted 370 to 269 to join the Health Professionals and Allied Employees/FNHP/AFT. A week before the election, management put "Vote No" on the nurses' computer screens—including those next to patient care areas where campaigning was not supposed to take place. Some nurses asked that the screen say simply, "Vote" but managers wouldn't go along. One enterprising nurse then created a screen saver that said "HPAE - Vote Yes," but that was taken down and "Vote No" stayed on the screens until the election, as if trying to hypnotize the nurses into following orders. It didn't work.

The victory at Cooper, one of the most prominent hospitals in southern New Jersey, was the latest in a string of organizing victories for HPAE. The union has grown from 5,000 members in 1996 to 8,000 today.

Last spring, 225 nurses at Meadowlands Hospital in Secaucus, N.J., joined the union, followed in June by 50 technicians.

Cooper Hospital put on a maximum effort to block the nurses' effort to organize, hiring one of the leading union-busting firms in the country: Adams, Nash and Haskell. The union estimates that management spent $2 million in its unsuccessful effort.

Many nurses felt it was typical of management's patronizing attitude to think that the nurses would be swayed by seeing "No" on their computer screens. "It's like they think I don't have a mind of my own," says Jean Lucas, a nurse in the intermediate maternal care unit who was active in the organizing committee.

A few days before the election, management mailed every nurse an anti-union video containing remarks like "There are no such things as unfair labor acts. Actually, I think employees have more rights than employers."

The story of the new union at Cooper Hospital, like many in health care, goes back to the mid-1990s when administrators, in response to managed care cutbacks, started reducing staff. Perhaps if they had involved the staff in finding ways to cope with the hospital's financial problems, things could have been different. Instead, they assigned more patients to each nurse, cut safety margins and started pulling nurses from one department to another to make up for shortages. Lucas remembers one 12-hour shift when she worked in four different departments. "I barely had a chance to introduce myself to a patient before I was whisked away and pulled somewhere else," she says.

Laura Spath, an intensive care unit nurse, suddenly found herself pulled to neonatal intensive care one day. "How helpful was I? Not very. I fed babies. I know very little about the work they do there."

Finally last summer, Cooper nurses asked HPAE for help in forming a union. The organizing moved slowly and deliberately at first, with dozens of small meetings of just a few people so everyone had plenty of time to talk. In March, 325 nurses signed a "mission statement" explaining why they were forming a union. Two months later, the nurses gave the National Labor Relations Board union cards from a large majority of the nurses and asked for an election.

Management responded with a state-of-the-art union-busting campaign that included high-pressure one-on-one meetings between nurses and their supervisors, compulsory group sessions and mailings about the dangers of unions in addition to the "Vote No" screen and the video.

But the nurses' organizing committee had prepared for the onslaught. They had held more than 50 meetings with small groups of nurses where everyone had plenty of time to talk about hopes and fears and find out what it would mean to have a union. The union busters found these nurses were not easily intimidated.

"Cooper was a major victory," says HPAE president Ann Twomey. "It's one of the largest and most prestigious hospitals in New Jersey, providing critical care and trauma services for the entire state. The Cooper nurses overcame immense obstacles to organize. They will help us all be more effective in fighting for quality patient care."

Despite the union's strong winning margin, the hospital has refused to start bargaining and instead has appealed to the NLRB to overturn the election.

But the nurses have already elected a negotiating committee and conducted surveys to determine bargaining priorities. The pro-union nurses formed a committee to reach out to those on the other side. Several former opponents have gotten involved in the preparations for negotiations.

Jean Lucas says life at the hospital is already better. She says that there's less friction between departments because nurses know each other and understand each department's special problems. "Just the unionizing process has brought people together," she says. "There's a new camaraderie. I'm talking to people I never talked to in 17 years."

SANDRA FELDMAN president, FNHP/AFT
TRISH GORMAN editorial department director
ROGER S. GLASS editor
PRISCILLA NEMETH managing editor (on leave)
ALAIN JEHLEN acting managing editor
MARY POWER BOYD senior associate editor
LAURA BAKER copy editor
JONI KETTER contributing editor
CHARLES GLENDINNING art director
SHARON WRIGHT production manager
SHARON FRANCOUR production support
SHAWNITRA JOHNSON production support
BARBARA TOBIAS production support

Healthwire (USPS 011536) is published six times a year—January/February; March/April; May/June; July/August; September/October; November/December by the Federation of Nurses and Health Professionals, a division of the American Federation of Teachers, 555 New Jersey Ave., N.W., Washington, DC 20001-2079
Telephone: 202/879-4491
Editorial: 202/879-4430.
http://www.aft.org
on AOL, keyword AFT
Letters to the editor are welcome.

Periodical postage paid at Washington, D.C.

POSTMASTER: Send address changes to: *Healthwire*, 555 New Jersey Ave., N.W., Washington, DC 20001-2079

Healthwire is mailed to all health care members of the AFT. Annual subscription price: $2.25 is included in membership and available only as a part of membership.

HEALTH *Wire*

WINNER

APEX '97
AWARDS FOR PUBLICATION EXCELLENCE

years and up to a total membership of some 1.2 million by 1999, as noted earlier (from only 210,000 in 1961), has until quite recently been the fastest-growing union in the nation. An almost comparable success story has been registered by the American Federation of Teachers, which increased (as also noted earlier) from 60,000 members in 1960 to 700,000 four decades later. And the labor movement can also take considerable encouragement from the octupling of members recorded by the American Federation of Government Employees during the 1960s and 1970s, although the size of this organization—with little growth in its primary potential membership market of defense installations—has not shown this level of expansion in more recent years. In 1999, it had about 200,000 members.

Even these statistics understate the degree of recent union penetration of the public sector, however. It was generally estimated at the time of this writing that at least another 3.5 million employees belonged to professional and civil service associations that were outside the official ranks of organized labor but in many cases distinguishable from bona fide unions only by their titles. Into this latter category would certainly fall the fast-growing and increasingly militant 2.2 million-member National Education Association, the heavy majority of whose members are now covered by collective bargaining agreements. So, too, would the Assembly of Government Employees (with an estimated strength of over 600,000 members in various state employee subunits), the American Nurses Association (representing the interests of almost 225,000 employees), and the Fraternal Order of Police (with over 150,000 members), all of these also having shown rapid rises in organizational size over the past few years.

One must freely acknowledge that organized labor still has a long way to go before its penetration of the public sector can be deemed to be anywhere near complete. Using only official union-membership figures, one can deduce that the 7.2 million unionized public employees constitute about 40 percent of the total membership potential. And even if all 3.5 million association members are included (and, as indicated earlier, not all of them should be, since an indeterminate although doubtless minority percentage of them are not bargained for collectively), the figure still comes to not much more than about 55 percent of the total public-sector employee population. It constitutes, in fact, the lowest percentage for public employees for any nation west of Germany and is significantly lower than the comparable statistics for Great Britain, Sweden, Norway, and Denmark (where over 75 percent of these employees are unionized), and even for our immediate neighbor to the north, Canada, where two-thirds of the public-sector workforce belongs to unions. But the gains of the recent past are nonetheless highly impressive and deserve exploration.

THE GROWTH OF PUBLIC-SECTOR UNIONISM: SOME EXPLANATIONS

In all likelihood, three factors have been particularly responsible for this new union thrust in the public sector.

❖ Legal Deveopments

First and probably foremost, *legal developments* since 1960 have given organized labor both a protection and an encouragement that were previously conspicuous by their absence. At the federal level, a highly influential event was President John F.

Kennedy's 1962 issuance of **Executive Order 10988**, constituting the first recognition ever on the part of the federal government that its employees were entitled to join unions and bargain collectively with the executive agencies for which they worked. Three types of union recognition were provided—informal, formal, and exclusive—depending on the percentage of employees in the bargaining unit represented by the union. And, if the latter could gain exclusive recognition (by showing that it represented at least 10 percent of the employees involved and then being selected or designated by a majority of employees within the bargaining unit), the employing agency was compelled to meet and confer regularly with such a union on matters affecting personnel policy and practices and working conditions.

The order did remove many key topics from the scope of this collective bargaining—among them, mandatory union membership, agency budgetary negotiations, and new technology—and it had certain deficiencies in the dispute-settlement area (in case of a bargaining impasse, should mediation efforts fail, the only available procedure was an appeal to a higher level of the agency's own management). But E. O. 10988, nonetheless, by attempting to provide organizational and bargaining rights for employees of the federal government in essentially the same way as these rights had been established for employees in the private sector almost three decades earlier by the Wagner Act, provided a significant stimulus to union growth not just in the federal employee province but, in short order, also at the state and local government levels. E. O. 10988 was the Magna Carta. Workers joined relevant governmental unions in droves.

The White House, moreover, liberalized its treatment of unions a very few years later. Richard M. Nixon's **Executive Order 11491**, effective as of January 1, 1970, abolished both informal and formal union recognition on the grounds that these two types had proved to have had little meaning. It provided, instead, that any union could gain exclusive recognition if selected by a majority of the bargaining unit employees in a secret-ballot election. It also created a three-member Federal Labor Relations Council to decide major policy matters and to administer and interpret the order itself, substituting these officials for the large potpourri of department heads who had handled—often quite inconsistently—these activities under E. O. 10988. And it gave the assistant secretary of labor for labor-management relations authority to settle disputes over the makeup of bargaining units and representation rights and to order and supervise elections: These matters had been handled by the particular federal agency involved.

E. O. 11491 also established an impartial Federal Services Impasses Panel to settle disputes arising during contract negotiations, by final and binding arbitration if necessary. As stated earlier, the old order had provided for no such impartial procedure in the case of bargaining deadlocks (except for mediation), effectively placing unions at the ultimate mercy of the federal agency with which they were negotiating (and, thus, allowing one labor leader to compare the whole process to "a football game in which one side brings along the referee"). Because federal employees lack the right to strike, the new system for arbitration by neutrals seemed both equitable and realistic.

For all this liberalization contained in E. O. 11491, Congress in 1979 enacted a law that supplanted it. For many years, indeed since President Kennedy's original executive order, the government unions had pressured Congress to provide a *statutory* basis for the federal labor relations program, and their persistence paid off when Congress enacted the Civil Service Reform Act of 1978, Title VII of which superseded E. O. 11491 in January of the following year. Though it carried forward the basic rights and duties of federal employees and agencies as contained in the executive order, it made a number of important changes in the federal labor relations program. Functions formerly performed by the Federal Labor Relations Council and the assistant secretary of labor were lodged in an independent **Federal Labor Relations Authority (FLRA)**. In large measure, the FLRA duplicates the functions of the National Labor Relations Board, which has jurisdiction in the private sector. By protecting the tenure of the members of the FLRA, and by making it independent from any existing federal agency, the law placed the new agency in a better position to administer objectively and effectively.

The new law also made a number of substantive changes. It expanded the scope of matters subject to negotiated grievance and arbitration procedures including, for the first time, employee discharge, demotion, and long-term suspensions. Upon a union's request, the federal agency involved is required to deduct dues of its members provided the employees sign the necessary dues checkoff authorization cards. And to balance the scales, official time (work time) may be used by employees representing the union in negotiations (including attendance at impasse-settlement proceedings) to the extent that management officials are on paid time.

At the state level, although the influence of the developments in Washington can be clearly detected, the trend toward giving legal protection to civil servants in their efforts to organize and bargain collectively has been even more pronounced. Prior to the enactment of the Kennedy order, only one state, Wisconsin in 1959, had extended such a right to public employees. By the time of this writing, virtually all other states had sanctioned collective bargaining for at least some types of public workers. Indeed, some 40 of them had enacted legislation conferring such protection upon all (or almost all) state and local employees, and laws in eight states (Alaska, Hawaii, Minnesota, Montana, Oregon, Pennsylvania, Vermont, and Wisconsin) even allowed—in different degrees—some strikes. Court decisions in three other states (Michigan, New Hampshire, and Rhode Island) had also effectively made the strike weapon a viable tool for some public workers in those jurisdictions.

And no signs of a reversal of either this trend or the significant increase in state and local employee-union membership that it has generated are on the horizon.

❖ The Lag of the Remuneration Package

A second factor behind the explosion in public-sector unionism has been the public servant's increasing unhappiness as the *remuneration package has fallen* further and further *behind* that of private employment. Wages in the two sectors had historically been quite comparable, but by the mid-1960s the gap, even going beyond that of the general union—nonunion discrepancy already touched on in this chapter, was fully in evidence. In general, public employees in these years earned from 10 to 30 percent less than their exact counterparts (whether these were electricians, laborers, stock clerks, or secretaries) in private industry, who perhaps worked down the street from them.

Even more jarring to the civil servants, however, was the lag in working conditions underpinning this wage package, since these conditions had for years been far *superior* in the public sector. For their traditionally comparable pay, the public servants had been asked to work shorter hours (with appreciably more liberal holiday and vacation entitlements than their private counterparts), had been given a degree of job security that almost no other workers possessed, and could look forward to a pension entitlement that in most instances would dwarf that of private-industry employees—if, in fact, the latter even had a pension expectation. By the 1960s, all these relative advantages had eroded, as public-sector fringe benefits and working conditions saw little further liberalization, while these areas in private industry first caught up with and then slowly eclipsed the public emoluments. If the public employees were not completely disgruntled in the face of this development, they were certainly—to paraphrase P. G. Wodehouse—a long distance from being gruntled. Increasingly, they turned to their newly legalized avenue of collective bargaining to redress what was viewed as a clear injustice.

❖ The Spirit of the Times

Third, and finally, one cannot disregard the *general spirit of the times* in explaining the rise of public unionism. These same growth years were at least initially marked throughout American society by a degree of social upheaval rare in the nation's history. No part of the established order was seemingly immune from attack, as blacks, Hispanics, women, gays, student activists, an increasingly broad spectrum of citizens opposed to the Vietnam War, and even older people organized—often militantly—to exert in support of their respective causes a collective pressure that could hardly be overlooked. The results were generally mixed. But sufficient progress was certainly made to bring home to many public employees who had avoided organization until that point the advantages to be gained by collective action.

❖ Other Possible Explanations

To this trio of key explanations, readers might care to add others of their choosing: the increasing vulnerability to unionization of many public-sector managers because of archaic personnel policies; a fear on the part of government workers in the latter, inflation-dominated years of this period that their jobs would be the first to be eliminated in the face of growing taxpayer resistance to the higher costs of public administration; the changing complexion of the government workforce itself, with an ever-higher percentage of younger and often more aggressive jobholders; and perhaps the sheer numerical growth in public employees, making them a more tempting target for the union organizer. In any case, however, the reasons for the successes of labor in the public-employee arena appear at the very least to have been understandable. As such, they seem destined to continue, certainly for a while.

THE PUBLIC-EMPLOYEE UNIONIST: THE STRIKE ISSUE

"If you treat public employees bad enough," said George Meany in 1974, on the occasion of the founding convention of the AFL-CIO's new Public Employee Department, "they'll go on strike and they'll get the support of the union movement." Meany, a man rarely accused of mincing words, also told the same audience that public workers involved in labor disputes should feel free to strike "any damn time you feel like going on strike."[26] This was not the first time that year that the (then) AFL-CIO chief executive had registered these sentiments. Nor did he depart from the views expressed by many other, if less influential, labor chieftains in advancing them. But the setting this time—the new department symbolized the conquests of the recent past by uniting under its aegis 24 AFL-CIO–affiliated unions representing more than 2 million workers—gave a special impact to his words.

Ironically, had Meany said exactly the same thing only a few years earlier, he would very likely have been either publicly vilified as a nihilistic demagogue or dismissed as a droll master of hyperbole (this being the same Meany who on an earlier occasion had offered his observation that "most college professors, when given a choice of publish or perish, tend to make the wrong decision"). For, throughout labor's long history in this country, public policy toward the public-sector strike had been clear, unequivocal, and resoundingly negative. Calvin Coolidge had deemed such work stoppages "anarchy": In a famous statement referring to the 1919 Boston police strike, he had also declared, "There is no right to strike against the public safety by anybody, anywhere, at any time"; Franklin D. Roosevelt had called them "unthinkable"; relevant government regulations (including E. O. 11491) for federal employees had historically banned the public-worker strike; and in the mid-1960s all states prohibited work stoppages of public employees, if not specifically by law at least by court decision. Public-employee organizations themselves showed their general agreement with this constraint by including, in almost all cases, total bans on work stoppages in their own constitutions.

What was past was definitely not prologue in this case, however. If, before 1960, public-sector strikes were all but unknown, and if, even as late as the year 1960, only 36 such strikes were recorded, the 1970 totals showed 412 of them. Strikes in the latter year included an unprecedented previously noted eight-day strike by the nation's postal employees (it was essentially over wages, leading one observer to comment that the government could end the stoppage by giving the strikers their wage increase, but mailing it to them) and another nationwide one by airport flight controllers. (For the National Association of Letter Carriers, its strike was the "defining moment," remembered and boasted of a quarter-century later in that union's major publication. See Exhibit 1-6.)

The trend was accelerating when Meany advanced his views on the subject, and it would not visibly diminish in the later years of the decade. An all-time record of 593 public-employee strikes actually took place in 1979, and as a publication of that year could assert, fairly enough in view of the reality so vividly communicated by the media:

> We may see firemen watching homes burn down as they pursue their labor relations goals, or nurses walking a picket line to achieve proper union recognition. Your local police may suddenly begin giving out traffic tickets for everything as they carry out a planned slowdown. ... Sanitation workers might leave your garbage to pile up in your driveway, or the guards at the correctional facility might decide to withhold their services. It may be the postal employees who become reluctant to handle your mail unless collective bargaining works for them, or the teachers who carry out a strike action to effect an increase. There are a dozen other examples of the criticality of labor relations in the public sector.[27]

Yet the harsh punishments all but universally called for by the various laws were essentially being ignored by civic authorities. (For example, in the federal government, any striker is subject to up to five years in jail plus a fine and dismissal, but as was pointed out in a reference to the postal and flight controllers' stoppages, no striker ever got close to Leavenworth or Joliet, and no striker has since.) It was, indeed, in recognition of this fact—that except in the rarest of instances, the anti-strike laws could be violated with impunity given the political realities—that the several states mentioned earlier had legalized the public strike for at least some workers. And, of potentially great significance, it was because of this awareness also that an increasing number of members of Congress appeared to be in basic agreement with the view of the new AFL-CIO department that *all* public-sector strikes except for those creating a demonstrable peril to the public health should be legalized.

On the other hand, not quite *every* public-sector strike has violated the laws with impunity. When the nation's 11,500 flight controllers waged a second strike 11 years later—in August 1981—President Ronald Reagan aggressively reacted by firing them and also by setting the wheels in motion for their union (**the Professional Air Traffic Controllers Organization, or PATCO**) to be removed as the controllers' legally recognized bargaining representative. PATCO, which displayed surprising ineptness in not trying to win support from other unions in advance of its stoppage and whose major demand (for higher wages than the controllers' current $35,000 to $40,000 annually and for shorter hours) was not one calculated to win much support from outsiders anyhow, was hardly typical in any of its actions. But Reagan's actions were well received by a heavy majority of all Americans, as has already been noted, and some experts thought that future political figures might heed a lesson here and act similarly in the years ahead. (A new union, the National Air Traffic Controllers Association, overwhelmingly won the right to represent the controllers in a 1987 representation election.)

❖ Arguments Regarding the Right to Strike

Whatever happens, the years ahead will presumably see a resolution of the inevitably emotion-laden issue of public-sector strikes. And, given the general ineffectuality of the present strike bans (PATCO notwithstanding), this resolution will quite probably be on the side of the right to strike except for (1) such clearly indispensable civil servants as police officers and firefighters and (2) cases in which the peril to health and safety is otherwise shown to exist; in these cases, most likely, binding arbitration by third parties will be utilized to resolve bargaining impasses.

Supporters of such a development—and in their ranks are many neutrals—contend that this right to strike would only recognize reality. They argue also that only the strike threat can guarantee that public officials will bargain in good faith. And they point out that the many private-sector unionists who perform jobs identical to those in the public arena (for example, transit employees, teachers, and maintenance workers), because they do have the right to strike, possess an inequitable bargaining advantage over their government counterparts.

Arguments on the negative (or antistrike) side focus on these factors: (1) In the private sector, employers can counter the strike weapon with a lockout of their own, but they can hardly do this as government officials, and hence the legalized public strike would create a large labor relations imbalance; (2) public pressures on public officials to end a strike are infinitely greater than those on the private administrators and thus the former are forced to capitulate more quickly, to the ultimate detriment of the community; and (3) the monopolistic nature of virtually all public-sector employment makes almost all of it "essential," and thus the public should be guaranteed against its legalized interruption.

Whatever the merits of these latter contentions and supplementary antistrike ones, the momentum definitely belonged to those taking the other side of the argument as this was being written—ironically, even as a widespread taxpayers' revolt was causing severe budgetary cuts at all levels of government and a definite if decreasing animus on the part of citizens to perceived public-employee excesses was taking a good deal of clout away from public-sector unions.

EXHIBIT 1-6

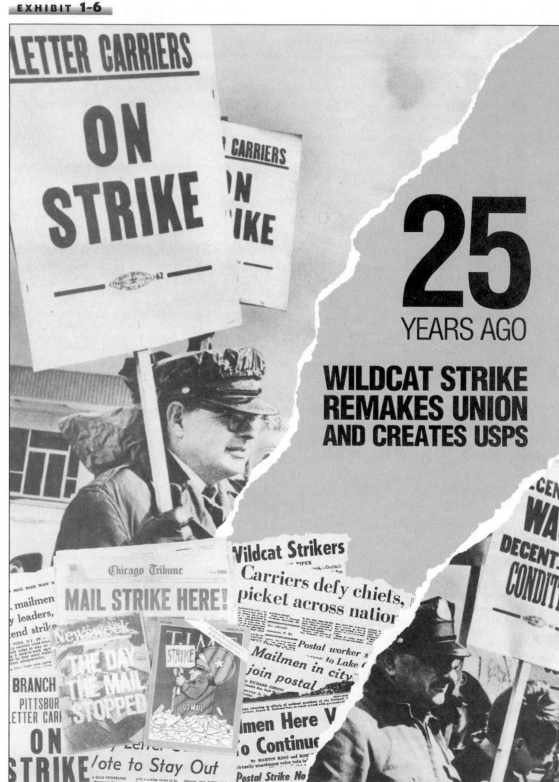

EXHIBIT 1-6 (continued)

THE POSTAL STRIKE OF 1970

MARCH MARKS THE 25th ANNIVERsary of the postal strike of 1970, an act of courage by letter carriers that shines today as the defining moment in NALC's emergence as a modern union dedicated to winning economic security and respect for its members.

First in New York City and then in hundreds of communities across the nation, tens of thousands of rank-and-file union members put their lives and livelihoods on the line—the picket line. Risking their jobs, facing criminal prosecution and jail sentences, letter carriers looked within themselves and found the fortitude to declare they had had enough.

Members of New York City Branch 36 are justly honored as the first to go out and the last to go back to work. Their bravery was a beacon and NALC members from coast to coast rallied to the cause—they, too, were tired of promises, tired of being impoverished, tired of being ignored or taken for granted. And, significantly, other craft employees climbed on board, honoring the wildcat picket lines and ultimately sharing in the fruits of victory—much-deserved pay increases, collective bargaining rights and an honest shot at a decent living.

The nation was stunned by what one columnist called "the revolt of the nice guys." The "dependable men in gray" had done the unthinkable.

As the walkout spread, the economic ripples widened—New York City accounted for 10 percent of the nation's mail—and the very fabric of society seemed at risk.

These "docile servants" had never "raised so much as a pinky in organized protest," one news magazine said. Now the anger was in the streets for all to see.

Letter carriers in Paterson, New Jersey give the victory sign on the first day of walkout, 25 years ago this month.
(UPI photo)

The articles that follow are a heart-felt "thank you" to the many active members and thousands of retirees who made the strike: Thank you for having the courage to take a stand and strengthen a union, and make a better life for more than 300,000 letter carriers and their families.

For newer NALC members, these pages offer some background on the conditions carriers faced a quarter-century ago and how events played out over eight days that opened a new era for the United States mail system and the National Association of Letter Carriers.

5

SOURCE: *The Postal Record*, March 1995, pp. 4–5.

PUBLIC EMPLOYEES AND HARDER TIMES

By the late 1980s and 1990s, some amount of spine-stiffening by politicians in their dealings with public-sector unions was inevitable. And the generous settlements of earlier years were now replaced in short order by hard-nosed bargaining by governmental officials—something that may well have led the unions themselves to agree with Oscar Levant's dictum that "a politician is a person who will double-cross a bridge when he comes to it." But that was clearly what the public wanted. As one seasoned labor lawyer had commented regarding the firing of the PATCO strikers, it "just put the frosting on the cake. It was all public employers needed to hear because they were beginning to feel more confident anyway about their ability to deal with unions."[28]

Republicans, not surprisingly, tended to be tougher in their labor relations—having little to lose in the way of labor support since they had won so little of it in the first place—than did Democrats. (Exhibit 1-7 illustrates the not particularly successful counterattack by the National Health and Human Service Employees and Service Employees International Union in the wake of severe 1999 budgetary cuts by New York's G.O.P. Governor George Pataki.) And although labor had initially chosen to fight unwelcomed treatment by public officials by engaging in more strikes than ever, in later years public resentment at the strikers had combined with the advent to the White House of Democrat Bill Clinton to cause some decrease in this activity in favor of union lobbying for more permissive labor legislation in individual states and cities as well as at the federal level. Given the basic union successes in public-sector bargaining in earlier years, there were grounds for union optimism, too. Under any conditions, it did not seem to be too much to hope that the current, newer, and not especially appealing situation would itself be replaced by a more responsible bargaining system, administered by parties whose maturity had been hastened by adversity, and fairer to all concerned.

SOME CONCLUDING THOUGHTS

It can be expected that managements will continue to oppose the concept of unionism and to resist new union inroads as energetically as ever, for the roots of this opposition are essentially rational ones as *judged by management values*. It also seems the safest of predictions that unions will continue to press for an ever-greater narrowing of the scope of management discretion, in the interests of obliging worker wants and needs as *they* view them. Indeed, in the years immediately ahead, the stresses between the parties seem destined to grow: The recent intensification of industrial price and technological competition (and, in the public sector, of severe budgetary pressures) has already pitted an accelerated employer search for greater efficiency against an equally determined union quest for increased job security. It is a certainty that occasional impasses will continue to be reached and that these will result in strike actions, as they have in the past.

There is both an irony and a serious threat for our system of free collective bargaining in the inevitability of future strikes. If labor relations progress has clearly been evident, the public has also increased its expectations in this area. It has become increasingly less tolerant of work stoppages, even as organized labor in its relatively weakened recent condition has engaged in fewer of these, and it regularly shows itself as favoring greater governmental control over union activities.

EXHIBIT 1-7

FIGHTING FOR SOCIETY'S SOUL ■

Budget Cut
FIGHT-BACK
Union defends health care from Pataki attack.

Our union fought back on several fronts this spring against Gov. Pataki's budget proposal to cut health care by $2.1 billion. "This is a fight for the soul of our society," says Pres. Dennis Rivera. "The people in power don't care about other human beings. Gov. Pataki is thinking of running for higher office, so although he has a $3.1 billion budget surplus, he wants to use it to cut taxes instead of maintaining decent health care. He wants to abuse us for his political purposes."

ACTIONS TAKEN IN THE BUDGET CUT BATTLE INCLUDED:

• **Lobby Day.** Some 2,000 SEIU members from 22 locals across the state rallied in Albany Feb. 23 for a budget cut Lobby Day. Before meeting with individual legislators they chanted "No cuts, no cuts!" as they were welcomed by Comptroller Carl McCall, State Senate Majority Leader Joseph Bruno and Assembly Speaker Sheldon Silver.

• **Home Care Unity.** Some 8,000 home care workers rallied at Madison Square Garden March 22 to kick off a unified home care campaign against budget cuts and for decent pay. Joining 1199ers at the rally were members of SEIU Local 32B-J-144. White House deputy chief of staff Maria Echeveste and former Mayor David Dinkins spoke. "The Clinton Administration is with you," said Echeveste. (See pages 10-11.)

• **Media Campaign.** The union joined the Greater N.Y. Hospital Assn. (GNYHA), religious leaders and community advocates in a media campaign against the cuts. Radio ads aired on 33 stations throughout the state. Direct mail went to 250,000 households.

• **Political Action Fund.** To help pay for the campaign, more than 18,000 members had signed up in mid-March for voluntary $5-a-month contributions to the 1199 Political Action Fund.

• **Mass Leafletting.** Members were scheduled to distribute leaflets March 30 at subway stations throughout the city in a joint New Century Movement campaign that includes the municipal and teachers unions. Similar actions were planned throughout the state.

• **Health Care for All.** Two thousand delegates in a Manhattan hotel ballroom March 5 to discuss fightback

strategy heard a telephone message from Sen. Charles Schumer. "Dennis Rivera, (GNYHA Pres.) Ken Raske and I are working together to prevent these cuts," said Schumer. "And then we'll move on to universal health care for all Americans."

• **Our Proposal.** SEIU N.Y. State Council Exec. Director Jennifer Cunningham testified at a March 4 State Senate hearing on the uninsured. She told how the Family Health Plus plan advocated by 1199 and GNYHA would provide health coverage to low-income working people. The program would be funded in part by the state's share in the tobacco settlement. New York State's non-elderly uninsured rose to 19.1% in 1996. The figure is over 25% in New York City.

SEVERAL 1199ERS SPOKE FEB. 23 AT THE ALBANY RALLY:

"Staffing with dignity is a right and understaffing is patient abuse," said Hugo Quinteros, a cook at Union Plaza Nursing Home for 21 years. "We should demand the attorney general's office bring charges against owners of understaffed homes."

"This isn't just about money," said Bronx Home Health attendant Helen Jones. "The elderly can't function without us. Let Pataki try doing the work we're doing." ▶

Members of 1199 and SEIU District 1115 demonstrated March 18 in Hauppauge, Long Island against budget cuts.

1199 NEWS 3

Source: *1199 News*, April 1999, p. 3.

Despite an ever-deeper penetration of governmental regulations (described in Chapter 3 and elsewhere in the pages that follow), our labor relations system—the public-sector obviously excepted—has thus far essentially remained in private hands. This preference for private decision making is consistent with the dominant values of our society, particularly the maximum freedom of action for both individuals and organizations. But the possibility that a tripartite labor relations system, with the government as a full-fledged participant, will ultimately supplant the present bipartite system can never be overlooked. Whether what is still free collective bargaining will be allowed to continue will depend entirely on our current system's ability to continue its progress sufficiently to satisfy the increasingly high level of public expectation. There is still much room for improvement in the relations between organized labor and the management community, and this fact makes the whole system as it currently exists a vulnerable one.

DISCUSSION QUESTIONS

1. "No one except union officers and union staff members would suffer one iota if unions were to be outlawed in the United States, and enormous numbers of people would gain immeasurably if this should happen." Discuss.

2. "There is no reason on earth why lower and even middle managers should not consider joining a labor union, and it is really just a fluke that they, at least to date, have not." Comment fully.

3. "From the labor point of view, there is an intrinsic unfairness in the fact that it is essentially only conflict that attracts attention from the media." How valid, in your opinion, is this statement?

4. "The blue-collar world is the only natural habitat of unionism in the United States, and union failures to date outside of this sector prove this statement conclusively." Do you agree? Why or why not?

5. "Managers resist unions for a variety of entirely logical and rational reasons, and, thus, they can be expected to continue this opposition indefinitely, since the reasons will presumably continue to be logical and rational." Comment with specifics.

6. More than a few public officials in recent years have argued that any police officer, firefighter, or sanitation worker who goes out on strike in defiance of the law should be fired on the spot. How does such a viewpoint accord with yours?

7. Under what, if any, circumstances would you personally consider joining a union?

8. It has occasionally been argued that the United States is experiencing the cult of the individual. Do you accept this position and, if so, do you think that its continuation would significantly hurt labor's efforts in the years immediately ahead?

MINICASES

 ## The White-Collar Union Organizer

"I have nothing against unions, mind you, but just give me one good reason why I should sign up with you," an office worker tells Office Employees International Union organizer Nancy Rogers.

"Anytime the production workers in this company get more money through their union, we nonunion folks in the office do, too, simply because the management doesn't want us to be tempted to become unionists. In fact, we might even be getting just a little bit extra so as to guarantee that we don't get any funny ideas.

"And more than that, everybody knows that unions are really just for manual workers. It's not appropriate for white-collar people like us to join them, which is why, except for a few malcontents, you just don't see office workers in unions. Maybe some day conditions will change here, but right now I don't see that it will help me in any way to be bargained for by some outside union lawyer or union leader. In fact, it might even hurt because unions, as we all know, want equal pay for equal work and have no rewards for individual merit. I don't want to boast, but I'm a very hard worker now. I'd be crazy to strain myself if we had a union contract."

If you were Rogers, what would you say in response to this employee?

#2 An Overture from a Business Agent

"As you know, the labor contract for the three unionized taxi companies in this city expires on Saturday night," Taxi Drivers Union business agent Monty Everest reminds taxi company owner Herbert King, "and since the centralized negotiations with the three of you have now collapsed, it looks like a strike is inevitable.

"But we like you. You're a gentleman who's always treated us fairly and with sensitivity, just like your dad did. Tell you what. Just give me $10,000 in cash and we'll merely stop work at one—or possibly both—of your competitors under what we'll call a 'selective strike.' Your guys can continue working and all you'll have to do is match the new master contract once we've negotiated it with the other firms. Your revenue won't stop at all; you'll probably get plenty of new business while the strike is on; and—who knows?—maybe one or both of the others won't even be able to survive the work stoppage and you'll be the winner on a permanent basis. You've got everything to gain and nothing to lose."

As King, how would you react to such an overture?

NOTES

[1] *New York Journal of Commerce*, February 7, 1851, as quoted in Neil W. Chamberlain, *The Labor Sector* (New York: McGraw-Hill, 1965), p. 341.

[2] Quoted in Herbert Harris, *American Labor* (New Haven, CT: Yale University Press, 1939), pp. 126–27.

[3] Sinclair Lewis, *Babbitt* (New York: Harcourt Brace Jovanovich, 1922), p. 44. (Rights for the British Commonwealth excluding Canada have been granted by Jonathan Cape Limited, Publishers, London, England, on behalf of the Estate of Sinclair Lewis.)

[4] Albert A. Blum, "Management Paternalism and Collective Bargaining," *Personnel Administration*, 26 (January–February 1963), p. 38.

[5] Unofficial data furnished by U.S. Department of Labor, Bureau of Labor Statistics.

[6] Ibid.

[7] *The New York Times*, October 17, 1999, p. A19.

[8] J. B. S. Hardman, *American Labor Dynamics* (New York: Harcourt, Brace & Co., 1928), p. 95.

[9] A. H. Raskin, "The Unions and Their Wealth," *Atlantic Monthly*, April 1962, p. 89.

[10] Wilfrid Sheed, "What Ever Happened to the Labor Movement?" *Atlantic*, July 1973, p. 69.

[11] *The New York Times*, August 31, 1997, p. F9.

[12] *International Teamster*, September 1960, p. 16.

[13] *The New York Times*, August 17, 1997, p. A28.

[14]*Wall Street Journal*, February 21, 1985, p. 1.

[15]*Wall Street Journal*, April 20, 1999, p. 1.

[16]*The New York Times*, September 1, 1999, p. A15.

[17]*Wall Street Journal*, March 24, 1988, p. 1.

[18]*Business Week*, July 19, 1999, p. 43.

[19]A. H. Maslow, *Motivation and Personality* (New York: Harper & Row, 1954).

[20]The most timeless of these studies are E. Wight Bakke, "To Join or Not to Join," in E. Wight Bakke, Clark Kerr, and Charles W. Anrod, eds., *Unions, Management and the Public* (New York: Harcourt Brace Jovanovich, 1960), pp. 79–85; and Joel Seidman, Jack London, and Bernard Karsh, "Why Workers Join Unions," *Annals of the American Academy of Political and Social Science*, 274, no. 84 (March 1951). See also Henry S. Farber and Daniel H. Saks, "Why Workers Want Unions: The Role of Relative Wages and Job Characteristics," in *Journal of Political Economy*, 88, no. 21 (1980), 349–69. Also instructive on the subject is Jeanne M. Brett's "Why Employees Want Unions," in Kendrith M. Rowland, Gerald R. Ferris, and Jay L. Sherman, *Current Issues in Personnel Management*, 2nd ed. (Boston: Allyn and Bacon, 1983).

[21]Seidman, London, and Karsh, "Why Workers Join Unions."

[22]Ibid.

[23]E. Wight Bakke, *Mutual Survival: The Goal of Unions and Management* (New York: Harper & Row, 1946), p. 7.

[24]Not all employers lament the "outside" aspects of unionization. Many prefer the more detached viewpoints of international union representatives who are removed from the tensions and political considerations involved in day-by-day local labor relations. Some managers welcome, in addition, the stabilization of labor terms among otherwise competitive employers that frequently accompanies wider-scale bargaining. The terms *international* and *national* are used interchangeably in this volume, as indeed they are used in practice.

[25]The most exhaustive study on the subject of "dual loyalties" is that of Father Theodore Purcell, conducted in the mid-1950s. Interviewing 202 workers in various departments at Swift and Company, he discovered that whereas at least 79 percent felt a definite allegiance to the union as an institution, 92 percent felt allegiance to the company. *Allegiance* was construed as an attitude of approval of the overall objectives of each institution rather than strict loyalty. See Theodore V. Purcell, *Blue Collar Man* (Cambridge, MA: Harvard University Press, 1960); and also *The Worker Speaks His Mind on Company and Union* (Cambridge, MA: Harvard University Press, 1953), by the same author. More recently, a 1975 poll of several thousand Burlington Northern Railroad employees (made in this case by the management itself) showed that workers with a "favorable attitude" toward their union also had a favorable attitude toward their boss to a large extent.

[26]*Wall Street Journal*, November 7, 1974, p. 29.

[27]Marvin J. Levine and Eugene C. Hagburg, *Labor Relations in the Public Sector* (Salt Lake City: Brighton, 1979), p. xv.

[28]*Wall Street Journal*, November 30, 1981, p. 34.

SELECTED REFERENCES

Applebaum, Eileen, and Rosemary Batt. *The New American Workplace: Transforming Work Systems in the United States*. Ithaca, NY: ILR Press. Cornell University, 1994.

Belman, Dale, Morley Gunderson, and Douglas Hyatt, eds. *Public Sector Employment in a Time of Transition*. Madison, WI: Industrial Relations Research Association, 1996.

Bok, Derek C., and John T. Dunlop. *Labor and the American Community*. New York: Simon & Schuster, 1970.

Budrys, Grace. *When Doctors Join Unions*. Ithaca, NY: ILR Press. Cornell University, 1996.

Cobble, Dorothy Sue. *Dishing It Out: Waitresses and Their Unions in the Twentieth Century*. Urbana: University of Illinois Press, 1991.

Coleman, Charles J. *Managing Labor Relations in the Public Sector*. San Francisco: Jossey-Bass, 1990.

Dunlop, John T. *Industrial Relations Systems*, (rev. ed.) Boston: Harvard Business School Press, 1993.

Freeman, Richard B., and James L. Medhoff. *What Do Unions Do?* New York: Basic Books, 1984.

Friedman, Allen, and Ted Schwarz. *Power and Greed*. New York: Franklin Watts, 1989.

Geoghegan, Thomas. *Which Side Are You On?* New York: Farrar, Straus & Giroux, 1991.

Goldfield, Michael. *The Decline of Organized Labor in the United States*. Chicago: University of Chicago Press, 1987.

Heckscher, Charles C. *The New Unionism*. New York: Basic Books, 1988.

Hoerr, John P. *And the Wolf Finally Came: The Decline of the American Steel Industry*. Pittsburgh: University of Pittsburgh Press, 1988.

Kerr, Clark, and Paul D. Staudohar, eds. *Industrial Relations in a New Age*. San Francisco: Jossey-Bass, 1986.

Kochan, Thomas A., Russell D. Lansbury, and John Paul MacDuffie. *After Lean Production: Evolving Employment Practices in the World Auto Industry*. Ithaca, NY: ILR Press, Cornell University, 1997.

Mantsios, Gregory, ed. *A New Labor Movement for the New Century*. New York: Garland, 1998.

Masters, Marick F. *Unions at the Crossroads: Strategic Membership, Financial and Political Perspectives*. Westport, CT: Quorum, 1997.

Moody, Kim. *An Injury to All: The Decline of American Unionism*. New York: Verso, 1988.

Nicholson, Nigel, Gill Ursell, and Paul Blyton. *The Dynamics of White-Collar Unionism*. New York: Academic Press, 1981.

Puette, William J. *Through Jaundiced Eyes: How the Media View Organized Labor*. Ithaca, NY: ILR Press, Cornell University, 1992.

Shostak, Arthur B. *Robust Unionism: Innovation in the Labor Movement*. Ithaca, NY: ILR Press, Cornell University, 1991.

Slichter, Sumner H., James J. Healy, and E. Robert Livernash. *The Impact of Collective Bargaining on Management*. Washington, DC: The Brookings Institution, 1960.

Staudohar, Paul D. *Playing for Dollars: Labor Relations and the Sports Business*. Ithaca, NY: ILR Press, Cornell University, 1996.

Strauss, George, Jack Fiorito, and Daniel G. Gallagher. *The State of the Unions*. Ithaca, NY: ILR Press, Cornell University, 1991.

Voos, Paula B., ed. *Contemporary Collective Bargaining in the Private Sector*. Madison, WI: Industrial Relations Research Association, 1994.

Walsh, John, and Garth Mangum. *Labor Struggle in the Post Office: From Selective Lobbying to Collective Bargaining*. Armonk, NY: M. E. Sharpe, 1992.

Zaniello, Tom. *Working Stiffs, Union Maids, Reds, and Riffraff: An Organized Guide to Films about Labor*. Ithaca, NY: ILR Press, Cornell University, 1996.

Zieger, Robert H., ed. *Organized Labor in the Twentieth-Century South*. Knoxville: University of Tennessee Press, 1991.

PART II The Environmental Framework

CHAPTER

2

The Historical Framework

*A*s is true of other established disciplines, there is still some controversy as to the returns inherent in the study of history. For every Shakespeare asserting that "what is past is prologue," or a Santayana who proclaims that "those who do not understand history are condemned to repeat its mistakes," there is a Henry Ford declaring that "history is a pack of tricks that we play on the dead" and that the field is, in fact, "bunk."

No one can claim to understand present-day institutions, however, without having at least some basic knowledge of their roots. It would make a considerable difference to those who are either hopeful or fearful that labor unions will ultimately fade from the industrial scene, for example, if unions were purely a phenomenon of the last few years (and thus potentially destined for extinction when environmental conditions change), rather than being—as they are—organizations of relatively long standing in the economy. Exhibit 2-1 indicates the ripe years of one union, the National Association of Letter Carriers; and, as the following pages will show, the Letter Carriers are far from the oldest of American unions. Exhibits 2-2 and 2-3 show the interest of two somewhat less ancient labor organizations, the Air Line Pilots Association and the Association of Flight Attendants, respectively, in their histories.

Similarly, only by recognizing what workers have expected of their unions in the past is one entitled even to begin to pass judgment on the present performance of organized labor. This chapter thus attempts to provide the reader with a necessary working knowledge of American labor history, as union membership rose (and sometimes fell) in the manner depicted in Exhibit 2-4.

THE EIGHTEENTH CENTURY: GENESIS OF THE AMERICAN LABOR MOVEMENT

If labor unions connote *permanent* employee associations that have as their primary goal the preservation or improvement of employment conditions, there were no such institutions in America until the closing years of the eighteenth century. Concerted actions of workers in the form of strikes and slowdowns were not unknown to the colonial period, but these disturbances were, without exception, spontaneous efforts. They were conducted on the spur of the moment over temporary grievances, such as withholding of wages. Generally unsuccessful, they were never undertaken by anything resembling permanent organizations.

In those years of simple handicraft organization, there were at least three reasons why workers did not join together on a long-term basis.

In the first place, the market for the employer's product was both local and essentially noncompetitive. Workers were thus allowed close social ties with the owner, often performing their work in the owner's home. In addition, they could maintain a comparatively relaxed pace of production in such an atmosphere.

Second, both the laws of supply and demand and government regulations allowed employees a large measure of job security at this time. Labor of all kinds, and particularly skilled craft labor, was in short supply in the colonies. A series of colonial labor laws carefully circumscribing the conditions under which employees could be discharged offered further protection to jobholders.

Third, the existence of ample cheap land in the West enabled the dissatisfied artisan or mechanic to move on should either local adversity or the spirit of adventure strike.

EXHIBIT 2-1

SOURCE: *The Postal Record*, August 1999, back cover.

    Ironically, however, the development of the frontier laid the groundwork for the birth of bona fide labor organizations. An expanded system of transportation built around canals and turnpikes was simultaneously linking the new nation's communities and allowing the capitalists of the late eighteenth century to enlarge their product markets into the beginnings of nationwide ones. The merchant who was unable

EXHIBIT 2-2

SOURCE: *Air Line Pilot*, July 1992, p. 56.

Prints of *Air Line Pilot*'s 60th Anniversary cover and the ALPA Code of Ethics, both suitable for framing, are available for $4 each including shipping and handling.

Send your requests to:
Air Line Pilot Cover, 535 Herndon Parkway
P.O. Box 1169, Herndon, VA 22070

to respond to the challenge was left by the wayside as competitive pressures forced each businessperson to find cost-cutting devices in the newly unsheltered atmosphere. The more imaginative employers located such devices: To decrease labor costs, they introduced women and children to their workplaces, farmed out work to prison inmates, and generally cut the wages of males who remained in their employ. For good measure, they frequently increased the hours in the workday (at no increase in pay) and hired aggressive overseers to enforce newly tightened work standards.

The less-skilled workers could react to these changes by moving to the frontier. Not having invested much in the way of time or education in learning the current job, such employees might also attempt to move occupationally to more desirable kinds of work. The skilled workers, on the other hand, had increasingly mastered the craft through years of apprenticeship and were no longer occupationally mobile.

Some skilled craftsmen did move to the frontier. But the extension of the product market did not free their new masters from the need to seek labor cost-cutting

EXHIBIT 2-3

SOURCE: *Flightlog*, Spring 1995, p. 13 (Association of Flight Attendants, AFL-CIO).

AFA HISTORY

A Half Century of MILESTONES

ASSOCIATION OF FLIGHT ATTENDANTS 50TH ANNIVERSARY 1945-1995

THIS YEAR, THE ASSOCIATION OF FLIGHT ATTENDANTS marks the 50th anniversary of the founding of its predecessor union, the Air Line Stewardesses Association (ALSA), on August 22, 1945. Here are some of the milestones that occurred during AFA's first half century of achievement.

1945 Air Line Stewardesses Association wins recognition as first union for flight attendants.

1946 First union contract raises United flight attendants' monthly pay to $155, limits duty hours, sets rest periods and establishes a grievance procedure.

1947 ALSA President Ada Brown, 30, marries and becomes a victim of United's no-marriage rule. Retires from career and union presidency.

1949 ALSA merges with the Air Line Pilots Association affiliate, the Air Line Stewards and Stewardesses Association (ALSSA).

1951 ALSSA represents 3,300 flight attendants at 24 small and large carriers. ▶ Pilots' opposition to union shop and flight attendants' desire to acquire a charter with the American Federation of Labor threatens ALSSA's relationship with ALPA.

1952 Civil Air Administration requires flight attendants on commercial aircraft as cabin safety professionals.

1960 ALPA creates two divisions, the Pilots Division and the Steward and Stewardesses Division. Nearly half of the nation's 8,700 flight attendants vote to affiliate with ALPA's S & S Division.

1964 Civil Rights Act passes. Flight attendants use Title VII of act to challenge discriminatory policies based on gender, race, age, weight, pregnancy and marital status.

1968 Average career for flight attendants lasts 18 months. ▶ Mandatory resignation at age 30-35 struck down.

1971 Pressed by AFA, courts prohibit airlines from refusing to hire males, find United's no-marriage rule illegal.

1973 Modern AFA is born when ALPA's S and S Division becomes the Association of Flight Attendants.

1974 Court rules Northwest Airlines must pay female flight attendants same scale as males.

1975 In court, AFA challenges requirement that flight attendants stop working upon pregnancy.

1978 Congress passes the Airline Deregulation Act, giving airlines unlimited authority over routes, scheduling and fare pricing.

1979 AFA litigation results in liberalizing airlines' weight policies.

1981 Nationwide AFA campaign helps kill FAA plan to reduce the number of cabin crew members.

1982 AFA represents 22,000 flight attendants at 18 carriers.

1984 Fulfilling a quest by AFA leaders since the union's founding in 1946, AFA is granted a charter by the AFL-CIO. ▶ AFA prodding results in new FAA rules requiring floor-level exit lights, less flammable cabin interiors and other cabin air safety breakthroughs.

1987 Years of pressure from AFA prompts FAA to issue a policy limiting number of passenger carry-on bags.

1988 Lobbying before Congress results in smoking ban on domestic flights of two hours or less.

1990 AFA petitions FAA to apply OSHA standards to flight attendants. ▶ Smoking ban goes into effect on all domestic flights.

1991 AFA hosts first international flight attendant symposium, sharing ideas with flight attendants from Australia, Austria, Canada, Denmark, Finland, France, Ireland, South Korea, Norway, Singapore, and Sweden.

1994 AFA CHAOS campaign of intermittent work stoppages upheld in court; results in landmark contract settlement at Alaska Airlines. ▶ USAir weight program suspended following litigation by AFA. ▶ FAA issues duty-time regulations for flight attendants.

1995 Representing 36,000 flight attendants at 23 airlines, AFA celebrates its first half century of union achievements.

FOR ERA

association of flight attendants
AFL-CIO

methods; suits tailored in Ohio competed now with those made in Boston. Nor could the craftsmen count any longer on advancing into the class of masters themselves; to enter the employer ranks it now took capital on a scale not ordinarily available to most wage earners. Basically, the skilled workers' alternatives were to passively accept the wage cuts and the harsh working conditions or to join in collective action against such employer innovations. Increasingly, by the end of the eighteenth century, they chose the latter course of action.

EXHIBIT 2-4

SOURCE: *Trade Union Membership in the United States for Selected Years.*

Year	Membership
1836	300,000
1865	200,000
1878	50,000
1897	447,000
1904	2,073,000
1917	3,014,000
1920	5,100,000
1930	3,400,000
1933	2,973,000
1941	10,200,000
1953	16,300,000
1965	18,250,000
1975	22,200,000
1996	17,000,000
1999 (est.)	16,200,000

SOURCE: Based on data provided by the U.S. Bureau of Labor Statistics.

THE FIRST UNIONS AND THEIR LIMITED SUCCESSES

These early trade unions—individually encompassing printers, carpenters, tailors, and artisans of similar skill levels—waged blunt attacks on the changes brought about by the extension of markets. Their members agreed on a wage level and pledged not to work for any employer who refused to pay that amount. In addition, most of these craft unions attempted to negotiate **closed shop** agreements, whereby only those who were union members in the first place would be employed at all.

Generally proving themselves willing to strike, if need be, in support of their demands, the early unions were at times surprisingly successful in achieving them. And the new worker aggressiveness that they symbolized was sufficient to bring on considerable countervailing action from the employers.

The masters turned to two sources: organization in employers' associations and aid from the courts. Societies of otherwise competitive master masons, carpenters, shoemakers, printers, and other employers of skilled labor were quickly established in most urban areas where union activity was pronounced, for the purposes of holding down wages and destroying labor combinations. The masters also turned to the judges and urged prosecution of their workers' organizations as illegal conspiracies in restraint of trade. The jurists were quickly convinced: The Journeyman Cordwainers (shoemakers) of Philadelphia were found guilty of joining in such a conspiracy by striking in 1806, and within the next decade a variety of similar court cases had also resulted in shattering defeats for the worker organizations. Not until 1842, indeed, with the famous *Commonwealth* v. *Hunt* decision in Massachusetts that strikes could be legal if they were undertaken for legal purposes, did the judges even begin to modify the harsh tenets of the "Cordwainer doctrine."

If the criminal conspiracy doctrine and the varying successes of the employer associations crimped the growth of the incipient labor movement, moreover, an economic event temporarily sent unionism into almost total collapse. In 1819, a major nationwide depression occurred and, as was to be no less the case in later nineteenth-century periods of economic reversal, labor organizations could not withstand its effects. Union demands that might be translated into employer concessions when the demand for labor was high could safely be dismissed by the masters with jobs now at a premium. Employers once again cut rates with impunity and showed little hesitation in dismissing workers who had joined unions in earlier years. Under the circumstances, the worker cry was "Every man for himself," rather than "In union there is strength," and virtually no union could, or did, survive mass desertion.

REVIVAL, INNOVATION, AND DISILLUSIONMENT

The return of economic health to the country by late 1822 was paralleled by a revival of unionism. Their bargaining power restored, skilled employees in the trades that had previously been organized once again turned to union activity.

More significantly, the process of unionization now spread to new frontiers, both geographic and occupational. Aroused by the same merchant-capitalist threats to living standards and status that had previously given incentive for collective bargaining to their East Coast counterparts, craftsmen in such newly developed cities as Buffalo, Cincinnati, and Louisville established trade union locals at this time. And new (and widely publicized) victories of the skilled worker unions in both the older and newer cities had by the mid-1830s generated the formation of unions among such previously nonunion groups as stonecutters, hatters, and painters.

It has been estimated that there were by 1836 some 300,000 American unionized workers, constituting 6.5 percent of the labor force.[1] One can only guess to what heights the total figures would have risen had not the following year brought a national economic depression that was even more severe than the business slump of 1819.

The hard times that began in 1837 were to last for almost 13 years. In the face of them, trade union activity vanished almost as completely as it had two decades earlier. Moreover, a new factor now arose to compound union ills: The 1840s saw waves of immigrants—themselves often the victims of economic adversity in such countries as Ireland, Germany, and England—enter the United States. American business conditions by themselves had been sufficient to wipe out most unions of the day, but this new source of job competition and low wages ensured that not even the strongest of unions could endure.

Now so severely frustrated in their economic actions and distrustful of the free enterprise system for having failed to safeguard their interests, some workers transferred their energies to a series of ambitious political schemes for redesigning the economy. Associationists set up socialistic agricultural communities; George Henry Evans preached the virtues of land reform through direct political action by workingmen ("Vote Yourself a Farm"); and still other advocates of a new social order promulgated producers' cooperatives—employee-owned industrial institutions—as the workingman's salvation.

None of these programs succeeded, however. As Dulles has observed, they did not "in any way meet the needs of labor. In spite of the enthusiastic propaganda, the answer to industrialization did not lie in an attempt to escape from it."[2]

THE LAYING OF THE FOUNDATION FOR MODERN UNIONISM AND SOME MIXED PERFORMANCES

With the return of prosperity in 1850, unions once again became a factor to be reckoned with. Profiting from the past, they shunned political diversions, concentrated on such now-traditional goals as higher wages, shorter workdays, and increased job security and regained much of their former membership.

The first major **national unions** were also established at this time. Construction of the first complex rail systems was now accelerating. As a result, not only were product markets once more widening but so too were labor markets, bringing workers within the same crafts and industries into direct economic competition with each other. National coordination to standardize wages, working conditions, membership rules, and bargaining demands was deemed necessary by labor leaders; the alternative was cutthroat competition among individual local unions, eager for new members and expanded work opportunities and, therefore, willing to undercut the terms of other locals (to the employer's distinct advantage). The International Typographical Union, the country's oldest permanent national, dates from 1852. By 1860, at least 15 other crafts had organized on a national basis.

The 1861 advent of the Civil War brought a new spurt in union membership growth, to a post-1836 high of over 200,000 unionists by the end of hostilities in 1865. Some of this organizational success was due to the labor shortages brought on by military mobilization: The economy's demand for labor commensurately increased, thus enlarging labor's bargaining power and union economic gains. There were undoubtedly at least two other reasons, however: (1) Wartime inflation always threatened to counteract the wage increases achieved by unions, and many workers (somewhat unsuccessfully) looked to collective bargaining as a force for staving off this menace; and (2) organized labor was further helped by the prolabor sentiments of President Abraham Lincoln, who firmly resisted employer and public pressure to intervene in the occasional wartime strikes and instead offered his opinion that "labor is the superior of capital and deserves much the higher consideration."

At war's end, however, the labor movement still constituted less than 2 percent of the country's labor force (as against the 6.5 percent in 1836) and had yet to make any real penetration into the factories of the land and their huge organizing potential. But the foundation for the unionism of the next 70 years had now been laid. Few skilled-worker types were totally unrepresented by unions in 1865: More than 200 local unions, individually encompassing such widely divergent craftsmen as cigar makers, plumbers, and barrel makers, were founded in the war years alone. In addition, the logical necessity of forming national unions had now been almost universally recognized by labor leaders, and some 30 new ones had been added to the several that had preceded the war.

Labor's momentum, moreover, was sustained in immediate postwar years. The war-generated nationwide prosperity continued virtually unabated until 1873 and, aided by its favorable economic conditions (as in earlier business booms), labor's bargaining strength again increased. New members were attracted by announcements of new union gains, but there were now also other reasons for the increased membership totals. The broader organizational foundations that had been laid prior to 1865, particularly in the multiplication of national unions, allowed both more efficient and more varied organizing campaigns. Moreover, the post–Civil War period unleashed formidable threats to the workingman in the form of (1) accelerated waves of immigrants (increasingly, now, from southern and eastern Europe) who were willing to work for low wages; (2) changing technology, with the machine downgrading many skill requirements and allowing the employer to substitute unskilled labor for craftsmen; and (3) the continued widening of the gap between wages and prices that had begun in the wartime years. Workers thus had more incentive to join in collective bargaining, and they acted upon it.

But business again collapsed in 1873, beginning a new period of deep depression that lasted for more than five years. In its wake, most of the local unions once more disappeared. Many of the nationals fared no better, but the greater financial resources and more diversified memberships of these broader organizations did allow them to offer greater resistance to the slump; not only did eleven of the nationals, in fact, weather these years but eight new nationals were established during this time. Consequently, for the first time, a depression did not completely stop unionization. Nonetheless, five-sixths of total union membership did erode in the 1873–1878 period; only 50,000 unionists remained in 1878.

Encouraged by the depression-caused weakening of unions, employers also turned—in the 1870s—to weapons of their own, in an all-out attack on what was left of organized labor. They engaged in frequent lockouts, hired spies to ferret out union sympathizers, circulated the names of such sympathizers to fellow employers through so-called blacklists, summarily discharged labor "agitators," and engaged the services of strikebreakers on a widespread scale.

Retaliating in kind, both unionists and nonunionized workers engaged in actions that for bitterness and violence were unequaled in American history. A secret society of anthracite miners, the Molly Maguires, terrorized the coal fields of Pennsylvania in a series of widely publicized murders and acts of arson. Railroad strikes paralyzed transportation in such major cities as Baltimore, Pittsburgh, and Chicago and, with mob rule typically replacing organized leadership as these ran their course, were most often ended only with federal troops being called out to terminate mass pillaging and bloodshed. Public opinion was almost always hostile to such activities, and lacking public support the demonstrations could not succeed. It is probably also true that employers were more easily enabled, by the general resentment directed toward worker groups for these actions, to gain still another weapon in their battle against unions: The labor injunction, first applied by the courts during a railway strike at this time, was to be quite freely granted—as Chapter 3 will bring out—by judges for more than five decades thereafter.

THE RISE AND FALL OF THE KNIGHTS OF LABOR

Prosperity finally returned in 1878, and with it union growth once again resumed. Over the next 10 years, 62 new national unions (or "international" unions, as many of these were now calling themselves, in recognition of their first penetration of the Canadian labor market) were established. Locals and city centrals also resumed their proliferation. Even more significantly, the early 1880s marked American labor's most notable attempt to form a single, huge "general" union, the **Knights of Labor**.

The Knights had actually been established before the depression. In 1869, a group of tailors had founded the organization's first local in Philadelphia. Its avowed goal was "to initiate good men of all callings"—unionists as well as those not already in unions, craftsmen, employers, the self-employed, and (unlike virtually all other labor organizations of the day) totally unskilled workers.

Surviving the depression as a secret society, the Knights abolished their assortment of rituals and passwords in the late 1870s and thenceforth openly recruited in all directions.

Such aggressiveness, combined with what now was the normal increase in union bargaining strength amid general economic prosperity, allowed a slow but steady growth of the order's membership. There were roughly 9,000 Knights in 1878 and over 70,000 by 1884. Then, following a major 1885 strike victory against the Wabash Railroad, the growth became spectacular. Workers of all conceivable types clamored for membership, and by mid-1886 there were 700,000 people in the wide-sweeping organization.

The aftermath of the Wabash strike was to be the high-water mark for the Knights, however. The leaders of the order proved wholly unable to cope with the gigantic membership increase, and as the new Knights sought to duplicate the Wabash triumph with one ill-timed and undisciplined strike after another, a steady stream of union defeats ensued. The very diversity of backgrounds among the members also drained the effectiveness of the organization: The old skilled trade unionists found little in common with the shopkeepers, farmers, and self-employed mechanics who shared membership with them, and they rapidly deserted the order. Nor did the presence of thousands of unskilled and semiskilled industrial workers, often of widely varying first-generation American backgrounds, add anything to group solidarity. Greatly discouraged by the schisms within their organization, many such workers soon followed the path set by the skilled tradesmen and left it.

Although each of the foregoing factors was undoubtedly influential in the Knights' rapid decline after 1886—to 100,000 members by 1890 and to virtual extinction by 1900—still another factor was probably even more responsible for the fall of the order. The system of values held by the Knights' leadership was considerably at variance with the values of rank-and-file Knights. For all their diversity and essential lack of discipline, the latter could (employers and the self-employed always excepted) at least unite on the desirability of higher wages, shorter hours, and improved working conditions. Under Knights president Terrence V. Powderly, however, these goals were significantly minimized in favor of such social goals as the establishment of consumer and producer cooperatives, temperance, and land reform. Even the strike weapon, despite its great success against the Wabash management and its popular appeal to Knights' members, was viewed with disdain by Powderly to the end; he considered it both expensive and overly militant. Why was this Knight different from all other Knights? The historical records lack a definitive explanation. But whatever the reason the philosophical gap between leadership and followers was, thus, a wide one, and Powderly was forced to pay the supreme penalty for perpetuating it. Ultimately, he was left with no one to lead.

By the late 1880s, a wholly new organization—the American Federation of Labor—had won over the mainstream of the Knights' skilled-trade unionists, and the once vast array of other membership types, disillusioned, was again outside the ranks of organized labor.

THE FORMATION OF THE AFL AND ITS PRAGMATIC MASTER PLAN

Almost from its inception in 1881, the American Federation of Labor was a highly realistic, no-nonsense organization. Even in that year, the more than 100 representatives of skilled-worker unions who gathered at Pittsburgh to form what was originally entitled the Federation of Organized Trades and Labor Unions (FOTLU) included many dissident Knights, disenchanted with Powderly's "one big union" concept and political-action emphasis. The rebels were already convinced that the future of their highly skilled constituents lay completely outside the catchall Knights. They recognized that such craftsmen possessed considerably greater bargaining power than other, less-skilled types of Knights members because of their relative indispensability to employers. Consequently, they were anxious to exercise this power *directly* in union–management negotiations. Powderly's idealistic legislative goals might be appropriate for workers who could not better their lot in any other way. But the goals seemed to many FOTLU founders to be a poor substitute for strike threats and other forms of economic action when undertaken by unionists who were not so easily replaceable. These early advocates of an exclusive federation of craft unions were also well aware of the fates of earlier organizations that had subordinated economic goals to political ones.

The basic issue that was to split irrevocably the craft unions from the Knights involved the jurisdiction of the national unions themselves. The dramatic spurt in Knights membership following the 1885 Wabash victory threatened to entirely submerge the craft "trade assemblies" and the parent national craft unions, which had thus far retained their separate identities within the order, in a throng of numerically superior semiskilled and unskilled workers. Nor would Powderly, never the compromiser, grant any assurances that the Knights would not violate the jurisdictions of the existing national unions. Rubbing salt into the nationals' wounds, the Knights' leadership even went so far now as to organize rival national unions.

The rupture was soon complete. In 1886, representatives of 25 of the strongest national unions met at Columbus, Ohio, transformed the somewhat moribund FOTLU into the American Federation of Labor (AFL), unanimously elected Samuel Gompers of the Cigar Makers as the AFL's first president, and thereby ushered in a new era for the American labor movement. Despite their moment of glory, the Knights were soon to begin their rapid decline—with some of the impetus toward their dissolution, to be sure, being directly lent by the secession of the skilled-worker nationals. For the next 50 years, the basic tenets of the AFL were to remain unchallenged by the mainstream of labor in this country.

Samuel Gompers, the Jewish immigrant from England who was to continue as president of the federation for all except one of the next 38 years,[3] has frequently been referred to as a supreme pragmatist, a leader convinced that any supposed "truth" was above all to be tested by its practical consequences. Careful consideration of the basic principles upon which he and his lieutenants launched the AFL does nothing to weaken the validity of that description. Essentially, Gompers had five such principles.

In the first place, the national unions were to be autonomous within the new federation: "The American Federation of Labor," Gompers proudly announced, "avoids the fatal rock upon which all previous attempts to effect the unity of the working class have split, by leaving to each body or affiliated organization the complete management of its own affairs, especially in its own particular trade affairs."[4] The leader of a highly successful national himself, Gompers felt particularly strongly that questions of admission, apprenticeship, bargaining policy, and the like should be left strictly to those directly involved with them.

Second, the AFL would charter only one national union in each trade jurisdiction. This concept of **exclusive jurisdiction** stemmed mainly from the unpleasant experiences of the nationals with rival unions chartered by the Knights. It was also, however, due to Gompers's deep concern that such competitive union situations would give the employer undue bargaining advantages by allowing him to pit one warring union against another.

Third, the AFL would at all costs avoid long-run reformist goals and concentrate instead only upon immediate wage-centered gains. As noted earlier, its founders were determined not to suffer the fates of earlier, reform-centered organizations: "We have no ultimate ends," asserted Gompers's colleague Adolph Strasser on the occasion of his testimony before a congressional committee at this time. "We are going on from day to day. We are fighting only for immediate objects—objects that can be realized in a few years."

Fourth, the federation would avoid any permanent alliances with the existing political parties and, instead, "reward labor's friends and punish labor's enemies." (A century later, these words had hardly been forgotten, as Exhibit 2-5 shows, and even today they are echoed and reechoed by labor leaders at countless political gatherings.) Gompers was willing, however, to accept help for the AFL from any quarter, with only one major exception: He had at one time been a Marxian Socialist, but familiarity had bred contempt and, long before 1886, he had permanently broken with his old colleagues. At the 1903 AFL convention, he was to announce to the relative handful of Socialists present. "Economically, you are unsound; socially, you are wrong; and industrially, you are an impossibility."[5] To the end, Gompers's philosophy was firmly capitalistic.

Finally, Gompers placed considerable reliance on the strike weapon as a legitimate and effective means of achieving the wages, hours, and conditions sought by his unionists. Shortly before his election to the AFL presidency in 1886, he had been one of the leaders of a general strike designed to obtain the eight-hour day. More than 300,000 workers had participated in this action, and almost two-thirds of them had achieved their objective through it. Gompers's own Cigar Makers, too, had rarely hesitated to resort to strikes when bargaining impasses had been reached. And, generally speaking, these demonstrations of economic strength had also been successful.

Profiting from the lessons of history, Gompers's federation, thus, represented a realistic attempt to adjust to an economic system that had become deeply embedded in the United States. National union autonomy, exclusive jurisdiction, "pure and simple" collective bargaining, the avoidance of political entanglements, and the use of strikes when feasible—these proven sources of union strength were to be the hallmarks of the new unionism. The federation would provide the definition of jurisdictional boundaries for each national and give help to all such constituent unions in their organizing, bargaining, lobbying, and public relations endeavors. But it would otherwise allow a free hand to its national union members as they pursued their individual goals. And the stress was to be on the needs of skilled workers, not on those of "good men of all callings," as the Knights had placed it: Some semiskilled and unskilled workers within a relatively few industries (such as mine workers and electricians, because of the strategic power of their national unions) were encouraged to join, but basically the AFL made no great efforts to organize workers with less than "skilled" callings and was to admit them only if they organized themselves and had no jurisdictional disputes with craft unions. So successful did this master

EXHIBIT 2-5

SOURCE: *The Laborer*,
July–August 1984,
back cover.

"Reward Our Friends, Punish Our Enemies!"
—Samuel Gompers

Register & Vote!

plan prove to be that it was not until the mid-1930s that its logic was in any way seriously questioned.

THE EARLY YEARS OF THE AFL AND SOME MIXED RESULTS

Even in the short run, the policies of the AFL were so attractive to the nationals that within a few years virtually all of them had become members of the new organization. Given this reception, the Gompers federation grew steadily, if not spectacularly: It counted 140,000 members in 1886; by 1889, the figure had risen to 278,000.

It is also noteworthy that the economic depression that swept the country between 1893 and 1896 did not drastically deplete union membership totals, as had been the case in earlier hard times. The new principles of Gompers, reflected at both the federation and national levels, gave labor significant staying power. Moreover, the now centralized control held by the nationals over their locals both lessened the danger that local monies would be dissipated in ill-advised strikes and provided the locals with what were normally sufficient funds for officially authorized strikes.

On the other hand, organized labor still had a severe problem to contend with in the 1890s: the deep desire of the nation's industrialists, now themselves strongly centralized in this era of trusts and other forms of consolidation, to regain unilateral control of employee affairs. Not since the 1870s had the forces of management been as determined, as formidable, or, particularly in the case of two widely heralded strikes of the time—waged against the predecessor of the United States Steel Corporation, the Carnegie Steel Company, at Homestead, Pennsylvania, in 1892 and against the Pullman Palace Car Company and various railroads in many places in 1894—as successful in opposing unionism. In both cases, each marked by considerable violence, the defeats were crushing ones for organized labor.

Other managers in turn, impressed by these two employer triumphs and at times alarmed by what they felt was the overly belligerent stance of the AFL unions, also became more aggressive in their battles with labor. Builders in Chicago, strongly united, completely ousted their workers' union representatives following a one-year 1899 strike. The employers in the job foundry industry banded together in the National Founders' Association, which successfully terminated not only longstanding Molders Union work rules but, for all practical purposes, the existence of the union itself. In addition, the general public tended to be no more sympathetic to the aims of the labor movement; symbolically, the president of Harvard University, Charles W. Eliot, "went so far as to glorify the strikebreaker as an example of the finest type of American citizen whose liberty had to be protected at all costs."[6]

Despite all these adverse factors, union membership growth in this period was unparalleled. From 447,000 unionists in 1897, the figure increased almost fivefold to 2,073,000 in 1904—a rate of expansion that has never been equaled since. The figures reflect the national prosperity of the day and the success of many of the national unions (their problems notwithstanding) in organizing their official jurisdictions along the lines of the AFL principles.

But the labor movement could not indefinitely withstand the continuing employer opposition, now augmented by a series of devastating court injunctions on the one hand and rival union challenges from leftist workingmen's groups on the other. Total union membership dropped to 1,959,000 in 1906, and even its ultimate growth to 3,014,000 by 1917 was quite uneven and—considering the fact that 90 percent of the country's labor force still remained unorganized—unspectacular.

Intensified employer campaigns for the open (nonunion) shop resulted in a number of notable union strike losses after 1904 in the meatpacking and shipping industries, among others. Violence often occurred—most drastically at the Colorado Fuel and Iron Company's Ludlow location (see Exhibit 2-6), when in 1914 eleven children and two women were found to have died of suffocation in a cellar beneath a strikers' tent that the state militia, summoned by the company, had set afire. These were also the peak years of **yellow-dog contracts** (under which employees promised in writing never to engage in union activities); labor spies; immediate discharge of

EXHIBIT 2-6

Source: *United Mine Workers Journal*, March–April 1999, p. 12.

It was April, 1914, and the UMWA's strike against mining giant Colorado Fuel and Iron Co. (CFI Co.) in Trinidad, Colo., over the company's refusal to recognize the union was in its sixth month. Tensions were high. Strikers and their families living in the tent colony of Ludlow feared the worst. A unit of the Colorado National Guard, which had been infiltrated by Baldwin-Felts agents hired by CFI, had encamped in the hills around Ludlow and the mood amongst them was decidedly anti-striker.

On the morning of April 20, based on a rumor that "someone" was being held against his will in the camp, the Guard commander ordered his men to advance and fire on Ludlow. The militiamen moved forward in a hail of bullets and miners began to return fire. Their wives and children took cover in cellars dug under the tents.

As the day and the shooting went on, an empty tent burst into flames and the fire spread to other tents.

At the end of the day, four strikers were dead. In addition, two leaders of the Ludlow colony were captured and shot—their bodies left in an open field for 48 hours. On the following day, searchers found two women and 11 children dead in a tent cellar—suffocated.

workers at the slightest evidence of union sympathies; and the use of federal, state, and local troops on a wholesale scale to safeguard company interests in the face of strike actions.

The courts, too, were not particularly restrained in their conduct toward unions. Injunctions banning specific union activities often appeared to unionists to be issued quite indiscriminately.

Still another threat to the established unions, in the years between 1904 and 1917, came from workers themselves. Sometimes impatient with what they considered to be the slow pace of AFL union gains, and sometimes wholly antagonistic toward the very system of capitalism, radical labor groups rose to challenge (without, as it turned out, very much success) the Gompers unions for membership and influence. This was the heyday of immigration into the United States—some 14 million newcomers, mainly from Europe, arrived in the first two decades of the twentieth century—and the European political socialism that many of the radical groups espoused found some recruits in this quarter.

Nonetheless, Gompers and the AFL could point with satisfaction to some major gains, gains that rested to a great extent on the outstanding organizing and bargaining successes of a few specific AFL member nationals, particularly in the building trades, the ladies' garment industry, and coal mining. Ironically, two of these unions (the International Ladies' Garment Workers and the United Mine Workers) owed much of their new strength to membership policies that took in many semiskilled and even unskilled workers, although skilled-worker needs were still emphasized (and although both these unions were definite exceptions to AFL union practice in their actions).

The AFL's further grounds for satisfaction rested on another irony: Despite the continuation of the policy against active involvement in politics, AFL lobbying activities at both the federal and state levels had been instrumental in the enactment of significant progressive labor legislation. Among other such achievements, by 1917 some 30 states had introduced workmen's compensation systems covering industrial accidents, and almost as many had provided for maximum hours of work for women. On the federal level, the 1915 LaFollette Seamen's Act had greatly ameliorated conditions on vessels, and the 1916 Owen-Keating Act had dealt a severe blow to child-labor abusers.

WARTIME GAINS AND PEACETIME LOSSES

From 1917 to 1920, the time of World War I and the months of prosperity following it, the AFL grew rapidly. The 3 million workers in the AFL unions on the eve of the hostilities increased to 5.1 million only three years later. During the war, military production, the curtailment of immigration, and the draft combined to create tight labor markets and thus gave unions considerable bargaining power and commensurate gains.

Even more significant, labor received for the first time official government support for its collective bargaining activities. The rights to organize and bargain collectively, free of employer discrimination for union activities, were granted AFL leaders by the Woodrow Wilson administration for the length of the war.

Despite this auspicious entrance into the 1920s, however, the decade was to be one of great failure for unionism. Total union membership rapidly dwindled from the 1920 peak of 5.1 million to 3.8 million three years later and, steadily if less dramatically declining even after this, hit a 12-year low of 3.4 million at the close of the decade. The drop is even more remarkable given the fact that the economy generally continued to flourish during this period; in every prior era of national prosperity, unions had gained considerable ground.

Nonetheless, there were understandable reasons for the poor performance of unionism in the 1920s. A combination of five powerful factors, most of them as unprecedented as organized labor's boom-period decline, was now at work.

First, after the beginning of the decade, prices remained stable, and, with workers generally retaining their relatively high wage gains of the 1917–1920 period, the cries of labor organizers that only union membership could stave off real wage losses fell on deaf ears.

Second, employers throughout the nation not only returned to such measures for thwarting unionization as the yellow-dog contract and the immediate discharge of union "agitators" but now embarked on an extensive antiunion, open-shop propaganda campaign.

The campaign, typically conducted under the slogan of the **American Plan**, portrayed unions as alien to the nation's individualistic spirit, restrictive of industrial efficiency, and frequently dominated by radical elements who did not have the best interests of America at heart. The public appeared to be impressed: To many citizens, organizations that could even remotely be construed as going against individualism and the free enterprise system in this day of laissez-faire Republicanism were highly un-American.

Third, many companies introduced what became known as **welfare capitalism**. Intending to demonstrate to their employees that unions were unnecessary, they established a wide variety of employee-benefit programs: elaborate profit-sharing plans, recreational facilities, dispensaries, cafeterias, and health and welfare systems of all kinds. Employee representation plans were also instituted, with workers thus being offered a voice on wages, hours, and conditions—the companies being thereby enabled to satisfy many grievances before they became major morale problems. Although the managements could withdraw the benefits at any time, and although the employee representatives normally had only advisory voices, union ills were undeniably compounded by these company moves.

In the fourth place, the courts proved themselves even less hospitable to labor unions than they had been in labor's dark days preceding World War I. Having denied in 1921 that the Clayton Act of 1914 exempted unions from the antitrust laws and the injunction, the Supreme Court proceeded to invalidate an Arizona anti-injunction law the same year and then struck down state minimum-wage laws as violations of liberty of contract in 1923. Encouraged by the implied mandate from Washington, lower-court judges now issued injunctions more freely than ever.

Fifth, and finally, some of the union losses were due to unimaginative leadership in the labor movement itself. Gompers died in 1924, and his successor, William Green, lacked the aggressiveness and the imagination of the AFL's first president. He and most of his AFL union leaders were nothing if not complacent.

On the eve of the Great Depression in late 1929, then, organized labor remained almost exclusively the province of the highly skilled worker minority, apathetic in the face of the loss of one-third of its members in a single decade, militantly opposed by much of the employer community, severely crimped by judicial actions, and often suspected by the general public of possessing traits counter to the spirit of America. It appeared to have a superb future behind it.

THE GREAT DEPRESSION AND THE AFL'S RESURGENCE IN SPITE OF ITSELF

The stock market collapse of October 1929 ushered in the most severe business downturn in the nation's history. By the depression's lowest point in 1933, a staggering 24.9 percent of the country's civilian labor force was out of work, compared with an unemployment rate of only 3.2 percent in 1929.

In 1933 union membership stood at 2,973,000—only 200,000 above the 1916 level. Given this severe loss of dues-payers, plus the necessity of sustaining strikes against the inevitable wage cuts of workers still employed, it is not surprising that many unions soon became as impoverished as their constituents.

It is surprising, however, that the mood of the workers themselves seemed to be one of bewildered apathy. The atmosphere was now marked by constant mortgage foreclosures. It was characterized by the fear of starvation on the part of many of those not working and the fear of sudden unemployment on the part of many of those still employed. Virtually all remnants of welfare capitalism were being abruptly terminated. Under these conditions, one might have expected a reincarnation of organizations seeking to overthrow the capitalistic system that was now performing so poorly. Some workers did indeed turn to such radical movements as Communism, but, in general, the nation seemed to have been shocked into inaction.

It is still more surprising, even considering its uninspiring performance in meeting the challenge of the 1920s, that the leadership of the AFL did not noticeably change its policies in these dark days. Through 1932, Green and the AFL executive council remained opposed to unemployment compensation, old-age pensions, and minimum-wage legislation as constituting unwarranted state intervention. They asked only for increased public-works spending from the government. So far was the AFL from the pulse of the general community at this time that, although the great bulk of union officials were and had long been Democratic party supporters, it refused, with scrupulous official neutrality, to endorse either candidate in the 1932 presidential election that swept Democrat Franklin D. Roosevelt into office with what was then the largest margin in American history.

Roosevelt's one-sided victory symbolized the country's (if not the AFL's) willingness to grant the federal government more scope for participation in domestic affairs than it had ever been given before. The business community, upon which the nation had put such a premium during the prosperous years of the 1920s, was now both discredited and demoralized. It had become painfully apparent, too, to the millions who had been steeped in the values of American individualism, that the individual worker was comparatively helpless to influence the conditions of the employment environment. In short, the depression allowed labor unions—which had been so greatly out of favor with the American people only a few years earlier—a golden opportunity for revival and growth, now with government encouragement.

❖ The Norris–LaGuardia Act

Even before the election, such a climate had resulted in one notable gain for unions. The **Norris–La Guardia** Act of 1932 satisfied a demand Gompers had originally made in a petition to the president and Congress some 26 years earlier: The power of judges to issue injunctions in labor disputes on an almost unlimited basis was now revoked. Severe restrictions were placed on the conditions under which the courts could grant injunctions, and such orders could in no case be issued against certain otherwise legal union activities. In addition, the yellow-dog contract was declared unenforceable in federal courts.

The 1932 act marked a drastic change in public policy. Previously, except for the temporary support that unions received during World War I, collective bargaining had been severely hampered through judicial control. Now it was to be strongly encouraged, by legislative fiat and—after Roosevelt took office in early 1933—by executive support.

❖ The National Industrial Recovery Act

Roosevelt and the first New Deal Congress wasted little time in making known their sentiments. The **National Industrial Recovery Act** (**NIRA**) of mid-1933, in similar but stronger language than that already existing in the Norris–La Guardia Act, specifically guaranteed employees "the right to organize and bargain collectively through representatives of their own choosing . . . free from the interference, restraint or coercion of employers." Almost overnight, thousands of laborers in such mass-production industries as steel, automobiles, rubber, and electrical manufacturing spontaneously formed their own locals and applied to the AFL for charters. By the end of 1933, the federation had gained more than a million new members.

The largest single gains at this time were registered by those established AFL internationals that had lost the most members during the 1920s and could capitalize on the new climate in public policy to win back and expand their old clientele. Both the men's and women's clothing unions fell into this category. Most impressive of all, however, was the performance of the United Mine Workers under their aggressive president, John L. Lewis. Lewis dispatched dozens of capable organizers throughout the coal fields, had signs proclaiming that "President Roosevelt wants you to join the union" placed at the mine pits, and not only regained virtually all his former membership but organized many traditionally nonunion fields in the Southeast. There were 60,000 Mine Workers at the time of the NIRA's passage; six months later, the figure had grown to over 350,000.

The employers, however, did not remain docile in the face of this new union resurgence. Many of them responded to the NIRA by restoring or instituting the employee representation plans of the previous decade. Such company unions, although bitterly assailed by bona fide unionists as circumventing the law's requirements concerning employer interference, spread rapidly. By the spring of 1934, probably one-quarter of all industrial workers were employed in plants that had them. Many other managements simply refused, the law notwithstanding, to recognize any labor organizations. On many occasions, this attitude led to outbreaks of violence, ultimately terminated by the police or by National Guard units.

❖ The Wagner Act

The National Industrial Recovery Act was itself declared unconstitutional by the Supreme Court early in 1935, but Congress quickly replaced it with a law that was even more to labor's liking. The National Labor Relations Act, better known (after its principal draftsman in the Senate) as the **Wagner Act**, was far more explicit in what it expected of collective bargaining than was the NIRA in two basic ways. First, it placed specific restrictions on what management could do, including an absolute ban on company-dominated unions. Second, it established the wishes of the employee majority as the basis for selection of a bargaining representative and provided that in cases of doubt as to a union's majority status, a secret-ballot election of the employees would determine whether the majority existed. To implement both provisions, it established a **National Labor Relations Board (NLRB)**, empowered not only to issue cease-and-desist orders against employers who violated the restrictions but also to determine appropriate bargaining units and conduct representation elections.

Considerably less than enthusiastic about the Wagner Act, many employers chose to ignore its provisions and hoped that it would suffer the same fate as the NIRA. They were to be disappointed: In 1937, the Supreme Court held that the 1935 act was fully constitutional.

THE CIO'S CHALLENGE TO THE AFL

Meanwhile, however, the AFL itself almost snatched defeat from the jaws of victory. The leaders of the federation clashed sharply as to the kind of reception that should be accorded the workers in steel, rubber, automobiles, and similar mass-production industries who had spontaneously organized in the wave of enthusiasm following the NIRA's passage. The federation had given these new locals the temporary status of federal locals, which meant that they were directly affiliated with the AFL rather than with one of the established national unions. The workers involved, however, wanted to form their own national **industrial unions** covering all types of workers within their industries, regardless of occupation or skill level. And this, obviously, meant a radical departure from the 50-year AFL tradition of discouraging nonskilled workers and essentially welcoming only **craft unions** (the mining and clothing industries, as noted earlier, always excepted because of their particular situations).

John L. Lewis, who had shown such initiative in expanding the ranks of his Mine Workers in the preceding months, led the fight for industrial unionism within the federation. He and his allies argued that changing times had now made skilled-craft unionism obsolete, that the AFL could no longer speak with any political power as long as it confined itself to what was (with the acceleration of mechanization and the replacement of craftsmen by semiskilled machine operators) a steadily dwindling minority of the labor force, and that, should the federation fail to assert its leadership over the new unionists, rival federations would arise to fill the vacuum. Holding perhaps the greatest oratorical powers ever possessed by an American labor leader (and very possibly the only one to begin sentences with "Methinks"), Lewis ridiculed the AFL president for not being able to decide the issue: "Alas, poor Green. I knew him well. He wishes me to join him in fluttering procrastination, the while intoning *O tempora, O mores*!" In a dramatic speech at the 1935 AFL Atlantic City convention, Lewis warned that should the federation fail to "heed this cry from Macedonia that comes from the hearts of men" and refuse to allow industrial unionism or to organize the millions still unorganized, "the enemies of labor will be encouraged and high wassail will prevail at the banquet tables of the mighty."

Lewis spoke to no avail. The convention was dominated by inveterate craft unionists, many of whom possibly believed that Macedonia was somewhere east of Akron and who at any rate were opposed to admitting what Teamster president Daniel Tobin described as "rubbish" mass-production laborers. The demands of industrial unionism were defeated by a convention vote of 18,024 to 10,933. And Lewis, never one to camouflage his emotions for the sake of good fellowship with his AFL colleagues, left Atlantic City only after landing a severe uppercut to the jaw of Carpenter Union president William L. Hutcheson in a fit of pique.

Within a month, Lewis had formed his own organization of industrial unionists. The Committee for Industrial Organization (known after 1938 as the Congress of Industrial Organizations) originally wanted only to "counsel and advise unorganized and newly organized groups of workers; to bring them under the banner and in affiliation with the American Federation of Labor." But the AFL, having already made its sentiments so clear, was to deny the new organization the latter opportunity; almost immediately, Green's executive council suspended the CIO leaders for practicing **dual unionism** and ordered them to dissolve their group. When these actions failed to dissuade the CIO, the AFL took its strongest possible action and expelled all 32 national member unions.

Lewis and his fellow founders were spectacularly successful in realizing their objectives. Armed with ample loans from the rebel nationals, aggressive leadership, experienced organizers, and, above all, confidence that mass-production workers enthusiastically *wanted* unionism, the AFL offshoot was able to claim almost 4 million recruits as early as 1937.

By 1941, even more remarkable conquests had been registered. One by one, virtually all the giant corporations had recognized CIO-affiliated unions as bargaining agents for their employees: all the major automobile manufacturers, almost all companies of any size in the steel industry, the principal rubber producers, the larger oil companies, the major radio and electrical equipment makers, the important meatpackers of the country, the larger glassmakers, and many others. Smaller companies that had also been unionized in this period could at least take comfort in the fact that they were in good company.

Still, the CIO's organizing campaigns were not welcomed by many of these companies with open arms. United States Steel recognized the CIO's Steel Workers

Organizing Committee without a contest in 1937 (because it feared labor unrest at a time when business conditions were finally improving). But the other major steel producers unconditionally refused to deal with unionism, the law notwithstanding. In 1941, the National Labor Relations Board ordered these companies to recognize what had by then become the United Steelworkers of America, but four years of company intimidation, espionage, and militia-protected strikebreaking—highlighted by a Memorial Day 1937 clash between pickets and police that resulted in the deaths of 10 workers, injuries to many more, and substantial damage to property—had then elapsed.

The use of professional strikebreakers often served as a particularly potent employer weapon in these years. Such temporary payroll members were entrusted with such missions as the conveying of the impression that the struck organization was actually operating (to demoralize those out on strike) and the inciting of violence (to encourage the public authorities to take action against the unionists). In pursuit of the first goal the strikebreaker might, for example, burn paper in a plant furnace so that the smoke of the chimney would give the appearance of plant production. Driving empty trucks to and from the plant was another frequently used ploy.

And these strikebreakers frequently adopted such tactics as the hurling of stones into picket lines and the spitting at strikers to provoke violence, facts that explain why such individuals were at times termed *agents provocateurs*. If the strikers were goaded into counterviolence, as they often were, the state militia or National Guard—rarely friendly to labor organizations—could then be summoned to the scene.

It was not the most honorable kind of occupation, and many of its practitioners in fact possessed criminal records. As one of them—the well-known professional strikebreaker Sam "Chowderhead" Cohen—once commented about his own lengthy record of imprisonment, "You see, in this line of work they never asked for no references."[7]

But where there was a will on the part of unionists there was generally a way. In some industries, workers turned to **sit-down strikes**—protest stoppages in which the strikers remained at their places of work and were furnished with food by allies outside the plant. Such stoppages, now illegal as trespasses upon private property, were of considerable influence in gaining representation rights for the unions in the automobile, rubber, and glass industries.

Nor, more significantly, was the AFL itself placid in the face of its new competition. Abandoning its traditional lethargy, it now terminated its "craftsmen only" policy and chartered industrial unions of its own in every direction. AFL meatcutters emerged to challenge CIO packinghouse workers for members at all skill levels within the meatpacking industry. AFL papermill employees competed against CIO paper workers. AFL electricians tried to recruit the same workers, from all quarters of the electrical industry, as did the CIO electrical-union organizers. And the story was much the same in textiles and automobiles. Aided by the same favorable climates of worker opinion and public policy that had originally inspired Lewis, and now also helped by improving economic conditions, the AFL actually surpassed the CIO in membership by 1941. By that time, however, the CIO had paid its parent the supreme compliment: It had modified its framework to include craft unionism as well as industrial unionism, and the lines separating the two rival federations had become permanently clouded.

At the time of Pearl Harbor, in December 1941, total union membership stood at 10.2 million, compared with the fewer than 3 million members of only nine years earlier. The CIO itself—representing some 4.8 million workers at this time—was destined to achieve little further success, as measured by sheer membership statistics; it would enroll only 6 million employees at its zenith in 1947 and then gradually retreat before the onslaught of a further AFL counterattack. But if Lewis's organization failed to live up to its founder's expectations as the sole repository of future union leadership, neither could it in any satisfactory way be described as a failure. When America entered World War II in late 1941, the labor movement not only was a major force to be reckoned with but, for the first time, was to a great extent representative of the full spectrum of American workers. And for this situation, the CIO's challenge to the AFL's 50 years of dominance deserves no small amount of credit.

WORLD WAR II

As in the case of World War I, the years after Pearl Harbor saw a further increase in union strength. Although the country's economic conditions had improved considerably in the late 1930s, only after the start of hostilities and the acceleration of the draft did a tight labor market arise to weaken employer resistance to union demands.

Other factors favorable to organized labor were also present. The federal government, sympathetic enough with the goals of unionism for almost a decade, now went even further in its tangible support: In return for a no-strike pledge from both AFL and CIO leaders, labor was granted equal representation with management on the tripartite War Labor Board, the all-powerful institution that adjusted collective bargaining disputes during this period. Unions further profited in the membership area from the fast growth of such wartime industries as aircraft and shipbuilding and the reinvigoration of such now crucial sectors as steel, rubber, the electrical industry, and trucking. By the end of the war in 1945, union ranks had been increased by more than 4 million new workers, or by almost 40 percent.

By and large, labor honored its no-strike pledge during hostilities. However, with the cost of living continually rising, and with the War Labor Board nonetheless attempting to hold direct wages in check (not always successfully, and frequently at the cost of allowing such "nonwage" supplements as vacation, holiday, and lunch-period pay), the incidence of strikes did increase steadily after 1942. Particularly galling to the general public were several strikes by Lewis's own Mine Workers, all in direct defiance of President Roosevelt's orders and all given substantial publicity by the media. (If anything, however, the strikes only cemented Lewis's popularity with his constituents. Even now he remains a latter-day legend with coal miners who never knew him. Exhibit 2-7 is a page that appeared almost a half-century after these strikes in the major publication of the Mine Workers. Lewis is the portly gentleman standing at the lower left.)

Managers, themselves regaining much of their lost stature with the stress on war production at this time, could also point to other evidence that labor had become "too powerful." The competition between the AFL and CIO, officially postponed for the duration of the war, in practice continued almost unabated. Such rivalry on occasion temporarily curtailed plant output, as unions within the two federations resorted to "slowdowns" and "quickie strikes" to convince employers of their respective jurisdictional claims. Instances of worker featherbedding—the receipt of payment for unperformed work—marked several industries, notably construction.

EXHIBIT 2-7

PORTAL TO PORTAL: As a result of the 1943 wartime strikes, some 500,000 miners won pay for time spent traveling from the mine mouth to the working face. The country's coal supply was never jeopardized, but the union was strongly criticized for striking a vital industry during wartime. The UMWA, led by President John L. Lewis, countered with an information campaign and refused to let the operators use the war as an excuse to further exploit them.

RANK-AND-FILE DISCIPLINE: During negotiations in 1941, President John L. Lewis calls for $1-per-day increase in wages for miners (above). In the fight for benefits, Lewis never went to the bargaining table alone—hundreds of thousands of miners gave him their undivided support. The wage and benefit victories achieved during Lewis' tenure as president from 1920 to 1960 were a direct result of rank-and-file solidarity and discipline. Across the country, miners would walk out of or return to the mines at his direction.

SOURCE: *United Mine Workers Journal*, August–September 1990, p. 31.

And members of the Communist Party, originally welcomed by some CIO unions because of their demonstrated organizational ability, had now gained substantial influence if not effective control within several of these unions, including both the United Automobile Workers and the Electrical, Radio, and Machine Workers.

The public's attention was also called, by forces unhappy with the labor movement's rapid growth, to union political strength. The AFL had not yet abandoned its traditional policy of bipartisanship, but Lewis had led the CIO actively into political campaigning and had, in fact, resigned his federation presidency when the CIO rank and file had refused to bow to his wishes and vote for Republican Wendell Wilkie in 1940. Under Lewis's successor, Philip Murray, and particularly through the direct efforts of Clothing Worker president Sidney Hillman, the CIO had become even more aggressive and influential—within the Democratic party. So effective had Hillman's CIO Political Action Committee become by this time that attacks upon it emanated from the highest of places: the House Un-American Activities Committee (with a membership unfriendly to Roosevelt) called it "a subversive . . . organization."[8]

The American man and woman in the street seemed to be impressed. By the end of the war in 1945, public opinion polls showed more than 67 percent of the respondents in favor of legislative curbs on union power.

PUBLIC REACTION AND PRIVATE MERGER

Organized labor fell even further from public favor in the immediate postwar period. Faced with income declines as overtime and other wartime pay supplements disappeared, with real wage decreases as prices rose in response to the huge pent-up consumer demand, and with layoffs as factories converted to peacetime production, workers struck as they had never done before. Although the violence of earlier-day labor unrest did not recur often, the year 1946 saw new highs established in terms of number of stoppages (4,985), and person-days idle as a percentage of available working time (1.43). By the end of the year, noteworthy stoppages (many of them simultaneously) had occurred in virtually every sector of the economy, including the railroads, autos, steel, public utilities, and even public education.

❖ The Enactment of Taft-Hartley

Such strikes were not well received by a frequently inconvenienced public that had already voiced reservations about union strength. The sentiments that the Wagner Act and other public policies of the 1930s had been too one-sided in favor of labor grew rapidly and soon became compelling. In 1947, a newly elected Republican Congress passed, over President Truman's veto, the **Taft-Hartley Act.**

Taft-Hartley drastically amended the Wagner Act to give greater protection to both employers and individual employees. To the list of "unfair" labor practices already denied employers were added six "unfair" *union* practices, ranging from restraint or coercion of employees to featherbedding. Employees could now hold elections to decertify unions as well as to certify them. Provisions regulating certain internal affairs of unions, explicitly giving employers certain collective bargaining rights (particularly regarding freedom of expression concerning union organization), and sanctioning government intervention in the case of national emergency strikes were also enacted.

A fuller discussion of Taft-Hartley is reserved for later pages; however, it might be added here that the 1947 act was at least as controversial as the Wagner Act had been. Its proponents, asserted that it "reinjected an essential measure of justice into collective bargaining." Less friendly observers of Taft-Hartley, including the spokespeople of organized labor, were less happy and hurled such epithets as "slave labor act" at it. That the act has proved generally satisfactory to the majority of Americans, however, may be inferred from the fact that more than five decades later Taft-Hartley, essentially unchanged from its original edition, remained the basic labor law of the land.

❖ Prelude to the Merger

It is tempting to argue that the American Federation of Labor-Congress of Industrial Organizations merger of 1955 was inevitable. The issue that had led to the birth of the CIO was, as noted, blunted even by the late 1930s when the AFL rapidly chartered its own industrial unions and the CIO began to recognize craft unions as part of its structure. But another 15 years were to elapse before merger became a reality, and significant differences still had to be bridged.

In the first place, the new unions that had been formed, first by the CIO and later by the AFL, were often meeting head-on in their quests for new members and enlarged jurisdiction. Any merged federation would have to resolve not only this kind of overlap but also the membership raiding that was frequently carried on by such rival unions.

Second, the conservative AFL leaders displayed deep hostility toward the Communist-dominated unions within the CIO. Such unions reached a peak in the immediate postwar months, when a special report of the Research Institute of America listed 18 of them in this category.

Finally, personalities played a role. Murray and Green were mutually suspicious leaders. Each was quite unwilling to take the initiative in any merger move that would involve subordination of influence to the other.

By 1955, however, most of these cleavages had been resolved. Murray, his patience with the Communist unions exhausted as they became more aggressive, had taken the lead in expelling most such unions from the CIO in 1949 and 1950. Murray's move cost the CIO an estimated 1 million members, but new unions were quickly established to assume the old jurisdictions, and Murray claimed to have regained most of the lost membership within the next two years.

Further preparing the way for ultimate merger were the 1952 deaths of Murray and Green, both suddenly and only 11 days apart. The two successors—Walter Reuther of the United Auto Workers, for Murray, and AFL secretary-treasurer George Meany, for Green—were relatively divorced from the personal bitterness of the earlier presidents.

And beyond these factors were growing sentiments on the part of both AFL and CIO leaders that only a united labor movement could (1) stave off future laws of the Taft-Hartley variety, (2) avoid the jurisdictional squabbles that were increasingly sapping the treasuries of both federations, and (3) allow organized labor to reach significant new membership totals for the first time since 1947.

In December 1955, culminating two years of intensive negotiations between representatives of the two organizations, the AFL-CIO became a reality. The new constitution respected the "integrity of each affiliate," including both its "organizing jurisdiction" and its "established collective bargaining relationships."

Consolidation of the rival unions was to be encouraged but was to be on a voluntary basis. And it was agreed that the new giant federation would issue charters "based upon a strict recognition that both craft and industrial unions are equal and necessary." With the act of merger, the open warfare that had first revitalized and then damaged the labor movement passed from the scene.

ORGANIZED LABOR SINCE THE MERGER

Although some observers predicted that the original 15 million membership total (two-thirds of it provided by the AFL) of the AFL-CIO would rapidly double, they were wrong. Four and one-half decades after the merger, the organization had fewer members than in 1955—some 13.3 million in 2000. The losses had not been confined merely to the federation, either. Labor had clearly been losing ground on all fronts in at least the later part of this period. The shrinkage had taken it from the just under 25 percent of the nation's labor force that unions represented in 1970 to the 13.9 percent representation at the end of the twentieth century.

❖ The Elusive White-Collar Sector

Several formidable obstacles undoubtedly serve to explain this situation. Paramount among them is, of course, the fact that blue-collar workers, traditionally constituting that sector of the labor force most susceptible to the overtures of the union organizer, have now been substantially organized. And this sector has, it will be recalled, been declining as a source of jobs in recent years. It remains to be seen whether new approaches, fresh leadership, and environmental changes adversely affecting worker morale can gain for organized labor the allegiance of the growing white-collar sector. As the statistics in the preceding chapter indicated, however, unions to date have not been spectacularly successful in recruiting this wave of the future.

❖ Labor and Public Opinion

Beyond this, labor's fall from public favor, which began in the 1940s and led initially to the enactment of Taft-Hartley, had yet to be arrested all these years later. Congressional disclosures of corruption in the Teamsters and several smaller unions in the late 1950s hardly improved labor's image. The AFL-CIO quickly expelled not just the Teamsters (who would not, in fact, be allowed to return until 1987) but all the offending unions. But the public seemed to be far more impressed by the disclosures than by the federation's reaction to them, as indeed had been the case following the CIO's expulsion of its Communist-dominated affiliates.

❖ Union Excesses

Union resistance to technological change, sometimes taking the form of featherbedding and insistence on the protection of jobs that seemed no longer to be needed (those of diesel firemen and certain airline and maritime employees, for example), also was anything but calculated to regain widespread public support. Nor was it easy to generate sympathy outside the labor movement on behalf of plumbers who threatened to strike for wage rates in excess of $50 per hour, electricians demanding a 20-hour workweek, and New York City transit workers seeking a 50 percent wage increase, a 32-hour workweek, and some 75 other demands. These few examples were among the extremes; most unionists showed considerably more concern for the welfare of their industries in the postmerger years. But such actions as the ones illustrated, being more newsworthy, attracted more attention. It is conceivable that, through this combination of factors ranging from corruption to excessive demands, countless potential union members had been alienated.

❖ Restrictive Legislation

The continuing lack of public confidence in unionism had also led, in the relatively recent past, to new legislation restricting labor's freedom of action. In particular, the **Landrum-Griffin Act** of 1959 stemmed from this climate and, directly, from the union-corruption revelations of Congress that were cited earlier. Among its other provisions, Landrum-Griffin guarantees union members a "bill of rights" that their unions cannot violate and requires officers of labor organizations to meet a wide and somewhat cumbersome variety of reporting and disclosure obligations. It also lays out specific ground rules for union elections, rules that have been deemed too inhibiting (as have most other parts of the act) by many labor leaders.

❖ More Responsible Employee Relations

It is perhaps also true that labor's conspicuous recent lack of success has stemmed from the fact that the new breed of manager has acted a great deal more responsibly in employee relations, thereby making the organization considerably less vulnerable to unionization. Objective and essentially uniform standards for discipline, promotion, layoffs, recalls, and a host of other personnel areas have now all but totally replaced even the palest efforts at tyranny, and in the face of the change relatively few workers seem to feel the need for a collective bargaining agency as a curb on supervisory ruthlessness.

❖ AFL-CIO Leadership Prior to 1995

And, perhaps foremost of all, labor's leadership in these many years has received much of the blame. George Meany, the bulldog-faced, cigar-chomping, tough-talking plumber from the Bronx who headed the AFL-CIO from its formation in 1955 until 1979, never seemed to be much concerned about the declining percentage of union members. He asserted with the candor that was as much a part of his personality as the bellicosity:

> To me, it doesn't mean a thing. I have no concern about it, because the history of the trade union movement has shown that when organized workers were a very, very tiny percentage of the work force, they still accomplished and did things that were important for the entire work force. The unorganized portions of the work forces have no power for the simple reason that they're not organized.[9]

Meany was much admired even by his enemies for his consistent and effective pursuit of progressive legislation. He was in the forefront of the successful effort to enact strong equal-employment-opportunities provisions into the Civil Rights Act of 1964, and throughout his 24 years at the federation's helm, he made labor a powerful voice for demanding more beneficent laws than had existed for the poor and the aged as well as for minorities. He also played a major role in staunchly backing U.S. foreign policy during the Vietnamese War even in the face of opposition to the hostilities by almost half of the U.S. population, and he strongly opposed totalitarian governments (especially communistic ones and that of Spain's fascist Francisco Franco) around the world. But as far as organizing the unorganized and enacting legislation that would directly benefit organized labor, he seemed to have an interest that could best be described as minimal. Not a young man at the time of the merger (he was then 61) and still AFL-CIO president at the age of 85, he was so solidly entrenched in the job that no one dared to take him on, all of the away-from-Meany rumblings about lack of organizing and labor lawmaking success notwithstanding.

Meany's successor, Lane Kirkland, head of the federation from 1979 to mid-1995, shared Meany's views on recruiting new members. "Frankly," he once said, "I don't care whether the salesmen are organized. If they want to be organized, fine. If they don't I don't feel any ideological compulsion to organize them. I don't feel any compulsion to organize foremen, plant managers, advertising men, hustlers, what have you."[10]

Kirkland was also admired in many quarters—especially for engineering the key role that the AFL-CIO played in toppling communist regimes in Eastern Europe (most conspicuously in Poland). But his critics asserted that foreign policy seemed to constitute almost the entire sphere of interest of this second president of the federation, and as the years went on with a notable lack of membership growth for organized labor the anti-Kirkland forces within the AFL-CIO became increasingly vocal on this count.

In the summer of 1995, Kirkland announced that he would seek a ninth two-year term at the federation's October convention in New York City, and the voices of dissent moved into high gear. In the first open challenge to a federation president since the AFL-CIO's founding, a coalition of international unions led by the fast-growing Service Employees International Union, the American Federation of State, County, and Municipal Employees, and the pivotal International Brotherhood of Teamsters chose a slate of candidates to oppose Kirkland and his supporters on the federation's governing executive council.

Under this pressure, Kirkland not only rescinded his October candidacy for reelection but resigned the presidency. The new interim president—Thomas R. Donahue, who had served for 16 years as AFL-CIO secretary-treasurer—immediately became a candidate for the top spot in the fall election. But in a bitter contest culminating in the voting in New York City, he lost by 1.6 million votes out of 13 million cast to the head of the Service Employees International Union (SEIU), John J. Sweeney.

❖ John J. Sweeney and a New Leadership Aggressiveness

The soft-spoken Sweeney, who had attracted much favorable attention over the past 15 years by—as noted in Chapter 1—almost doubling the size of his union (thereby making the SEIU the best organizing performer of all U.S. international unions), immediately promised to bring labor back to life. He called for recruiting new union members on an "unprecedented scale," as well as for greatly beefing up AFL-CIO political action so as to generate prolabor legislation both nationally and at the state level. He also promised to see to it that more minorities and women played major AFL-CIO leadership roles: Blacks now accounted for 15 percent of union membership and Hispanics 8 percent, and both figures were rapidly rising; women had increased their percentage of union membership from 33 to 40 percent in the past decade.

In furtherance of this last objective, Sweeney and his supporters were instrumental in getting the convention to vote to expand the executive council from 35 to 54 members, with 10 of the 19 new slots being reserved for women and minorities. This action resulted in the female/minority percentage on the council rising from 17 percent to 27 percent. Linda Chavez-Thompson, who had served as national vice president on the council since 1988, when she became the first Hispanic woman to be elected to it, was now elected to the new post of AFL-CIO executive vice president and thus became the second-in-command of the federation. And concrete plans to create a new Women's Department within the AFL-CIO were also announced.

The recruitment of millions of new union members was, Sweeney insisted, at the highest level of urgency because, without this, labor's influence in both the economy and the political arena would continue to wane. As Service Employees president, he had shifted a third of his international's budget into organizing, and in the first years of his federation presidency he convinced many of his AFL-CIO member unions—the majority of whom in recent decades had spent, if anything at all, no more than about 3 percent of their budgets on this activity—to devote at least 10 to 20 percent of their budgets to organizing. The federation itself in these early Sweeney years spent over 20 percent of its $95 million annual budget on coordinating multiunion membership drives and, occasionally, in direct organizational efforts of its own. And in the last years of the twentieth century labor also turned to such long-neglected populations as college students and other young people in recruiting and training those who would themselves be union organizers. Several thousand such workers were rapidly enlisted in labor's cause, significant numbers of them as unpaid volunteers.

Results were definitely achieved—among health care workers, service workers, and public employees, in particular. In 1998, the Service Employees International Union added over 60,000 new members, for the best organizing year in its history, and in the process signed up more hospital workers than it had in the previous five years combined. The American Federation of State, County, and Municipal Employees and the American Federation of Teachers have both in recent years, as noted earlier in this book, also made significant gains. In 1999, indeed, the federal government's Bureau of Labor Statistics announced that for the first time in years union membership in the previous year had actually increased, if by the relatively small total of 101,000. The AFL-CIO asserted that the BLS statistic actually understated union successes because it only considered as union members those workers whose local had ratified a contract and who were paying dues. It declared that over 475,000 new workers had been recruited into union ranks through organizing efforts in 1998, but that only a minority of them had come under a contract by December 31 of that year, and that some had lost their jobs when companies closed or cut back.

But, even at that, labor's overall percentage of the labor force had continued to drop—to 13.9 percent—in the face of an economy that by creating almost 3 million new jobs each year was forcing unions to do even better just to stay even.

It can fairly be said, whatever the future may bring, that labor's new emphasis on organizing that began in late 1995 and continues now has marked a radical departure from the lassitude of the previous four decades and has at least the potential to turn union membership around, perhaps in a significant way. In stark financial terms, the possible returns to unions are anything but minuscule. If labor were to duplicate the Sweeney SEIU formula and commit a third of its collective $5 billion annual estimated income (mainly from membership dues) to organizing, the

$1.67 billion each year would greatly outstrip the estimated $1 billion that employers annually spend to fight unionizing efforts, even without recognizing the countless hours of unpaid volunteer efforts in pursuit of adding to the organizing totals.[11]

Sweeney's third area of emphasis, the political arena, has already paid some dividends. Labor spent an estimated $35 million, mainly on television and radio ads, in the 1996 elections to help defeat 18 Republican congressional incumbents. In so doing it almost gained control of the U.S. House of Representatives for the Democrats, and the new Congress was, if hardly prounion, at least much more restrained in its moves to crimp union activities than national legislative bodies immediately prior to it had been. Republicans who had vowed revenge by, for example, curbing union ability to spend dues money on politics and letting employers give time off instead of paying overtime, were unable to marshal sufficient support. In 1998, instead of the TV and radio ads, unions emphasized grassroots volunteer union member get-out-the-vote efforts, and saw labor's share of the electorate soar to 22 percent from 14 percent in the last nonpresidential election year in 1994. Such an outpouring of labor votes greatly helped Democrats to pick up five House seats. The same year in California, a major union victory was the solid defeat of the so-called Proposition 226, which would have done what the House Republicans had tried to do two years earlier in curbing the political spending of labor.

Encouraged by all of this, the AFL-CIO alone planned to spend some $40 million in the year 2000 elections, with at least $20 million more being earmarked for year 2000 political activities by the international unions. It was probably too much for labor to hope that a newly elected post-2000 U.S. Congress would combine with a Democratic president to change labor laws to make unionization easier and otherwise significantly help unions. But, as in the case of the new emphasis on union organizing, the potential for large labor gains after years of anemia definitely existed on the political front, too.

SOME CONCLUDING THOUGHTS

At least one factor emerges clearly from a reading of U.S. labor history. And it suggests that the more pessimistic predictions about unionism's future may well be without foundation.

Organized labor has been surrounded by conditions at least as bleak as those confronting it today many times in its long history. And on each occasion it has proved equal to the challenge. It fully recovered from disastrous economic depressions that at various times wiped out most of its membership. It survived the inroads of reformers who temporarily succeeded in divorcing it almost entirely from its collective bargaining functions. It overcame devastating victories won by employers and formidable weapons in the hands of the courts. It incurred deeply rooted public disfavor, particularly in the 1870s and 1920s, and ultimately surmounted it. And at perhaps the two most critical junctures of all—(1) in the 1880s, with the rapid disintegration of the Knights and their "one big union" concept, and (2) on the eve of the Great Depression, when an apathetic AFL remained almost strictly interested in highly skilled workers despite mammoth membership losses and concerted attacks from without—a Gompers and a Lewis could emerge to lead unionism to heights previously thought unreachable.

It is entirely possible that labor's remarkable staying power has been due to the simple fact that to many workers, from the early nineteenth century to the present, there really has been no acceptable substitute for collective bargaining as a means of maintaining and improving employment conditions. Whatever its deficiencies, the labor union has offered millions of employees in our profit-minded society sufficient hope that their personal needs would be considered to warrant their taking out union membership. At the very least, these employees have concluded that the only theoretical alternative to collective bargaining—individual bargaining—has for them been no real alternative at all.

Thus, as the earliest pages of this book have indicated, the strongest of cases can be built that collective bargaining is here to stay—and most probably in the highly pragmatic "bread-and-butter" form from which its successes have always emanated, although presumably with some future structural changes to accommodate future institutional needs just as it has made these in the past.

From this it follows that we need to find, not an alternative to labor–management relations, but ways of *improving* the process that now exists. And the latter can be located only after we fully understand both this process and the framework in which it operates. Toward such understandings such a book as this is, of course, directed.

DISCUSSION QUESTIONS

1. "Without the rise of the merchant-capitalist in this country, there could have been no genuine labor movement." Comment.
2. It has been said that "unions are for capitalism for the same reason that fish are for water." Elaborate upon this statement, drawing from the historical record.
3. Explain the following paradox: Until relatively recent years, skilled workers who enjoyed comparatively high levels of income and status constituted the main source of union membership.
4. "If the Knights of Labor expired because it could not fulfill any function, the American Federation of Labor succeeded because it could admirably fulfill many functions." Elaborate, qualifying this statement if you believe that qualifications are needed.
5. One scholar of labor history has offered as his opinion that "even with the New Deal . . . union development experienced, not a marked mutation, but a partial alteration and expansion in leadership, tactics, and jurisdiction. The adjustment in basic union philosophy was neither profound nor completely permanent." Do you agree?
6. If a Gompers and a Lewis could emerge to rescue unionism at critical times in the past, cannot a case be made that there is nothing basically wrong with organized labor today that imaginative leadership could not cure? Discuss fully.
7. "American unionism has very definitely been a war profiteer." Do you agree or disagree?

MINICASES

 ## The Frustrated Labor Historian

Dr. Horace P. Karastan, Distinguished Professor of Labor Relations History at the University and a widely recognized authority in his field, had readily accepted the invitation to speak at the upcoming winter banquet meeting of the Newspaper

Owners' Roundtable. Forty-five minutes had seemed to him to be somewhat on the meager side to properly accommodate the topic that he had been asked to handle— "American Labor Union History from the Eighteenth Century to the Present." But thoughts of the considerable remuneration that he would receive for this brief stint allowed him to forget his compunctions and he approached the date of the banquet with his customary optimism.

Unexpectedly, and sadly from Karastan's point of view, the two speakers who preceded him at the microphone (a United States Congressman and a woman from the Internal Revenue Service) each consumed far more than the 15 minutes that *they* had been allotted. And the professor, originally scheduled to be presented to the audience at 8:15 P.M., did not get the floor until 9:10 P.M. The last words that he heard the Roundtable program chairman use in introducing him were "whose topic for the next few minutes will be 'The Three Most Important Events in American Labor Union History.'"

What would you, as Dr. Karastan, now say to the audience—and why?

#2 A Vote of No Confidence

MEMORANDUM TO: Sara Yayvo, Chairperson, Department of Business Administration
FROM: Harold O. West-Sackville, Associate Professor and Chairperson, Departmental Curriculum Committee
SUBJECT: Proposed Abolition of Labor History Course
After considerable thought, some of it frankly quite painful, I have come to the conclusion that when subjected to any kind of close scrutiny a course in American Labor History such as our BA 487 falls short of justifying itself in our curriculum by some distance.

Enrollments, as you know, have never been particularly gratifying for this elective offering, but since neither person who has taught BA 487 has been known as a crowd-pleaser I don't attach too much weight to this factor by itself. What concerns me much more is the fact that in no way can our graduates *use* the information that they get in this course: Unlike essentially anything else that we offer, there is simply *no practical value* in the material that is covered in this full-semester experience.

Not one of our other advanced courses in the Human Resource Management area—Wage and Salary Administration, Selection, HR Planning, and Collective Bargaining itself—is open to such an indictment; in all cases, their carryover to the real world is obvious. And the same can be said for all of our many offerings, at both the survey course and advanced course levels, outside of HRM—in Marketing, Production, Finance, Quantitative Business Analysis, and General Management. They are nothing if not relevant to the everyday life of the manager.

BA 487 stands out as the exception like an orange in a bag full of apples. And while I write at this moment only as an individual in making known my desire to see it dropped from our curriculum, I intend to make such a recommendation to my full committee when we next meet (on October 21) and, hopefully, thereafter to our full faculty.

Thanks for the backing that I know I have from you in adopting this position.

Do you agree or disagree with Professor West-Sackville's sentiments?

NOTES

[1]Foster Rhea Dulles, *Labor in America*, 2nd rev. ed. (New York: Thomas Y. Crowell, 1960), p. 59.
[2]Ibid., p. 81.
[3]In 1895, he lost his try for reelection by a narrow margin and had to wait a year before he could return to office.
[4]Philip Taft, *Organized Labor in American History* (New York: Harper & Row, 1964), p. 117.
[5]*AFL Convention Proceedings*, 1903, p. 198.
[6]Joseph G. Rayback, *A History of American Labor* (New York: Free Press, 1966), p. 215.
[7]R. R. R. Brooks, *When Labor Organizes* (New Haven: Yale University Press, 1937), p. 146.
[8]Rayback, *A History of American Labor*, p. 386.
[9]Haynes Johnson and Nick Kotz, *The Unions* (Washington, DC: Washington Post Co., 1972), p. 175.
[10]Ibid., p. 176.
[11]*Business Week*, February 17, 1997, pp. 58–59.

SELECTED REFERENCES

Anderson, Carlotta R. *All-American Anarchist: Joseph A. Labadie and the Labor Movement*. Detroit: Wayne State University Press, 1998.

Atleson, James B. *Labor and the Wartime State: Labor Relations and Law During World War II*. Urbana: University of Illinois Press, 1998.

Blackwelder, Julia Kirk. *Now Hiring: The Feminization of Work in the United States 1900–1995*. College Station: Texas A&M University Press, 1997.

Boyle, Kevin. *The UAW and the Heyday of American Liberalism, 1945–1968*. Ithaca, NY: ILR Press, Cornell University, 1995.

Cobble, Dorothy Sue, ed. *Women and Unions: Forging a Partnership*. Ithaca, NY: ILR Press, Cornell University, 1993.

Eisenberg, Susan. *We'll Call You If We Need You: Experiences of Women Working Construction*. Ithaca, NY: ILR Press, Cornell University, 1998.

Finley, Joseph E. *The Corrupt Kingdom: The Rise and Fall of the United Mine Workers*. New York: Simon & Schuster, 1972.

Fraser, Steven. *Labor Will Rule: Sidney Hillman and the Rise of American Labor*. New York: Free Press, 1991.

Galenson, Walter. *The CIO Challenge to the AFL: A History of the American Labor Movement, 1935–1941*. Cambridge, MA: Harvard University Press, 1960.

Gompers, Samuel. *Seventy Years of Life and Labor: An Autobiography*. Edited and introduced by Nick Salvatore. Ithaca, NY: ILR Press, Cornell University, 1984.

Goulden, Joseph C. *Meany*. New York: Atheneum, 1972.

Hoerr, John. *We Can't Eat Prestige: The Women Who Organized Harvard*. Philadelphia: Temple University Press, 1997.

Horowitz, Roger. *"Negro and White, Unite and Fight!"* Urbana and Chicago: University of Illinois Press, 1997.

Juravich, Tom, William F. Hartford, and James R. Green. *Commonwealth of Toil*. Amherst, MA: University of Massachusetts Press, 1996.

Kaufman, Bruce E. *The Origins and Evolution of the Field of Industrial Relations in the United States*. Ithaca, NY: ILR Press, Cornell University, 1993.

Kingsolver, Barbara. *Holding the Line: Women in the Great Arizona Mine Strike of 1983*. Ithaca, NY: ILR Press, Cornell University, 1989.

Kochan, Thomas A., Harry C. Katz, and Robert B. McKersie. *The Transformation of American Industrial Relations*. New York: Basic Books, 1986.

Letwin, Daniel. *The Challenge of Interracial Unionism*. Chapel Hill and London: University of North Carolina Press, 1998.

Lynd, Staughton, ed. *"We Are All Leaders"*. Urbana and Chicago: University of Illinois Press, 1996.

Malkiel, Theresa Serber. *The Diary of a Shirtwaist Striker*. Ithaca, NY: ILR Press, Cornell University, 1990.

Rachleff, Peter. *Hard-Pressed in the Heartland: The Hormel Strike and the Future of the Labor Movement*. Boston: South End Press, 1993.

Scranton, Philip. *Endless Novelty: Specialty Production and American Industrialization, 1865–1925*. Princeton, NJ: Princeton University Press, 1997.

Selvin, David F. *A Terrible Anger: The 1934 Waterfront and General Strikes in San Francisco*. Detroit: Wayne State University Press, 1996.

Sloane, Arthur A. *Hoffa*. Cambridge, MA: MIT Press, 1991.

Solden, Norbert C., ed. *World of Women's Trade Unionism: Comparative Historical Essays*. Westport, CT: Greenwood Press, 1985.

Stepan-Norris, Judith and Maurice Zeitlin. *Talking Union*. Urbana and Chicago: University of Illinois Press, 1996.

Stromquist, Shelton and Marvin Bergman. *Unionizing the Jungles*. Iowa City: University of Iowa Press, 1997.

Wilson, Joseph F. *Tearing Down the Color Bar: A Documentary History of the Brotherhood of Sleeping Car Porters*. New York: Columbia University Press, 1989.

Zieger, Robert H. *American Workers, American Unions, 1920–1985*. Baltimore: Johns Hopkins University Press, 1986.

3

The Legal Framework

OF KEY
CONTENTS

- A century and a half of judge-made law and why labor didn't like it
- The Norris–La Guardia Act of 1932 and the start of a new era for unionism
- The Wagner Act of 1935 and why the modern American labor movement can be said to have begun with it
- The Taft-Hartley Act of 1947 and the public's less positive sentiments toward unions
- The Landrum-Griffin Act of 1959 and yet another change in the thrust of labor law
- The Reagan-Bush labor legacy and at least a slight tilt toward labor in the Clinton era
- The recent and controversial issue of permanent replacements for strikers

$\mathcal{A}$s previous pages have suggested, today's managers are hardly free to deal with unions in any way that they want. A growing body of federal and state laws and the judicial and administrative interpretations of those laws now govern the employer. Legislation today has much to say about management's role in union organizational campaigns and its bargaining procedures in negotiating contracts once a union has gained recognition. It is also outspoken about the acceptable contents of the employer's labor agreements and even its actions in administering those agreements. As is also true of the union, whose conduct is at least equally regulated by public policy, the management can scarcely afford to be poorly informed in the area of labor law.

If the laws have become extensive, however, they have also become complex. Labor lawyers have been forced to undertake herculean tasks in attempting to assess what is legal and what is not in collective bargaining. And inconsistent interpretations of the labor statutes—stemming from the National Labor Relations Board, the various state and lower federal judiciaries, and the Supreme Court itself—continue to mark the field. There is, in fact, some justification for those who have termed the last major piece of federal labor legislation, the Landrum-Griffin Act of 1959, the "Lawyers' Full Employment Act."

But if it is impossible to state the exact constraints on union–management relations that the law now imposes, at least what might be described as currently useful generalizations can be offered. If the lessons of labor history have greatly influenced the nature of the bargaining process as it exists today, the ever-greater thrust of the laws has had an equally pervasive effect.

THE ERA OF JUDICIAL CONTROL

In view of the present scope of labor legislation, it is ironic that well into the twentieth century employers were virtually unrestrained by law from dealing with unions as they saw fit. There was, as we have seen, almost no statutory treatment of labor–management relations from the days of the American Revolution until the Great Depression of the 1930s. Instead, individual judges exercised public control over those relations. And the courts' view of union activities was, for the most part, as unsympathetic as was that of most managements of the times.

The employers' traditional weapons for fighting labor organizations—formal and informal espionage, blacklists, and the very potent practice of discharging "agitators"—were normally left undisturbed by the judges. However, if the members of the judiciary believed that union activities were being conducted either for "illegal purposes" or by "illegal means," they were generous in extracting money damages from the unions and in ordering criminal prosecution of labor leaders.

The qualifications for illegality varied to some extent from court to court. In general, however, most aggressive union activities of the day—strikes to obtain agreements whereby the employer would employ only union members (the closed shop), picketing by "strangers" (those not in a direct superior–subordinate relationship with the employer), and the secondary boycott (the exercise of economic pressure against one company to force it to exert pressure on another company that is actually the subject of the union's concern)—were held to be illegal. Many courts went even further. Throughout the 1920s, such remarks as "Judicial actions against even peaceful picketing are merely declaratory of what has always been the law and the best practice in equity" flowed freely from the judges. And although it was President Calvin Coolidge who asserted that "the business of the United States is business," the remark could readily have emanated from most members of the judiciary well into the third decade of this century. The courts, viewing their primary role as that of protecting property rights, allied themselves with few exceptions squarely with the employer community to neutralize the power of organized labor.

Fully as welcome to employers, too, was the extensive court use of the **injunction**. This device, a judicial order calling for the cessation of certain actions deemed injurious, was often invoked by the judges following employer requests for such intervention. To unionists, such restraining orders seemed to be issued quite indiscriminately. Even the relatively detached observer of legal history, however, would very likely conclude that it did not seem to take much to convince the judges that union activities should be curbed: The jurists issued their restraining decrees almost as reflex actions; and strikes, boycotts, picketing—virtually any form of union "self-help" activity—thus ran the risk of being abruptly ended if in any way present or imminent damage to the employer's property could be shown. (Exhibit 3-1 indicates labor's intense hostility toward the injunction. The cartoon happened to have appeared in a recent publication of the National Association of Letter Carriers, but its counterparts have been published in countless labor periodicals for many decades.)

THE NORRIS–LA GUARDIA ACT OF 1932

Despite its 1932 date, the Norris–La Guardia Act is of considerably more than historical interest. As is true of the later labor laws that will be discussed in this chapter, most of its provisions continue today to govern labor relations in interstate commerce.

At the time of its passage, however, the act was particularly noteworthy. Not only did it constitute the first major federal legislation to be applied to collective bargaining, but—as stated earlier—it marked a significant change in public policy *from repression to strong encouragement of union activity*. Implemented in the final days of the Hoover administration, it owed its birth mainly to the widespread unemployment of the times and to a general recognition that only through bargaining collectively could many employees exercise any satisfactory influence on their working environments. It also stemmed, however, from popular sentiment that justice had not been served by allowing the courts their virtually unlimited authority to issue injunctions in labor disputes.

Accordingly, the act greatly narrowed the scope of the courts for issuing such injunctions. Peaceful picketing, peaceable assembly, organizational picketing, payment of strike benefits, and a host of other union economic weapons were now made nonenjoinable. Also enacted within the new law were procedural requirements for injunctions issued on other grounds.

Even more symbolic of the major shift in public policy was the act's assertion that it was now necessary for Congress to guarantee to the individual employee "full freedom of association, self-organization, and designation of representatives of his own choosing, to negotiate the terms and conditions of his employment . . . free from interference, restraint, or coercion of employers." All the federal labor laws passed since 1932 have embodied this same principle.

EXHIBIT 3-1

SOURCE: *The Postal Record*, June 1999, p. 8.

Cartoon parody of anti-labor judge features this order: "INJUNCTION. Strikers are forbidden use of the so-called public sidewalk or going near the premises of their so-called jobs, and shall not interfere with any so-called man or woman who may try to take the bread and butter from the mouths of themselves or their families or both, thereby interfering with the bosses' profits."

Nor was the new treatment of unionism destined to be confined only to the federal arena. Within a short period of time, 20 states (including almost all the major industrial ones) had independently created their own "little Norris–La Guardia Acts" to govern labor relations in intrastate commerce.

Norris–La Guardia and its state counterparts did not by themselves, however, greatly stimulate union growth. They clearly expanded union freedoms and placed legal limits on judicial capriciousness, but they did little to restrain employers directly in their conduct toward collective bargaining. Only the previously cited yellow-dog contract arrangement, whereby managements had been able to require nonunion membership or activity as a condition of employment, was declared unenforceable by the 1932 act. Otherwise, employers remained at liberty to fight labor organizations by whatever means they could implement, despite the ambitious language of Norris–La Guardia.

THE WAGNER ACT OF 1935

It remained for the National Labor Relations Act of 1935, more commonly known as the Wagner Act, to alter this situation by putting teeth in the government's pledge to protect employee collective bargaining rights. The Wagner Act, it will be recalled, accomplished this through two basic methods: (1) It specifically banned five types of management action as constituting **unfair labor practices**; and (2) it set forth the principle of majority rule for the selection of employee bargaining representatives and provided that, should the employer express doubt as to the union's majority status, a secret-ballot election of the employees would determine if the majority existed. It also created an independent, quasi-judicial agency—the National Labor Relations Board (NLRB)—to provide the machinery for enforcing both these provisions. Exhibits 3-2 and 3-3 constitute the key documents currently being used by the

EXHIBIT 3-2

FORM NLRB-501 (8-83)		FORM EXEMPT UNDER 44 U.S.C. 3512
UNITED STATES OF AMERICA NATIONAL LABOR RELATIONS BOARD **CHARGE AGAINST EMPLOYER**	**DO NOT WRITE IN THIS SPACE**	
	Case	Date Filed

INSTRUCTIONS: File an original and 4 copies of this charge with NLRB Regional Director for the region in which the alleged unfair labor practice occurred or is occurring.

1. EMPLOYER AGAINST WHOM CHARGE IS BROUGHT

a. Name of Employer	b. Number of workers employed

c. Address (street, city, state, ZIP code)	d. Employer Representative	e. Telephone No.

f. Type of Establishment (factory, mine, wholesaler, etc.)	g. Identify principal product or service

h. The above-named employer has engaged in and is engaging in unfair labor practices within the meaning of section 8(a), subsections (1) and (list subsections) _____ of the National Labor Relations Act, and these unfair labor practices are unfair practices affecting commerce within the meaning of the Act.

2. Basis of the Charge (be specific as to facts, names, addresses, plants involved, dates, places, etc.)

By the above and other acts, the above-named employer has interfered with, restrained, and coerced employees in the exercise of the rights guaranteed in Section 7 of the Act

3. Full name of party filing charge (if labor organization, give full name, including local name and number)

4a. Address (street and number, city, state, and ZIP code)	4b. Telephone No.

5. Full name of national or international labor organization of which it is an affiliate or constituent unit (to be filled in when charge is filed by a labor organization)

6. DECLARATION

I declare that I have read the above charge and that the statements are true to the best of my knowledge and belief.

By _____   _____
  (signature of representative or person making charge)   (title if any)

Address _____ _____ _____
                                                   (Telephone No.)   (date)

**WILLFUL FALSE STATEMENTS ON THIS CHARGE CAN BE PUNISHED BY FINE AND IMPRISONMENT
(U. S. CODE, TITLE 18, SECTION 1001)**

NLRB for these two activities, respectively. Exhibit 3-4, a cartoon that originally appeared in 1935, conveys organized labor's jubilation at the time of the Wagner Act's passage.

❖ Employer Unfair Labor Practices

The five employer unfair labor practices, deemed "statutory wrongs" (although not crimes) by Congress, have been modified to some small extent since 1935, as noted later. They remain, however, a significant part of the law of collective bargaining to this day, and they constitute an impressive quintet of "thou shalt nots" for employers who might otherwise be tempted to resort to the blunt tactics of prior eras in an effort to undermine unionism. The Wagner Act (1) deemed it "unfair" for managements to "interfere with, restrain, or coerce employees" in exercising their now legally sanctioned right of self-organization; (2) restrained management representatives from dominating or interfering with either the formation or the administration of labor unions; (3) prohibited employers from discriminating "in regard to hire or tenure of employment or any term or condition of employment to encourage or discourage membership in any labor organization"; (4) forbade employers to discharge or otherwise discriminate against employees simply because the latter had filed unfair labor practice charges or otherwise offered testimony against management actions under the act; and (5) made it an unfair labor practice for employers to refuse to bargain collectively with the duly chosen representatives of their employees.

In the years since 1935, the NLRB and the courts (to which board decisions can be appealed by either labor relations party) have had ample opportunity to make known their interpretations of all five of these provisions. In dealing with some of them, both public bodies have been quite consistent in their decisions. In other cases, however, the board members and judges have had some difficulty in issuing rulings that seem fully compatible with prior rulings on the same subject. But the judges have at least generally proved themselves to be reluctant to reverse the original NLRB decisions when these have been appealed to the courts: Historically, the board has been backed by the judiciary more than 80 percent of the time. And the inconsistencies would in most cases appear to stem more from the changing membership of the five-member board through the years and from inherent difficulties in the words of the laws themselves than from this "opportunity for appeal" factor.

Relatively clear-cut decisions have been rendered by the NLRB and courts in two of the five areas:

1. The interpreters of the Wagner Act have consistently held a wide variety of employer practices to be in violation of the "interfere with, restrain or coerce employees" section. Among other management actions, bribery of employees, spy systems, blacklisting of union sympathizers, removal of an existing business to another location for the sole purpose of frustrating union activity, and promises by employers of wage increases or other special concessions to employees should the latter refrain from joining a union have all historically constituted "interference" contrary to the act. The same can be said of board and court treatment of employers who have threatened to isolate ("like a rotten apple," in one case) prounion workers, engaged in individual bargaining with employees represented by a union, or questioned employees concerning their union activities in such a way as to tend to restrain or coerce such employees. When satisfied that any such violations have occurred, the board has issued cease-and-desist orders against the guilty employer with no hesitation. And when it has found that employees have been discharged unlawfully in the process, the NLRB has most frequently required their reinstatement with full back pay.

Particularly in this area, the courts have proved unwilling, by and large, to reverse board decisions upon appeal, moreover, and the fact that failure to "cease and desist" after the courts have called for this action constitutes contempt of court has at times dissuaded employers from carrying an appeal to the courts in the first place.

2. The board and courts have also had no apparent difficulty in deciding what constitutes evidence of employer discrimination related to the fourth unfair labor

EXHIBIT 3-3

FORM NLRB-652
(5-80)

UNITED STATES OF AMERICA
NATIONAL LABOR RELATIONS BOARD

STIPULATION FOR CERTIFICATION UPON CONSENT ELECTION

Pursuant to a petition duly filed under Section 9 of the National Labor Relations Act, as amended, and subject to the approval of the Regional Director for the National Labor Relations Board (herein called the Regional Director), the undersigned parties hereby agree that the petition is hereby amended to conform to this Stipulation and that the approval of this Stipulation constitutes a withdrawal of any Notice of Representation Hearing previously issued in this matter, and further AGREE AS FOLLOWS:

1. SECRET BALLOT.—An election by secret ballot shall be held under the supervision of the said Regional Director, among the employees of the undersigned Employer in the unit defined below, at the indicated time and place, to determine whether or not such employees desire to be represented for the purpose of collective bargaining by (one of) the undersigned labor organization(s). Said election shall be held in accordance with the National Labor Relations Act, the Board's Rules and Regulations, and the applicable procedures and policies of the Board.

2. ELIGIBLE VOTERS.—The eligible voters shall be those employees included within the unit described below, who were employed during the payroll period indicated below, and also employees who did not work during said payroll period because they were ill or on vacation or temporarily laid off, employees in the military services of the United States who appear in person at the polls, employees engaged in an economic strike which commenced less than 12 months before the election date and who retained their status as such during the eligibility period and their replacements, but *excluding* any employees who have since quit or been discharged for cause and employees engaged in a strike who have been discharged for cause since the commencement thereof, and who have not been rehired or reinstated prior to the date of the election, and employees engaged in an economic strike which commenced more than 12 months prior to the date of the election and who have been permanently replaced. At a date fixed by the Regional Director, the parties, as requested, will furnish to the Regional Director an accurate list of all the eligible voters, together with a list of the employees, if any, specifically excluded from eligibility.

3. NOTICES OF ELECTION.—The Regional Director shall prepare a Notice of Election and supply copies to the parties describing the manner and conduct of the election to be held and incorporating therein a sample ballot. The parties, upon the request of and at a time designated by the Regional Director, will post such Notice of Election at conspicuous and usual posting places easily accessible to the eligible voters.

4. OBSERVERS.—Each party hereto will be allowed to station an equal number of authorized observers, selected from among the nonsupervisory employees of the Employer, at the polling places during the election to assist in its conduct, to challenge the eligibility of voters, and to verify the tally.

5. TALLY OF BALLOTS.—As soon after the election as feasible, the votes shall be counted and tabulated by the Regional Director, or Board agent or agents. Upon the conclusion of the counting, the Regional Director shall furnish a Tally of Ballots to each of the parties.

6. POSTELECTION AND RUNOFF PROCEDURE.—All procedures subsequent to the conclusion of counting ballots shall be in conformity with the Board's Rules and Regulations.

7. RECORD.—The record in this case shall be governed by the appropriate provisions of the Board's Rules and Regulations and shall include this Stipulation. Hearing and notice thereof, Direction of Election, and the making of Findings of Fact and Conclusions of Law by the Board prior to the election are hereby expressly waived.

practice. They long ago concluded that such management actions as the layoff of an employee shortly after his testimony before the board and the discharge of a woman worker immediately after her husband had filed unfair labor practice charges (on other grounds) against the company could be taken as discriminatory, and they have consistently ruled in this direction ever since. The board has further concluded, apparently also without much hesitation, that management's belief that charges filed

EXHIBIT 3-3

(continued)

8. COMMERCE.—The Employer is engaged in commerce within the meaning of Section 2 (6) and (7) of the National Labor Relations Act, and a question affecting commerce has arisen concerning the representation of employees within the meaning of Section 9 (c). *(Insert commerce facts.)*

9. WORDING ON THE BALLOT.—Where only one labor organization is signatory to this agreement, the name of the organization shall appear on the ballot and the choice shall be "Yes" or "No." In the event that more than one labor organization is signatory to this Stipulation, the choices on the ballot will appear in the wording indicated below and in the order enumerated below, reading from left to right on the ballot, or, if the occasion demands, from top to bottom. *(If more than one union is to appear on the ballot, any union may have its name removed from the ballot by the approval of the Regional Director of a timely request, in writing, to that effect.)*

First.

Second.

Third.

10. PAYROLL PERIOD FOR ELIGIBILITY - THE PERIOD ENDING_____

11. DATE, HOURS, AND PLACE OF ELECTION.—

12. THE APPROPRIATE COLLECTIVE-BARGAINING UNIT.—

                    (Employer)

By _____
              (Name)   *(Date)*

                     (Title)

Recommended:

         (Board Agent)   *(Date)*

Date approved _____

                              Regional Director,
                     National Labor Relations Board.

GPO : 1981 O – 351-733

                (Name of Organization)

By _____
              (Name)   *(Date)*

                     (Title)

            (Name of other Organization)

By _____
              (Name)   *(Date)*

                     (Title)

Case No._____

EXHIBIT 3-4

SOURCE: *United Mine Workers Journal*, June 1992, p. 6.

by an employee are false in no way justifies its taking punitive action against the employee. On the other hand, considerably fewer cases have had to be decided concerning this fourth unfair practice than any of the others, presumably because employers have themselves recognized that violations here are normally quite obvious to all concerned and have therefore refrained from taking such action in the first place.

Interpretation seems to have been somewhat more difficult when the issues have involved the three other portions of the employer unfair labor practice section.

1. The restriction on employer discrimination "in regard to hire or tenure of employment or any term or condition of employment to encourage or discourage membership in any labor organization" has clearly made it unlawful for employers to force employees who are union members to accept less desirable job assignments than nonunionists or to reduce the former type of employee's pay because of the union affiliation. Similarly, it is obvious that managements that demand renunciation of union membership as a condition of continued employment or of promotion within the nonsupervisory ranks do so only at their peril. But the legality of other types of employer conduct has proved to be anything but clear-cut.

Where, for example, there is conclusive evidence that a union member employee has falsified an employment application and thus failed to reveal a previous criminal record, can the person properly be discharged for that offense? Not always, according to at least one NLRB decision covering exactly this situation. Here, the board cited the company's "antiunion bias," its knowledge of the employee's union activities, and its treatment of nonunion employees who had committed comparable offenses, in deciding that the company's official reason for the discharge was only a pretext for discrimination against union members.[1] Cases of this kind have proved to be thorny ones for the board and the courts and have often caused considerable flows of adrenalin on the part of employers.

2. The proviso restraining management representatives from dominating or interfering with both the formation and the administration of labor unions—included because of Congress's unhappiness with the widespread creation of employer-influenced company unions in the years preceding 1935—has been the basis of much litigation since that date. Obviously, when an employer has control over the union sitting on the other side of the bargaining table, genuine bargaining cannot take place. But determining just when an employer has such control has proved to be no easy matter. Among specific management actions that the board and courts have looked unfavorably upon as evidence of employer control have been the following: the solicitation of union membership by supervisory employees, the employer's payment of membership dues for all employees joining the union, and an employer gift to a union of $400 and the right to operate a canteen that made a monthly profit—none of these managerial moves being especially notable for their subtlety. On the other hand, interpretations have found nothing unlawful in the mere fact that, for example, a labor organization limits its membership to employees of a single employer; the test for unfair practice pivots exclusively upon the question of which party *controls* the organization, and in a case such as this only much closer inspection can reveal whether the employer is in violation of the law.

In late 1992, the board dealt a major blow to *nonunion* employers who might be tempted to thwart union organizing drives by establishing employer-dominated labor organizations. Electromation Inc., an Indiana manufacturer of electrical parts, did—the board concluded—just that when it established five "action committees" of up to six workers and one or two managers to delve into such matters as working conditions and pay scales.[2]

The Teamsters, who had at the time been trying to organize Electromation, successfully convinced the board that the company had violated the Wagner Act not only because the "action committees" were to deal with traditional bargaining issues but also because the management had set the committee objectives and basic operating procedures. The company was quick to appeal the board's decision but had no success in reversing it.

3. The fact that the 1935 legislation said little more on the subject of an employer's "refusal to bargain collectively with the representatives of his employees" than can be gleaned from those words perhaps guaranteed that controversies would result from this last section of the Wagner Act's "Rights of Employees" section, and this has indeed been the case. As such new topics for potential bargaining as pensions, health insurance, seniority, and subcontracting have arisen in the years since 1935, the NLRB and courts have been freely called upon to make known their opinions as to what must be bargained by employers, and what need not be. The courts have also been asked for a more precise definition of "bargaining" itself than the act provided. The issue is still far from resolved, and with new possibilities for bargaining constantly emerging, perhaps it never fully will be. But the board and judicial decisions of the past six and one-half decades have at least ambitiously attempted to shed light on the scope for employer action in this area, and certain statements can now be made with some authority.

In a nutshell, there are today many **mandatory subjects of bargaining** with which the employer must deal in good faith. Such subjects include wages; hours of employment; health insurance; pensions; safety practices; the grievance procedure;

procedures for discharge, layoff, recall, and discipline; seniority; and subcontracting. Managers are not required to make concessions or agree to union proposals on any of these (or various other) subjects. They are obligated, however, to meet with the union at reasonable times and with the good-faith intention of reaching an agreement. On **nonmandatory or voluntary subjects**—those that are lawful but not easily related to "wages, hours and other conditions of employment"—employers are not so obligated and are free to refuse to bargain about them.

Where there is a duty to bargain, the employer must supply—upon union request—information that is "relevant and necessary" to allow the labor representatives to bargain "intelligently and effectively." The NLRB and courts have ruled, for example, that a union is entitled to information in the employer's possession concerning wage rates and increases on the grounds that it cannot deal intelligently with the subject without such information. Similarly, if a management claims financial inability to honor the union's demands, it must stand ready to supply the union with authoritative proof of that inability.

The employer's duty to bargain also entails the duty to refrain from taking unilateral action on the mandatory subjects. Managements that have announced a wage increase without consulting the employees' designated representatives, or have subcontracted work to another employer without allowing their own union a chance to bargain the matter, violate this portion of the law.

Yet the apparent finality of such remarks as these is highly deceptive. Not only is considerable uncertainty left as to what else is a mandatory subject for bargaining (beyond the specific topics cited and the few others that the NLRB and judges have thus far dealt with affirmatively) and what is nonmandatory, but the question of what constitutes "the good-faith intention of reaching an agreement" on the employer's part is left an open one.

It remains to be seen what further subjects the board and courts will ultimately assign to the mandatory category. A union demand for moving allowances for workers transferred by the company? A proposal that all production workers be placed on a salaried basis, rather than being paid by the hour? A request by the labor organization that all foreign production of the company's product be terminated? Guarantees by the company that pension funds will be invested in low-cost housing for union employees? Each of these demands has been raised on several occasions in actual bargaining situations in recent years. Except for the first, company negotiators have been notably reluctant to accommodate any of them, or numerous similarly ambitious union proposals. Yet every one of them and dozens of others not even dreamed of yet by labor organizations may well ultimately go before the interpreters of public policy.

The board members and judges, lacking any clear-cut guidance from the Wagner Act, will not necessarily find such questions easy to resolve. It at least appears safe to predict that the books have not yet closed on the list of mandatory topics; most of the subjects with which employers are now required to deal in good faith are themselves relative newcomers to such status.

Indeed, a previous edition of this book declared with absolute confidence that (among other situations forbidden them) unions could not make the prices charged by employers for food in plant cafeterias and vending machines subject to the bargaining process. A mere four years from the time that those words were written, the U.S. Supreme Court made them obsolete by ruling, in a case involving the Ford Motor Company, that employers could in fact be required to bargain over such prices (and related services, too). Speaking for the Court, Justice Byron White said that "the availability of food during working hours and the conditions under which it is to be consumed are matters of deep concern to workers, and one needn't strain to consider them to be among those 'conditions' of employment that should be subject to the mutual duty to bargain."[3] Nothing is guaranteed except change.

In 1989, the NLRB dealt with the compulsory testing of employees for drugs and alcohol, a fast-growing problem. The board ruled that preemployment testing was not a subject of mandatory bargaining.[4] Until job applicants were hired, they were not part of the bargaining unit or covered by the labor agreement, it said. But the agency also said that testing of *current* employees was a mandatory issue of bargaining.[5] The clear purpose of the testing program was that employees failing the test would be disciplined, possibly discharged. Before implementing such a rule, the employer must bargain with the union.

The steadily increasing types of tests adopted by the board and courts for "good faith"—for example, whether employer delaying tactics were used in the bargaining, some evidence of management initiative in making counterproposals, and employer willingness to accommodate completely routine demands (such as the continued availability of plant parking spaces)—have often been attacked for their naïveté, if not for the spirit behind them. Anyone who thinks that such tests by themselves can definitively reveal whether good faith has actually occurred at the bargaining table would probably believe almost anything.

At the very least, however, it is obvious that in being forced to plug the existing gaps in the Wagner Act's "refusal to bargain" interpretations, representatives of public policy have projected themselves more and more into the labor–management arena in the years since 1935, undoubtedly to an extent that was never contemplated when Wagner was passed.

❖ Employee Representation Elections

Despite all the interpretative difficulties that have been involved in the employer unfair labor practice provisions, the latter clearly were—and are—widesweeping in their implications for collective bargaining. However, they still represent an *indirect* approach to the protection of employee bargaining rights: By themselves, they restrict employer action in the labor relations area, but they say nothing explicit about the key question of initial union recognition.

The authors of the Wagner Act were well aware of this gap and proceeded to deal directly with the issue in another section of the act, that pertaining to the **secret-ballot election**. As noted previously, the NLRB was authorized to conduct such an election should the employer express doubt that a majority of its employees had chosen to be represented by any union at all. Prior to this time, a union could gain recognition from an unreceptive employer only through the successful use of such economic weapons as the strike and boycott.

As this part of the act now stands, the board can conduct a **certification election** if requested to do so by a single employee, by a group of employees, or by a labor organization acting for employees. In any of these three cases, the petition must be supported by "a substantial number of employees" who desire collective bargaining representation, and it must allege that the employer refuses to recognize such representation. Employers may also petition for such an election, presumably with the objective of proving that the employees do *not* desire union representation or for various reasons of scheduling strategy (such as trying to get the board to hold the election at the time least favorable to the union).

It is also possible for an election to involve two or more unions, each claiming "substantial" employee support. The employees then have the choice of voting for any of the unions on the ballot or for "no union." If none of these choices (including "no union") wins a majority of the votes cast, a runoff election is then conducted between the two choices that have received the highest number of votes. (Exhibit 3-5 shows the NLRB form now used for all petitions requesting a representation election.)

In administering this portion of the law, the NLRB itself ultimately framed a few further rules. Should any union win an NLRB-conducted election and then execute a valid contract with the employer, rival unions may now not seek bargaining rights (through a subsequent election) for a period of three years following the effective date of the contract or for the length of the contract—whichever is the shorter. However, the victorious union is still not guaranteed its bargaining rights for this period of time: If the employees themselves have second thoughts about the desirability of retaining the union's services, they can—after one year—petition the NLRB for a **decertification election**. A majority vote in this election rescinds the union's bargaining agency.

Unions lose a majority of decertification elections and, thus, their right to bargain. In 1970, according to the National Labor Relations Board's annual report for that year, they won only 30.2 percent of some 301 decertification elections. In 1980, an unprecedented total of 902 such contests took place, and workers voted for retention of the union in a mere 25 percent of them. By the late 1990s, with some 700 of these elections being held annually, unions were continuing to lose three out of four. (Organized labor is, however, doing far better than this in *new* certification elections. It is currently winning about half of the roughly 3,200 such elections that are conducted each year. However, this is somewhat lower than the 55 percent certification election victory registered by unions until the 1970s, so even here there is some cause for concern in the labor movement.)

Employers cannot legally start the decertification process, but antiunion consultants are amply available—in fact, as noted earlier, they constitute a new growth industry by themselves—to help management make the environment "right" for decertification. Forcing the union to go out on a costly strike is only one example. And something of a process of contagion may also abet the changes of a given union's being thrown out at times: Employers who become aware that a competitor across town or downstate has become nonunion may be encouraged to try and do, through decertification, the same.

Although winning an election has historically been the most common way for a union to secure bargaining rights, in about 1 percent of all union organizing campaigns, the NLRB has not insisted that the election be held. If a union gets a majority of the bargaining unit employees to sign union membership authorization cards and the employer then engages in a serious unfair labor practice (such as the discharging of union sympathizers), the election requirement is waived. The board's theory here is that the union would have won the election were it not for the employer's conduct. In 1969, the Supreme Court—agreeing with the theory—sustained it in *NLRB* v. *Gissel Packing Company.*

For a time the NLRB certified unions even without demonstrating majority support when employers committed "outrageous and pervasive" unfair labor practices during the organizational campaign. In 1984, however, the Reagan board, in a case involving Gourmet Foods, abolished that policy, ruling that it would not grant bargaining rights under any circumstances unless a union signed up a majority of employees within the bargaining unit.

EXHIBIT 3-5

FORM NLRB-502
(5-85)

FORM EXEMPT UNDER 44 U.S.C. 3512

UNITED STATES GOVERNMENT
NATIONAL LABOR RELATIONS BOARD
PETITION

DO NOT WRITE IN THIS SPACE	
Case No.	Date Filed

INSTRUCTIONS: Submit an original and 4 copies of this Petition to the NLRB Regional Office in the Region in which the employer concerned is located. If more space is required for any one item, attach additional sheets, numbering item accordingly.

The Petitioner alleges that the following circumstances exist and requests that the National Labor Relations Board proceed under its proper authority pursuant to Section 9 of the National Labor Relations Act.

1. PURPOSE OF THIS PETITION *(If box RC, RM, or RD is checked and a charge under Section 8(b)(7) of the Act has been filed involving the Employer named herein, the statement following the description of the type of petition shall not be deemed made.)* **(Check One)**

☐ **RC-CERTIFICATION OF REPRESENTATIVE** - A substantial number of employees wish to be represented for purposes of collective bargaining by Petitioner and Petitioner desires to be certified as representative of the employees.

☐ **RM-REPRESENTATION (EMPLOYER PETITION)** - One or more individuals or labor organizations have presented a claim to Petitioner to be recognized as the representative of employees of Petitioner.

☐ **RD-DECERTIFICATION** - A substantial number of employees assert that the certified or currently recognized bargaining representative is no longer their representative.

☐ **UD-WITHDRAWAL OF UNION SHOP AUTHORITY** - Thirty percent (30%) or more of employees in a bargaining unit covered by an agreement between their employer and a labor organization desire that such authority be rescinded.

☐ **UC-UNIT CLARIFICATION** - A labor organization is currently recognized by Employer, but Petitioner seeks clarification of placement of certain employees: *(Check one)* ☐ In unit not previously certified. ☐ In unit previously certified in Case No. _____ .

☐ **AC-AMENDMENT OF CERTIFICATION** - Petitioner seeks amendment of certification issued in Case No. _____
Attach statement describing the specific amendment sought.

2. Name of Employer	Employer Representative to contact	Telephone Number

3. Address(es) of Establishment(s) involved *(Street and number, city, State, ZIP code)*

4a. Type of Establishment *(Factory, mine, wholesaler, etc.)*	4b. Identify principal product or service

5. Unit Involved *(In UC petition, describe **present** bargaining unit and attach description of proposed clarification.)*	6a. Number of Employees in Unit:
Included	Present
	Proposed *(By UC/AC)*
Excluded	6b. Is this petition supported by 30% or more of the employees in the unit? * ____ Yes ____ No *Not applicable in RM, UC, and AC

(If you have checked box RC in 1 above, check and complete EITHER item 7a or 7b, whichever is applicable)

7a. ☐ Request for recognition as Bargaining Representative was made on *(Date)* _____ and Employer declined recognition on or about *(Date)* _____ *(If no reply received, so state).*

7b. ☐ Petitioner is currently recognized as Bargaining Representative and desires certification under the Act.

8. Name of Recognized or Certified Bargaining Agent *(If none, so state)*	Affiliation
Address and Telephone Number	Date of Recognition or Certification

9. Expiration Date of Current Contract, If any *(Month, Day, Year)*	10. If you have checked box UD in 1 above, show here the date of execution of agreement granting union shop *(Month, Day, and Year)*

11a. Is there now a strike or picketing at the Employer's establishment(s) Involved? Yes ____ No ____	11b. If so, approximately how many employees are participating?

11c. The Employer has been picketed by or on behalf of *(Insert Name)* _____ , a labor organization, of *(Insert Address)* _____ Since *(Month, Day, Year)* _____

12. Organizations or individuals other than Petitioner *(and other than those named in items 8 and 11c)*, which have claimed recognition as representatives and other organizations and individuals known to have a representative interest in any employees in unit described in item 5 above. *(If none, so state)*

Name	Affiliation	Address	Date of Claim *(Required only if Petition is filed by Employer)*

I declare that I have read the above petition and that the statements are true to the best of my knowledge and belief.

_____
(Name of Petitioner and Affiliation, if any)

By _____
(Signature of Representative or person filing petition) _____ *(Title, if any)*

Address _____
(Street and number, city, State, and ZIP Code) _____ *(Telephone Number)*

WILLFUL FALSE STATEMENTS ON THIS PETITION CAN BE PUNISHED BY FINE AND IMPRISONMENT (U. S. CODE, TITLE 18, SECTION 1001)

The Wagner Act actually let unions gain recognition as bargaining agents by yet another route. The NLRB could certify a union as exclusive representative of all employees in the designated bargaining unit (as in the case of representation elections, designated by the board after hearing arguments as to what this unit should be from both the union and the management) if in a so-called **card check** cards signed by members of the potential unit showed that the union was backed by a majority of all the workers. This gave labor two distinct advantages: Elections could not be delayed by employer legal maneuvering, and managements could not harass or intimidate workers regarding upcoming elections because no elections would in fact be held. Fully one-third of all union certifications in the years immediately after the passage of Wagner were, indeed, granted on this basis, and it is still possible today for unions to prevail as representative in exactly this manner. Ever since 1947, however, employers must also agree to the procedure for the certification to be granted, and for understandable reasons relatively few managements have been willing to do so.

On the other hand, in the late 1990s the United Food and Commercial Workers added more than 100,000 new members through card checks, the Hotel and Restaurant Employees Union increased its membership from 18,000 to almost 50,000 in Las Vegas alone through this mechanism, and the Service Employees International Union relied on the card checks to unionize over 40,000 janitors. At the time of this writing, unions—their attention again turning to massive organizing efforts after years of neglect in this area—were optimistic that many more membership gains could be registered in such a fashion.

FROM THE WAGNER ACT TO TAFT-HARTLEY

As established by the Wagner Act, then, the scope of National Labor Relations Board activities was to be twofold. The board was charged with investigating employer unfair labor practices, and it was given the authority to conduct employee representation elections.

The NLRB's members (appointed by the president, subject to confirmation by the Senate) and its various regional officials outside Washington, even in their earliest years of existence, undertook both of these assignments zealously. By 1947, they had processed almost 44,000 unfair labor practice cases, running the gamut in their decisions from dismissing complaints as having no merit to issuing cease-and-desist orders against guilty employers. In the area of representation cases, the board was even more active. Almost 60,000 such cases were dealt with between 1935 and 1947. In addition to determining whether elections should be held and conducting such elections if the answer was in the affirmative, the NLRB often had the further duty of deciding the type of unit appropriate for the particular labor relationship (such as employer, craft, or plant).

Although its activities were necessarily controversial, as was the act sanctioning them, there is general agreement today that in this 12-year period the board performed its basic mission of protecting the right of employees to organize and bargain collectively quite creditably. Even at the time, many contemporaries had been impressed; as in the case of Norris–La Guardia, "little Wagner Acts" were soon enacted in many states to govern labor relations in intrastate commerce.

The modern labor movement in this country can, in fact, justifiably be said to have begun in 1935. Union membership totals boomed after that year, owing in no small measure to the Wagner Act and its state counterparts. Other factors were, of course, also responsible: the improving economic climate, the generally liberal sentiments of the times, the keen competition between the American Federation of Labor and the newly born Committee for Industrial Organization, and dynamic union leadership. And it is equally true that prior legislation—not only Norris–La Guardia but also the ill-fated National Industrial Recovery Act of 1933—had paved the way for the new era and had independently led to much spontaneous union organization before 1935. But it is no less a fact that employers could still legally try to counteract unionism by almost any means except the yellow-dog contract and the arbitrary injunction process—up to and including sheer refusal to grant the union recognition under any circumstances—before the passage of the Wagner Act. It is extremely doubtful that organized labor could have grown as it did—from 3.6 million unionized workers in 1935 to more than 14 million by 1947—without the Wagner Act's protection.

Certainly, public opinion as registered in Congress did not debate this last point. The average citizen gradually turned against unionism in the mid-1940s, blaming existing public policy for the union excesses of the times, most notably for the postwar strike waves. As the preceding chapter described, this view ultimately became a compelling one: Congress overrode President Truman's veto and passed the Taft-Hartley Act of 1947, thereby stilling the cries that the Wagner Act had become too one-sided in favor of labor.

THE TAFT-HARTLEY ACT OF 1947

With the advent of Taft-Hartley, officially known as the Labor–Management Relations Act, a new period in public policy toward labor unions began: that of *modified encouragement coupled with regulation*. Much as the Wagner Act was to a great extent designed to fill gaps in Norris–La Guardia, which nonetheless was not repealed and remains a part of the legal environment of collective bargaining to this day, Taft-Hartley amended but did not displace the Wagner Act. Wagner, essentially as adjusted by the 1947 legislation, governs labor relations today.

Indeed, the old unfair employer practices were continued virtually word for word by the new legislation. The only significant changes were that the closed shop (and its requirements that all workers be union members at the time of their hiring) was no longer allowed and that the freedom of the parties to authorize the *union shop* (which, as noted earlier, allows the employer to hire anyone but provides that all new employees must join the union after a stipulated period of time) was somewhat narrowed. The intention of this amendment was related to the third employer unfair labor practice: In its ban on employer hiring and job condition discrimination in order to encourage or discourage union membership, the Wagner Act had authorized employers to enter into union and closed-shop agreements. The changes clearly symbolized public policy's new attitude toward unions.

Far more indicative of the public's less enthusiastic sentiments toward unions, however, were those portions of Taft-Hartley that dealt with (1) *unfair union labor practices*, which were now enumerated and prohibited in the same way that the employer practices had been; (2) *the rights of employees as individuals*, as contrasted with those rights that employees now legally enjoyed as union members; (3) *the rights of employers*, a subject the Wagner Act had glossed over in its concentration on employer duties; and (4) *national emergency strikes*. To some extent, other major parts of the new law—those relating to internal union affairs, the termination or modification of existing labor contracts, and suits involving unions—also demonstrated a hardening of congressional attitudes toward labor organizations. We shall consider these various provisions separately.

❖ Unfair Union Labor Practices

Going the framers of the Wagner Act one better, Taft-Hartley enumerated six labor practices that the unions were prohibited from engaging in. Labor organizations operating in interstate commerce were now officially obliged to refrain from (1) restraining or coercing employees in the exercise of their guaranteed rights to themselves refrain from union activities; (2) causing an employer to discriminate in any way against an employee in order to encourage or discourage union membership; (3) refusing to bargain in good faith with the employer about wages, hours, and other employment conditions; (4) certain types of strikes and boycotts; (5) charging employees covered by union-shop agreements initiation fees or dues "in an amount which the board finds excessive or discriminatory under all the circumstances"; and (6) engaging in featherbedding, the requirement of payment by the employer for services not performed. (Exhibit 3-6 illustrates the major document currently being used by the NLRB to enforce the portion of the law that covers these six practices.)

As in the case of the unfair employer labor practices, interpretative difficulties have marked the subsequent treatment of some of those provisions.

The first two of the six provisions have perhaps had the greatest influence on collective bargaining, and, undoubtedly a good one, in the years since the enactment of Taft-Hartley.

1. The ban on union restraint or coercion of employees in the exercise of their guaranteed bargaining rights also entails a union obligation to avoid coercion of employees who choose to refrain from collective bargaining altogether. What constitutes such restraint or coercion? The many rulings rendered by the NLRB and courts since 1947 have at least indicated that such union actions as the following will always run the risk of being found "unfair": the stating to an antiunion employee that the employee will lose his job should the union gain recognition; the signing with an employer of an agreement that recognizes the union as exclusive bargaining representative when in fact it lacks majority employee support; and the issuing of clearly false statements during a representation election campaign. Union picketline violence, threats of reprisal against employees subpoenaed to testify against the union at NLRB hearings, and activities of a similar vein are also unlawful.

This first unfair union practice also extends to the coercion of the employer in the latter's selection of its own bargaining representative. Post-1947 rulings have stated, for example, that unions cannot refuse to deal with former union officers who represent employers or insist on meeting only with the owners of a company rather than with the company's attorney. On the other hand, unions have every right to demand that the employer representative with whom they deal has sufficient authority to make final decisions on behalf of the management; the interpreters of public policy have clearly understood that to have this any other way would be to frustrate the whole process of bargaining.

2. The Taft-Hartley provision that makes it unfair for a union to cause an employer to discriminate against an employee in order to influence union membership has a single exception: Under a valid union-shop agreement, the union may lawfully demand the discharge of an employee who fails to pay his or her initiation fee and periodic dues. Otherwise, however, unions must exercise complete self-control in this area. They cannot try to force employers to fire or otherwise penalize workers for any other reason, whether these reasons involve worker opposition to union policies, failure to attend union meetings, or refusal to join the union at all. Nor can a union lawfully seek to persuade an employer to grant hiring preference to employees who are satisfactory to the union. Subject only to the union-shop proviso, Taft-Hartley sought to place nonunion workers on a footing equal to that of union employees.

3. Occupying more or less middle ground in its degree of influence upon the labor relations process stands the third restriction on union practices, pertaining to

EXHIBIT 3-6

FORM EXEMPT UNDER
44 U.S.C. 3512

FORM NLRB-508
(5-81)

UNITED STATES OF AMERICA
NATIONAL LABOR RELATIONS BOARD
CHARGE AGAINST LABOR ORGANIZATION OR ITS AGENTS

DO NOT WRITE IN THIS SPACE

Case No.

Date Filed

INSTRUCTIONS: File and original and 3 copies of this charge and an additional copy for each organization, each local, and each individual named in item 1 with the NLRB Regional Director of the Region in which the alleged unfair labor practice occurred or is occurring.

1. LABOR ORGANIZATION OR ITS AGENTS AGAINST WHICH CHARGE IS BROUGHT

a. Name

b. Union Representative to Contact

c. Telephone No.

d. Address (street, city, state and ZIP code)

e. The above-named organization(s) or its agents has (have) engaged in and is (are) engaging in unfair labor practices within the meaning of section 8(b), subsection(s) _____ of the National Labor Relations Act, and these
(list subsections)
unfair labor practices are unfair labor practices affecting commerce within the meaning of the Act.

2. Basis of the Charge (be specific as to facts, names, addresses, plants involved, dates, places, etc.).

3. Name of Employer

4. Telephone No.

5. Location of Plant Involved (street, city, state and ZIP code)

6. Employer Representative to Contact

7. Type of Establishment (factory, mine, wholesaler, etc.)

8. Identify Principal Product or Service

9. No. of Workers Employed

10. Full Name of Party Filing Charge

11. Address of Party Filing Charge (street, city, state and ZIP code)

12. Telephone No.

13. DECLARATION

I declare that I have read the above charge and that the statements therein are true to the best of my knowledge and belief.

By _____
(signature of representative or person making charge)

_____
(title or office, if any)

Address _____

_____   _____
(telephone number)   (date)

WILLFULLY FALSE STATEMENTS ON THIS CHARGE CAN BE PUNISHED BY FINE AND IMPRISONMENT
(U. S. CODE, TITLE 18, SECTION 1001)

union refusal to bargain. Here, clearly, Taft-Hartley extended to labor organizations the same obligation that the Wagner Act had already imposed on employers.

To many observers, the law's inclusion of this union bargaining provision has meant very little; unions can normally be expected to pursue bargaining rather than attempt to avoid it. Nevertheless, the NLRB has used it to some extent in the years since Taft-Hartley to narrow the scope of permissible union action. The board has, for example, found it unlawful under this section for a union to strike against an employer who has negotiated, and continues to negotiate, on a multiemployer basis, with the goal of forcing that employer to bargain independently. It has also found a union's refusal to bargain on an employer proposal for a written contract to violate this part of the law. To the employer community, in short, at least some inequities seem to have been corrected by this good-faith bargaining provision.

4. The fourth unfair union practice has given rise to considerable litigation. Indeed, of all six Taft-Hartley union prohibitions, the ban on certain types of strikes and boycotts has proved the most difficult to interpret. Even as "clarified" by Congress in 1959, this area remains a particularly murky one for labor lawyers.

Briefly, Section 8(b)(4) of the 1947 act prohibits unions from striking or boycotting if such actions have any of the following three objectives: (1) forcing an employer or self-employed person to join any labor or employer organization or to cease dealing with another employer (secondary boycott); (2) compelling recognition as employee bargaining agent for another employer without NLRB certification; (3) forcing an employer to assign particular work to a particular craft.

Particularly in regard to the secondary boycott provision, it does not take much imagination to predict where heated controversy could arise. To constitute a secondary boycott, the union's action must be waged against "another" employer, one who is entirely a neutral in the battle and is merely caught as a pawn in the union's battle with the real object of its concern. But when is the secondary employer really neutral and when is he an "ally" of the primary employer? The board has sometimes ruled against employers alleging themselves to be "secondary" ones on the grounds of common ownership with that of the "primary" employer and, again, when "struck work" has been turned over by primary employers to secondary ones. But board and court rulings here have not been entirely consonant.

In its other clauses, too, the Taft-Hartley strike and boycott provision has led to intense legal battles. When is a union, for example, unlawfully seeking recognition without NLRB certification and when is it merely picketing to protest undesirable working conditions (a normally legal action)? Is a union ever entitled to try to keep within its bargaining unit work that has traditionally been performed by the unit employees? On some occasions, but not all, the board has ruled that there is nothing wrong with that practice. The histories of post-1947 cases on these issues constitute a fascinating study in the making of fine distinctions.

Last, and least in the magnitude of their effect, stand the relatively unenforceable provisions relating to union fees and dues and to featherbedding.

5. The proscription against unions charging workers covered by union-shop agreements excessive or discriminatory dues or initiation fees included, it will be recalled, a stipulation that the NLRB could consider "all the circumstances" in determining discrimination or excess. Such circumstances, the wording of the Taft-Hartley Act continues, include "the practices and customs of labor organizations in the particular industry and the wages currently paid to the employees affected." Without further yardsticks and depending almost exclusively on the sentiments of individual employees rather than on irate employers for enforcement, this part of the act has had little practical value. In one of the relatively few such cases to come before it thus far, some years ago, the board ruled that increasing the initiation fee from $75 to $250 when other unions in the area charged only about one-eighth of

that amount was unlawful. In another case, it was held that the union's uniform requirement of a reinstatement fee for ex-members that was higher than the initiation fee for new members was *not* discriminatory under the act.

6. The sixth unfair labor practice for unions has proved even less influential in governing collective bargaining: Taft-Hartley's prohibition of unions from engaging in featherbedding. The board has ruled that this provision does not prevent labor organizations from seeking *actual* employment for their members, "even in situations where the employer does not want, does not need, and is not willing to accept such services." Mainly because of this interpretation, the antifeatherbedding provision has had few teeth; the union would be quite happy to have the work performed, and the question of need is irrelevant. Employer spokespersons for some industries, entertainment and the railroads in particular, have succeeded in convincing the public that their unwanted—but performing—workers are featherbedding, but under the interpretation of the law as this now exists they are engaging in inaccuracies.

Even these least influential of the six union prohibitions, however, clearly indicate the philosophy in back of Taft-Hartley—in the words of the late Senator Robert A. Taft, "simply to reduce special privileges granted to labor leaders."

❖ The Rights of Employees as Individuals

In other areas, too, the act attempted to even the scales of collective bargaining and the alleged injustices of the 1935–1947 period. Taft-Hartley, unlike Wagner, recognized a need to protect the rights of individual employees against labor organizations. It explicitly amended the 1935 legislation to give a majority of the employees the right to refrain from, as well as to engage in, collective bargaining activities. It also dealt more directly with the question of individual freedoms—even beyond its previously mentioned outlawing of the closed shop, union coercion, union-caused employer discrimination against employees, and excessive union fees.

◆ **Right-to-Work Legislation.** Perhaps most symbolically, Taft-Hartley provided that should any state wish to pass legislation more restrictive of union security than the union shop (or, in other words, to outlaw labor contracts that make union membership a condition of retaining employment), the state was free to do so. Many states have proved themselves as so willing: Twenty-one states, mainly in the South and Southwest, now have so-called **right-to-work legislation**. Advocates of such laws, which will be discussed at greater length in Chapter 9, have claimed that compulsory unionism violates the basic American right of freedom of association; opponents of right-to-work laws have pointed out, among other arguments, that majority rule is inherent in our democratic procedure. There has thus far, however, been an impressive correlation between stands on this particular question and attitudes toward the values of unionism in general. People opposed to collective bargaining have favored right-to-work laws with amazing regularity. Prounionists seem to have been equally consistent in their attacks on such legislation. Although it is difficult, if not impossible, to measure objectively the labor relations effects of right-to-work laws, there is consensus on one point: Such laws make it more difficult to organize a union and to maintain one once formed. This condition tends to attract industry to right-to-work states to take advantage of a comparatively union-free work environment with lower wages and general conditions of employment.

◆ **Direct Presentation of Grievances.**   Also designed to strengthen the rights of workers as individuals was a Taft-Hartley provision allowing any *employee* the *right to present grievances directly* to the employer without intervention of the union. The union's representative was to be given a chance to be present at such employer–employee meetings, but the normal grievance procedure (with the union actively participating) would thus be suspended. Few employees have thus far availed themselves of this opportunity: The action can clearly antagonize the union, and, because the employer's action is normally being challenged by the grievance itself, the employee may have a formidable task ahead. There is no sense in making two enemies right off the bat.

◆ **Restricted Dues Checkoff.**   Finally, the act placed a major restriction on the fast-growing **dues checkoff** arrangement. Through this device (which will also be discussed in more detail later), many employers had been deducting union dues from their employees' paychecks and remitting them to the union. Managements were thus spared the constant visits of dues-collecting union representatives at the workplace, and unions had found the checkoff to be an efficient means of collection. Under Taft-Hartley, the checkoff was to remain legal, but now only if the individual employee had given his or her own authorization in writing. Moreover, such an authorization could not be irrevocable for a period of more than one year. This restriction has hardly hampered the growth of the checkoff; today it is provided for in over 95 percent of all labor contracts, compared with an estimated 40 percent at the time of Taft-Hartley's passage. The new legal provision has undoubtedly minimized abuse of the checkoff mechanism, however. (Exhibit 3-7, drawn from a current labor agreement between the International Paper Company and the United Paperworkers International Union, shows typical dues checkoff language.)

❖ Other Employee Rights

Employees have gained other rights based on the language of Taft-Hartley or by NLRB and court construction. *When a labor agreement requires membership in a union as a condition of employment*, and should a member protest the stance of the union in political elections or lobbying activities, the U.S. Supreme Court has held that the union must rebate to the member that proportion of his or her dues allocated for political purposes. The union member who supports the Republican candidate for political office, for example, has the right to have rebated the portion of dues spent for political purposes when the organization supports the Democratic candidate.

   This dues rebate policy originally surfaced under the Supreme Court's interpretation of the Railway Labor Act, which covers labor–management relations only on the railroads and airlines. But, in 1988, the Court established the same rule for unionized employees covered by Taft-Hartley. The new policy could injure unions much more seriously than merely making dues rebates to political dissenters. In *Communications Workers of America* v. *Beck*, the Supreme Court held that dues-paying nonunion employees (as in agency shop arrangements, explained in Chapter 9) can demand a rebate for *any* union expenditure not related strictly to collective bargaining.

   Thus, union expenses for organizing, some publications, certain litigation, and educational functions are now placed in jeopardy. In addition, unions may no longer select an arbitrary figure—5 percent, for example—for rebate purposes, as some

EXHIBIT 3-7

ARTICLE 4

DEDUCTION OF UNION DUES

4.1 Deduction of Union Dues

Subject to the provisions of State and Federal laws, the Company agrees to make a payroll deduction of the normal monthly union dues and a one time union initiation fee, provided there is on file with the Company a copy of a voluntary authorization as shown below, properly filled out, signed by the employee and countersigned by an official of the local Union.

The payroll deduction of Union dues shall be made only on the second payday of each month.

The total amount collected shall be transmitted to the Local Union financial secretary, marked "For Deposit Only." The Local Union will be supplied each month with the names of its members from whose earnings Union dues have been deducted. The authorization of Union dues deduction shall be in the following form:

Form A

CHECK-OFF AUTHORIZATION

I hereby voluntarily assign to my Local Union affiliated with the United Paperworkers International Union from any wages earned or to be earned by me, the amount of my monthly membership dues and initiation fee in said Union.

I authorize and direct my employer to deduct such amounts from my pay each month and to remit the same to the order of the financial secretary of my Local Union in accordance with the terms of this Agreement.

This assignment, authorization and direction shall be irrevocable for a period of one year from the effective date of the Agreement, or until the termination date of said Agreement, whichever occurs sooner, and I further agree and direct that this assignment, authorization and direction shall be automatically renewed and shall be irrevocable for successive periods of one year each or for the period of each succeeding applicable collective bargaining Agreement with the Union whichever shall be shorter, unless written notice is given by me to the Company and the Union not more than thirty days or less than ten days prior to the expiration of each period of one year or of each applicable collective bargaining Agreement, whichever occurs sooner.

Date_____ Signature of Employee_____

Name[Print]_____ UPIU Local No._____

Address_____ City and State_____

Social Security No. _____

Employed By_____ Department_____

---

have done in the past. *Beck* commands that unions keep detailed records specifying what portion of the dues is in fact spent for collective bargaining purposes and what part for unrelated activities. Should the policy be fully applied to funds spent on organizational campaigns, the impact could be serious for labor organizations. The degree of organization within an industry or trade has a direct bearing on the ability of unions to negotiate wages and working conditions. It is hard to believe that organizational efforts do not constitute a collective bargaining activity.

In the years since the *Beck* decision was rendered, some workers have successfully reclaimed some of their dues. But by and large a massive logjam at the NLRB, with which employees who feel that they are being maltreated under *Beck* by not getting rebates must file unfair labor practice charges, has developed: By 1999, over

250 *Beck*-related cases awaited NLRB resolution and the number was still climbing. Board members, in defense of their failure to act speedily here, were pointing out that the *Beck* issue is a highly complex one, and that they lack both statutory guidance and any kind of board precedent on the topic; critics of the board's slow approach argued that this simply showed an NLRB willingness to flout a judicial mandate and its prounion bias in trying to keep workers from enforcing their rights.

Taft-Hartley confers a special benefit on professional employees, who under its terms are defined in part as those whose work is primarily intellectual in character and who utilize considerable judgment and discretion in the performance of their jobs. When employees meet requirements of the definition, the NLRB must poll them in a special election to determine whether they desire to be represented by a rank-and-file union, by an organization composed exclusively of professionals, or by no union. Whatever their verdict, the board must comply with their wishes. Thus, the agency may not place professional employees in a bargaining unit composed of production and maintenance employees unless a majority of the professionals polled vote for that kind of representation. Over the years the NLRB has struggled with the definition of professional employees. It has held that a college degree does not necessarily place the person in the professional category, and that the lack of a college degree does not automatically exclude the employee. Rather than formal educational achievement, what counts is the kind of work the employee actually performs on the job. In the professional category, for example, the board has included non-college-trained plant engineers, time study specialists, and employees who estimate the needs and cost of material used by their employers. In the nonprofessional category, the NLRB has placed—not without some controversy—general accountants, newspaper journalists, radio and television announcers, and singers.

Finally, pursuant to a mandate incorporated in Taft-Hartley, the NLRB under certain circumstances permits craft employees (electricians, machinists, carpenters, plumbers) to break away from an industrial bargaining unit and establish their own unions. In each case, the NLRB will consider the specific situation involved before ruling on separate craft union representation. In one case, the agency denied separation of a group of craft employees from the production workers unit on the grounds that the work of the skilled employees was so highly integrated into the productive process that a strike of the skilled group would cause a shutdown of the entire plant.[6] In another case, the NLRB permitted a group of craft employees to break out of the industrial unit because the evidence demonstrated that their work was not closely integrated. Equally important was the fact that the industrial union did not represent the craft employees fairly in collective bargaining.[7] As expected, industrial unions, because of loss of membership, and employers, because of the problems involved in dealing with many unions in the same plant, normally argue that craft employees should not be separated. Despite these claims, however, under the proper set of circumstances, the NLRB permits craft employees to select their own bargaining agent.

❖ The Rights of Employers

In still a third area, Taft-Hartley circumscribed the union's freedom of action in its quest for industrial relations equity. In this case, it explicitly gave employers certain collective bargaining rights.

Although employers were still required to recognize and bargain with properly certified unions, they could now give full freedom of expression to their views concerning union organization, as long as there was "no threat of reprisal or force or promise of benefit." Thus an employer may now, when faced with a representation election, tell employees that in his opinion unions are worthless, dangerous to the economy, and immoral. An employer may even, generally speaking, hint that the permanent closing of the plant would be the possible aftermath of a union election victory and subsequent high union wage demands. Nor will an election be set aside, for that matter, if the employer plays upon the racial prejudices of the workers (should these exist) by describing the union's philosophy toward integration, or if the employer sets forth the union's record in regard to violence and corruption (should this record be vulnerable) and suggests that these characteristics would be logical consequences of the union's victory in that plant—although the board has attempted to draw the line here between dispassionate statements on the employer's part and inflammatory or emotional appeals. An imaginative employer can, in fact, now engage in almost any amount of creative speaking (or writing) for employees' consumption. The only major restraint on the employer's conduct is that he must avoid threats, promises, coercion, and direct interference with the worker-voters in the reaching of their decision. And two lesser restrictions also govern: The employer may not hold a meeting with employees on company time within **24 hours** of an election; and the employer may never urge employees individually at their homes or in the office to vote against the union (the board has held that the employer can lawfully do this only "at the employees' work area or in places where employees normally gather").

An employer may avoid these two minor restrictions by holding a **captive audience meeting** before the 24-hour limit on company property and during working time. And the employer need not give equal time to the union to reply to the employer's statements. At such meetings, with all the employees assembled, the employer by the use of representatives has an excellent opportunity to influence the vote in the impending election. In a case involving the J. P. Stevens Company, the NLRB moved further to protect the right of employers to hold effective captive audience meetings. At a Stevens meeting a number of employees sympathetic to the union got up and asked questions. When they refused to sit down and stop asking questions, the company discharged them and the NLRB subsequently sustained the discharges.[8]

In an effort to balance the opportunity of unions to reach the employee, the NLRB has ruled that within seven days after an election is scheduled the employer must make available to a regional director of the agency the names and addresses of the employees eligible to vote in the election. Then the list is furnished to the union. In other words, instead of granting unions equal time at captive audience meetings, the agency has provided unions with an alternative method of contacting employees—home visitation and letter writing. However, unions claim that these techniques do not measure up to the effectiveness of the captive audience meeting and that the captive audience doctrine is one factor explaining why unions currently lose many NLRB elections.

Under Taft-Hartley, what is more, employers may lock out their employees when an impasse occurs in collective bargaining after the union has gained certification rights. At times, employees are willing to work on a day-to-day basis after the labor agreement expires. Under the law, however, the employer may use the lockout to shock employees into accepting management's last offer. Even if employees are willing to work after the contract expires, the employer may deny them this opportunity and lock them out of the facility. The only qualification on this right is that the employer must have engaged in good-faith collective bargaining prior to the lockout. What makes the employer's lockout right even more effective is that it is all right to continue to operate with temporary replacements. Under these circumstances, the locked-out employees are under pressure to capitulate to the employer's final contract offer.

❖ National Emergency Strikes

Of most direct interest to the general public, but of practical meaning only to those employers whose labor relations can be interpreted as affecting the national health and safety, are the **national emergency strike** provisions that were enacted in 1947. As in the case of most Taft-Hartley provisions, these remain unchanged to this day.

Sections 206 through 210 of the act provide for government intervention in the case of such emergencies. If the president of the United States believes that a threatened or actual strike affects "an entire industry or a substantial part thereof" in such a way as to "imperil the national health or safety," he is empowered to take certain carefully delineated action. He may appoint a board of inquiry to find out and report the facts regarding the dispute. The board is allowed subpoena authority and can thus compel the appearance of witnesses. It cannot, however, make recommendations for a settlement. On receiving the board's preliminary report, the president may apply, through the attorney general, for a court injunction restraining the strike for 60 days. If no settlement is reached during this time, the injunction can be extended for another 20 days, during which period the employees are to be polled in a secret-ballot election as to their willingness to accept the employer's last offer. The board is then to submit its final report to the president. Should the strike threat still exist after all these procedures, the president is authorized to submit a full report to Congress, "with such recommendations as he may see fit to make for consideration and appropriate action."

By 2000, the national emergency provisions of the law had been invoked 34 times and 27 injunctions had been issued. On five occasions the president did not elect to seek injunctions, and twice federal district courts turned down the president on the grounds that the strikes did not imperil the national health or safety. But much of the earlier excitement and controversy about this feature of Taft-Hartley has subsided. The last attempt to use it was in 1977 when a court refused President Carter's request for an injunction in a coal strike. An injunction was issued for the last time in 1972. The major explanation is the lessening of power of labor organizations within industries in which injunctions were previously issued.

In 2000, for example, less than 20 percent of the coal industry was organized in contrast with a much more impressive 80 percent of that sector in the 1940s and 1950s. From 1960 to 2000, Teamster membership in the enormously important trucking industry fell from 500,000 to about 150,000. Given these circumstances, the national emergency dispute provisions of Taft-Hartley are more or less a relic of labor relations law.

Even the mammoth 1997 strike of 185,000 Teamsters against United Parcel Service (UPS) did not, in fact, appear to meet the traditional presidential intervention standard. Because Federal Express, the U.S. Postal Service, and a variety of other unionized and nonunionized delivery providers could, and did, pick up much of the UPS slack, President Clinton refused to intervene here on these grounds. (Cynics, however, pointed out that the Teamsters' huge flow of political contributions had in recent years generally gone to Clinton's Democrats and that intervention would probably have helped UPS far more than it would have aided the union.)

❖ Other Taft-Hartley Provisions

Taft-Hartley also devoted attention to *internal union affairs*, the first such regulation in American history. Its impetus came not only from the previously cited communist taints attached to several unions but also from the fact that, in the case of a few other labor organizations, lack of democratic procedures and financial irregularities (often involving employer wrongdoing as well) had become glaringly evident. Accordingly, the act set new conditions for unions thenceforth seeking to use the NLRB's services: (1) All union officers were obligated to file annual affidavits with the board, stating that they were not members of the Communist Party; (2) certain financial and constitutional information had to be filed annually by unions with the secretary of labor; and (3) unions (as well as corporations) could no longer contribute funds for political purposes in connection with any federal election. The affidavit requirement, judged to be ineffective, was repealed in 1959. The other stipulations were allowed to remain in force until that date, when they were only slightly amended and then substantially enlarged upon (as further discussion will indicate). Essentially, aside from what unionists vocally termed a nuisance value, the provisions are notable for the first recognition of public policy that some internal regulation of the union as an institution was in the public interest—and as a harbinger of more such regulation to come.

Another Taft-Hartley provision that has upset some union leaders involves the *termination or modification of existing labor contracts*. Applicable to both labor organizations and employers, it requires the party seeking to end or change the agreement to give a 60-day notice to the other party. The law further provides that, during this time period, the existing contract must be maintained without strikes or lockouts. In addition, the Federal Mediation and Conciliation Service and state mediation services are to be notified of the impending dispute 30 days after the serving of the notice. Workers striking in violation of this requirement lose all legal protection as employees in collective bargaining, although the law also asserts that "such loss of status for such employee shall terminate if and when he is reemployed" by the employer.

In some instances, leaders of labor organizations have found it both difficult and politically unpopular to restrain their constituents from violating this provision. Unionists have also pointed out that the scheduling prerequisites for striking have deprived their organizations of some economic power, at least insofar as the element of surprise is concerned. Yet many representatives of both parties would undoubtedly agree that these provisions have let mediators intervene before it is too late to help and have generally aided in the resolution of disputes by allowing more time for thoughtful consideration of what is involved. From the point of view of the public interest, it is on this basis that the effectiveness of the notice provisions should be judged.

Section 301 of Taft-Hartley decreed that "*suits for violations of contracts* between an employer and a labor organization representing employees in an industry affecting commerce" could be brought directly by either party in any U.S. district court. Labor agreements, in short, were to be construed as being legally enforceable for the first time in American history. Damage suits are not calculated to increase mutual trust or offset misunderstandings between the parties in labor relations, however, and unions and managements have generally recognized this fact. Consequently, relatively few such suits have come to the courts in the years since this provision was enacted. Many contracts today, in fact, contain agreements *not* to sue, a perfectly legal dodge of Section 301.

Though employer suits against unions under Section 301 for violation of no-strike provisions have been comparatively infrequent, the U.S. Supreme Court has established some applicable policies. Only the union, and not an individual member or officer, is liable for any damages assessed in court proceedings. Also, a national union is not responsible for damages when its local unions engage in such strikes, assuming that the national has neither provoked nor encouraged the illegal cessation of work. Local unions do not normally have huge treasuries, and employers would much prefer to recover damages from the nationals. But absent specific contractual language allowing them to do the latter (something that national unions have understandably rarely agreed to), employers are simply out of luck in these situations.

❖ Coverage of Private Hospitals

In 1974, Congress extended the coverage of Taft-Hartley to private nonprofit hospitals and nursing homes. This was no small matter. More than 3 million employees now work in almost 4,000 such nonprofit institutions, and some 83 percent of all private hospitals in the United States are not operated for profit. Before 1974, only proprietary (profit-making) health care institutions were covered by the National Labor Relations Act and thus came under the NLRB's jurisdiction.

Whatever benefit organized labor could derive from this change in organizing its large and rapidly growing worker market was not immediately apparent. Typically, the NLRB decided prospective bargaining units on a case-by-case basis and could be counted on to issue findings that lumped most occupational categories in a simple broad group for purposes of a potential union election. Thus, such diverse worker types as salaried physicians, registered nurses, X-ray technicians, physical therapists, maintenance employees, and business office clerks would all be found to be part of a single "appropriate" unit. And hospital managements could rather readily play upon the lack of common identities to divide and conquer any union hopes of winning a representation election.

In 1989, however, a less conservative board concluded two years of hearings on this increasingly incendiary topic by ruling that thenceforth separate elections for each of eight private hospital groups could routinely be held. Doctors, registered nurses, all other professional employees, technicians, skilled maintenance workers, business office clerical employees, guards, and all other nonprofessionals could now each vote to have their own bargaining units, regardless of the wishes of the other groups.

Hospital managements, through their umbrella American Hospital Association, immediately sued to overturn this union victory. They argued that the NLRB did not have the legal authority to do anything but decide such matters on a case-by-case basis. But their effort failed: In 1991, the Supreme Court unanimously affirmed the board action of two years earlier.[9]

In the years since then, unions have aggressively wooed health care workers and have already had much success. By the late 1990s, for example, they were annually filing almost 10 times as many petitions for union elections as they had in 1989 and winning almost 60 percent of these health care worker elections (compared with the previously noted 50 percent figure for all union elections). They were capitalizing on the job insecurities and real income reductions that had increasingly come to the world of the health care employee as employers had themselves been confronted with rampant competition and escalating costs and had to make tough moves involving their payrolls.

By 2000, New York City's Local 1199 of the National Health and Human Service Employees had grown from minuscule totals to the whopping 200,000 membership noted in the previous chapter, and the head of its nursing home division was confidently predicting that the organization would in the relatively near future represent 75 percent of the nursing home workers in the New York metropolitan area. In a two-and-one-half-year period in the late 1990s, Beverly Enterprises—the nation's biggest nursing home operator—encountered 28 organizing drives throughout the country and managed to defeat labor in only nine of these. Nurses and nurses aides were joining up in droves, some of them in such successful operations as Local 1199. (Exhibit 3-8, an 1199 product, pinpoints several reasons why this union is so optimistic as to the future. Exhibit 3-9 shows a happy group of 1199

EXHIBIT 3-8

SOURCE: *1199 News*, January–February 1995, pp. 12–13. The artists were João Paulo and Elanora Castaño Ferreira.

EXHIBIT 3-9

SOURCE: *1199 News*, May 1999, front cover.

organizers and staffers celebrating the recruitment of some new members in a fairly typical organizing month in the last year of the twentieth century and Exhibit 3-10 also relates to an 1199 victory.) In 1999, the Service Employees International Union gained the right to represent 74,000 Los Angeles County health care workers, labor's biggest single organizing victory since 1937 (when 112,000 General Motors workers joined the United Automobile workers).

Although only about 7 percent of the nation's approximately 600,000 physicians and surgeons were unionized at this writing, the ranks of unionized doctors had nonetheless grown by 80 percent in the past three years. A sign of what might be coming in the face of unhappiness with the power of HMOs may also lie in the 1999 decision of the elite American Medical Association (AMA) to form a union for doctors in what the AMA called "an attempt to level the playing field with powerful managed-care organizations."[10]

❖ Administrative Changes in the Law

Taft-Hartley also enlarged the NLRB from three to its current total of five members (no more than three of whom can be from any one political party) and, in the interests of a faster disposition of cases, authorized the board to delegate "any or all" of its powers to any group of three or more members. In addition, the office of independent general counsel was created within the NLRB, to administer the prosecution of all unfair labor practices. This last change was made to satisfy the increasingly bitter

EXHIBIT 3-10

SOURCE: *1199 News*, January–February 1999, p. 12.

charges (particularly from employers) that the same individuals had exercised both prosecution and judicial roles.

As the NLRB machinery now operates, the board members and general counsel delegate most of their work in processing the 35,000 unfair labor practice charges filed annually and conducting the 1,500 representation elections each year to more than 600 NLRB attorneys and other professionals in more than 50 offices scattered throughout the country. The general counsel supervises this work, and the board members' efforts are thus saved for those issues appealed to it from the regional level.

From what has been said, it is obvious that the NLRB has considerable authority to apply the provisions of the law. What the legislation does is to establish broad guidelines, but it is up to the agency to apply the law to particular situations. In the vast majority of the cases, the courts have sustained the decisions of the board on the grounds that the agency possesses expertise that should be given full credit by the judiciary. It follows, therefore, that how the law will be applied depends to a great extent on who sits on the board. It is a matter of common sense that presidents will choose members who generally represent the philosophy of the nation's chief executive office and thus over the years, employers and unions alternately have been bitterly critical of board policies. In general, unions have criticized the policies of Republican-appointed NLRB members, and employers have displayed the same attitude toward the board when directed by appointees of Democratic chief executives. Possibly providing for permanent tenure for board members in the same manner as federal judges are appointed for life would be a more palatable arrangement for both sides.

THE LANDRUM-GRIFFIN ACT OF 1959

As might have been expected, the Taft-Hartley Act generated considerable controversy. In the years immediately after its passage, labor leaders bitterly assailed the new law as being—in addition to a "slave labor act"—a punitive one. Taft-Hartley supporters, on the other hand, frequently referred to the act as a "Magna Carta" for both employers and employees and widely praised its efforts to "equalize bargaining power." Unable to see any appropriateness in these latter remarks, spokespersons for organized labor, until roughly a decade ago, in turn responded by pressing for the repeal of the act—or occasionally, for its drastic amendment—in every session of Congress. Their complete failure to realize this goal and their recent unwillingness even to pursue it attests to the basic acceptance of Taft-Hartley's provisions in the recent past by the American public, as well as to labor's concern that an even less desirable law might be the outcome.

The framers of public policy themselves, however, did not long remain satisfied that existing labor legislation was fully adequate to uphold the public interest. In 1959, the national legislature passed another significant law, the Landrum-Griffin Act (officially, the Labor-Management Reporting and Disclosure Act). This act was the direct outgrowth of the unsatisfactory internal practices of a small but strategically located minority of unions, as revealed by Senate investigations, and it can be said to have marked the beginning of quite *detailed regulation* of internal union affairs, going far beyond the Taft-Hartley treatment of this subject.

❖ Landrum-Griffin's "Bill of Rights"

Under Landrum-Griffin provisions, as noted earlier, union members are guaranteed a **"Bill of Rights"** that their unions cannot violate, officers of labor organizations must meet a variety of reporting and disclosure obligations, and the secretary of labor is charged with the investigation of relevant union misconduct.

The Bill of Rights for union members is an ambitious and wide-sweeping one. It provides for equality of rights concerning the nomination of candidates for union office, voting in elections, attendance at membership meetings, and participation in business transactions—all, however subject to "reasonable" union rules. It lays down strict standards to ensure that increases in dues and fees are responsive to the desires of the union membership majority. It affirms the right of any member to sue the organization once "reasonable" hearing procedures within the union have been exhausted. It provides that no member may be fined, suspended, or otherwise disciplined by the union except for nonpayment of dues, unless the member has been granted such procedural safeguards as being served with written specific charges, given time to prepare a defense, and afforded a fair hearing. And it obligates union officers to furnish each of their members with a copy of the collective bargaining agreement, as well as full information concerning the Landrum-Griffin Act itself. In a 1989 case, the U.S. Supreme Court made it clear that the Bill of Rights section protects union members' right to free speech. An elected union representative was removed from office because he spoke out against a dues increase. Ruling the action illegal, the high court held that the union action violated the free speech guarantee of Landrum-Griffin.[11]

❖ Union Election Provisions

Not content to stop here in prescribing internal union conduct, the 1959 legislation laid out specific ground rules for *union elections*. National and international unions must now elect officers at least once every five years, either by secret ballot or at a convention of delegates chosen by secret ballot. Local unions are obligated to elect officers at least once every three years, exclusively by secret ballot. As for the conduct of these elections, they must be administered in full accordance with the union's constitution and bylaws, with all ballots and other relevant records being preserved for a period of one year. Every member in good standing is to be entitled to one vote, and all candidates are guaranteed the right to have an observer at the polls and at the ballot counting.

❖ Trusteeship Provisions

Landrum-Griffin also made it more difficult for national and international unions to place their subordinate bodies under trusteeships for purely political reasons. The trusteeship, or the termination of the member group's autonomy, has traditionally allowed labor organizations to correct constitutional violations or other clearly wrongful acts on the part of their locals. The Senate investigations preceding Landrum-Griffin had found, however, that this device was also being used by some unions as a weapon of the national or international officers to eliminate grassroots opposition per se. Accordingly, the act provided that trusteeships could be imposed only for one of four purposes: (1) to correct corruption or "financial malpractice";

(2) to assure the performance of collective bargaining duties; (3) to restore democratic procedures; and (4) to otherwise carry out the "legitimate objects" of the subordinate body. Moreover, the imposition of a trusteeship, together with the reasons for it, was now to be reported to the secretary of labor within thirty days and every six months thereafter until the trusteeship was terminated.

❖ Union Officer Qualification Provisions

The extent of Landrum-Griffin control of the internal affairs of unions is perhaps best illustrated by the act's policing of the kind of person who can serve as a union officer. Persons convicted of serious crimes (robbery, bribery, extortion, embezzlement, murder, rape, grand larceny, violation of narcotics laws, and aggravated assault) are barred for a period of five years after conviction from holding any union position other than a clerical or custodial job. The period of exclusion may be shortened if the person's citizenship rights are fully restored before five years or if the U.S. Department of Justice decides that an exception should be made.

A fair question to ask is whether this policy should be applied to officers of other kinds of institutions, such as business, government, universities, and churches. On the surface, at least, it would appear that if government controls the moral character of union officers, it should apply the same policy across the board. To do otherwise makes it appear that union officers are being held to a higher standard of personal conduct than is required of, say, corporation officials. Shouldn't a corporation official who has been convicted of a serious crime, including violations of the nation's antitrust and pure food and drug laws, be treated in the same way as a union officer?

❖ Financial Requirements

To curb financial corruption, the law requires that union officers must each year file reports with the secretary of labor containing the purpose for which union funds are spent. The objective is to discourage union officers from using the organization's treasury for items of a personal nature. Since financial reports are made available to union members, they can learn whether their dues are being used for the good of the membership. Should it be determined that a union officer has used union funds for personal items, the law authorizes court suits to recover the money from the officer. If a report is not filed, or if the information contained is not true, the responsible union officer is subject to criminal penalties. Outright embezzlement of union funds may, of course, also result in imprisonment or fines or both. In addition, all union officers must be bonded by a private bonding company in which the union has no interest.

❖ Provisions Relating to Employer Activities

Although most of Landrum-Griffin was aimed at union behavior, the act does include provisions that cover employer activities. Landrum-Griffin made employers responsible for reporting annually to the secretary of labor all management expenditures directed at influencing employee collective bargaining behavior. Employer bribery of union officers and other such blunt tactics had actually constituted federal crimes since the passage of Taft-Hartley, but the new act expanded the list of unlawful employer actions. Bribes by companies to their own employees so that they do not exercise their rights to organize and bargain collectively were added to the list of crimes. So, too, were many forms of employer payment aimed at procuring information on employee activities related to labor disputes. Violations by employers of their reporting obligations invite the same criminal penalties as are provided for union representatives.

In a way, the law attempted to fill the gap created by union-membership apathy. It can be argued that a more effective way to promote union democracy and financial responsibility would be by active participation of members in union affairs. The members of any union, local or international, have it in their power to require that their organizations adhere to democratic procedures and financial responsibility through the existing internal machinery of their unions. It is debatable that the federal government should protect union members against abuse by the organization when these members are not particularly concerned as to how their unions in fact operate.

But few would now argue for repeal of the legislation. Even union opposition to Landrum-Griffin has subsided. Control of the internal affairs of unions by government is now established. Possibly, no law will convert unions into models of democracy; still, the effect of the law has eliminated some of the more flagrant abuses of undemocratic practices and financial irresponsibility. For example, in 1969, the United Mine Workers held an election to choose its international officers. This was the first such national election ever conducted in this union in over 40 years, and it is not likely that it would have been held in the absence of the law's requirements. Undoubtedly, too, the act has curtailed the activities of the comparatively small number of union officers who would regard the union's treasury as something to be used for their personal aggrandizement. Although there still exist some undemocratic practices and corruption in unions, there have been fewer flagrant instances of such conduct since the passage of the legislation. If nothing else, the law has educated union officers as to their responsibilities to their members. To this extent, the law has apparently accomplished its major objectives and does for union members what they have failed through apathy to do for themselves.

PUBLIC POLICY IN RECENT YEARS

❖ The Thrust of the NLRB in the 1980's and Early 1990s

If the labor movement was something less than enthusiastic about Landrum-Griffin, moreover, it was to be absolutely incensed by what public policy would do to it in the 1980s and early 1990s. By the middle of the 1980s, a major report of the AFL-CIO could assert that "the norm is that unions now face employers who are bent on avoiding unionization at all costs and who are left largely free to do so by a law that has proven to be impotent and a Labor Board that is inert."[12] And the then Federation President Lane Kirkland, going even further, was regularly declaring in these years that it would not be a bad thing if the collective bargaining statutes were done away with altogether and the parties allowed to go back to their pre-Wagner Act "law of the jungle," as he called it. (Exhibit 3-11 conveys labor's general sentiments about the evenhandedness of government in the early 1990s.)

The four basic laws of collective bargaining—Norris–La Guardia, Wagner, Taft-Hartley, and Landrum-Griffin—had not, of course, changed a bit in these years.

EXHIBIT **3-11**

Source: *The Guild Reporter*, January 10, 1992, p. 8.

What had changed, as it often had in the past and assuredly will in the future, was the makeup of the major interpreter of these laws, the NLRB. And a scant half-decade after applauding a host of decisions rendered by the relatively liberal Jimmy Carter–era board, labor was in fact virtually united in its animosity toward the NLRB as controlled by appointees of Ronald Reagan and then George H.W. Bush.

Few opinions from unionists regarding the newly turned conservative board were notable for their moderation. The president of the United Food and Commercial Workers had asked rhetorically, "If we cannot get fairness from the board, why fool with it?"[13] A staff attorney for the United Automobile Workers had given vent to his opinion that "the board is no longer a neutral agency. It's trying to give management the maximum amount of freedom."[14] The veteran general counsel of the International Ladies Garment Workers, to cite only one more of a myriad of markedly antiboard observers, had announced that "we're dealing with a board whose tilt to management is the most pronounced in my [thirty-one-year] experience."[15]

Such sentiments had been inspired by more than a dozen sharp reversals of pro-labor Carter board precedents by the Reagan and Bush appointees.

Among other actions, the newer NLRB had ruled that employers could move work being performed by union workers to a nonunion facility during the life of a labor agreement that didn't specifically prohibit such a move. It had also declared that these employers need not bargain on the move at all even with such a specific prohibition if the move was due to factors other than labor cost considerations. In addition, the NLRB had reduced protection for employees that labor believed had been granted by the Wagner Act by holding that for an activity to be "concerted" and, thus, covered by that act at least two workers had to be involved. As noted earlier in this chapter, it had declared that it would no longer order an employer to bargain with a union unless the labor organization could prove that it represented a majority of the employees, even in the face of outrageous unfair labor practices by management.

Reversing other precedents of a few years earlier, the newer NLRB provided employers more leeway to interrogate individual employees about their union sympathies; curtailed the scope of the statute by refusing to certify a union composed of teachers in schools related to a religious organization, but not directly operated by the church or synagogue; made it more difficult to have an adverse arbitration decision reversed by the board when it previously deferred to arbitration; and, in cases that particularly irritated the labor movement, made it unlawful for unions to impose fines on employees who resigned from the unions before working during a strike and refused unions the right to enforce bylaws forbidding union members to resign during a strike.

The courts showed no more willingness to overturn these NLRB actions than it had in years past, and one judicial decision caused the labor movement particular consternation. In 1984, the Supreme Court ruled unanimously in *Bildisco Manufacturing* that a company that had filed for bankruptcy could cancel its labor agreement without having to prove that the contract would cause it to go entirely broke. If the employer could show merely that the labor pact "unduly burdened" its prospects for recovery and that it had made "reasonable" efforts to bargain with the union for labor cost savings, it had no further relations obligations, said the court. Even in its weakened 1980s condition, labor had enough friends in Congress to reverse this rather one-sided decision a few months later, and employers now have to convince a bankruptcy court that they would go out of business without contract termination prior to being allowed such relief. The fact that the court decision could have been rendered in the first place, however, still rankled unionists years later.

❖ The Gould Era

Only the severest of the prophets of doom in the labor movement expected such unfriendly public policy actions as these to continue indefinitely, and they didn't. In the later Reagan years, after the initial hard-lining Reagan appointees left the NLRB as their five-year terms expired, the agency started to become more evenhanded. And this trend continued through the Bush era, although none of the controversial earlier board decisions were actually set aside. Then, the 1992 election of Democrat Bill Clinton to the White House ushered in a new tilt at the NLRB that was far more to labor's liking.

The new NLRB chairman, former Stanford law professor William B. Gould IV, in fact, had made no bones at all about his unhappiness with the legal treatment of organized labor in recent times: "The plight of many workers coupled with the inability of unions to represent them at the bargaining table," he asserted, "erodes the fabric of democratic institutions and is profoundly worrisome to all who value a system of checks and balances in the workplace."[16] Because of such sentiments, his nomination encountered much hostility in the Republican-controlled Senate and he was not confirmed until March 1994—and then with the highest negative vote (58 to 38) of any Clinton nominee.

But Gould and his now-Democratic-controlled board went to work with a vengeance once in office. In its first six months, the Gould agency went to the federal courts 67 times to reinstate workers who had been fired for union activities (more than the combined total of the previous two years). In its first two years, it authorized requests for some 200 federal injunctions (including one in 1995 that ended a major league baseball strike), three times the rate of the prior decade.

Between his installation and his departure in the summer of 1998, Gould also made a host of management enemies by announcing with his Democratic board colleagues his support for letting workers vote by mail on whether to be represented by a union, for recognizing unions without elections (regardless of employer acquiescence) when 60 percent of employees had signed up and paid dues, and for allowing modified collective bargaining when just 20 to 30 percent of the employees had indicated a desire to unionize. These rather radical ideas never came to fruition but other Gould board actions applauded by labor did—most importantly the implementation of a procedure in which NLRB administrative law judges could issue decisions in a day or two after hearing a representation or unfair labor practice case instead of waiting their customary several months to write a decision. (Gould argued that delay generally operated to penalize labor in its efforts.) House Republicans in turn threatened to slash Gould's board budget by 30 percent and relented only somewhat: His 1998 budget was still $2 million less than his first year's budget had been.

❖ Other Labor Victories

Labor also won two major victories away from the NLRB in the Gould years, although both amounted to the removal of threats to its well-being as opposed to any enlargement of union powers.

In late 1995, the Supreme Court unanimously decided in *Town & Country Electric, Inc.* that employers couldn't discriminate against paid union organizers who sought jobs for the purpose of organizing nonunion firms. Such a practice is known as **salting** of a company's labor pool. In reviewing applicants for electrician positions at a Minnesota construction project, a nonunion company had refused to interview 10 of 11 union members, and the one unionist who was hired was quickly discharged. The Court here sustained a prior NLRB ruling that the union applicants were "employees" for legal purposes; consequently, they enjoyed the protection of the National Labor Relations Act and, therefore, could not be discriminated against on the grounds of union activity or affiliation. (Obviously, the court went on to say, employers could still discipline and discharge union organizers who violated company rules and regulations just as they could discipline and discharge any worker.)

And in late 1996 Clinton killed a business-supported bill, promulgating a so-called **Teamwork for Employees and Management (TEAM) Act,** that would have given employers greater leeway in establishing labor–management teams to address such issues as productivity, quality control, and health and safety. Both houses of Congress had passed the bill, and more than 600 corporate chief executives had signed a letter asking the president to join them in supporting it. Clinton, however, announced that the TEAM Act would effectively repeal that portion of the Wagner Act prohibiting company-dominated unions. His veto stood because neither the House nor the Senate had passed the bill with the two-thirds majority needed to override such a White House action.

❖ Another NLRB Change in Emphasis

With the Republicans continuing to hold power on Capitol Hill, the NLRB took on a more probusiness tone in the last years of the century. Two Republican hard-liners replaced more moderate GOP appointees, and Gould's successor as chairman, veteran NLRB staffer John C. Truesdale, although one of the three Democrats in this Clinton board, was far more to the employer community's liking (although this admittedly didn't take much) than had been the former Stanford professor. He vowed to "stay out of political maters" and to concentrate on reducing the board's enormous case backlog, not an easy task in itself because the budgetary constraints had led to a significant drop in staff size in the Gould era. No new attorney had been hired in five years and most other staff members who had left NLRB employ in these years had also not been replaced. With so many friends in Congress, business once again appeared to be in the ascendancy on the national labor relations scene.

PERMANENT REPLACEMENTS FOR STRIKERS: ANOTHER WORRY FOR LABOR

In bestowing its various forms of protection on employee collective bargaining, the Wagner Act quite clearly allowed union members the right to strike without losing their jobs. Employers could not—and cannot—in any way punish striking union members, much less fire them, for taking such action.

But a mere three years after this landmark legislation was passed, a U.S. Supreme Court decision essentially negated this stricture. In 1938, the Court ruled that employers could hire **permanent replacements** for workers who were striking for economic reasons such as increased pay or benefits or for improved working conditions, as opposed to unfair labor practices. In such strikes as the former—and most strikes by far, of course, have significant wage-benefit-working condition components—managements can achieve exactly the same result as a mass discharge of their workers would have simply by awarding the jobs of the strikers to new employees. Only if the courts find that the employer has engaged in an unfair labor practice can the strikers regain their jobs and accrued pay. Otherwise, the most that a striking worker can hope for is a preferential claim to the job that he or she has lost *after* the replacement has retired or for some other reason vacated the position.

For more than four decades after 1938, the replacement-worker strategy was nonetheless used very sparingly by managements. Employers feared retaliation not only directly by organized labor but from unionized suppliers and prounion consumers. Considerations of public relations, community relations, the costs and uncertainties of recruiting and training the new workers, and even possible governmental intervention on the side of the striking union also acted as deterrents. Nor was the chance of violence by the strikers themselves to be casually dismissed. Between 1938 and 1981, only some 200 cases of permanent replacement action were officially recorded.

It was the previously noted illegal strike of 11,500 air traffic controllers in mid-1981 and President Ronald Reagan's immediate authorization of permanent replacements for these strikers that finally gave the policy a huge shot in the arm. Thenceforth, as Mine Worker President Richard L. Trumka could point out, "any businessman could . . . say, 'The President did it so it must be O.K.'"[17] With this extreme kind of action having come from the highest elected official in the land, employers no longer had to worry about governmental intervention on the side of organized labor in such situations—at least as long as friends like Reagan were in power.

Nor by the 1980s were managements oblivious to two other developments that were not only continuing but seemed to be accelerating. One was the declining influence of unions, making potential retaliation in cases of permanent replacement less likely. The other was a general wage stagnation in the economy; it was creating a sizable supply of nonunion workers who were making far less than the incomes realized by many of their unionized counterparts and who were therefore presumably quite able to be attracted to these bargaining unit positions should they become available.

In recent years, replacement workers have been hired with increasing frequency. Some of the companies embracing the tactic—Continental Airlines, the New York *Daily News*, Greyhound, Eastern Air Lines, and Boise Cascade, among many others—were in dire financial straits at the time and vehemently argued that they had no choice in the matter if they wished to survive. But other employers—most notably, Caterpillar, the world's largest manufacturer of construction equipment— have been quite profitable.

What's more, use of the weapon has often been surprisingly effective. Not long ago, Caterpillar's mere threat of hiring permanent replacements broke a bitter five-month Automobile Worker strike within days. In Maine, International Paper, when confronted by another acrimonious strike, had no trouble finding many more candidates for replacement jobs than were needed despite relatively low unemployment and the fact that the replacements were offered hourly rates that were less than 70 percent of what the strikers had gotten. Within a year, the company had reduced its workforce by almost 20 percent and abolished premium pay. Two years later, 80 percent of the workforce was made up of replacement workers.

With such successes, the replacement strategy has gained a remarkable number of employer converts in the recent past. In 1985, 15 percent of 132 managements that had experienced strikes said that they would use permanent replacements. In 1989, about 23 percent of such employers did.[18] (In both years, about 15 percent actually hired the replacements.) In a 1992 survey of a much larger group of employers (most of whom responded strictly hypothetically), 32 percent said that they would definitely replace the strikers and an additional 48 percent said that they would "consider" replacing their old employees to keep operating.[19] In 1995, a whopping 82 percent of large unionized employers said they would hire replacements if struck, and, although only 25 percent of these declared that the replacements would be permanent, an additional 57 percent said that they hadn't decided this issue of permanence one way or the other.[20] Random samplings of employers five years after that have indicated that the percentage has, if anything, grown.

Nor has organized labor been able to remove this very real threat by getting Congress to declare it, in the style of *Bildisco*, illegal. A labor-backed **Workplace Fairness bill** that would have done so got the highest possible legislative priority from unions in the 1991–1992 session of the national legislature. But its margin of victory in the House (247–182) was too small to override an expected veto by President George H.W. Bush. In the Senate, the bill's backers could not even muster the 60 votes needed to head off a Republican-led filibuster and the bill died there. And in 1994, although Democrat Bill Clinton had replaced Bush and the veto was no longer a threat to labor (and the House passed the same bill by a 230 to 190 margin), the Senate again, now by 53–46, voted to prevent a vote. After the November 1994 elections had produced a national Republican congressional landslide, most labor leaders bowed to reality and acknowledged that the Workplace Fairness bill was, for the foreseeable future, dead. Unions did derive some consolation when Clinton in 1995 signed an executive order that banned the use of permanent striker replacements by government contractors, but this was a rather minimal gain.

SOME CONCLUDING THOUGHTS

What are some reasonably safe conclusions based on the long experience of public policy recited on these pages? The first conclusion must be that public policy toward organized labor has changed significantly over the years. It has moved from legal repression to strong encouragement, then to modified encouragement coupled with regulation, and, finally, to detailed regulation of internal union affairs in an environment that unions see (despite a temporary prolabor swing of the pendulum at the NLRB in the mid-1990s) as increasingly antilabor. It seems a safe prediction not only that further shifts in this public policy can be expected, but also that these changes, as was not always the case in earlier times, will depend for this direction strictly on the acceptability of current union behavior to the American public.

This point is particularly important to the unionists of today. Especially since 1937, when it held the Wagner Act wholly constitutional, the Supreme Court has permitted the legislative branch of government the widest latitude to shape public policy. Congress and the state legislatures are judicially free to determine the elements of the framework of labor law. To most citizens, such a situation is only as it should be; our judiciary is expected to interpret law but not to make it, and we generally expect actions of the legislative branch to be voided only when the particular statute clearly and unmistakably violates the terms of the Constitution. But since today the polls, and not the courts, do constitute the forum in which our policies toward labor are determined, and since the public has in the recent past apparently increased its level of aspiration as to union behavior, labor organizations have been forced amid their adversity to become increasingly conscious of the images they project. Such a situation accounts to a great extent for the growing union stress on such nontraditional labor concerns as charity work, college scholarships, Scout troops, and Little League teams, which will be discussed in the next chapter. It also accounts for the entire labor movement's uneasiness whenever strikes arousing the public ire or such notable black marks as convictions of Teamster leaders occur. And it undoubtedly has been one major factor in leading to more maturity and self-restraint on the part of some labor leaders at the bargaining table. As Chapter 1 noted, however, whether this progress will continue sufficiently and in time to satisfy the increasingly high level of public expectation and thereby ward off further laws of the Taft-Hartley and Landrum-Griffin variety remains an unanswered question.

Second, every law since Norris–La Guardia has expanded the scope of government regulation of the labor–management arena. To the curbs on judicial capriciousness enacted in 1932 have been added, in turn, restrictions on employer conduct, limitations on union conduct, and governmental fiats closely regulating internal union affairs. Most of the other parts of the later laws—for example, Taft-Hartley's modification of the Wagner Act's closed- and union-shop provisions—represent ever-finer qualifications of the freedom of action of both parties. Given both the electorate's impatience with the progress of collective bargaining and Congress's apparently deep-seated reluctance to decrease the scope covered by its laws, future legislation can be expected to move *further* in the direction of government intervention. This should hold true whether the future laws are enacted with the implicit goal of "helping" or of "hurting" unions.

Individual value judgments clearly determine the advisability of such a trend. But if one believes that stable and sound industrial relations can be achieved only in an environment of free collective bargaining, wherein labor and management—the parties that must live with each other on a day-to-day basis—are allowed to find mutually satisfactory answers to their problems, there is cause for concern. Government policy that limits this freedom strikes at the very heart of the process.

This is not to say that the more recent labor statutes are entirely barren of provisions that are valuable additions. The unfair union labor practices relating to restraint and coercion of employees and to union-caused employer discrimination are clearly a move in the right direction. So, too, are Taft-Hartley's curbs on strikes and boycott activity engaged in at times by some unions for the objective of increasing the power of one union at the expense of other labor organizations, despite all the litigation that has surrounded these curbs since 1947. Nor does the requirement that unions bargain collectively embarrass anyone except the union leader who is uncooperative and recalcitrant.

At the same time, however, the government intervention in regard to such issues as union security, the checkoff, and the enforcement of the collective bargaining agreement (to cite but three), and the decreasing scope for union and management bargaining-table latitude in general, do raise the question of ultimate government control over *all* major industrial relations activities. For one who believes in free collective bargaining, the increasing reach of the statutes may be steering labor policy in a very dangerous direction.

Third, even if one does conclude that the gains of our present dosage of government regulation outweigh its losses and inherent risks, this hardly proves that the current statutes and their interpretations constitute the most *appropriate* ones to meet each specific labor relations topic now being dealt with.

Finally, and probably also as an inevitable consequence of the increased coverage of public policy, labor laws have become anything but easy to comprehend. The inconsistent NLRB and judicial rulings that have plagued them in recent years may be based to some extent on philosophical and political differences, but they undeniably also stem from the built-in interpretative difficulties in the laws themselves.

What constitutes refusal to bargain? When are employers discriminating in regard to "hire or tenure of employment or any term or condition of employment" to influence union membership? What constitutes unlawful union recognition picketing? It is hard to disagree with the commonly heard lament of unionists and labor relations managers that it has become ever more risky to state definitively what is legal in bargaining relationships and what is not; and the most valuable information available to the management or labor union representative who is concerned with labor law may very possibly be the telephone number or address of an able labor attorney. But, given the dimensions of this law today, however unpalatable many of its tenets may be to one or the other party, and whatever dangers may be inherent in present trends, managers and unionists who are *not* concerned with public policy remain so only at their peril.

DISCUSSION QUESTIONS

1. Why, do you think, did the courts so squarely ally themselves with the employer community and against organized labor from the days of the American Revolution until the Great Depression of the 1930s?
2. "The Norris–La Guardia Act conferred no new rights on workers. It merely adjusted an inherently inequitable situation." Comment.
3. Comment on the truth of this statement: "There was great need for the Wagner Act. Its sole defect lay in the fact that it was not slightly broadened from time to time to regulate a few union practices of dubious social value."
4. It has been argued that whatever deficiencies may have accompanied the Taft-Hartley Act, it did "free workers from the tyrannical hold of union bosses." Do you agree?
5. Do you feel that the Wagner Act or the Taft-Hartley Act has been more influential in leading to the current status of organized labor in this country?
6. "In the last analysis, the public must judge the relative merits of the collective bargaining process." Discuss.
7. If all existing national labor legislation could instantly be erased and our statutory regulation could then be completely rewritten, what would you advocate as public policy governing labor relations—and why?
8. Whether or not you agree with the exact scope and specific wording of the present laws, do you consider these laws to be essentially equitable to both management and labor?
9. "If union members were to attend union meetings regularly and take an active role in the operation of the union, there would be no need for Landrum-Griffin." Defend your position, whatever it may be.
10. What do you believe to be the most important right that the Taft-Hartley Act offers (a) the employee, (b) the employer? In each case, defend your selection.

MINICASES

 A Question of Definition

After some professors at Deer Valley University (DVU) show an interest in collective bargaining and invite a national representative of the American Association of University Professors (AAUP) to visit their campus and explain to them and their colleagues how to go about holding a union representation election, the university administration makes an announcement. The faculty members had better forget the whole thing, it says, because DVU is a "private institution" and the AAUP is consequently deprived of all legal protection in its unionizing activities.

The professors immediately circulate an irate written rejoinder, asserting that the university is not private but "state-related" and, thus, quite entitled to the coverage of the state's "little Taft-Hartley" labor law. The institution, they point out, currently derives one-quarter of its annual revenues from the state, and four of its 28 trustees are appointed by the governor (the other 24 are designated by vote of the board of trustees itself).

Who, in your opinion, is right—and why?

#2 Alleged Union Paranoia

Two weeks before a scheduled union representation election, a supervisor drives three times past a union meeting that is attended by about 80 employees. After the union loses the election, by the wide margin of 140 to 63, it asks the NLRB to set the latter aside on the grounds that the supervisor's actions constituted an obvious attempt to find out who was at the meeting and, thus, an implicit "threat of reprisal," prohibited by Taft-Hartley. The management tells the board that the union is being "paranoid" and that the connection between the supervisor's driving and reprisal is far too tenuous to prove anything illegal. The supervisor, it says, was "simply curious" as to who was attending and how large the overall crowd was. And, it asserts, he drove by entirely on his own, in no way at the behest of his supervisors.

If you were on the NLRB, would you set aside the election? Why or why not?

NOTES

[1] *Photoswitch*, 99 NLRB 1366 (1962).
[2] *Nielsen Lithographing*, 1991–92 CCH NLRB, 16, 992.
[3] *Ford Motor Company* v. *NLRB*, 441 U.S. 488 (1979).
[4] *Cowles Media Co. Star Tribune Division*, 295 NLRB No. 63 (1989).
[5] *Johnson-Bateman Co.*, 295 NLRB No. 26 (1989).
[6] *Firestone Tire & Rubber Company*, 222 NLRB 1254 (1976).
[7] *Buddy L. Corporation*, 167 NLRB 808 (1967).
[8] *J. P. Stevens*, 219 NLRB 850 (1975).
[9] *American Hospital Association* v. *NLRB*, Case No. 90–97, April 23, 1991.
[10] *The New York Times*, June 24, 1999, p. 1. The union will work to recruit only the approximately 200,000 doctors who are medical residents or otherwise salaried employees. To unionize self-employed physicians and surgeons, the AMA must first persuade Congress to let such doctors bargain collectively, as they cannot now do.
[11] *Sheet Metal Workers' Local 75* v. *Lynn*, 86 S. Ct. 1940, January 17, 1989.
[12] AFL-CIO, Committee on the Evolution of Work, *The Changing Situation of Workers and Their Unions* (Washington, DC: AFL-CIO, 1985), p. 10.
[13] *Business Week*, June 11, 1984, p. 122.
[14] *The New York Times*, February 5, 1984, Sec. F, p. 4.
[15] *Wall Street Journal*, January 25, 1984, p. 35.
[16] *Business Week*, August 16, 1993, p. 12.
[17] *The New York Times*, January 27, 1991, p. A1.
[18] *The New York Times*, January 27, 1991, p. A23.
[19] *Wall Street Journal*, April 20, 1992, p. A3.
[20] *Business Week*, April 10, 1995, p. 66.

SELECTED REFERENCES

Baer, Walt. *Labor Union Representatives: Allowed and Prohibited Practices*. Jefferson, NC and London: McFarland, 1992.

Dougherty, James L. *Union-Free Labor Relations: A Step-by-Step Guide to Staying Union Free*. Houston: Gulf, 1980.

Ernst, Daniel R. *Lawyers Against Labor: From Individual Rights to Corporate Liberalism*. Urbana and Chicago: University of Illinois Press, 1995.

Finkin, Matthew W. *The Legal Future of Employee Representation*. Ithaca, NY: ILR Press, Cornell University, 1994.

Flanagan, Robert. *Labor Relations and the Litigation Explosion*. Washington, DC: The Brookings Institution, 1987.

Forbath, William E. *Law and the Shaping of the American Labor Movement*. Cambridge, MA: Harvard University Press, 1991.

Friedman, Sheldon, Richard W. Hurd, Rudy Oswald, and Ronald L. Seeber, eds. *Restoring the Promise of American Labor Law*. Ithaca, NY: ILR Press, Cornell University, 1994.

Getman, Julius. *The Betrayal of Local 14; Paperworkers, Politics, and Permanent Replacements*. Ithaca, NY: ILR Press, Cornell University, 1998.

Gold, Michael Evan. *An Introduction to Labor Law, Revised*. Ithaca, NY: ILR Press, Cornell University, 1998.

Gould, William B. IV. *A Primer on American Labor Law*, (3rd ed.). Cambridge, MA: MIT Press, 1993.

Hill, Marvin F., Jr., and James A. Wright. *Employee Lifestyle and Off-Duty Conduct Regulation*. Washington, DC: Bureau of National Affairs, 1993.

Kaufman, Bruce E., ed. *Government Regulation of the Employment Relationship*. Ithaca, NY: ILR Press, Cornell University, 1998.

Lawler, John J. *Unionization and Deunionization*. Columbia: University of South Carolina Press, 1990.

Leslie, Douglas L. *Labor Law in a Nutshell*, (2nd ed.). St. Paul, MN: West, 1986.

Levitt, Martin Jay, with Terry Conrow. *Confessions of a Union Buster*. New York: Crown, 1993.

Malin, Martin H. *Individual Rights within the Union*. Washington, DC: Bureau of National Affairs, 1987.

Morris, Charles J., ed. *American Labor Policy: A Critical Appraisal of the National Labor Relations Act*. Washington, DC: Bureau of National Affairs, 1987.

Schlossberg, Stephen I., and Judith A. Scott. *Organizing and the Law*, (4th ed.). Washington, DC: Bureau of National Affairs, 1991.

Weiler, Paul C. *Governing the Workplace: The Future of Labor and Employment Law*. Cambridge, MA: Harvard University Press, 1990.

Witney, Fred, and Benjamin J. Taylor. *Labor Relations Law*, (7th ed.). Englewood Cliffs, NJ: Prentice Hall, 1996.

CHAPTER

4

Union Behavior: Structure, Government, and Operation

OUTLINE OF KEY CONTENTS

- Why national unions do and sometimes don't belong to the AFL-CIO
- The somewhat complex structural organization of the AFL-CIO
- The major interests and activities of the AFL-CIO
- The relationship between national and local unions
- What national unions do beyond providing service to local unions
- How national unions are governed and why, even though they hardly grow rich on the salaries of their offices, national union officers generally like the work
- The government and basic characteristics of local unions
- The financial status of unions

$\mathcal{O}$rganized labor in the United States has a structure that is anything but simple. The AFL-CIO is a federation that contains many different units exercising different duties and authority. Sixty-eight of the 121 national (or international, as—it will be remembered—they are interchangeably called) unions in the country belong to the AFL-CIO and account for roughly 13.3 million of the nation's 16.2 million unionized workers. But the other 53 of these, essentially all relatively small ones in terms of membership, do not. National unions, in turn, are themselves subdivided into regions or districts for more efficient management and administration. And, although the vast majority of the country's approximately 43,000 local unions belong to national unions, several hundred of them do not and are commonly described as independent unions.[1] Finally, some unions are craft in character, others industrial, and some are both craft and industrial.

Because unions are also not similar in terms of heritage, size, geographic location, the personalities of their officers, and the kinds of workers who are members, it should be expected that they will differ widely in terms not only of their governments but also of their day-to-day operations. Some (perhaps most notably the Automobile Workers and the Newspaper Guild) both before and after Landrum-Griffin have been models of democracy. A few (including both the Teamsters and the Laborers until democratic procedures were forced on them by governmental consent decrees not long ago) have historically been quite autocratically administered. Unions are different in terms of the intensity of their political activities, although events of the past few decades have made virtually all labor organizations conscious of a need to become active in political campaigns. Some unions have engaged in considerably more social activities of the type alluded to earlier in this book than have others. Above all, unions vary in terms of their internal rules, dues and initiation fees, and qualifications for membership. Thus, although the following pages will feature common principles and trends, it should be recognized that there are many exceptions to them.

THE AFL-CIO

❖ Relationship to National Unions

The decision of the former American Federation of Labor and Congress of Industrial Organizations to unite forces into a consolidated AFL-CIO in 1955 was made by the affiliated national unions of the two federations; the officers of the AFL and the CIO did not themselves have the power to bring about such a consolidation. This observation demonstrates a very important principle of the structure of the American labor movement—the national unions are autonomous. The federation can exist only as long as the national unions that belong to it agree to stay in this labor body.

The relationship of the national unions to the federation is like the relationship of member nations to the United Nations. No nation *must* belong to the United Nations; any nation *may* withdraw from the international organization at any time and for any reason whatsoever. Nor does the United Nations have the power to determine the internal government of any of its affiliates, its tax laws, its foreign policy, the size of its military establishment, or any other national matters. Nations affiliate and remain members of the world body for the advantages that the organization allows in the pursuit of world peace and for other purposes, but they continue to exercise absolute sovereignty in the conduct of their own affairs.

The same is true of the relationship of the AFL-CIO to its 68 affiliated national unions. A union belongs to the federation because of the various advantages of affiliation, but the national union is autonomous in the conduct of its own affairs. Each union determines its own collective bargaining program, negotiates its contracts without the aid or intervention of the federation, sets its own level of dues and initiation fees, and may call strikes without any approval from the AFL-CIO; nor, conversely, can the federation prohibit a strike that an affiliated member desires to undertake.

❖ Merger of AFL-CIO Affiliates

Moreover, the federation cannot force a merger of two of its affiliates that have essentially the same jurisdiction. For example, the International Brotherhood of Electrical Workers of the old AFL and the International Union of Electronic Workers of the old CIO have virtually identical jurisdictions in manufacturing. It may seem logical that these two national unions should merge their forces and in the process further consolidate with the smaller, independent United Electrical Workers; in fact, all three of them have in recent years discussed such a consolidation. To date, however, the conversations have produced no action, and perhaps they never will. As a president of the American Federation of State, County, and Municipal Employees once observed:

> Mergers and consolidations are, of course, easier to talk about than to bring about. At stake are the bread-and-butter questions that always impede institutional change: What will happen to the elected officers, the paid staff, the local and regional structures, and the assets and traditions to which all unions, meek or mighty, cling? There still would be jobs and titles. But even the most selfless politician (and we labor leaders are, after all, political creatures) often sees himself as peerless when it comes to occupying a union presidency. The power, the payroll, the trappings—these are the real obstacles.[2]

On the other hand, two or even more unions within the AFL-CIO may merge voluntarily if they do desire to do so, and, since 1955, some 90 of them have. In the past decade alone there have been almost 50 such consolidations.

Most of these combinings have seen the absorption of a small labor organization by a much larger one (for example, the 1991 merger of the 2,000-member Train Dispatchers with the 50,000-member Locomotive Engineers; the 1992 coming together of the 9,000 Broadcast Technicians and the close-to-600,000-member Communications Workers; and the 1995 merger of the 35,000 Newspaper Guild members with the same Communications Workers). But some considerably more impressive ones have also taken place: the 1993 amalgamation of the 130,000 members of the Retail, Wholesale, and Department Store Union and the million-member United Food and Commercial Workers (although at this writing separate union identities were still maintained); the 1995 merger of the Amalgamated Clothing and Textile Workers (200,000 constituents) with the International Ladies' Garment Workers (about 155,000) to form what was officially named in 1996 the Union of Needletrades, Industrial and Textile Employees (UNITE); and the United Rubber

Workers (98,000 members) merger with the United Steelworkers (565,000 at that time), also in 1995.

Plans for an even more formidable merger, this one involving *three* major unions, were in fact also announced in 1995. The United Automobile Workers, the International Association of Machinists, and the United Steelworkers—among them, in that year, representing nearly 2 million workers—revealed that they had agreed to merge by the year 2000, creating what would be by far the largest U.S. industrial union. Although in this case many details remained to be worked out and although in early 2000 it looked as though the mammoth new organization might miss its timetable by a year or even two years, it seemed equally clear that the new megaunion was not far down the road.

Steadily rising administrative costs have motivated many of these merger actions. Even now, after all of the mergers of the 1990s, almost half of the federation's 68 national unions have fewer than 50,000 members and thus fall below what AFL-CIO officials have estimated to be the minimum dues-paying base necessary to support effective action, while another 17 AFL-CIO affiliates have under 100,000 members and are also often hard-pressed for cash. In other cases, technological change or the changing desires of the marketplace have simply made a union obsolete, and the merger becomes a device to provide a respectable burial. Examples in this latter category are the Cigar Makers, whose remaining 2,500 members merged with the Retail, Wholesale, and Department Store Union a while ago, and the Sleeping Car Porters, who disappeared by merger into the Brotherhood of Railway and Airline Clerks some time back.

In still other situations, the growth of the managerial conglomerate—with ownership spanning several different product markets—has been the spur. The Tobacco Workers and Bakery and Confectionery Workers merger and the absorption by the Steelworkers of not only the Mine, Mill, and Smelter Workers but also the Aluminum Workers and District 50 of the Mine Workers can all be explained on this latter basis. The mergers were triggered by a desire to match the bargaining strength of employers whose own boundaries had themselves been significantly expanding. Obviously, such a multifaceted conglomerate as the LTV Corporation (to use only one example), which today controls—among other operations—Jones & Laughlin Steel, Youngstown Sheet and Tube, Kentron International, Lykes Bros. Steamship, Continental-Emsco, and Vought Corporation, could not be met on equal terms by narrowly jurisdictioned unionism.

Some observers of the trend now predict that within another decade the federation will be composed of only 15 to 20 large unions—perhaps one for the communications field, one for retailing, another single union for the metal trades, and so on. Should this actually come to pass, the U.S. labor movement would more closely resemble organized labor in most European countries, which have in fact only about 15 unions apiece.

It must be stressed again, however, that all mergers under the decentralized AFL-CIO system have been voluntary. The affiliated unions decide their own fates, and each of them can pursue its own objectives, conduct its own affairs, and devise what policies and programs it desires to follow without intervention by either the federation or any other national union. Least of all can any outsider compel the unions to merge.

Nor, for that matter, can the AFL-CIO compel them to *stay* merged. Although most mergers are permanent, some simply don't work out and, usually by mutual agreement of the merging parties, the arrangement terminates. In 1976 the Pottery Workers merged with the Seafarers International Union in what many observers viewed as a wedding that was as appropriate as, say, a newspaper industry merger between the *Christian Science Monitor* and the *Jewish Daily Forward* would be. Less than two years later, their differences too major to overcome, the two unions effected an institutional divorce. In 1982, the same Pottery Workers, with barely 11,000 members at that point, merged with the 85,000-member Glass Bottle Blowers. When last heard from this time, they were still happily married.

❖ Enforcement of Federation Rules

The AFL-CIO constitution does contain certain rules of conduct that a national union must respect if it desires to remain a member of the federation. Each affiliate must pay to the federation a per capita tax that on January 1, 2000 stood at 50 cents per member per month. No union may "raid" the membership of any other affiliate, nor may it be officered by communists, fascists, or members of any other totalitarian group. Among other rules, an affiliate is obligated to conduct its affairs without regard to "race, creed, color, national origin, or ancestry." Each affiliate is further expected "to protect the labor movement from any and all corrupt influences."

The practical question immediately arises as to what powers the AFL-CIO may exercise when an affiliated national union does not comply with these and various other rules of the federation. If the AFL-CIO had wide-sweeping powers over the national unions, the federation officers could swiftly compel the errant union to correct its improper conduct. The union could still belong to the federation, but its violation of the federation's constitution would be abruptly terminated. The realities of the situation, however, are such that the federation is not empowered to correct violations by exercise of such power. It can do no more than suspend or expel a national union that persists in the violation.

The expulsion weapon has been used in several instances, but never rashly. Before the AFL-CIO expelled the Teamsters Union in 1957 to begin a separation that would endure for 30 years, for example, that union was put on notice that it stood in flagrant violation of the anticorruption provision of the federation's constitution. AFL-CIO officials instructed the Teamsters that they would face expulsion unless certain of their national officers were removed and the corrupt practices eliminated. Only when the Teamsters adamantly refused to comply did the AFL-CIO convert the threat into actuality and take the ultimate step of expelling the union from its ranks. And even though the United Automobile Workers actually withdrew from the AFL-CIO in 1968 (and would not return until 1981) because of that union's claim that the AFL-CIO was not doing enough in organizational work and had not been militant enough in areas of social affairs, the federation technically expelled the UAW only on the entirely understandable ground that it had refused to pay its per capita dues.

Moreover, as a practical matter, the federation is compelled to use even this amount of authority sparingly and with discretion. The expulsion of the Teamsters was prompted by the corrupt practices of union officers who were highly visible to the public. The AFL-CIO could not tolerate such a situation in the light of the existing public clamor against dishonest union leadership and practices; it was fully aware that the retention of the Teamsters would reflect adversely on *every* affiliated union. One would be naïve, however, to believe that all unions scrupulously adhere to the letter and spirit of each rule incorporated in the federation's constitution. It is, for example, common knowledge that a few affiliated unions still discriminate against minority group members, although in recent years much progress has been made in eliminating such practices. Despite this improvement, however, some unions still prohibit minorities from joining, fail to represent them impartially in collective bargaining, and otherwise discriminate against them. Such practices, of course, conflict not only with legality, (above all, the Civil Rights Act of 1964) but also with the AFL-CIO constitutional proscription against racial discrimination. But the federation is faced with a major dilemma under such circumstances: If it were to expel each union found to be in any way discriminating, the size of the federation would be reduced and its influence as a labor body would be accordingly impaired. In fact, to date no union has been expelled from the federation for racial discrimination; about all the federation officers have done has been to use moral suasion to deal with the problem. Such an approach has not yet been particularly effective in many cases, but to do more would jeopardize the entire federation.

Member-union autonomy is also evident from the ease with which national unions have left the federation voluntarily. Several affiliates—including the Mine Workers, Lithographers, and Radio and Television Directors—have pulled out of the larger body with impunity, saving their considerable per capita tax money in the process.

Why, then, do most national unions seek to belong to the federation? What do they get for their money?

❖ Advantages of Affiliation

By far the chief benefit associated with membership is protection against **raiding**. One provision of the AFL-CIO constitution states that "each such affiliate shall respect the established collective bargaining relationship of every other affiliate and no affiliate shall raid the established collective bargaining relationship of any other affiliate." This means that once an affiliated union gains bargaining rights with a management, no other union affiliated with the federation may attempt to dislodge the established union and place itself there instead. Such a stricture frees unions from the task of fighting off raids from sister unions of the federation. Time and money conserved in this way can be used to organize the unorganized or to devote to other union programs. Unions that violate the no-raiding provision of the constitution may realistically expect to be expelled from the AFL-CIO; and because mutual self-interest of all members is involved, the amount of raiding has in fact decreased sharply since the formation of the federation.

Thus, before a union withdraws voluntarily from the AFL-CIO or engages in conduct that could result in expulsion, the officers of the union must weigh the consequences of operating outside the federation as these consequences concern proneness to raiding. Such considerations have been particularly influential in maintaining AFL-CIO membership for most smaller and weaker nationals, whom protection against raids benefits to a greater degree than it does larger national unions. But considerations of the money, time, and energy involved in counterattacking raiding attempts have also convinced most larger nationals of the wisdom of continued federation membership.

Federation membership involves still other advantages. With the federation as the spearhead, the union movement has comparatively more power in the political and legislative affairs of the nation and labor's impact upon elections and congressional voting is correspondingly greater than if each national union went its own way. In addition, by coordinating political efforts, the federation can use union funds, and such other sources of political persuasion as letter-writing campaigns, more effectively. Moreover, the AFL-CIO helps national unions in organizing campaigns, although the nationals are expected to bear the chief responsibility for new organization. And affiliated national unions also receive some help from the federation in the areas of legal services, educational programs, research, and social activities.

On the other hand, in the best tradition of Gompers, the federation does not negotiate labor agreements for the affiliated national unions. It is not equipped to render such services; nor do the autonomous national unions desire such intervention. In only one way does a national union directly benefit on the collective bargaining front from its membership in the federation: A framework is provided whereby unions that bargain in the same industry or with the same company can consolidate their efforts. A large company such as General Electric, for example, bargains with many different unions, and affiliated unions that deal with General Electric can thus more easily adopt common collective bargaining goals (such as uniform expiration dates of labor agreements and the attainment of similar economic benefits) than would be the case without the availability of federation coordination. The joint bargaining endeavors over the past few decades of (most often) 12 major unions with General Electric (and subsequently with Westinghouse) have been in fact conducted under AFL-CIO auspices, through the coordinating efforts of the federation's increasingly active Industrial Union Department, and this has been true of several other joint union efforts, which are summarized in the next chapter under "Coordinated Bargaining and Multinationals."

❖ Structure and Government of the AFL-CIO

The supreme governing body of the federation is its *convention*, held once every two years. Each national union, regardless of size, may send one delegate to the convention, and unions with more than 4,000 members may send additional delegates in proportion to their size. Each national union delegate casts one vote for every member represented, an arrangement that allows larger unions, such as the Teamsters and the Food and Commercial Workers more influence in the affairs of the convention.

The decisions and policies adopted by the convention are implemented by the AFL-CIO *executive council*, composed of the president, secretary-treasurer, and 52 vice presidents of the federation. The vice presidents are elected at the convention and are usually selected from the presidents of the affiliated national unions. Only the president of the federation and its secretary-treasurer devote full time to the affairs of the organization, however; the vice presidents meet with the executive council at least three times a year but spend most of their time presiding over their own national unions.

Among its chief duties, the executive council interprets and applies the federation constitution; plays a "watchdog" role in legislative matters that affect the interests of workers and unions; assembles, through a full-time staff of legal and economic experts, the data needed for testimony before congressional committees; keeps in contact with the many federal agencies that have authority in the labor field; and ensures that the federation is kept free from undesirable influences. If it suspects that a union or its officers are in violation of the federation's constitution, it may investigate the matter, and if it finds that the charges are valid, it may, by a two-thirds majority, vote to suspend the guilty union. It may also recommend the ultimate penalty of expulsion of the union, but only the full convention may actually expel the union from the federation.

The executive council also selects six of its membership who, along with the AFL-CIO president and secretary-treasurer, constitute the federation's *executive committee*. This smaller group meets every two months and has the major function of advising and counseling the president and secretary-treasurer on issues involving the federation and its policies. Only the president and the secretary-treasurer receive a salary for their duties. All other federation officers serve without salary, although they are compensated by the federation for their expenses when attending to federation business.

A fourth decision-making body within the federation is the AFL-CIO *general board*, which consists of all members of the executive council and one principal officer of each of the national and international unions and the affiliated departments (to be described in a minute). Usually, the affiliated national union designates its chief officer as its representative to serve on the general board, which must meet at least once a year and may meet more often at the discretion of the federation's president. Its chief duty is to rule on all questions and issues referred to it by the executive council.

As for *standing committees*, the federation constitution requires the president to appoint a number of them, and AFL-CIO custom dictates that each committee chairperson be president of a national union and that all members be active trade unionists. At present, such committees (which are in all cases supplied with full-time professional staffs) deal with such issues as civil rights, community services, economic policy, education, ethical practices, international affairs, legislation, political education, public relations, research, safety and health, and veterans' affairs. The federation's growing scope of interests is illustrated by the character of these committees, some of which are relatively new and virtually all of which clearly extend well beyond strictly trade union affairs.

Nine constitutional *departments*, groupings for unions with strong common interests, are currently in existence: Building Trades, Industrial Union, Maritime Trades, Metal Trades, Union Label, and—most recently—Professional Employees, Public Employees, Food and Beverage Trades, and Working Women. National unions may belong to more than one of these departments, and many of them with memberships in two or more areas of interest do exactly that (for example, the International Brotherhood of Electrical Workers, with some members who work in the building trades and others who work in factories), but in each case the national is required to pay to the respective department a per capita tax based on the number of its members whose occupations or jobs fall under the department's jurisdiction. These dues are in addition to those the national union pays as a condition of belonging to the AFL-CIO.

Each department is concerned with problems of its particular industry. Such problems can involve collective bargaining issues, new organizational drives, legislative matters, or more specialized areas with which the unions of a particular branch of industry are uniquely confronted. The Union Label Department, for example, has as its primary objective the education of the consuming public with regard to the desirability of purchasing union-made goods. It is composed of all AFL-CIO affiliates that stress use of a union label to show that union members produced the product; to many union members, and to many supporters of unionism also, such a label is particularly persuasive before a purchase is made. (Exhibit 4-1 shows two efforts of this AFL-CIO unit.)

❖ State and City Bodies

Even though most of the activities of the AFL-CIO are centered in Washington, the federation has also established state and city bodies to deal with problems at the state and municipal levels. There are now state bodies in each of the 50 states and one in Puerto Rico; on the city level, the federation has created city centrals in some 745 communities.

Note that these state and city central bodies are established *directly* by the AFL-CIO; they are not created by the national unions affiliated with the federation or by local unions that belong to these national unions. Local unions that belong to national unions affiliated with the AFL-CIO may join a state or a city central body, but the national union must be affiliated with the AFL-CIO; and should a national

EXHIBIT 4-1

Don't Buy ✗ National Boycotts
National boycotts sanctioned by AFL-CIO. As published by *Label Letter*, Union Label & Service Trades Department, AFL-CIO—July/August 1999

Apparel & Accessories

MASTER APPAREL
Men's and boys' pants. Labels include Botany 500, Hills and Archer, and Blair • *Electronic Workers*

Building Materials & Tools

BROWN & SHARPE MFG. CO.
Measuring, cutting and machine tools and pumps • *Machinists*

OREGON STEEL
(CF&I's parent company) operates plants in Portland; Napa, Calif., and Camrose, Alberta, Canada and CF&I STEEL in Pueblo, Colo., which does business as ROCKY MOUNTAIN STEEL MILLS. Products include railroad rails, seamless pipe, steel plate for railroad cars, ships and other heavy equipment, and large welded pipe for oil and gas pipelines. All plants continue to be operated by strike-breakers. • *United Steelworkers of America*

JET EQUIPMENT & TOOLS, INC.
Auburn, Wash., distributor of "JET" brand metal- and woodworking power and hand tools for home and commercial use • *Teamsters*

SOUTHWIRE CO.
Commercial and industrial wire and cable; Do-It-Yourself brand homewire • *Electrical Workers*

Miscellaneous

BLACK ENTERTAINMENT TELEVISION
BET cable television, Action pay-per-view, BET on Jazz • *Electrical Workers*

REGAL CINEMAS AND COBB THEATERS
Movie-theater chain operating 2,000 screens in 22 states, including: Ala., Ark., Calif., Del., Fla., Ga., Ind., Ky., La., Md., Miss., N.J., N.Y., N.C., Ohio, Okla., Penn., S.C., Tenn., Va., Wash., and W.Va. • *Intl. Alliance of Theatrical Stage Employees*

R.J. REYNOLDS TOBACCO CO.
Cigarettes: Best Value, Camel, Century, Doral, Eclipse, Magna, Monarch, More, Now, Salem, Sterling, Vantage, and Winston; plus all Moonlight tobacco products • *Bakery, Confectionery & Tobacco Workers*

STRAITS FURNITURE CO., JACKSON, MS
• *Electronic Workers*

WELLS FARGO BANK
Wells Fargo, which operates in 10 states in the West, is the lead bank in a consortium of banks that is providing OREGON STEEL with a $125-million revolving line of credit, which, the USWA (*United Steelworkers of America*) asserts, has helped prolong the dispute. • *United Steelworkers of America*

Food & Beverages

CALIFORNIA TABLE GRAPES
Table grapes that do not bear the UFW label on carton or crate • *Farm Workers*

DIAMOND WALNUT CO.
Diamond brand canned and bagged walnuts and walnut pieces • *Teamsters*

FARMLAND DAIRY
Milk sold under the Farmland Dairy label in stores in Connecticut, New Jersey and New York • *Teamsters*

MT. OLIVE PICKLE CO. IN NORTH CAROLINA
The nation's second largest pickle packer refuses to recognize unionized farm workers • *Farm Labor Organizing Committee*

Transportation & Travel

ALITALIA AIRLINES
Air transport for passengers and freight • *Machinists*

BEST WESTERN— GROSVENOR RESORT
Hotel in Lake Buena Vista, Fla. • *Hotel Employees & Restaurant Employees*

CROWN CENTRAL PETROLEUM
Gasoline sold at Crown, Fast Fare and Zippy Mart stations and convenience stores • *Oil, Chemical & Atomic Workers*

FOUR POINTS BY SHERATON
Hotel in Waterbury, Conn. • *Hotel Employees & Restaurant Employees*

HOLIDAY INN SUNSPREE HOTEL
Hotel in Kapaa, Hawaii • *Longshoremen & Warehousemen*

NEW OTANI HOTEL & GARDEN
Hotel in downtown Los Angeles • *Hotel Employees & Restaurant Employees*

SOURCE: Courtesy of Union Label and Service Trades Department, AFL-CIO.

union be expelled from or withdraw voluntarily from the federation, its local unions lose membership in the state and city central bodies. Thus, when the Teamsters Union was expelled from the AFL-CIO, the locals of this union were expelled from the state and city units.

Similar to the AFL-CIO, also, the state and city bodies have no executive power over their affiliated unions. They do not engage in collective bargaining, call or forbid strikes, or regulate the internal affairs of their affiliated local unions. Instead, the chief concern of the state and city bodies is political and educational activities. They lobby for or against legislation, offer testimony before state legislative committees, and promote political candidates favored by organized labor. Almost all state organizations now hold schools for representatives of their affiliated unions—the classes being taught by union officials, university instructors, government officials, and, on some occasions, representatives of the business community. The city bodies, in addition to participating in similar legislative and educational activities, engage in a wide variety of community service work—promoting the United Way, Red Cross, and similar community projects, among other endeavors. In many cities and towns, such bodies have sponsored Boy Scout and Girl Scout troops and Little League baseball teams, as well as art institutes, musical events, day-care centers, and even the purchase of Seeing-Eye dogs for blind people. Although genuine altruism doubtless motivates many of these good deeds, so, too, does the need for an improved public image which is today so keenly felt by many unionists.

❖ Functions and Problems of the Federation

◆ The AFL-CIO and Politics
For all that the AFL-CIO voluntarily abstains from doing or is restricted by its constitution from attempting, there can be no denying the aggressiveness with which the federation pursues the activities it does undertake. In the political arena, this is particularly true. As do most other major interest groups in the United States, the federation now employs a large corps of full-time lobbyists whose mission is to exert pressure upon members of Congress to support legislation favored by the AFL-CIO and to oppose those bills the federation regards as undesirable. Its principal officers themselves frequently testify before congressional committees and make public declarations of federation political policies. And, by its very dimensions, the federation provides a powerful sounding board for all of organized labor. Ostensibly, when the president of the AFL-CIO speaks, he represents some 13.3 million union members and their families, 68 national unions, 43,000 local unions, 51 state federations (including the one in the Commonwealth of Puerto Rico), and over 700 citywide labor bodies. No other labor leader can claim as much attention and exert as much influence. He and other important federation officials are regularly invited by members of Congress and heads of federal agencies dealing with labor matters to specify labor's position on vital issues of the day. And it is doubtful that representatives of any other interest group make as many appearances at the White House as do members of the AFL-CIO high command, certainly when the Democrats, traditional wooers of labor, are in power.

At times of federal and state elections, the federation's role is equally important. The federation's **Committee on Political Education (COPE)** coordinates the political action of organized labor during such periods. This political arm of the federation operates at the national, state, and local levels, where (since the Taft-Hartley law, as we know, forbids unions to contribute union dues to political candidates) it raises money on a voluntary basis from union members through so-called political action committees (PACs). Some of this money is given directly to political candidates who are regarded as friends of labor; the rest is spent on radio and TV programs of a political nature, the publication of voting records of candidates who have previously served in elective offices, the distribution of campaign literature, and kindred activities.

It is difficult to assess exactly how effective the federation has been in the political arena, since both successes and failures are amply in evidence. In 1980, for example, an estimated 44 percent of all union members voted for Ronald Reagan, whose candidacy was about as welcome to the bulk of the AFL-CIO leaders as Martin Luther King's would have been to the Ku Klux Klan,[3] and in 1984 some 46 percent did so. In 1988, well over 40 percent of unionized Americans continued the pattern by voting for Republican George H.W. Bush, another national politician whose AFL-CIO leadership support was conspicuous by its absence. In 1992, although some 60 percent of unionists voted the way COPE had urged them to (for victorious Democrat Bill Clinton), the other 40 percent voted either for loser Bush or for loser Ross Perot and, either way, once more went counter to the AFL-CIO's strongly held preference.

Roughly the same situation was true in 1996: Presidential contender Robert Dole, almost as conservative a Republican as Reagan had been, got only slightly less union support than had Bush in 1992, as Clinton won reelection. And on the eve of the 2000 race for the White House, 33 percent of all union members in a poll conducted for the federation backed the Republican front-runner (Bush's son, George W. Bush), and another 20 percent described themselves as being undecided in a potential contest involving the AFL-CIO–endorsed Al Gore.[4]

In congressional elections, the labor success rate was markedly more impressive than this presidential election statistic in the years prior to 1994. Between the mid-1970s and 1994, COPE endorsed roughly 400 candidates either for the House or the Senate in each biennial election and between 65 and 80 percent of these candidates won each time. In 1994, labor-backed House candidates had only a 55 percent success rate and Senate aspirants did even worse: They garnered a meager 39 percent victory percentage. And at the state level, the 1994 returns were even bleaker: Only 25 percent of gubernatorial candidates with COPE support won their elections. ("Disgusted voters threw the rascals in," said the AFL-CIO in a grim post-election statement.) But the union successes in the 1996 and 1998 congressional elections—as Chapter 2 has noted, labor's efforts almost gained control of the House for the Democrats in 1996 and greatly helped Democrats pick up five House seats in 1998—marked a return to the earlier kind of union box score. In 1998, the federation could boast that 76 percent of union members who received union literature voted, at all levels of government, for the labor-backed candidate.[5]

Even before the recent emphasis on political action by AFL-CIO president John J. Sweeney, COPE did not, under any conditions, think small. In all election years, it could and can regularly be counted on to recruit as many as 125,000 volunteers to work on community political activities. The federation estimates that such volunteers in recent elections have placed over 10 million telephone calls from more than 20,000 telephones (operating at COPE offices, local union and council offices, and the private homes of union members) during registration and get-out-the-vote campaigns, and that they have distributed hundreds of COPE films and millions of campaign leaflets. In recent years, freshman Democrats in the national House have received on the average well over 40 percent of their political-action committee funds from COPE, while veteran Democrats have gotten almost one-third of their political-action committee monies from this source. (With exceptions, Republicans are about as popular with labor as the Grim Reaper and do not normally attract any COPE support at all.) COPE activity is, in short, something that neither its friends nor its foes can ignore.

The political objectives of organized labor and the federation are varied in character. The AFL-CIO supports legislation that strengthens the role of organized labor in collective bargaining, organizational drives, strikes, picketing, and boycotting. To these ends, it has, for example, consistently advocated such measures as the repeal of state right-to-work legislation (which bans union shops) and has lobbied for other changes in the federal and state laws that would strengthen the use of union self-help methods such as boycotts and picketing in labor's direct relationship with business. It has also, however, regularly supported bills favoring health care reform, a higher minimum wage, more comprehensive unemployment compensation statutes, a sounder financial footing for Medicare, and more effective public education—measures intended to benefit all workers of the nation and their families rather than strictly those within the ranks of unionism. The AFL-CIO today fully recognizes that many of these less parochial objectives cannot be achieved through face-to-face union–management collective bargaining and has, consequently, supported such measures as the ones cited to gain additional leverage in its efforts to improve the status of the American wage earner.

◆ **Research Efforts**   Beyond the legislative and political function, the federation carries out a massive research program—the results of which are embodied in its regular publications, above all the weekly *AFL-CIO News*, as well as in special bulletins, briefs for the courts of the nation, and a series of pamphlets, monographs, and books. Through these varied publications, the federation tries to keep union members and others abreast of labor developments from the union point of view.

◆ **Organizational Drives**   Another important function is that of promoting new organization. Although the basic responsibility for such organization falls on national unions, the federation also organizes on its own and helps affiliated unions in their organizational drives. When the AFL-CIO organizes a union by itself, it charters such a local union directly with the federation in much the same fashion that the old AFL did in the 1930s. There are 102 such directly affiliated labor unions now in existence, and through its field officers the AFL-CIO bargains contracts for these local unions and aids them in time of strikes and other difficulties with management. In return, members of such locals pay dues directly to the AFL-CIO. This collective bargaining function for directly affiliated local unions should not, however, be confused with the principle already established: The AFL-CIO does not bargain collectively for affiliated national unions or for locals that belong to such affiliated national unions. Moreover, most of these directly affiliated local unions are ultimately assigned by the federation to a national union that has appropriate jurisdiction over the jobs and occupations of its members.

◆ **Foreign Affairs**   Until quite recently, the AFL-CIO also spent significant resources on anti-Communist efforts. Still influenced considerably by many former cold warriors who had themselves spent much of their long careers fighting

Communism, in the mid-1990s the AFL-CIO was spending one-third of its $100 million annual budget on four foreign affairs institutes that were geared primarily to this purpose. Given both the rapidly declining influence of Communism and labor's many problems in the United States, this was simply too much for many AFL-CIO national union leaders: "[The federation leadership] spends an extraordinary amount of time dealing with Eastern Europe while we're going to hell in a handbasket," complained one of these national leaders in 1995 in a typical showing of dissatisfaction.[6]

Few federation members have begrudged the financing of such standard efforts as teaching foreign labor leaders how to recruit new members and better administer their unions. But some of the AFL-CIO's more aggressively anti-Communist activities—the development of moderate labor movements in the Philippines, Nicaragua, and El Salvador to prevent allegedly Communist unions there from gaining strength, for example—have been criticized for both their ambitiousness and their direction.

As a result of such outcries (and the previously cited 1995 involuntary resignation of federation president Kirkland, which to a large extent resulted directly from these outcries), the AFL-CIO in more recent times has downplayed its anti-Communist efforts and diverted much of the money spent on these activities into organizing and political action.

Some of the diverted dollars have also had a global reach—particularly into lobbying efforts to derail so-called **fast-track authority** on the part of U.S. presidents to negotiate foreign trade pacts with low-wage nations without congressional amendments or codicils. In both 1997 and 1998, the federation played a major role in blocking a vote on President Clinton's bid for fast-track ability to negotiate such trade agreements with several Latin American nations, and it has favored politicians whose stand on this job-threatening issue duplicates its own. Sometimes member unions have gone their own way on this issue: The Teachers, Service Employees, and State, County, and Municipal Workers, for example, have understandably not felt as menaced by cheap foreign labor as have the Steelworkers, Automobile Workers, and Machinists. And some unions have accepted the argument of fast-trackers that free trade opens up foreign markets to more American goods, thus creating a net gain for U.S. workers. But the federation has responded to the majority of its 68 member unions in steadfastly resisting, through political action, the granting of fast-track authority as much as it can.

♦ The Federation and Cyberspace   To enlist rank-and-file support in such activities as these, the AFL-CIO in late 1999 announced an ambitious new cyberspace program. Working with a start-up company based in Massachusetts, it planned to offer to its 13.3 million members in the near future heavily discounted computers and monthly on-line service that, at less than $14.95, would cost about 30 percent less than what many on-line services were currently charging. By making these more affordable, the federation hoped not only, as Sweeney asserted, to help "bridge the gap between the technological haves and have-nots," but to give union families "new ways to connect with one another and to make their voices heard." The possibilities for labor gains were gigantic: "Can you imagine," as the president of the Communications Workers put it, "being able to instantly ask (by e-mail message) millions of union members to refuse to buy a product or to bombard elected officials with e-mail in protest?"[7] The AFL-CIO, which had generally been slow to embrace high technology, was about to make up for lost time.

THE NATIONAL UNION

❖ Relationship to Locals

If the national union is quite autonomous in the conduct of its affairs, the story is quite different when one examines the relationship between the national union and its local unions. Although there are many exceptions, most national unions exercise considerable power over their locals. Before a local union may strike, it must normally obtain the permission of the national union. And, should the local union strike in defiance of national union instructions, the national union can withhold strike benefits, refuse to give the local union any other form of aid during the strike, and in extreme cases even take over the local on a trusteeship basis. In addition, all local collective bargaining contracts must be reviewed by the national officers before they may be put into force. And all national union constitutions today contain provisions that establish standards of conduct and procedures for the internal operation of their locals—usually, the dues that the locals may charge, the method by which their officers may be elected and their tenures of office, the procedures for the discipline of local union members, the conduct of union meetings, and other rules of this kind.

The nationals are, quite understandably, particularly interested in supervising their locals when the members of the locals work for companies that sell their products in national product markets—an ever-increasing number. Nationals desire that companies over whose employees they have jurisdiction and that compete in national product markets operate under common labor-cost standards. They are less likely to exercise close control over the unions whose members produce for local markets—for example, in the construction industry, because the labor costs involved in the construction of a building in one city do not directly compete with those affecting the construction of a building in another.

❖ Service in Collective Bargaining

The national exercises much of its influence over the local through the service that the national union provides its locals in the negotiation of labor agreements. To understand this national–local relationship, however, one should not regard the negotiation service of the national union as a function that is performed against the will of the local union. On the contrary, local unions not only generally desire and expect the help of the national union when they negotiate labor agreements with the employer, but should the national either refuse to provide these services or perform them in an ineffective way, the local union members and their officers can be counted on to be sharply critical of the national union. The officers of the national could safely assume, in fact, that such a disgruntled local union would attempt to take political reprisal against the officers of the national in the next election of national officers.

The chief reason for the local union's desire for help from the national union in collective bargaining involves the complexities of contemporary bargaining. As will be made more evident in future chapters, many of the issues of collective bargaining have become increasingly intricate. Most contracts focus on such involved items as technological change, pension plans, insurance programs, production standards, subcontracting, and complicated wage incentive programs. And the modern process is obviously made more difficult because of the character of the laws of labor relations. In short, it takes an expert to negotiate these days.

For effective representation, it is necessary to find people who are knowledgeable and experienced and have a professional understanding of collective bargaining, but few local unions are fortunate enough to include such people in their membership. Each local union elects a negotiating committee, but the members of such committees typically work full time on their regular jobs. They simply do not have the opportunity to keep abreast of current developments in collective bargaining and to make a searching study of the problems involved in the negotiation of the difficult issues. On the employer side, moreover, there are normally management representatives who are well trained and equipped to negotiate. Many of them have received special training in labor relations, and some devote full time to the problems of negotiation and administration of collective bargaining contracts.

Indeed, without the services of the national union, there would be a sharp disparity of negotiating talent at the bargaining table. In this light, it is easy to understand why the local union does not regard the intervention of the national union at the bargaining table as an invasion of the rights of the local, but rather views this service as indispensable.

Most national unions have well-qualified people to render this service: the so-called **staff representatives**, who devote full time to union affairs. They are hired by the national union, paid salaries and expenses for their work, and expected to provide services to the local unions of the national. All of them are union members, and they normally reach their position of staff representative by having demonstrated their ability as union members and local union officers. They are not, however, elected to their jobs but are hired because of their special talents.

Although the staff representatives perform a variety of duties, such as organizing new facilities, engaging in political action work at times of federal and state elections, directing strikes, and representing the union and its members before federal and state labor agencies, helping the local unions to negotiate labor agreements constitutes one of their primary functions.[8] Staff representatives gain much bargaining experience because they normally service several local unions, and in the course of one year they may be called upon to negotiate many different labor agreements, thus getting on-the-job training that serves as an invaluable asset to them when they confront a specific management at the bargaining table. Many national unions also send their staff representatives to special workshops and seminars, some of which are held on university campuses and are taught by specialists in the labor education field, for additional training. Moreover, the staff representative is invariably backed up by experts within the national union. Almost every national union has several departments that concentrate on the major issues involved in collective bargaining. For example, the United Automobile Workers not only has special departments that deal with pensions, health insurance, and wage systems (among others) but also has recently created a department specifically mandated to coordinate the union's relationships with automakers owned entirely or in part by foreign companies. The Air Line Pilots Association has, among its large variety of specialized subunits, ones that individually focus on discipline and discharge, economic and financial analysis, engineering and air safety, Federal Aviation Administration legal actions, and retirement and insurance. The specialists assigned to these national departments may be called on freely by the staff representatives, should their services be needed.

❖ The Regional or District Office

Staff representatives may work out of the headquarters of the national union, but more frequently they are assigned to a regional or district office. Almost every national union divides the nation into regions or districts, and locals of the national union that are located in the geographical area or the district obtain services from their respective district offices. District 30 of the United Steelworkers is reasonably typical: Headquartered in Indianapolis, it covers most of Indiana and Kentucky and is administered by a district director elected by the local unions of the district. About 20 staff representatives are assigned by the national union to District 30 and work under the immediate supervision of the district director.

Each staff representative services about seven local unions. The representative attends the local union meetings, works closely with the negotiating committees, and attempts to understand the values and objectives of the members. The representative is the liaison between the national and the local union and in this capacity can do much to influence the local in the acceptance of national union collective bargaining policies. In such a role, moreover, the staff representative can serve as a mediator between local unions and the national when differences arise between them.

A good staff representative wins the confidence of local officers and members, and the local union will thus rely heavily on this individual's counsel in collective bargaining matters. The representative can exert great influence on the local to reject or accept the last offer of an employer. Frequently this person can even provoke a strike or prevent one by the way in which he or she reports to the local union and makes recommendations to the members.

❖ Multiemployer Bargaining

Although most multiemployer bargaining is in relatively small bargaining units in local product markets, at times national unions bargain with employers on a multiemployer basis. That is, a number of managements band together as a unit to negotiate with the national union. Employers find this structure of collective bargaining valuable because it prevents a given union from "whipsawing" each employer: Usually, under a multiemployer bargaining structure, each employer is comparatively small in size and unimpressive in financial resources, and the managements compete fiercely; in the absence of multiemployer collective bargaining, the union could pick off one employer at a time. Such employer-association–national-union collective bargaining is found in industries such as clothing, coal, shipping, and trucking—all of which contain large measures of the unstabilizing factors noted.

When multiemployer collective bargaining exists and where the product market is not a local one, the national officers themselves typically bargain for the contract, and the local unions play a comparatively passive role—a situation that also holds at the other extreme, when unions bargain with corporate giants (such as General Motors and UPS). The national unions negotiate the agreement in the latter instance because no one local union could possibly measure up to the strength of these companies. Bargaining logic dictates that in both cases the national rather than the local play the paramount labor relations role.

❖ Additional National Union Services

Beyond providing considerable help in the negotiating of labor agreements, the national renders other valuable services to its local unions. It usually awards benefits to employees on strike, although the actual amount of money paid in strike benefits is invariably modest. Approximately $150 weekly (usually awarded to strikers with a minimum number of dependents, with other strikers getting less) constitutes the ultimate in union generosity. Even this, of course, is dispatched only until the strike fund is exhausted and assumes that beneficiaries take their turn on the picket line when and if asked to do so. More important, the national union intervenes with the strikers' creditors so that the homes, automobiles, furniture, and other holdings of the union members will not be repossessed. Furthermore, it ensures that no striking employee or his or her family goes hungry, even if this guarantee involves the actual distribution of food to the strikers.

Management should be aware that unions these days do not lose strikes because of hunger or unpaid bills. If there are insurance premiums to be paid, doctors to see, mortgages or rent to be paid, or school tuition to be met, the national unions will see to it that the worker does not suffer. This is true despite the obvious fact that the national unions do have financial limitations. However, all nationals do under normal circumstances have the resources to assure that the minimum physiological needs of their member-workers are met, and many larger unions are quite amply financed. As it went into its 1999 negotiations with the three major automobile manufacturers, for example, the UAW operated with a $750 million strike fund. In addition, if a national union does run out of money, labor custom dictates that other national unions and perhaps the AFL-CIO itself will lend it funds to finance the strike. This was the case in 1994 when the Teamsters struck the long-haul trucking industry and again in 1997 when 185,000 IBT members walked off their jobs at UPS.[9] Sometimes, too, other nationals will spearhead drives for outright donations from their members to the families of strikers elsewhere—as the Mine Workers (UMWA) did to alleviate hardships of Rubber Workers, Automobile Workers, and Paperworkers—all in Decatur, Illinois—in 1995. (See Exhibit 4-2.)

The national union also aids the locals in the **grievance procedure** and in **arbitration**, both of which will be discussed in detail in Chapter 6. Normally, the staff representative represents the local in the last step of the grievance procedure. Along with the local union grievance committee, the staff representative attempts to settle the grievance to the satisfaction of the complaining worker, and if the case does ultimately go to arbitration, the staffer very often directly represents the grievant. In general, whether they win or lose their arbitration cases, staff representatives present the union's case very effectively. This fact is often offered by labor leaders as one reason why unions employ lawyers less frequently than do employers when cases go to arbitration. There is no need to incur the expense if the staff representative can do the job as competently as an attorney.

Of course, at times local unions *are* in need of an attorney, as when the local union has a case that requires testimony in the courts. For example, employers may sue a union for breach of contract, or workers may be indicted because of violence in picketing. When attorneys are needed, the local union can normally obtain the services of the national union's legal staff, whose members, although invariably paid less than comparable lawyers who work for corporations, are frequently highly competent and usually quite dedicated to the union movement.

EXHIBIT **4-2**

DECATUR
Let's Make Their Fight Our Fight

Today in Decatur, Illinois, some 4,000 union families are fighting for their lives. They are the members of the United Rubber Workers at Bridgestone/Firestone who have been on strike for more than 9 months, the members of the United Auto Workers at Caterpillar who have been on the picket line even longer and workers at A.E. Staley, members of the United Paperworkers, who have been locked out since June 1993.

Though the details of each of their battles are different, what isn't is the fact that they need our support . . . now.

UMWA members in Illinois—together with other unions—have already been actively supporting our brothers and sisters in Decatur. But it will take the backing of the entire labor movement to beat Caterpillar, Staley and Bridgestone/ Firestone once and for all.

UMWA families know better than anyone that solidarity makes the difference. Together, let's make their fight our fight.

To support the Decatur workers, please send checks made payable to:

UMWA Decatur Strikers' Aid Fund
1220 S. Park Ave., Suite D
Herrin, IL 62948

The fact that the local does so readily receive such services from its national constitutes the reason why the vast majority of local unions belong to a national union. Less than 2 percent of all locals are not so affiliated and all these "independents" (except for the relative handful of them belonging directly to the AFL-CIO and thus enabled to make use of the federation's services) must rely on their own resources, whereas the many local unions that do belong to nationals can use the considerable resources of the latter.

❖ Other Functions of the National Union

Although national union officers and staff representatives devote the major share of their time to providing services to the local unions, the range of the national union's activities includes many other important functions.

• Organizing the Unorganized   Today, the major concern of all unions is, as we know, that of increasing membership, and the chief burden for this also falls to the national union staff representatives, upon whom constant pressure is exerted to organize nonunion operations. In some national unions, not only the advancement but even the continued job tenure of the staff representative is determined by the latter's success in organizing such places.

The task is hardly an easy one. Most nonunion employers can be counted upon to wage a fierce fight against organization. Many employees who are not members of unions do not want a labor union because management provides them with many of the benefits they would receive if organized. And the staff representative's organizing mission becomes even more difficult if attempts are made to organize in the South or in small communities regardless of sectional location. In any event, the representative must make contacts among the workers, convince them of the value of unions, and dispel notions that unions are corrupt or otherwise undesirable institutions. Many workers are ready to believe the worst about organized labor, and staff representatives often admit that these conceptions are difficult to erase. "Today," one veteran said a while ago, "the workers insult you, they spit at you, they throw [union membership] cards in your face." And, as one union leader could point out from his own unhappy experiences, even such institutions as church-administered hospitals can become formidable foes when faced with union organizers: "The Little Sisters of the Poor," as the president of the Hospital and Health Care Employees could observe, "can be hard as nails."[10]

Moreover, the potential union member of today most often lacks the background in unionism that his or her parents may have had and typically neither uses the word *worker* as a self-description nor feels any sense of identity with what unions still often call the "working class." Even otherwise friendly employees often equate unions, as was pointed out earlier in this volume, with manual workers, and although this is by definition no obstacle if the target workforce is made up of construction workers or truck drivers, it can clearly handicap organizers who go after the growing body of office, professional, and other non-blue-collar types.

Staff representatives are thus forced to use their powers of imagination, and any understanding of law and psychology that they might have, to the fullest. The representative may initially attempt to organize "from inside," through the informal leaders in the enterprise. The next step may be to visit workers in their homes, distribute leaflets, and arrange organizational meetings. Subsequently, the representative must counteract whatever management does to block the organizational attempt; even in today's more enlightened atmosphere, some employers warn employees of dire consequences if they organize, tell their employees that unions exist only to collect dues for the personal benefit of the union "bosses," and—the organizing tactic laws cited in Chapter 3 notwithstanding—on occasion even threaten workers with loss of their jobs if a union is established, as well as promise them benefits if they reject the union. A while ago, the Farah Manufacturing Company was organized by the Amalgamated Clothing Workers (not yet merged with the Textile Workers) following a two-and-one-half-year struggle that included a boycott of Farah products. The victory, however, came only after a National Labor Relations Board administrative law judge had criticized Farah for carrying on "a broad-gauged antiunion campaign consisting of glaring and repeated violations" of the National Labor Relations Act and acting as if "there were no act, no board and no Ten Commandments."

There are other formidable obstacles for the organizer. If the employer is located in a comparatively small community, there may be a concerted attempt among the leaders of the community to keep the union out. The employer may have good friends who run the newspaper, the radio and TV stations, the chamber of commerce, and the local stores, and these power centers may join forces to do what they can to keep the union from gaining a foothold. It is not uncommon for the clergy in a town to be enlisted in the fight against the union, for that matter.

Tenaciousness is thus a firm prerequisite for the staff representative to have. Victories, at least in recent years, have often taken considerable time to achieve. In mid-1996, the United Farm Workers and one of the country's larger lettuce growers, Red Coach, signed a labor agreement—after almost 18 years of acrimony and stalemate. Some years earlier, J. P. Stevens and Co. (the second largest textile manufacturer in the nation) signed a contract with the Amalgamated Clothing and Textile Workers in the culmination of a 17-year concerted organizational campaign by that union. (Stevens, the real-life backdrop for the 1979 film *Norma Rae*, had fought the union so aggressively that a New York court had branded it "the most notorious recidivist in the field of labor law," and the NLRB had cited it 22 times for violating the federal labor statutes.) These two examples are, of course, among the more extreme, but organizational campaigns are almost always measured in years, not months, and a labor organizer without a good deal of patience is poorly equipped for the job. (Exhibit 4-3 shows a successful organizing "game plan" developed by one national union, the American Federation of State, County, and Municipal Employees.)

◆ **National Unions and Politics** Another major function of the national union concerns political action, although the nationals vary widely in the vigor that they display in this regard. The Teamsters, Communications Workers, Food and Commercial Workers, and Laborers have been among the heaviest hitters here. All four of them in recent years have, in fact, ranked in the top 10 of donation givers to the Democratic Party, with the Teamsters more than once in the past decade raising over $10 million, primarily through voluntary $1-per-week contributions to the union's political-action committee. Other especially politically active national unions are the State, County, and Municipal Employees, Automobile Workers, Letter Carriers, Mine Workers, Teachers, and Steelworkers. At the other end of the spectrum, many of the building trades unions have rarely shown much interest in this area.

The trend, however, is definitely in the direction of more rather than less activity. As has already been noted, national leaders understand that the success of the

EXHIBIT 4-3

ORGANIZING

The International Union's external organizing drive — AFSCME in Motion — is picking up momentum. And it works. So say supervisors at the Los Angeles County Metropolitan Transportation Authority who followed the AIM game plan.

LOS ANGELES

First-line and senior supervisors at Los Angeles County's Metropolitan Transportation Authority had tried again and again for more than a decade to form a union, but to no avail.

Frustration finally turned to elation in April. Armed with a fresh, new approach — the AIM organizing model — the 475 supervisors in the unit finally became part of the AFSCME family.

'Proud To B

SOURCE: *Public Employee*, July–August 1999, pp. 18–20.

EXHIBIT 4-3   (continued)

"We're proud to be AFSCME," declares one of them, James Adams, a self-proclaimed agitator who has worked at MTA for nearly 25 years and currently is a bus transit operations supervisor. "Now we have a real chance to level the playing field, rather than sit on the sidelines, accepting layoffs and budget cuts," he says.

Adams says the time was ripe for intensifying the organizing effort last October, when many of the workers were ready to organize with AFSCME.

AIMING TO SUCCEED. Adams, along with Barbara Service, Kevin McGraff and other workers, approached AFSCME Council 36 Organizing Coordinator Karleen George for assistance. George introduced them to the International's new external organizing model — AFSCME in Motion. The workers' application of the AIM principles was a textbook example of how to conduct a successful campaign. (See sidebar).

The AIM model looks at not only winning a representation election, but settling a bargaining unit's first contract.

Initially, as outlined in the organizing model, the workers took care not to tip off their employer about the drive. To determine the level of interest, they developed a list of employee names and addresses, mapping out the workplace to target potential leaders and front-line activists interested in joining the union.

Armed with solid support and information, the workers held their first organizing committee meeting. It drew 75 workers — 15 percent of the unit — who volunteered to be part of the organizing effort. AIM recommends obtaining 10 to 15 percent of the workforce on the committee, which has the task of signing up at least 65 percent of the unit as union supporters to help ensure a successful outcome in the election.

Several weeks later, after one-on-ones and visits to nearly 20 MTA worksites, the committee signed up 72 percent of the workforce and filed a petition for a representation election in February.

THUMBS UP AND DOWN. Service, a 28-year MTA worker who works as rail

Los Angeles County MTA personnel high-five over their AFSCME victory. From left: Paul Alleyne, Bob Parreco, Sonny Abrego, John Lowrie, Jon Harting, Jacky Lee, and O'neal McDaniels.

Photos: Paul Rodriguez

EXHIBIT 4-3 (continued)

Fernando Hernandez, a transit operations supervisor, at work.

MTA Rail Transit Operations Supervisor Barbara Service tests doors of a commuter train, making sure everything is safe for citizens of Los Angeles.

transit operations supervisor, believes one-on-ones — personal contact between employees supporting the union and their peers in the workplace — made the difference in getting workers to sign up.

Service says some long-time managers were reluctant to join because they thought the effort was futile, while others, frustrated because they had not received a raise since 1992, doubted the value of paying union dues. "So we had to keep the pressure on with the concrete facts: that AFSCME has a fine tradition of winning better wages, working conditions and benefits for its members," she says.

Organizing activist and transit operations supervisor Fernando Hernandez says he, too, ran into opposition along the way, with workers citing retaliation and/or demotion as reasons why they were hesitant to join the union. "It was a collective effort, scrambling to get as many people to sign up as possible, he says. He told workers they needed union protection, citing a 1993 incident in which upper management officials assured employees in Hernandez' unit they would not be affected by layoffs, only to hand out termination papers to seven workers the next day.

Equipment maintenance supervisor Robert Torres, by contrast, didn't face a lot of opposition

in his organizing efforts. He set up a table outside the Gateway Building, passed out leaflets, answered questions and signed up members whenever he had time off from work. "I signed folks up left and right. ... I have a reputation of getting the job done, no matter what it is," he says, proudly bragging that as a former bus maintenance worker for over 20 years, none of the buses he serviced ever failed an inspection. MTA has a fleet

of 2,200 buses and a variety of other rail services, including rapid and trolley transportation.

Senior Supervisor Michael Turf says that what really convinced him to sign up was the fact that as a member, he would have ownership in the union.

AIM REALLY WORKS. The workers indeed made the campaign happen, noted George, by following many of the organizing model's guidelines. They ran into periodic glitches, specifically ploys by MTA management to derail or stall their efforts.

The committee first had to convince MTA to waive the public utility code that does not allow supervisors in California to organize. (The state law governing collective bargaining by units of local government, on the other hand, allows supervisors to unionize, as do public employee laws in 20 other states.)

Then MTA did not want the supervisors under one bargaining unit, so the organizing committee compromised by agreeing to two separate units.

In the representation election, a whopping 84 percent of those eligible voted: First-line supervisors cast 324-37 ballots for the union and second-line managers voted 29-2.

Over a thousand more workers at the MTA are ready to organize. Administrative support and professional and technical employees are targeted for the next phase of the organizing drive.

The AIM model makes it clear that securing a first contract, not simply winning a representation election, is the ultimate goal of an organizing campaign.

George noted that the organizing committee that provided the base for the election victory stepped right in to prepare for bargaining their first contract. Committee members are now divided into five separate groups to work on contract language: seniority, grievance procedure, retirement, salary, and wages and benefits.

Hernandez, who serves on the seniority committee, says having AFSCME on our side "feels like a ton of bricks has been lifted off our shoulders. We now have a future with AFSCME."

By Venida RaMar Marshall

Main Ingredients in AIM, AFSCME's Organizing Model

AFSCME IN MOTION
ORGANIZING TOGETHER, GROWING STRONGER

The AIM Model works because it draws from the efforts of successful employee organizing campaigns all around the country. The document was the collective effort of 60 organizers from councils and locals around the country, as well as the International.

The model sets the stage for a winning campaign by pointing out what others have learned by trial-and-error: That certain elements are key in a successful effort "from first contact to first contract." Those elements include:

- Thorough preparation
- One-on-one organizing
- Strong committees, giving workers ownership of the campaign
- Strong majority support for the union
- Fast-paced campaigns
- Involvement by current members in organizing new members
- Message discipline, projecting the reasons for unionizing even in the face of employer resistance
- Sound decisions at each stage

The publication — AFSCME in Motion: Organizing Together, Growing Stronger — is available to AFSCME councils and locals upon request from the International Department of Organizing and Field Services, 1625 L Street, N.W., Washington, D.C. 20036-5687 or telephone (202) 429-1260.

union depends in large measure on the fashioning of a favorable legal climate for new organization and for the implementation of traditional trade union weapons when conflicts arise with employers. Moreover, a growing number of national unions share the belief of AFL-CIO leaders that the political programs of organized labor in such areas as social security, medicine, low-cost public housing, and full employment are in the best interests of the nation as a whole.

But sometimes the political activity is more tailored to the specific membership. The Association of Flight Attendants, for example, some time ago began a campaign to persuade the Federal Aviation Administration to tighten its rules limiting carry-on luggage in the interest of flight safety. Exhibit 4-4 shows the questionnaire that was sent to the union's 33,000 members as a supplement to this effort. Members could return it, postage prepaid, to the office of the national president. Exhibits 4-5 and 4-6 depict recent special efforts of the Mine Workers and Teamsters, respectively, to generate the support of politicians for their particular causes.

When the national union officers are politically motivated, they are normally aggressive in exerting pressure on the local unions and their members to take an active role in political affairs. Their union newspapers are filled with political news, voting records of the candidates, and the union point of view when elections are impending. National unions also arrange political rallies, purchase radio and television time to get the national's story across to the members and the public, and issue a barrage of political leaflets and pamphlets. In some national unions, during the weeks before important elections, the staff representatives are ordered to suspend negotiations, grievance meetings, and arbitrations and devote their full time to political work. The fact that each national union employs many staff representatives—in such large unions as the Automobile Workers and the State, County, and Municipal Employees, the numbers run into the hundreds—serves as an important advantage; and if the staff representatives are adroit and hardworking, the favored political candidate can benefit greatly from such support.

EXHIBIT 4-4

AFA Membership Survey on Carry-on Baggage Problems

Name of Carrier: _____

How well do you think the carry-on baggage program at your carrier is working?
    Very well ❑   Well ❑   Poorly ❑   Very Poorly ❑

If you do not think it is working well, please rate the following problems by writing the appropriate number (1,2,3 as indicated) in the space provided:
    ① Major Problem   ② Minor Problem   ③ Not a Problem

    a. __Passengers bringing overly large bags on board.   **e.** __Closing of door before baggage is stored.
    b. __Passengers bringing overly heavy bags on board.   **f.** __Flight attendants not rejecting/removing bags.
    c. __Passengers bringing too many bags on board.   **g.** __Company resistance to removing bags from planes.
    d. __Lack of baggage screening before boarding.

If you experienced a carry-on baggage problem in May or June, 1992, please describe the incident.
Date _____   From _____   To _____   Aircraft Type_____

Description: _____

_____

_____ Your name *(optional)* _____

EXHIBIT 4-5

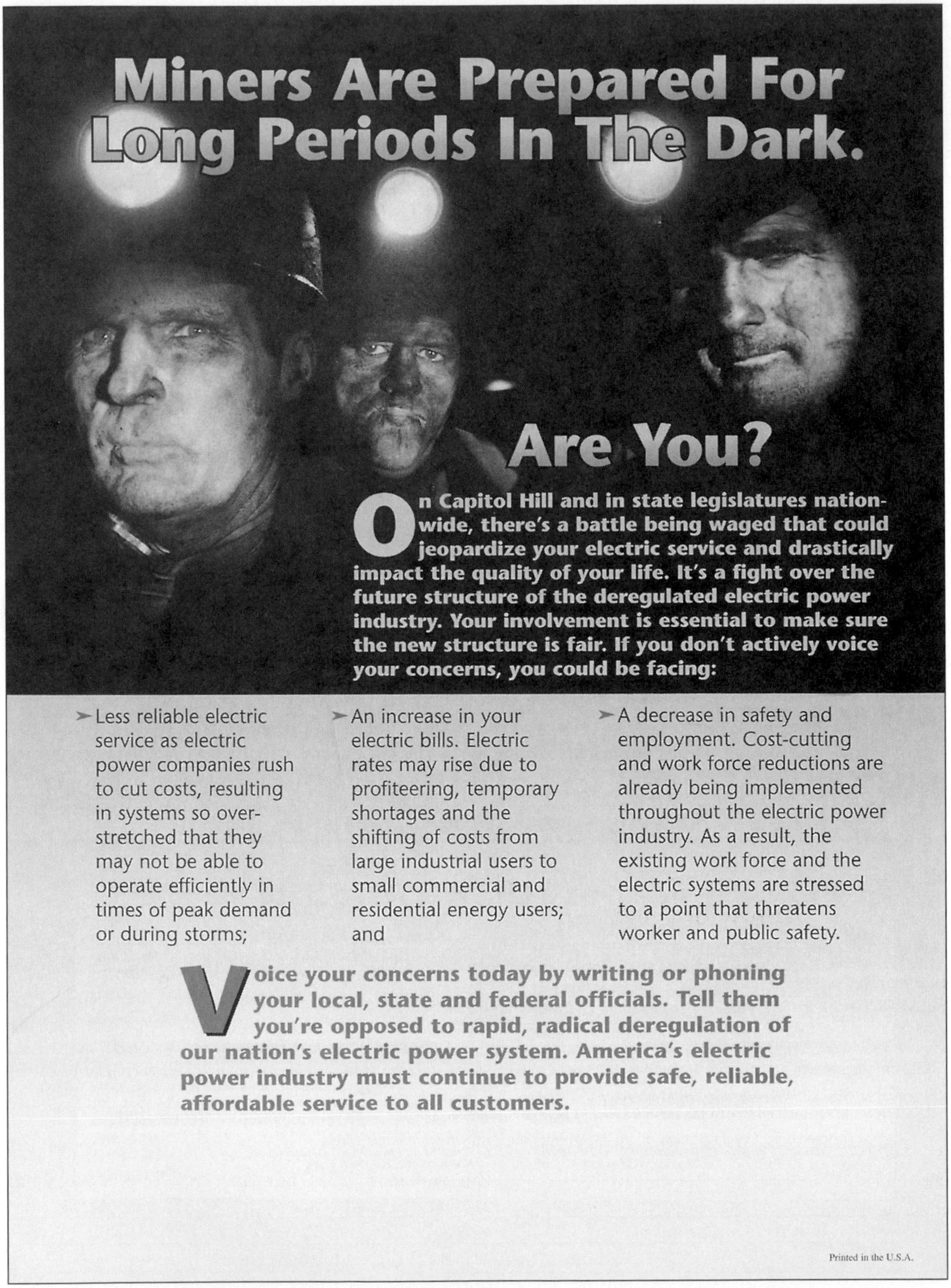

Miners Are Prepared For Long Periods In The Dark.

Are You?

On Capitol Hill and in state legislatures nation-wide, there's a battle being waged that could jeopardize your electric service and drastically impact the quality of your life. It's a fight over the future structure of the deregulated electric power industry. Your involvement is essential to make sure the new structure is fair. If you don't actively voice your concerns, you could be facing:

➤ Less reliable electric service as electric power companies rush to cut costs, resulting in systems so over-stretched that they may not be able to operate efficiently in times of peak demand or during storms;

➤ An increase in your electric bills. Electric rates may rise due to profiteering, temporary shortages and the shifting of costs from large industrial users to small commercial and residential energy users; and

➤ A decrease in safety and employment. Cost-cutting and work force reductions are already being implemented throughout the electric power industry. As a result, the existing work force and the electric systems are stressed to a point that threatens worker and public safety.

Voice your concerns today by writing or phoning your local, state and federal officials. Tell them you're opposed to rapid, radical deregulation of our nation's electric power system. America's electric power industry must continue to provide safe, reliable, affordable service to all customers.

Printed in the U.S.A.

SOURCE: *United Mine Workers Journal*, May–June 1998, back cover.

EXHIBIT 4-6

SOURCE: *The Teamster*, April 1999, back cover.

By some estimates, in fact, national unions spend a much greater portion of their resources on such noncash "in-kind" contributions to friendly political campaigns than they do on direct cash contributions to candidates of their choice through political-action committees. In a recent presidential election year, for example, an informal estimate was that unions gave $35.5 million to political candidates and about $200 million more in such in-kind help as free printing and voter registration drives.[11]

◆ **Other Activities** Depending on their size and leadership policies, national unions perform other functions. Some arrange educational programs for their staff representatives and local union officers. Most of the courses in these programs deal exclusively with such practical aspects of labor relations as how to bargain labor agreements and the best way to handle grievances. At times, however, the courses deal with foreign affairs, taxation, economics, government, and other subjects not directly related to the bread-and-butter issues of trade unionism.

In addition, some national unions administer vacation resorts for their members, award university scholarships to children of members, organize trips to foreign nations, and—as noted earlier in this volume—sponsor a variety of social functions that are similar to those maintained by the state and city labor bodies but more tailored to the specific interests and aptitudes of the particular national union's members.

In recent years, there has also been a trend on the part of some nationals to engage in media campaigns to build a more favorable institutional image and often to attract members directly as well. Television, radio, billboard, and newspaper projects of some magnitude have been conducted by such unions as the Automobile Workers (who, among other approaches, have taken a page from the slogan of Honda, a UAW organizing target in Ohio, by advertising, "They make it simple. We make it fair."), Garment Workers (whose ads feature actual members of the union singing about looking for the union label), Communications Workers, Teachers, and an increasing number of others.

Sometimes, too, a desire to counteract damaging publicity has been the spur. In the wake of news that three former Northwest Airlines pilots were found guilty of drunken flying (leading to such widespread jokes as "How many Northwest pilots does it take to fly a plane? Three and one-fifth"), the Air Line Pilots created a 30-second television spot and a half-dozen 60-second radio commercials that depicted pilots as models of calm conscientiousness.

And no less well aware that sometimes the best defense is a solid offense, labor's public relations efforts have also not ignored occasional black marks on the record of the *employer* community. A few years ago the Teamsters announced with considerable fanfare that its (then) $6 billion Central States Pension Fund had stopped using E. F. Hutton & Co. as a stockbroker, because Hutton had pleaded guilty to a check overdrafting scheme, and under the terms of the fund's existing consent decree with the Labor Department it was banned from dealing with individuals or corporations guilty of a crime. For the union, itself the recipient of so much negative publicity for decades that in the eyes of many citizens the word *Teamster* was roughly equated with the word *hoodlum*, even a little revenge was sweet.

❖ Government of the National Union

When a national union is formed, a constitution is adopted that spells out the internal government and procedures of the union. Virtually every constitution provides that a convention should be held, and it designates this convention as the supreme authority of the union just as the AFL-CIO's constitution mandates that the federation's convention serve as *its* uppermost authority. Under the rules of most national unions, each local union sends delegates to the convention, with the number of delegates permitted each local being dependent upon the local's paid-up membership totals. Hence, as in the AFL-CIO, the larger locals are more influential than the smaller units. Within most unions the locals range in size from several thousand to a literal handful of members in some locals that have contracts with small employers.

Ordinarily, the chief officers of the local unions are elected as delegates, although in the very large locals, which have the opportunity to send many delegates, rank-and-file members are chosen because the quota cannot be filled by the officers alone.

Many rank-and-filers consider being sent to a convention a definite plum, and not simply for the honor involved. Union conventions tend to be reasonably elaborate affairs, although few national get-togethers have remotely approached the level of tastelessly conspicuous consumption that the Teamsters reached at their 1986 convention in Las Vegas. There, following unlimited free drinks and a seemingly inexhaustible supply of top-quality caviar, shrimp, beef, and pastries, 300-pound IBT president Jackie Presser (who had been indicted the previous week for allegedly embezzling union funds) was wheeled into the Caesar's Palace ballroom on a golden sedan chair by four men dressed as Roman centurions. Like a Roman emperor in a Hollywood extravaganza, Presser reached out from a semireclining position to touch the many hands extending toward him as colored floodlights played upon the scene and a voice on the loudspeaker mellifluously declared, "Hail, Caesar." (Another party that was reputed to cost $600,000 was thrown at this same convention and was understandably viewed as an anticlimax.)

Even the Teamsters have, indeed, moved some distance from that ostentation. A recent convention featured nothing much more expensive than run-of-the-mill chicken, cold soup, and cheesecake, had no side extravaganzas at all, and took place in the staid, family-oriented environment of Florida's Disney World.

But almost all national conventions, which are usually held in resort locations, do offer some luxuries and pageantry. When the delegates lose time from work, the local union normally pays their lost wages, and the convention often lasts a week or so, allowing a welcome change of pace from what is often a humdrum employment life. Many delegates, even at their own expense, take their families along and look on the entire experience as money well spent. (Exhibit 4-7 shows both light and serious moments at a recent convention of the National Association of Letter Carriers.)

Although under the terms of the Landrum-Griffin Act the delegates must be chosen by secret ballot, the officers of the nationals themselves may be selected in either of two ways: In about three-fourths of the national unions, the constitution requires that the principal officers (president, vice president, and secretary-treasurer) be elected by the convention. In the others, the officers are elected by a direct referendum in which each member of the union may cast a ballot. Some of the largest unions follow the latter procedure, including the Steelworkers, the Clothing and Textile Workers, and the Machinists, but, even among the larger unions, most utilize the convention election system.

Union business dealt with at national conventions, in addition to the election of chief officers, runs a wide gamut. At a recent convention of the UAW, for example, the 2,500 delegates were asked to consider avenues for improving job security of their members in upcoming negotiations with the Big Three automobile makers and ways of making the diminished UAW budget (diminished because the union had lost some 400,000 members in the previous five years) go further in the field of organizing. They also pondered the authorization of a major new lobbying effort designed to rebuild America's basic industries (including, needless to say, the automotive sector). Cutting membership contributions to the union's hefty strike fund, from 30 percent of each member's monthly dues to 15 percent, was another item on the agenda.

Special problems of the various locals are also aired, and this provides an excellent opportunity for an exchange of ideas and experiences and for otherwise breaking down the provincialism of the local unions; delegates from a large local union in, say, Chicago can learn of the problems of a small local in a small southern community, for example. The convention also permits local union officers to display themselves to their best advantage. Most of them would like to rise in the union hierarchy, and the convention offers a testing ground for their talents. A rousing speech by a local union president may attract the attention of the delegates, and this favorable showing can stand the local person in good stead later when an attempt at higher office is made.

The actual business of the convention may be initiated either by the national officers or by the delegates. Decision making takes the form of resolutions, proposals, and reports on which the delegates vote. As in any large convention, the officers have a distinct advantage in this respect because the president appoints the

EXHIBIT 4-7

National Association of Letter Carriers
61st Biennial Convention
Las Vegas, Nevada   July 27-31, 1998

President Sombrotto's keynote address set the tone for the convention. At left, delegates show their serious— and not-so-serious—sides. From top, the Convention Chronicle was must reading; lighter moments brought laughter, but serious thought also was common (bottom).

2 THE POSTAL RECORD

SOURCE: *The Postal Record*, September 1998, pp. 2 and 5. Photos by Ray Crowell.

EXHIBIT 4-7 (continued)

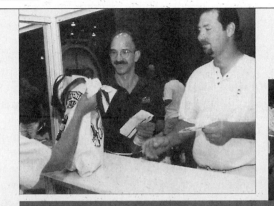

With more than 9,100 delegates, the pace at registration ranged from steady to hectic, whether delegates were having their credentials checked (r.) or collecting souvenir bags containing convention schedule, reports and other information.

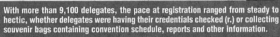

SUNDAY REGISTRATION AND ROUND-UP

A welcoming reception Sunday offered Old West entertainment, including rope tricks, music and line-dance lessons, to more than 5,500 delegates and family members. Victuals and liquid refreshment also were provided.

Good cheer filled the room for the full three hours of Sunday's Old West-themed welcoming reception as delegates greeted brothers and sisters from far and wide, setting a congenial tone for the week's deliberations.

This youngster knew what to do with his souvenir 61st Biennial Convention bandana. The red-and-white bandanas were distributed at the entrance to the "NALC Roundup."

SEPTEMBER 1998 **5**

committees that bring important issues before the delegates and is in a position to select members for these committees whom the leadership knows are favorable to the national officers' point of view. On the other hand, a determined local union, or even individual delegates who feel strongly about their cause, can bring to the attention of the convention a resolution, a recommendation, or even an amendment to the constitution. There is a limit, in fact, to how far any national president can go in bottling up the resentment of determined delegates. And, particularly if a delegation from a local can enlist the support of delegates from other locals, there is an excellent chance that the entire convention will hear its point of view. For all the authority and control that the nationals exert over the locals, if national officers gain the enmity of a sufficient number of local unions, the delegates of these locals can band together and cause an upheaval at the convention; and, if the issues are of extreme importance, the resentment of these locals could result in a change in national union leadership. Thus, the local unions do have a political check against their national officers. There is a line that the latter can cross only at the risk of losing their jobs.

In short, as long as the national union holds regularly scheduled conventions, the democratic process has an opportunity of working. The convention provides the forum where the policies, behavior, and competency of the national union officers can be evaluated, and the key to the democratic operation of a national union therefore lies in the regularity with which conventions are held. More than half the national unions hold conventions either annually or biennially, and most of the rest hold them every three or four years. A small number of national unions, however, simply do not hold conventions at all, and this clearly eliminates almost entirely any practical opportunity for the local unions to participate in the government of their unions. Nothing in the Landrum-Griffin Act requires unions to hold regular and reasonably frequent conventions. The law does require that the union membership be afforded the opportunity to elect its national officers at least every five years, but a union managed by autocrats can legally avoid the holding of conventions indefinitely.

❖ National Union Officers

◆ **Responsibilities**   The chief of the national union is, of course, its president. He or she administers the organization with the assistance of such other major officers as the vice president (or vice presidents), secretary-treasurer, and members of the executive board. The latter group is ordinarily composed of the district or regional directors (who, in some national unions, are also called vice presidents), and its members have a variety of official tasks. They are responsible for enforcing the constitution of the national, implementing its policies, filling national officer positions when these become vacant, and voting on matters referred to them by the president, among their other duties. Normally, they meet regularly and frequently, according to the provisions of their constitution, and on occasion also meet at the call of the president to deal with some pressing problem. Because the members of the executive board are from all over the nation and have direct supervision of the locals in their particular districts, the board mechanism provides an excellent way for the national union officers to learn of the problems of all locals throughout the country. Likewise, it provides a channel for communicating policies of the national union to its locals and membership.

In some unions, however, executive boards merely rubber-stamp decisions of the national officers. This is true most often when a president, either by union custom or because of the person's particular personality, is allowed to exercise autocratic leadership. It is safe to say, however, that in most unions the executive board directs the affairs of the union and establishes the union's basic policies, which the president is then obliged to carry out. The exceptions in recent years have in fact generally been succeeded in office by leaders who appear to have taken extra efforts to alter the old images of power imbalance and to encourage the executive boards to participate more fully in policy-making decisions.

The history of the nation's largest union, the International Brotherhood of Teamsters (IBT), over the past decade well illustrates this last phenomenon. Ronald R. Carey became the reform candidate president of the union in 1992 following the first direct one-member, one-vote election in that union's long history, and he was nothing if not responsive to his now democratically elected executive board. For at least four decades, IBT chief executives had generally operated with complete disdain for their boards. Carey's immediate predecessor, William J. McCarthy, had gone so far as to rig the bidding on the contract to print the monthly Teamsters' magazine so that his son-in-law could get the $3.6 million business. All of the five other Teamster presidents who had served since 1952 (three were sent to prison for crimes of various kinds, partly explaining the high turnover) had at best been benevolent autocrats. Nepotism had been a way of life in these years, and all that it had typically taken for these IBT leaders to remove any real or potential rivals from the post had been a command from the presidents to the board members. Nor had the boards given the presidents any trouble at all concerning the national political arena. In all but one of the 10 White House campaigns in these 40 years, the Teamster boards had endorsed conservative Republicans without batting an eyelash simply because the various Teamster chief executives had informed the board members that this was their personal desire.

Carey, whose first announcement as president-elect was that he would cut the existing IBT presidential salary—at $225,000 the highest of any union leader—to $175,000, had campaigned on a platform of "returning the union to the members." Once in office he sold not only the ostentatious limousine but also two jets that his predecessors had flaunted. Unlike them, he flew only by coach. With the consent of his executive board, he forced a strict budget on a union that had never known one. By the previously described government-imposed anticorruption machinery, he eased out most of the remaining mob-connected members of the bureaucracy that he had inherited. That his career as IBT president also ended in disgrace—in 1997, he was barred from running for reelection by a court-appointed monitor on the grounds that he had supported a plan in which over $700,000 in union funds had been improperly diverted to his presidential campaign the previous year—does not detract from the new tone of executive board participation and quasi-democracy that he set.

Nor should the experience to date of the man who was elected in 1998 to succeed Carey, James P. Hoffa, do so. The son of James R. Hoffa—the colorful, effective, and popular strongman who ran the Teamsters from 1957 to 1971, went to prison for jury tampering and mail and wire fraud, and vanished in 1975 in what was generally viewed as a mob-ordered murder—the younger Hoffa has also proven himself to be a far more participative manager than any of the pre-Carey presidents (including his father) ever were. As attentive to the executive board as was Carey, he also won plaudits in his early presidential years for returning much decision-making power to the Teamster regional councils and local unions, and for appointing a respected federal prosecutor to oversee what Teamsters hoped to be a final internal cleanup of the union, which has been under governmental supervision since 1989.

All responsible, devoted, and active national union presidents have a difficult job. One day they may be negotiating a contract with a major corporation and the next day speaking at an important meeting of the union or to the members of some other labor organization. They are also, typically, obligated to testify before congressional committees, preside over the union's executive board meetings, and travel to foreign nations as participants in international labor organization bodies. They are expected to take an active role in important national political elections, constantly put pressure upon the staff representatives to organize nonunion plants, mollify managements that are disgruntled because of wildcat strikes or other forms of unauthorized union behavior, and perform a variety of other duties that may be of major importance or strictly routine in character but that also take up a great deal of time. The management of even a small or medium-sized national union is a difficult one; the job becomes immensely more complicated and difficult in a large union.

The union president, moreover, is constantly torn between duties of a pressing character and, in many cases, must make the hard decision alone and hope it is the right one. As any chief executive, the president bears the ultimate responsibility for the organization's efficient, honest, and prudent management. Above all, he or she must satisfy the membership, and at times this is a much more difficult job than dealing with management.

♦ **Remuneration**   For all of this, union presidents hardly grow rich on the salaries of their offices. Even leaders of the largest unions rarely make more than $125,000. Although in a recent year the president of the Air Line Pilots Association (many of whose members themselves received six-figure incomes) earned $192,000—$500 less than AFL-CIO president Sweeney currently makes—and although a handful of other union top officials approached that relatively affluent level, these numbers were easily balanced by the salaries of the presidents of major unions such as the Automobile Workers, Communications Workers, Clothing and Textile Workers, Mine Workers, Rubber Workers and Oil, Chemical and Atomic Workers. In these organizations, the salary range was between $75,000 and $100,000. It is also clear that money was not the motivator, either, for the president of the United Electrical Workers (UE): Limited in what he could get by the union's constitution to no more than the highest weekly wage in the industry, he earned in 1996 a far from staggering $27,083 plus an equally unimpressive expense allowance. (The UE, nothing if not egalitarian, has a leaflet that asserts that "a boss-size salary can give you a boss-eye point of view. Champagne tastes can soon make you forget how important a 50 cent beer can be.") At the extreme of financial self-denial was Farm Worker president Cesar Chavez, the recipient before his death not long ago of a paltry $5,645.

It is certainly true that a few national leaders have taken things too far, financially speaking, while in office. Before the passage of the Landrum-Griffin Act, for example, Teamster president David Beck succumbed to an urge to buy items of a personal nature in copious amounts and charge them to his union. In more recent years, the authoritarian Mine Workers president W. A. "Tony" Boyle also flagrantly misused union money for his personal benefit. And, although receiving pay from the holding of several union jobs simultaneously is not in itself illegal—in the Teamsters, it was almost a way of life for the top officials and even now at least 10 IBT leaders currently get paychecks from at least three positions—some element of good judgment might be brought into question when the total derived incomes go well into the six-figure area. The same can be said of the practice in some unions (the Laborers, most conspicuously) of placing relatives in high-paying jobs with no seeming correlation of such placements to any merit on the part of the relatives.

Yet these latter situations are definitely the exceptions. And, under any conditions, the most handsomely remunerated union official is many light-years in income away from such corporate chief executives as Michael Eisner of Walt Disney, Mel Karmazin of CBS, and Sanford Weill of Citigroup, who in 1998 got from their organizations (in all cases, primarily from options) $575.6 million, $201.9 million, and $167.1 million, respectively, whereas all CEOs at large public companies made an *average* $10.6 million.[12] With almost no exceptions, union leaders don't even remotely approximate the average $133,672 pay that outside *directors* at the nation's 200 largest industrial and service companies averaged in 1999—to say nothing of the $409,500 that directors at Sun Microsystems in 1998 raked in, or the $362,448 that board members at Compaq Computer also got in 1998.[13]

Workers pay the salaries of their union officers, however. And the employee who earns $21,000 in a good year may still think of a $75,000 salary as being exorbitant. However, an objective assessment must turn more toward a conclusion that the typical national union leader is, if anything, underpaid given his responsibilities. When measured by his own very formidable list of duties, even the president of the Air Line Pilots does not seem to be getting an unreasonable salary.

♦ **Tenure in Office** Although modestly paid, the national president wants to keep the job. Union leaders have power and prestige and play an important role in our society. Many presidents do indeed remain in office for considerable lengths of time, and some of them stay in the chief executive chair for so long that memory does not recall another president. Daniel J. Tobin was president of the Teamsters for 45 years; William L. Hutcheson, of the Carpenters for 41 years (immediately following which his son Maurice moved into that union's presidential office for a full additional two decades); and John L. Lewis, of the Mine Workers for 40 years. James C. Petrillo, president of the Musicians, gave up his job, involuntarily at that, only when he grew so old and feeble that it is doubtful that he had the strength to play his instrument. Only a relative handful of unions—including the Automobile Workers, Steelworkers, and Machinists—have any provision for compulsory retirement of their national officers, and, if national union board meetings can no longer be confused with "a collection of a wax museum," youth does not exactly hold sway in them, either. Richard L. Trumka, a lawyer and third-generation miner who was elected in 1982 at age 33 to head the 180,000-member United Mine Workers, was even in 1995, when he resigned his presidency to become AFL-CIO secretary-treasurer, the youngest leader of a major union in the United States. Only a handful of other national presidents are even below the half-century mark and most are in their sixties or beyond.

It is not difficult to explain why national union leaders do so often stay in power for years. Once in office, they possess sufficient leverage to minimize centralized opposition and to make it extremely difficult for new candidates to present themselves to the membership in an effective manner. The point has been made that when conventions are not held regularly and frequently, it is difficult for a new face to get much backing.

In addition, staff representatives are hired by the national union and can usually be removed at the pleasure of the national officers. It would take rare courage for a paid representative to oppose the incumbent president, and the tendency is, in fact, understandably in the other direction. Furthermore, most incumbent presidents get personal mileage out of their union newspapers. The editor of the national union newspaper is also a hired person and subject to control of the national officers. Any upstart candidate could not expect much favorable publicity, if indeed the candidate received any publicity at all, in the union press. As Wilfrid Sheed once commented, "The [president] controls the newspaper and assorted promo material, which is likely to feature pictures of himself peering knowingly into a mine face or welding machine, like a bishop at a confirmation. (In the Steelworkers, I'm told, a man could go mad staring at I. W. Abel. It's worse than *Muhammed Speaks*.)"[14] Exhibit 4-8 portrays Letter Carrier president Vincent R. Sombrotto in a light hardly calculated to hurt him with the membership. His picture actually appeared 14 times in this issue of his union's *Postal Record* magazine. Exhibit 4-9 comes from the major publication of the Teamsters and contains four of the seven photographs of newly elected IBT chief executive Hoffa that were produced in that issue of *The Teamster*, as well as a variety of carefully chosen words for rank-and-file consumption.

In short, the incumbent national officers have a political machine that tends to perpetuate them in office. However, it would be incorrect to believe that this is the only reason for long tenure of office. Sophisticated union members understand that frequent changes of national union officers and open displays of factionalism weaken the position of the union against management in collective bargaining. Beyond this, a national union officer may have genuinely earned reelection to office over the years because the officer has been doing a good job for the membership. A national union president who is devoted, honest, courageous, and competent does not need a political machine to be reelected. Most national union officers fall within this category, and representatives of management should not regard national union officers as incompetent people who hold office only because of political machination.

THE LOCAL UNION

❖ Where the People Are

Although we leave for the last an analysis of the local union, it does not follow that the latter is the least important of the labor bodies in the union movement. On the contrary, it could be argued successfully that for the individual union member, the local union is the most important unit of all. In a sense, the federation, the national union and its district organizations, and the other labor bodies discussed previously are administrative and service organizations. Although they carry out a variety of significant activities, as we have seen, no union member really "belongs" to such larger bodies. Unionists are members of these organizations only by reason of their membership in a local union, are geographically close only to the local, and largely condition their loyalty toward the total labor movement by what they perceive to happen within the confines of the local union. Many union members do not, for that

EXHIBIT 4-8

SOURCE: *The Postal Record*, September 1999, front cover. Photo by Bill Burke.

EXHIBIT 4-9

Interview

Teamster Magazine Interview With

Jim Hoffa

Q How do you account for your convincing election victory? Why do you think you won?

A Our campaign went to the rank and file with a simple message: unify our union, restore its financial integrity, and return it to greatness. We pledged to end the corruption at the International, stop deficit spending, start aggressive organizing campaigns and cut the fat while keeping the muscle. Obviously, that is what the members want and what we intend to deliver.

Q This was a hotly contested election with a lot of negative attacks against you and your slate. How will you heal the

rifts and reunite the rank and file behind you?

A We have already begun the process of unifying our union. Our campaign won over officers and members in key areas that were against us in 1996, such as New York, Pennsylvania, and California. The members gave us a clear mandate: they want us to end the civil war in the Teamsters. They want the union's officers to stop fighting each other, roll up their sleeves and go to work on behalf of all Teamsters. It is time to start healing the wounds and that process is well under way.

Q The IBT's finances are in shambles. The Teamster treasury has fallen from

$154 million to $1 million in the last seven years. Where did the money go?

A That's a question we intend to find the answer to. Actually, far more dues money is involved. The union has a yearly income of more than $80 million. When you add this to the $154 million decline in assets, about $700 million of the members' dues was spent by the previous administration. We know that too much went to bloated payrolls and far-out political schemes that didn't benefit the membership. Moreover, at least $1 million was illegally used by the Carey slate in the 1996 election. I will not compromise on my pledge to do everything possible to recover these funds. We intend to file a lawsuit

2   THE TEAMSTER

Source: *The Teamster*, April 1999, pp. 2–3.

EXHIBIT 4-9 (continued)

against Ron Carey and others that participated in looting our treasury. We have only seen the tip of the iceberg regarding this embezzlement scandal.

Q Explain some of your ideas for putting the Teamsters financial house in order.

A I plan to work with General Secretary Treasurer Tom Keegel to ensure that the Teamsters will have a balanced budget in the first year of our administration. Employees hired by the Carey administration who were not actually doing their jobs will be dropped from the payroll and, from now on, Teamster paychecks will go only to staff who work hard for the members. We intend to cut the fat and keep the muscle — and do this without any dues increase.

Q Critics warn that under your leadership, the Teamsters will revert to an undemocratic union. How do you respond to this charge?

A It's nonsense. The Hoffa slate is totally committed to the direct election of union officers and the principle of "one man, one vote." Without direct election of officers, I would have never had a chance to run for General President. We will never return to the previous system of elections.

Q Big Business says that critics of NAFTA are overstating the job losses associated with the free trade law. What is your position?

A NAFTA was a huge mistake that put far too many American jobs on the fast track across the Rio Grande into Mexico. It has been destructive to our standard of living because it put us in a race to the bottom by asking American workers to compete with people who will work for $8 a day in Mexico. NAFTA is an invitation to corporations to move plants from the United States to Mexico for greater savings and profits. Well, I believe we have to keep good jobs in this country. I should also

point out that a recent study by the Department of Transportation revealed that Mexican trucks are completely unsafe. NAFTA opens the door for Mexican trucks to run anywhere on our highways in the year 2000. I don't think Americans are going to tolerate having these trucks, with unsafe equipment and dangerous cargo, on our highways. This will also lead to layoffs of thousands of American truck drivers who work hard and play by the rules. We cannot allow the Clinton administration to open our borders to these unsafe trucks.

Q Your election has fueled speculation that the Teamsters will tilt more toward the Republican Party and away from the Democrats. Will we see a truly bipartisan union?

A I have articulated this goal ever since I began running. The Teamsters union can not be taken for granted by either party anymore. We will support those who endorse an agenda that helps working families have better lives, regardless of party affiliation.

Q The Teamsters' strike against UPS was viewed by most observers as a win for the union. How will you approach labor management relations?

A I will take a militant approach in contract negotiations and we will continue to involve the membership in their contract battles. Teamster negotiators will fight to win the best possible contracts to give our members what they need and want. We are already drawing up plans for the important carhaul agreement and are preparing for it as if we were going to war.

Q Suppose your father was here today. What advice would he give you to lead the IBT into the next millennium?

A My father always said one thing **"TRUST THE MEMBERS."** I trust the members and their

infinite wisdom. They are tired of the rhetoric, personal attacks, and name calling. The members put us in office because they want to belong to a union that works hard for them, one they can be proud of. When they pay their dues they expect a strong union that fights for them. My father would be proud to see me restore the members' confidence in their leadership as I take this strong, proud union into the next century.

matter, even know the names of their national and federation officers, but they do know their local union president, business agent, and stewards. They know them because they see them where they work and because these are the people who handle the union members' day-to-day problems.

❖ Local Union Officers

Although some locals are formed before the employer is organized, a local union normally comes into existence when there is organization of an employer. After it has organized and secured bargaining rights, it typically applies for and receives a national union charter. This document establishes the local's affiliation with the national union and entitles the local to its services, and by the same token it subjects the local to the rules and discipline of the national union. Depending on the unit of organization, a local union may be confined to a single plant or several plants of a single company or may include workers of a single occupation, such as electricians, nurses, or musicians, who perform their duties in a given geographic area.

There is absolutely no correlation between the size of a national union and number of locals. The Teamsters, with 1.4 million members, have 560 locals, but the Steelworkers, considerably smaller with a membership of 500,000, have almost 3,000 locals. And although the Food and Commercial Workers have chartered 750 locals to support their 1 million constituents, the Railroad Signalmen have 170 locals for their 10,000 members, allowing those who belong to the latter union the unusually small member-to-local ratio of about 59 to 1.

Once the local is established, the members, in accordance with their bylaws (which are usually specified in the national union constitution), elect their officers—typically a president, vice president, secretary-treasurer, and several lesser officials. Since such election procedures almost invariably allow direct participation by all union members, the local union officers are elected on a much more democratic basis than are those chosen to lead the national union. Moreover, the union member knows much more from firsthand experience about the local union candidates for office than he or she does about the national union officers. The vast majority of local union officers, in fact, work at regular jobs along with the other union members and are under constant and often highly critical observation by them. Both democracy and a far higher turnover rate for local officers than for the union's national officials also stem from the fact that the local union officer, unlike the national union president, has little if any patronage to dispense. Local leaders do not have a paid staff as does the national counterpart; nor, generally speaking, can the local officer make use of any other powers of patronage or the purse, since neither exist in any measure.

In general, the local union officers even work without pay. In only the large local unions are such officers reimbursed for their work, and, even then, their salaries tend to approximate the wages they would have earned from their employers. And in the relatively infrequent instances when the local union president and secretary-treasurer do receive some compensation for their duties even when they are full-time employees in the plant, the amount of money is comparatively small. For example, in Bloomington, Indiana, one local's secretary-treasurer receives the far from awesome salary of $5,000 per year for taking care of the books, making financial reports, answering all correspondence, and assuming a volume of other miscellaneous duties. The size of his job is measured by the fact that the local has over 2,200 members and by the union's requirement that all his duties must be conducted on his own time.

There *are* local leaders who do far better than this. Gus Bevona, the longtime president of a New York City Service Employees local representing 55,000 janitors and doormen, in 1997 made a staggering $531,529—or 17 times what his average constituent earned: $365,401 was his salary for serving as the local's president; the rest came his way for serving both as president of a related local and on a board of his international union. Frank Wsol, head of a Chicago Teamsters local in 1997, was paid $428,745 by his local union and $44,324 for his work as vice president of Teamsters Joint Council 25 in Chicago.[15] But for every Bevona or Wsol, there are thousands of local officers whose financial rewards are either nominal or nonexistent.

A fair question, then, is why union members desire to acquire and retain local union officer jobs. Despite their meager incomes, they must perform a variety of duties and assume considerable responsibility, and they are constantly being pressured by the membership under whose direct surveillance they labor.

A leading reason is that the local union officers acquire prestige and status in the company and in the community. Virtually all people desire recognition once lower needs have been relatively well satisfied, and the attainment of a local officer's job accomplishes this objective for some workers.

Another reason may involve the local union officer's devotion and dedication to the union movement. "In general," Koziara, Bradley, and Pierson have concluded from their study of this topic, those who become union officers "are people who believe unions have a meaningful function to perform in our society."[16] If the local officer really believes in unions, he or she has the opportunity of making the movement work by carrying out the position's duties in an honest and effective manner.

Still other union members may genuinely court the competitive character associated with the office: The local union officers deal with the employer on a day-to-day basis, and many of the dealings regularly involve what some workers view as "the struggle" with management.

Finally, the reason may be a political one, involving the future of the local union officer in the national union. As stated, national union officers are elected officials, and staff representatives are union members who are hired by the national union. Thus, to go up the ladder, the union member must normally start at the local union level; a local union officer's job is commonly the first step in the long and hard pull toward the top. The large majority of all current national union officers and staff representatives have held a local union officer's job at some earlier period of their careers.

❖ Functions of the Local Union: Relations with Management

The duties of local union officers are dependent, of course, upon the functions of the particular local union, but unless contracts are negotiated on a multiemployer basis or with a very large organization, local union officers directly negotiate the labor agreement with the employer. If the national union staff representative often aids the local in carrying out this function and usually plays a highly visible role in the process, the fact remains that the local union officers who are also involved in negotiations are directly responsible to the members of the local union. The staff representative, a hired hand, does not face political defeat if he or she exercises poor judgment or fails to negotiate a contract that the membership feels is suitable. Should a contract, however, hurt the local union members, it is very likely that in the next election the local union officers will be changed. Because of its local character, factionalism in the local is, in fact, a constant problem. It is comparatively easy for a dynamic, aggressive, and ambitious newcomer to use a poor contract as a weapon to dislodge an incumbent officer.

Another important function of the local is that of handling grievances, complaints filed during the life of a labor agreement because the agreement has allegedly been violated. In fact, most of the union's time is devoted to this task; the labor agreement is negotiated only periodically, but, through the grievance procedure, it must be administered every day. To this end, each local union has a number of stewards—usually one steward to a department of the organization, elected by the union members of that department—who serve as administrative personnel.

In most plants, the members also elect a chief steward to be chairperson of the grievance committee. At the lower steps of the grievance procedure, the worker's complaint is handled by the department steward, and, normally, the local union president or chief steward does not enter the picture until the grievance has reached the higher levels. But at the last step of the grievance procedure, the local union president and the union grievance committee (composed of the chief steward and several other stewards) will most often negotiate the grievance, typically with the staff representative of the national union also being present. Moreover, if a grievance goes to arbitration for a binding decision by a mutually chosen outsider, the local union president and the union committee will attend the hearing, and, although at this forum the national staff representative usually presents the union's case, the representative depends heavily on the local union officers and the committee for the data that will be offered to the arbitrator.

It is difficult to overestimate the vital importance of the effective use of the grievance procedure as a function of the local union. To the union member who has a grievance, the handling of that grievance means more than what the union secured in the collective bargaining agreement. This is particularly true when the grievant complains against a discharge or against an alleged employer violation of an important working condition.

In this capacity, however, the local union officers are also vulnerable. Take, for example, a grievance that, though important to the employee, does not have merit. If the local president tells this to the union member, the president risks offending a constituent. And if this happens frequently and with many different workers, the union members can demonstrate their resentment in the next election. This appears completely unfair and senseless, but it is what the local union officers have to contend with and explains why they frequently take up grievances that do not have merit.

At times, too, the local officers are forced to deal with "borderline" grievances—complaints that may or may not have merit but that, for a variety of reasons, the local union officers cannot persuade the employer to grant. Often, the local does not want to risk losing the grievance in arbitration. It, therefore, refuses to handle the grievance, and the job now is to pacify the employee, who may have some justification for being resentful—not an easy mission when the grievance deals with an important issue and has some basis under the labor agreement. Consequently, the local officials may change their minds and take such grievances into arbitration, hoping for the best; if the arbitrator denies the grievance, the local officers can always use the arbitrator as the scapegoat. In spite of an effective presentation at the arbitration hearing, however, the disgruntled union member may still blame the union officers. Fortunately, unions win their share of grievances in the grievance procedure and in arbitration, and in the campaign before the next election the local union officer can point with pride to successes and minimize or explain away defeats. Victory has many fathers and mothers, but defeat is almost always an orphan.

❖ Judicial Procedures

Another function of the local union is that of disciplining union members who are alleged to have violated union rules. As does every organization, unions have standards with which members must comply. These standards are incorporated by the national union's constitution and are duplicated in the local union's bylaws. A union member who violates any of these rules may be disciplined by the local union membership in the form of a reprimand, a fine, suspension, or, in extreme cases, expulsion from the union.

Commonly proscribed standards of conduct that frequently merit expulsion include the promotion of dual unionism (when a union member seeks to take the local out of one national union and place it in another—true treason in unionism!), participating in an unauthorized or "wildcat" strike, misappropriating union funds, strikebreaking, refusing to picket, sending the union membership list to unauthorized persons, circulating false and malicious reports about union officers, and providing secret and confidential information to the employer. Under the official rules of some unions, a member may also be expelled because of membership in a communist, fascist, or other totalitarian group. One may quarrel with the justice or fairness of one or more of these rules, but the fact remains that they must be obeyed, since they have been adopted by the union at large. From the union point of view, each of them pertains to an important area of conduct.

The procedures used at the local level to enforce the rules of the union differ widely, but the following would probably reflect most local union procedures: Any union member may file charges against any other member, including the local union officers. When this occurs, the president has the authority to appoint a so-called trial committee, composed of union members belonging to the local in question and normally including officers, stewards, and rank-and-file members who take an active role in the affairs of the union. The trial committee has the job of investigating the complaint, holding a hearing if it believes that the charge has substance, and reaching a decision that it will ultimately present to the entire local union body for final determination. To protect against a political situation within the local where favorites of the local union officers, or the officers themselves, may not be brought to account for a violation, the union members initiating the charge may appeal to the national union. Thus, a "not guilty" verdict, the dismissal of charges by the local union officers, or the pigeonholing of complaints does not necessarily end the disciplinary process.

After its investigation of the charges, the local union's trial committee holds a hearing at which the accused member is present. The accused may select another union member to act as spokesperson. As in most other private or semiprivate organizations, the union member may not hire a defense lawyer while the case is being processed within the union, but witnesses are called, and cross-examination is permitted. And, although no oath is administered for the same reason (since the hearing is not in a court of law), union members who deliberately lie or who grossly misrepresent the facts may themselves be charged with a violation. After the hearing, the trial committee reports its decision and the reasons for the verdict to the local union membership. At this point, the membership may adopt, reject, or modify the committee's decision. At times, the trial is in effect reheld before the local membership, since some members might desire to review the evidence that the trial committee used to arrive at its decision.

If the decision is "not guilty," the member or members who filed the charge may appeal to the executive board of the national union. By the same token, when the decision of the local goes against the charged union member, that member may appeal to the national and, under the provisions of virtually every constitution, the member can also ultimately appeal the decision of the national officers to the national convention.

On the surface, this judicial procedure appears fair and calculated to protect the accused union member. It would seem that the accused receives a full and fair hearing and gains further protection through provisions for the right of appeal. In practice, however, there have been instances of serious abuses of the local union judicial procedure, although, with some 43,000 locals to consider, it is absolutely impossible to make any kind of accurate judgment of the relative extent to which abuse has existed, and any opinion is sheer speculation.

It was because of such union actions, however, that the Landrum-Griffin Act specified that no member could be disciplined, fined, or expelled without having first received a written list of charges, a reasonable time to prepare the defense, and a full and fair hearing. Today, if these legal standards are violated, a union member may bring suit in the federal courts for relief. Under the law, the union member may not go to court before attempting to settle the case through union procedures, although to check dilatory union tactics the law also specifies that if the internal procedure consumes longer than four months the union member need not exhaust the internal remedies of the union before going to court.

In 1957, the same year that the Teamsters were expelled from the AFL-CIO for alleged domination by "corrupt influences," the United Automobile Workers (UAW)—who had led this expulsion action—dealt with the problem of abuse in the disciplinary procedure in a different manner. The UAW established a **Public Review Board**, composed of seven citizens of respected reputation and impeccable integrity and having no other relationship with the union. Usually, such citizens have been nationally known members of the clergy, the judiciary, or academia, and in the years since the board's creation they have actively pursued their official charge of ensuring "a continuation of high moral and ethical standards" within the UAW. They have investigated all credible complaints, from allegations of individual member wrongdoing to charges by individual members that their union representatives have not adequately handled a grievance, and generally have done so to the full satisfaction of all concerned.

Experience has shown, indeed, that the board—which is empowered to reverse UAW executive board decisions that have upheld the discipline of union personnel—has been quite willing to make such reversals when it has believed that such a reversal has been justified. To date, few other unions have, however, followed the pattern of the UAW. If each national union were to establish such an agency, and if each agency were allowed the same freedom to act that has been granted the UAW Public Review Board, there clearly would be less need for legislation to protect the status of union members.

❖ Political Activities

Although the AFL-CIO and national union officers and staff representatives play an effective role in lobbying and in supporting candidates in their campaigns for political office, it can be argued with much justification that the political efficiency of the union movement depends above all upon the vigor of the local. After all, the number of federation and national officers and staff representatives is very small in comparison with the number of local union members. And much of the legwork during the national and state elections must necessarily be performed by local union members if it is to be performed at all on any large scale.

Nonetheless, the degree to which local unions participate in politics is often determined by the basic philosophy of the national union. If the national union officers do not want their union to engage in politics, or if they merely go through the motions of indicating such a preference, the local unions of the nationals will reflect this kind of leadership. On the other hand, when the national union officers do take an active role in the political affairs of the nation, the local unions typically respond by placing a major emphasis on such political action of their own. However, even when the national unions do cajole their locals into taking this active role in politics, the members themselves may or may not follow the instructions of the national union officers, and the national's efforts must consequently be geared in two directions: toward the local leadership and toward the local membership.

If a constant problem of the national union that is politically inclined is thus to motivate the locals to follow its example, even within the ranks of such active unions as the UAW and the Food and Commercial Workers, there are many dozens of local unions that either refuse to participate or participate in a half-hearted way. Locals of less politically conscious nationals often show even greater reluctance. Moreover, just because the AFL-CIO leadership or a national union president supports a candidate for elective office, this does not mean that every union member will vote that way. Some may not vote at all, of course, and postelection analyses of union member districts show that many others vote for the opposite candidate, as the millions of unionist votes for the Republican presidential nominees in the last several races for the White House, noted earlier, vividly illustrate. There is no permanent labor vote, as is sometimes claimed by people who view the political participation of the union movement as an evil.

Nonetheless, a local union that takes an active role in politics can be of great help to a favored candidate, and, in a close election, the support can tip the scales in the candidate's favor. The local union will encourage each member to register and to cast a ballot at election time. Prior to the election, it will do all in its power to "educate" the union member as to how to vote, through publications, meetings, house-to-house visits, and other forms of active political activity. In addition, the local union may legally make expenditures from union dues for such purposes as the holding of meetings of a political character and the publication and distribution of politically inspired newspapers and leaflets, although (as stated earlier) only money that is raised on a voluntary basis from the membership can be contributed directly to the people running for political office.

❖ Other Functions and Problems

Beyond the major functions discussed earlier, local unions at times engage in a variety of social, educational, and community activities.

♦ Community Activities   Of late, as in the case of higher labor bodies, this area has become increasingly important. Union leaders realize that the welfare of their members depends in part on a progressive and well-run community. How the schools are run, for example, is of vital interest to the local unionist who must pay taxes to operate the schools and who may have children attending the schools. As in the case of city labor bodies, representation of local union officials on United Way committees, Red Cross drives, and similar endeavors is also increasing in frequency. Moreover, unions recognize that the public image of organized labor, which has been tarnished in recent years, tends to improve to the extent that unions engage in such community services. Labor's various forms of participation in community service programs demonstrate that union members are not only collectively a socially oriented group but also individually responsible and interested citizens of the community. Likewise, the integration of unions in community work tends to lessen the tensions between management and organized labor. If a union leader can work effectively with management representatives on the school board or in the United Way drive, there is a better chance for harmonious labor relations at the workplace.

♦ Educational Programs   Many local unions also conduct regularly sponsored and generally effective educational programs for the benefit of their officers and stewards. As noted previously, the need for these programs arises primarily from the complexity of the contemporary labor–management relationship, but it also stems to a great extent from the brisk turnover of the local union officers and stewards. Some of the programs are sponsored by the national unions, although in many cases the local itself arranges the educational program. In fact, no union is considered modern today unless it has devised a well-planned educational program for its leadership. Such educational programs frequently bring to the surface workers of talent and high native intelligence. Through education, not only are they capable of doing a better job for their membership and acting more responsibly and rationally at the bargaining table, but education tends to make them more useful citizens. Of at least as much practical interest to many workers, union members who acquire such measures of education tend to rise more rapidly to important jobs at both the local and national levels. (The Letter Carriers, by no means alone among unions, has put considerable recent emphasis on strengthening steward and local union leader development. Exhibit 4-10 is illustrative.)

♦ Membership Attendance at Meetings   One of the most important problems of the local is that of interesting the membership in attending regular monthly meetings of the union. Attendance at these meetings is frequently very poor, and the problem is not easy to solve. The vast majority of union leaders sincerely want their members to turn out at the meeting. They believe that the union has nothing to hide and that, by regular attendance and discussion at meetings, the members become more active, tend to be more devoted, and in general allow the local to deal with both employers and representatives of the public from a considerably stronger position than would otherwise be the case. The fact remains, however, that union members normally stay away from their meetings in droves; for the regular monthly

EXHIBIT 4-10

Salt Lake City Branch 111 President Steve McNees (l.) and V.P. Tom McPartland advise Steward Karl Lopez.

From basics to buddies, branches back up stewards

"It's the toughest job in the union, being a steward. On the front line, every day. Here it is, right in your face. You know you don't have all the answers, but the members are counting on you and management's leaning on you. It's a load."

That's the take from John DiTollo, president of Pittsburgh Branch 84 and chairman of NALC's Board of Trustees, and few union leaders—no matter what craft or trade, local or national level—would disagree.

To help stewards shoulder that load, NALC branches have developed systems for training and support, not only to make stewards more effective but also to help keep these volunteers from "burning out."

The union's 15 National Business Agents provide the foundation for steward training in their regions. They often run special steward programs at state training seminars and conventions, regional rap sessions or in special classes conducted at the request of a branch.

Each NBA has three nationally trained steward trainers, who attended a weeklong teaching techniques program in 1995 that was arranged by NALC's Education Department and held at the George Meany Center near Washington. Those trainers and their NBAs often use material from the NALC Steward Training Program. The program contains dozens of interactive teaching units addressing such basic steward skills as organizing the members, steward rights and duties, and grievance investigation, writing and negotiation.

Classes for all levels

In Pittsburgh, the branch offers regular training classes for the 95 stewards who look out for

more than 2,200 active members. "We engage some pros from Penn State's labor education department or the local community college, give them our NALC materials, and have them organize a series of four or five courses," DiTollo said.

The programs, held each spring and fall, run one night a week for six weeks, three hours a session. The content varies—basic skills, contract knowledge, grievance procedure, even arbitration training.

"We look at our group and see what's most appropriate. If we have a lot of newer stewards, we'll go with basic training," DiTollo said.

With a veteran group, new material is introduced, such as a program on NALC history and labor movement issues—something that might seem far afield from a steward's daily grind, but helps keep "old-timers" fresh and interested.

For completing the course, the stewards get continuing education certificates from the college and frequently a celebratory dinner.

Coaching and mentoring

Another branch that makes a major effort to recruit and support stewards is Salt Lake City Branch 111. The approach is based on the idea of "mentoring," where prospective stewards are identified and recruited, then supported and counseled by veteran branch leaders.

While the system demands a commitment from branch leaders, it does not represent a major financial drain and can be adapted by branches of any size. (Salt Lake City has 26 stewards and 14 alternates serving nearly 750 active members.) Branch 111 President Steve McNees and Vice President Tom McPartland outlined the program in detail for a report in the Summer 1996 *NALC Activist*.

As described by McPartland, who developed it, the mentoring process involves four steps: targeting, marketing, protecting and godfathering.

First, branch leaders target people who show the potential to be good stewards—signs that include "good intuition, street smarts and common sense," McPartland said. Often these are members who face a work crisis of their own and show interest in how their problem is resolved.

Once identified, these prospects get the "marketing" pitch, assurances that as stewards they can be effective and get things done. This includes delegating them minor responsibilities within the branch along with steward duties. It also features coaching the new activists to ensure they succeed in each task and giving them public recognition for their achievements.

Protecting new stewards is vital. McPartland noted management too often decides to push new stewards around, such as making them fight for steward's time. That means leaders must be prepared to step in on their behalf when needed.

Godfathering is an extension of the protection process, where branch leaders work to develop a personal relationship with the fledglings and create a level of confidence and comfort so the steward always has a place to turn when the inevitable frustrations of the work create intolerable pressures and stress.

The investment of time by branch leaders pays dividends both by improving service to members and injecting fresh enthusiasm to carry the union forward, McPartland said.

Other branches also have effective, if less elaborate, strategies for supporting stewards, with an emphasis on training at the top of the list. State association meetings also are a good place to share ideas about how to support and sustain NALC's steward backbone. And no matter what the size of the branch, all stewards deserve one more thing—a hearty "thank you." ✉

12 POSTAL RECORD

SOURCE: *Postal Record*, March 1997, p. 12.

meetings, only about 5 to 10 percent of the membership turns out (even a smaller percentage is common enough, especially in large locals); and one wonders why there has been so much said about union democracy when the union member does not seem sufficiently interested to participate in the affairs of his or her own union. When unions are poorly managed, when corruption exists, when leadership is second-rate, the fault is essentially that of the union member who does not care enough to attend the regular union meeting.

Thus, although from the days of the earliest unions labor organizations have undertaken a variety of measures (ranging from more convenient hours to the incorporation of social activities into the meeting schedule) to encourage attendance, in all these years unions have not found the solution to the problem of worker apathy toward attendance at meetings, and there is every likelihood that it will persist in the future. The only notable exception involves meetings at which a strike vote is scheduled to be taken. In general, the union members will turn out at this time because this issue of striking or working is, of course, of crucial importance.

On the other hand, management should not interpret poor attendance at the regular monthly meetings to mean that in crisis situations the members will not support their union. In a showdown, the typical union member will actively support the union; a management that makes a decision to chance a strike solely on the grounds of poor attendance at union meetings makes a very unwise choice. The members will invariably rally to the union's cause when there are issues involved that vitally affect their welfare, no matter how little interest they have demonstrated in the day-to-day operation of their local at more peaceful times.

UNION FINANCES

Chief expenditures of unions include the payment of salaries for full-time officers and staff representatives, travel expenses, clerical expenses, office equipment and supplies, arbitration fees, and rent or mortgage payments for office space and the union hall. Beyond this, the strike fund must be built up to pay strike benefits when needed.

At the international level, where the lion's share of the dollars is spent, most of the money paid out goes to staff members who provide direct and indirect services. It has been estimated that in the case of the United Automobile Workers, for example, about 85 percent of the spending is for this purpose. In a recent year, the UAW's research budget was approximately $700,000; its 16-member Washington staff spent about the same amount; the union's public relations expenditures were running at an annual rate of just over $1 million; and this fifth-largest union in the country was even financing a six-member staff of safety experts who were flying around the country on request from local unions to check for hazards.

The Teamsters spend even more lavishly on services. Some 550 staff persons employed in 15 different departments at the block-long union headquarters in Washington work in such fields of endeavor as lobbying, education (including the administration of a 40,000-volume library), communications (including the issuance of an impressively packaged monthly publication, *The Teamster*), and a large legal department (itself supervising the activities of some 400 Teamster lawyers scattered throughout the country). They also staff a research wing (to compile information, above all, to back up contract bargaining demands), a steadily growing health and safety unit, an organizing department, and an electronic data-processing department that supplies computer support nationwide to the several hundred Teamster locals.

At times, people are impressed by the relatively large amounts that unions collect in dues and initiation fees, forgetting that the union dispenses formidable amounts of money to meet its bills. By some estimates, the annual income of American unions from all sources—special assessments and earnings from investments, as well as the regular monthly dues paid by constituents, and initiation fees—amounts to about $5 billion. And there is little question that $5 billion looks like a lot of money, particularly when you don't have it. But when one considers the net worth of unions, a more accurate picture is gained. Such worth, for all unions in the United States, still remains under the $1 billion mark and in no way comes close to paralleling the wealth of corporations, at least three dozen of which have net assets that *individually* exceed this billion-dollar figure. Incomewise, too, organized labor is a relative pygmy in relation to business: The 10 most profitable U.S. corporations alone had profits of $40 billion in 1998, and the nation's top 500 industrial corporations in that same year racked up a mammoth $3 trillion in sales. (The recent financial dimensions of one, not untypical labor organization, the Association of Flight Attendants, are reproduced as Exhibit 4-11.)

EXHIBIT 4-11

ASSOCIATION OF FLIGHT ATTENDANTS FINANCIAL STATEMENTS 1998

Dear AFA Members:

The report on this page represents AFA's financial status as of December 31, 1998, as audited by an independent accounting firm. The report is comprised of several sections that should be viewed as a whole in order to create an accurate picture of AFA's financial position.

The *Independent Auditor's Report* expresses the opinion of the accounting firm Squire, Lemkin and O'Brien that AFA's financial records are properly maintained and that the audit fairly reports the Union's financial condition.

AFA's assets and liabilities and our total net worth are described in the *Balance Sheets*. The *Statement of Revenue and Expenses* shows the income that AFA received from dues, initiation fees and interest, and how it was spent. *The Statement of Changes in Member's Equity* specifies growth in designated and undesignated equity. Designated monies comprise our Reserve Fund.

Finally, the *Statement of Cash Flows* shows the movement of cash in and out of AFA, and reconciles the year-to-year changes in assets and liability balances to net cash received. Notes that accompany this audit provide information relevant to AFA's business, and are an integral part of the financial statement.

Our Union's financial operations are directed by AFA's highest governing body, the Board of Directors, which is made up of the elected Local Presidents from each AFA carrier. Every year the Board meets in October to confirm AFA's agenda and approve a budget for the ensuing year.

AFA experienced an adequate financial year, ending in a surplus of $32,249, and increased total members' equity, an indication of AFA's financial strength, to $2.175 million.

The deficit of 1997 continued to affect our operation throughout 1998 and into 1999. Fortunately, increased growth in revenue has helped to offset this and, barring any major unforeseen developments, we anticipate a substantial increase in equity for year end 1999.

In solidarity,
Paul G. Mac Kinnon
International Secretary-Treasurer

FINANCIAL STATEMENT AND REPORT OF INDEPENDENT AUDITORS
DECEMBER 31, 1998

Board of Directors
Association of Flight Attendants
Washington, D.C.

We have audited the accompanying balance sheets of the Association of Flight Attendants as of December 31, 1998 and 1997, and the related statements of revenue and expenses, changes in members' equity and cash flows for the years then ended. These financial statements are the responsibility of the Association's management. Our responsibility is to express an opinion on these financial statements based on our audits.

We conducted our audits in accordance with generally accepted auditing standards. Those standards require that we plan and perform the audits to obtain reasonable assurance about whether the financial statements are free of material misstatement. An audit also includes assessing the accounting principles used and significant estimates made by management, as well as evaluating the overall financial statement presentation. We believe that our audits provide a reasonable basis for our opinion.

In our opinion, the financial statements referred to above present fairly, in all material respects, the financial position of the Association of Flight Attendants as of December 31, 1998 and 1997, and the results of its operations and its cash flows for the years then ended in conformity with generally accepted accounting principles.

Squire, Lemkin & O'Brien, LLP
Rockville, Maryland 20852

March 10, 1999

SOURCE: *Flightlog*, No. 2, 1999, pp. 10–11.

EXHIBIT 4-11 (continued)

ASSOCIATION OF FLIGHT ATTENDANTS
BALANCE SHEETS

FOR THE YEARS ENDED DECEMBER 31,

ASSETS	1998	1997
CURRENT ASSETS:		
Cash and cash equivalents	$ —	$ 250,141
Member dues and other receivables, net of allowance for doubtful accounts of $136,220 in 1998 and 1997	1,716,475	1,543,653
Member and employee advances	95,197	77,993
Prepaid expenses	117,665	113,177
TOTAL CURRENT ASSETS	$ 1,929,337	$ 1,984,964
DESIGNATED CASH AND INVESTMENTS	2,145,768	2,348,542
PROPERTY AND EQUIPMENT	1,188,977	1,045,079
OTHER ASSETS	48,848	39,217
TOTAL ASSETS	$ 5,312,930	$ 5,417,802

LIABILITIES AND MEMBERS' EQUITY	1998	1997
CURRENT LIABILITIES:		
Cash overdraft	$ 296,065	$ —
Line of credit	319,395	550,000
Current portion of notes and capital lease obligations payable	49,359	162,837
Accounts payable and accrued expenses	1,555,121	1,411,834
Accrued flight pay loss	597,786	890,000
Advance payments for dues	78,166	76,176
TOTAL CURRENT LIABILITIES	$ 2,895,892	$ 3,090,847
OTHER LIABILITIES:		
Notes and capital lease obligations payable, net of current portion	185,886	141,317
Deferred revenue	56,090	42,825
TOTAL LIABILITIES	$ 3,137,868	$ 3,274,989
COMMITMENTS AND CONTINGENCIES		
MEMBERS' EQUITY:		
Undesignated	$ 29,294	$ (205,729)
Designated for union reserves	2,145,768	2,348,542
TOTAL MEMBERS' EQUITY	$ 2,175,062	$ 2,142,813
TOTAL LIABILITIES AND MEMBERS' EQUITY	$ 5,312,930	$ 5,417,802

The accompanying notes are an integral part of these financial statements.

STATEMENTS OF REVENUE AND EXPENSES

FOR THE YEARS ENDED DECEMBER 31,

	1998	1997
REVENUE:		
Member dues and service charges, net of credits and refunds of $309,620 and $286,666 in 1998 and 1997, respectively	$ 16,308,127	$ 15,263,420
Miscellaneous	68,143	5,548
TOTAL REVENUE	$ 16,376,270	$ 15,268,968
EXPENSES:		
Negotiations	$ 1,173,179	$ 1,410,810
System Board	804,833	935,745
Master Executive Council	2,247,784	2,198,879
Local Executive Council	2,498,050	2,310,970
Seminars, Meetings and Committees	339,999	372,535
Accounting and Membership	869,135	825,043
Air Safety and Health	298,241	361,477
Communications	326,660	353,228
Employee Assistance Program	149,953	140,222
Organizing	931,454	247,018
Programs and Services	617,330	428,932
Administration	2,687,075	3,140,185
Outside Legal Support	408,601	177,851
Legal Administration	2,179,863	2,173,143
Affiliations	365,637	316,106
Special Projects	184,618	278,699
Research	409,317	403,703
TOTAL EXPENSES	$ 16,491,729	$ 16,074,546
EXCESS EXPENSES OVER REVENUE BEFORE OTHER INCOME	$ (115,459)	$ (805,578)
OTHER INCOME:		
Investment income	$ 130,987	$ 152,166
Unrealized gain (loss) on investments	16,721	(2,229)
TOTAL OTHER INCOME	$ 147,708	$ 149,937
EXCESS REVENUE OVER EXPENSES (EXPENSES OVER REVENUE)	$ 32,249	$ (655,641)

The accompanying notes are an integral part of these financial statements.

STATEMENTS OF CHANGES IN MEMBERS' EQUITY

FOR THE YEARS ENDED DECEMBER 31,

	1998			1997		
	Undesignated	Designated Reserves	Total	Undesignated	Designated Reserves	Total
MEMBERS' EQUITY, BEGINNING OF YEAR	$ (205,729)	$ 2,348,542	$ 2,142,813	$ 558,516	$ 2,239,938	$ 2,798,454
Excess revenue over expenses	(77,065)	109,314	32,249	(790,373)	134,732	(655,641)
Transfers	312,088	(312,088)	—	26,128	(26,128)	—
MEMBERS' EQUITY, END OF YEAR	$ 29,294	$ 2,145,768	$ 2,175,062	$ (205,729)	$ 2,348,542	$ 2,142,813

The accompanying notes are an integral part of these financial statements.

EXHIBIT 4-11 (continued)

ASSOCIATION OF FLIGHT ATTENDANTS FINANCIAL STATEMENTS 1998

STATEMENTS OF CASH FLOWS

FOR THE YEARS ENDED DECEMBER 31,

	1998	1997
CASH FLOWS FROM OPERATING ACTIVITIES:		
Cash received from members	$ 16,218,703	$ 15,205,473
Interest received	132,392	144,679
Cash paid to members, suppliers and employees	(16,293,101)	(15,419,499)
Interest paid	(49,336)	(26,121)
NET CASH PROVIDED BY (USED IN) OPERATING ACTIVITIES	$ 8,658	$ (95,468)
CASH FLOWS FROM INVESTING ACTIVITIES:		
Net decrease (increase) in appropriated cash and investments	$ 218,090	$ (103,346)
Purchases of property and equipment	(376,529)	(382,642)
(Increase) decrease in deposits	(9,631)	6,362
Proceeds from sale of equipment	—	17,350
NET CASH USED IN INVESTING ACTIVITIES	$ (168,070)	$ (462,276)
CASH FLOWS FROM FINANCING ACTIVITIES:		
Principal payments of long-term borrowing	$ (156,189)	$ (211,904)
Net advances (repayments) on line of credit	(230,605)	550,000
NET CASH PROVIDED BY (USED IN) FINANCING ACTIVITIES	$ (386,794)	$ 338,096
NET DECREASE IN CASH AND CASH EQUIVALENTS	$ (546,206)	$ (219,648)
CASH AND CASH EQUIVALENTS, BEGINNING OF YEAR	250,141	469,789
CASH AND CASH EQUIVALENTS (CASH OVERDRAFT), END OF YEAR	$ (296,065)	$ 250,141

RECONCILIATION OF EXCESS REVENUE OVER EXPENSES TO NET CASH PROVIDED BY (USED IN) OPERATING ACTIVITIES:

	1998	1997
Excess revenue (expenses) over expenses (revenue)	$ 32,249	$ (655,641)
Reconciliation adjustments:		
Depreciation and amortization	319,911	260,245
Bad debt expense	—	15,220
Loss on sale of equipment	—	8,983
Realized and unrealized (gains) losses	(16,721)	2,229
Changes in assets and liabilities:		
Member dues and other receivables	(172,822)	(90,081)
Member and employee advances	(17,204)	(6,770)
Interest receivable	1,405	(7,487)
Prepaid expenses and inventory	(4,488)	57,610
Accounts payable and accrued expenses	143,287	271,877
Accrued flight pay loss	(292,214)	16,213
Advance payments for dues	1,990	(10,691)
Deferred revenue	13,265	42,825
NET CASH PROVIDED BY (USED IN) OPERATING ACTIVITIES	$ 8,658	$ (95,468)

The accompanying notes are an integral part of these financial statements.

NOTES TO FINANCIAL STATEMENTS

FOR THE YEARS ENDED DECEMBER 31, 1998 and 1997

Note 1. Summary of Significant Accounting Policies

Organization and Other Matters—The Association of Flight Attendants (the Association) is a labor union representing the flight attendants of a number of commercial airline companies in the collective bargaining process to enhance working conditions, rates of pay and employee benefits. The Association also actively works to secure additional federal safety regulations for the airline industry and provides legal representation for Title VII class action suits for its members. The Association is a member of the AFL-CIO.

The Association is a not-for-profit organization, which qualifies as a tax-exempt organization under Section 501(c)(5) of the Internal Revenue Code.

Cash and Cash Equivalents—For purposes of the statements of cash flows, the Association considers highly liquid debt instruments purchased with a maturity of three months or less to be cash equivalents except for those amounts that have been set aside to fund the designated equity, as disclosed in Note 2.

Investments—Marketable securities are shown at aggregate market value.

Property and Equipment—Furniture and equipment is stated at cost. Equipment under capital leases is stated at fair value at the date of acquisition. The Association provides for depreciation of furniture and equipment using the straight-line method over estimated lives of three to ten years. Equipment under capital leases and leasehold improvements are amortized over the lives of the respective leases.

Member Dues and Service Charges—Member dues revenue consists of dues withheld from the members' wages (direct check off) and subsequently remitted to the Association by the employer, and of billings made by the Association to individual flight attendants not using direct check off. Service charges paid by nonmembers covered under Association representation are handled in the same way as dues. The allowance for doubtful accounts represents that amount of individual dues billings which, based on historical data, is estimated to be uncollectible.

The Association uses the accrual method of accounting under which revenue is recognized as earned and expenses are recognized as incurred. Revenue from member dues and service charges is recorded as being earned over the period of membership. Annual dues received in advance of the membership year are deferred and recognized as revenue in the year to which they apply.

Flight Pay Loss—The Association reimburses members for pay lost while engaged in union business and therefore absent from their regular jobs. Flight pay loss is either paid to members or reimbursed to members' employers for wages paid by the employers. Vacation time dedicated to performing union business also is reimbursed by the Association.

Note 2. Designated Funds—The Board of Directors has designated members' equity in the minimum amount of $1,000,000 to provide a financial base for the Association.

Under the Board's minimum reserve policy, the cash funds and accumulated earnings thereon are required to be invested in treasury bonds and high-grade corporate or municipal bonds or equities, bank certificates of deposit and government-insured mortgage loans, in accordance with investment liquidity requirements stated in the constitution and bylaws. The following summarizes the aggregate cost and market value of the investments at December 31:

	1998	
	Cost	Market Value
Commercial money market accounts	$ 19,509	$ 19,509
U.S. Agency and Corporate obligations	1,983,949	1,981,730
ULLICO, Inc.	100,000	114,800
Interest receivable	29,729	29,729
Totals	$ 2,133,187	$ 2,145,768

	1997	
	Cost	Market Value
Commercial money market accounts	$ 316,362	$ 316,362
U.S. Agency and Corporate obligations	1,905,187	1,892,806
ULLICO, Inc.	100,000	108,240
Interest receivable	31,134	31,134
Totals	$ 2,352,683	$ 2,348,542

Note 3. Concentration of Credit Risk—Financial instruments which potentially subject the Association to concentration of credit risk include cash deposits with commercial banks. The Association's cash management policies limit its exposure to concentrations of credit risk by maintaining cash accounts at financial institutions whose deposits are insured by the Federal Deposit Insurance Corporation (FDIC). Cash deposits could exceed the FDIC insurable limit of $100,000 during various times throughout the year. However, through its commercial bank, the Association systematically invests excess funds in overnight repurchase agreements collaterized by U.S. Government Obligations, thereby minimizing its exposure.

Note 4. Property and Equipment—As of December 31, 1998 and 1997, property and equipment consisted of the following:

	1998	1997
Furniture and equipment	$ 2,118,397	$ 1,846,943
Equipment under capital leases	548,012	541,836
Software	274,987	165,237
Leasehold improvements	72,127	68,523
Totals	$ 3,013,523	$ 2,622,539
Less, Accumulated depreciation and amortization	1,824,546	1,577,460
Property and equipment, net	$ 1,188,977	$ 1,045,079

EXHIBIT 4-11 (continued)

Depreciation and amortization expense for the years ended December 31, 1998 and 1997 was $319,911 and $260,245, respectively.

Noncash investing and financing activities, which are not disclosed in the statements of cash flows for the year ended December 31, 1997, include the purchase of telephone equipment valued at $138,259 under a capital lease. For the year ended December 31, 1998, noncash investing and financing activities included the purchase of copiers valued at $122,000 under capital leases. Equipment was traded in on the leased equipment with a book value of $24,275 and an outstanding lease obligation of $32,720 at the date of the trade in.

Note 5. Notes and Capital Lease Obligations Payable—As of December 31, 1998 and 1997, the Association was obligated under the following notes and capital leases:

	1998	1997
Capital leases for equipment acquisition with monthly payments aggregating $5,883, ($7,801 in 1997) including interest at 5% to 14%, secured by equipment with a net book value of $247,184, expiring 2003	$ 235,245	$ 217,433
Note payable—payable $5,714 per month including interest at 5%, expiring November 1998, unsecured	—	66,721
Note payable - payable $10,000 per annum due semi-annually plus interest at 7%, expiring November 1998, unsecured	—	20,000
Totals	$ 235,245	$ 304,154
Less, Current portion	49,359	162,837
Long-term portion	$ 185,886	$ 141,317

Future obligations under the notes and capital lease obligations are as follows:

	Capital Leases
1999	$ 68,810
2000	59,885
2001	59,885
2002	59,885
2003	40,449
Totals	$ 288,914
Amount of lease payments representing interest	53,669
Totals	$ 235,245

As of December 31, 1998, the Association had available two lines of credit for $650,000. One line bears interest at the Libo Rate plus 1.0% and the other bears interest at a rate equal to the three month London Interbank offered rate plus 75 basis points. The lines of credit are secured by the accounts receivable. At December 31, 1998, $115,108 and $204,287 were outstanding on the lines of credit, respectively.

The Association maintained a line of credit for the year ended December 31, 1997 in the amount of $650,000. The line bore interest at the Libo Rate plus 1%. The outstanding balance was $550,000 at December 31, 1997.

Interest expense for the years ended December 31, 1998 and 1997 was $49,336 and $26,121, respectively.

Note 6. Commitments and Contingencies—The Association entered into an eleven year lease dated November 11, 1996 for office space for its Washington, DC headquarters. The lease term began July 1, 1997, and monthly payments under the lease are $39,217 for the first five years of the lease and $42,293 thereafter. The accompanying financial statements include a lease security deposit of $39,217. The base rent is subject to adjustment for 30 percent of increases in the CPI (up to 2 percent) and for pass throughs of a ratable share of increases in operating expenses and real estate taxes. The landlord provided a build out allowance up to $645,925.

The lease provides for one renewal option for five years. Monthly rental under the renewal option will be set at the prevailing market rate for comparable office space at that time.

In addition, the Association is committed under various field office leases. The lease terms range from three to seven years. The leases call for aggregate monthly rental of $15,511. Certain of the leases base rents are subject to increases in the CPI and for pass throughs of a ratable share of increases in operating expenses and real estate taxes. The future minimum lease payments due under these leases are included in the schedule below. The Association is committed under certain other facility leases on a month-to-month basis with no specific expiration dates.

Minimum future lease payments under this lease are as follows:

	Field Offices	Headquaters	Total
1999	$ 176,049	$ 470,603	$ 646,652
2000	179,969	470,603	650,572
2001	151,831	470,603	622,434
2002	144,251	489,058	633,309
2003	147,135	507,513	654,648
Thereafter	24,603	2,283,804	2,308,407
Totals	$ 823,838	$ 4,692,184	$ 5,516,022

Rent expense for the years ended December 31, 1998 and 1997 was $836,328 and $689,195, respectively.

In addition, the Association is committed under various operating leases for equipment. The lease terms range from two to five years. The minimum future lease payments under these leases are as follows:

1999	$ 16,726
2000	15,658
2001	12,696
2002	10,455
2003	1,482
Total	$ 57,017

The Association is party to an agreement with the AFL-CIO under which the Association has granted a license to the AFL-CIO, which has in turn sub-licensed Household Bank (Nevada) N.A. (Household) to use the Association's name, trademarks, and membership mailing lists in connection with Household's financial services programs. The accompanying financial statements include approximately $26,190 and $14,335 of royalties representing amounts earned during 1998 and 1997, respectively. Payment of royalties under so called "affinity card" programs has been the subject of litigation between the Internal Revenue Service and certain not-for-profit organizations engaged in such programs. Insofar as the taxability of income earned under such arrangements has not been conclusively determined by the courts, the accompanying financial statements include no provision for income taxes which could ultimately be payable on this income.

The Association serves in a variety of functions with respect to retirement and employee benefit plans maintained by the employer airlines. The fiduciary responsibilities held by the Association range from those of Plan Administrator for one plan to joint board member with employer airlines on several other plans. The Association maintains liability insurance with respect to its responsibilities in these capacities.

The Association is party to various claims and legal actions arising in the ordinary course of business. In the opinion of legal counsel, no significant adverse financial impact on the Association is anticipated.

Note 7. Retirement Plan—The Association maintains a Cash or Deferred Profit Sharing Plan (the Plan) qualifying under Section 401(k) of the Internal Revenue Code. Under the terms of the Plan, which covers substantially all employees, eligible employees may elect to defer a portion of their compensation which is then contributed to the Plan. The Association, pursuant to a Letter of Agreement with the Union of Staff Employees, is required to make a matching contribution of each employee's deferral contribution and has the discretion to make a contribution of a percentage of the salary of all eligible employees.

Retirement plan expense related to this Plan for 1998 and 1997 was $300,708 and $274,968, respectively.

Note 8. Dues/Service Charge Obligations—The Association has established procedures in order to comply with the U.S. Supreme Court rulings in Ellis v. Brotherhood of Railway, Airline and Steamship Clerks and Chicago Teachers Union, Local No. 1 v. Hudson. The rulings require that a union set aside and return a portion of the service charges paid to the union by individuals who object to the use of their payments for activities which are not directly related to collective bargaining, contract administration, grievances or representative functions ("arguably unrelated activities"). In accordance with the Association's procedures, a separate interest-bearing escrow account has been established, into which has been placed a percentage of objectors' service charges reflecting the percentage of the Association's expenditures for arguably unrelated activities. The balance in that account as of December 31, 1998 and 1997 was $3,442 and $3,442, respectively.

During 1998, the Association participated in an arbitration hearing, which affirmed the Association's determination that 7.2% of its 1997 expenditures were for arguably unrelated activities. The percentage of expenditures in 1998 for arguably unrelated activities has not been calculated as of the date of this report.

Note 9. Post-retirement Benefits—The Association sponsors a defined benefit post-retirement health care plan that covers personnel meeting the eligibility requirements. Those requirements are, (1) coverage under the Association's health care plan at retirement, (2) 15 or more years of service and (3) attainment of age 55. The post-retirement health care plan is noncontributory. The Association will pay one half of the cost of group health insurance for three years after retirement of eligible personnel.

The following sets forth the plan's funded status reconciled with the amount included in the Association's balance sheet at December 31, 1998:

Approximate present value of estimated accumulated post-retirement benefit obligation	$ 530,830
Plan assets	—
Accumulated post-retirement benefit obligation in excess of plan assets	$ 530,830
Unrecognized transition obligation	424,664
Accrued post-retirement benefit cost	$ 106,166

For measurement purposes, a 12 percent annual rate of increase in the per capita cost of covered health care benefits was assumed for 1998 and thereafter. The health care cost trend rate assumption has a significant effect on the amounts reported. A discount rate of 6 percent was used in determining the present value of the accumulated post-retirement benefit obligation. The estimated accumulated post-retirement benefit obligation is being amortized against earnings over twenty years.

A substantial majority of union members now pays dues that come out to roughly two hours' wages per month, and two major unions—the Steelworkers and the Automobile Workers—have in fact officially set their monthly dues figures at exactly this two-hour level, thereby building automatic increases into the dues structure. Initiation fees—by definition, a one-shot affair—tend to be in the $50 to $100 range, with only a small handful of unionists (primarily in the building trades, airline pilot profession, and similarly highly remunerated groupings) being charged more than $200 in such fees by their labor organizations.

In light of all that has been said about the functions of unions, the amount of money the typical member pays is thus comparatively small. Nonetheless, like everyone else, the union member desires maximum and ever-improving services for the least cost possible. In particular, union leadership must be very careful when it seeks to raise the monthly dues. Even a modest increase of a dollar per month could cause an upheaval among the membership. With increasing expenses and sometimes declining memberships, unions *must* at times raise dues if they desire to maintain the same level of services for their membership, but this is a step normally taken only as an extreme last resort. Unions have often laid off staff representatives and otherwise tried to curb expenses drastically before requesting even a modest dues increase.

SOME CONCLUDING THOUGHTS

The American labor movement is vast and complicated, but its elements fit together in a systematic fashion and provide the framework for the carrying out of the basic functions and objectives. In a day of increasing union dependence upon the sentiments of the general public, particularly as these sentiments are translated into legislative actions, the objectives have increasingly encompassed social and community activities that clearly extend well beyond labor's traditional campaigns for improved "property rights" on the job itself. These more broadly based endeavors can in no way be expected to diminish in the years ahead, for the advantages for the labor movement that can potentially be derived from them are certain to continue.

Yet this newer emphasis should not obscure either the pronounced strain of "bread-and-butter" unionism that has marked organized labor throughout its history or the internal union political considerations that continue to generate this more basic behavior. If unions are, by and large, not fully democratic, they are nonetheless highly political in nature. The union leader must above all be conscious of the general wishes of the constituents. And these wishes, particularly at the lower levels of the union structure where the collective bargaining process itself takes place, continue to be closely related to wages, hours, and conditions.

Just as internal political considerations have dictated national union autonomy within the AFL-CIO, so too have such considerations led to the complete responsiveness of virtually all national union executives to at least the most pressing desires of local unionists, and to such commonly observed phenomena as the high turnover rates of local officers themselves.

It has often been said that a union "is a political animal operating in an economic framework." The story of a union that a while ago sent its hospitalized management adversary a basket of fruit with a card stating that the "members of Local 25 wish you a speedy recovery by a vote of 917 to 648" may or may not be fictitious: Corroboration is now impossible. But unions are by any standard highly "political." And no one who loses sight of this most fundamental labor relations factor can truly appreciate union behavior. Union members do have the ultimate control of their labor organizations—however much in practice union *leadership* has been the catalyst of the programs of the union—and the leadership can never ignore this fact of life.

DISCUSSION QUESTIONS

1. J. B. S. Hardman once described labor organizations as being "part army and part debating society." What considerations on his part might have led to this description?

2. It has been argued in many nonlabor quarters that it is socially undesirable for unions to take the initiative in organizational campaigns and that the public interest is served only when unorganized workers initially seek out the union. Is there anything to be said for this point of view? Against it?

3. "There are both advantages and disadvantages to AFL-CIO affiliation for national unions." Comment.

4. "The increasing sophistication and enlightenment of modern top business executives in dealing with their subordinates has led to a state of affairs wherein managements today are more democratic than unions." Do you agree? Why or why not?

5. "Unions are no less private institutions than country clubs or Masonic lodges, and as such should be no more subject to government regulation of their internal affairs than these other organizations." The present thrust of the laws notwithstanding, is there any validity to this argument?

6. Albert Rees has pointed out that it is "paradoxically true that the presence of strong unions may improve the operation of democratic processes in the general national or state government even if the internal political processes of the union are undemocratic." Explain this paradox.

7. Daniel Bell, the former labor editor of *Fortune* magazine, once commented that in taking over certain power from management, "the union also takes over the difficult function of specifying the priorities of demands—and in so doing, it not only relieves management of many political headaches but becomes a buffer between management and rank-and-file resentments." Is there any justification for such a comment?

MINICASES

 #1 The Independent International

The Space Workers International Union withdrew voluntarily from the AFL-CIO in 1978, ostensibly because of a difference in organizing philosophy with the leadership of the federation at that time but actually because of personality differences between the Space Workers' president in those days and the then AFL-CIO president, the late George Meany. Its present officers have recently been assured, through informal overtures made to them by federation officials, that the international's return would be very much welcomed.

The Space Workers' current president, Homer T. Molloy, and a definite majority of the international's 24-member executive board see no particular advantage in reaffiliating and are, therefore, inclined to let the union remain independent. But the board does vote unanimously to allow its popular First Vice President George C. Adams, who strongly favors a return to the federation, speak in defense of his position at its next meeting (scheduled for one month from now). In private conversation, however, Molloy warns Adams that "you don't stand a prayer, George, unless you can come up with some new arguments for reaffiliation: We've heard all the old ones."

What case, if you were Adams, would you build at the board meeting?

 ## Qualifications for Union Office

In a 1977 decision* involving the United Steelworkers of America, the U.S. Supreme Court by a split vote upset a union rule requiring candidates for local union office to have attended at least one-half of a local's regular meetings for the three years preceding the election. Under the union's rule, 96.5 percent of the members of the local were disqualified from union office. In its decision, the high court stressed that national labor legislation (and specifically the Landrum-Griffin Act of 1959) was designed to promote union democracy without interfering unduly with union internal affairs. It said:

> Applying these principles to this case, we conclude that . . . the anti-democratic effects of the meeting attendance rule outweighs the interests urged in its support. . . . An attendance requirement that results in the exclusion of 96.5 percent of the members from candidacy for union office hardly seems to be a "reasonable qualification" (as required by Landrum-Griffin) consistent with the goal of free and democratic elections. A requirement having that result obviously severely restricts the free choice of the membership in selecting their leaders.

The minority of the Court believed the attendance rule to be a reasonable qualification. It criticized the majority for using a statistical test. The rule was reasonable, it said, because it could encourage attendance at meetings, guarantee that candidates for office had a meaningful interest in the union, and assure that the candidates had a chance to become informed about union affairs.

Do you agree with the majority or the minority here, and, in either case, why?

*Local 3489, United Steelworkers v. Usery, 429 U.S. 305 (1977).

NOTES

[1] A number of such "independents" nonetheless belong to the AFL-CIO as federal locals.

[2] *Washington Post*, October 14, 1973, p. C1.

[3] A slight irony is the fact that Reagan was the first U.S. chief executive who was at one time a union president. He was head of the Screen Actors Guild from 1947 to 1952 and again in 1959.

[4] *The New York Times*, September 11, 1999, p. A9.

[5] *The New York Times*, October 13, 1999, p. A19.

[6] *Business Week*, February 13, 1995, p. 44.

[7] *The New York Times*, October 11, 1999, p. C1.

[8] A major exception to all these remarks involves craft unions in local product market industries; here, local business agents are normally elected to perform such duties.

[9] In this regard, it should also be appreciated that striking workers usually have income sources beyond the aid that they might receive from their own or other unions. Some get welfare payments. Some have working spouses, or they themselves can rather easily find full-time or part-time jobs. In two states—New York and Rhode Island—strikers are eligible for unemployment compensation. And, although credit can hardly be called an income source, the fact that this is the age of widespread charge accounts must also be placed into the equation.

[10]*The New York Times*, January 7, 1982, p. A18.
[11]*Wall Street Journal*, March 24, 1992, p. A16.
[12]*Business Week*, April 19, 1999, p. 72.
[13]*Wall Street Journal*, October 29, 1999, p. B1.
[14]Wilfrid Sheed, "What Ever Happened to the Labor Movement?" *Atlantic*, July 1973, p. 62. Abel was president of the union until June 1977, when he retired.
[15]*The New York Times*, March 14, 1999, p. WR5.
[16]Karen S. Koziara, Mary I. Bradley, and David A. Pierson, "Becoming a Union Leader: The Path to Local Office," *Monthly Labor Review*, February 1982, p. 46.

SELECTED REFERENCES

Barling, Julian, Clive Fullagar, and E. Kevin Kelloway. *The Union and Its Members*. New York and Oxford: Oxford University Press, 1992.

Bronfenbrenner, Kate, Sheldon Friedman, Richard W. Hurd, Rudolph A. Oswald, and Ronald L. Seeber, eds. *Organizing to Win: New Research on Union Strategies*. Ithaca, NY: ILR Press, Cornell University, 1998.

Bullush, Jewel, and Bernard Bullush. *Union Power in New York*. New York: Praeger, 1984.

Chaison, Gary N. *Union Mergers in Hard Times*. Ithaca, NY: ILR Press, Cornell University, 1996.

Crowe, Kenneth C. *Collision: How the Rank and File Took Back the Teamsters*. New York: Charles Scribner's Sons, 1993.

Daniels, Gene, Roberta Till-Retz, Larry Casey, and Tony DeAngelis. *Labor Guide to Local Union Leadership*. Englewood Cliffs, NJ: Prentice Hall, 1986.

Dubofsky, Melvyn, and Warren Van Tine, eds. *Labor Leaders in America*. Urbana and Chicago: University of Illinois Press, 1987.

Dunlop, John T. *The Management of Labor Unions: Decision Making with Historical Constraints*. Lexington, MA: Lexington Books, 1990.

Form, William. *Segmented Labor, Fractured Politics: Labor Politics in American Life*. New York: Plenum, 1995.

Ginzberg, Eli. *The Labor Leader*. New York: Macmillan, 1948.

Heldman, Dan C. and Deborah L. Knight. *Unions and Lobbying: the Representation Function*. Arlington, VA: Foundation for the Advancement of the Public Trust, 1980.

Hutchinson, John. *The Imperfect Union: A History of Corruption in American Trade Unions*. New York: Dutton, 1972.

La Botz, Dan. *Rank-and-File Rebellion*. New York: Verso, 1990.

Mangum, Garth, and John Walsh. *Union Resilience in Troubled Times*. Armonk, NY: M. E. Sharpe, 1994.

Quaglieri, Philip L. *America's Labor Leaders*. Lexington, MA: Lexington Books, 1989.

Shostak, Arthur B., ed. *For Labor's Sake: Gains and Pains as Told by 28 Creative Inside Reformers*. Lanham, MD: University Press of America, 1995.

Wallihan, Jim. *Union Government and Organization*. Washington, DC: Bureau of National Affairs, 1985.

PART III Collective Bargaining

CHAPTER 5

At the Bargaining Table

179

*H*owever much specific unions may differ, virtually all of them share at least the same primary objective. Whatever in the way of concrete demands may be sought from the employer, the union's major goal is to negotiate with the employer a written agreement covering both employment conditions and the union–management relationship itself on terms that are acceptable to the union. But the employer, too, must be able to live with these terms, and it is because of this second requirement that the 50,000 labor negotiations that take place every year in the United States almost unavoidably contain stresses and strains; more for one party—not only in the economic areas of the contract but, as will be seen, in many of the so-called institutional and administrative areas—all but invariably means less for the other. Moreover, the labor–management tensions are *recurrent* in their nature because contracts are regularly renegotiated—most commonly, today, every three or four years. No contractual issue can thus ever be said to have been permanently resolved.

There is always a certain glamour to any interorganizational bargaining situation, particularly when such conflicts as those just mentioned can be anticipated. Labor–management negotiations constitute no exception to this rule, and the process of arriving at a labor relations agreement has actually been viewed in a number of colorful ways.

The process has been depicted as (1) a poker game, with the largest pots going to those who combine deception, bluff, and luck, or the ability to come up with a strong hand on the occasions on which they are challenged or "seen" by the other side; (2) an exercise in power politics, with the relative strengths of the parties being decisive; and (3) a debating society, marked by both rhetoric and name calling. What is done at the union–management bargaining table has also been caricatured in a somewhat less dramatic way—as (4) a "rational process," with both sides remaining completely flexible and willing to be persuaded only when all the facts have been dispassionately presented.[1]

All these characteristics have marked most negotiations over a period of time. The increasing "maturity" of collective bargaining implies enlargement of the rational process, but it is doubtful that there can ever be such a thing as complete escape from the other elements.

And a number of additional factors will also, almost inevitably, have a bearing upon the conduct of the negotiations. Items such as the personalities and training of the negotiators, the history of labor relations between the union and management, and the economic environment operate to influence what happens at the bargaining table.

Some negotiators try to bluff or outsmart the other side; others would never even think of employing such tactics. Some employer or union representatives try to dictate a labor contract on a unilateral basis—"take it or else"—but most bargainers recognize that such an approach is ultimately self-defeating. In most instances, unions presenting their original proposals will demand much more than they actually intend to get, and managements' first counterproposals are usually much lower than the employers are actually prepared to offer. In other situations, however, managements and unions do not engage in these practices to any appreciable extent, and original proposals and counterproposals are relatively realistic. Representatives of employers and labor organizations differ in education, experience, and labor relations philosophy.

There are still other sources of variation. In some negotiations, the predominant feature might be union factionalism; in others, disagreement between management officials concerning objectives and policies. The history of labor relations in one situation might reveal that each side has had implicit faith in the other. In other negotiations, because of past experience, the bargaining might be conducted in a climate of mutual distrust, suspicion, and even hatred. Certainly, if the objective of the parties is to find a solution to their mutual problems on the basis of rationality and fairness, the negotiations will be conducted in an atmosphere quite different from one in which the fundamental objective of the union is to "put management in its place" or in which the chief objective of the employer is to weaken or even destroy the union.

Two other preliminary remarks are in order. First, because so many variables do have a bearing on the negotiations, a portion of the following discussion highlights some procedural practices that might help to minimize the possibility of strikes, and to promote better labor relations. Nonetheless, if labor relations have been harmonious in the past, and if negotiations have been conducted with a minimum of discord, there is little reason to change procedures. "Let sleeping dogs lie" is a sound principle of collective bargaining negotiations.

Second, there has been a marked change in the general atmosphere of negotiations in relatively recent years. Thirty-five years ago, bargaining sessions frequently involved a tussle between table pounding, uninformed, and generally ill-equipped people. The side that came out better was often the one whose representatives shouted more loudly or that could use overt power threats more effectively. Each side's taking the adamant position of "take it or else" was frequently a foregone conclusion, and deceit was anything but unknown at the table.

At present, however, collective bargaining is most commonly an orderly process in which employee, employer, and union problems are discussed relatively rationally and settled more or less on the basis of facts. There is less and less place in bargaining sessions for emotionalism and name calling. Nor do many negotiators use trickery, distortion, misrepresentation, or deceit. Advantages gained through such devices are temporary, and the side that sinks to such low levels of behavior can expect the same from the other party. Certainly, one objective of collective bargaining sessions should be the promotion of rational and harmonious relations between employers and unions. To achieve this, those to whom negotiations are entrusted should have the traits of patience, friendliness, integrity, and fairness. If each party recognizes the possibility that it may be mistaken and the other side right, a long stride will have been taken.

PREPARATION FOR NEGOTIATIONS

By far the major prerequisite for modern collective bargaining sessions is preparation for the negotiations. Both sides normally start to prepare for the bargaining table long before the current contract is scheduled to expire, and in recent years the time allotted for such planning has steadily lengthened. A year or even 18 months for this purpose has become increasingly observable in both union and management quarters.

❖ The Growing Complexities of Contracts

The now general recognition of the need for greater preparation time rests on the previously cited fact that contents of the typical labor agreement have undergone a major transformation in the comparatively recent past. In recognizing and attempting to accommodate new goals of the parties, contracts have steadily become more complex in the issues they treat. Exhibit 5-1, the table of contents for a recently bargained agreement between the United Food and Commercial Workers and the General Foods Corporation, indicates the wide range of topics now dealt with by the typical contract. Exhibit 5-2, the index to the present contract between the National Association of Flight Standards Employees and the U.S. Department of Transportation, shows a few unique issues as well as a far larger number of now standard ones. And note the variety of complicated topics cited even in Exhibit 5-3's brief summary of the 1995 bargaining between the Screen Actors Guild and the American Federation of Television and Radio Artists, negotiating jointly, and the Alliance of Motion Picture and Television Producers.

Take, for example, wage clauses—which have appeared in essentially all contracts since the days of the earliest unions. Today they make anything but easy reading. Where such clauses once noted little more than the schedule of wages (generally the same for all workers within extremely broad occupational categories) and the

EXHIBIT 5-1 **Table of Contents from a Recently Negotiated Bargaining Agreement between the United Food and Commercial Workers and the General Foods Corporation.**

TABLE OF CONTENTS

TABLE OF CONTENTS

EXHIBIT 5-2   Index to the Present Contract between the National Association of Flight Standards Employees and the U.S. Department of Transportation

EXHIBIT 5-3

SAG/AFTRA BOARDS APPROVE TENTATIVE FILM-TV AGREEMENT

The combined SAG/AFTRA Board of Directors approved the new Theatrical and Television pact on May 9, and the new contract will be sent to union members in the next few weeks for ratification.

After a marathon 25-hour bargaining session in Los Angeles, the Screen Actors Guild and the American Federation of Television and Radio Artists reached a tentative agreement on March 24, with the Alliance of Motion Picture and Television Producers, and on May 5 with the networks for a new three-year contract for theatrical and television film performers. These early talks started February 7. They were initiated well in advance of the contract's expiration to help insure a smooth flow of production without any interruption.

After some hard bargaining, the unions, the AMPTP and the networks reached an agreement that covers virtually all film and primetime TV production. Performers will receive a 10.9% increase in minimum wages compounded over three years, and a .5% increase in employer contributions to the unions' pension and health plans. The new contract also provides improved affirmative action language covering disabilities. SAG/AFTRA negotiators were also able to address an issue of preeminent concern: new networks. The agreement will generate increases in original employment for guest stars who appear on emerging networks. Residuals at Fox have also seen a significant increase.

Despite management's attempts to erode hard-fought gains for extra performers, SAG and AFTRA won substantial pay increases for all Background Performers & Stand-Ins, which will bring the West Coast general extra daily rate to $86.00 by the third year of the contract – representing a 32 percent increase.

The new tentative agreement must now be submitted to the full memberships of both unions for a referendum vote, prior to the old contract's expiration date of June 30.

SAG National Executive Director Ken Orsatti (right) reaches a tentative agreement with AMPTP head Nicholas Counter after a marathon bargaining session in Los Angeles.

PHOTO BY JORDAN DERWIN

SOURCE: *Call Sheet*, Summer 1995.

hours to be worked for those wages, in recent years they have become far lengthier and considerably more complicated. Today subsections relating to labor-grade job classifications, rate ranges, pay steps within labor grades, differentials for undesirable types of work, pay guarantees for employees who are asked to report to work when no work is available for them, and a host of other subjects are commonplace in contracts. And most of these subsections spell out their methods of operation in detail.

Nor can the question of hours any longer be disposed of cavalierly. The extension of premium pay for work on undesirable shifts, holidays, Saturdays, and Sundays has increased the room for further bargaining. In addition, the contract must resolve the question of remuneration for hours worked in excess of a "standard" day or week: All nonexempt workers in interstate commerce today receive, by law, time-and-one-half pay after 40 hours in a single week, but an increasing number of contracts have more liberal arrangements from the worker's viewpoint. And having opened these issues to the bargaining process, the parties must now anticipate a whole Pandora's box of further related issues: Do workers qualify for the Sunday premium when they have not previously worked the full weekly schedule? Where employees are normally required for continuous operations or are otherwise regularly needed for weekend work (firefighters, maintenance workers, and security guards in certain operations, for example), can they collect overtime for work beyond the standard week? The bargainers on both the labor and the management side must prepare their answers, and their defenses of these answers, to such questions and many similar ones; all may reasonably be expected to arise during the actual bargaining. And this necessity for anticipation is no less true merely because a previous contract has dealt with these matters, for each party can count on the other's lodging requests for *modifications* of the old terms in the negotiations.

The same can be said concerning the wide range of employee benefits, from paid vacations to pension plans, which have increased dramatically over the past two decades. This benefit list promises to become even lengthier. Job insecurity in an age of rampant competition and changing market demands should lead to increased income-security devices. Collectively bargained profit-sharing plans have received some recent impetus as either partial or total substitutes for wage increases at such companies as General Motors, Ford, DaimlerChrysler, Uniroyal, and Navistar and may now—after years of achieving only a foothold in industry—realistically be expected to spread. But it is even more likely that the continuous liberalization in the existing benefits, and the attendant costs and administrative complexities involved in all of them that have marked the history of each since its original negotiation, will continue. No one is more aware of this fact than the experienced labor relations negotiator.

Finally, increasingly thorny problems have arisen at the bargaining table regarding the so-called administrative clauses of the contract. These provisions deal with such issues as seniority rights, discipline, rest periods, work-crew and workload sizes, the subcontracting of work, and a host of similar subjects that vary in importance with the specific industry. All these topics involve, directly or indirectly, employment opportunities; and, therefore, treatment of them has become ever more complicated in a competitive industrial world that pits a management drive for greater efficiency and flexibility against a commensurately accelerated union search for increased job security.

Fuller discussion of all these areas is reserved for Chapters 7 through 10. Even the cursory treatment offered here, however, offers ample evidence that bargaining the "typical" contract necessitates far more sophistication than in an earlier, less technical age. Labor agreements can no longer be reduced to the backs of envelopes, and ever more specialized subjects confront labor negotiators. Accordingly, the need for thorough and professional preparation well in advance of the bargaining is no longer seriously questioned by any alert union or management.

❖ Sources of Information

In today's increasingly data-conscious society, much general information can aid the parties in their advance planning. The U.S. Department of Labor's Bureau of Labor Statistics is a prolific issuer of information relating to wage, employee benefit, and administrative clause practices—and not only on a national basis but for many specific regions, industries, and cities. Many employer groups stand ready to furnish managers with current and past labor contracts involving the same union with which they will be bargaining, as well as other relevant knowledge. International unions perform the same kind of function for their local unions and other subsidiary units where the bargaining will be on a subinternational basis. (Exhibit 5-4 from the Newspaper Guild's major publication illustrates some of that union's handiwork in this regard, and Exhibit 5-5 shows the wide range of activities embraced by the Research Department of the Association of Flight Attendants.) And for both parties

EXHIBIT 5-4

Copy desk rates top reporters in 59 contracts

MINIMUM WEEKLY pay rates for experienced copy editors as of June 1, 1994, were higher than those for experienced reporters under terms of 59 of more than 120 Guild contracts at daily and Sunday papers in the United States, Canada and Puerto Rico, according to a list compiled by TNG's Collective Bargaining Department.

The differentials ranged from $3 to $88.27 a week.

Under 17 of the contracts, less experience was required for the copy editor top minimum than for the reporter top. Under four of the contracts, more experience was required for the copy editor top. Under six of the contracts, the higher copy editor minimum was a "flat" rate, not based on experience in the job.

Under two contracts not on the list—Philadelphia and Vancouver—top minimums for reporters and copy editors are the same but less experience was required to reach the copy editor top.

The list does not reflect deferred increases or raises from settlements concluded since June 1, 1994. Rates from contracts in Canada are stated in Canadian dollars; the others in U.S. dollars.

	Weekly Top Minimums				Weekly Top Minimums		
	Copy editor-After	Reporter-After	Differential		Copy editor-After	Reporter-After	Differential
Albany, N.Y., Times-Union	$ 683.22—4 yrs.	$ 678.22—4 yrs.	$5.00	Ottawa Citizen	1,057.95—2 yrs.	991.16—5 yrs.	48.59
Allentown, Pa., Call	745.01—4 yrs.	727.13—4 yrs.	17.88	Pawtucket, R.I., Times*	615.90—1 yr.	610.00—4 yrs.	5.90
Baltimore Sun, Evening Sun (2)	946.00—6 yrs.	916.00—5 yrs.	30.00	Pittsburgh Post-Gazette	912.00—3 yrs.	898.00—5 yrs.	14.00
Battle Creek, Mich., Enquirer*	349.00—5 yrs	346.00—5 yrs.	3.00	Portland, Me., Press Herald*	674.00—3 yrs.	666.60—4 yrs.	7.40
Boston Herald	801.50—2 yrs.	791.63—4 yrs.	9.87	Pottstown, Pa., Mercury	765.32—flat	701.05—5 yrs.	64.27
Brantford, Ont., Expositor	853.31—2 yrs.	817.95—4 yrs.	35.36	Providence Journal-Bulletin	851.70—4 yrs.	835.19—4 yrs.	16.51
Brockton, Mass., Enterprise*	644.52—1 yr.	609.27—4 yrs.	35.25	Salem, Mass., News	629.56—5 yrs.	610.61—4 yrs.	18.95
Buffalo News	893.08—5 yrs.	883.42—5 yrs.	9.66	San Diego Union-Tribune*	859.01—6 yrs.	832.76—6 yrs.	26.25
Chicago, Sun-Times	988.36—5 yrs.	955.90—5 yrs.	32.46	San Francisco Chronicle, Examiner (2)	919.94—6 yrs.	887.44—6 yrs.	32.50
Denver Post	753.00—5 yrs.	738.00—5 yrs.	15.00	San Jose Mercury-News	904.94—6 yrs.	887.44—6 yrs.	17.50
Denver Rocky Mountain News	880.00—5 yrs.	873.00—5 yrs.	7.00	Scranton, Pa., Times, Tribune (2)	691.59—3 yrs.	677.09—3 yrs.	14.50
Detroit News	761.54—4 yrs.	750.54—4 yrs.	11.00	Seattle Post-Intelligencer	779.68—flat	773.67—4 yrs.	6.01
Eugene, Ore., Register Guard	815.70—6 yrs.	799.81—5 yrs.	15.89	Seattle Times	779.28—5 yrs.	773.69—5 yrs.	5.59
Fall River, Mass., Herald-News	698.45—1 yr.	683.71—4 yrs.	14.74	Sheboygan, Wis., Press	664.65—2 yrs.	646.39—5 yrs.	18.26
Hamilton, Ont., Spectator	973.00—4 yrs.	935.00—4 yrs.	38.00	Sioux City, Iowa, Journal	561.82—5 yrs.	541.64—4 yrs.	20.18
Harrisburg, Pa., Patriot, News (2)	653.75—4 yrs.	623.75—4 yrs.	30.00	St. Louis Post-Dispatch	946.26—5 yrs.	933.76—5 yrs.	12.50
Jersey City Jersey Journal*	681.19—flat	650.03—4 yrs.	31.16	Terre Haute, Ind., Tribune-Star	459.92—5 yrs.	438.02—5 yrs.	21.90
Kenosha, Wis., News	719.00—5½ yrs.	660.00—5½ yrs.	59.00	Toledo, Ohio, Blade	862.91—2 yrs.	824.08—4 yrs.	38.83
Kingston, N.Y., Daily Freeman	590.07—4 yrs.	573.82—4 yrs.	16.25	Toronto Globe & Mail	1,134.68—6 yrs.	1,120.22—6 yrs.	14.46
Kitchener-Waterloo, Ont., Record	979.00—5 yrs.	946.00—5 yrs	18.00	Toronto Star	1,133.68—6 yrs.	1,101.78—6 yrs.	31.90
Lansing, Mich., State Journal*	595.00—5 yrs.	579.85—5 yrs.	15.14	Victoria Times-Colonist	1,079.07—2 yrs.	1,032.23—5 yrs.	46.84
London, Ont., Free Press	995.00—5 yrs.	949.00—5 yrs.	46.00	Washington Post	1,010.07—4 yrs.	921.80—4 yrs.	88.27
Lowell, Mass., Sun*	679.18—1 yr.	638.00—4 yrs.	41.18	Waterbury Republican-American	633.46—1 yr.	590.94—5 yrs.	42.52
Lynn, Mass., Item	659.65—flat	608.00—4 yrs.	15.65	Waukegan, Ill., News-Sun*	659.14—5 yrs.	653.56—5 yrs.	5.58
Malden, Mass., Daily News-Mercury*	539.25—flat	514.25—3 yrs.	25.00	Wilkes-Barre, Pa., Citizens' Voice*	491.00—1 yr.	479.00—4 yrs.	12.00
Manchester, N.H., Union Leader	756.23—6 mo.	746.23—3 yrs.	10.00	Windsor, Ont., Star	964.78—5 yrs.	948.48—5 yrs.	16.30
Monessen, Pa., Valley Independent	545.00—3 yrs.	453.00—5 yrs.	69.00	Woodbridge, N.J., News Tribune	641.45—2 yrs.	624.08—4 yrs.	17.37
Monterey, Calif., Herald	768.00—6 yrs.	753.00—6 yrs.	15.00	Woonsocket, R.I., Call*	563.36—4 yrs.	560.07—4 yrs.	3.29
Montreal Gazette	1,128.00—5 yrs.	1,086.00—5 yrs.	42.00	York, Pa., Daily Record	595.50—flat	566.49—4 yrs.	17.09
Norristown, Pa., Times Herald	698.92—5 yrs.	683.44—5 yrs.	15.48	* Rates from previous/expired contract.			

SOURCE: *The Guild Reporter*, January 20, 1995, p. 7.

EXHIBIT 5-5

AFA's Research Department:

Behind-the-Scenes Support and Analysis

Surveys, bargaining, informational picketing, roadshows, media events, lobbying — these are some of the many activities that go into achieving Union contracts and legislation to benefit AFA members.

You may have participated in some of these activities, read about them in *Flightlog*, or even seen them on the news. Yet you may not know that behind the scenes, AFA's Research Department is providing vital information and analysis to bolster the Union's efforts.

"The Research staff's expertise in flight attendant contract issues, corporate financial analysis, and retirement and insurance issues makes them an invaluable resource for the basic functions of the Union," said AFA National President Dee Maki. "From bargaining and organizing to arbitrations and legislative efforts, the department provides the necessary facts and figures to help us reach our goals."

Negotiations: From Questionnaire to Contract

As AFA negotiating committees begin preparations for bargaining, the Research Department staff prepares to assist the committees and their National Bargaining Representatives (NBRs) with the arduous process of achieving a contract.

Before contract talks begin, the department helps the bargaining team write a questionnaire to determine which issues are most important to the members. The Research staff then tabulates and analyzes the responses to provide useful information on members' priorities. "We had no experience with surveys," said Jacki Pritchett, MEC president at newly-

organized American Trans Air. "Research helped us go over the issues, develop the survey, and advised us on how to best utilize the results we got back."

The department also analyzes carriers' financial health, an important factor throughout contract talks. "Airline managements usually 'cry poverty' at the table, claim they can't afford any contract improvements, or ask for concessions to stay afloat," according to AFA Research Director Mary Converse. "By analyzing a carrier's financial reports filed with the Securities and Exchange Commission and the Department of Transportation, the department staff provides AFA bargaining committees with an objective assessment of the company's financial status."

In recent negotiations, spiraling healthcare costs have brought severe management pressure to slash benefits. Research staffers with expertise in retirement and insurance issues help negotiating committees evaluate their benefit plans, both to propose improvements and to design cost-effective ways of maintaining existing coverage. This is how flexible healthcare spending accounts, now in place at United

Photo by Earl Dotter

Research Department staff at work (l to r): Secretary Vicki Pratt, Benefits Research Analyst Antoinette Corbin-Taylor, Benefits Specialist Laurie Borman and Research Analyst Theresa McGlauflin. Not pictured: Director of Research Mary Converse.

EXHIBIT 5-5 (continued)

and Aloha, were established. If requested, department staff will also participate in bargaining for benefits.

Comprehensive Bargaining Support

There can be many twists and turns to negotiations, and the Research Department assists at every step. The department routinely develops comparisons of pay and workrules; provides graphs or charts for newsletters or roadshows; calculates the cost of wage or benefit proposals; and provides information about flight attendant contracts at other airlines. These are vital to effective negotiations.

Department staff "is always willing to help and has, therefore, been a tremendous asset to us in our current round of collective bargaining at USAir," said USAir Council 67 President and Negotiating Committee Chair David Alexander. "They have assisted in everything from the construction and processing of a topnotch negotiations survey, to the compilation of essential industry-wide comparisons covering a host of relevant negotiating topics."

In addition, the department undertakes unique, carrier-specific projects. For example, as members at United prepared for a possible strike last year, the department researched visa requirements for cabin crews who might be stranded at foreign layovers, and determined whether London-based flight attendants would be eligible for continuation of health insurance benefits like their U.S.-based counterparts.

Arbitration, Organizing and Legislative Affairs

The Research Department also provides support in areas beyond bargaining. • With contract violations by carriers occurring more frequently, the department provides increasing support to AFA attorneys in arbitrations. • Graphs, charts and comparisons prepared by the department are utilized by AFA's Organizing Department to show prospective members the superior pay, benefits and work rules provided by AFA contracts. Most recently, this vital information helped flight attendants at American Trans Air and Simmons Airlines make their decision to join AFA. • Legislatively, the department researches information for AFA testimony, and reviews contracts to determine the possible impact of proposed legislation. Recently, the department critically analyzed FAA and management estimates of the cost impact of the flight/duty time bill.

Training and Special Projects

Besides providing insurance and retirement expertise, the Research Department trains local committees in these areas. At an upcoming training this summer, AFA members will learn more about which healthcare cost-containment measures to anticipate in negotiations, comparisons of pension plans, and proposed legislation on benefits issues. Two similar trainings in 1990 met with enthusiastic member response.

In addition, the department carries out special, one-of-a-kind projects.

Research Department Publications

The department keeps AFA leaders and members better informed through several specialized publications.

• **Sourcebooks for negotiations.** *The Summary of Flight Attendant Agreements, The Summary of Health & Welfare Plans,* and *The Summary of Retirement Plans* provide an instant reference on how contracts and benefits compare among flight attendant groups. Single-carrier flight attendant Unions which lack research departments also subscribe to these one-of-a-kind reference books.

• **Research Reports,** for bulletin board posting, briefly cover such topics as the male/female earnings gap, flight attendant productivity, the Union advantage for benefits and pay, and airline industry trends.

• **Retirement and Insurance Newsletter,** a new publication, informs R&I committees about benefits issues.

• **AFA Perspectives** informs AFA leaders about issues of concern to our Union. Recent articles have discussed weight policies and healthcare reform. The state of the airline industry and women's special problems in retirement programs will be covered in an upcoming issue.▲

• The department calculated the back pay owed to each of 127 Aloha flight attendants in settlement of a 1983 concessions "snap-back" dispute involving lost wages and vacation since 1983, plus interest. (As a result, affected members received checks averaging approximately $1,000 per flight attendant, totalling more than $125,000.) • Prior to the Gulf war, the department researched the status of life, health, and accidental death insurance at each AFA carrier to see if any plans included waivers for acts of war that would put our members at risk of working without adequate insurance coverage. • The department undertook lengthy research to select the best company and to design the most useful plan for Long-Term Disability for AFA members and associate members. As a result, AFA was able to implement this benefit in 1990.

Maintaining the Vital Information Flow

Like a computer system in a busy airport control tower, AFA's Research Department keeps up the vital information flow which enables the Union to function at its best.

"I don't know how we would have gotten along without the Research Department," said United Strike Coordinator Susan Miller (UAL 09). "They helped our Bargaining Committee refine our proposals. So much of what we requested, comparisons and other information, was part of the step-by-step process leading to the final contract proposal. During the course of negotiations, they also provided information for various leaflets we passed out on the consumer price index and the impact of inflation after five years with no pay raise."

The Research Department's work is an important backdrop to the other work the Union does, and is an invaluable benefit of AFA membership.▲

SOURCE: *Flightlog,* January–March 1992, pp. 6–7 (Association of Flight Attendants, AFL-CIO).

there is also no shortage of facts emanating from such other sources as the Federal Reserve Board, the U.S. Department of Commerce, private research groups, and various state and local public agencies.

Each bargaining party may also find it advisable to procure and analyze information that is more specifically tailored to its needs in the forthcoming negotiations. Most larger unions and almost all major employers today enlist their own research departments in the cause of such special data-gathering projects as the making of community wage surveys.

On occasion, outside experts may also be recruited to make special studies for one of the parties; much of the bargaining stance taken by the Maintenance of Way Employees not long ago, for example, rested on a painstaking analysis of employment trends in that sector of railroading, conducted at union expense by a highly respected University of Michigan professor. As a preliminary to the 1994–1995 baseball negotiations, the players commissioned an analysis of the 28 clubs' financial data by a well-known Stanford University economist: His study concluded that the owners had underestimated their expected 1994 revenues—$1.78 billion—by anywhere from $50 million to $140 million (predictably, the managements dismissed this conclusion as "biased").[2]

Many managements have also made major use of the research services of academicians and other outsiders on an ad hoc basis. In multiemployer bargaining situations, whether or not an official employers' association actually handles the negotiations, the same premium on authoritative investigation has become increasingly visible.

The computer, of course, has also become an invaluable assistant to both parties in these preparations. Costs, revenues, and other key information can now be calculated in seconds instead of minutes, hours, or even days. Reliability in such calculations is much more likely than in prior eras of paper-and-pencil mathematics. Alternatives can be summarized and studied with much more assurance that the list is both logical and comprehensive.

The list of uses to which such research can be put is literally endless. Depending on its accuracy and stamp of authority, it can be used to support any stand, from a company's avowal that certain pension concessions would make it "noncompetitive" to a union's demand for increased cost-of-living adjustments. The management may find support for a desired subcontracting clause in the revelation that the union has been willing to grant the same clause to other employers. The union may gain points in its argument for a larger wage increase by mustering the bright outlook for the industry that has been forecast by the Commerce Department.

On the other hand, where poker, power, or debating traits mark the bargaining, and the "rational process" of appeal to facts counts for little, the whole effort may seem a fruitless one. And even amid the most elaborate fact-gathering efforts, very serious differences of opinion, naturally, can still be expected to emerge: In negotiations a few years ago, for example, the four U.S. Postal Service unions asserted with statistics that their wage and benefit demands would add $11 billion to that agency's $20 billion wage bill while the Postal Service management's figures showed a $14.6 billion increase (for a difference that exceeded the gross national products of many nations).[3] Tense 1997 negotiations between 9,000 American Airlines pilots and the parent AMR Corporation were made all the more ticklish by the union's insistence that its "bare minimum" demands would cost "only" $315 million more than a tentative pact that its members had just rejected whereas by the employer's mathematics the added expenses would amount to $600 million and guarantee that the airline would be noncompetitive.[4] For that matter, in the 1998 bargaining between Northwest Airlines and its pilots, the parties couldn't even agree on the *current* average salary of the pilots. The company insisted that it was $133,000; the union, $120,000.[5]

Negotiators who approach the bargaining table without sufficient factual ammunition to handle the growing complexities of labor relations, however, operate at a distinct disadvantage. The burden of proof invariably lies with the party seeking contractual changes, and in the absence of facts, "proof" is hard to come by.

❖ Other Prerequisites for Bargaining

As painstaking a task as the fact-accumulation process may seem to be, far-sighted managements and labor leaders recognize that considerably more must be done to adequately prepare for bargaining. Increasingly, the top echelons within both union and management circles have come to appreciate the necessity of carefully consulting with lower-level members of their respective operating organizations before framing specific bargaining table approaches. Supervisors, industrial engineers, union business agents, union stewards, and various other people may never become directly involved in the official negotiation sessions,[6] and the distance separating them from the top of the management or union hierarchy is usually a great one. But the growing maturity of labor relations has brought with it a stronger recognition by the higher levels of both organizations that the success or failure of whatever agreement is finally bargained will always rest considerably upon the acceptance of the contract by such people. In addition, unless the official negotiators are well informed on actual operating conditions in advance of the bargaining, there is every chance that highly desirable modifications in the expiring agreement will be completely overlooked.

On the management side, since the daily routines of the operating subordinates require their close contact with the union, such people are in a position to provide the bargainers with several kinds of valuable information. They can be expected to have knowledgeable opinions as to what areas of the expiring contract have been most troublesome; they can, for example, provide an analysis not only of grievance statistics within their departments but of employee morale problems that may lie behind the official grievances that have been lodged. They presumably have some awareness as to the existing pressures on the union leadership, and their knowledge of these political problems can help management anticipate some of the forthcoming union demands. They may be able to assess how the union membership would react to various portions of the contemplated management demands.

Not to be dismissed lightly, either, is the fact that this process of consultation allows lower managers genuine grounds for feeling some sense of participation in at least establishing the framework for bargaining. The employer thus stands to gain in terms of morale, as well as in information.

For the union, the need for thorough internal communication may be even more vital. The trend to centralization of bargaining in the hands of international unions has in no way lessened the need of the union officialdom to be responsive to rank-and-file sentiments. It has, however, made the job of *discovering* these sentiments, and incorporating them into a cohesive bargaining strategy, considerably harder; and "middlemen" within the union hierarchy must be relied upon to perform this assignment. Thus, business agents, grievance committee members, and other lower union officials can play a key role even when negotiations themselves have passed upward to a higher union body, for only they are in a position to take the pulse of the rank and file.

The long list of widely varying and frequently inconsistent rank-and-file demands cannot, however, be passed upward to the international level without some adjustment. Most internationals screen these workers' proposals—inevitably giving more weight to those of important political leaders at the lower levels than to those stemming from totally uninfluential constituents—through committees composed of the subordinate officials at successively higher levels within the union hierarchy. Ultimately, a "final" union contract proposal may be placed before the membership of each local, or at least before representatives of these locals, for their official stamps of approval. And here again, the support of lower union officialdom is vitally needed by the union negotiators—to rally rank-and-file support behind the finalized union demands and to gain membership willingness to strike, if need be, in support of those demands. Aside from the fact that the local unionists may be as well equipped to help the negotiators plan their strategy as are their management counterparts, local leaders who have been bypassed in the consultation process do not typically make loyal supporters of the union's membership-rallying effort.

Finally, both legal and (on many occasions) public relations considerations now clearly demand a major place in preparation for bargaining. Specialists in both these areas must be engaged and utilized by both sides to ensure that bargaining demands will be compatible with the labor statutes and that public support (or, at the very least, public neutrality) will be forthcoming if it is needed. The legal ramifications of present-day trucking contract negotiations, for example, have necessitated for the involved union the employment of a huge corps of lawyers, who have become collectively known as the "Teamsters' Bar Association." Through their high levels of remuneration former Teamster president James R. Hoffa could claim to have "doubled the average standard of living for all lawyers in the past few years," although the personal legal problems of Hoffa accounted for some of the high statistics. For the importance of public relations to both parties in the railroad industry, one need look no further than to the myriad full-page newspaper advertisements placed separately over the past two decades by the railroad unions and managements to state their respective labor relations cases to the general citizenry in advance of the bargaining. (Exhibit 5-6 shows a public relations effort, presumably worked on sometime before the parties actually reached their impasse, produced during the 1994–1995 hockey dispute. This ad was placed in 29 newspapers, including *The New York Times* and the *Philadelphia Inquirer*).

For both management and union, bargaining preparation also involves more mundane matters. Meeting places must be agreed upon and the times and lengths of the meetings must be decided. Ground rules regarding transcripts of sessions, publicity releases, and even "personal demeanor" (a designation that in labor relations can deal with a spectrum extending from the use of profanity to appropriate attire for the negotiators) are sometimes drawn up. Payment of union representatives at the bargaining table who must take time off from work as paid employees of the employer must also be resolved. Only on rare occasions have the parties reached a major prebargaining impasse on such issues as these, but if relations are already strained between union and management such joint decision making can be a time-consuming and even an emotion-packed process.

The latter condition was certainly the case a few years ago, for example, when the large earth-moving equipment producer Caterpillar Inc. and the United

EXHIBIT 5-6

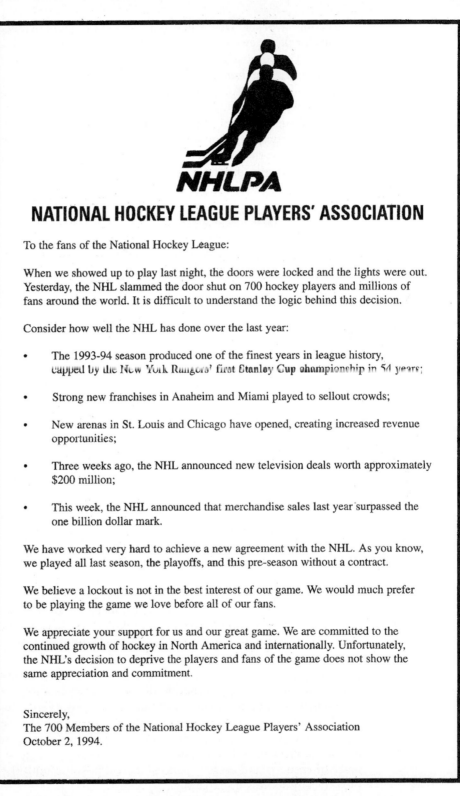

NHLPA

NATIONAL HOCKEY LEAGUE PLAYERS' ASSOCIATION

To the fans of the National Hockey League:

When we showed up to play last night, the doors were locked and the lights were out. Yesterday, the NHL slammed the door shut on 700 hockey players and millions of fans around the world. It is difficult to understand the logic behind this decision.

Consider how well the NHL has done over the last year:

- The 1993-94 season produced one of the finest years in league history, capped by the New York Rangers' first Stanley Cup championship in 54 years;

- Strong new franchises in Anaheim and Miami played to sellout crowds;

- New arenas in St. Louis and Chicago have opened, creating increased revenue opportunities;

- Three weeks ago, the NHL announced new television deals worth approximately $200 million;

- This week, the NHL announced that merchandise sales last year surpassed the one billion dollar mark.

We have worked very hard to achieve a new agreement with the NHL. As you know, we played all last season, the playoffs, and this pre-season without a contract.

We believe a lockout is not in the best interest of our game. We would much prefer to be playing the game we love before all of our fans.

We appreciate your support for us and our great game. We are committed to the continued growth of hockey in North America and internationally. Unfortunately, the NHL's decision to deprive the players and fans of the game does not show the same appreciation and commitment.

Sincerely,
The 700 Members of the National Hockey League Players' Association
October 2, 1994.

Automobile Workers were still deadlocked in a dispute over where to hold the negotiations for their new contract just 48 hours before these critical talks were supposed to begin. The company was holding out for its hometown of Peoria, Illinois. The union was arguing that such a site would give the employer an unfair advantage not only in ready access to its headquarters but in the prospect of homecooked evening meals. It was proposing instead the "neutral" location of St. Louis. Objective observers suggested that both sides simply wanted to show who was boss from the outset. (The company won in this tense battle of wills, as it by any standard won in the negotiations themselves, although only after a bitter five-month strike and after Caterpillar's threat of permanently replacing the strikers.)

THE BARGAINING PROCESS: EARLY STAGES

No manager who is prone to either ulcers or accepting verbal statements at face value belongs at the labor relations bargaining table. Negotiations often begin with the union representatives presenting a long list of demands in both the economic and noneconomic (for example, administrative clause) areas. To naïve managements, many of these avowed labor goals seem at best unjustified and at worst to show a complete union disregard for the continued solvency of the employer. Although extreme demands, such as a new golf course and free transportation in company cars to and from work for all employees, are rarely taken seriously, the management negotiators may be asked for economic concessions that are well beyond those granted by competitors and noneconomic ones that exhibit a greater use of vivid imagination than that shown by Penn and Teller, Monty Python, and Woody Allen combined.

A while ago, for example, the local police association in Rockville Centre, Long Island, demanded from its employer municipality 85 concessions, including a gymnasium and swimming pool; 17 paid holidays, including Valentine's Day and Halloween; and free abortions. And these public servants hold no record for ambitiousness. The union leader Walter Reuther used to open automobile bargaining with so many holiday demands that on one occasion his management counterpart at General Motors is alleged to have asked, "Walter, wouldn't it be faster if you merely listed the days on which you would like to work?"

The experienced management bargainer, however, takes considerable comfort in the fact that the union is, above all, the *political* animal that the preceding chapter has depicted: There is no sense in the union leaders' alienating constituents by throwing out untenable but pet demands of the rank and file (beyond what the various screening committees have been able to dislodge) when the employer representatives stand fully ready to do this themselves and thus to accept the blame. This is particularly true when the pet union demands originate from influential constituents or key locals within the international; alienation of such sources is a job for which the employer representatives, not being subject to the election procedure, are better suited.

There are other logical explanations for the union's apparent unreasonableness. Excessive demands allow leverage for trading some of them off in return for management concessions. In addition, the union can camouflage its true objectives in the maze of requests and thereby conceal its real position until the proper time—a vital ploy for any successful bargaining.

Beyond this, labor leaders have frequently sought novel demands with the knowledge that these will be totally unacceptable to managements in a given bargaining year, but with the goal of providing an opening wedge in a long-range campaign to win management over to the union's point of view. Only in this light can, for example, Reuther's demand for supplementary unemployment benefits in the early 1950s be understood. Much more recently, "30 and out," or retirement after 30 years of service in the automotive industry regardless of age, had a similar genesis. Originally the managements in each case essentially accepted the initial union demands subject to only one condition: that implementation of what the union wanted had to be done over their dead bodies. After several years of pondering each request (and concluding that neither involved any important sacrifice of principle), however, the employers recognized both demands as desires for novel but completely acceptable kinds of employee benefits. They returned to the bargaining table fully prepared to grant them in return for union concessions in other economic areas.

Finally, since contract negotiations frequently extend over a period of weeks (on occasion, months), the union can gain a buffer against economic and other environmental changes that may occur in the interval. Technically, either party can introduce new demands at any time prior to total agreement on a contract, but the large initial demand obviates this necessity.

There is thus a method in the union's apparent madness. Demands that seem to managements to be totally unjustified and even disdainful of the enterprise's continued existence may, on occasion, be genuinely intended as union demands; far more often, however, they are meant only as ploys in a logical bargaining strategy. They are to be listened to carefully but not taken literally.

In fact, if imitation is the sincerest form of flattery, there is ample evidence that some managements have increasingly come to appreciate the strategic value of the large demand. Many employer bargainers have, in recent years, engaged in such **blue-skying** in their counterproposals, and for many of the same reasons as unions have. As a result of the premium placed on exaggerated demands and equally unrealistic counterproposals, however, the positions of the parties throughout the early negotiation sessions are likely to remain far apart.

Standing in the way of early agreement, too, is the fact that these initial meetings are often attended by a wide variety of "invited guests" from the ranks of each organization. Given a large and interested audience of rank-and-file unionists, or a union negotiating committee that is so large as to be totally unable (and unexpected) to perform the bargaining function but is nonetheless highly advisable from a political point of view, the actual union bargainers sometimes find it hard to refrain from using creative but wholly extraneous showmanship. Management representatives, too, frequently succumb to a temptation to impress their visiting colleagues as to their negotiating "toughness." And when lawyers or other consultants are engaged by either party to participate in the bargaining sessions, the amount of acting is often significantly expanded.

Even amid the theatrics and exaggerated stances of these early meetings, however, there is often a considerable amount of educational value for the bargainers. The excessive factors still do not preclude each party from evaluating at least the general position of the other side and from establishing weaknesses in the opposing position or arguments. Frequently, indeed, if negotiators are patient and observing at this point, they will be able to evaluate the other side's proposals along fairly precise qualitative lines. Thus, during the first few sessions when each side should be expected to state its position, it can often be discerned which demands or proposals are being made seriously and which, if any, are merely injected for bargaining position. Such information will be of great help later on in the negotiations.

Actually, the principle of timing in negotiations is very important. There are times for listening, speaking, standing firm, and conceding; there are times for making counterproposals, compromising, suggesting. At some points, "horse-trading" is possible; at others, taking a final position is called for. There is a time for an illustration, a point, or a funny story to break ominous tension, and there is likewise a time for being deadly serious. Through experience and through awareness of the tactics of the other side, negotiators can make use of the time principle most effectively.

THE BARGAINING PROCESS: LATER STAGES

After the initial sessions are terminated, each side should have a fairly good idea of the overall climate of the negotiations. Management should now be in a position to determine what the union is fundamentally seeking, and the union should be able to recognize some basic objectives of management. In addition, by this time, each side should have fairly well in mind how far it is prepared to go in the negotiations. Each party to the negotiations in secret internal sessions should establish with some degree of certainty the maximum concessions it will be prepared to make and the minimum levels it will be willing to accept. Negotiators will be in a better position to bargain intelligently if certain objectives are formulated before the negotiations enter into the "give-and-take" stage. However, even at this stage it is not wise to take extreme positions and to appear inflexible in the approach to the problems under discussion. Skilled negotiators who are striving to avoid a strike—and this is the attitude of the typical management and union—will remain flexible right down to the wire. It is not a good idea to climb too far out on a limb, since at times it may be difficult, or at least embarrassing, to crawl back to avoid a work stoppage.

In fact, after the original positions of the parties are stated and explained, skilled negotiators seldom take a rigid position. Rather than take a definite stand on a particular issue, experienced negotiators (often, where negotiation units are large, through the use of subcommittees to focus upon the major bargaining issues individually before these are dealt with at the main bargaining table) "throw something on the table for discussion and consideration." The process of attempting to create a pattern of agreement is then begun. In this process, areas of clear disagreement are narrowed whenever they can be, mutual concessions are offered, and tentative agreements are effected. Counterproposals are frequently offered as "something to think about" rather than as the final words of the negotiators. In this manner, the parties are in a better position to feel one another out as to ultimate goals. By noting the reaction to a proposal thrown on the table for discussion and by evaluating the arguments and the attitudes in connection with it, negotiators can make a fairly accurate assessment of the maximum and minimum levels of the other side.

Actually, flexibility is a sound principle to follow in negotiations, because the ultimate settlement between managements and unions is frequently in the terms of "packages." Thus, through the process of counterproposals, compromise, and the like, the parties usually terminate the negotiations by agreeing to one package selected from a series of alternative possibilities of settlement. The package selected will represent most closely the maximum and minimum levels acceptable to each of the parties. The content of the various packages will be somewhat different, because neither side in collective bargaining gets everything it wants out of a particular negotiation. The maintenance of flexibility throughout the negotiation allows certain patterns of settlement to be established over which the parties can deliberate.

The package approach to bargaining is particularly important in reference to economic issues. Once the parties obtain an agreement on a total cost-per-hour figure, it becomes a relatively uncomplicated task to allocate that figure in terms of such matters as basic wage rates, supplements to wages, and wage inequities. The more difficult problem, of course, is to arrive at a total cost-per-hour figure. If, for example, through the process of bargaining, the parties established $1.80 per hour as the level of agreement, they might finalize the money agreement in terms of $1.22 per hour basic wage increase, $.20 per hour to correct any wage inequities, $.19 per hour to improve the insurance program, and $.19 per hour to increase pensions. Other subdivisions of the $1.80 would be possible depending upon the attitudes of the parties and their objectives in the negotiations.

❖ Trading Points and Counterproposals

In establishing the content of the alternative packages, experienced negotiators employ a variety of bargaining techniques. Two of the most important are trading points and counterproposals. These procedures are best explained by illustrations.

♦ Trading Points   Let us assume that management employs the **trading point** procedure. The first prerequisite in the use of this technique is to evaluate the demands of the union. Evaluation is necessary not only along quantitative lines but also along the line of the "intensity factor," which requires an assessment of the union demands to determine which of them the union is most anxious to secure. Management representatives should make mental notes of these strongly demanded issues as the negotiations proceed. For example, after a few sessions it may become apparent that the union feels very strongly about securing the union shop. At the same time, the labor organization also demands a $1.50 per hour wage increase and three additional paid holidays. Use of the trading point technique in this situation may be as follows: Management agrees to the union shop but insists that, in return for this concession, the union accept a $.70 per hour increase and just one more paid holiday.

Labor organizations also employ the trading point technique, as illustrated by the following example. Assume that, during the course of the negotiations, the union representatives sense that management will not concede to the union demand for a reduction of the basic workweek from 40 hours to 36 hours. Assume further that the union feels that the issue is not worth a strike. Under these circumstances, the union may be able to employ the hours issue as a trading point. Let us say that, along with the hours demand, the union has insisted upon also securing a union shop and a $1.40 per hour increase in pay. After the union presses the hours issue vigorously for some time (as part of the strategy, it may, of course, threaten a strike over the issue), the union negotiators agree to withdraw the hours demand in return for obtaining the union shop and the wage increase.

♦ Counterproposals   **Counterproposals** are somewhat different from trading points. They involve the compromise that takes place during the bargaining sessions. As a matter of fact, the use of counterproposals is one element that the National Labor Relations Board will consider to determine whether management and labor unions bargain in good faith. However, under the established rules of the board, employers and unions do not have to make *concessions* to satisfy the legal requirement of bargaining in good faith: The implementers of public policy are more interested in whether there have been *compromises*. The union may request four weeks' vacation with pay for all employees. Management might counter by agreeing to three weeks' vacation with pay for employees with 10 years of service and two weeks for the remainder. A union may demand a $1.44 per hour increase, and management may agree to a $.70 per hour increase. At times three or four counterproposals may be made before a final agreement is reached on an issue of collective bargaining.

❖ Costing Out the Contractual Changes

It is suicidal, needless to say, for either party to proceed without a firm understanding of the costs of the contemplated changes. And these costs encompass more than just the additional direct payroll expenses. They also include changes in costs that directly stem from the added payroll costs—in the FICA contributions, for example. Nonpayroll costs such as the employer's annual payments for health insurance and life insurance and nonwork paid time such as any additional holidays, vacations, or sick leave allowances must also be taken into account. Exhibit 5-7 illustrates costing of the labor contract. Stephen Holoviak's *Costing Labor Contracts and Judging Their Financial Impact* and Bruce Morse's *How to Negotiate the Labor Agreement*, both of which are fully cited in the selected references at the end of this chapter, are valuable for a more thorough discussion of costing.

EXHIBIT 5-7

Costing the Labor Contract

CHANGES IN COSTS

I. Direct Payroll—Annual

    Straight-time earnings—36¢ per hour general increase
        100 employees
        $100 \times 2,080 \text{ hrs.} \times 36¢ =$
    Premium earnings, second-shift established differential—10¢ per hour
        30 employees involved
        $30 \times 2,080 \text{ hrs.} \times 10¢ =$
    Overtime: Overtime costs increased by increased straight-time rate, average
        straight-time rate increase 36¢
        $36¢ \times 12,000 \text{ overtime hrs.} \times .5 \text{ overtime rate} =$
    Bonus—none
    Other direct payroll cost increases
        Total Increase in Direct Payroll Costs =

II. Added Costs Directly Resulting from Higher Payroll Costs—Annual

    F.I.C.A.—5.85% times increase in average straight-time earnings below $42,000
        annually
        100 employees
        $100 \times 36¢ \times 5.85\% \times 2,080 =$
    Federal and state unemployment insurance tax
        Number of employees $\times 4,200 \times$ tax rate (2.5%) =
    Workmen's compensation
        (Total cost or estimate)
    Other
        Total Additional Direct Payroll Costs =

EXHIBIT 5-7

(continued)

III. Nonpayroll Costs—Annual

    Insurance—company portion

        Health insurance, no change

        Dental insurance, none

        Eye care, none

        Life insurance—added employer contribution

            $100 per year

            $100 × 100 employees =

    Pension Costs

        Fully vested pension reduced from 25 years and age 65 to 20 years and

            age 62

        Estimated additional cost per year =

    Miscellaneous

        Tuition reimbursements

        Service rewards

        Suggestion awards

        Loss on employee cafeteria

        Overtime meals

        Cost of parking lots

        Company parties

        Personal tools

        Personal safety equipment

        Personal wearing apparel

        Profit sharing

    Other

        Total Additional Nonpayroll Costs, Annual =

IV. Changes in Nonwork Paid Time

    Holidays—2 new holidays added to 6 already in contract

        100 employees × 8 hrs. × 2 holidays × Average new wage

            ($3.96) =

    Vacation, new category added—4 weeks (160 hours annual vacation) with 20 or

        more years service; former top was 3 weeks after 15; average number of

        employees affected annually, 15

        15 × 40 × Average new wage ($3.96) =

    Paid lunchtime—paid 1/2 lunchtime added to contract

        100 employees × 1/2 hr. × days worked yearly (236) × Average new wage

            ($3.96) =

    Paid washup time, none

    Coffee breaks, no change

    Paid time off for union activity—new, one hour per week per shop

        steward

        10 shop stewards × Average new wage shop stewards ($4.20) × 1 hr. × 52

            weeks =

    Paid sick leave

    Paid time off over and above workmen's compensation paid time, none

    Jury-service time off, no change

    Funeral-leave time off, no change

    Paid time off for safety or training, no change

    Other

        Total change in Hours Paid For but Not Worked, Annual =

EXHIBIT 5-7

(continued)

SOURCE: Adapted from Reed C. Richardson, *Collective Bargaining by Objectives: A Positive Approach*, 2nd ed., 1985, pp. 85–86, Reprinted by permission of Prentice Hall, Inc., Upper Saddle River, NJ.

V. Financial Data Derived from Costing Out

Total increase in contract costs
   I + II + III

Average total increase in contract costs per employee payroll hour
   I + II + III ÷ 2,080 hours

Average total increase in direct payroll costs per man-hour
   I + II ÷ 2,080 hours ÷ 100 employees

Average total increase in nonpayroll costs per payroll-hour, per employee
   III ÷ 2,080 hours ÷ 100 employees

Average total increase in nonwork paid time per payroll-hour per employee
   IV ÷ 2,080 hours ÷ 100 employees

Average total increase in direct payroll costs per prod. (worked) hour (per employee)
   I + II ÷ 1,888 hours ÷ 100 employees

Average total increase in nonpayroll costs per prod. (worked) hour (per employee)
   III ÷ 1,888 hours ÷ 100 employees

Average total increase in nonwork paid time per prod. (worked) hour (per employee)
   IV ÷ 1,888 hours ÷ 100 employees

THE BARGAINING PROCESS: FINAL STAGES

There is almost no limit to the ingenuity that skilled negotiators use in attempting to create an agreement pattern. At more sophisticated bargaining tables, even highly subtle modes of communication may do the trick while at the same time allowing the party making a concession to suffer no prejudice for having "given in." Carl Stevens, for example, has pointed out that

> in some situations, silence may convey a concession. This may be the case, for example, if a negotiator who has frequently and firmly rejected a proposal simply maintains silence the next time the proposal is made. The degree of emphasis with which the negotiator expresses himself on various issues may be an important indication. The suggestion that the parties pass over a given item for the present, on the grounds that it probably will not be an important obstacle to eventual settlement, may be a covert way of setting up a trade on this item for some other. . . . The parties may quote statistics (fictitious if need be) as a . . . way of suggesting a position, or they may convey a position by discussing a settlement in an unrelated industry.[7]

Yet, however much the gap between the parties may be narrowed by such methods, even the most adroit bargainers frequently reach the late stages of negotiations with the complete contract far from being resolved. Given the potential thorniness of many of the individual issues involved, this should not be surprising; more than bargaining sophistication and flexibility is still generally required to bring about agreement on such delicate substantive topics as management rights, union security, the role of seniority, and economic benefits. And the fact that the bargainers seek an acceptable package that in some way deals with *all* these issues clearly makes the assignment a much more complicated one than it would otherwise be.

❖ The Strike Deadline

It is the *strike deadline* that is the great motivator of labor relations agreement. Exactly as most students hand in their term papers just before the deadline set by the professor for doing so, most taxpayers fill out their Internal Revenue Service forms in the days immediately prior to midnight on April 15, and most Christmas shoppers do their Christmas shopping in the last week before that holiday, deadlines produce action. This is no less true in union–management contract negotiations. Labor deadlines can always be extended, but they usually aren't: They are typically viewed as urgent, so much so that in some negotiations (as in recent Ford-UAW bargaining) the negotiators face fines (here, $5 per minute for the UAW bargainers) should they arrive late.

As the hands of the clock roll around, signaling the imminent termination of the old contract, each side is now forced to reexamine its "final" position and to balance its "rock bottom" demands against the consequences of a cessation of work. And, with the time element now so important, each party can be counted upon to view its previous bargaining position in a somewhat different light.

For example, paid holiday demands, which once seemed of paramount importance to the union, may now appear less vital when pursuing them is likely to lead to the complete *loss* of paid holidays through a strike. The labor leaders may also conclude now that, although the union membership has authorized the strike should this prove necessary, a stoppage of any duration would be difficult to sustain—through either lack of membership esprit de corps or union resources that are insufficient to match those of management.

On its part, the management may also prove more willing to compromise as the strike deadline approaches. Up until now, it has sought to increase its net income by improving its labor-cost position. Now the outlook is for a *cessation* of income if operations stop.

These threats, in short, bring each party face to face with reality and can normally be expected to cause a marked reassessment of positions. The immediacy of such uncertainty generates a willingness to bridge differences that has not been in evidence at the bargaining table before.

The final hours before time runs out are, therefore, commonly marked by new developments. Frequent caucuses are held by each party, followed by the announcement from a caucus representative that his or her side is willing to offer a new and more generous "final" proposal. Leaders from each side often meet with their counterparts from the other side in informal sessions that are more private and have fewer participants than the official sessions themselves. These are also likely to result in new agreements. And sometimes, in these last moments, one side will successfully suggest to the other that language relating to an especially sticky issue be intentionally left unclear, or even omitted altogether, with an unwritten "understanding" between the parties serving as a less inflammatory substitute. Stevens has described the implications of the deadline in the following terms:

> The approach of the deadline revises upward each party's estimate of the probability that a strike or lockout will be consequent upon adherence to his own position. . . . An approaching deadline does much more than simply squeeze elements of bluff and deception out of the negotiation process. It brings pressures to bear which actually change the least favorable terms upon which each party is willing to settle. Thus it operates as a force tending to bring about conditions necessary for agreement.[8]

And the imminence of the deadline can foster positive attitudes, as well as positive actions, between the parties: Its approach dramatically brings home to both groups that each will pay major costs and thus emphasizes the existence of a common denominator. The potential consequences of not settling tend to be so unsettling to the parties that they, most of the time, now settle.

❖ Why Strikes Occur at All

Strikes do, however, occur. Sometimes the impasse leading to a work stoppage stems from a genuine inability of the parties to agree on economic or other terms; the maximum that the management feels it is able to offer in terms of dollars and cents, for example, is below the minimum that the union believes it must gain in order to retain the loyalty of its members. Or, where rank-and-file ratification is required to put the contract into effect, the negotiators may misjudge membership sentiments, bargain a contract that they feel will be fully acceptable to the membership, and then see their efforts overturned by the members' refusal to approve what they have negotiated.

On other occasions, inexperienced or incompetent negotiators fail to evaluate the importance of a specific concession to the other side and refuse to grant such a concession where they would gladly have exchanged it for a strike avoidance. At times, pride or overeagerness causes bargainers to adhere to initial positions long after these have become completely untenable.

And, in rare instances, one or even both of the parties may actually *desire* a strike—to work off excessive inventories, to allow pent-up emotions a chance for an outlet, or for various other reasons.

A few years ago, the managements of three Bell Telephone companies—Bell Atlantic, Pacific Telesis, and Nynex—were anything but dismayed when 157,000 members of the Communications Workers struck them. There was little disruption of phone service as sophisticated computer switches and elaborate software systems routed billions of calls and the Bells could save the entire salaries of the striking employees: On the basis of an average union annual wage of $25,000, they had realized more than $75 million in savings after merely one week of the strike and presumably were something less than exhilarated after that as, in various locations, the strikers returned to their jobs.

And it is widely believed among students of major league baseball's labor relations that at least one or two of the four bargaining impasses in that sector in the 1980s and 1990s could be mainly attributed to a desire for a strike on the part of many owners. The latter had consistently agreed that the players had been ruining the game by getting too much money and that only a hard line against such excesses—even at the cost of letting, if need be, an entire season go down the tubes—could save America's national pastime. From 1994 to 1995, as noted earlier, much of an entire season was in fact erased: A 234-day strike wiped out, among other things, the 1994 League Playoffs and World Series and the first three weeks of the next season, and if the players clearly must accept some of the responsibility for this unprecedented stoppage, it seemed to many insiders that the owners should be credited with even more of a hand in triggering and maintaining it.

Unions, too, have been known to favor a strike to a settlement without one, at least on occasion. When 57,000 members of the Machinists Union halted work on $80 billion worth of aircraft at Boeing not long ago, most of these workers welcomed the inactivity as allowing them a needed rest. They had been under pressure to turn out one new commercial jet every day, four times the pace of just two years earlier, and many had complained of exhaustion from seven-day workweeks and mandatory overtime. (In this situation, some analysts also believed that Boeing itself was happy to see the strike take place: It would ultimately fill the entire $80 billion in orders, anyhow, since these orders were firm ones, and the work stoppage allowed it, no less than the employees, to enjoy a bit of a "breather.")

And, while on the surface the National Hockey League Players Association derived little tangible benefit from its 10-day strike against the team owners in 1992 beyond some marginal gains in bonus money for playoff games and for individual awards, many of these unionists felt that the strike still was eminently justified. After a quarter-century of peaceful contract renegotiations, they believed, a work stoppage was imperative just to show the managements that it *could* happen.

The strike incidence has been almost steadily declining in the United States since the beginning of the 1960s, and strikes today, as noted earlier, idle only about one-tenth of 1 percent of total available working time. As long as workers are free to engage in work stoppages, however, it is realistic to expect that they will occasionally do so.

CRISIS SITUATIONS

It would be strange, as a matter of fact, if there were not *some* crisis items involved in *any* particular negotiation. In the typical situation, some issues will be extremely troublesome, and they will severely tax the intelligence, resourcefulness, and good faith of the negotiators. Actually, if both sides sincerely desire to settle without a strike, a peaceful solution of any problem in labor relations can usually be worked out. As previously implied, the possibility of a work stoppage is increased when both sides are not sincere in their desire to avoid industrial warfare or when one of the parties to the negotiation is not greatly concerned about a strike. If negotiators bargain on a rational basis, keep open minds, recognize facts and sound arguments, and understand the problems of the other side, crisis situations can be avoided or overcome without any interruption to operations or any impairment of good labor relations.

❖ Bypassing the Difficult Issues

One way to avoid a state of affairs where negotiations break down because of a few difficult issues is to bypass those issues in the early stages of the bargaining sessions. It is a good idea to settle the easy problems and delay consideration of the tough ones until later in the negotiations. In this way, the negotiation keeps moving, progress is made, and the area of disagreement tends to be isolated and diminished. Thus, at the early stages, the parties might agree to disagree on some of the items. If only a few items are standing in the way of a peaceful settlement toward the close of the negotiations, there is an excellent chance for full agreement on the contract. Moreover, what might appear to be a big issue at the beginning stages of the negotiations might, of course, appear comparatively insignificant when most of the contract has been agreed upon and when time is running out. (Nonetheless, contingency plans must inevitably be made just in case. Exhibit 5-8 shows the many variables that may well have to be dealt with.)

EXHIBIT 5-8

One Major Corporation's Emergency Plan Checklist for Strike Situations

1. Fuel Oil
2. Food Services
3. Trash Removal
4. Janitorial Supplies
5. Mail Delivery
6. Maintenance Supplies
7. Security Equipment
   - Cameras and Film and Tape Recorder
   - Police and Guard Service
   - Keys and Locks
   - Passes and Parking Lots
   - Portable Radios
   - Flashlights/Binoculars
   - Extension Cord
8. First Aid
9. Standby Facilities
10. Sleep-in Arrangements
11. Mechanical Maintenance
12. Electrical Maintenance
13. Emergency Transportation
14. Switchboard Operations
15. Supervisory Shift Coverage
16. Picket Line Instruction
17. Observer Teams and Forms
18. Salaried employee assignments-If/When permitted to enter facility
19. Communication Tree
20. Radio Stations to listen to
21. Vendor Notification
22. Payroll Distribution
23. Warehousing Requirements
24. Mailing Lists—labels/envelopes
25. Emergency Personnel Team
26. Hazardous Material Storage
27. Fire Brigade Team
28. Removal of necessary equipment/systems information
29. Return of all leased vehicles
30. Obtain all keys from union employees
31. Contact local police
32. Contact fire department
33. Check all locks on buildings
34. Check perimeter lighting of buildings
35. Establish location for Company-owned vehicles

❖ Human Relations Mistakes

At times, crisis situations are created not as a result of the merits of certain issues but because some negotiators make mistakes in human relations. For example, it is good practice to personalize the things that are constructive, inherently sound, and defensible, and to depersonalize the items that are bad, destructive, or downright silly. Under the former situation, the union or the management, as the case may be, commends the other party, by saying "That is a good point," or "The committee definitely has an argument," or "Bill certainly has his facts straight." In the latter situation, it is sound policy to deal with the merits of a situation. Thus, in the face of a destructive or totally unrealistic proposal, the reaction of the other side might be something like this: "Let's see how this proposal will work out in practice if we put it into the labor agreement." It is elementary psychology that people like being commended and dislike being criticized. If this is recognized, rough spots and danger areas in the negotiations may be avoided.

❖ The Advance Framing of Alternatives

Another way to avoid crisis situations is to be prepared in advance of negotiations to propose or accept alternative solutions to a problem. For example, suppose that the union desires to incorporate an arrangement into the labor agreement making membership in the union a condition of employment. In mapping its overall strategy for the negotiation, the union committee might decide first to propose a straight union shop but be prepared, in the face of strong management resistance, to propose a lesser form of union security. Suppose, for another illustration, that an employer wants to eliminate all restrictions on the assignment of overtime. It plans first to suggest that the management should have the full authority to designate any workers for overtime without any limitation. At the same time, it is prepared to suggest some alternative solution to the problem in the event that this proposal appears to create strong resistance. For example, it may propose that seniority be the basis for the rotation of overtime insofar as employees have the capacity to do the work in question. If both sides are prepared in advance to offer or to accept alternative solutions to particular problems, there will be less possibility for the negotiations to bog down. Instead, they will tend to keep moving to a peaceful climax. The momentum of progress is an important factor in reaching the deadline in full agreement on a new contract.

❖ Joint Study Groups

One additional procedure is available to minimize the chances of negotiation breakdowns. It has already been pointed out that many of the topics of contemporary collective bargaining are complicated and difficult. Issues such as working rules, pension plans, insurance systems, and production standards require study and sometimes are not suitable for determination in the normal collective bargaining process. As contract termination deadlines approach, a strike may result simply because not enough time has been allowed for *jointly* attacking these particularly complicated matters in a rational, sound, workable, and equitable manner. All the *unilateral* preparation in the world still does not dispose of the problem. The parties are, however, at liberty to consider such issues by the use of a joint study group, composed of management and union representatives *during the period of the new contract*. At times, managements and unions may see fit to invite disinterested and qualified third parties to aid them in such a project. The joint study group does not engage in collective bargaining as such; its function, rather, is to identify and consider alternative solutions. But, by definition being freed from the pressure of contractual deadlines, such a group can gain sufficient time to study these necessarily difficult issues in a rational manner.

To work effectively, the joint study group should be established soon after a contract is negotiated; it should be composed of people who have the ability to carry out appropriate research and the necessary qualities to consider objectively and dispassionately the tough issues confronting labor and management. These are no small prerequisites, but such a procedure has worked successfully in industries such as basic steel, and modified versions of it are also currently being used with beneficial results in the automobile, glass, rubber, and aluminum industries. There is no reason to believe that other collective bargaining parties, including those bargaining on an individual plant basis, could not also profit from it in avoiding crisis situations.

❖ Mediation

Some parties have found the **mediation** process helpful when crisis situations are reached in negotiations. The Federal Mediation and Conciliation Service (FMCS) of the U.S. government, and state conciliation services, make mediators available to unions and employers. The Federal Service maintains regional offices in New York, Philadelphia, Atlanta, Cleveland, Chicago, St. Louis, and San Francisco, as well as field offices and field stations in many other large industrial centers. It employs some 300 mediators, whose services are available without charge to the participants in the collective bargaining process, and it currently mediates about 20,000 labor disputes a year.

Sometimes, the parties prefer private citizens in the mediation role: Long after his tenures as Richard Nixon's FMCS director and Gerald Ford's Secretary of Labor, William J. Usery, Jr. was requested by the involved unions and managements to help resolve major coal strikes (which he did with remarkable success in both 1990 and 1993) and major league baseball's 1994–1995 bargaining impasse (one of the rare Usery failures); in 1994, former Virginia Governor Gerald Baliles was helpful in easing a stormy conflict between US Air and its pilots' union.

Mediation is based on the principle of voluntary acceptance. Suggestions or recommendations made by the mediator may be accepted or rejected by both or either of the parties to a dispute. Unlike an arbitrator, the mediator has no conclusive powers in a dispute. This person's chief value is a capacity to review the dispute from an objective basis, to throw fresh ideas into the negotiations, to suggest areas of settlement, and at times to serve to extricate the parties from difficult and untenable positions. The profession constitutes, as one of the nation's more active mediators once observed,

> the public or private exercise of the last alternative. It is not repression. It is not dictation or decision-making for others. It is third-party participation in the bargaining process to minimize the external manifestations of conflict and to maximize the chances of agreement. It is intended to hasten agreement in the least offensive way. A mediator's lack of the customary forms of power is his greatest asset. The power of persuasion can be more potent than the powers of compulsion or suppression.[9]

But if the successful mediator must obviously be impartial, this does not by any means demand that he always be neutral. "He is," as Walter E. Baer once wrote, "not merely a badminton bird to be knocked back and forth between the parties. When he thinks a proposal is completely out of line, he tells the parties so. When the situation dictates, he offers positive leadership."[10] Under any conditions, the mediator is a potentially valuable appendage to the bargaining table process when the results of that process lead to crisis situations.

TESTING AND PROOFREADING

When all issues under consideration have been resolved, the contract should then be drafted in a formal document. Many unions and managements permit lawyers to draft the formal contract. No objection is raised against this practice provided that the lawyer writes the document so that it can be understood by all concerned. A lawyer does not perform this function effectively by including in the contract a preponderance of legal phraseology. Such a contract will serve to confuse the people affected by its terms.

Regardless of who writes the final document, the author or authors should draft the agreement in the simplest possible terms. No contract is adequately written until the simplest, clearest, and most concise way is found to express the agreement reached at the bargaining table. Whoever drafts the agreement should recognize the basic fact that unfamiliar words and lengthy sentences will cause confusion once the document is put into force and may lead to unnecessary grievances and arbitration. Hence, it is sound practice to use words that have special meaning at the place of work or in the industry. Some contracts wisely include illustrations to clarify a particular point in the agreement. It is of particular value to explain in detail the various steps of the grievance procedure, and just what employees are entitled to as benefits. The contract is designed to stabilize labor relations for a given period. It is not drawn up for the purpose of creating confusion and uncertainty in the area of employer–employee relations.

Before signatures are affixed to the documents, the negotiators should have the contract test-read for meaning. No person who was associated with the negotiations should be used; each individual's interpretation will be colored by his or her participation in the negotiations. A better practice is to select someone who had no part in the conference. For this purpose, the union may utilize a shop steward or even a rank-and-file member. An office employee, such as a secretary, or a supervisor can serve the same purpose for management. If those who are to administer the contract were not parties to the negotiation, such people should also be used for testing purposes; this is an excellent opportunity for them to determine whether they understand the provisions before they attempt to administer the document. If the testing indicates confusion as to meaning, the author must rewrite the faulty clause or clauses until the provision is drafted in a manner that eliminates vagueness.

The final step before signing is the proofreading of the document by each negotiator. Particular attention should be given to figures. Misplacing a decimal point, for example, can change a sum from 1 percent to one-tenth of 1 percent. Human errors and typographical mistakes are inevitable, and the proofreading of the contract should have as its objective the elimination of any such errors.

The signing of the contract is an important occasion. Newspapers and television stations may be notified of the event. Pictures may be taken to be inserted in management house organs and union publications. The tensions of the negotiation terminated, the parties to the conference may well celebrate. They have concluded a job that will affect the welfare of many employees, the position of the labor union, the operation of the business, and, indeed, sometimes the functioning of the entire economy. They have discharged an important responsibility. Let us hope that they did it well!

COORDINATED BARGAINING AND MULTINATIONALS

An employer who must bargain with not just one but a number of different unions can frequently capitalize on a built-in advantage to the situation. There often exists the possibility of dividing and conquering the various unions by initially concentrating upon the least formidable of them, gaining a favorable contract from it, and then using such a contract as a lever from which to extract similar concessions from the other unions. Recent corporate trends toward merger have increased such occurrences, not only by bringing together under one company umbrella a large number of unions but also, generally, by augmenting management bargaining strength as a consequence of the greater resources now provided the company. But even without mergers, many companies have—whether because of historical accident, union rivalry, or planned and successful management strategy—enjoyed this ability to play off one union against another, often even gaining widely divergent contract expiration dates (thus blunting the strike threat of any one union) in the process.

In recent years, many unions so affected have sought to offset their handicap by banding together for contract negotiation purposes in what has come to be known as **coordinated bargaining**. The concept, which has no rigorous definition but which universally denotes the presentation of a united union front at the bargaining table and often also involves common union demands, was first applied with any degree of formality in the 1966 General Electric and Westinghouse negotiations (and has been reapplied there in each triennial negotiation ever since). By the late 1990s, it had also been used by organized labor as a weapon in bargaining with Union Carbide, Campbell Soup, the major companies in the copper industry, American Home Products, Olin, and General Telephone, among others.

Such union attempts to change the traditional bargaining structure had, understandably, been received with something less than enthusiasm by the managements involved. Many had felt that it made no sense at all for them to expose themselves to more all-encompassing work stoppages just because their employees had selected different unions as their bargaining agents in different units of the company. Ironically, however, the management opposition *had* led to strikes, and some of these had been quite lengthy. At Union Carbide, a dozen plantwide strikes had occurred, with the shortest of them lasting 44 days and the longest going 246 days. The bulk of the copper industry was shut down for more than eight months. One set of General Electric negotiations was marked by a strike of more than three months' duration. Nor could it be said, at the time of this writing, that particularly impressive union victories had been recorded by the new labor strategy. In general, unions that had not previously cooperated had found it hard to adjust to a policy requiring the sublimation of their own often intensely desired demands for the common good. In addition, the uncertain legal status of coordinated bargaining had remained a force to be reckoned with for organized labor.

At the moment, cooperation between unions is, at least in the opinion of the U.S. Court for the Second Circuit (New York), "not improper, up to a point." But the absence of a clear-cut Supreme Court ruling to dispose of this issue once and for all has meant that the legally permissible boundaries of coordinated bargaining remain unclear.

Generally speaking, spokespersons for those unions that have thus far used the coordinated bargaining approach seem to be encouraged by its results for their specific situations and optimistic about its general growth prospects, but at the same time they appear to be realistic in assessing its general applicability. They know that it is no magic answer to the challenges of bargaining, but they do generally believe that as corporations become more diverse and complicated this mechanism, still a very young one, will become more finely tuned and more effective.

On the other hand, the long-lasting failure of the United Steelworkers to form a genuinely strong multiunion coalition to bargain with the major copper companies because of internal schisms cannot be overlooked as a guide to the future, either. Many copper unionists, both leaders and rank and file, have vocally preferred their bargaining here to be at the local level and have been especially fearful that the Steelworkers would force "carbon copies" of its settlements elsewhere on them.

Whatever the future may bring, coordinated bargaining has grown relatively little lately. Although trying to advance it now consumes about 25 percent of the AFL-CIO Industrial Union Department's (IUD) $6 million annual budget and such bargaining does currently affect a not inconsequential 750,000 employees, IUD officials freely admit that they had hoped for greater growth in the more than three decades since the concept was first applied. Company resistance and union parochialism are generally given most of the blame by the latter, who continue to view the recent corporate merger trend with much alarm.

Nor is organized labor happy about another growing phenomenon—that of the U.S.-based **multinational**, or corporation operating plants in various countries. For many years, unions have watched fearfully as such firms—attracted by a combination of tax concessions, lower-cost labor abroad, and accessibility to vital materials—have expanded their employment well beyond not only the borders of the United States but also, quite probably, the reach of U.S. labor law. By any estimate, thousands of jobs each week are being exported in this fashion by U.S.-based multinationals, and it is of no consolation at all from the viewpoint of displaced workers (or those who because of the exporting have never been employed at all) that multinationals often make huge sense if corporate return on investment is the criterion applied.

The UAW was the first major union to be touched by this threat, long before other labor organizations noted any grounds for alarm. But UAW president Walter Reuther's advocacy of "one big global union" was all but universally believed to be unrealistic. Given the continuing absence of international collective bargaining laws, the wide disparity in union strengths and ideologies throughout the world, the millions of totally unorganized workers, and interunion rivalries, it still is. American labor's counterattack to date has essentially been confined only to loose consultation with the unions and union federations abroad. And if the rationales for worldwide bargaining expiration dates, global strikes and boycotts, and international exchanges of information have all been intensively discussed, after many years no move toward genuine international collective bargaining at the global level can be even remotely detected.

It is not very conceivable that the American labor relations systems and its NLRB protection will prove to be of much help to unions even though their target employers are American-based themselves (in most cases). Actions taken by U.S. unions could well turn out to be illegal secondary boycotts, and most American laws could hardly be expected to bind Japanese, British, or German workers in any event. A potent adversary for unionism, the multinational is something that to date has caused only frustration for the labor movement in the United States.

BOULWARISM: A DIFFERENT WAY OF DOING THINGS

It can be argued with some justification that, for all its ultimate ability to effect a contract with which both parties can live for a fixed future period of time (even on the relatively infrequent occasions when a strike interrupts the negotiations), the conventional bargaining pattern is a highly inefficient one. With its exaggerated opening demands, equally inflated counterproposals, and particularly its seeming inability to motivate the parties into making satisfactory concessions until the fixed strike deadline is approached, it consumes the time and talents of many people for weeks, if not months, in a role-playing exercise that is often theatrical and almost always heavily laced with ritual. Could not the parties, it could well be asked, devise a system that comes to the point more quickly and deals with reality from the very beginning? The General Electric Company (GE) for many years had no doubts that such a system could be initiated. Its bargaining approach for almost three decades attempted to do exactly that.

From the 1940s until the 1970s GE religiously pursued a policy of (1) preparing for negotiations by effecting what company representatives described as "the steady accumulation of all facts available on matters likely to be discussed"; (2) modifying this information only on the basis of "any additional or different facts" it was made aware of, either by its unions or from other sources, during the negotiations (as well as before them); (3) offering at an "appropriate," but invariably a very early, point during the bargaining "what the facts from all sources seem to indicate that we should"; and (4) changing this offer only if confronted with "new facts." In short, the company attempted "to do right voluntarily," if one accepts its own description of the process. It alternatively engaged in a ruthless game of "take it or leave it" bargaining, if one prefers the union conclusion.

Aided by a highly favorable combination of circumstances—chief among them the presence of several competing unions, major internal friction within its most important single union (the International Union of Electrical Workers), a heavy dependence of many of its communities on the company as the primary employer, and an abundance of long-service (and thus less mobile) employees—GE was highly successful with this policy, known as **Boulwarism** after former GE Vice President of Public and Employee Relations Lemuel R. Boulware, until the late 1960s. With essentially no exceptions, the company offer in its original form was transformed into the ultimate labor contract. Constantly communicating to both its employees and the general citizenry of the various General Electric communities on the progress of the negotiations as these evolved—another major part of the Boulwaristic approach—the company could point with pride to the value of its policy.

For their part, GE's unions attacked Boulwarism not only as an unethical attempt to undermine and discredit organized labor but as an illegal endeavor in refusing to bargain. Triggered by charges lodged by the IUE following the 1960 negotiations, the NLRB did in fact (in 1964) find the company guilty of bad-faith bargaining in those negotiations. And almost five years later the U.S. Court of Appeals at New York upheld this NLRB ruling, as did the U.S. Supreme Court shortly thereafter by refusing to disturb that decision. But the facts on which these judicial actions were taken were, of course, those pertaining only to 1960, and it appeared that Boulwarism itself was far from dead.

By 1969, however, other changes had started to work against Boulwarism. The long-competitive GE unions had (as mentioned earlier) been able to coordinate their efforts. The IUE itself had been rescued from its intramural warfare by a new slate of officers. The GE communities had broadened their industrial bases and, hence, were no longer as dependent as they had been on the company's goodwill. And the high number of long-service employees on the GE payrolls had, by the normal processes of attrition, been greatly reduced. These factors all served to lessen the company's ability to transfer its offer in pristine form into the final contract. In 1969, a long and bitter strike did motivate GE to adjust its offer somewhat, with the strike itself being the only visible "new fact" in the picture. And in the 1973 negotiations, the original company offer was also modified in the course of the negotiations. Both the 1969 and 1973 changes were relatively minor and seemed to lie far more in the packaging than in the substance, but they presaged a new approach to the bargaining.

In the years after the mid-1970s, this new approach came to total fruition. Triennial bargaining sessions were all conducted without one serious accusation of Boulwaristic practice being levied at the company. And, although an armed truce philosophy could still be said to characterize the relationship, the old "doing right voluntarily/take it or leave it" strategy was completely supplanted by the far more typical pattern of proposals, counterproposals, and ultimate compromises in all of these contract negotiations.

Yet there remained at GE executives who believed that the old ways, having given the company so much success for so long, had been prematurely relinquished. They hoped that Boulwarism could still be drawn upon in GE labor relations. And it is of relevance, too, that more than a few other managements had at least partially utilized the Boulwaristic pattern in *their* bargaining in the more recent past. Employers at AMF, Timken, Allis-Chalmers, J. P. Stevens—and those in the worlds of both professional baseball and professional football—had acknowledged some indebtedness to the approach even in the 1990s. Many smaller and less visible organizations had also embraced Boulwarism in these years, without any fanfare at all.

Whether or not such efforts as the latter represented anachronisms or—with the tougher recent stance of management in general—the shape of things to come, Boulwarism even at the time of this writing thus could not be entirely disregarded. Whatever its deficiencies, it was at least a different concept that, certainly in the case of one major corporation, for a time operated with enormous efficiency. Such successes, however temporary, are never totally forgotten.

SOME FURTHER COMPLEXITIES

Generalizations such as those offered in the bulk of this chapter cannot, of course, do justice in accounting for a *specific* contract settlement or strike. To appreciate adequately the complexities and variations involved in the negotiation process, one must turn to the interdependent variables that are apt to be influential in determining bargaining outcomes.

The *current healths of both the economy and the industry*, for example, have been of major effect in determining the relative settlements of the United Automobile Workers and major car manufacturers for years. In 1967, when automobile-company production and profitability set new all-time records and the general economy was booming, the management quest for uninterrupted production led the companies to grant terms that dwarfed all earlier times. In 1970, company costs were way up and sales (owing primarily to foreign car inroads) were way down at the same time that union members felt themselves badly hurt by inflation. A strike (at General Motors, the target employer of the UAW) was probably inevitable as a result, and the union, even after 67 days of striking, achieved a settlement that was so relatively unexciting to its members that for a while its ratification was in definite doubt. In 1973, a rather intermediate year for both the economy and the industry, union gains were moderate. In 1976, the economy and the industry had rebounded nicely from a lean period a year earlier, and the union fared well indeed, particularly with the negotiation of an additional 12 days off with pay annually to counter any future threats of unemployment.

In 1979, an average economy produced average gains. In the bargaining of the 1980s and early 1990s, hard times unknown to the industry since the 1930s generated mammoth economic concessions (to be described in Chapter 7) from the union in its desperate quest for maximum job retention. In the late 1990s, and particularly in 1999, red-hot sales led to mammoth profits for the companies and their desire to have labor peace was such that the UAW extracted contracts that were the most generous in decades. (Nor were the GM, Ford, and DaimlerChrysler workers in these boom years themselves very anxious to strike: They were receiving sizable profit-sharing checks and lucrative overtime opportunities. The last thing that they wanted, too, was a cessation of such financial rewards.) A Rip Van Winkle awakening after many years could without much difficulty discover how the overall economy had fared in the interval (assuming that he cared to, of course) simply by learning the extent of union successes while he was asleep.

Paradoxically, in 1983, when most unions were relatively pleased to come away with wage increases of 6 percent per year, Eastern Airlines granted the Machinists a whopping 32 percent over three years—not because it was rolling in wealth, however, but because it was so relatively poverty-stricken that it simply could not afford a strike: By its own admission, a strike would have caused severe cash problems for it within two weeks.

On the other hand, the shoe industry has been plagued by consistently poor economic conditions for many of its individual employers for years, and, in the face of this variable and its persuasive logic, the Shoe Workers have shown considerable bargaining self-restraint for over two decades. And when the Brewery Workers struck several breweries in 1981, they undoubtedly regretted the actions (forced on the leadership by militant memberships) far more than did the employers: The industry had been hard hit by too great a beer-making capacity and slumping sales—particularly, indeed, involving several of the struck facilities—and, not urgently needing the plants in operation, the managements basically felt no great pressures to settle. (Even the entertainment industry, for decades seemingly immune to the consequences of national economic slumps, is, at least at times these days, very much affected, as Exhibit 5-9, drawn from the quarterly journal of the Screen Actors Guild, demonstrates.)

Technological innovations—running a wide gamut from turbojet aircraft to computerized newspaper typesetting—have been the primary cause of many recent major bargaining stalemates and subsequent strikes, as even the cursory follower of current events is well aware. Recently, the Screen Actors Guild and the American Federation of Television and Radio Artists struck for a share of the industry's profits on videocassettes and videodiscs, something that they could hardly have done a few years earlier when these new forms of technology were barely visible and anything but lucrative.

EXHIBIT 5-9

GUILD AFFAIRS

Riding Out the Recession

BY ROBERT CAIN
SAG HOLLYWOOD DIRECTOR OF RESEARCH

By now it has become distressingly apparent that the entertainment industry is not, as many of us had hoped, recession-proof. Until the current recession began early last year, the conventional wisdom held that in times of economic distress Americans turn more often to filmed entertainment for relief from their troubles.

The statistics do not, unfortunately, support this comforting but questionable theory. Movie theater admissions in 1991 fell to their lowest level in almost two decades. Television advertising revenue, the engine that drives the network business, suffered a dramatic decline of 6.7 percent, the first drop since 1971. And more than 20 entertainment companies were forced into bankruptcy by withering business conditions. Screen Actors Guild members, for their part, faced the triple whammy of a shrinking employment base, falling salaries, and an expansion in membership which heightened the competition for work. All in all, it was a pretty tough year.

Total income under the four basic SAG contracts fell by 2.2 percent to $1.08 billion, the biggest year-to-year drop since the disastrous box-office year of 1971. Television, theatrical, and industrial earnings all declined, by 6.8%, 4.4%, and 12.6% respectively (*see chart below*). The one bright spot was commercial earnings, which rose 3.7% last year; although the number of job opportunities in commercials diminished, this trend was more than offset by the significant increases in session and use fees implemented with the new SAG contract in February 1991.

Fewer Jobs, Smaller Checks

Actors had to get by with fewer jobs, smaller residuals checks, and reduced salaries at every level. But the tough earnings climate did little to dissuade new members from joining the ranks, and the roster of dues-paying SAG members swelled by 3.2%. When coupled with the 2.2% contraction of the total income pie, this resulted in a 5.3% decline in the average member's earnings, from $12,596 in 1990 to an estimated $11,920 last year.

Actors at the top of the earnings scale were hit just as hard as those at the bottom — the number who earned over $100,000 fell last year by 5.2%, from 2,261 to 2,144. New York actors suffered perhaps the most, since the studios' production boycott of the Big Apple halted all television and film production until May. Female performers also experienced a tougher time than their male counterparts, particularly in commercials, as advertisers tend to revert to more conservative, male-dominated ad campaigns during times of economic uncertainty. All told, almost two-thirds of all SAG actors earned less in 1991 than they did in the previous year.

Fortunately, history has shown that the entertainment industry, and SAG in particular, are remarkably resilient. In the past decade SAG earnings have experienced two major setbacks: the 1982 recession, and the 1988 writers' strike. In the year following each slowdown, earnings vigorously rebounded, by 22.6 percent in 1983, and 17.7 percent in 1989. Several encouraging indicators point to the likelihood of a similar rebound in the next 12 to 18 months: the broadcast networks' combined ratings and shares are up substantially over last year; home video continues to boom; and the global appetite for American entertainment product shows no sign of diminishing.

(continued ⟶)

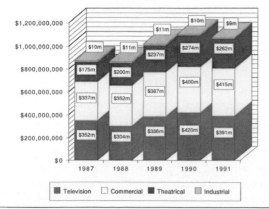

★ **SAG EARNINGS BY CONTRACT** ★
1987-1991

■ Television ☐ Commercial ■ Theatrical ☐ Industrial

SOURCE: Screen Actor, Spring 1992, p. 12.

EXHIBIT 5-9 (continued)

A Chill In Film & TV Residuals

A *winter's worth of reruns barely keeps us warm*

A year-end report reveals that SAG residuals from theatrical films, television films and television series totalled $190.4 million in 1991, a modest 5.5% increase from 1990 (data on commercial and industrial residuals were not yet available at press time). This represents a dramatic slowdown from the double-digit increases of recent years. Reruns of television series — on network, syndicated, cable, and foreign TV — accounted for half of the residuals earned; ancillary markets for theatrical films generated 40%; and reuse of TV movies provided the remaining 10% (*see chart below*). The share of residuals generated by foreign sales continues to grow, now accounting for an estimated 20 to 25 percent of all film and TV residuals.

Residuals have become an increasingly essential component of SAG members' income. The $190 million in film and TV residuals accounted for almost one-third (29.2%) of all film and TV earnings in 1991, up from 26% just two years ago. The residual check, which was once merely a welcome supplement to acting pay, is now the only means for many actors to keep food on their tables. That is why the SAG contract negotiating committee rejected the broadcast networks' demands for an 80 percent roll-back of network rerun residuals.

There is no question that the networks had a tough year in 1991, but it is equally evident that SAG members suffered right along with them. A substantial cut in residual pay at this point would be excessively punitive, and would hurt actors far more than it would help the networks. SAG's Board and staff have always considered these residuals to be sacrosanct in the past, and will continue to do so in the future. ■

— Robert Cain

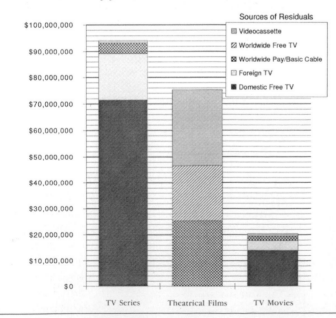

★ SAG 1991 FILM & TV RESIDUALS ★

Sources of Residuals
- ▨ Videocassette
- ▨ Worldwide Free TV
- ▨ Worldwide Pay/Basic Cable
- ☐ Foreign TV
- ■ Domestic Free TV

A 1992 announcement by American Telephone & Telegraph that by the end of 1994 it would replace as many as one-third of its unionized operators with a computerized voice-recognition technology developed by AT&T's Bell Laboratories for a while made relations between that giant organization and its two largest unions especially unpleasant. (In this case cooler heads ultimately prevailed, however, and the unions agreed in their new contract that the real enemy was the competition and that the technological changes that had already resulted in job losses of some 100,000 since the breaking up of the Bell System in 1984[11] were the price to be paid if the employer was to remain competitive in a global market.)

And the introduction of new Boeing jetliners, requiring only two-member cockpit crews that replaced planes requiring three-person crews, has fostered much pilot unrest at many airlines in the past few years. Delta and Continental have had particularly sticky problems over such staffing, problems that as of the year 2000 remained unresolved and that threatened to explode into strike situations at any time.

The influence of other major variables can be illustrated. The *relative strengths of the two sides* can be decisive in particular negotiations as in the case of the management of New York City's Jacob K. Javits Convention Center and the several enormously powerful unions representing its employees. By the late 1990s, exhibitors at the center were used to being charged $50 (by the Teamsters) to retrieve a packing crate, $70 (by the Electrical Workers) to plug in a lamp, and a formidable $200 (by the Carpenters) to install a prefabricated booth that, absent union work rules, could have been assembled by the exhibitors themselves without tools. From its opening in 1986, the center had taken to union strike threats like a fish to land and its philosophy of peace at any cost had caused these and scores of other aberrations.

Likewise, America's 40 or so major waterfronts are all unionized. The International Longshoremen's Association (ILA) controls the movement of hundreds of billions of dollars worth of goods on the East and Gulf Coasts and the International Longshore and Warehouse Union (ILWU) does the same on the West Coast. Any interruption in the loading and unloading of ship cargoes by the 40,000 dockworkers involved could be ruinous to the employers, both because of rotting perishables at the piers and through a diversion of shipments to waterfronts that have not been struck. Consequently, strikes are rare, but just as understandably, union incomes are by any standard high. With overtime, West Coast port workers were in 1999 earning between $99,016 (the level for longshoremen) and $156,251 (the stipend for foremen, who are also members of the ILWU), [12] and their East and Gulf Coast counterparts lagged behind these figures by only a little. High school diplomas are not required to hold the bulk of these jobs, but a willingness to support the union and to vote to go out on strike in the case of a negotiations impasse is very helpful.

Conversely, Xerox has held virtually all the power in *its* labor negotiations, above all because it has convinced its union—the Amalgamated Clothing and Textile Workers—of its sincerity in threatening to move significant copier production overseas because of 20 percent lower wage rates abroad. Not long ago, the union agreed to let the company use large numbers of part-time and temporary employees at a modest $8 per hour (well below scale) in an effort to keep the work in Rochester, New York, and the future will presumably see more such concessions.

Some negotiations have not been easily resolved because of *political problems within the union*. In 1995, the newly elected head of the Long Island Railroad unit of the Brotherhood of Locomotive Engineers seemed determined to prove his hard-line credentials and thereby increase the size of his militant faction within the union. On this basis, he held out for a larger wage increase than most of the railroad's 11 other unions had received and an Engineer walkout (that, taking place on the eve of the long Memorial Day weekend, was particularly ill-received by the public) was the result.

In 1995, too, a civil war between two groups within the National Basketball Association players union led in large measure to the lockout of these employees. The union leader had strong supporters from one segment within the union, but another gained the ascendancy by convincing a player majority that their top representative was running the union (as one insider said) "like a banana republic" and would as easily sell his members out at the bargaining table as look at them. Convinced, the players refused to ratify his negotiated agreement and the lockout followed.

The Major League Umpires Association has in recent times been torn by a rift between member umpires who have supported the supremely self-confident union chief Richie Phillips and those who have not. Phillips, who had successfully led his members through three strikes and a lockout over the past two decades, stumbled in 1999. He persuaded his constituents to resign en masse as a pressure tactic in that year's contract negotiations, but the strategy backfired. The two major leagues permanently accepted the resignations of one-third of the 68 umpires, while most of the others returned to work, and the resulting bitterness between the pro-Phillips and anti-Phillips forces has only seemed to grow as Phillips's future with the union remains in definite doubt. At this writing, it was quite unclear to the employers (the two leagues) just how future negotiations with the association would be conducted, and with whom.

And 1999 also saw the chances of a New York City subway and bus strike greatly increased because of a bitter internal battle between the Transport Workers Union president and a militant faction that wrongly convinced many of the members that a strike would not be illegal. Only a last-minute settlement averted what would, at the height of the Christmas shopping season, have been a major problem for some 3.5 million New Yorkers.

A *failure to accurately assess the other side's strengths* can sometimes explain things. That the Teamsters extracted huge concessions from United Parcel Service in their 15-day 1997 strike that cost UPS an estimated $600 million in lost revenue has been widely credited to three miscalculations by the management. For one, UPS thought that ongoing governmental investigations into the campaign financing of Teamster president Ronald Carey would diminish his effectiveness in the bargaining: they did not, although they ultimately led to his resignation as IBT leader. For another, the management believed that the unsavory reputation of the Teamsters as a hoodlum-infested and possibly mob-controlled organization would guarantee an absence of public support for the union. However, the public, perhaps because it saw the UPS-driver strikers as integral and welcome members of the community, instead roundly backed the strikers. And, for a third, UPS seemed to underestimate the willingness of the 185,000 Teamster members actually to participate in a work stoppage. (A union spokesperson was later to comment that the company "tried to define the fight as whether UPS employees would be loyal to UPS or loyal to the union.") There was no hesitation at all on the part of the unionists either to go out or to stay out. [13]

Similarly, a 191-day 1998–1999 lockout that involved the National Basketball Association and its players union, and cost the league almost $1 billion in revenues and the players roughly $500 million in salaries, stemmed to a large extent from the NBA's underestimation of the union's solidarity. Mindful of the lack of togetherness of the players in the previous negotiations, the owners simply couldn't believe, before it actually happened, that the union members would in a concerted way be willing to walk away from all that money. They had anticipated that any work stoppage, if forthcoming at all, would be a very brief one.

Unions have also shown inadequacies in the assessment area. Believing that the McDonnell Douglas Corporation would do almost anything to avoid a strike in 1996, the Machinists Union put 32 *new* demands on the table in the very last pre-deadline hours. The management felt that all of this was quite unreasonable and granted none of the 32 demands. The 6,400 involved unionists, to the surprise of at least many of them, had no option but to strike.

Hostility between different unions may, of course, also cause problems, as in much of the past decade when the three biggest postal unions (the Postal Workers, the Letter Carriers, and the Mail Handlers) were for a while barely on speaking terms. (By the late 1990s, the Postal Workers and the Letter Carriers had gotten together to agree on something: the irresponsibility of the Mail Handlers in prior negotiations for accepting a U.S. Postal Service offer providing lump-sum bonuses in lieu of wage increases and authorizing lower wages for new workers.) This situation has made the achievement of labor peace quite elusive for the Postal Service as it has sought to negotiate contracts that would be fair to all parties.

Heterogeneity among managements in an industrywide bargaining situation may also play a large role in complicating negotiations. The team owners in major league baseball, for example, have widely varying degrees of financial strengths. By and large, they are strong-willed property holders, and personal animosities abound. Some of this friction, indeed, cannot be divorced from the financial factors (for example, many American League owners harbor a suspicion that their National League counterparts—on the whole, a wealthier class—are selfishly resistant to needed changes in the game). Other rifts are not as clearly rooted to money: The owner of the Atlanta Braves, for example, is unpopular in the inner circles because of his "unpredictability." Either way, negotiating a contract that will be acceptable to a majority of these mutually suspicious owners has been anything but easy for the owners' chief negotiator. This is in enormous contrast to the union side, where unity has generally existed.

In professional sports, too, the 1994–1995 major league hockey lockout was in large measure caused by the wide financial gulf between rich and poor ownerships. Such big-market teams as the New York Rangers, Toronto Maple Leafs, and Detroit Red Wings—all enormously profitable—had no real objection to sharing some of their increasing wealth with their players (at least if the alternative was a work stoppage and thus no revenues for a while). Small-market teams—such as the Hartford Whalers (who had lost $26 million in the previous two years) and the Buffalo, Winnipeg, and Edmonton franchises—felt that taking a hard line toward the players' union was their only recourse. Blaming the richer teams for having escalated player salaries to the point at which they could no longer afford them, the small marketers ultimately prevailed, but ownership enmities continue to this day.

The *personalities* of labor and management representatives often have a major bearing on the outcome. The painful concessions that nine striking unions granted the late British press baron Robert Maxwell in 1991 to end a five-month strike at the *New York Daily News* stemmed from a consensus among these unions that Maxwell's proffered purchase of the sick paper was the *News*'s only alternative to extinction. But the concessions could also be in good measure explained by the sheer force of personality of the swaggering, egocentric Maxwell: "He can charm the birds out of the trees," one of Maxwell's labor antagonists later said (although the labor leader added "and then shoot them").

In like vein, what was believed to be the longest strike in U.S. history was settled in 1992, when Park-Ohio Industries, Inc., announced its intentions of naming Edward Crawford—a man very much respected by the striking United Automobile Workers for his integrity and industrial relations competencies—as its new chairman and chief executive officer. (The announcement ended a labor dispute that had, rather amazingly, lasted nine years and the union shortly thereafter told the media that the *Guinness Book of World Records* was in fact looking into the situation as a precondition of awarding the parties' inclusion in that publication.)

And a major reason why the International Association of Machinists (IAM) settled peacefully with Boeing in mid-1999 was that IAM officials were concerned that a disruptive strike just as the company had finally succeeded in meeting its ambitious production goals could cost the well-liked company CEO Philip M. Condit his job and force the union to deal with a much more hard-line management replacement. Condit, showing why he was held in such high esteem by the Machinists, made it doubly easy for the union to avoid striking by engineering an offer that was seen as so liberal by some Boeing investors that they were apprehensive, but analysts generally agreed that the new pact was not unjustified given the Seattle-based company's situation at the time.

In professional football, on the other hand, an eight-week 1982 strike clearly had many causes—not the least of them a deep desire on the players' part to move away from being the least well paid of all major league athletes—but a widespread belief by the owners that the chief negotiator for the 1,500 players was nothing if not power-hungry undoubtedly prolonged it. The owners, not exactly shrinking violets themselves as individuals, strongly resented Edward R. Garvey's aggressiveness and adamancy. They ultimately took their last offer directly to the players, undercutting Garvey's base, and were successful in this tactic.

Personalities of management negotiators have been known to trigger problems, too. A short-lived but highly disruptive 1985 Transport Workers strike against Pan American World Airways was not exclusively due to the style of Pan Am's major bargainer—the airline's economic problems also played a role—but it owed a heavy indebtedness to the abrasive, acerbic approach of this vice president for industrial relations, C. Raymond Grebey. "He can anger twenty-eight people by just walking into the room," one observer of these negotiations told the press.[14] And one ranking unionist would say only, "You can't print what I would call Grebey."[15] (Mr. Grebey was the chief negotiator for the major league baseball team owners from 1978 to 1983 and as such is to this day also held responsible by some for helping to bring about the 1981 stoppage in that industry.)

And, although a bitter, long-lasting 1989 strike against the now-vanished Eastern Airlines that was waged by all three of its major unions (the Pilots, the Machinists, and the Flight Attendants) had many causes, the enmity that the strikers had for Francisco A. Lorenzo, the intense and demanding chairman of Eastern's parent Texas Air Corporation, was a dominant factor. Lorenzo, who had been able to slash his air fares considerably only by draining resources from the airline and taking a hard line on labor costs was, in the opinion of the Air Line Pilots, "the embodiment of evil." The leader of Eastern's Machinists went so far as to call the entire strike "a Frank Lorenzo strike." And picket lines across the country vilified the chief executive as a "corporate buccaneer," carried placards with a bull's-eye over Lorenzo's face, and chanted, "Eastern, yes! Lorenzo, no!" Lorenzo retaliated by blaming the union leaders for all of Eastern's considerable financial problems and the personal feuding for months made meaningful negotiations impossible.

In the airlines industry, also, years of labor–management mistrust at American Airlines that culminated in hundreds of American pilots calling in sick in early 1999 (forcing hundreds of flights to be canceled and hundreds of thousands of passengers to be inconvenienced) certainly had some large connection to former American CEO Robert L. Crandall, a hard-lining and combative executive whose unquestioned strengths did not extend to labor relations. Two years after his departure, the personal animosity that many pilots held toward him seemed to have been rather unfairly transferred to his successor.

SOME CONCLUDING THOUGHTS

The preceding examples are only a few of the many that could have been chosen to illustrate each category of variable. In any given contract negotiation, one factor might be of major importance—or of no significance at all. The degree of importance of each also, of course, changes over time. And, clearly, many (or none) of these variables can be at play at one time on the bargainers. Contract negotiation is, in short, no more susceptible to sweeping statements than are the unions and managements that participate in the process.

The foregoing *has* indicated, however, that the negotiation of the labor contract in the contemporary economy is a complex and difficult job. The negotiators are required to possess a working knowledge of trade union principles, operations, economics, psychology, statistics, and labor law. They must have the research ability to gather the data necessary for effective negotiations. Negotiators must be shrewd judges of human nature. Often effective speaking ability is an additional prerequisite. Indeed, the position of the negotiator of the modern contract demands the best efforts of people possessing superior ability. Today's collective bargaining sessions have no place for the uninformed, the inept, or the unskilled.

DISCUSSION QUESTIONS

1. Assume that a large, nationwide company is negotiating a contract at the present time. What economic, political, legal, and social factors might be likely to exert some influence on these negotiations?
2. It has been argued by a union research director that "a fact is as welcome at a collective bargaining table as a skunk at a cocktail party." Do you agree?
3. Evaluate the statement that "in the absence of a strike deadline, there can be no true collective bargaining."

4. What might explain the frequently heard management observation that "highly democratic unions are extremely difficult to negotiate with?"
5. How do you account for the fact that the joint study approach still remains confined to a relative handful of industries?
6. From the viewpoint of society, is there anything to be said in favor of strikes?
7. Of all the personal attributes that this chapter has indicated are important for labor relations negotiators to have, which single one do you consider to be the most important, and why?
8. "Successful labor contract bargaining should no longer be viewed as an 'art.' It is far more appropriate today to refer to it as a 'science.'" Discuss.

MINICASES

 ## Trying to Strike a Balance

In order to bargain for the health and safety of employees, the Oil, Chemical and Atomic Workers Union demanded that several employers disclose the generic names of chemical substances used or produced, as well as the medical records of employees. The employers refused, claiming that disclosure would both invade the privacy of employees and compromise trade secrets. With some limitations, the NLRB in 1982 held that the employers did not bargain in good faith when they refused to divulge such information.* While upholding the union's request, the board asserted that few matters could be of greater concern to employees "than exposure to working conditions potentially threatening their health, well-being or their very lives."

However, the board also ruled that the employers could conceal individual employee identities before turning over the medical records and also that the managements did not have to disclose the generic names of chemicals that constituted proprietary trade secrets. Thus, the NLRB attempted to strike a balance between conflicting interests: the employer's desire to protect both worker privacy and trade secrets and the union's need for material information about potentially life-threatening work conditions.

How do you feel about this NLRB decision?

 ## An Advocate of Boulwarism

"I don't care a bit that Boulwarism is long gone at General Electric," says Susan B. ("Ralph") Grishaver, labor relations vice president at the Grand Junction Light Company ("Let There Be Light"). "It's a terrific way of dealing with the union.

"It's not only honest, since the employer literally lets everything hang out, but efficient—because it eliminates all of the wasteful ritual of hyperbolic opening demands and far-out counterproposals. The ridiculous unwritten rule that no agree-

Minnesota Mining & Manufacturing Co., 261 NLRB 27 (1982).

ment will be reached until the strike deadline two months or more down the road is, of course, done away with, too. And it remains completely legal.

"You tell me one thing wrong with it as a strategy for us to use in our 2000 negotiations, in fact. I think that we should seriously consider trying it."

As Grishaver's colleague, how would you advise her?

NOTES

[1]John T. Dunlop and James J. Healy, *Collective Bargaining*, rev. ed. (Homewood, IL: Richard D. Irwin, 1955), p. 53.

[2]*The New York Times*, August 25, 1994, p. B9.

[3]These union demands, needless to say, constituted only the opening union position. As the next section of this chapter will show, there are reasons for such hyperbole. The parties ultimately settled for an estimated $3.5 billion increase.

[4]*Business Week*, February 17, 1997, p. 38.

[5]*Wall Street Journal*, August 28, 1998, p. B4.

[6]Whether they do depends on the scope of the negotiations, however. Where the bargaining is on the local level (as opposed to areawide, industrywide, or nationwide bargaining), the business agent (for example) will very likely be an active union participant in the formal sessions. The same can be said for many management superintendents.

[7]Carl M. Stevens, *Strategy and Collective Bargaining Negotiation* (New York: McGraw-Hill, 1963), pp. 105–6.

[8]Ibid., p. 100.

[9]William E. Simkin, *Mediation and the Dynamics of Collective Bargaining* (Washington, DC: Bureau of National Affairs, 1971), p. 357.

[10]Walter E. Baer, *Labor Arbitration Guide* (Homewood, IL: Dow Jones-Irwin, 1974), p. 94.

[11]*Wall Street Journal*, March 4, 1992, p. A4.

[12]*Wall Street Journal*, July 8, 1999, p. A2.

[13]See *Wall Street Journal*, August 21, 1997, p. A16, for an excellent elaboration of all three points.

[14]*Business Week*, January 21, 1985, p. 40.

[15]*Wall Street Journal*, March 6, 1985.

SELECTED REFERENCES

Brecher, Jeremy. *Strike!* Rev. and updated ed. Boston: South End Press, 1997.

Cohen, Herb. *You Can Negotiate Anything*. Secaucus, NJ: Lyle Stuart, 1980.

Cohn, Samuel. *When Strikes Make Sense—and Why*. New York: Plenum, 1993.

Dunlop, John T., and Arnold M. Zack. *The Mediation and Arbitration of Employment Disputes*. San Francisco: Jossey-Bass, 1997.

Fisher, Roger, and William L. Ury. *Getting to Yes*. Boston: Houghton Mifflin, 1981.

Goldman, Alvin L. *Settling for More: Mastering Negotiating Strategies and Techniques*. Washington, DC: Bureau of National Affairs, 1991.

Holoviak, Stephen J. *Costing Labor Contracts and Judging Their Financial Impact*. New York: Praeger, 1984.

Kagel, Sam, and Kathy Kelly. *The Anatomy of Mediation: What Makes It Work*. Washington, DC: Bureau of National Affairs, 1989.

Kennedy, Gavin. *Field Guide to Negotiation*. Boston: Harvard Business School Press, 1994.

Kolb, Deborah M. *The Mediators*. Cambridge, MA: MIT Press, 1983.

Lax, David A., and James K. Sebenius. *The Manager as Negotiator*. New York: The Free Press, 1986.

Lewicki, Roy J., and Joseph A. Litterer. *Negotiation*. Homewood, IL: R. D. Irwin, 1985.

Loughran, Charles S. *Negotiating a Labor Contract: A Management Handbook*, 2nd ed. Washington, DC: Bureau of National Affairs, 1992.

Morse, Bruce. *How to Negotiate the Labor Agreement*. Southfield, MN: Trends, 1984.

Raiffa, Howard. *The Art and Science of Negotiations.* Cambridge, MA: Harvard University Press, 1982.

Simkin, William E., and Nicholas A. Fidandis. *Mediation and the Dynamics of Collective Bargaining,* 2nd ed. Washington, DC: Bureau of National Affairs, 1986.

Stevens, Carl M. *Strategy and Collective Bargaining Negotiation.* New York: McGraw-Hill, 1963.

Ury, William. *Getting Past No.* New York: Bantam Books, 1991.

Walton, Richard E., Joel E. Cutcher-Gershenfeld, and Robert B. McKersie. *Strategic Negotiations.* Boston: Harvard Business School Press, 1994.

Wever, Kirsten. *Negotiating Competitiveness.* Boston: Harvard Business School Press, 1995.

Zack, Arnold M. *Public Sector Mediation.* Washington, DC: Bureau of National Affairs, 1985.

Zack, Arnold M., and Richard I. Bloch. *Labor Agreement in Negotiation and Arbitration.* Washington, DC: Bureau of National Affairs, 1983.

CHAPTER

6

Administration of the Agreement

*W*hen agreement is finally reached in contract negotiations, the bargainers frequently call in news reporters and photographers, smilingly congratulate each other (as the cameras snap), and announce their satisfaction with the new contract. The exact performance, of course, varies from situation to situation. In general, however, such enthusiastic phrases as "great new era" and "going forward together for our mutual benefit" are often heard.

There is a minimum of sham in these actions. Public relations are, as has been stressed at several earlier stages in this book, important to both sides, and both management–stockholder and union leader–union member relationships are also not overlooked by the management and union participants, respectively, as they register their happiness with their joint handiwork. But typically the negotiators are genuinely optimistic about what they have negotiated: Compromise and statesmanship have once again triumphed.

It will be some time, however, before one can tell whether this optimism is justified. The formal signing of the collective bargaining agreement does not mean that union–management relations are terminated until the next negotiation over contract terms. No contract—whether it involves marriage, insurance on an automobile, or terms and conditions of employment—is any better than its administration. And it is a safe prediction that problems—many of them, in fact—will arise involving the *application* and the *interpretation* of the various clauses in the labor agreement.

The application of the contract is, in fact, a daily problem. Representatives of the two parties normally devote a considerably larger share of their time to the administration of the labor agreement than to its negotiation. Moreover, the climate of labor relations in the workplace will be determined to a large extent by the manner in which management and union representatives discharge their obligations in the day-to-day application of the labor contract.

The source of many administrative problems is in the language of the agreement. Owing to the conditions under which bargaining takes place, many contractual clauses are themselves written in rather broad terms. The day-to-day job in labor relations is to apply the *principles* of the contract.

Many problems can arise under a single clause. A contract may limit the right of management to discharge for "just cause," for example, and an employee is discharged for talking back to a supervisor in harsh terms. Is this just cause within the meaning of the agreement? In another case, a seniority arrangement may provide that the employee with the longer service will get the better job, provided that he or she has ability to perform the job equal to that of any other employee who desires the position. A worker who has been on the payroll for 18 years bids for a higher-rated job, is turned down, and a more junior employee wins the promotion. Has the contract been ignored? Or the parties may have agreed that employees will be expected to perform jobs falling within their job description. An emergency arises, and the management directs some employees to work outside their job description. Did the employer violate the agreement? Or the labor agreement provides that wage rates of new jobs are to be established in a manner that is equitable in terms of comparable jobs. Does a rate established for such a job in fact compare fairly with that for kindred jobs?

These illustrations suggest the multitude of problems that can arise on a day-by-day basis. Practically every provision in a collective bargaining contract can be the basis for controversies that must be resolved.

GRIEVANCE PROCEDURE

Problems such as those posed in the preceding paragraphs are handled and settled through the grievance procedure of the labor contract, which is both an orderly and a peaceful mechanism. It is thus infinitely superior to a system that would allow a strike or lockout every time that one side or the other believed that the contract had been violated. Recognizing this virtue, hundreds of thousands of grievances alleging contractual violations are filed annually in the United States and work stoppages are ruled out pending the grievance procedure's following its prescribed course.

A grievance is an official complaint that the contract has been violated. What makes it official depends on the further understanding of the parties (e.g., it must be reduced to writing on Form 117), and the exact specifics of this can vary widely from relationship to relationship. What is universal, however, is the basic character of the grievance procedure: It is an instrument designed to resolve the day-to-day problems *bilaterally* at, if need be, *successively higher levels* of the union and management hierarchies.

What also does not vary significantly any place is that the vast majority of all grievances are filed by unions on behalf of themselves or on behalf of one or more bargaining unit members. This one-sidedness of grievance activity has nothing to do with any greater combativeness or militancy on the part of unions as compared with the behavior of management. It can be explained exclusively by the definition of *grievance* itself. Unions do not administer employee benefits, make promotion decisions, subcontract work, or discharge employees. Only managements take these and similar actions; thus, only managements are most often in a position to be seen as violating the labor agreement. Managements, as a labor relations maxim has it, act and unions react—except on the relatively rare occasions when employers charge unions with such contractual violations as encouraging a slowdown or causing damage to property during a work stoppage. In the latter situations, the grievance roles are understandably reversed.

❖ Grievances Illustrated

Here is a concrete example of a grievance. Monadnock Swift, a rank-and-file member of Local 1000, had been employed by the Ecumenical Bagel Company for a period of five years. His production record was excellent, he caused management no trouble, and during his fourth year of employment he received a promotion. One day, he began preparations to leave the plant 20 minutes before quitting time. He put away his tools, washed up, got out of his overalls, and put on his street clothes. O. Leo Leahy, an assistant foreman in his department, observed Swift's actions. He immediately informed Swift that he was going to the front office to recommend his discharge. The next morning, Swift reported for work, but Leahy handed him a pay envelope that, in addition to wages, included a discharge notice. The notice declared that the company discharged Swift because he made ready to leave the plant 20 minutes before quitting time.

Swift immediately contacted his union steward, Norman Conquest. The steward worked alongside Swift in the plant and, of course, personally knew the assistant foreman and foreman of his department. After Swift told Conquest the circumstances, the steward believed that the discharge constituted a violation of the collective bargaining contract. A clause in the agreement provided that an employee could be discharged only for "just cause." Disagreeing with the assistant foreman and the front office, the steward felt that the discharge was not for just cause.

The contract covering the employees of Ecumenical contained a carefully worded grievance procedure that provided that all charges of contract violation must be reduced to writing. Consequently, the steward and the discharged worker filled out a "grievance form," describing in detail the character of the alleged violation.

The steps in processing the complaint through the grievance procedure were also clearly outlined in the collective bargaining agreement. First, it was necessary to present the grievance to the foreman of the department in which Swift worked. Both Conquest and Swift approached the foreman, and the written grievance was presented to him. The foreman was required to give his answer on the grievance within 48 hours after receiving it. He complied with the time requirement, but his answer did not please Swift or the steward. The foreman supported the action of the assistant foreman and refused to recommend the reinstatement of Swift.

Not satisfied with the action of the foreman, the labor union, through Conquest the steward, resorted to the second step of the grievance procedure. This step required the appeal of the complaint to the superintendent of the department in which Swift worked. Again the disposition of the grievance by management's representative brought no relief to the discharged employee. Despite the efforts of the steward, who vigorously argued the merits of Swift's case, the department superintendent refused to reinstate the worker. Hence, the second step of the grievance procedure was exhausted, and the union and the employee still were not satisfied with the results.

Actually, the vast majority of grievances are settled in the first two steps of the grievance procedure. This is a remarkable record, indicating the fairness of employers and labor unions. The employer or the union charged with a contract violation may simply admit the transgression and take remedial action, or the party charged with violating the collective bargaining agreement may be able to persuade the other party that, in fact, no violation exists. Frequently, the two parties work out a compromise solution satisfactory to all concerned.

In the Swift case, however, the union refused to drop the case after the complaint was processed through the second level of the grievance procedure. Grievance personnel for the third step included, from the company, the general superintendent and his representatives, and, for the labor union, the organization's plantwide grievance committee. The results of the negotiations at the third step proved satisfactory to Swift, the union, and the company. After 45 minutes of spirited discussion, the management group agreed with the union that discharge was not warranted in this particular case. Management's committee was persuaded by the following set of circumstances: Everyone conceded that Swift had an outstanding record before the dismissal occurred. In addition, the discussion revealed that Swift had inquired of the department foreman whether there was any more work to be done before he left his bench to prepare to leave for home. The foreman had replied in the negative. Finally, it was brought out that Swift had had a pressing problem at home that he claimed was the motivating factor for his desire to leave the plant immediately after quitting time.

The grievance personnel reached a mutually satisfactory solution of the case after all the factors were carefully weighed. Management repeatedly stressed the serious consequences to production efficiency if a large number of workers prepared to leave the plant 20 minutes before quitting time. Recognizing the soundness of this observation, the union committee agreed that some sort of disciplinary action should be taken. As a result, it was concluded that Swift would be reinstated in his job but would be penalized by a three-day suspension without pay. In addition, the union committee agreed with management's representatives that better labor relations would be promoted if a notice were posted on the company bulletin boards stating that all workers would be expected to remain at their jobs until quitting time. Union and company grievance personnel were in agreement that the notice should also declare that violations would be subject to penalty. Thus, the grievance procedure resulted in the amicable solution of a contract violation case.

What would have occurred, however, if the company and the labor union had not reached a satisfactory agreement at the third step of the grievance procedure? In this particular contract, the grievance procedure provided for a fourth step. Grievance procedure personnel at the fourth step included, for the company, the vice president in charge of industrial relations or a representative, and, for the union, an officer of the international union or a representative. It is noteworthy that this particular contract provided four chances to effect a mutually satisfactory disposition of a complaint alleging a contract violation.

All collective bargaining contracts do not provide for the same structural arrangements as the one described in the Swift case. Some contain only three steps while others may have as many as five; in still others, the time limits may be different; or the particular management and union personnel participating at the various steps of the grievance procedure may be somewhat different (as in Exhibit 6-1, illustrating a different but still quite common third-step situation). If their structural arrangements vary slightly from contract to contract, however, the fact remains that the essential characteristics of grievance procedures are similar. All have as their basic objective the settling of alleged contract violation cases in a friendly and orderly manner. In each there is provided a series of definite steps to follow in the processing of grievances. A certain time limit is placed on each step, and an answer to a grievance must be given within the allotted time. Failure to comply with the time limits could result in the forfeiture of the grievance by the errant party. For example, if a union fails to appeal a grievance within the stipulated time limit, the employer may deny the grievance on that basis. In cases that go to arbitration, the arbitrator may under appropriate circumstances hold that, since the union did not comply with the time limit, the grievance is not arbitrable. That is, the arbitrator may deny the grievance on those grounds and without inquiry into the merits of the employee's complaint. *(Case 1, found at the end of this chapter, deals with the time limit problem. It is the first of 10 cases offered by this volume to illustrate specific problems in labor relations.)*

GRIEVANCE PROCEDURE: ITS FLEXIBILITY

Since management officials and union officers make up grievance procedure personnel, people intimately connected with the work will decide whether a particular pattern of conduct violates the terms of the collective bargaining agreement. Obviously, these people are in a favored position to make such a determination. Frequently, some of them helped negotiate the contract itself. And such participation should result in a clear understanding of the meaning of particular contract terms. Not only do grievance procedure personnel normally possess a thorough and firsthand knowledge of the meaning of the contract, but they can be expected to be well aware of the character of the conduct alleged to be a violation. Grievance cases are at times complex in nature. The line dividing lawful from unlawful conduct under a collective bargaining contract is not always sharply drawn, but the men and women on the front lines of labor relations are best equipped to make such a distinction.

EXHIBIT 6-1

Local 117
Record of Grievance

Date: _____ June 8, 1999

Name _____ Raymond R. Mellish _____   Home Phone _____

Address _____   Status: Regular____Seasonal____

Date of Hire _____   Pay Rate _____   Job Class _____

Department _____   Supervisor _____

NATURE OF COMPLAINT (Give dates) ___ I was discharged for fighting on company property. I feel that this is unfair and unjustified because the company does not fire everyone for fighting. I ask to be reinstated with back pay and seniority. _____

_____

_____

_____

_____

Steward or Business Representative ___ Rupert Psmith _____

COMPANY RESPONSE: ___ Grievance denied. Rule #39 in the "Employee Handbook" outlines the amount of discipline to be administered for violation of this rule. This grievance is untimely. Incident occurred on 5/4/99.

Date 6/9/99 **Plant Manager** ___ Joss Weatherby ___

The local people should also be well aware of the environmental context in which the alleged violation occurred. Weight can be given to human or economic factors. This does not mean that an "explainable" violation will go unchallenged. However, the grievance procedure personnel might resolve an explainable violation in a different manner from one in which no extenuating circumstances were involved.

In addition, since grievance procedure personnel are closely associated with the circumstances, they are in an excellent position to anticipate the effects of the disposition of a grievance on employers, on the union, on union leadership, and on plant operations. To promote sound industrial relations, management and union grievance procedure personnel, as noted, frequently compromise on the solution of grievance cases. It is not unknown for management to allow the union to "win" a grievance case to bolster the prestige of union leadership in the eyes of union membership; the state of industrial relations may be improved when union leaders have the confidence of the membership. On the other hand, a labor union may refuse to challenge a management violation of a contract when the employer engages in conduct absolutely essential to operations.

Contrary to the seniority provisions of an existing collective bargaining contract, for example, an employer recently laid off longer-service employees and retained shorter-service employees. Such action constituted a direct violation of the particular contract. However, the union representatives agreed with the management, when the case was resolved through the grievance procedure, that the retention of the shorter-service workers was vital to the continued operation of a crucial department. Union and management grievance procedure personnel concluded that had the longer-service workers been retained and the shorter-service employees been laid off, the organization and all of its employees would have suffered great damage.

It is not intended here to create a false impression of the operation of the grievance procedure. Certainly, the mechanism does not function to condone employer, employee, or union violations of contracts. In the overwhelming number of cases disposed of through the grievance procedure, practices inconsistent with the terms of the agreement are terminated. At times, retroactive action must be taken to implement rights and obligations provided for in the contract. Thus, the employer may be required to reinstate with back pay a worker who had previously been discharged in violation of the discharge clause of the labor agreement. Or perhaps a union caused damage to the employer's property while on strike; to comply with a particular contract provision, this union might be required to pay the management a certain sum of money.

But it is still true that the grievance procedure is singularly adaptable for the settlement of contract disputes to the maximum satisfaction of all concerned. Interests of all parties can be considered. The procedure's flexible and personalized character permits compromise when this is deemed the best way to settle a particular grievance. Extenuating circumstances can be given weight. Precedent can be utilized or disregarded, depending on the particular situation. Solutions to problems can be reached that will serve the basic interests of sound industrial relations. These observations lead to one conclusion: Resort to the grievance procedure provides management and unions with the most useful and efficient means of contract enforcement.

❖ Grievance Procedure and Harmonious Labor Relations

Depending on the attitudes of the management and the union, the grievance procedure can also be used for functions *other* than the settlement of complaints arising under the labor agreement. Many parties, for example, use the grievance machinery to prevent grievances from arising as well as to dispose of employee, union, and employer complaints. Major grievances are viewed here as symptomatic of underlying problems, and attempts are jointly made to dispose of these problems to prevent their future recurrence. In other cases, the parties may utilize the scheduled grievance meeting time, after the grievance itself has been dealt with, to explore ways of improving their general relationship and also as an avenue of bilateral communication on matters of interest to both institutions (such as new employer plans, the economic prospects for the industry, or the upcoming union election).

In the last analysis, in fact, the grievance procedure should be regarded as a device whereby managements or unions can "win" a grievance only in the most narrow of senses. It should also be viewed as a means of obtaining a better climate of labor relations.

This objective is not realized when representatives of management look upon their obligations under the grievance procedure as burdensome chores, as wastes of time, or as necessary evils. It is not attainable to the extent that unions stuff the grievance procedure with complaints that have no merit whatsoever under the contract, something that most unions fully appreciate (many union manuals for stewards and grievance committee members, indeed, explicitly contain statements such as "After you have thoroughly investigated the case, if you decide that no grievance exists, it is your duty to the worker and the union to state this, and to take time to explain why"). It cannot be achieved when the parties regard the procedure as a method to embarrass the other side or to demonstrate authority or power. Nor can opportunities for more harmonious labor relations through the use of the grievance procedure be realized to the extent that the system is used to resolve internal political conflicts within the union or the management. If the grievance procedure does not contribute to a better labor relations climate, the fault lies not with the system, but with the representatives of unions and management who either misunderstand or distort the functions that the procedure plays in the industrial relations complex.

ARBITRATION

The vast majority of problems that arise as the result of the interpretation and application of collective bargaining contracts are resolved bilaterally by the representatives of management and the labor organization. Through the process of negotiation, the parties to a contract manage to find a solution to grievances at some step in the grievance procedure. Such a record testifies to the utility of the grievance procedure as a device for the speedy, fair, and peaceful solution of disputes growing out of the application of the contract. It also shows rather clearly that the great majority of management and union representatives understand fully the purpose of the grievance procedure and discharge their responsibilities on the basis of good faith.

Indeed, in healthy union–management relationships, the great bulk of grievances is disposed of at the lower levels of the procedure. This is as it should be; were most such complaints merely bucked up the union and management hierarchical ladders, the time and efforts of the more broadly based officials would be hopelessly drained. Lower-step settlement also helps maintain the status of lower supervision and assures that the grievance is allowed treatment by the people who are apt to be most familiar with the circumstances under which it arose.

Under even the most enviable of labor relationships, however, there will undoubtedly be some grievances that prove themselves completely incapable of being solved by *any* level within the bilateral grievance procedure. Each party genuinely believes that its interpretation of the contract is the right one, or the parties remain in disagreement as to the facts of the case.

There may also, on occasion, be less commendable reasons for a stalemate. The union leadership may feel that it cannot afford to "give in" on an untenable grievance because of the political ramifications of doing so. Management may at times prove quite unwilling to admit that the original employer action giving rise to the grievance was in violation of the contract, even though in its heart it realizes that the union's allegation is right. The union may, the remarks previously offered in this connection notwithstanding, seek to "flood" the grievance procedure with a potpourri of unsettled grievances, with the hope of using the situation to gain extracontractual concessions from the employer. The employer may, in turn, seek to embarrass the union leadership by making it fight to the limit for any favorable settlement. The union may want to get rid of an incumbent manager and use the existence of a large number of unresolved grievances as a weapon in its campaign to convince higher management that the unwanted manager is a poor administrator. And grievances involving such thorny issues as discipline, work assignment, subcontracting, job classification, and management rights are sometimes accompanied by emotional undercurrents that make them all the more difficult to resolve by the joint conference method of the grievance procedure. Given all these possibilities, it is, in fact, a tribute to the maturity of labor–management relations that more than 90 percent of all grievances are settled by the joint process.

Nonetheless, some contractual provision must be made by the parties to handle the relatively few issues for which the grievance procedure proves unsuccessful—those occasions upon which the parties to the labor contract are still in disagreement over a problem arising under the contractual terms after all bilateral steps in the grievance procedure have been exhausted. To break such deadlocks, the parties have the opportunity to resort to the arbitration process. An impartial outsider is selected by the parties to decide the controversy. This person's decision is invariably stipulated in the contract as being "final and binding upon both parties."

❖ The Growth of Arbitration

As a method of dispute settlement, arbitration is anything but new. King Solomon was an arbitrator some three thousand years ago. Arbitration (sometimes with more than one arbitrator) was also used to settle disputes between towns in ancient Greece and was an accepted avenue for resolving controversy in ancient Babylon, the early Islamic civilization, and under Roman law. The Confucian Chinese used it, too, and so did the medieval Germans. In the United States, George Washington showed his high regard for the concept by providing for binding arbitration in his will (should any disputes arise concerning the intent of the latter).

As American unionism grew, the advantages of arbitration became visible in this sector, also. Above all, it was seen that the arbitrator could resolve the labor dispute in a peaceful manner. In the absence of arbitration, the parties might use the strike or lockout to settle such problems, a process that not only could be costly to the management, the union, and the employees but also would tend to foster embittered labor relations. Impressed by these arbitral facts of life, 99 percent of all U.S. labor agreements provide for arbitration as the final step in the grievance procedure. This national percentage is significantly greater than it was in the early 1930s, when fewer than 8 to 10 percent of all agreements contained such a clause. And even by 1944, arbitration provisions had been included in only 73 percent of all contracts.

A major Supreme Court decision in 1957—in the *Lincoln Mills* case—gave the concept a significant shot in the arm.[1] The Court ruled here that an employer could not refuse to arbitrate unresolved grievances when the labor agreement contains an arbitration clause: "Plainly," the justices said, "the agreement to arbitrate grievance disputes is the *quid quo pro* for an agreement not to strike."

And in 1960, the highest court in the land handed down three other decisions, all involving the United Steelworkers of America, that provided even greater backing of the arbitration process. These decisions are commonly referred to as the Trilogy cases.[2]

THE TRILOGY CASES

In the *Warrior & Gulf Navigation* case, which stemmed from a union grievance claim that the company had violated the contract by improperly subcontracting out some maintenance and repair work, the Court held that, in the absence of an express agreement excluding arbitration of a disputed activity, it would direct the parties to arbitrate a grievance. The Court stated that a legal order to arbitrate would thenceforth not be denied "unless it may be said with positive assurance that the arbitration clause is not susceptible to an interpretation that covers the asserted dispute. Doubts should be resolved in favor of coverage."

More precisely, the courts will not decide that a dispute is *not* arbitrable unless the parties have taken care to *expressly remove* an area of labor relations from the arbitration process. This could be accomplished by providing, for example, that "disputes involving determination of the qualifications of employees for promotion will be determined exclusively by the employer and such decision will not be subject to arbitration." But, needless to say, not many unions would agree to such a clause, since management would then have the unilateral right to make determinations on this vital phase of the promotion process.

In its ruling, the *Warrior & Gulf Navigation* decision eliminated a course of action that some managements had followed. When faced with a demand by a union for arbitration, some employers had frequently gone to court and asked the judge to decide that the issue involved in the case was not arbitrable. On many occasions, the courts had agreed with the management, with the effect of sustaining the employer position in the grievance and denying the union an opportunity to get a decision based on the merits of the case.

In *Warrior & Gulf Navigation*, the Supreme Court ordered arbitration because the contract did not *specifically* exclude the disputed activity (subcontracting) from the arbitration process. It stated:

> A specific collective bargaining agreement may exclude contracting-out from the grievance procedure. Or a written collateral agreement may make clear that contracting-out was not a matter for arbitration. In such a case a grievance based solely on contracting-out would not be arbitrable. Here, however, there is no such provision. Nor is there any showing that the parties designed the phrase "strictly as a function of management" to encompass any and all forms of contracting-out. In the absence of any express provision excluding a particular grievance from arbitration, we think only the most forceful evidence of a purpose to exclude the claim from arbitration can prevail, particularly where, as here, the exclusion clause is vague and the arbitration clause quite broad.

One additional important point must be emphasized to understand the significance of this decision. Though the court may direct arbitration, it will not determine the merits of the dispute. A federal court decides only whether the grievance is arbitrable, but the private arbitrator has full authority to rule on its merits. As the Supreme Court stated in *Warrior & Gulf Navigation*, "Whether contracting out in the present case violated the agreement is the question. It is a question for the arbiter, not for the courts." This principle was reaffirmed in 1986 by the Court in *AT&T Technologies* v. *Communications Workers.*[3]

In the second case, *American Manufacturing*, the issue of arbitrability was also involved, but in a different way. The American Manufacturing Company argued before a lower federal court that an issue was not arbitrable because it did not believe that the grievance had merit. Involved was a dispute concerning the reinstatement of an employee on his job after it was determined that the employee was 25 percent disabled and was drawing workmen's compensation. The lower federal court sustained the employer's position and characterized the employee's grievance as "a frivolous, patently baseless one, not subject to arbitration." When the U.S. Supreme Court reversed the lower federal court, it held that federal courts are limited in determining whether the dispute is covered by the labor agreement and that they have no power to evaluate the merits of a dispute. It stated:

> The function of the court is very limited when the parties have agreed to submit all questions of contract interpretation to the arbitrator. It is then confined to ascertaining whether the party seeking arbitration is making a claim which on its face is governed by the contract. Whether the moving party is right or wrong is a question of contract construction for the arbitrator. In these circumstances the moving party should not be deprived of the arbitrator's judgment, when it was his judgment and all that it connotes that was bargained for.

Essentially, this means that the courts may not hold a grievance to be nonarbitrable even if a judge believes that a grievance is completely worthless. It is up to the private arbitrator to make the decision on the merits of a case. The arbitrator may dismiss the grievance as being without merit, but this duty rests exclusively with the individual arbitrator, and not with the courts.

In the third case, *Enterprise Wheel & Car Corporation*, a lower federal court reversed the decision of an arbitrator on the grounds that the judge did not believe that his decision was sound under the labor agreement. The arbitrator's award directed the employer to reinstate certain discharged workers and to pay them back wages for periods both before and after the expiration of the collective bargaining contract. The company refused to comply with the award, and the union petitioned for the enforcement of the award. The lower court held that the arbitrator's award was unenforceable because the contract had expired. The Supreme Court reversed the lower court and ordered full enforcement. In upholding the arbitrator's award, the Court stated:

> Interpretation of the collective bargaining agreement is a question for the arbitrator. It is the arbitrator's construction which was bargained for; and so far as the arbitration decision concerns construction of the contract, the courts have no business overruling him because their interpretation of the contract is different from his.

The significance of this last decision is clear. It shows that a union or a management may not use the courts to set aside an arbitrator's award. The decision, of course, cuts both ways: It applies to both employers and labor organizations. Whereas the other two decisions definitely favor labor organizations, this one merely serves to preserve the integrity of the arbitrator's award. Thus, even if a judge believes that an arbitrator's award is unfair, unwise, and not even consistent with the contract, that judge has no alternative except to enforce the award.

With the Trilogy decisions, private arbitration had come very much of age, its integrity fully established by the judiciary. The most fanatic devotee of the process really could have asked for nothing more.

And with such enthusiastic Supreme Court backing, as well as the growth of the labor movement in these years, the volume of arbitration cases increased sharply over the next quarter-century. In 1980, arbitrators serving under the auspices of the Federal Mediation and Conciliation Service (FMCS) issued 7,539 awards, compared with 2,849 in 1970 and only half the latter number in 1960. In 1986 the award total climbed to 9,286. Since then, however, the annual number of FMCS awards has steadily stayed in the 4,500 to 5,000 range, a situation attributable to at least some extent to the decline in union membership but not helped at all either by some post-Trilogy judicial rulings.

❖ Post-Trilogy Developments

In 1974, the pendulum started to swing slightly in the other direction, with the Supreme Court's *Alexander* v. *Gardner-Denver* decision.[4] Other decisions from the bench over the next decade also detracted to some extent from the Trilogy.

In *Gardner-Denver*, the high court held that an arbitrator's decision is not final and binding when Title VII of the **Civil Rights Act of 1964** is involved. That legislation, in force since 1964 and subsequently broadened by amendments to it, prohibits discrimination in all employment decisions on the basis of race, color, religion, national origin, disability, or sex. An arbitrator had sustained the discharge of a black employee on the grounds that he was terminated for just cause. The employee had claimed, however, that he had been discharged for racial reasons in violation of Title VII. Lower federal courts upheld the decision of the arbitrator, in line with the Trilogy doctrine. However, the Supreme Court remanded the case to the federal district court to determine whether or not the employee's rights under Title VII had been violated. What *Gardner-Denver* means, therefore, is that if an employee loses a case in arbitration, the employee may still seek relief from the courts, provided that Title VII rights are involved.

In 1976, the Supreme Court decided *Anchor Motor Freight*,[5] which also represents a departure from the finality of an arbitrator's award. In this case, the Court held that an arbitrator's decision is subject to reversal by a federal court when a union does not provide fair representation to employees involved in the arbitration. An employer discharged eight truck drivers for allegedly submitting inflated motel receipts for reimbursement. Their union took the discharges to arbitration, but the union failed to heed the drivers' request to investigate the motel employees. After the arbitration, in which the discharges were sustained, evidence turned up that a motel clerk was the guilty party. He had been making false entries in the motel register and pocketing the difference.

Thereupon, the drivers sued the employer and the union. A lower federal court upheld the arbitrator's award on the basis of *Enterprise Wheel*. However, the U.S.

Supreme Court ruled that when a union fails to provide fair representation to employees involved in arbitration, they are entitled to an appropriate remedy. Obviously, the truck drivers were not discharged for just cause, and elementary fairness should dictate their reinstatement to their jobs with full back pay. The arbitrator's award should not stand in the way of providing justice to the discharged employees. *Anchor Motor Freight* put the union on notice. In effect, the Court has said that the courts have the authority to upset an arbitration award when a union commits a gross error in the representation of employees in arbitration or otherwise fails to live up to its arbitration responsibilities.

Then, in 1981, the Supreme Court ruled that an arbitrator's decision involving rights established by the Fair Labor Standards Act may be reviewed and reversed by the federal courts,[6] and thereby, when taken in conjunction with *Gardner-Denver*, implicitly gave a clear signal that arbitration decisions are not final and binding when the issue falls within any labor law.

And in 1984, the high court once again determined that an employee's claim, based on statutory rights, is not foreclosed by an arbitration award. In *McDonald* v. *City of West Branch, Michigan*,[7] a police officer—a union steward—was discharged for allegedly participating in a sexual assault on a minor. An arbitrator sustained the discharge, finding that McDonald was discharged for just cause. Asserting that his discharge was in reprisal for his activities as a union steward, the police officer sued in federal district court requesting that damages be assessed against the chief of police and other city officials. His suit alleged a violation of Section 1983 of the Civil Rights Act of 1871, claiming that his discharge violated his First Amendment rights of freedom of speech and association and freedom to petition the government for redress of grievances. A federal district court permitted McDonald to proceed with his suit and a jury eventually awarded him an $8,000 judgment against the police chief. On appeal by the city, however, a federal appeals court reversed the lower court's decision, finding that the First Amendment claim was an unwarranted attempt to litigate a matter already decided by the arbitrator.

In a unanimous decision, the U.S. Supreme Court reversed the federal appeals court, finding that arbitration was not the proper forum to address issues involving statutory and constitutional rights. Following its earlier decisions, the high court stated that,

> although arbitration is well suited to resolving contractual disputes, our [earlier decisions] compel the conclusion that it cannot provide an adequate substitute for a judicial proceeding in protecting the federal statutory and constitutional rights that Sec. 1983 is designed to safeguard.

One should not believe, however, that the high court intends to undermine the arbitration process just because of these decisions. It would not be correct to conclude that they demonstrate the Court's intent to upset arbitration decisions on a wholesale basis. In fact, the courts have in these same post-Trilogy years also sustained an NLRB policy that makes private arbitration an even more important feature in labor relations.[8] In 1971, the NLRB held, in *Collyer Insulated Wire*,[9] that it would defer some cases to arbitration even though they contained elements of unfair labor practices. In these cases, contractual provisions were arguably involved, and the NLRB believed that private arbitrators not only could decide whether the contract was violated but also could determine the unfair labor practice issue. Though this *Collyer* decision has been criticized on the grounds that the NLRB should not abandon its statutory duty to enforce the Taft-Hartley Act, the fact remains that the doctrine makes arbitration an even more viable instrument for the settlement of labor–management disputes.

And in *Misco*, a 1987 case, the Supreme Court further underscored the integrity of arbitration awards.[10] An employee was discharged for possessing marijuana on plant premises. An arbitrator reinstated him with full back pay on the basis that the company had insufficient evidence to prove that he violated the rule against drug use and/or possession. After the employer moved to vacate the award as contrary to public policy, lower federal courts upset the arbitrator's decision. A federal appeals court held that reinstatement would violate the public policy "against the operation of dangerous machinery by persons under the influence of drugs or alcohol."

Reversing the lower courts and upholding the arbitrator's decision, the high court ruled that "absent fraud by the parties or the arbitrator's dishonesty, reviewing courts in such cases are not authorized to reconsider the merits of the award, since this would undermine the federal policy of privately settling labor disputes by arbitration without governmental intervention." As for reversal on the basis of public policy, the Court significantly limited the federal courts by saying that such action is justified only when policy is well defined, dominant, and ascertained by reference to laws and legal precedents, rather than general consideration of supposed policy. In other words, a court may not use its subjective judgment of what constitutes public policy, or what the policy ought to be.

For the arbitrator, the Trilogy, *Collyer*, and *Misco* decisions are equally important. Private arbitrators bear an even greater degree of responsibility as they decide their cases. Not only is the post one of honor, in which the parties have confidence in the arbitrator's professional competency and integrity, but the arbitrator must recognize that for all intents and purposes his or her decision is completely "final and binding" upon the parties. Indeed, if the system of private arbitration is to remain a permanent feature of the American system of industrial relations, arbitrators must measure up to their responsibilities. Should they fail in this respect, managements and unions would simply delete the arbitration clause from the contract and resolve their disputes by strikes or by going directly to court. These are not pleasant alternatives, but the parties may choose these routes if they believe that arbitrators are not discharging their responsibilities in an honorable, judicious, and professional manner. Arbitrators should not feel so smug as to believe that their services are indispensable to labor unions and employers. They are as expendable as last year's calendar.

❖ Limitations to Arbitration

If employers and unions support the arbitration process as an accepted method of disposing of disagreements relating to problems arising under the terms of a labor contract already in existence, there is almost no approval on the part of industry and organized labor for using arbitration as the means of breaking deadlocks in the negotiations of *new* agreements. Most employers and unions would rather have a work stoppage than refer such disputes to arbitration, chiefly because of the parties' extreme aversion to having an outsider determine the conditions of employment, the rights and obligations of management, and the responsibilities and rights of the union. Employers and unions almost invariably believe that, since the labor agreement will establish their fundamental relationship, they should have the full authority to negotiate its terms. For these reasons, the use of arbitration during the negotiation stage of a labor contract is rare.

It is also important to note that in the United States the system is one of *private and voluntary arbitration.* That is, the government does not force the parties to include arbitration clauses in their labor agreements. They do so voluntarily as they negotiate the latter. Either party can refuse to incorporate any arbitration provisions at all, as has been the case in the building construction industry, where the duration of the job is deemed too brief to make use of a neutral feasible, and in some of the trucking industry, where the Teamster hierarchy has traditionally insisted that neutrals "attempt to please both sides and actually please nobody."

Equally significant is the fact that arbitrators are private rather than government officials. Most of them are lawyers and college professors. As a matter of fact, the Federal Mediation and Conciliation Service and some state agencies that provide mediation services will not permit their mediators to serve as arbitrators.

❖ Characteristics of Arbitration Hearings

Since the decision of the arbitrator *is* final and binding, arbitration is quite different from mediation. The parties are completely free to accept or reject the recommendations or suggestions of the mediator. But whether the arbitrator rules for or against a party to the arbitration, that decision *must* be accepted. This is true even when the losing side believes that the decision is not warranted by the labor agreement, by the evidence submitted in the hearing, or on the basis of fairness or justice. Frequently, an arbitrator's decision will establish an important precedent that must be followed by the employer, the union, and the employees. At times the party that suffers an adverse ruling in an arbitration case will attempt to change, during the next labor contract negotiations, those sections of the labor agreement that proved to be the basis of the decision. Obviously, the side that is benefited by the decision will be reluctant to alter those features of the labor agreement that were interpreted and applied by the arbitrator.

These considerations tend to show the seriousness of arbitration as a tool of labor relations. When the decision to arbitrate is made, the employer and union representatives are undertaking a deep responsibility. To discharge this responsibility in a competent and intelligent manner, they must put the arbitrator in such a position that the latter can make a decision in light of the evidence and of the relevant contractual clauses. Consequently, the parties have the obligation of preparing fully before coming to the hearing. This means the accumulation of all evidence, facts, documents, and arguments that may have a bearing on the dispute. Careful preparation also means the selection of witnesses who can give relevant testimony in the case. Management and union representatives should leave no stone unturned in preparing for the arbitration.

At the arbitration hearing, each side will have full opportunity to present the fruits of its preparation. Normally, although arbitration hearings are much more formal than grievance procedure negotiations, they are considerably less formal than court proceedings. In addition, the rules of evidence that apply in the courts of the land do not bind the conduct of the arbitration. This means that the hearing can be conducted not only more informally but also much faster than a case in court. However, the parties should not be deluded into believing that the arbitrator's decision will not be based on evidence and facts. Even though the arbitration proceedings might be regarded as semiformal, arbitration cases are not won on the basis of emotional appeals, theatrical gestures, or speechmaking. The arbitrator is interested in the facts, the evidence, and the parties' arguments as they apply to the issues of the dispute. Such material should be developed in the hearing through careful questioning of witnesses and the presentation of relevant documents.

The parties cannot, moreover, take too much care to make sure that they have presented *all* evidence that might support their case. Representatives of unions and managements who have dealt with a problem in the grievance procedure, and who therefore are fully aware of all the facets of a case, will at times not fully present their case because they believe that the arbitrator is likewise familiar with the facts and issues. Unless prehearing briefs are filed by the parties, it should be recognized that the arbitrator knows absolutely nothing about the case at the time of the hearing. It is the responsibility of the parties to educate the arbitrator about the issues, the facts, the evidence, the arguments, and the relevant contractual clauses. Clearly, if the arbitration process is to have a significant positive value, the parties to the arbitration must discharge their obligations fully and conscientiously. They must be indefatigable in their efforts to prepare for the arbitration and absolutely thorough in the presentation of their case to the arbitrator.

❖ Responsibilities of the Arbitrator

The arbitrator, of course, is the key person in the arbitration process, possessing the cold responsibility for the decision in the case. The arbitrator decides, for example, whether a discharged employee remains discharged or returns to work, which of two workers gets the better job or whether the employer placed a correct rate on a new job. Few members of the profession have ever rendered a decision that even remotely approximates in its direct financial ramifications one that was handed down a while ago by arbitrator Sidney A. Wolff. In a case involving the Pabst Brewing Company and the Teamsters, Wolff ordered Pabst to negotiate a new plant-closing settlement that cost it some $18 million in back pay. Even an award of the magnitude cited in Exhibit 6-2 (a "victory" to the union involved but not reason for celebration to the employer) is unusual; decisions directly involving less than a very few thousand dollars are much more typical. But arbitration is always of critical importance to everyone who is a party to it—or at least those who are asked to arbitrate must operate under that assumption—and it is beyond argument that one of the most important jobs that a person can receive is the assignment by an employer and a union to an arbitration case.

❖ Ethical Considerations

In discharging their responsibilities, arbitrators are expected to adhere to a strict code of ethics. The decision must be based squarely on the evidence and the facts presented. The arbitrator must give full faith and credit to the language of the labor contract at the time of the case. It should be recognized by all concerned that the language of the labor agreement binds the employer, the union, the employees, *and the arbitrator*. It is not within the scope of the arbitrator's authority to decide whether a particular contractual clause is wise or unwise, desirable or undesirable. The arbitrator's job is to apply the language of a labor contract as he or she finds it in a particular case. To follow any other course of action not only would be a breach of faith to the parties but also would create mischief with the labor agreement. The arbitrator must regard the collective bargaining contract as a final authority and give it full respect. If a case goes against a party because of the language of the contract, the responsibility for this state of affairs lies not with the arbitrator but with the parties who negotiated the agreement.

EXHIBIT 6-2

SOURCE: *1199 News*,
September–October
1998, p. 29.

Pathmark Arbitration Victory

Pathmark pharmacists who helped win
$1.75 million settlement include (l-r)
Oliver Coutrier, Martha Wainer (front),
James Fitzgerald and Ira Hauer.

1199 pharmacists at Pathmark stores
won an arbitration victory in June totaling $1.75 million in back pay and
benefit and pension contributions.

The settlement brings about
$12,000 to each of the 140 pharma-
cists affected by the ruling.

Pathmark violated the union
contract when it hired part-timers to
do work previously performed by
full-time pharmacists, ruled the arbitrator. She said that whatever its intention, Pathmark could not violate
a 30-year past practice without
union consent.

"When Pathmark management
announced its intention to eliminate
overtime, we asked for a temporary
moratorium and an opportunity to
discuss different options," says Ira
Hauer, a Pathmark pharmacist and
delegate in the Shirley, Long Island
store for 11 years. "Management was
not interested in negotiations."

In March, 1997, Pathmark instituted its new policy and the union
followed with a class action grievance. Management refused to
budge. Members continued to apply
pressure, holding demonstrations at
several Pathmark stores.

"We had an unbeatable team,"
Hauer says. "We were united. Pharmacist Steve Shalat produced a
newsletter that kept everyone informed. Organizer Laurie Vallone
worked long hours and did in-depth
research. Attorney Dan Ratner made
a brilliant presentation at the hearing. Pathmark was overmatched."

"This victory sends a clear message to management that our contracts are sacred," says Exec. VP
Mike Rifkin.

The committee that worked on
the grievance included Organizer
Vallone, Hauer, Oliver Coutrier,
Marty Wainer, Jim Fitzgerald and Jeff
Haupmann.

If the language of the contract is clear-cut and unequivocal, the arbitrator's job
is not too difficult. Under these circumstances, the award will favor the party whose
position is sustained by the precise contractual language. Of course, there are not
many cases of this type, since, if the language is clear-cut and precise, the dispute
should not have gone to arbitration. It should have been resolved in the grievance
procedure on the basis of the contractual language.

❖ Past Practice

What complicates the problem is contractual language that is subject to different
shades of meaning. That is, impartial people could find that the language involved
may be reasonably interpreted in different ways. Under these circumstances, what is
called past practice—the way in which the language has been applied in the past—
serves as the guide for construction of the ambiguous contractual language.

The idea behind past practice is that both parties have knowledge of the practice
and both expect that the practice will be honored as the basis of administration of

the relevant language. Thus, when the arbitrator is confronted with language that is ambiguous, the decision will normally be based on the evidence demonstrating practice. However, if the language is unambiguous and unequivocal, and the practice conflicts with the clear-cut contractual language, the arbitrator will normally base the decision on the language rather than on the practice. Unequivocal contractual language supersedes practice when the two conflict.

Also, arbitrators generally recognize that past practice should not be used to restrict management in the changing of work methods required by changing conditions. Thus, past practice is normally not used to prevent management from changing work schedules, work assignments, workloads, job assignments, and the number of workers needed on the job. The key to such an arbitration principle is that changing conditions have made the practice obsolete. Of course, there may be written contractual language that would forbid the management's making such changes in work methods. Under these circumstances, the arbitrator's decision would be based on the written contractual language; but past practice would not normally be used to block management action when conditions change. Despite these limitations, past practice is frequently used as the basis for arbitrator decisions, particularly, as stated, when contractual language is subject to different shades of meaning.

❖ "Fairness"

Much has been said and written about the necessity of the arbitrator's being "fair" in making a decision. A decision is fair only when it is based on the evidence of a case and the accurate assessment of the relevant provisions of the labor agreement. Furthermore, fairness does not mean charity, compromise, or an attempt to please both sides. At times, a management and a union arbitrate a number of different grievances in one hearing. An arbitrator who deliberately decides to compromise or "split" the grievances is not worthy of the confidence of the parties. An arbitrator who is a "splitter" not only violates the ethics of the office but also causes untold confusion and damage to the parties. What managements and unions desire in arbitration is a clear-cut decision on each grievance, based on the merits of each dispute; they do not want splitting. They are invariably unhappy with an award that appears to have been shaped from the formula $AA = (E + U)/2$, where $AA =$ arbitrator's award, $E =$ employer's position, and $U =$ union's position. The parties can divide by 2 themselves and presumably have no desire to go to the trauma, expense, and uncertainty of the arbitration process for this kind of result (even while recognizing that on occasion—rare occasion—it is nonetheless inevitable).

Compromise or "horse trading" of grievances may be accomplished in the grievance procedure. However, once grievances are referred to arbitration, every one of them must be decided on its own merits. Clearly, a "split-the-difference" approach to arbitration can do irreparable harm to the parties, the collective bargaining contract, and the arbitration process. Managements and unions would quickly lose confidence in arbitration if cases were decided not upon their merits but upon the determination of the arbitrator to "even up" his or her awards.

In fact, before hearing a case, each arbitrator normally takes a solemn oath of office to decide the dispute on the evidence, free from any bias. Any arbitrator who transgresses this oath by striving to decide a case on a split-the-difference formula has absolutely no business serving as an arbitrator. A famous and respected baseball umpire once said he called them as he saw them. Even though umpiring a baseball game is quite different from arbitrating a labor dispute, and although the qualifications for baseball umpires are quite different from those for arbitrators in labor relations, the homely statement "call them as you see them" has real significance for arbitration of any kind of dispute.

❖ Other Responsibilities of Arbitrators

Additional responsibilities and personal qualities are required in the person serving as an arbitrator. The latter not only must be incorruptible, free from any bias, and aware of the principles of arbitration but also must have a deep and well-rounded understanding of labor relations. It takes more than honesty and integrity to serve effectively as an arbitrator. Arbitrators who are not trained in labor relations matters, even though they may be paragons of virtue, can cause enormous damage to the parties by decisions that do violence to the collective bargaining contract.

At the hearing, the arbitrator should treat both sides with the dignity and the respect that are characteristic of the judicial process. The arbitrator should be patient, sympathetic, and understanding. Experienced arbitrators do not take advantage of their office by being arrogant or domineering. Arbitrators who have a tendency to exaggerate their own importance should be aware of the fact that arbitration, although important, plays a distinctly minor role in the overall union–management relationship. The arbitrator should permit each side to the dispute the fullest opportunity to present all the evidence, witnesses, documents, and arguments that it desires. While a desire for relevancy is, as Justice Oliver Wendell Holmes once wrote, a "concession to the shortness of life," experienced arbitrators frequently lean over backward to permit the introduction of evidence that may or may not be relevant to the dispute. This procedure is better than a policy that could result in the suppression of vital information.

The arbitrator also has the responsibility for keeping the hearing moving. When there is a deliberate or unconscious waste of time by either or both of the parties, the arbitrator is obligated to take remedial action. This does not mean that he or she should not permit recesses, coffee breaks, or the occasional telling of a humorous story; what it means is that part of the arbitrator's fee is earned by conducting a fair, orderly, thorough, and speedy hearing. To this end, the arbitrator, while at all times demonstrating the qualities of patience and understanding, must remain in full *control* of the hearing.

Perhaps J. Paul Getty was overdoing it a bit in declaring that "the meek shall inherit the earth but not its mineral rights," yet there is at least some relevancy in that observation to arbitral obligations. Anyone who unwittingly or by design attempts to take over the hearing must be dealt with courteously but firmly. Of course, if the arbitrator is not experienced, is unsure, or for some reason cannot or will not make definite decisions, the hearing can get out of hand.

The arbitrator also has an obligation to the witnesses called upon to give testimony in the hearing. Even though they should be subject to searching examination, the arbitrator should make sure that they are treated in a courteous manner by the examining party, or by the arbitrator if the latter finds it necessary to ask questions of witnesses to clarify a point. The arbitrator should not permit witnesses to be "badgered" or insulted. Even in cross-examination, where the examining party has more leeway with witnesses than it does in direct examination, they should be treated with decorum.

Finally, the arbitrator has a responsibility to the parties relative to the award. One significant advantage of arbitration is the comparatively fast disposition of disputes. Thus, the arbitrator has an obligation to get the decision in the hands of the parties in a prompt manner after the end of the hearing. Unless unusual conditions are involved, the American Arbitration Association requires awards to be submitted not more than 30 days from the date of the hearing. The Federal Mediation and Conciliation Service is less demanding of arbitrators appointed under its jurisdiction and allows 60 days.

Of course, when the parties elect to file posthearing briefs, as they do in about 75 percent of all cases, the arbitrator's time tolls from the receipt of such briefs. Similarly, when a court reporter has been engaged by one or both of the parties to render a stenographic transcript of the hearing (something that happens in roughly 25 percent of all arbitrations), the clock does not start to run on the arbitrator until the latter has been furnished with a copy of the transcript. Whatever the circumstances, however, the deadline should be scrupulously observed by the arbitrator. In fact, in discharge cases the interests of the parties would be best served by decisions rendered even more promptly than in other types of cases, perhaps in about 15 days. Arbitrators who are constantly late in their awards do a disservice to the arbitration process. As a matter of fact, under the FMCS rules, the failure of an arbitrator to render timely awards may lead to removal from the FMCS roster.

❖ Awards and Opinions

The award should be clear and to the point. There should be no question in the minds of the parties as to the exact character of the decision in the case. If the grievance is denied, the award should simply state that fact. Under these circumstances, some arbitrators in the decision also mention the contract provision or provisions that the employer did not violate. For example, in a work-assignment case, the award might read as follows:

> The grievance of Mr. Elmer Beamish, Grievance No. 594, is denied on the basis that the company, under the job descriptions for Tool- and Die-makers, Class A, Code 286, and for Maintenance Men, Class A, Code 263, and without violating Article XVI of the Labor Agreement, may properly assign either category of employees to repair the classes of machinery in question in this case.

When a case is decided in favor of the union, the award should clearly and specifically direct the employer to take action to bring it into compliance with the contract. In addition, to avoid any misunderstanding, the decision should require the action within a certain number of working days after the receipt of the award. As an example, the award might read as follows:

> Within three working days after the receipt of this award, the Company is directed to place the grievant, Kay Serasera, into the job of Spray Painter, Class "B," Labor Grade No. 7, and to make her whole for any financial loss that she suffered because of the refusal of the Company to permit her to roll into the aforementioned job on the grounds that the Company violated Article IX, Section 7, Paragraphs A and B of the Labor Agreement.

In addition to the incorporation of a clear award, arbitrators are charged with the responsibility of writing an opinion to support their decision. Although technically opinions are not required to explain a decision, the fact is that arbitrators almost universally write an opinion. What is more important in this connection, the parties expect their arbitrators to write them, and so do agencies such as the Federal Mediation and Conciliation Service and the American Arbitration Association, which submit to managements and unions the names of arbitrators.

In the opinion, the arbitrator sets forth the basic issues of the case, the facts, the positions and arguments of the parties, and the reasons for the decision. The arbitrator deals with the evidence presented in the case as it relates to each decision. Arbitrators are frequently extraordinarily careful to deal in an exhaustive manner with each major argument and piece of evidence offered by the losing side. Obviously, the arbitrator has an obligation to tell the losing side just why it lost the case. Since normally the losing side will be very disappointed with the decision, the arbitrator should at least indicate in a careful manner the reasons for the adverse ruling. This will probably not make the losing side feel any better, but at least an opinion that is carefully written and covers thoroughly the major arguments and areas of evidence will demonstrate that the character of an arbitration opinion is a guide to the amount of time, energy, and thought the arbitrator has put into the case.

❖ The Arbitrator as Scapegoat

Being asked to arbitrate can be a heady, invigorating and ego-bolstering experience. And busy arbitrators accordingly receive positive reinforcement as to their labor relations desirability on a regular basis. But it is not a popularity contest, and anyone who plies this craft can expect at times to be placed in the position of scapegoat by the losing party, which may find it politically preferable to criticize the decision as a poor one rather than accepting blame for either poor presentation or poor screening of the grievance. The arbitrator neither has to stand for union election or worry about advancement as a manager.

The arbitrator will normally not hear of the blame placing because his or her relationship with the parties generally ceases once the decision is rendered. Once in a great while, however, a letter will arrive informing the neutral that he or she rendered a particularly incompetent decision and is a disgrace to the profession. Most arbitrators can take this very much in stride and recognize that such criticism, even if genuine (as opposed to politically motivated) comes with the territory.

But those whose skin is not as thick as it should be do understandably take umbrage: One so-constituted fellow arbitrator told one of the authors when asked if he ever tried at a hearing to help—in the interests of rendering justice—a party that was obviously doing a poor job presenting its case, "Are you kidding? I sit in the arbitrator's chair when that happens and think to myself, 'You're sinking? Here's a rock! Drown!!!'"

❖ The Years Ahead

In the years immediately ahead, it is safe to predict, the caseloads of labor–management arbitrators will still contain many of the traditional issues. It is, however, an equally safe bet that such emerging topics as alcohol and drug use by employees and AIDS will increasingly find their way into arbitration. *(An employer requirement that employees injured on the job must submit to a drug test is the subject of Case 2.)* In the public sector, privatization—the transfer of governmental functions to the private sector—will raise subcontracting controversies between public employers and labor organizations to a dimension and complexity not encountered in the past. Modern workplace surveillance technology such as video cameras, closed circuit television, and video display terminals make employer monitoring easier and more efficient: In increasing frequency, arbitrators will be called on to decide disputes pitting the right of employers to use such devices against an employee insistence on a right to privacy.

And in 1990, Congress provided a new and challenging problem for the arbitration community. It passed the **Americans with Disabilities Act (ADA)**. Undoubtedly the most difficult problem confronting arbitrators under the statute is the requirement that employers must make "reasonable accommodation" for employees with physical or mental disabilities. A few arbitrators have refused to deal with the issue on the grounds that problems arising under ADA are not proper for arbitration and should be determined by governmental agencies, commissions, or the courts. But a vast number of contracts contain a provision that prohibits an employer from discriminating against employees. And many arbitrators have held that employers discriminate against employees should they fire a disabled employee without making a reasonable effort to accommodate such employee. Yet, what is a "reasonable effort" is not easily, at times, ascertained with precision. In sum, as we move into the new century, arbitrators will tread new and challenging paths as they explore problems that were thought about either scarcely or not at all in past years.

❖ Selection of the Arbitrator

After the parties decide to arbitrate a dispute, the problem of the selection of the arbitrator arises. To solve this problem, most labor agreements provide that the parties will select the arbitrator from a panel of names submitted by the **Federal Mediation and Conciliation Service** or the **American Arbitration Association**. When called upon by the parties to an arbitration, these agencies will supply the management and the union with a list of names, and the parties, in accordance with a mutually acceptable formula, will select the arbitrator from the list. Under some labor agreements, the Federal Mediation and Conciliation Service and the American Arbitration Association have the authority to select the arbitrator on a direct-appointment basis in the event that none of the names on the panel is acceptable.

The Federal Mediation and Conciliation Service (FMCS) is a governmental agency that is administered independently from the U.S. Department of Labor. It maintains a roster of arbitrators totaling about 1,700. About 60 percent are lawyers or law professors. Thirty percent are college professors not in law schools. The remainder are a mixed bag, mainly members of the clergy and former management and union officials who have shed their partisan roles. Upon the selection of the arbitrator, the service withdraws from active participation in the case, and the relationship thereafter is between the parties and the arbitrator, although (as Exhibit 6-3 shows) the latter must ultimately file a report with the service.

Unlike the FMCS, the American Arbitration Association (AAA) is a private organization. In its formative years, it devoted itself almost exclusively to the promotion of commercial arbitration, but since 1937 its Voluntary Labor Arbitration Tribunal has become increasingly active in labor disputes. In addition to furnishing the parties with arbitrator-selection aid similar to that of the Mediation Service, it administers arbitration hearings in accordance with a number of formalized rules. The association's panel of available arbitrators currently contains about 1,500 names, although most of the work is actually done by fewer than 500 active arbitrators, and the heavy majority of these are the same people who are listed on the FMCS roster. It, too, keeps reasonably close tabs on its arbitrators (as Exhibits 6-4 and 6-5 indicate).

EXHIBIT 6-3

FMCS FORM R-19
(Revised June 1984)

FEDERAL MEDIATION AND CONCILIATION SERVICE
WASHINGTON, D.C. 20427

Form Approved
OMB No. 23-R0004

ARBITRATOR'S REPORT AND FEE STATEMENT

FILE NO. _____ ARBITRATOR _____ DATE OF AWARD _____

1. COMPANY _____
                          (Name)   *(City)*   *(State)*   *(Zip Code)*

2. UNION _____
                          (Name)   *(Local No.)*   *(Affiliation)*

3. ISSUES: *(Please check either a or b, and complete c and d)*

a. ☐ New or reopened contract terms

b. ☐ Contract interpretation or application

c. Issue or Issues *(Please check only one issue per grievance)*

   1. ☐ Discharge and disciplinary actions

   2. ☐ Incentive rates or standards

   3. ☐ Job evaluation

   4. ☐ Work assignment

   5. ☐ Job classification

   6. Seniority:

      ☐ a. Promotion and upgrading

      ☐ b. Layoff, bumping and recall

      ☐ c. Transfer

      ☐ d. Other

   7 Overtime:

      ☐ a. Overtime pay

      ☐ b. Overtime distribution

      ☐ c. Compulsory overtime

      ☐ d. Other

   8. ☐ Union officers—superseniority and union business

   9. ☐ Strike or lockout issues *(excluding disciplinary actions)*

10. ☐ Vacations and vacation pay

11. ☐ Holidays and holiday pay

12 ☐ Scheduling of work

13. ☐ Reporting, call-in and call-back pay

14. ☐ Health and welfare

15. ☐ Pensions

16. ☐ Other fringe benefits

17. Scope of agreement:

   ☐ a. Subcontracting

   ☐ b. Jurisdictional disputes

   ☐ c. Foreman, supervision, etc.

   ☐ d. Mergers, consolidations, accretion, other plants

18. ☐ Working conditions, including safety

19. ☐ Severance pay

20. ☐ Rate of pay

21. ☐ Discrimination

22. ☐ Management rights

23. ☐ Job posting & bidding

24. ☐ Wage issues

25. ☐ Arbitrability of grievances

26. ☐ Miscellaneous

d. Was arbitrability of grievance involved? ☐ Yes ☐ No If yes, check one or both ☐ Procedural ☐ Substantive

4. HEARING:

a. Were briefs filed? ☐ Yes ☐ No If yes, give date _____

b. Was transcript taken? ☐ Yes ☐ No

c. Number of grievances _____

d. Dates of Hearing: _____ _____

e. Date of grievance _____

f. Was there any waiver by parties on date the award was due?
                ☐ Yes ☐ No

5. FEES AND DAYS: For services as Arbitrator

No. of Days: _____ + _____ + _____ = _____ × $ _____ = $ _____
              Hearing   *Travel*   *Study*   *Total*   *Per Diem Rate*   *Total Fee*

Expenses: Transportation $ _____ + Other $ _____ = $ _____
                                                                    Total Expense

Amount payable by Company $ _____

                                                            TOTAL $ _____

Amount payable by Union $ _____

6. PANEL: If tripartite panel or more than one arbitrator made the award, check here _____

7. Date of this report _____ Signature _____

(Please attach to this report copies of the submission agreement and the award)

Please do not write below this line

DATE CLOSED: _____   **REVIEWED BY:** _____

EXHIBIT 6-4

American Arbitration Association

VOLUNTARY LABOR ARBITRATION TRIBUNAL

In the Matter of the Arbitration between

CASE NUMBER:

AWARD OF ARBITRATOR

THE UNDERSIGNED ARBITRATOR(S), having been designated in accordance with the arbitration agreement entered into by the above-named Parties, and dated and having been duly sworn and having duly heard the proofs and allegations of the Parties, AWARDS as follows:

_____

Arbitrator's signature (dated)

STATE OF

COUNTY OF

} SS.:

On this   day of   , 19   , before me personally

came and appeared

to me known and known to me to be the individual(s) described in and who executed the foregoing instrument and   he   acknowledged to me that   he   executed the same.

EXHIBIT 6-5

Make check payable to, and mail directly to, the Arbitrator

ARBITRATOR'S BILL
This bill is submitted on behalf of the Arbitrator

ARBITRATOR_____ Case No._____

ADDRESS _____ No. of Grievances_____

_____

Appointed from List ☐   Administrative Appointment ☐

UNION

EMPLOYER

To be filled out by the Arbitrator

ARBITRATOR'S COMPENSATION

Number of hearing days_____ @ $ _____ $ _____

Study and preparation days___ @ $ _____ $ _____

Other (specify)_____ @ $ _____ $ _____

FEE TOTAL $ _____

ARBITRATOR'S EXPENSES

Transportation $ _____

Hotel $ _____

Meals $ _____

Other (specify) $ _____ $ _____

TOTAL $ _____

Payable by Employer $ _____

Payable by Union $ _____   Arbitrator's Soc. Sec. No._____

Date _____   Signature_____

AAA Signature_____

AAA-116   **DO NOT PAY UNLESS AAA SIGNATURE IS AFFIXED**

There is no obligation on the parties to use either the FMCS or the AAA, of course, and some relationships avoid both organizations in their selection of arbitrators. They contact directly someone of their own choosing, draw upon the names on arbitration panels of individual states (although not all states have such panels), or even designate a person of unimpeachable integrity to select an arbitrator for them. What satisfies one relationship may not satisfy another, and in this activity as in so many others in our system of private collective bargaining, it is a case of different strokes for different folks.

Regardless of the method, the majority of labor contracts provide some definite procedure for the appointment of the arbitrator. At times, managements and unions find that in practice they cannot agree on any arbitrator when the contract merely states that an arbitrator "mutually acceptable" to the parties will decide the dispute. It is sound procedure to incorporate some method for the selection of arbitrators by an outside agency when the parties are unable or unwilling to agree on a neutral on a mutual-acceptance basis.

❖ Permanent Versus Ad Hoc Arbitrators

In about 10 percent of situations, employers and unions solve the problem of selection by appointing a **permanent arbitrator** under the terms of a labor agreement. Under this arrangement, one person will decide every dispute that is arbitrated. However, managements and unions are not in agreement on the use of a permanent arbitrator as against the **ad hoc method of selection,** in which a different arbitrator may be chosen for each case. Some employers and unions, as a matter of policy, will use a different arbitrator for each dispute; others find it a better practice to use the same arbitrator. The permanent arbitrator is used most frequently when a management has a number of different locations. Such a procedure makes for uniformity of labor policy within the different operating units of the enterprise.

Actually, there are advantages and disadvantages to each method. Perhaps the chief argument in favor of the ad hoc method is that the parties will not be "stuck" with an arbitrator whom they do not want. The parties can simply dispense with an arbitrator who proves incompetent or otherwise unqualified, even though it appears unlikely that a management and a union would have selected such a person to arbitrate on a permanent basis in the first place. Balancing the chief advantage of the ad hoc system are several disadvantages. The time and effort required to select an arbitrator for each case delay the rapid disposition of the grievance, sometimes to the detriment of employee morale. At times, out of desperation, a person who has little or no experience or real qualifications is selected to serve as an arbitrator. Such a choice may be made because he or she is the only person available who has not handed down an award somewhere at some time that the employer or the union did not like. Moreover, because each new arbitrator must be educated in the local conditions, a comparatively long period may sometimes be required to conduct the hearing.

Perhaps the chief disadvantage of ad hoc arbitration, however, is the fact that this method does not assure consistency in decisions or the application of uniform principles to contract construction. No arbitrator is bound by any other arbitrator's decisions or principles of contractual construction. Consequently, disputes involving fundamentally the same issues could be resolved in as many different ways as there are arbitrators chosen to decide cases. Thus, there is no assurance that a particular decision will bring stability to labor relations. It may have precedent value only until the next time the issues involved in the case are tested before another arbitrator.

The latter consideration indicates the greatest advantage of the selection of permanent arbitrators. The parties have the assurance of consistency and uniformity of decisions and consistent contractual interpretation. As a result, precedent will be established, the parties will know what to expect, and cases dealing with essentially the same issues as contained in a grievance previously decided in arbitration can be settled in the earlier stages of the grievance procedure. In addition, the permanent arbitrator becomes familiar with the labor agreement, the technology, and the "shop language." This means that cases can frequently be expedited much more effectively than under circumstances of ad hoc arbitration.

Perhaps the chief disadvantage of the permanent selection method is that the parties involved may tend to arbitrate more disputes than are absolutely necessary, rather than first exhausting the possibilities of settling them in the grievance procedure. This is particularly true when arbitrators are paid a set fee for a year and are obligated to arbitrate any and all cases submitted to them.

This possibility, of course, is a serious charge against the permanent selection method. As stated before, arbitration should be employed only after the parties have honestly exhausted every possibility of settling disputes in the grievance procedure. One method that might be effective in obtaining the advantages of the permanent method without incurring the possible disadvantages of excessive arbitration would be to compensate the permanent arbitrator on a per diem or a per case basis, rather than on an annual fee basis. In the last analysis, however, the amount of arbitration needed by a management and a union depends on the attitudes of the parties rather than on the method of selection or the procedure of payment.

ARBITRATION COSTS AND TIME LAG

In recent years, arbitration has been criticized as being unduly expensive and involving too much time, but beyond these two criticisms the process has always been criticized for other reasons. Parties complain when they lose a case that they believe should have been decided in their favor. That criticism may not have much validity, but justified censure involves an arbitrator who ignores unambiguous contractual language and thereby rewrites the labor agreement. At times, opinions are confusing, leading to unnecessary discord between the parties; and, indeed, there are instances where the opinion does not even reflect the award. As at least one dissatisfied party has said, "We won everything except the decision." Sometimes arbitrators include so-called dicta (gratuitous remarks not required for a decision in a case) in their opinions, which could lead to serious problems the next time a labor agreement is negotiated. And, obviously, it is understandable why the losing side believes it has been treated unjustly when the arbitrator does not conduct a fair and impartial hearing, or fails to deal with major arguments, or ignores material evidence.

However, the most vocal criticism recently has pertained to the costs and the delays associated with arbitration. Even though alternatives to arbitration—a strike or court enforcement of a labor agreement—would be far more expensive, arbitration costs, at least on the surface, appear to be quite high.

In 1999, arbitrators serving under the jurisdictions of either the Federal Mediation and Conciliation Service or the American Arbitration Association charged on the average bit over $600 per day and total arbitrator billings to the parties (who normally shared these billings equally) was almost $3,000. Payment for the time that the arbitrator devoted to analyzing the evidence and writing the opinion entered, of course, into the total, as did any expenses incurred by the arbitrator—for travel, hotel, meals, and secretarial services in particular. But beyond the fee and expenses of the arbitrator, there are other costs. Some parties use lawyers (employers now do so in over three-quarters of all arbitrations and unions in over half of theirs). Court reporters (as noted, currently present at about one-quarter of all hearings) do not do their work as a public service, either, but fully expect to be paid. And the nonattorney personnel on each side of the arbitration table (the arbitrator, to symbolize the neutrality of the position, usually sits at the table's head) also must be remunerated.

There are ways to cut arbitration costs. Grievances that are of minimal importance to the parties, particularly those that go to arbitration for political and tactical purposes, should be eliminated from the process. Other suggestions include the use of local arbitrators to save on expenses, elimination of court reporters and attorneys when they are not necessary, and the consolidation of grievances of the same type to be determined in one hearing. To reduce costs, the parties may instruct their arbitrators not to write an opinion but merely to issue an award. The writing of an opinion takes considerable time, even after the arbitrator has carefully reviewed the evidence and has reached a decision. Of course, there is genuine value in a carefully written opinion, as pointed out earlier, but there are cases in which the merit of cost saving outweighs the advantages of an opinion.

One delay is not attributable to arbitrators or the process but to dilatory tactics of the parties. This involves the time before arbitration is requested on a grievance. One of this book's authors a while ago was asked to decide a case in which three years had elapsed before the parties invoked the arbitration process. Although such an incredible delay is not usual, grievances commonly vegetate for many months before the parties decide to take them into arbitration.

The time-lag criticism properly starts from the point at which the parties request arbitration. And in recent years, both the FMCS and AAA have consistently reported that more than 200 days have on the average elapsed from the time the parties requested a panel of arbitrators until the award was issued. This is much too long, and the parties understandably wonder in such circumstances if the process really constitutes a viable forum for the disposition of grievances in arbitration. One consequence of the delay is the lowering of the morale in the workplace, in the same way that the morale of students suffers when their teachers take much too long in returning examination papers. Employees become impatient waiting for the award; their resentment could have an adverse impact on the quantity and quality of their work, and, frequently, they badger their union representatives about the problem. Employers could also suffer a large financial loss (should they lose their case) if the arbitrator directs a monetary remedy for a contractual violation.

One way to deal with the time problem is for the parties to use comparatively new arbitrators rather than requesting the services of so-called mainline, or veteran, arbitrators. Since the latter group receives the lion's share of the cases, its members may be unable to provide prompt hearing dates. It is not unusual for 90 or 100 days to elapse between the appointment of the arbitrator and the day of the hearing. It follows that arbitrators with small caseloads might be able to offer more prompt hearing dates. The problem, of course, is to convince the parties to use new arbitrators rather than those with considerable experience. It is true that there is no substitute for experience, but it is equally true that new arbitrators could be just as qualified as those who have been in the profession for many years and who have handled a great number of cases. Many veteran arbitrators would agree with this and would encourage employers and unions to provide opportunities for the comparatively newer arbitrators.

To avoid the delay associated with the use of arbitrators from the FMCS or the AAA, a growing number of employers and unions are making use of a *permanent panel* of arbitrators. That is, they choose a number (seven is modal) of arbitrators when they negotiate the labor agreement; when grievances are ready to be arbitrated, one of the members of the panel is selected through some agreed-upon procedure. This could save considerable time, since the use of the traditional agencies for the selection of arbitrators necessitates some delay: A letter goes from the parties to the Federal Mediation and Conciliation Service or the American Arbitration Association; the agency then sends a panel of arbitrators to the parties; additional time elapses while the parties decide which of the arbitrators on the panel is to be used; then they write the appointing agency of the choice; the agency notifies the arbitrator; and then the arbitrator must write the parties to arrange a hearing date. A whopping 60 or more days can easily go by between the time that a request for arbitration is made and the appointment of the arbitrator. By the use of the permanent panel, most of this delay is avoided. A telephone call or a single letter sent directly to the selected arbitrator is all that is needed.

Not only could costs be reduced by relieving the arbitrator of the responsibility of writing an opinion, but the same practice is a time saver. The time lag could be further reduced by eliminating stenographic transcripts of the proceedings and posthearing briefs. (One of the authors for some years served on a permanent panel of arbitrators of a major airline and a labor organization in which, by contractual agreement, transcripts and posthearing briefs are expressly prohibited.) Transcripts and posthearing briefs delay the process; it is not unusual to wait a month or longer for a transcript and then another month for the briefs. In the "normal" case, these are not really needed. The arbitrator simply takes his or her own notes at the hearing and provides the opportunity to the parties to offer an oral argument at the close of the hearing. To be fair about it, however, there are some cases in which a transcript is valuable, and a posthearing brief could be helpful to the arbitrator in reaching a decision.

Finally, there is the matter of the dilatory arbitrator. As stated before, it is customary, and indeed directed by the FMCS and the AAA, that an arbitrator's decision is due within a specified number of days after the close of the hearing or the filing of posthearing briefs and receipt of transcript. Unfortunately, there are arbitrators who take much longer than this allowed time—chiefly because they are handling so many cases that they cannot meet this deadline.

❖ Mini-Arbitration

First applied in the basic steel industry in 1971, **mini-, or expedited, arbitration** has been adopted by other employers and unions, including the U.S. Postal Service and the postal labor organizations, the League of New York Theatres and Actors' Equity, and the UAW and the automobile manufacturers. The chief value of the mini-arbitration process is the sharp reduction of the time element and costs. Under the steel plan, the hearing must be held within 10 days after the appeal to arbitration is made, and the arbitrator's decision must be made within 48 hours after the close of the hearing. No transcripts or briefs are permitted, and the arbitrator is expected to provide the parties with a short but precise award. Costs are also much lower than in regular arbitration. A fee is paid only for the hearing day, and this fee is only about $300 for each party per case. Sometimes it is even less than that.

To provide for such rapid service at an economical charge, the steel corporations and the United Steelworkers of America use a battery of about 200 inexperienced arbitrators, including a significant number of minorities and women. The panel includes relatively young lawyers and local university faculty. One advantage of the new process, therefore, is to train new arbitrators.

Indeed, this spinoff from the miniprocess is of significant value to arbitration. Arbitrators may not as yet, to paraphrase one unhappy observer's previously cited remark regarding labor leaders, look like a wax museum collection when they hold a meeting, but the bulk of the profession is hardly made up of youngsters nowadays. Many still-active arbitrators entered the field on the strength of their experiences in the War Labor Board days of World War II or the wage stabilization of the Korean War and are now nearing the end of their careers. Unless newcomers can rather quickly be developed at this point, the field will be in some trouble.

Not all cases, however, are disposed of in the miniprocess—only, in general, those of the simpler and more routine type—with the regular arbitration process still being used for those cases of difficult nature and representing substantial interest to the parties. Normally, cases suited for the expedited procedure are those involving individual and not contractual disputes. In addition, either the employer or the union may demand that a case go through the regular arbitration process. Indeed, even during an expedited hearing, the parties may transfer the case to regular arbitration should it be discovered that the issue is more complex than originally believed.

In any event, the miniprocedure has generally worked successfully in the several sectors where it has been tried. Undoubtedly, there is a place for it within our system of labor relations. It provides a swift and inexpensive forum for the determination of grievances that are well within the capability of inexperienced arbitrators. And it is likely that the process will spread. The most difficult problem is to determine which grievances should go the mini- and which the regular arbitration route; but this problem is not insoluble, since skilled and mature labor relations representatives on both sides can easily spot those grievances that can best be handled through the expedited procedure.

Finally, the parties and expedited arbitrators must take due care that the desire for speed should not sacrifice the judicial nature of the arbitration process. Whether expedited or regular, arbitration is a judicial process where thoughtful consideration of the evidence controls the outcome of the case. To purchase speed at the price of quality undermines the integrity of arbitration.

❖ Grievance Mediation

Another alternative is available to employers and unions who desire to reduce costs and time delay associated with regular arbitration. This is called **grievance mediation,** a procedure that combines elements of both mediation and arbitration. After the final step of the internal grievance procedure, the parties have the option of resorting to this procedure rather than regular arbitration. An experienced arbitrator is used, but one who possesses the skills and temperament of a mediator. After hearing the circumstances of a dispute, he or she first seeks to assist the parties in reaching a mutually satisfactory settlement. At this stage of the proceedings, the focus is on the problem that caused the grievance and not necessarily on the labor agreement. To be sure, the labor agreement establishes the limits within which a settlement can be reached. Nonetheless, by this approach there is ample room for innovative problem solving. The procedure is very informal. Witnesses relate their versions in narrative fashion, and cross-examination normally does not take place. No briefs are submitted, and no record of the proceedings is made. So brief is the procedure that several grievances may be handled in one day.

If a settlement is not achieved through this initial step, the mediator-arbitrator issues an advisory opinion as to how the grievance would likely be decided if it were to go to conventional arbitration. This opinion is immediate, oral, and nonbinding. Should the parties accept the opinion, the grievance is resolved on that basis. If they do not, the parties are free to proceed to regular arbitration. Of course, in such an arbitration, the person who handled the grievance may not serve as arbitrator. Nothing that was said by the parties at the previous step, including the advisory opinion, may be used in the regular arbitration.

The grievance mediation process, although still not used extensively, has definitely been growing since the 1980s. Word of consistently good results with it in the unionized worlds of both bituminous coal mining and education has led to the insertion of grievance mediation in the current labor contracts of such dissimilar employers as AT&T, the Chicago Transit Authority, Continental Telephone, and Teledyne Motors. Almost three thousand grievances have now been referred to such mediation, and about 80 percent of those have been successfully resolved. Inexpensive and often surprisingly efficient, it will presumably never replace arbitration, but it should be considered by employers and unions who have extensive arbitration.

SOME CONCLUDING THOUGHTS

Just as it is a tribute to the maturity of union–management relations that more than 90 percent of all grievances are settled jointly, it speaks volumes about this maturity that all but a handful of parties are willing to let impartial outsiders render final and binding decisions on the relatively few occasions in which the grievance procedure is deadlocked.

Arbitration's acceptability must be taken as a healthy development. The process may not be as fast, as inexpensive, or as "just" as the parties might desire. And other dangers and defects—as has been pointed out—also exist. But for unions and managements, arbitration is far preferable to its only two alternatives—a) resort to strikes and lockouts and b) going directly to the courts—as an effective means of conflict resolution. And the fact that both sides are willing in the case of stalemated grievances to turn to this entirely civilized, eminently peaceful process in which each necessarily transfers its power to an outsider is by any standard impressive.

DISCUSSION QUESTIONS

1. "The handling of workers' grievances on the job is perhaps the single most important function of modern unionism." How accurate is this statement?
2. It is generally agreed that a low grievance rate does not necessarily prove the existence of good union–management relations and that a high grievance rate does not necessarily prove the existence of poor relations between the parties. Why might the grievance statistics be misleading as a guide to the quality of the relationship?
3. From the employer's viewpoint, what advantages and disadvantages might there be in reducing a grievance to writing?
4. It has been argued that "a genuine grievance requires an airing, even if it is not strictly in order under the existing contract." What considerations, again from the employer's point of view, might justify this opinion?

5. Why might (a) a management or (b) a union prefer *not* to have an arbitration provision in the contract?

6. Some labor relations scholars have pointed out that although it is often said that "arbitration is an extension of collective bargaining," it is also frequently held that "arbitration is a judicial process." What are your own feelings regarding these two apparently inconsistent descriptions?

7. Given the fact that arbitrators have no compulsion to follow any other arbitrator's award or line of reasoning, how do you account for the fact that there are available at least three widely distributed publications that feature arbitration awards from all over the country? On the surface, would it not appear that such publications are a waste of time and money, since each arbitrator is in effect a law unto himself or herself?

8. How could the present system of labor contract administration, as described in general terms in this chapter, be improved?

9. Beyond the authors' ideas to reduce arbitration delays and costs, can you offer additional suggestions to accomplish this goal?

10. Do you believe that arbitrators, like doctors and lawyers, should be certified by government before they are permitted to arbitrate labor cases? Why or why not?

MINICASES

#1 A Dissenting View Regarding Arbitration

Years ago, the colorful and controversial leader of the International Brotherhood of Teamsters, Jimmy Hoffa, explained his adamant opposition to arbitration as follows:

> Even if it takes one or two hours or longer [for the management and the union] to work out a [grievance] settlement among ourselves we are better off, knowing the business as we do from both sides, than to submit a grievance to some third party who attempts to please both sides and who actually pleases nobody. In my opinion, the best method of settling grievances is to leave open the end for final settlement and, if we cannot mutually agree, either for the employer to lock out the union or for the union to strike the employer. If we don't come out with a completely satisfactory settlement we come out with a settlement both sides can live with and one which doesn't change the terms of the contract.

What do you think of this argument?

#2 An Embarrassing Incident for the Arbitrator

Professor Grover Harrison has been jointly selected as impartial ad hoc arbitrator by a union and management, none of whose principals he has ever met. Eating his breakfast alone in a booth in the dining room of the hotel in which the hearing will shortly be held, he overhears the following words emanating from the next booth:

Well, of course, it's not the truth, but if we're to have any chance of winning this thing, we'd damned well better consistently stick to our claim that the supervisor on at least one occasion made lewd and suggestive remarks to Mary. She can be counted on to testify this way at the hearing, and she's a good enough liar so that there's no chance of her being shaken in the cross-examination.

If you were Harrison, what (if anything) would you now do?

NOTES

[1] *Textile Workers* v. *Lincoln Mills*, 353 U.S. 488 (1957).
[2] *United Steelworkers of America* v. *Warrior & Gulf Navigation Co.*, 363 U.S. 574 (1960); *United Steelworkers of America* v. *American Manufacturing Co.*, 363 U.S. 564 (1960); *United Steelworkers of America* v. *Enterprise Wheel & Car Corp.*, 363 U.S. 593 (1960).
[3] *AT&T Technologies* v. *Communications Workers*, 106 S. Ct. 1415 (1986).
[4] *Alexander* v. *Gardner-Denver Co.*, 94 S. Ct. 1011 (1974).
[5] *Hines* v. *Anchor Motor Freight*, 424 U.S. 554 (1976).
[6] *Barrentine* v. *Arkansas-Best Freight System, Inc.*, 450 U.S. 728 (1981).
[7] *McDonald* v. *City of West Branch, Michigan*, 104 S. Ct. 1794 (1984).
[8] *Nabisco, Inc.* v. *NLRB*, 479 F (2d) 770 (CA 2, 1973).
[9] 192 NLRB 837 (1971).
[10] *United Paperworkers International Union* v. *Misco*, 108 S. Ct. 364 (1987).

SELECTED REFERENCES

Bales, Richard A. *Compulsory Arbitration.* Ithaca, NY: ILR Press, Cornell University, 1997.

Brand, Norman, ed. *Discipline and Discharge in Arbitration.* Washington, DC: Bureau of National Affairs, 1988.

Coleman, Charles J., Theodora T. Haynes, and Marie T. Gibson McGraw. *Labor and Employment Arbitration: An Annotated Bibliography, 1991–1996.* Ithaca, NY: ILR Press, Cornell University, 1997.

Dunlop, John T., and Arnold M. Zack. *The Mediation and Arbitration of Employment Disputes.* San Francisco: Jossey-Bass, 1997.

Elkouri, Frank, and Edna Elkouri. *How Arbitration Works,* 5th ed. Co-edited by Edward P. Goggin and Marlin M. Volz. Washington, DC: Bureau of National Affairs, 1997.

Gleason, Sandra E., ed. *Workplace Dispute Resolution: Directions for the Twenty-First Century.* East Lansing: Michigan State University Press, 1997.

Hauck, Vern E. *Arbitrating Race, Religion, and National Origin Discrimination Grievances.* Westport, CT: Quorum, 1997.

Hill, Marvin, Jr., and Anthony V. Sinicropi. *Evidence in Arbitration,* 2nd ed. Washington, DC: Bureau of National Affairs, 1987.

_____, *Remedies in Arbitration,* 2nd ed. Washington, DC: Bureau of National Affairs, 1991.

Lewin, David, and Richard B. Peterson. *The Modern Grievance Procedure in the United States.* Westport, CT: Quorum 1988.

Loughran, Charles S. *How to Prepare and Present a Labor Arbitration Case.* Washington, DC: Bureau of National Affairs, 1996.

Schoonhoven, Ray J., ed. *Fairweather's Practice and Procedure in Labor Arbitration,* 3rd ed. Washington, DC: Bureau of National Affairs, 1991.

St. Antoine, Theodore J., ed. *The Common Law of the Workplace: The Views of Arbitrators.* Washington, DC: Bureau of National Affairs, 1998.

Zack, Arnold M. *A Handbook for Grievance Arbitration.* New York: Lexington Books and American Arbitration Association, 1992.

Zimny, Max, William F. Dolson, and Christopher A. Barreca, eds. *Labor Arbitration: A Practical Guide for Advocates.* Washington, DC: Bureau of National Affairs, 1990.

Arbitration Cases

As in the eight other arbitration cases that follow in later chapters, the two arbitration cases presented here are drawn from our own experiences. They are actual cases, but because arbitration is a confidential process, the names of the employers and unions have been deleted. We have also used fictitious names for the witnesses, and some of the dates have been changed.

In five of the cases, you will play the role of arbitrator. To reach a proper decision, be sure that you fully understand the basic facts and contractual provisions. Clearly establish the reasons for your decision in each case. In the discussion of these cases, at the instructor's discretion, the actual arbitrators' decisions may be disclosed to the class. These decisions can be found in the *Instructor's Manual*.

In the other five cases, the relevant factual background and material contractual language as well as the arbitrator's decision are presented. Students are urged to read the cases. A great deal can be learned about the practical day-to-day problems of labor relations and how a professional arbitrator handles cases by faithful study of them. Whether you agree with a decision is not really important. Rather, the value is to learn how arbitrators apply and interpret contractual language, evaluate evidence, apply commonly accepted principles of contractual construction and arbitration practices, and defend their decisions with what they would like to believe is logical and unassailable reasoning.

If you would like to read additional arbitration cases, thousands have been published by the Bureau of National Affairs, *Labor Arbitration Reports*, and Commerce Clearing House, *Labor Arbitration Awards*. These services have been available for many years. (In keeping with the confidentiality of the arbitration process, the employer and the union involved must agree to publication.) However, the published cases represent only a small percentage of the cases decided by arbitrators; the vast majority are found only in the private files of the arbitrators and the parties.

Each of the ten cases has been placed at the end of the chapter in which reference to the case is made. Carefully selected questions follow the cases that include the arbitrator's decision. If you can answer the questions adequately, you should have a good understanding of the case. In the other cases, your problem is this: If you had been the actual arbitrator, what would have been your decision and why?

Time Limits: The Case of Absenteeism

Cast of Characters

Queen   Union's Attorney
Smith   Employer's Attorney

[*A* "cast of characters" in this form does not appear in actual arbitration decisions. It is used here, and in the other cases in this volume, to aid in the reading of the cases. In keeping with the principle of confidentiality of the arbitration process, all names are fictitious.]

Should a union fail to comply with the time limits stipulated in the grievance procedure, it could lose a grievance that might have merit. Likewise, depending on the contractual language involved, an employer who ignores time limits could be required to grant a grievance that otherwise might not have merit. Time limits are incorporated into the grievance procedure to ensure that a grievance will be processed properly. To accomplish this purpose, both sides are under a time pressure to keep the grievance moving expeditiously through the various steps of the grievance procedure.

This case involves time limits established in the contract and their application to a grievance filed to protest discipline under the employer's attendance program. In 1988, the employer unilaterally established a so-called no-fault attendance program. Under it, employees receive "points" when they are absent or tardy or leave their shift early. The reason for or circumstances of the breach do not matter. Unless exempted by the system, all absences are unexcused, and points are given to the employee. What counts is the number of absences in a given time period and not the reason for or cause of the absence. The program established the penalty for a given number of points: eleven (11) points calls for a three- (3) day suspension, and fifteen (15) points results in discharge. Although no actual employee was disciplined under the program, the union moved the case to arbitration to determine whether it could file grievances pertaining to the program and how the time limits established in Section 18 of the contract would apply to such grievances.

For example, assume that an employee receives a three- (3) day suspension on November 25, 1999, that neither the Union nor the employee files a grievance to protest the suspension, and that the time limit to file a grievance is within five (5) days after the event occurs. On July 20, 2000, the employee wants to file a grievance protesting the November 25, 1999, suspension because on July 20, 2000, she is discharged for absenteeism. If the November 25, 1999, suspension is eliminated, the employee will not have sufficient points for discharge. Despite the failure to grieve the suspension within five (5) days after November 25, 1999, and despite the five- (5) day time limit, the Union believes it has the right to file a grievance to knock out the suspension. Thus, the Union's position is that regardless of when a point is assessed against an employee, and despite time limits in the contract, it has the right to file a grievance and protest the discipline on its merits. (It would argue that the suspension of November 25, 1999, was not issued for just cause.) Needless to say, the employer disagrees, claiming that grievances protesting points under the attendance program must be filed within the time limits established in the grievance procedure.

The preceding scenario is hypothetical; as noted, no employee was actually disciplined. Rather, this case involves the interpretation and application of material contractual language, particularly Section 18. In most cases involving the interpretation and application of contractual language the union has the burden of proof. By presenting competent evidence, it must prove that the employer violated the labor agreement. In cases in which an employee has been discharged, however, the burden of proof shifts to the employer. It must prove by competent evidence that the employee engaged in the conduct that resulted in the discharge.

Neither the employer nor the union presented a witness in this case. To say the least, this is very unusual in arbitration. Nonetheless, the parties believed witnesses were not necessarily given the character of the case. Instead, the attorneys argued their clients' positions. They agreed, however, to a stipulation of facts, which means that both parties agreed that the events in the stipulation actually occurred (or did not occur). An arbitrator, of course, is bound by stipulations mutually agreed to by the parties.

INTRODUCTION

Grievance and Company Answer

On May 17, 1997, the Union filed Grievance No. 97–07, which generated this proceeding. It stated:

> In a letter dated May 13, 1997, the Company notified Local 280 that the Union's response to the Company's position on Grievance 96–17 was unacceptable. The Company's position is that the Union adhere to Section 18, Paragraph 7, and either withdraw the grievance or send it to arbitration. The Union and Company negotiated and agreed to Section 18 of our Labor Agreement. The Union did not negotiate, nor are we in agreement with, the Company's "no-fault" absentee program. The Company has stated time and time again that points under the program are simply a recordkeeping device and are not punitive. Thus, no matter what the reason, or how severe or compelling the incident that precipitated the absence was, a point is issued. The Company's position now that they will use Section 18, Paragraphs 7 and 15 time limits to bar the Union, when discipline is issued, from bringing up all the points issued leading up to the discipline, is unreasonable and violates our Contract. The Union demands that when discipline is issued under the "no-fault" program all the points be open to the grievance procedure and the time limits in Section 18 not apply.

Denying the grievance on June 18, 1997, the Employer stated:

> The union has filed this grievance because it does not agree with the no-fault attendance program that has been in place in excess of 10 years! Under the

program, points are accumulated without making subjective decisions about what is a good and what is a bad reason to be absent. Credits are also assigned for good attendance.

People who are awarded discipline under the program can challenge the accuracy of the company's records back to the previous time that discipline was awarded. If they are awarded discipline and they disagree with a point that was assessed, they must do so in accordance with Section 18. If they grieved it at the time it was awarded, they have already been made aware of the point and they can't grieve it again.

There is a big difference between challenging the accuracy of records and challenging the merit of what does and does not constitute an absence that is assigned a point. To allow the union to prevail in its opinion that every point from inception can be grieved would be in conflict with Section 18.

No employee was a direct party under Grievance No. 97–07. Instead this was a class action or policy grievance. Material to the case are the following provisions of the Labor Agreement, effective August 1, 1996, and scheduled to expire August 1, 1999.

SECTION 18–ADJUSTMENT OF GRIEVANCES

Should differences arise between the management and the union or its members employed by the company as to the meaning and provisions of this agreement, or should any local trouble of any kind arise in the plant, there shall be no strikes, stoppages, or suspension of work on the part of the union or its members or a lockout on the part of the company, and such differences shall be settled and disposed of in the following manner:

•••

Beginning with Step two (2) above, all grievances shall be placed in writing and replies thereto shall be in writing. The union will file grievances within five (5) days of their discovery and in no case more than twenty (20) days from its occurrence. Grievance meetings shall be set by mutual agreement and will not be unduly delayed.

•••

Grievances must be appealed in writing from Step 3 to arbitration within sixty (60) days after the date on which the company's answer is given.

•••

SECTION 20–MANAGEMENT RIGHTS

The management of the company's operation and direction of the working force, including but not limited to the right to employ, retire, promote, discipline, and discharge employees, to assign work and transfer employees, to increase and decrease the working force, to establish production methods and standards to determine products to be handled and produced, manufactured, or sold, to schedule production and to make such reasonable rules and regulations in connection with the company's operations and the conduct and duties of its employees as are deemed advisable, is the exclusive right of management, provided these rights are not used for the purpose of discriminating or to avoid the other provisions of this agreement.

SECTION 22—SENIORITY

Seniority shall be bargaining-unit–wide for those jobs which were certified by the National Labor Relations Board. Layoff and reemployment rights shall be governed by unitwide seniority.

Employees shall have no seniority during the first thirty (30) working days. Seniority shall date to the original hiring date after completing thirty (30) working days.

Employees may claim temporary job openings by seniority provided they can perform the job without training.

Employees will lose all seniority rights if they:

1. Voluntarily quit.
2. Are discharged for just cause.

• • •

ISSUE

Is the Company's position correct that the Union must satisfy the time limits incorporated in Section 18 of the contract? If not, what should the remedy be?

BACKGROUND

No-Fault Progressive Discipline System

On June 1, 1988, the employer unilaterally established a progressive discipline system for absenteeism and tardiness. It is based on a so-called no-fault program in which points are given to employees who are absent or tardy or who leave their shifts early. In such a system, the reason for an absence or tardy reporting is not generally considered for purposes of discipline. Rather, the issue is the number of infractions in a given time period. The absentee program is currently in effect. It states:

Absences for all other reasons and tardiness or leaving early will be considered to be *UNEXCUSED* [emphasis in original] and subject to the discipline scale on the following basis:

- Unexcused Tardy (with notification 30 minutes or more prior to shift start)—1/2 POINT
- Unexcused Tardy (without notification 30 minutes or more prior to shift start)—1 POINT
- Unexcused Absence—1 POINT
- Leave Early (after midpoint of shift)—1/2 POINT
- Leave Early (before midpoint of shift)—1 POINT

Next, the program established the discipline employees receive based upon the number of points acquired:

Action	Accumulated Points
Verbal warning	7
Written warning	9
3-day suspension	11
5-day suspension	13
Termination of employment	15

Under the program, one (1) point is deducted from an employee's point total for any thirty- (30) day calendar period worked during which no absentee occurrences take place. An employee does not receive discipline for the first six (6) points that he or she accumulates. When an employee reaches the seventh (7th) point and receives the verbal warning, all seven (7) points are open to challenge on the basis of accuracy or on their merits regardless of time limits.

The following shows the discipline of employees under the program between 1994 and February 2, 1999, the date of the arbitration:

Verbal warnings	63 (approx.)
Written warnings	46 (approx.)
3-day suspensions	14 (approx.)
5-day suspensions	25 (approx.)
Terminations	0

Practice and Collective Bargaining

In the grievance's original form, the parties stipulated as follows:

The Company has a consistent practice of rejecting grievances which have been filed in an untimely manner, including grievances challenging discipline under this Attendance Policy.

During the arbitration, however, the parties agreed to eliminate the word *consistent*. Attorney Smith said:

In an off-the-record conversation, the parties agreed to amend stipulation number ten by striking the word *consistent*. So stipulation number ten as amended would read as follows: "The company has a practice of rejecting grievances which have been filed in an untimely manner, including grievances challenging discipline under this attendance policy."

The Parties also stipulated that in pre–Labor Agreement negotiations held in 1993

The Union requested discussion and resolution of problems with Company's "no-fault" Attendance Program.

Obviously, the Union's request was denied (and was later withdrawn), and the attendance program was implemented. Apparently the Union did not raise the issue again later during the negotiations that resulted in the current contract, which covered the period August 1, 1996 through August 1, 1999.

POSITIONS OF THE PARTIES

Both parties submitted posthearing briefs to support their respective positions in this case. In this regard, the Union argued:

In the case being arbitrated (Grievance No. 97–07), the Union seeks a ruling that it has the right under the collective bargaining agreement, when contesting discipline under the Company's attendance policy, to show that any one or more of the prior "points" received by the disciplined employee should not have been given to the employee and thus that the employee should not be regarded as having the number of points relied upon by the Company as the basis for the present discipline.

An example might clarify the Union's position further. Assume that the Company's record shows that an employee has accumulated 11 points.

Under the previous table, 11 points calls for a three-day suspension. This employee has never grieved any prior point, but now grieves the three-day suspension he has been given, contending that the suspension is without just cause. It is the Union's position that the Union should be able to contest the merits or propriety of the 11th point *and* every prior point counted by the Company in arriving at a decision that the employee now has 11 points and merits a suspension. The reason is that the employee must have received 11 justifiable points before he can properly receive a three-day suspension under the policy; if any one of those 11 points marked against him was unjustified, then his suspension [is] without just cause. If the Union should establish that point no. 8, for example, should not have been given to the employee, then the three-day suspension would be unjust and should be set aside, since the employee should be regarded as having 10 points instead of 11. It should be noted that in that scenario the Union would not be asking for any remedy per se for the Company's violation of the employee's rights in wrongfully issuing point no. 8 to him; instead, the Union would contest point no. 8 solely in order to show that current discipline based on the employee's record having shown 11 points is improper. (Emphasis in original)

On its behalf, the Company asserted:

Every aspect of this case, . . . legal, equitable, factual and contractual . . . compels a ruling that this Arbitrator is without the authority to issue a blanket or "advisory" determination that the time limits of Section 18 do not apply to attendance policy grievances.

The Company submits, of course, that the rather absurd position taken by the Union in this dispute must be summarily rejected. In any event, any request by the Union for an advisory opinion should be rejected pending the filing of a "real" case or controversy.

Due to an apparent desire to wear both a belt and suspenders, these parties, in Section 18, provided that "the Union *will file* grievances within five (5) days of their *discovery* and *in no case* more than twenty (20) days from its *occurrence*." [Emphasis added] By using such words, these parties clearly intended that the involved clauses be mandatory or directory, not discretionary.

Also, the parties placed the typical restraints on an arbitrator thereby rendering this Arbitrator powerless to ignore or overlook these jurisdictional and mandatory timing guidelines.

Arbitrators generally support an employer claim of late grievance filing unless there is evidence of a waiver, estoppel or a continuing violation.

With respect to the issue of timeliness, the involved agreement is quite clear. *The requirement of timeliness is a jurisdictional prerequisite;* and the Arbitrator should not ignore Section 18's time limits in any given case, real or hypothetical, absent evidence that the Company waived or otherwise acquiesced in any late filing of any grievance. *Since this case arose in a hypothetical vacuum*, there can be no evidence of waiver, estoppel or continuing violation. This Company should not be saddled with a requirement that it excuse explicit contractual grievance filing requirements due to employee whim. Such a standard is not only unfair to the Company but also to the other employees whose untimely grievances (as stipulated in Joint Exhibit 5) have been consistently denied and rejected. In addition, this Union should not be permitted to exact from this Arbitrator a general, declaratory, or advisory determination which surgically removes from Joint Exhibit 1 a clear grievance filing, jurisdictional requirement. As a gentle reminder, this is not a live case . . . there is no discipline of any employee in this case . . . and there is no burning building. (Emphasis in original)

To the extent necessary and appropriate for purposes of this case, additional arguments raised by the parties in their briefs will be quoted in the following portion of this decision.

THE ARBITRATOR'S EVALUATION OF THE EVIDENCE

Burden of Proof: Section 18 Time Limits

Since no employee was disciplined, the dispute is a case involving the interpretation and application of contractual language. It follows, therefore, that the Union bears the burden of demonstrating that the employer violated the terms of the labor agreement by instituting the no-fault attendance policy.

And given the circumstances of the case, the Union bears an extraordinarily *heavy* burden to prove that its case should prevail. Time limits are written in clearcut and unambiguous language in Section 18, which states:

The union *will file* grievances within five (5) days of their discovery and in no case more than twenty (20) days from its occurrence. (Emphasis added)

It goes on to say:

Grievances *must be appealed* in writing from Step 3 to arbitration *within sixty (60) days* after the date on which the company's answer is given. (Emphasis added)

Such unambiguous and unequivocal language binds all concerned in the dispute. It does not provide for any exception, condition, or modification of its terms. Despite the clarity of the language, the Union requests the arbitrator to ignore that language and find timely a grievance protesting a point no matter when the penalty was given. As long as the point was issued to impose discipline, no matter its failure to protest within the stipulated time limits, the union position is that Section 18 time limits do not apply. As the Union indicated in the last sentence of the grievance in question, No. 97–07:

The Union demands that when discipline is issued under the "no-fault" program all the points be open to the grievance procedure and the time limits in Section 18 not apply.

To grant the Union's position, the arbitrator would violate the parameters of his allowable area of authority. Once more in unambiguous contractual language, the parties restricted the power of arbitrators. Section 18 provides:

The decision of the arbitrator shall be binding and conclusive upon both parties to the agreement. Such decision shall be within the scope and terms of this agreement, *but shall not change any of its terms or conditions*, nor deprive the company or union of any rights expressly or impliedly reserved herein. (Emphasis added)

Would not the arbitrator change the terms or conditions expressed in the contract should he permit the Union to file grievances and arbitrate regardless of time limits?

Early in his career the arbitrator established his respect and fidelity to contract language. Thus:

> If the language of an agreement is clear and unequivocal, an arbitrator generally will not give it a meaning other than that expressed. As Arbitrator Fred Witney has stated, an arbitrator cannot "ignore clear-cut contractual language," and he "may not legislate new language, since to do so would usurp the role of the labor organization and employer."*

Over the years, the arbitrator has used this most fundamental and venerable arbitration principle to grant or deny a countless number of grievances. What if the shoe were on the other foot? Suppose that, in another case, unambiguous contractual language supported the Union's position and that an arbitrator ignored such language, denying the grievance on the basis of factors not germane to the terms of the contract. What would be the Union's attitude under such circumstances? It would be incensed, and rightfully so!

Past Practice

True, at times a party to a contract loses a right established by unambiguous contractual language. This could occur when an employer or union by its action or inaction permits a practice to develop that is inconsistent with the language. Under these circumstances, an arbitrator may hold that the party waived its right to the benefits of the clear-cut language. This does not occur frequently, of course, because a party will not permit a practice to nullify clear-cut contractual language.

In the case at hand, the evidence demonstrates that the employer at no time waived its right under the time limits provision of the contract. In fact, the parties stipulated, as indicated earlier, that the Company has a "practice of rejecting grievances which have been filed in an *untimely manner, including grievances challenging discipline under this Attendance Policy.*"

Indeed, the Union has not supplied a scintilla of evidence to support its cause in this proceeding. It has not produced even one instance in which the Company handled a grievance on its merits despite the Union's noncompliance with the time limits.

In sum, therefore, there is no conflict between the crystal-clear contractual language and practice. As a consequence, we have the company's position supported by unequivocal contractual language and past practice.

Contractual Negotiations

A maxim of the arbitration process is that a party should not gain in arbitration what it failed to achieve at the bargaining table. Application of this principle is an additional burden that the Union must bear.

As said earlier, the Union proposed but failed to obtain in the 1993 contract negotiations "discussion and resolution of problems with the Company's 'no-fault' Attendance Program."

Given the Union's position in this case, no mystery exists as to what the Union wanted to achieve from such discussions. It wanted then what it seeks in this dispute: the right to use the grievance procedure including arbitration regardless of the time limits established in Section 18.

---

*As reported in Frank Elkouri and Edna Elkouri, *How Arbitration Works*, 4th ed. (Washington, DC: Bureau of National Affairs, 1985, pp. 348–49. (Citations omitted.)

In sum, the employer's position is supported by unambiguous and unequivocal contractual language, past practice, and contract negotiations. The Union consequently must raise arguments which it hopes would justify ignoring such factors to win a favorable decision in this forum.

Impact on Labor–Management Relations

In the Union's judgment, should the Company prevail in this proceeding, it would result in a deleterious impact on labor–management relations. This would be the case because each time a point is given the employee would be required to file a grievance, possibly carrying it to arbitration. Employees would be compelled to do this in order to comply with the Section 18 time limits. This is a major, if not the major, contention that the Union presents in its quest for a favorable decision.

To be sure, the Union argument is legitimate, certainly not fatuous, and is worthy of serious consideration. Even the employer does not want a multiplicity of grievances arbitrated:

> We do not want marathon, multiple, out-of-control arbitrations as the union suggests will happen under the company's position.

With full deference to the Union and its counsel, the Union's fear is not rooted in reality. Its speculative and gloomy prediction did not occur. Clearly, the deluge of arbitrations did not take place. The attendance program has been in effect for about eleven (11) years. For an equal period of time, the time limits in the grievance procedure have been in effect. In all that time, documentable at least since 1994, *no employee has been terminated under this attendance Program.* What occurred is that employees managed to improve their attendance as they moved through the progressive disciplinary system. From that point of view, the program has been a smashing success. Productivity increased as employees improved their attendance, and there was no deluge of arbitrations as the Union now fears. Given that the factors now are the same as they were in the past, there is no reason to believe that the attendance program will result in the dire prediction that the Union envisions in future years.

Other factors make the Union's speculation difficult to believe. In error, the Union claims:

> Minimally, at least the 39 instances which did result in loss of pay would have had to be grieved and arbitrated. Adding such a burden to all involved—the employee, the Union and the Company—would be more destructive than helpful. Reason and flexibility should prevail rather than the policy suggested by the Company.

Starting in July 1998, suspended employees, for either three (3) or five (5) days, no longer lose their wages and they are permitted to work, but the suspensions remain in their records. Thus, loss of pay, standing by itself, would not be a reason for arbitration.

The Union does not take into consideration the professionalism and expertise of its officers. Indeed, the Union is a very sophisticated labor organization led by knowledgeable national and local union officers. They know when a grievance under the attendance program has or does not have merit. Maybe there could be instances of close calls as to whether a grievance would have merit. But by and large, the Union officers know as much as the Company officials about the merits of grievances.

In addition, the Union fails to recognize that the first six (6) instances of absence are fully grievable regardless of the time limits, provided that the employee files a timely grievance to protest the seventh (7th) point. Under these circumstances, all seven (7) points are subject to challenge for accuracy and on their merits:

Mr. Queen:	Now, I would like to ask for the purpose of clarification one or two questions of the company or Mr. Smith.
	Mr. Smith has said on several occasions that if the employee gets seven points and that is what leads to a verbal warning, that the employee or the union, if they wanted to challenge that, could challenge the accuracy of all seven points.
	I would like to clarify what *accuracy* means. Does that mean only clerical accuracy in recording points, or are you saying . . .
The Arbitrator:	The way I understood it, it would be the merits of the points.
Mr. Queen:	That's what I want to make sure.
Mr. Smith:	No, we are saying that points at the seven-point stage, the verbal warning stage, all seven points are subject to challenge.
The Arbitrator:	On merits.
Mr. Smith:	Merits and accuracy.

In other words, for the first six (6) points there is no need to file grievances or for the union to seek arbitration. Regardless of the time limits of Section 18, such points may be challenged by the employee or union whenever an employee receives the seventh (7th) point.

Reasonableness of Attendance Program

Not even the Union claims that the employer may not establish a no-fault attendance program. Under Section 20, Management Rights, the employer has the authority to establish unilaterally such a program. Among other rights, the provision establishes the employer's right "to make such reasonable rules and regulations in connection with the company's operations."

Standing alone, a no-fault attendance program is inherently reasonable. In increasing numbers, employers and unions have adopted such programs because they eliminate the subjective judgment of supervisors to penalize employees for absenteeism leading to charges of discrimination. Indeed, in the case at hand, the no-fault system has been in effect for about eleven (11) years. During those years the Union has not challenged the Company's authority to institute such a system on a unilateral basis.

In this proceeding, the Union still does not challenge the Company's right. Rather, it claims that the program is unreasonable because the employer's position is that the Union must comply with the time limits established in the Grievance Procedure. In this respect, the Union directs attention to the fact that the Company's exercise of any right found in Section 20 (Management Rights) may not be used "for the purpose of discriminating or to avoid the other provisions of this agreement." Section 22 protects employees against unjust discharge. Therefore, argues the Union, by forcing employees to comply with the Grievance Procedure time limits, the employer violated Section 20 of the contract because the employer exercised its rights in an unreasonable manner.

With due respect, the Union ignores the unmistakable fact that the contract contains time limits written in the most unambiguous manner possible. They were agreed to by the Union and the Company. The analysis of that issue has been presented earlier in this decision and no need exists to repeat it at this point.

How can an employer, or union for that matter, exercise its rights unreasonably when such rights are established by the unambiguous terms of a contract? How can the Company act unreasonably when the Labor Agreement in plain and clear language establishes the time limits in question? How can anyone be a lawbreaker when the action is fully supported by express and unambiguous language?

Another factor demonstrating that the attendance program is reasonable is that an employee may be absent for a variety of reasons and not receive points. Some excusable reasons are absences for work-related injuries, vacations, holidays, jury duty, and funeral and military leave. In this way, the program takes into account uncontrollable events in the lives of employees requiring absence.

Special Review by Plant Manager

In addition, the program contains a catch-all provision calling for special review conducted by the plant manager. It says:

> Prior to the termination of employment of any employee, the purpose of this review will be to evaluate the employee's entire employment history, attendance pattern, reasons for absences, employee efforts to improve, length of service, or any other criteria that he/she deems relevant and of sufficient weight to justify additional consideration.

Indeed, the special review practice would cover the scenario designed by the Union: An employee rushes into a burning building saving the lives of several people. At a ceremony in which the city administration awards him a medal, the Mayor speaks too long, and the employee is late for work. The Company gives him half a point under the attendance program.

Assuming that the employee was discharged because of the half-point, and assuming that, in the Grievance Procedure, Company officials denied the grievance, demonstrating conduct that would put them in first place for meanness and lack of common sense, the case goes before the plant manager for special review. Where would we find a plant manager of any company who would not reverse the discharge? Any manager would undoubtedly reverse it and probably would censure lower management for complete lack of judgment.

Conclusion and Award

After carefully reviewing the record and the parties' arguments, I can only decide that the Union's position does not have merit and must be denied. As said at the outset, the Union had a most difficult task to overcome obstacles to a favorable decision. Unambiguous language in the grievance procedure requires that challenges to discipline under the attendance program must be filed during the stipulated time limits.

By strict language, the arbitrator does not have the authority to eliminate the time limits.

Past practice and contractual negotiations favor the employer's position.

Union contentions designed to overcome those matters were not acceptable. In particular, the Union contended that denial of its position would result in paralysis of the Grievance Procedure, including a deluge of arbitration cases that could possibly bankrupt the Union. This was a major, if not the major Union contention. At the minimum, it would strain relations between the parties.

Substantial reasons, as detailed in this decision, shed considerable doubt upon this Union argument. In the final analysis, the Union only speculates that that state of affairs will actually result. In *eleven (11) years, the deluge of grievances and arbitration cases did not exist.* Since that was not the case in the past, why should it come about in the future, particularly since the no-fault absentee program and the Grievance Procedure time limits are exactly the same?

One final word is in order. In no way does the arbitrator express any opinion about the equitability or desirability of the Union or employees' position. Maybe employees and the Union should have the right to file grievances and invoke arbitration of past absentee offenses regardless of the time limits contained in the Grievance Procedure. Whether contractual language is fair or unfair, wise or unwise, or just or unjust may not be used to fashion an arbitration decision.

When either an employee or union finds contractual language, and particularly unambiguous contractual language, to be burdensome, relief must be sought at the bargaining table and not in arbitration.

Appeals to an arbitrator's sense of fairness or justice will not be successful. As the United States Supreme Court ruled:

> The draftsmen may never have thought of what specific remedy should be awarded to meet a particular contingency. Nevertheless, an arbitrator is confined to interpretation and application of the collective bargaining agreement; *he does not sit to dispense his own brand of industrial justice.* He may of course look for guidance from many sources, yet his award is legitimate only so long as it draws its essence from the collective bargaining agreement. When the arbitrator's words manifest an infidelity to this obligation, courts have no choice but to refuse enforcement of the award.* (Emphasis added)

Award of Arbitrator

Grievance No. 97–07, dated May 17, 1997, is denied on the grounds that the Union and/or employee challenging discipline under the attendance program must comply with time limits in Section 18 of the Labor Agreement.

Questions

1. Evaluate the reasons that the arbitrator used to find the attendance program reasonable under the contract, including the employer's position that grievances protesting discipline must conform to the time limits established in the grievance procedure.
2. If you were representing the Union, explain how you would criticize the arbitrator's decision.
3. Do you agree with the arbitrator's statement that since there was no deluge of grievances and arbitrations in the past, there is no reason to believe that there would be in the future? Why or why not?
4. How do you believe the arbitrator's decision will affect the parties when they negotiate a new labor agreement?

---

*United Steelworkers of America v. Enterprise Wheel & Car Corp., 363 U.S. 593 (1960).

Injury on the Job: The Case of Drug and Alcohol Testing

Cast of Characters

Wang   Company Director of Industrial Relations
Houseman International Union Representative

*A*ll of us should know that the use of illegal drugs and abuse of alcohol are critical problems of society. Untold billions of dollars have been spent to curb the use of illegal drugs, and apparently with limited success. Since the workplace reflects society, it is not surprising that drugs and alcohol constitute a major problem for employers, unions, and employees.

This case demonstrates how some employers have tried to curb the use of illegal drugs and alcohol. The company unilaterally instituted a rule requiring employees who have a job-related injury to undergo drug and alcohol testing. Employees who refuse to take the test or who show positive results are subject to discharge. In the case, the union charged the employer with violation of the Labor Agreement, especially Article XI(b). At the heart of its position is that the contract requires negotiation and agreement between the employer and union before new or modified Plant Rules can be imposed.

A few days after it had filed the grievance, the union filed an unfair labor practices charge against the employer with the National Labor Relations Board. By putting the rule in effect unilaterally and without bargaining with the union, the employer, the union charged, had violated the law by refusing to bargain in good faith. The NLRB deferred the case to arbitration under the *Collyer* doctrine. (In this chapter, there is discussion of *Collyer,* and it should be read and understood for purposes of this case.)

As the decision shows, the arbitrator held that the employer did not violate the contract or the National Labor Relations Act. As you read the case, determine why the arbitrator held that plant rules are not part of the contract and, therefore, that a new rule or modification of an existing rule need not be negotiated but may be announced by the employer on a unilateral basis. Most important of all, determine why the arbitrator held that postaccident drug and alcohol testing is neither a new nor a modified rule. Finally, establish how the arbitrator ruled that the company did not violate the National Labor Relations Act.

INTRODUCTION

This case surfaced when the Company, on May 3, 1997, unilaterally adopted a policy requiring a drug and alcohol test when an employee had a work-related injury or illness. In protest, the Union filed Grievance Number 05-9729, dated May 5, 1997, which stated:

> Violation of Contract Art. XI Para B. Changing plant rules or adding plant rules that have not been agreed upon by both Parties.

> For settlement of the grievance, the Union requested:

> Remove plant rule that was posted on 5-4-97 pertaining to testing injured employees. It is unfair and unreasonable.

On May 7, 1997, the Employer denied the grievance, contending that its action did not violate the Labor Agreement. On May 13, 1997, the Union filed an unfair labor practices charge against the Company alleging a violation of Section 8(a)(1) and Section 8(a)(5) of the National Labor Relations Act. The charge stated:

> On or about May 3, 1997 the Employer unilaterally implemented mandatory drug and/or alcohol testing for employees with a work-related illness or injury. Within the last 6 months the above-named Employer, by the above and other acts, interfered with, restrained and coerced employees in the exercise of rights guaranteed in the Act.

Catalogued Case Number 25-CA-22524, it was deferred to arbitration by the Regional Director, Region 25, National Labor Relations Board.

LABOR AGREEMENT (MAY 1, 1995)

ARTICLE I—RECOGNITION

(b) Management of the plant and the direction of the working forces, including the right to hire, suspend or discharge for just cause, except as expressly limited by this Agreement, and the right to establish production standards, transfers, or layoffs, due to lack of work, and in general, all other functions of Management, unless expressly limited by this Agreement, are reserved to and are vested exclusively in the Company.

ARTICLE VIII—WORKING CONDITIONS

(a) The Union agrees for its members to abide by all reasonable shop rules, as drafted by the Company and posted on the bulletin board, and violation of said rules shall subject the violator to action on the Company's part, commensurate with the seriousness of the violation.

•••

ARTICLE XI—AMENDMENTS TO THE AGREEMENT

(a) This Agreement constitutes the full and complete understanding and agreements of the parties hereto, and all differences, claims and demands existing between the parties are considered settled and finally determined by the Agreement. No amendments, changes or modifications shall be made except by an instrument in writing duly ratified by the Local Union and signed by the authorized agents of the parties hereto.

(b) Amendments, changes or modifications made during the term of the Agreement shall be reduced to writing and become a part of this Agreement effective on the date signed by the authorized agents of the parties to this Agreement.

Any existing amendments, changes, or modifications shall be reviewed and if agreed to, be incorporated as part of this Agreement on its effective date.

C.   Causes for Immediate Discharge

•••

3. Possession or use of intoxicating liquors or narcotics on Company property or reporting to work or working under the influence of either. POSSESSION OF AN ILLEGAL DRUG(S) ON COMPANY PROPERTY SHALL INCLUDE ONE (THOSE) FOUND AND CONFIRMED BY A DRUG TEST OF THE EMPLOYEE'S PERSON. THE SUBSTANCE OF THIS RULE ALSO APPLIES TO A LEGAL PRESCRIPTION DRUG(S) NOT OBTAINED BY PHYSICIAN'S ORDER. [Emphasis in original]

•••

ISSUE

1. Under the circumstances of this case, did the Company violate Article XI, Paragraph b or any other provision of the Labor Agreement? If so, what should the remedy be?
2. Under the circumstances of this case, did the Company violate Section 8(a)(1) or Section 8(a)(5) of the National Labor Relations Act? If so, what should the remedy be?

BACKGROUND

Drug and Alcohol Policy Prior to May 3, 1997

Prior to May 3, 1997, employees were tested for controlled drug substances or alcohol when the Company had reasonable or just cause for the procedure. Regarding this issue, Wang testified:

Before the current policy became effective, employees would be tested for drugs after an accident when we had reasonable cause to believe the employee was under the influence of drugs or alcohol.

Some employees who had accidents, said Wang, were not tested.

Houseman confirmed the policy by saying that the Employer tested employees for drugs or alcohol when there was "just cause" to believe that employees were under the influence, for example by exhibiting observable characteristics such as slurred speech, staggering, glassy eyes, and smell.

Notice of May 3, 1997

On May 3, 1997, the Company announced the policy that generated this arbitration. It stated:

Effective Monday, May 3, 1997, a new plant rule will be added to the procedure governing the examination and/or treatment of work-related injuries or illnesses that require attention, examination or treatment at a facility outside of our plant (i.e., clinic, hospital or doctor's office). These work-related injuries will require the employee to submit to a drug and/or alcohol test at the time the attention, examination, or treatment is being given. The drug and/or alcohol test, which could be given in the form of urinalysis, blood alcohol or breathalyzer, will be paid for by the Company.

If an employee refuses to submit to the test, or if the employee tests positive for alcohol (beyond the legal threshold), illegal drugs, or legal drugs for which the employee has no prescription, the employee may be terminated and Worker's Compensation benefits may be denied.

Wang explained why the Employer adopted the policy. U.S. Department of Labor studies demonstrate that about 12 percent of the nation's labor force test positive for illegal drugs. An employee who uses drugs or alcohol is four times as likely to have a job-related accident as an employee who does not. Users of drugs and alcohol are five times as likely to file Worker's Compensation claims as are nonusers. Between 1989 and 1996, accidents in the Employer's plant increased to the extent that its Worker's Compensation premiums increased from $25,000 annually to approximately $200,000.

Since the policy became effective, 10 employees had been tested for drugs and alcohol after an accident. All 10 employees had tested negative and returned to work.

POSITIONS OF THE PARTIES

Both parties submitted comprehensive posthearing briefs to support their respective positions. To the extent necessary and appropriate for purposes of this case, arguments contained in them will be referenced in the following portion of this decision.

EVALUATION OF THE EVIDENCE

Parties' Bargaining History

At stake in this dispute is the determination of whether the Company policy implemented May 3, 1997, violated a provision of the Labor Agreement. In the Union's view, testing of employees for drugs or alcohol after a job-related accident constitutes a new plant rule or a modification of an existing rule, and such rules must be negotiated. There is no question that prior to establishing the policy the Employer neither notified the Union nor bargained with it. Instead, the Company, by unilateral action, put the policy into effect.

The gravamen of the Union's position rests upon the proposition that Plant Rules are part of the Labor Agreement and any changes must be negotiated. Plant Rule C3, as changed by the May 3, 1997, policy, is invalid in the Union's opinion because such a change was not negotiated.

To support this position, the Union highlights the collective bargaining history of the parties. In 1985, the parties executed a Memorandum of Agreement regarding attendance policy for employees. The last sentence of the document states:

This memorandum is entered into and made a part of the Plant Rules as attached to the Labor Agreement on this 7th day of August, 1985.

On this basis, the Union contends:

Testimony at the hearing by the company shows the rules were not printed in the agreement until 1989. Further testimony was they were a separate document which was given to each employee. As such, the phrase signed by the parties in 1985 "... PART OF THE PLANT RULES AS ATTACHED TO THE LABOR AGREEMENT ..." could only have one meaning, that being the rules are part of the agreement. (Emphasis in original) (Union Posthearing Brief, p. 6)

To the contrary, the Memorandum refers strictly to Plant Rule B1, which states "repeated absenteeism and/or tardiness for any reason" subjects an employee to discipline. The document *does not make* Plant Rules a part of the Labor Agreement.

Referring to the contract negotiations of 1985, the Union directs attention to Items 13 through 15 of the Employer's negotiation agenda. They stated:

13. *Memorandum of Understanding*—Attendance Policy, Delete.
14. Discuss Smoking Policy.
15. Discuss Alcohol and Drug Testing.

No question exists that the attendance policy was negotiated by the parties. The best evidence is that Article XI, Section (6), Amendments to the Agreement, provides for mutual agreement to make "amendments, changes or modifications" during the term of the agreement. Thus, the parties agreed to a Memorandum of Agreement, entitled "Attendance Control Program, Plant Rule B, Article I."

Items 14 and 15, dealing respectively with smoking policy and alcohol and drug testing, carry the denotation "discuss." Clearly, to discuss an issue does not mean to negotiate or bargain on the matter. Compare the Company's proposal to discuss smoking and drug and alcohol policy with the other items on its agenda. For the other items, the Employer used the words *amend* and *delete*. For example, the Employer proposed to amend Section 3(j) to read (j) Retirement and to delete Section 3(a)(3) of Article VII. In total, fifteen items appeared on the Company's agenda. Of that number, two are identified as "discuss"; the others say "amend" or "delete," indicating the Company's willingness to bargain over those issues.

In sum, nothing in the history of negotiations demonstrates that Plant Rules are part of the contract or that bargaining is necessary to change them.

Change in Plant Rule C3: November, 1995

Reference was made to the unilateral change the Company made in Plant Rule C3 when it sent its draft of the 1995 contract to the printer. The Employer added the following language:

Possession of an illegal drug(s) on Company property shall include one (those) found and confirmed by a drug test of the employee's person. The substance of this rule also applies to a legal prescription drug(s) not obtained by physician's order.

After the Union discovered the change, it objected because the change had not been negotiated. Houseman testified that Wang had assured the Union that the added language only clarified the previous Rule and that the testing procedure would not change. Given this assurance, the Union dropped its objection. The last sentence of the posted notice stated:

This wording does not mean or imply that we are changing any drug testing policy or procedure.

On this basis, the Union asserts:

THE COMPANY AGAIN NEGOTIATED AND LOCKED INTO THE EXISTING TESTING PROCEDURES IN NOVEMBER 1995. (Emphasis in original) (Union Posthearing Brief, p. 8)

This argument could have merit provided we find that the May 3, 1997, policy constituted a new rule or a modification of an existing rule. We shall reach that issue later on in this decision.

Negotiations of 1995

In the 1995 negotiations, the Company's agenda included the employees' obligation to report accidents regardless of whether they resulted in injury; a smoking policy to permit smoking in the plant except in areas designated nonsmoking; a requirement that employees follow safety rules; and a moving of the penalty for leaving assigned job duties or immediate work area without permission of supervision from Plant Rule C to Plant Rule B.

As Union Exhibit 5 demonstrates, for each Plant Rule the document says "on Wednesday, April 17, 1995, the Company and the Union agreed . . ." When the Company drafted the changes in the 1995 contract, including the Plant Rules changes, the Union used that phrase in the membership ratification meetings.

Under these circumstances, the Union contends that Plant Rules are negotiated by the parties, claiming:

> The actions of the parties to negotiate rule changes and to allow the ratification of the rules by the members requires the rules be construed as being part of the agreement. (Union Posthearing Brief, p. 7)

Testing the validity of the Union's argument requires that certain conditions be kept in mind. Before 1989, Plant Rules appeared in a special document and were distributed to employees on that basis. Since 1989, they are included in the contract booklet. Wang testified that it was his decision to include them in the contract booklet for "ease and convenience." Plant Rules, however, appear *after* the signature page. In the current contract, the signatures of the parties' representatives appear on page 58. Following that page, in a series of unnumbered pages, the Plant Rules appear. They are *not* included as a Memorandum of Understanding as is the Attendance Control Program. As stated earlier, Article XI, Section (b) provides that the Labor Agreement may be changed during its effective period only by a written document signed by the authorized agents of the parties. If the Plant Rules are part of the contract, as the Union contends, they should either appear before the signature page or be reduced to a Memorandum of Understanding and signed by the authorized representatives of the parties.

In regard to the issue under consideration, Wang testified regarding the Plant Rules in question, stating:

> In 1995, before reaching a tentative agreement, I told the Union "this is what we are going to do."

Regarding the 1995 negotiations, the Union asserts:

> Again, in 1995, the company brought demands for change to rules to the negotiation table. These are found in union Exhibit 4 as items 17 and 18. The union also brought a demand to modify the attendance policy to the bargaining table in 1995 Union Exhibit 3 page two last item.
>
> The demands brought by the parties to two negotiations were discussed and either agreed to by the parties or abandoned by the originating party.
>
> If the rules were not considered a part of the agreement then it would not be likely that two different company negotiators would bring demands for rule changes to the bargaining table, discuss the changes desired, modify or abandon their demands based on discussion with the union. (Union Posthearing Brief, pp. 6–7)

With full respect to the Union and its advocate, the evidence does not support the argument. In only one way did the Employer later change its original position. It removed the "near miss" from Plant Rule B9. Clearly, this change does not prove that Plant Rules are part of the contract and negotiable. Even when rules are unilaterally established by an employer, it may very well provide notice to the labor organization, discuss the rules, and accept suggestions from the union. Although the circumstances of the removal of "near miss" from Plant Rule B9 are not in the record, they probably resulted from a Union suggestion.

In addition, the record does not demonstrate the basic elements of collective bargaining. It lacks evidence of counterproposals and compromises, the essence of the process. In fact, nothing in the record demonstrates that the Union objected to any of the Plant Rules announced by the Company in the 1995 contract sessions. Nothing in the record shows that the Union offered counterproposals or compromises to the Company's changes in Plant Rules.

In short, as demonstrated by the record, the Employer announced the Plant Rule changes in the 1995 negotiations and the Union simply agreed to them. The evidence does not demonstrate that Plant Rules are negotiable or that they are not an exercise of Company rights established in Article I, including the authority of management to direct the working forces.

Given the evidence, it is not correct to find as does the Union that "THE COMPANY SHOULD NOT BE GIVEN WHAT IT FAILED TO ACHIEVE IN NEGOTIATIONS." (Emphasis in original) (Union Posthearing Brief, p. 7)

The argument is not valid because the evidence shows that Plant Rules have not been negotiated. Equally, the Company never proposed in negotiations to test employees for drugs and alcohol after having an accident. If it made such a proposal, and withdrew it after the Union objected, the Union's argument would have merit.

That Plant Rules in the past have not been negotiated, and are not a part of the contract, does not necessarily mean that the grievance does not have merit. In this dispute, we are concerned with Plant Rule C3 requiring a drug and alcohol test after an accident. Additional issues must be considered before determining whether Plant Rule C3 is valid under the contract, or in the alternative, violates its terms.

Management Rights

Consideration should be given to Article I, paragraph b, the Management Rights provision. It states:

> Management of the plant and the direction of the working forces, including the right to hire, suspend or discharge for just cause, except as expressly limited by this Agreement, and the right to establish production standards, transfers, or layoffs, due to lack of work, and in general, all other functions of Management, unless expressly limited by this Agreement, are reserved to and are vested exclusively in the Company.

Clearly, within the scope and meaning of this provision, Management has the right to adopt reasonable measures to protect the safety of the workers. As noted earlier, employees who use alcohol or illegal drugs have a four times greater chance to have accidents than those who do not. On this basis, in the interest of maintaining a drug-free work environment, the Employer's decision to adopt a postaccident alcohol and drug testing policy is supported by the Management Rights provision.

True, in exercising its rights under the provision, the Company may not adopt a policy that *conflicts with any express provision of the contract*. To put it in other terms, Management may direct the working forces *except as expressly limited by the Agreement."* (Emphasis supplied)

In its grievance, the Union alleges that the Employer violated Article XI, paragraph b, which states that any amendment, change, or modification made during the effective period of the contract must be reduced to writing and signed by the authorized representatives of the parties.

Clearly, that language does not forbid the Company from adopting the policy in question. Not when, as previously held, the Employer has the unilateral right to adopt reasonable measures to protect the safety of the work force. Given that finding, the provision relied upon by the Union (Article XI, paragraph b) may not be construed *to expressly prohibit* the Employer's right and responsibility to adopt reasonable rules to maintain a drug-free work environment. Later on we shall address the issue determining whether the postaccident testing policy is reasonable.

Application of Article VIII, Section 4

Under this provision, the Union agreed that its members would abide by all reasonable shop rules, as drafted by the Company and posted on bulletin boards. It further agreed that violators of the rules shall be subject to discipline commensurate with the seriousness of the violation. In support of its position, the Company relies on Section 4, asserting:

> In addition, we and the Union specifically bargained that its members were to abide by the reasonable shop rules, *as drafted by the Company* and that violation of the said rules would result in disciplinary action. (Emphasis in original) (Employer Posthearing Brief, pp. 21–22)

In other words, Plant Rule C3 requiring a drug and alcohol test following an accident is a rule drafted by the Company. Violators shall be subject to discipline, including discharge.

Not so, asserts the Union, because the accident feature modifies Plant Rule C3, and "THERE IS NO CONTRACT PROVISION GIVING THE COMPANY THE RIGHT TO MODIFY THE RULES." (Emphasis in original) (Union Posthearing Brief, p. 10) It asserts further:

> There exists at page 54 of the agreement Section 4, a general working condition which states "the union agrees that its members will abide by all reasonable shop rules, as posted on the bulletin board . . ." THIS LANGUAGE DOES NOT SAY THAT THE COMPANY MAY MODIFY ANY EXISTING RULE. (Emphasis in original) (Union Posthearing Brief, p. 10)

To close the circle, the Union claims that the Arbitrator does not have the authority to affirm modification of rules. It points to the restrictions on the power of arbitrators selected by the parties. In this regard, Article V, Fourth Step, states:

> The jurisdiction of the arbitrator shall be limited to the interpretation and application of the provisions of this Agreement and the arbitrator shall have no power to change, modify or alter any provisions of this Agreement.

On this basis, the Union argues:

> The company position on the other hand requires the arbitrator to change, modify or alter a provision of the agreement. As shown above what the company really seeks here is to have the arbitrator give them a right to modify existing rules unilaterally. There is no right specified for them to do so. As a result, it would mean the Section 4 provision they point to as defense of their actions has to have the term "or modified" added by virtue of final and binding arbitration interpretation, so it would then be read ". . . reasonable shop

rules, as drafted OR MODIFIED by the company and posted . . ." (Emphasis in original) (Union Posthearing Brief, p. 13)

To be sure, if the disputed language of Plant Rule C3 requiring a drug and alcohol test after an accident constitutes a modification of the rule, the Union's argument could have merit. It could be valid to assert that the Company does not have the power to modify an existing rule in the absence of bargaining and that the Arbitrator does not have the authority to approve modification of an existing rule.

Before resolving the parties' conflict, the following comments are appropriate. If the Company has the right to adopt a new rule, it should follow that the Employer has the equal right to adopt a reasonable modification of the rule. In addition, since Union members must abide by all reasonable rules drafted by the Employer, it should follow that the Union waived its right to bargain concerning any reasonable plant rule or a modification of the rule unilaterally established by Management.

Rule C3: Testing After an Accident

In any event, where the Union's basic argument fails is that Rule C3 requiring postaccident drug and alcohol testing is *neither a new rule nor a modification of an existing rule*. Instead, it is an *enforcement technique* of Plant Rule C3. The substance of the rule is not changed or altered. The rule pertaining to possession or the use of intoxicating liquors or narcotics on Company property or reporting to work under the influence of either is not changed. Possession or use of drugs or alcohol are grounds for immediate dismissal; this is the heart and essence of the rule. To more effectively enforce the rule, the Employer posted a notice on November 19, 1995, requiring a drug and alcohol test of the employee's person to confirm possession or use. Thus, the May 3, 1997, policy was not the first time an actual test was to be performed on an employee's person to determine whether the employee was in violation of the rule.

In addition, the penalty for violation of Plant Rule C3 is not altered by the testing technique. Whatever may be the penalty for violation remains the same before and after May 3, 1997. The purpose of Rule C3 is to enhance the Employer's right and responsibility to investigate accidents. Postaccident testing improves the Company's right and responsibility to provide a safe working environment for its employees.

Reasonableness of Postaccident Testing

Even when an employer has the unilateral right to establish work rules and to enforce such rules, the employer's action must meet the standard of reasonableness. In the Union's view, postaccident testing is unreasonable and should be invalidated on that basis. The Union argues:

> A general test of reasonableness is whether the rule is reasonably related to a legitimate objective of management.
>
> The primary stated objective of Mr. Wang is the reduction of costs specifically, reducing Worker's Compensation costs. The operation of the rule at this facility has rendered the rule unreasonable. According to Wang, there have been ten accidents involving medical treatment. All ten have had drug or alcohol tests administered. All ten have come back negative. Ten tests more than would have been required have now been administered. Thus, costs have increased. All of the tests were negative so there have been no Worker's Compensation cost reductions. The net effect is the rule has added costs. (Union Posthearing Brief, p. 12)

The obvious problem with this argument is that the Union totally ignores the *deterrent* resulting from the postaccident testing policy. When employees understand that they will be tested for drugs and alcohol should they have an accident, it is a matter of common sense that they will be less likely to consume alcohol or to use narcotics. That is why many private employers and the federal government have such a policy in place.

The Union contends:

> The company also wants to reduce the incidents of accidents. There is no evidence or testimony by the employer that the incidents have reduced in number. (Union Posthearing Brief, p. 12)

This is sheer speculation on the part of the Union. It could also be speculated that in the absence of the policy there may have been more accidents.

Another contention of the Union is equally unpersuasive, asserting:

> Another objective of the company is to provide a safer place for employees to work. There already exists a rule and enforcement procedure for prohibiting drug or alcohol related activity. If the observation for physical conditions requiring a test are administered diligently by the supervisor, unsafe conditions of drug or alcohol influence will [be] minimized by removal of those under the influence from the work environment prior to an accident. (Union Posthearing Brief, p. 12)

It ignores the situation in which an employee has used alcohol or illegal drugs but has not exhibited the physical characteristics. The Union does not take into consideration that people are different in terms of tolerance to alcohol and narcotics.

Once again, the Union failed to take into consideration the deterrent of this policy when it argued:

> If on the other hand there has been an accident and injury has occurred, the effect of testing does not enhance employees' safety as the safety of the injured employee has already been breached. Thus this objective is not achieved as the testing is not preventive or abating of accidents but rather it is punitive after the fact. (Union Posthearing Brief, p. 12)

We stress that when employees understand that a test will be taken should there be an accident, they will be less likely to consume alcohol or drugs. As objective studies have demonstrated, an employee who uses illegal substances is four times more likely to have accidents. To the extent that employees cease such use because of the postaccident testing policy, there would be a sharp drop in accidents.

With due respect, the Union has turned the argument around when it says:

> The company's knowledge that tests under these conditions are arbitrary and capricious is evidenced by the fact that people are put immediately and directly back to work before the results of the test are known. (Union Posthearing Brief, p. 12)

Indeed, it would be arbitrary and capricious if the Employer did not permit *capable employees to return to their jobs after testing.* Wang testified:

> If an employee has an accident, after the test he returns to work if capable. If the doctor certifies the injury is not serious, we let him return to work the same day as the accident.

The point is that the test was made. The physician certified that the injury was not serious enough to keep the employee from working. Indeed, it would be very arbitrary for the Company to keep such an employee from working, perhaps for several days, while the urine or blood samples are being processed.

In the event of illness, the Employer would have difficulty in establishing whether an illness is work-related. An employee could easily get a respiratory condition because of conditions other than the job. Thus, in the administration of the policy, it would be much more difficult to establish that an illness is work-related compared with an accident. Should the Employer fail to establish that an illness is job-related, the employee under the policy should not be tested. It is significant that in its comprehensive posthearing brief, the Employer does not deal in substance with work-related illnesses. In contrast, it mentions "postaccident" testing many times.

Finally, the program places a minimal burden on an employee. Understand that the policy comes into effect only when he/she suffers a job-related accident requiring examination and/or treatment at a facility outside the plant. It is not a policy in which every accident and/or injury calls for testing. In addition, it is appropriate to say that a nonuser of alcohol or narcotics has nothing to fear from the program. If the employee is a user, and that is disclosed by the test, even the Union would presumably agree that such an employee should be penalized. In that condition, the user jeopardizes his own and others' safety.

Despite potential difficulties in the administration of a job-related illness, the program as a whole, including its enforcement, meets the test of reasonableness. To be sure, the Arbitrator carefully considered the Union's contentions, but these did not demonstrate the program to be unreasonable, arbitrary, capricious, or discriminatory.

Conclusion: No Contract Violation

The preceding analysis and careful consideration of the parties' contentions lead to the conclusion that the Employer did not violate Article XI, paragraph b, or any other material provision of the Labor Agreement. Consistent with its right and obligation, the Company implemented a reasonable policy in the effort to establish a drug-free work environment. Such a policy benefits all concerned: bargaining unit employees, Management personnel, Union, and Company.

In short, on the basis of the evidence, Grievance Number 05-9729, dated May 5, 1997, does not have merit and must be denied.

What remains, therefore, is a determination of whether the instant decision is consistent with or repugnant to the National Labor Relations Act.

Application of National Labor Relations Act

Section 7 of the National Labor Relations Act states:

> RIGHTS OF EMPLOYEES. Sec. 7. Employees shall have the right to self-organization, to form, join, or assist labor organizations, to bargain collectively through representatives of their own choosing, or to engage in other concerted activities for the purpose of collective bargaining or other mutual aid or protection, and shall also have the right to refrain from any or all of such activities except to the extent that such right may be affected by an agreement requiring membership in a labor organization as a condition of employment as authorized in section 8(a)(3).

Under the terms of Section 8(a)(1), it is an unfair labor practice for an employer "to interfere with, restrain, or coerce employees in the exercise of the rights guaranteed in Section 7." Section 8(a)(5) makes it unlawful for an employer "to refuse to bargain collectively with the representatives of his employees."

Since the Employer did not bargain with the Union prior to implementing the postaccident testing policy, the Union filed unfair labor practice charges against it with the National Labor Relations Board (NLRB). It asserted that the Company violated Section 8(a)(1) and Section 8(a)(5) of the statute.

To support its position, the Union cites *Johnson-Bateman,* 295 NLRB 180 (1989). In that case, similar to the case at hand, the employer unilaterally established a policy requiring employees to take a drug and alcohol test if treated for a work-related injury. As here, refusal to submit to the test may result in termination. Finding the policy to be a mandatory subject of collective bargaining, the NLRB held that Johnson-Bateman violated the law. The Board ruled:

> Accordingly, in light of all the above considerations, we conclude that drug/alcohol testing of employees who require treatment for injuries received while on the job is a mandatory subject of bargaining; that the Union has not waived its right to bargain with the Respondent about this subject; and that the Respondent's unilateral implementation of the requirement for such testing, without providing the Union with prior notice and an opportunity to bargain, violated Section 8(a)(5) and (1) of the Act, as alleged.

On the basis of *Johnson-Bateman,* the Union cautions the Arbitrator by saying:

> The Union asserts that a finding by the Arbitrator which carries with it a remedy continuing the testing of employees for drugs or alcohol after involvement in an accident or being treated for an industrial illness is repugnant to the Act. (Addendum to Posthearing Brief)

To support its position, the Union could also have cited *Coastal Chemical,* 304 NLRB 556 (1991). In that case, as here, the employer unilaterally instituted a new rule requiring drug testing following job-related injuries. Using *Johnson-Bateman* as precedent, the NLRB held the company's action unlawful under national labor policy. To defend its action, Coastal Chemical stressed that it had a preemployment drug-testing policy, but the NLRB held that it was too far a "leap" from existing policies to subject employees to that postemployment drug test for the employer not to have consulted the employees' bargaining agent.

What the Union ignores, however, is that since *Johnson-Bateman,* the NLRB has deferred drug-testing procedure cases to arbitration under the *Collyer* doctrine. (192 NLRB 837 (1971))

In *Inland Container Corporation* (298 NLRB 715 (1990)), the employer, as here, unilaterally established a policy requiring drug-testing procedures. Since the employer did not bargain prior to implementation of the rule, the labor organization filed unfair labor practice charges. While deferring the dispute to arbitration, the NLRB ruled:

> In conclusion, we find not only that there are not impediments to deferral, but also that deferral will fulfill the Act's mandate to foster the practice and procedure of collective bargaining. Although the complaint alleges that the respondent has failed to meet its bargaining obligations by unilaterally implementing its substance abuse policy, we find that deferral will foster the Act's mandate by requiring the parties to abide by their agreed to method of resolving such disputes through the grievance and arbitration procedure.

In *Bath Iron Works* (302 NLRB 898 (1991)), the employer, as here, unilaterally established a substance-abuse policy that called for drug-testing procedures. An arbitrator sustained the policy, but an Administrative Law Judge held that the decision was "repugnant to the purposes and policies" of the National Labor Relations Act.

Previous to the implementation of the drug-testing procedure, Bath Iron Works had in effect a plant rule providing discharge for the "use, possession, distribution, sale or offering for sale of narcotics, dangerous drugs including marijuana or alcoholic beverages on company premises at any time." Under its changed policy, the rule stated:

Being on Company premises under the influence of alcohol, narcotics or dangerous drugs including marijuana *or refusing to submit to a test administered by the medical department to determine such influence.* (Emphasis added)

First Offense: Five (5) days off
Second Offense: Discharge

In his decision, the arbitrator held that the testing procedure was not a "substantial or significant departure" from the existing rule, but, rather, a "particularization and methodological implementation of the preexisting rules."

While reversing the Law Judge, and deferring to the arbitration decision, the NLRB said

That . . . acquiescence in previous unilateral changes does not necessarily operate as a waiver of a Union's right to bargain changes for all times. . . . When changes in existing plant rules, however, constitute mere particularizations of or delineations of means for carrying out an established rule or practice, they may in many instances, be deemed not to constitute a "material substantial and significant change."

In the case at hand, the arbitrator held that the postaccident testing procedure is an enforcement technique of the preexisting rule, or, as said in *Bath Iron Works,* that the testing procedure constitutes "mere particularizations of or delineations of means for carrying out an established rule or practice."

In a 1993 case, the NLRB, while reversing the General Counsel, deferred to an arbitration award upholding the employer's unilateral right to implement a drug and alcohol testing procedure at its nuclear generating facility. *Southern California Edison Co.* (310 NLRB No. 211, April 30, 1993)* An arbitrator held that the testing procedure was reasonably related to safety considerations and that the program violated neither the labor agreement nor the National Labor Relations Act. Opposing deferral to the arbitrator's decision, the General Counsel held that it was "repugnant to the purposes and policies" of the National Labor Relations Act.

In the labor agreement, a provision stated:

The Company reserves the right to draft reasonable safety rules for employees and to insist on the observance of such rules. The Union may submit suggestions to the Company labor relations division concerning plant conditions and revision and enforcement of safety rules.

In his decision, the arbitrator held that the challenged drug tests were directly related to safety considerations. He also ruled that the union waived its right to protest against employer unilaterally promulgated safety rules because it agreed to the safety provision. Rejecting the General Counsel's position, the NLRB held that the arbitrator's decision was not repugnant to the statute or "palpably wrong."

---

*The Board distinguished *Johnson-Bateman* from *Southern California Edison Co.* on the grounds that in the former case "no party sought deferral of the charge to arbitration."

It is recognized, of course, that the Employer in this case is not a nuclear generating facility. Nonetheless, accidents do occur in the plant. Without contradiction from the union, Wang testified:

> Our Company is a dangerous place to work. We have had many accidents, some of them serious.

In comparing safety considerations between a nuclear generating facility and this Company, it is a matter of degree and not of substance. All manufacturing facility employers, regardless of size, have the right and the obligation to protect their work force against injury.

As noted, in *Southern California Edison Co.*, the arbitrator held that the labor organization waived its right to protest against reasonable rules relating to safety because it agreed to the aforecited safety provision. In the case at hand, the arbitrator suggested that it would not be unreasonable to hold that the Union also waived its right to protest because it agreed to Article VIII, Section 4 in which the Union agreed that "its members will abide by all reasonable shop rules as drafted by the Company."

It should also be repeated that the Employer's alcohol and drug testing program is contemplated and protected by the Management Rights provision of the Labor Agreement.

This decision satisfies the standards established in *Spielberg Manufacturing Co.* (112 NLRB 1080 (1955)). The arbitration proceedings were fair and regular; the parties agreed to be bound by the Arbitrator's award; the unfair labor practice issue was expressly presented by both sides in the hearing; the unfair labor practice issue was specifically treated in this decision; and the Arbitrator's decision is not repugnant or palpably wrong to the purposes and policies of the National Labor Relations Act as administered and enforced by the National Labor Relations Board.

In sum, under the circumstances of this case, and in light of the evidence, the Employer violated the terms of neither the Labor Agreement nor the National Labor Relations Act.

Award of Arbitrator

1. Grievance No. 05-9729, dated May 5, 1997, filed by the Union, is denied on the grounds that the Company did not violate Article XI, Section (b), and/or any other relevant provision of the Labor Agreement under the circumstances of this case.
2. The Company did not violate Section 8(a)(1) or Section 8(a)(5) of the National Labor Relations Act.

Questions

1. Do you agree or disagree with the arbitrator's finding that the rule in question (Plant Rule C3) was a reasonable exercise of the employer's right and duty to promote safety in the plant? Whatever your position, present cogent arguments to support it.
2. Explain why the arbitrator held that the postaccident testing for drugs or alcohol is neither a new rule nor a modification of an existing rule.
3. What is the major argument that the arbitrator used to find that plant rules are not a part of the Labor Agreement?
4. Evaluate the following union argument: "Testing is not preventive or abating of accidents but rather it is punitive after the fact."

Wage Issues under

Collective Bargaining

*A*lmost all contract negotiations pivot upon, and most grievances and arbitrations thus ultimately deal with, four major areas: (1) wages and issues that can be directly related to wages; (2) employee benefits or economic "fringe" supplements to the basic wage rate; (3) "institutional" issues that deal with the rights and duties of employers and unions; and (4) "administrative" clauses that treat such subjects as work rules and job tenure. In this chapter and the three that follow it, each of these areas will be discussed in turn. As in the preceding chapter, arbitration cases will also be used, where appropriate, to illustrate particular problems.

Job security considerations are currently running a close second to wage issues as the most vexatious bargaining table problem, but wage and wage-related considerations historically have been the leading overt cause of strikes. During the past decade, for example, controversies over wages have been either the exclusive or the primary cause of almost 40 percent of the nation's work stoppages.[1]

This record highlights the vital character of wage negotiations in collective bargaining and also suggests that in the area of wages much can be done to decrease management–labor conflict substantially.

In fact, as is the case perhaps with no other area of collective bargaining to that extent, wage problems test the skill of negotiators. The latter are, as we know, now confronted with a legion of wage issues, including the establishment of the basic wage rate, wage differentials, overtime rates, and wage adjustments during contractual periods, as well as with the thorny problems involved in the negotiation of the so-called fringe, or supplemental, wage payments, which will be discussed in the next chapter. It is hoped that the following discussion of some of the principles, practices, and trends concerning these several wage and wage-related areas will contribute to a better understanding of them.

DETERMINATION OF THE BASIC WAGE RATE

If union and management representatives are exhibiting an ever-greater willingness to deal with factual information at the bargaining table, there is still no single standard for wage rate determination that has anything approaching a "scientific" base. Both of the bargaining parties, in fact, commonly utilize at least *three different* such standards, each of which has definite advantages from the viewpoint of achieving an "equitable" settlement but also significant limitations: the comparative norm, ability-to-pay, and standard-of-living criteria.

❖ Comparative Norm

The basic idea behind the **comparative norm** concept is the presumption that the economics of a particular collective bargaining relationship should neither fall substantially behind nor be greatly superior to that of other employer–union relationships; that in short it is generally a good practice to keep up with the crowd, but not necessarily to lead it.

The outside observer would very probably agree with this principle, at least on the surface. When a management is operating with a highly competitive product or in highly competitive labor markets, there is safety for employee relations in keeping labor costs and wage rates consistent with the local and industrial pattern but not necessarily any need to exceed this pattern. Unions tend to maintain harmony and contentment among the rank and file as long as wage conditions are competitive; on the other hand, it is at times quite difficult and embarrassing for union leaders to explain to the membership why their economic terms of employment are not at least equivalent to those of other people in the labor market area or in the industry who appear to be performing essentially the same job duties. In short, the comparative norm principle is often valid for economic, sociological, and psychological reasons.

Thus, the parties frequently make a careful and comprehensive study of the community and industry wage structure before negotiations begin and then compare those rates with the rates in existence at the location involved in the negotiations. The strategic implications of such comparisons, already cited in Chapter 5, are quite obvious. If the employer's rates are below the community or industry pattern, the union can be expected to argue for a wage increase on that basis. When the rates are in excess of the pattern, the employer has an argument *against* a wage increase.

Notwithstanding these considerations, there are limitations to this approach. Even though economic forces are at work that tend to place employers operating within the same industrial grouping on the same economic footing, many other factors may place such managements on different economic levels.

In the troubled U.S. basic steel industry, for example, it would not have taken much of a wage increase not long ago to put such financially ill smaller producers as Wheeling-Pittsburgh and McLouth entirely out of business. And Bethlehem, Armco, and LTV, among the larger companies, were not rolling in wealth, either. The wolf was much farther from the door, on the other hand, at USX, Inland, and National. The United Steelworkers, representing employees at all of these producers, increasingly recognized these realities, and to preserve jobs it necessarily granted various forms of economic relief to the harder-pressed producers in separate company-by-company negotiations.

Only in recent years has the union been forced to grant such individual treatment: The steel producers, in their generally healthy state before the rise of competition from low-wage foreign steel and nonunion domestic minimills, wanted to remove wages from competition. Consequently, starting in the 1950s, they bargained jointly with the union for a single industrywide basic steel manufacturer contract. But the nation's steel *fabricating* firms, with very different financial and market circumstances historically not only from the producers but (often) from each other, have *always* tried to strike their own wage bargains with the union in company-by-company negotiation. The inevitable result, even before the breakup of the industrywide bargaining and obviously all the more so now, has been a wide variety of wage levels in what is nonetheless still referred to as the steel industry.

In the rubber industry, too, there has been a significant breaking away from pattern bargaining in recent times. As in steel, the major rubber companies had more or less identical contracts with their major union (the United Rubber Workers), although in rubber they historically bargained these separately with a pattern developing after one company settled. Until the 1980s, none of them was in significant financial trouble and, therefore, none felt a pressing need to strike its own bargain with the union. But General Tire, hard-pressed to pay its bills, broke away from this pattern some 16 years ago and since then has paid lower wages. And Bridgestone/Firestone (a unit of Japan's Bridgestone Corp.) in 1994 adamantly refused—after years of losses—to follow pattern agreements that the URW signed at both Goodyear and Michelin North America (a unit of France's Groupe Michelin) and after a bitter 10-month strike won a special wage scale that was very much to its liking. Moreover, nontire members of the rubber industry—the highly competitive footwear manufacturers (although some tire companies also manufacture footwear)—have historically settled with the union for considerably less than the pattern established with the major rubber companies.

Other examples would include the larger meatpackers, who, despite the ill health of their industry, have generally been better equipped to support higher wage levels than have their smaller competitors. However, even within the ranks of the major packers, wage-paying capacities differ, and in the late 1990s Hormel workers were averaging $10 per hour while Armour employees—represented by the same union, the United Food and Commercial Workers—averaged a rather minimal $7. In the automobile industry, General Motors produces many more of its own parts than do either Ford or DaimlerChrysler. Because the outside parts suppliers for Ford and DaimlerChrysler are mostly nonunion and pay lower wages, GM has somewhat higher labor costs than its two competitors. Lately it has received some economic dispensation (although not nearly as much as it has demanded) in its bargaining with the United Automobile Workers on these grounds.

Such situations should be recognized before one accepts the proposition that the comparative norm principle of wage determination should be used as the exclusive, or the most desirable, standard for wage settlements in collective bargaining.[2]

❖ Other Factors Regarding the Use of the Comparative Norm

There are at least four other factors to be considered in regard to the comparative norm principle. *First*, not only do employers within a given industry at any given time have unequal capabilities to meet economic demands, but frequently it is quite difficult to classify an organization in a particular industrial grouping for wage comparison purposes. In 1991, agricultural implements manufacturer Caterpillar refused to follow terms that the UAW had negotiated with its counterparts Deere and Case, claiming that it was in a very different industrial category. No settlement of the strike that ensued (beginning in 1994) was reached until 1998, when it was generally agreed that Caterpillar had not only convincingly made its point but had won a significant victory in the contract that was finally negotiated.

What's more, some firms may logically be classified in two or more industries because of the products they manufacture or the services they provide. Likewise, even if a firm is classified within a particular industry, there are frequently significant subgroupings in each major industrial classification. Within the oil industry, for example, there are large, medium, and small producers of oil, and producers can be classified considerably further in terms of exact product and nature of operations. Such complicating circumstances illustrate the difficulty of classifying a particular employer in a particular industry or in a segment of an industry for purposes of wage determination.

A *second* limitation involved in the use of the comparative norm wage principle for collective bargaining is the fact that interorganizational comparisons of jobs are not always feasible because a job title at one place might designate a set of duties that has little or nothing in common with those embraced by an identically entitled job somewhere else. What the job specifications for an employee classified as "subassembler,B" in one plant call for may be quite different from what a person known as "subassembler,B" in another plant does. And the same goes for "electronics engineers" (who, surprisingly enough, bake bread and are paid on an hourly rate in one Euclid, Ohio, place of employment), "football coach" (at Florida State and Penn State, the men with those titles can, within limits, name their incomes; at a middle school, the same title holder might get an extra $1,500 and be relieved of six hours of weekly classroom duties during the football season), and even "professor" (a title that earlier in American history, sometimes designated a man who played the piano in a house of ill repute). Job titles have not been standardized in the world of work and the usefulness of the comparative norm wage principle is proportionately reduced.

This wage criterion is limited in its applicability by still a *third* complication. It is difficult to use the principle when comparing workers who are within the same job classification but who are paid by different systems of wage payments. Some workers are paid on a straight hourly rate basis, others on an individual incentive system, and still others on a group incentive plan. The kind of wage system in operation can in itself have a significant impact on wage rates.

Briefly described, incentive wages constitute a method of wage payment by which earnings are geared more or less directly to actual output instead of to time spent on the job. Employees are thus granted a relatively clear-cut financial motivation to increase their outputs, essentially by increasing the effort on which such outputs depend.

On the other hand, determination of the actual rate of pay for each "piece" or unit of output is, of course, open to union–management controversy; the management's conception of an appropriate rate is typically somewhat less liberal than is the union's. And the problem is compounded when the original job on which the rate has been set is in any way "modified" (as virtually all jobs ultimately are because of a host of factors ranging from worker-implemented shortcuts to management job reengineering) and each party seeks a new rate that is beneficial to its own interests.

Some unions have historically opposed such plans from their inception, through fear of management rate cutting (for example, artificial reconstruction of the job in order to pay it a lower rate) and because of a deeply harbored suspicion that there is nothing "scientific" to *any* established rates. But managements that have yielded too readily to union requests for higher rates have also suffered, in inequities between earnings and effort and in consequent problems involving not only finances but also employee morale. Increased automation of industry to the point where many workers cannot control their output rates has caused some further deemphasis of incentive plans in recent years. However, about one-quarter of all production plant workers in the United States continue to be paid under such plans, and it is obvious that the presence of such workers can make the comparative norm principle severely misleading.

Fourth, and finally, consideration must be given to the existence of the wide variety of fringe benefits previously cited. These benefits are not distributed equally throughout industry. Thus, it could be wrong to conclude that workers in different organizations are not equal in terms of net economic advantage where one group earns a lower basic wage rate but surpasses another group in terms of paid holidays and vacations, pensions, health coverage, and other benefits.

These considerations do not mean that the comparative norm principle is of no value in collective bargaining. Its utility is demonstrated by its widespread use. But bargainers who utilize this avenue of wage comparisons without recognition of the several problems and limitations involved in its implementation do so only at their peril.

Perhaps the near future will see the spread of some sort of compromise on the principle, possibly along the lines of a contract negotiated not long ago by the Teamsters and Pony Express. It recognizes the advantages of relative uniformity on wages by stipulating a floor below which Pony Express cannot fall but simultaneously acknowledges the negatives by allowing local unions to negotiate wage rates above that minimum.

❖ Ability to Pay

A second leading criterion involved in wage determination under collective bargaining is the **ability** of the employer (or industry, where negotiations are on an industrywide basis) **to pay** a wage increase. The outcome of wage negotiations is frequently shaped by this factor, and many strikes occur where there is disagreement between management and union negotiators relative to the wage-paying capacity of the enterprise.

The level of profits is one indicator of the wage-paying ability of the management involved in the negotiations. If a management is earning a "high" rate of profit, union representatives will frequently claim that it can afford all or most of the union wage demand. If the employer is earning a "low" rate of profit, management negotiators will frequently argue that the place does not have the financial capacity to meet the demands. But the heart of this controversy is, clearly, the determination of what constitutes a rate of profits sufficient to meet a given union wage demand. No economic formula can answer this question with precision and exactness.

Nor, sometimes, can unions be expected to accept a management claim of *in*ability to pay even when there clearly are *no* profits. The nation's sixth largest airline, Continental Airlines, didn't, for example, operate in the black for even one year between 1986 and 1996. In 1994, it lost a mammoth $613.3 million. But its 3,800 unionized pilots resoundingly rejected a 1995 company offer that would boost captains' pay by 38 percent over five years and raise overall compensation by $200 million in that period. The pilots thought that a variety of large severance packages to Continental executives who had been let go over the past year ($2.8 million to the dismissed CEO, $874,219 to a terminated senior vice president, and $364,000 to a departing executive vice president, among other eye-catching payments) showed that the company could do better for *them*. The pilots' union president, who pointed out that these executive severance dollars could easily have paid the salaries of all 45 pilots who had been laid off over the past few months, declared that "to work these compensation deals at a company that's been having problems is obscene."[3]

❖ Other Ability-to-Pay Considerations

As in the case of the preceding criterion, the problem is complicated by further considerations. In the *first* place, it is not certain whether a given rate of profits earned by a company over a given time in the past will hold for the future. Further profits may fall or rise depending on the behavior of a number of economic variables that are themselves uncertain: Changes in sales, output, productivity, price, managerial efficiency, and even the state of international relations will all have an influence. Thus, a wage rate negotiated in light of a given historical profit experience may not be appropriate in the future. Moreover, if profits are to be used as an indicator of the firm's ability to meet a given wage demand, consideration must be given to anticipated government tax structures. The wage-paying ability of the firm may be quite different before and after the payment of the federal income tax and other taxes, as many business administrators can testify. Tax programs are never static for very long.

Second, the use to which an organization intends to put its profits also has a vital bearing on this problem. Since profits are frequently used to promote capital growth and improvement, the future plans of the enterprise itself must receive consideration by the negotiators. The problem of whether profits should be used for growth and improvement, for lower commodity price, or for higher wages is one of the most troublesome issues in industrial relations. Concepts of "fair treatment"— always subjective—are inevitably involved. And so are a host of fundamental business decisions whose optimal resolution is vital to the very survival of the organization. Dealing with this determinant of wages alone is, in short, anything but child's play.

Third, although the level of profits is an important factor in the determination of a firm's ability to pay wages, it is not the only factor. Other considerations that have an important bearing are the ratio of labor costs to total costs, the amount of money expended for the financing of fringe benefits, and the degree of elasticity of demand for the firm's product or service.

The ratio of labor costs to total costs particularly conditions the ability of a firm to afford increased wage rates. An employer is in a better position to grant higher wages when the firm's labor costs represent a comparatively small part of the total costs. For example, a 10 percent increase in wage rates will result in a 1 percent increase in total costs when wage costs are 10 percent of total costs (as they are, for example, in portions of the petroleum industry). Where, however, wage costs are 60 percent of total costs (as in the trucking industry), a 10 percent increase in wage rates will result in a 6 percent increase in total costs. This illustration, of course, is based on the assumption that there is no increase or decrease in labor productivity after the wage rates are negotiated. If output increases faster than the wage rise, labor cost per unit of production tends to decrease. The reverse is true when labor productivity does not increase with higher wages.

Moreover, the ratio of labor cost to total cost cannot by itself be taken as conclusive evidence of the wage-paying ability of a particular firm. Firms with a low labor cost do not necessarily have the capacity to pay higher wages. By the same token, it would not be accurate to conclude that firms with a high labor cost can never afford wage increases. All that can be said with some degree of accuracy is that if all economic variables were held constant, a firm with a low labor-cost ratio could afford to pay higher wages more easily than a firm with a high labor-cost ratio.

As in the case of the comparative norm principle, it should also be emphasized that an employer's total wage bill includes not only direct wage costs but also costs incurred in providing employees with nonwage economic benefits. Employer payments for such benefits have been rising rapidly, as Chapter 8 will relate with documentation. Today, after a rise of about 1 percent of payroll per year in terms of national average over the past two decades, benefits consume over 41 percent of the typical employer's labor payout—although hardly uniformly, with some organizations being far more tightfisted in this area than are others. (A recent survey of 1,057 larger employers by the U.S. Chamber of Commerce found, for example, that the benefit payments ranged from less than 18 percent of payroll to more than 65 percent.)

The ease with which a company can pass on the costs of a wage increase in the form of higher prices to other firms or to the consuming public is still another determinant of its wage-paying ability. Some firms (in the brewing and cigarette industries, for example) operate in a highly competitive selling market. Under these circumstances, it is very difficult, if not impossible, for an employer to shift the burden of a wage increase to the consumer. Even a slight increase in price could result in a significant decrease in sales, since consumers would simply buy from other sellers. To the degree that a firm sells its products in a highly competitive market, it will find strong consumer resistance to price increases. In contrast, some companies (for example, major league sports teams in virtually all cities and newspaper publishers in single-newspaper cities) operate in monopolistic markets. Under these circumstances, managements have a greater degree of freedom to raise prices without experiencing a sharp decrease in sales. This would be particularly true where the product in question is sold under conditions of inelastic demand. Such a demand characteristic would apply to goods that are necessities or to those for which there are few satisfactory substitutes. Thus, if a company is operating in a monopolistic market and is selling a product for which the demand is relatively inelastic, it has an excellent opportunity to shift the costs of wage increases to other firms or to the general public in the form of higher prices.

Negotiators at times take advantage of such an economic environment. Wage increases are agreed upon, and the result is higher prices. From the public's point of view, it would be much more desirable if unions and employers could work out an arrangement whereby wages could be increased without price increases. Certainly, a wage agreement that increases the prices of basic economic commodities and thereby generates a general inflation of the price level cannot be regarded as socially sound.

❖ Wage and Price Controls

Throughout history, governments confronted with major inflationary movements have imposed some kind of limit on wage and price increases. Almost four thousand years ago, King Hammurabi of Babylonia set the annual wages of field workers at eight gur (75 bushels) of corn and those of herdsmen, whose job was presumably less valuable to society, at six gur (56.25 bushels). The Roman Emperor Diocletian in A.D. 301 established price maximums for transportation by camel and for artichokes and he meant business: Anyone caught charging more was put to death. In the United States, a wage and price controls program during World War II was itself a major industry: It needed 60,000 full-time officials and almost five times that many volunteer checkers for its implementation.

In more recent decades, on more than one occasion, the executive branch of the federal government has also turned to labor-related controls in an effort to thwart large rises in the general level of prices. In the last four decades, three presidents have promulgated so-called voluntary wage-price guidelines, and in a 1971–1973 program of the Nixon administration mandatory wage and price controls were imposed.

In most of these experiences, single figures were announced as the maximum allowable annual increase in pay: 3.2 percent in the noninflationary early 1960s under Presidents Kennedy and Johnson; 5.5 percent in base pay plus another 0.7 percent for certain fringe benefits in 1971 to 1973; and 7.0 percent in President Carter's program of the late 1970s (in 1980, a range of 7.5 to 9.5 percent was substituted by Carter). In all of these, exceptions were permitted for "special circumstances," a term that to most observers appeared to mean roughly the same as "political pressures." None of these programs achieved anything approaching complete success in holding down inflation, and in retrospect most of them can be judged to have been definite failures insofar as any beneficial long-run effect on the economy is concerned. Most scholars agree that while mandatory controls can restrain wages for a short while, they also cause shortages, bureaucratic complexities, inequities, and—sooner or later—inflationary explosions. Most agree, too, that guidelines alone are not much more than cosmetic attempts, conveying the impression of governmental concern but frequently doing little else.

Organized labor opposed all of the attempts in one way or another. The 3.2 percent Kennedy-Johnson guidelines were attacked as inequitably "freezing" worker shares in the income-distribution pie at their existing levels, in the absence of a convincing reason why such wage income shares should not be *increased*. And unionists also viewed with some alarm the increased governmental intervention involved, as did their counterparts on the management side. One labor leader said that the 3.2 percent figure was "as welcome to organized labor as 3.2 beer."

Nixon's mandatory arrangement was not, at least as the majority of union leaders saw it, at all fair, either. AFL-CIO president Meany described it as "window dressing for the benefit of business profits" and labor generally argued with some justification that the program was enforced neither fairly nor effectively.

And the AFL-CIO felt so strongly that President Carter's officially "voluntary" program could not legally withhold federal government contracts from firms not in compliance with Carter's guidelines, as the government was in 1979 threatening to do, that it filed suit in federal court requesting that such a practice be enjoined as violating the Procurement Act of 1949. Unsuccessful in this activity, labor subsequently confined its attack to public pronouncements, once again arguing that the controls inequitably favored profits over wages (a charge that, with prices escalating at about 13 percent annually in 1979 and 1980, gained considerable nonlabor support). The AFL-CIO announced that it *would* support a mandatory wage and price controls program (although "for the duration of the emergency only") because if truly mandatory, the latter would impose "equal sacrifices" on all citizens.

With inflation very much under control after the early 1980s, no further governmental programs of this kind were in the immediate offing. History having a way of repeating itself, however, any predictions that such federal controls would not sooner or later—amid rapidly rising prices—be tried again would be rash. And so very likely, too, would be any bets either that labor would support such controls or that the controls would be very successful in dampening inflation in any long-term way.

❖ Standard of Living

Orientation of the plant wage structure to community and industry levels and ability to pay are not the only criteria utilized for wage determination in contemporary industry. Many management and, particularly, labor representatives are concerned with the problem of the adequacy of wages to guarantee workers "a decent standard of living." Disagreements arise, however, as to what constitutes such a standard.

The problem is most often resolved by personal judgment and opinions of the negotiators. More objective information is, however, at the disposal of the parties, and it has frequently been used to support demands and counterdemands at the bargaining table.

The most widely publicized source of standard-of-living data was that published by the U.S. Department of Labor's Bureau of Labor Statistics (BLS). Unfortunately, after 1982, because of budget constraints, the Department of Labor ceased publishing this information. However, when adjustments are made for the rate of inflation since 1983, it is still useful as a general guide to establish the standard of living and many negotiating parties use it even now. First developed in 1946 to 1947 at the request of Congress, and revised periodically since that time, the BLS's "City Worker's Family Budget" attempted to describe and measure a "modest but adequate standard of living." It was necessarily selective, restricting itself to a measurement of the income needed by a family of four (a 38-year-old employed husband, a wife not employed outside the home, and two children of school age—a 13-year-old boy and an 8-year-old girl), living in a rented dwelling in a large city or its suburbs. By studying the prices of a "representative list of goods and services" presumably purchased by such families, for about 40 representative cities (weighted according to their population), the BLS showed the cost of "a level of adequate living standards prevailing in large cities of the United States in recent years."

To make the City Worker's Family Budget more relevant, the Bureau of Labor Statistics provided levels for three standards of living—low, intermediate, and high. Naturally, employees who earn sufficient wages to live at the high level enjoy more of the good things of life than do those whose wages can claim only the goods and services at the low level.

The low budget recently required an annual outlay of close to $22,000; the intermediate one demanded just under $34,000; and the high budget called for almost $49,000. Food costs had increased about 4 percent in each of the budgets over the past few years. But since they absorbed a larger percentage of total living costs at the lower-budget level, these food costs clearly had a greater influence there, making it less likely that the lower-budget families would eat much in the way of quality foods on any sustained basis.

Not unexpectedly, the amount required varies considerably depending on the city involved. In a recent year, an income of $33,477 in San Diego would have gone no further than one of $25,000 in the far-less-expensive Atlanta. New York City is more than twice as costly as the average city in the United States, and Boston, Washington, Philadelphia, and Los Angeles are about one-third more expensive than the average. Houston, Kansas City, Phoenix, and New Orleans, on the other hand, are relative bargains. In all cases, however, the overall weighted averages at the time of this writing were sufficiently beyond those earned by most workers to make the budget an attractive bargaining weapon for union negotiators. Labor spokespersons had not been hesitant about arguing the "need" for substantial wage increases to reach the budgeted levels while also pointing out that the overall weighted average was required to meet the necessities of life, pay taxes, and enjoy a few amenities—but that it contained no allowance for luxuries or savings.

Employers, equally logically, had taken bitter exception to the City Worker's Family Budget. They had argued that the items used in computing the budget were far too generous to warrant the description "modest but adequate"; frequently cited in this regard were the budget's annual allowance for gifts and contributions and certain of its provisions for furniture, appliances, automobiles, and recreation. In addition, they pointed out that wage earners do not have uniform responsibilities in terms of dependents (with many, of course, having no dependents) and that many families have more than one wage earner.

The arguments and counterarguments can be expected to continue indefinitely, without mutual agreement as to their validity; the line of demarcation between "luxury" and "necessity" has never been susceptible to exact location, and the concept of "decency" allows much room for emotion. Moreover, despite the use of the standard-of-living criterion at the bargaining table, it does not carry as much weight as the other wage factors previously noted in this chapter. After all, a management that simply cannot pay wages that will realize the "modest but adequate standard of living" may be entirely sympathetic to the worker's needs, but the cold realism of economic life will not persuade it to grant the additional wages. Likewise, a union will not stop at the level of wages required of the budget if it can get more from the employer because of the operation of the comparative norm; indeed, under these circumstances, the union will probably argue that the items of the budget are too meager.

But use of such standard-of-living information is still to be preferred to total recourse to personal opinion on the subject. The data may not be accepted, but even in rejecting them the recalcitrant party is forced to deal with information that is more objective than mere individual sentiment.

COST OF LIVING: ESCALATOR AND WAGE-REOPENER ARRANGEMENTS

In addition to the comparative norm, ability-to-pay, and standard-of-living principles, experienced negotiators pay close attention in wage negotiations to the status of the *cost of living*. This economic phenomenon is important because trends in the cost of living have an important bearing upon the real income of workers. Increases in the cost of living at a given level of earnings result in decreased capacity of workers to buy goods and services. By the same token, real income tends to increase with decreases in the cost of living at a given wage level. Real income for a particular group of workers also increases for a time when money wages increase faster than the cost of living.

As a matter of fact, during the soaring inflation in the 1978–1981 period, the cost of living was the major determinant for wage negotiations, as union leaders raced to keep up with higher and higher prices to protect the real income of their members. Of course, to the extent that wage rates exceeded productivity, negotiated wages aggravated the inflation problem. If the lessons of inflation teach us anything, it is that a stable price level is the way to achieve the negotiation of noninflationary wage rates.

It is beyond the scope of this volume to analyze the multitude of factors that influence the cost of living in the American economy. This cost is affected by a variety of forces, including the general climate of business activity, productivity, the financial and monetary policies followed by financial institutions, the rate of new investment, and the propensity of consumers to spend money, as well as by the wage policies that are followed under collective bargaining itself. Government policies relating to interest rates, tariffs, the lending capacity of national banks, taxation and agriculture also have an impact upon the cost of living. And, of course, as we have come to realize in recent years, energy costs can constitute another important factor. When the OPEC nations increased the cost of oil from about $5 per barrel at the beginning of the 1970s to more than seven times that figure by the end of the decade, the effect was an increase not only in gasoline prices but also in prices of other goods manufactured by petroleum-chemical industries, in transportation and heating costs of all users, and ultimately in the prices of almost all goods and services. By the same token, the rapid deterioration of oil prices in the later 1980s and 1990s significantly dampened the level of price increases.

The uncertain character of the forces determining the cost of living makes it very difficult to predict with certainty its future trends. The difficulty inherent in using the cost of living as a determinant in wage negotiations is simply this: Wages are negotiated for a *future* period, whereas the cost-of-living data are *historical* in character. It is a comparatively simple task to adjust wages for historical trends in the cost of living if this is the desire of the negotiators. The criterion is of limited usefulness, however, in the attempt to orient wage rates to future trends in the consumer price index (CPI) (whose basic movements in a recent year are illustrated by Exhibit 7-1).

The CPI, regularly prepared and published by the federal government's Bureau of Labor Statistics, is the measure that unions and managements almost universally use in their wage bargaining. It is based on the prices of food, clothing, shelter, fuel, drugs, transportation fares, doctors' and dentists' fees, and other goods and services that people purchase for everyday living. The compilers of the CPI keep the quantity and quality of these items basically unchanged over time so that only price changes will be measured.

But if compiling the CPI can be done with reasonable precision, predicting its future movement is quite another matter. As most other attempts to envision what lies ahead, forecasts about future price movements—as important as they are to both the real income of employees and the financial position of employers—can be way off base. Recognizing the latter situation as a fact of life, some labor relations parties have adopted one or both of two procedures—escalator clauses and wage reopeners—in an effort to adjust for it.

❖ Escalator Clauses

The philosophy behind the incorporation of so-called **escalator clauses**, also known as cost-of-living adjustment (COLA) provisions, in labor agreements is that wages of workers should rise and fall automatically with fluctuations in the cost of living. The escalator first attained national prominence in the 1948 General Motors–United Automobile Workers collective bargaining agreement. As a result of the anticipated price inflation growing out of the Korean War, many other managements and unions soon negotiated similar arrangements, and by 1952 these covered about 3.5 million workers.

Since 1952, use of the wage-escalator clause appears to have depended to great extent on the upward movement of the cost-of-living index. By 1955, for example, three years of comparatively steady prices had elapsed, and the number of workers covered by such escalator clauses had dropped considerably, to about 1.7 million. In 1956, on the other hand, the consumer price index moved strongly forward, and a study conducted late in that year estimated that approximately 3.5 million workers were once again covered by escalator arrangements.

EXHIBIT 7-1

Consumer Price Index for All Urban Consumers (CPI-U): Selected Areas, All Items Index

(1982-84=100, unless otherwise noted)

All items

CPI-U	Pricing Schedule (1)	Indexes				Percent change to Feb. 1999 from--			Percent change to Jan. 1999 from--		
		Nov. 1998	Dec. 1998	Jan. 1999	Feb. 1999	Feb. 1998	Dec. 1998	Jan. 1999	Jan. 1998	Nov. 1998	Dec. 1998
U.S. city average	M	164.0	163.9	164.3	164.5	1.6	0.4	0.1	1.7	0.2	0.2
Region and area size (2)											
Northeast urban	M	171.2	171.2	171.4	171.6	1.5	0.2	0.1	1.5	0.1	0.1
Size A - More than 1,500,000	M	172.2	172.2	172.5	172.4	1.4	0.1	-0.1	1.8	0.2	0.2
Size B/C 50,000 to 1,500,000 (3)	M	102.6	102.5	102.6	103.0	1.6	0.5	0.4	1.0	0.0	0.1
Midwest urban	M	160.1	159.8	160.4	160.5	1.6	0.4	0.1	1.8	0.2	0.4
Size A - More than 1,500,000	M	161.3	161.0	161.6	161.8	1.8	0.5	0.1	2.0	0.2	0.4
Size B/C - 50,000 to 1,500,000 (3)	M	102.4	102.3	102.6	102.6	1.0	0.3	0.0	1.4	0.2	0.3
Size D - Nonmetropolitan (less than 50,000)	M	154.7	155.0	155.5	155.6	1.9	0.4	0.1	1.7	0.5	0.3
South urban	M	159.6	159.6	159.9	160.0	1.4	0.3	0.1	1.5	0.2	0.2
Size A - More than 1,500,000	M	158.6	158.3	158.9	158.9	1.4	0.4	0.0	1.5	0.2	0.4
Size B/C - 50,000 to 1,500,000 (3)	M	102.8	102.8	102.9	103.0	1.4	0.2	0.1	1.4	0.1	0.1
Size D - Nonmetropolitan (less than 50,000)	M	160.0	160.4	160.8	160.9	1.9	0.3	0.1	2.1	0.5	0.2
West urban	M	165.8	165.8	166.4	166.9	2.3	0.7	0.3	2.1	0.4	0.4
Size A - More than 1,500,000	M	166.5	166.5	167.3	167.8	2.6	0.8	0.3	2.4	0.5	0.5
Size B/C - 50,000 to 1,500,000 (3)	M	103.5	103.4	103.6	103.8	1.5	0.4	0.2	1.3	0.1	0.2
Size classes											
A (4)	M	148.5	148.4	148.9	149.0	1.8	0.4	0.1	2.0	0.3	0.3
B/C (3)	M	102.8	102.7	102.9	103.0	1.3	0.3	0.1	1.3	0.1	0.2
D	M	159.9	160.2	160.6	160.7	1.8	0.3	0.1	1.8	0.4	0.2
Selected local areas (5)											
Chicago-Gary-Kenosha, IL-IN-WI	M	165.4	165.1	166.1	166.4	2.0	0.8	0.2	2.0	0.4	0.6
Los Angeles-Riverside-Orange County, CA	M	163.4	163.5	164.2	164.6	2.2	0.7	0.2	2.0	0.5	0.4
New York-Northern N.J.-Long Island, NY-NJ-CT-PA	M	174.7	174.7	175.0	175.1	1.4	0.2	0.1	1.7	0.2	0.2
Boston-Brockton-Nashua, MA-NH-ME-CT	1	173.3	--	174.1	--	--	--	--	1.7	0.5	--
Cleveland-Akron, OH	1	160.8	--	160.6	--	--	--	--	1.5	-0.1	--
Dallas-Fort Worth, TX	1	154.0	--	155.0	--	--	--	--	1.9	0.6	--
Washington-Baltimore, DC-MD-VA-WV (6)	1	102.4	--	102.8	--	--	--	--	1.8	0.4	--
Atlanta, GA	2	--	161.6	--	161.9	1.5	0.2	--	--	--	--
Detroit-Ann Arbor-Flint, MI	2	--	161.2	--	161.2	1.7	0.0	--	--	--	--
Houston-Galveston-Brazoria, TX	2	--	146.1	--	146.6	0.3	0.3	--	--	--	--
Miami-Fort Lauderdale, FL	2	--	161.1	--	161.4	0.7	0.2	--	--	--	--
Philadelphia-Wilmington-Atlantic City, PA-NJ-DE-MD	2	--	169.0	--	168.6	1.0	-0.2	--	--	--	--
San Francisco-Oakland-San Jose, CA	2	--	167.4	--	169.4	3.8	1.2	--	--	--	--
Seattle-Tacoma-Bremerton, WA	2	--	169.4	--	170.6	2.5	0.7	--	--	--	--

1 Areas on pricing schedule 2 (see Table 10) will appear next month.
2 Regions defined as the four Census regions. See map in technical notes.
3 Indexes on a December 1996=100 base.
4 Indexes on a December 1986=100 base.
5 In addition, the following metropolitan areas are published semiannually and appear in Tables 34 and 39 of the January and July issues of the CPI Detailed Report: Anchorage, AK; Cincinnati-Hamilton, OH-KY-IN; Denver-Boulder-Greeley, CO; Honolulu, HI; Kansas City, MO-KS; Milwaukee-Racine, WI; Minneapolis-St. Paul, MN-WI; Pittsburgh, PA; Portland-Salem, OR-WA; St. Louis, MO-IL; San Diego, CA; Tampa-St. Petersburg-Clearwater, FL.
6 Indexes on a November 1996=100 base.
-- Data not available.

Note: Index applies to a month as a whole, not to any specific date.

SOURCE: U.S. Department of Labor, Bureau of Labor Statistics.

The figure has waxed and waned ever since. Inflation was minimal in the early 1960s, and by 1965 only about 2 million workers were covered. But the enormous surge of prices in the 1970s and first two years of the 1980s again stimulated the growth of cost-of-living escalator clauses: By 1983 almost half of all major union contracts (the only ones studied) had them. Since that peak percentage, the frequency has steadily declined: In the low-inflation late 1990s, only about one-quarter of the 5.7 million workers subject to these major contracts were covered.

Historically, managements have been anything but enthusiastic about the escalator concept. They have voiced fears that prices could not be commensurately raised without undesirable effects on profits. They have also argued what they view as the inequities of a system that allows workers to benefit without effort of any kind on their part. The CPI ignores the fact, for example, that consumers often counter price rises in individual items by purchasing less of the more costly items and more of items that are cheaper (e.g., they buy more margarine and less butter if margarine becomes relatively less expensive than butter). It may understate the influence of the growing percentage of sales that take place at discount stores. Other managers opposing its use have stressed the potential inflationary ramifications of the escalator. And, above all, employers have attacked the constant "freezing" of cost-of-living allowances into basic wage rates: Most labor contracts ultimately make such allowances a permanent part of rates when the agreements are renegotiated, and to many workers the allowances are, consequently, really additional wage increases temporarily couched in other terms. Not only do cost-of-living allowances realistically become a part of basic wage rates, but frequently they are also "rolled" into pay for vacations, holidays, and other employee benefits tied to basic wage rates. Thus, not only are employers' direct wage costs increased, but so are their costs associated with a variety of fringe benefits. One need look only to where COLAs exist today to see this absence of pro-COLA sentiment on the part of managements: They are all but exclusively in the unionized sector of the economy, leading to a definite conclusion that employers have tolerated COLAs only when, because of union bargaining power, they have had to.

On the other hand, unions have favored the COLA concept through the years and, indeed, even when forced to give back compensation previously won at the bargaining table in distressed industries in recent years (a topic that is treated later in this chapter), have chosen to give up COLA only as a very last resort.

Inflation has not been the only generator of COLA clauses. A second, if lesser, impetus has been the lengthening of the durations of labor contracts. In 1948 about 75 percent of collective bargaining agreements were for one year or less; today a minuscule 1 percent of all contracts are of this length, with a whopping 21 percent of the agreements being for four or more years (up from 5 percent in 1986 and 9 percent in 1989). Most contracts by far (some 70 percent of them) have three-year terms.[4] Longer-term contracts lend greater stability to labor relationships, and by definition they reduce the problems of negotiation and the traumas of frequent strike threats. However, as contracts are negotiated for longer periods of time, negotiators must recognize the necessity of providing some method for the adjustment of wages during the contractual period. Some authorities believe that increasing awareness of this situation, together with the continuation of the trend to contracts of longer duration, will lend greater allure to the escalator formula, even in the face of continuing managerial opposition to the whole idea.

❖ How Escalators Work

Although there is a wide variety of escalator arrangements, all contain a number of common principles. The most significant characteristic of the escalator formula is its automaticity. For the duration of the labor agreement, wage changes as related to cost of living are precisely determined by the behavior of a statistical index—almost always the consumer price index. Wages are increased or decreased in accordance with comparatively small changes in this index. For example, the labor agreement might provide, as most of them currently do, for a $.01 per hour adjustment of wages for every 0.3-point change in the CPI.

Each escalator arrangement specifies the time at which the CPI is reviewed. At the time of the review, a determination is made as to whether the index increased sufficiently to trigger a wage increase. Of the workers covered by escalators in 1999 quarterly reviews were by far the most common, covering about 50 percent compared with about 25 percent each for annual or semiannual reviews. Though a matter of only academic interest in a period of inflation, escalator provisions normally specify the floor to which wages can fall in response to a decline in the cost-of-living index. On the other hand, the escalator formula does not normally contain a *ceiling* on wage increases occasioned by increasing prices. Only about 20 percent of the workers covered by the arrangement are currently subject to a ceiling, also called a **cap,** on their cost-of-living wage increases. When the labor agreement provides for a cap, it means that wages can increase by only a certain specified amount during the contractual period regardless of the size of the increase in the consumer price index. Needless to say, when a cap appears, the employer and not the union insisted on it at the bargaining table. An escalator arrangement containing a cap enhances the employer's ability to estimate the firm's labor costs for the contractual period. Employer resistance, of course, increases during periods of economic recession. This occurred during the economic recession of the early 1980s. Faced with declining sales, employers demanded caps on the operation of COLAs.

Finally, the escalator method of wage adjustment is often accompanied by a definite and guaranteed increase in wages for each year of a multiyear labor agreement. Such an increase is popularly called the **annual improvement factor**. These increases are not offset by any increase generated by an escalator clause. By the same token, any increase triggered by an escalator clause is not reduced by the payment of the annual improvement factor. For example, a recent three-year contract negotiated by one union states:

> Effective as of April 24, 1998, and April 23, 1999, each employee covered by this Agreement shall receive an annual improvement factor of twenty cents ($.20) per hour added to his or her hourly rate.

Those employees are guaranteed the 20-cent increase on each anniversary date of the agreement regardless of the results of the escalator provision. As expected, in a labor agreement that does not contain an escalator clause, the annual improvement factor normally calls for a higher increase than in a contract that includes a cost-of-living adjustment provision. In the former situation, it is understandable that union leaders press for a much higher annual increase, recognizing that inflation affects adversely the real income of the members. When an escalator clause is contained in the contract, the union's leaders need not be so aggressive in the matter of the annual improvement factor.

However, it should be noted that the operation of escalator arrangements *does not* provide employees with 100 percent protection against inflation. From 1968 to 1977, the average escalator yield met only 57 percent of the inflation occurring during those years. In not one year did the yield match the CPI increase. This will come as a genuine surprise to many who believe, in error, that escalator provisions provide the employee full protection against the ravages of inflation.

Moreover, in more recent years COLAs have actually *cut* wage rates in some industries. In giving economic relief to such financially ailing sectors as steel, aluminum, and (for a while) automobiles and trucking, unions often surrendered fixed wage increases and agreed to make pay increases fully dependent on COLAs. But the "engines of inflation," as COLAs were called in the years of high inflation prior to 1982, were reduced to what the editors of *Business Week* could accurately call "little more than sputtering outboards"[5] in the minimal annual inflations after that time. In fact, in some cases—the automobile, aluminum, and can industries most notably—the price index on which the quarterly adjustment was contractually made actually dropped once or twice and employees had to surrender past wage gains on these occasions.

Such occurrences as the last, however, were anomalies. Prices have virtually always risen—even in quarterly periods and except for only two years, both during the Great Depression, from year to year throughout the century. Sporadic periods of high inflation have been regular problems in the United States, as elsewhere, for many decades. Only the most naïve of employees could possibly believe that inflation is now permanently under control. And, given these circumstances, it seems a safe prediction that, despite management opposition to COLAs and the present minimal levels of price increases, COLAs—and generally ones without caps, at that—will continue their frequent appearances in labor—management contracts.

❖ Wage Reopeners

A second method for wage adjustments during the life of a labor agreement involves a provision that permits either the employer or the union to **reopen** labor agreements **for wage issues** at stated intervals. It is not exactly commonplace, but 8 percent of all contracts do have such a mechanism, and the percentage is greater in agreements that are for four years or more. Wage negotiations are typically permitted in these circumstances once each year.

Two major characteristics of the wage-reopening clause arrangement distinguish it from the escalator principle as a method of wage adjustment. The most important involves the fact that where the escalator arrangement provides for an *automatic* change in wages based on a definite formula, under wage reopeners the parties must *negotiate* wage changes. This could be an advantage or a disadvantage, depending on the particular circumstances of a given collective bargaining relationship. In addition, the wage-reopener arrangement can be utilized to take into account determinants of wages other than the cost of living. The fact that both the escalator and the reopener arrangements are frequently used in industry indicates that both procedures apparently fill the needs of employers, employees, and unions. What may be suitable for one collective bargaining relationship, however, clearly might be unsuitable for another management and union.

To invoke a wage-reopening clause, collective bargaining contracts require that the party that desires to change wages give a written notice to the other party within a specified period. Under the terms of the Taft-Hartley law, as we know, a party to a collective bargaining agreement desiring to modify or terminate the agreement must give 60 days' notice of its intention to do so. Following such notice, the law declares that there may be no lockout or strike "for a period of sixty days . . . or until the expiration date of such contract, whichever occurs later." Employees who engage in a strike during this period lose their status as employees under Taft-Hartley and have no legal right to be reinstated.

A wage-reopener provision is to be used only to negotiate a new wage structure. Some employers and unions use the opportunity to gain changes, however, in other areas of the labor agreement, using the wage issue as the pretext. For example, a union might strike ostensibly for wages but send a message to the employer that the strike would terminate were the employer to grant certain concessions to the union, say in the matter of the application of the seniority provisions. Such tactics are not necessarily very subtle. They can, however, be potent.

WAGE DIFFERENTIALS

Under certain circumstances, collective bargaining contracts provide for different rates of wages for different employees performing the same kind of work and holding down the same types of jobs. Such differentials are completely lawful except when used by the parties to discriminate on the basis of race, color, religion, sex, national origin, age, or anything else forbidden under the various antidiscrimination laws of the land. To many employers (as well as to unions), moreover, utilization of the "nondiscriminatory" differentials appears mandatory to ensure an adequate supply of willing employees for work under arduous or otherwise unpleasant conditions.

The most common of these differentials involves premium payment for work on relatively undesirable shifts—in the late afternoon, evening, night, and early morning hours. Practically all workers scheduled on late shifts receive extra pay.

In addition, under most contracts there is now a graduated increase in compensation for working the second and third shifts. All but a tiny fraction of workers in establishments where there is a third, or "graveyard," work schedule now receive a rate for it that is higher than that received by second-shift workers. But second-shift workers themselves have received relatively significant premiums for their acceptance of these working hours: Premium rates for second-shift work are often as high as 10 percent above first-shift rates. Premiums often up to 10 percent of second-shift rates are the general rewards for the graveyard-shift workers.

The rationale for the shift differential is quite easy to understand. When an employee works a less common shift, there is obvious interference with family life and with full participation in the affairs of society. In Western society, the school system, recreational activities, and cultural pursuits assume that employees work during the day. Since working the odd hours tends to interfere with family and societal affairs, the premium is designed to compensate the employee for this sacrifice. And although it is a fact of industrial life that some employees may actually prefer to work the afternoon or midnight tour (under these circumstances, the employee reaps a net benefit for the shift differential premium), the overwhelming majority of employees prefer the day shift, and thus the shift differential will undoubtedly always be a common feature in the collectively bargained wage package.

Under many collective bargaining contracts, special premiums are also provided for workers who handle certain supervisory or instructional duties, especially demanding tasks, or particularly hazardous, dirty, or otherwise undesirable work.

For these jobs, extra pay is again granted as a premium to the basic wage rate of the worker concerned. For example, under one current agreement in the Midwest, a $2.70 per hour premium is paid to employees who are engaged in "dirty work." Such work is spelled out in the labor agreement and includes, among other possibilities for premium-rate reimbursement, "work in oil tanks where not cleaned out." Another labor agreement provides for the regular overtime rate for employees engaged in hazardous work. This provision covers employees working at elevations "where there is danger of a fall of 50 feet or more."

In addition to these *premium*-rate practices, many collective bargaining contracts allow *lower* differentials for other situations. A number of agreements provide lower rates for workers who are handicapped, temporary, or learners. Such differentials are rooted in the belief that these qualities make workers comparatively less productive, and even the federal government, recognizing the persuasive economic logic involved, has gone along with this employer argument to the extent of exempting such workers from the minimum wage laws. Abuses have occasionally been in evidence, however: Some "temporary" employees turn out, upon closer inspection, to be deserving of 25-year pins; and some "handicapped" employees appear to have nothing more than a proneness to getting hay fever. Such situations notwithstanding, employer good faith in regard to these workers is far more the rule than the exception, and the differential can be defended on the grounds that the alternative to a lower rate of remuneration for such employees is, most often, unemployment.

Until passage and implementation of the Civil Rights Act of 1964, some contracts also contained lower wage rates for women than for men and for minorities than for white employees. For women, the practice was traditionally defended on such presumed grounds as a lesser productivity of women than men, a female inability to do all the tasks performed by men in accomplishing a job, and the argument that the employment of women at times involves extra costs not incurred when men are employed. Racial discrimination per se appears to have motivated the minority differential, although some of the lower-productivity claims used to defend lower women's wages were also heard. Neither type of differential is, understandably, promulgated by labor contracts governed by the act, although whether the practices involved continue is subject to employer and union compliance, which goes well beyond the official wording of their agreements.

OVERTIME AND FLEXTIME

❖ Overtime

Collective bargaining agreements invariably establish a standard number of hours per day and per week during which employees are paid their regular rate of pay. For hours worked in excess of the standard, however, employers are required to pay employees overtime rates. By far the most common standards found in labor agreements are eight hours per day and forty hours per week, with only a fraction of labor agreements establishing standards differing from that formula. In the wearing apparel, printing, and publishing industries, a number of agreements do provide for a basic seven- to seven-and-one-half-hour day and 35-hour workweek; and in the food-processing, retail, and service industries some contracts establish a standard 44-hour week; but these remain the exceptions.

The fact that the **Fair Labor Standards Act** of 1938 provides a basic 40-hour week has undoubtedly caused the adoption of a 40-hour standard workweek under collective bargaining. Labor agreements that provide for a basic workweek in excess of 40 hours without premium overtime pay presumably do not fall within the scope of this legislation, or within the reach of the many state wage and hour laws that regulate this activity within individual states for their intrastate commerce. On the other hand, nothing in the federal wage and hour law prohibits employers and unions from negotiating a workweek of *fewer* than 40 hours. In addition, the Fair Labor Standards Act places no restriction on employers who desire their employees to work *more* than 40 hours in a workweek, other than that the employees who work more than 40 hours must be paid at least one and one-half times their regular rate of pay for all hours in excess of 40 hours.

The vast majority of labor agreements provide overtime rates of exactly one and one-half times the regular rate of pay for employees who work in excess of 40 hours per week, thus offering a not surprising conformity to the provisions of the Fair Labor Standards Act, but a relatively small number of labor agreements do call for overtime rates of greater than time and a half, most frequently double time. With respect to hours worked in excess of the *daily* standard, most labor agreements also provide for time and a half, although some labor agreements provide for double time after a certain number of hours are worked or after a stipulated hour of the day or night. For example, some employers and unions have agreed that double time should be paid if employees work more than four hours' overtime on any one workday. In this connection it should be noted that—since the Fair Labor Standards Act does not establish a basic workday—if employees are to be paid for working hours in excess of a certain number per day, the parties to the collective bargaining contract must negotiate this objective.

Most labor agreements prohibit the *pyramiding* **of overtime**. This means that weekly overtime premiums are not required for hours for which daily overtime premiums have already been paid; moreover, many contracts provide that only one type of overtime premium can be paid for any one day.

But it's not always as simple to administer the pyramiding prohibition as the bare contractual language might indicate that it should be. For example, under a labor agreement that recognized employee birthdays as holidays, mandated time and a half payment for work performed on a holiday, and banned the pyramiding of overtime premiums, a worker was paid holiday pay at time and a half for the first eight hours that he worked on his birthday and overtime pay at time and a half for another four hours that he worked immediately after the first eight. His union agreed at the ensuing arbitration that the first eight hours should have been counted in calculating the weekly overtime because these hours were compensated not as overtime work but as holiday work. The arbitrator, dismissing the employer's argument that such action would amount to pyramiding, agreed with the union in his ruling.[6]

In another set of circumstances that was not so clear-cut, an employee of Safeway Stores worked Sunday and the following five days under a contract that not only called for double time for Sunday work and time and a half for all hours beyond 40 in a given workweek, but also prohibited "the pyramiding of overtime and/or premium pay." The worker was paid double time for his Sunday work but was denied time and a half for the sixth day. The employer explained to him that to do so would be pyramiding of the two kinds of pay. But the arbitrator concluded that the double-time pay for the Sunday was really "a penalty against the employer" for such scheduling, not premium pay and, because in his opinion it would not constitute pyramiding, he awarded time and a half for the sixth day.[7]

In most relationships, the employer also has the right to force employees to work overtime. *(Case 3 deals with compulsory overtime.)* However, labor agreements and arbitration decisions typically establish certain standards that employers must follow before discipline can be assessed against employees who refuse to work overtime. For example, in the absence of some dire emergency—a flood in the plant, perhaps—the employer must give proper notice and not grab an employee for overtime just as the person is about to clock out. Also, the employer must accept a "reasonable" excuse from an employee who refuses to work overtime. Of course, what is reasonable is subject to controversy, and arbitrators are often called on to apply the concept in light of the particular facts of a case. Should an employee be excused from overtime because he was scheduled to be the best man at a wedding? This was the basic issue involved in a case handled by one of the authors. When the employee refused, he was suspended for three days. How would you decide this issue if you were the arbitrator?

As in the case of the shorter-hour workweek, the issue of compulsory overtime invariably pops up during periods of excessive unemployment. Because unemployment was so high during the recession of 1975—the frightening level of 9.2 percent was reached during that year—some unions pressed for a flat prohibition against any overtime in an attempt to preserve job opportunities. Not many of them succeeded in this goal. They were more successful in negotiating voluntary overtime provisions; that is, the employee could refuse the assignment without facing discipline. This development was dramatically highlighted in the 1973 basic automobile industry labor agreement. For the first time in that industry, production employees under certain circumstances gained the right to turn down overtime without penalty. Compulsory overtime was a major strike issue, and only by compromise on it did the automobile corporations and the UAW avoid open conflict. During the severe recession in the early 1980s—unemployment reached 10.8 percent in 1982—some unions again attempted to forbid all overtime, once more without notable success. However, a step in this direction occurred when, at General Motors and Ford, the UAW negotiated a $.50 an hour penalty charged to the company for every hour of overtime beyond 5 percent of straight-time hours worked. This penalty discourages scheduling of overtime, and all penalty money goes into a fund for retraining.

The national unemployment figure overall has been anything but formidable in recent years. In April 2000, it stood at a tame 3.9 percent, for example. But the healthy statistic has invariably masked the double-digit unemployment in many of the manufacturing industries that have historically been heavily unionized, and the spread of penalties such as the automotive one in these sectors certainly cannot be entirely discounted.

Moreover, the employer's overtime authority has rarely been an unrestricted one. Contracts frequently provide that overtime work must be shared equally within given classifications of employees, or at least that overtime is to be rotated equally "as far as is practicable." Some agreements limit overtime to regular employees as against seasonal, temporary, part-time, or probationary employees.

By the same token, however, under many agreements, penalties may be assessed against employees who refuse to work overtime. Such penalties range from discharge to ineligibility to work overtime at the next opportunity. But, for most workers, such penalties have little meaning because they *want* to work overtime, at least within limits. For all that has been said regarding union pressures for overtime discouragement, the premium earnings even of overtime at time and a half remain sufficiently attractive to individual employees on most occasions to make the ineligibility penalty a significant one.

Indeed, a prolific source of grievances and even arbitration is the employee complaint that the employer has improperly, under the labor agreement, failed to offer employees the opportunity to work overtime. Where the grievance is found to have merit, the employer typically has the obligation of paying the employee the amount of money he or she would have earned on the overtime tour of duty.

The employee, of course, has nothing to lose by filing such grievances, even if the worker would have refused the assignment if offered the opportunity to work overtime. If the opportunity has *not* been offered, the employee can file a grievance and possibly get paid for work the grievant never intended to do in the first place. For these reasons, employer representatives are very careful to assure that eligible employees are afforded the opportunity to work the overtime. When a supervisor makes an error in this regard, the employer may be faced with the situation of paying for the same work twice and at premium rates. To say the least, the organization's chief financial officer would take a dim view of that state of affairs! (Exhibit 7-2 illustrates a reasonably typical overtime provision.)

EXHIBIT 7-2

ARTICLE 31. OVERTIME

Section 1

Employees who are required to work overtime will be compensated in accordance with applicable laws and regulations.

Section 2

The Employer agrees to make a reasonable effort to distribute overtime equitably among qualified and available employees, consistent with the specialized skills and abilities necessary for the work to be performed. Adequate records of overtime will be maintained by the Employer and will be available to the Union upon request.

Section 3

In the assignment of overtime, the Employer agrees to provide an employee with as much advance notice as the situation permits. Consideration will be given, in light of the workload involved and the ready availability of other qualified employees willing to accept the assignment, to an employee's request to be excused from an overtime assignment.

Section 4

Callback overtime shall be a minimum of 2 hours.

Section 5

The Employer agrees to make a reasonable effort consistent with operational needs to avoid situations involving callback overtime or requiring employees to work overtime on their regularly scheduled days off.

Section 6

An employee performing overtime work on his/her regularly scheduled day off shall be guaranteed 4 hours of work.

❖ **Flextime**

A relatively recent innovation in collective bargaining involves letting employees select within limits their daily work schedules. These newer schedules are popularly called **flextime**. Under this innovation, all employees still must work eight hours per day. However, they have more flexibility in selecting their starting and quitting times. Typically, there is a daily fixed schedule during that all employees are expected to work. This period, called **core time**, may range between four and six hours per day. Surrounding the core time, employees may select the starting and quitting times. For instance, core time may be established between 10 A.M. and 3 P.M. During those five hours all employees must work. Then within certain limits the employee may select a starting and a quitting time. For example, the schedule may require that all hours be worked between 6 A.M. and 6 P.M. An employee may elect to start at 10 A.M. and work until 6 P.M. or may elect to start at 7 A.M. and work until 3 P.M. to complete the eight-hour day. Thus, employees may adjust their starting and quitting times in accordance with their personal needs and preferences. Of firms surveyed by a management association not long ago, almost 40 percent permitted at least some of their workers to help determine their own schedules, which is double the percentage of a decade ago.

Some employers, indeed, have eliminated even core time. U.S. West, with continuous operations, lets its payroll members set any hours that they want subject only to the approval of their supervisors. Equifax, Inc. allows its employees to come to and leave the workplace anytime between 7:30 A.M. and 9:30 P.M. as long as they are on the job for 7.5 hours each workday. At NCNB Corporation, a bank holding company headquartered in Charlotte, North Carolina, workers can leave on both Thursdays and Fridays at noon and can make up the hours on evenings of the same or other weekdays.

Unions have not been overly enthusiastic about flextime schedules, although this attitude is changing to make organizations more attractive particularly to women with children, who often find that such a schedule fits their personal needs. But, in general, unions look at flextime as a managerial tool to reduce the need for overtime payment and to increase the intensity of the work pace. They have frequently charged supervision with having encouraged employees to "volunteer" for a schedule to avoid the need for overtime. If flextime is to spread in the United States, objections raised by organized labor will have to be resolved. And, of course, even if employees and their unions are willing, some employers may find flextime scheduling an impossibility. To produce effectively under certain types of technology and operations, all employees must be present at the same time.

JOB EVALUATION AND JOB COMPARISON

Thus far we have been dealing with *general* changes in the level of wages under collective bargaining. The comparative norm, ability-to-pay, standard-of-living, and cost-of-living principles—as well as the principles relating to wage differentials and overtime rates—rather than affecting any particular jobs apply either to all jobs or to all jobs that fall within certain widely delineated areas (for example, night work, "dirty work," and overtime work).

Another important problem, however, involves the establishment of *relative* wage rates (or rate ranges) for each particular job, so that wage differentials are rationalized (jobs of greater "worth" to the management are rewarded by greater pay) and the overall wage structure is stabilized on a relatively permanent basis.

Essentially, employers adopt one of two methods to achieve this goal: (1) job evaluation and (2) what, for lack of a universally accepted descriptive designation, might be best described as "job comparison."

❖ Job Evaluation

Job evaluation in its broadest sense is actually used by all employers. It occurs whenever the management decides that one job should be paid more than another, and this is *invariably* done by organizations in the sense that some jobs obviously do deserve more pay than do others.

In the more technical sense in which it is used here, however, job evaluation requires a more systematic approach. Briefly, job evaluation—through the use of thorough job descriptions and equally detailed analyses of those descriptions—attempts to rank jobs in terms of their (1) skill, (2) effort, (3) responsibility, and (4) working condition demands on the jobholder. Each job is awarded a certain number of points, according to the degree to which each of these four factors (or refinements of them) is present in it, and the total number of points consequently assigned to each job (usually on a weighted-average basis, depending on the importance of each factor) determines the place at which the particular job falls in the job hierarchy of the employer. Wage rates or ranges are then established for all jobs falling within a single total point spread (usually called a "labor grade") of this hierarchy. All jobs awarded between 250 and 275 points, for example, might constitute labor grade 4 and be paid whatever wages are called for by this labor grade.

Many managements have found the appeal of such a system to be irresistible. In addition to simplifying the wage structure through the substitution of a relatively few labor grades for individual job listings, it allows the employer a basis for defending particular wage rates to the union and provides a rational means for determining rates for new and changed jobs (through using the same process for these jobs and then slotting their point totals into the hierarchy of labor grades). At least three-quarters of all American managements probably make use of such a system today.

This growth of job evaluation, at least for unionized companies, has nonetheless been accomplished only in the face of rather adamant union opposition. Only a few unions—most notably the Steelworkers—have done anything but strongly attack the system. Virtually all others have voiced deep suspicion of the technique itself and have decried the reduced possibilities for union bargaining on individual wage rates allowed by job evaluation.

Why, then, has this method of evaluation spread so pervasively to industry? E. Robert Livernash years ago conveyed an authoritative opinion that remains valid:

> In part, unions have been bought off. Objection was not strong enough to turn down evaluation if an increase in the rate structure was also involved. . . . In part, unions became willing to accept less bargaining over individual job rates. . . . Unions found that job evaluation did not freeze them out of a reasonable voice in influencing the wage structure and continuous wage grievances became a union problem. Particularly when accompanied by formal or

informal joint participation in the evaluation process, the technique became acceptable.[8]

Unions, on those grounds, have been far more receptive to the concept than a mere reading of their official statements would lead one to believe.

❖ Job Comparison

Job comparison is, in many cases, the manager's answer to intransigent union opposition to job evaluation where this remains a force. It has also been utilized by many employers whose job structures do not appear complex enough to warrant job evaluation or (in some cases) where the management itself is divided on the worth of the evaluation technique. Although it has certain refinements, it most frequently involves (1) the establishment of an appropriate number of labor grades with accompanying wage rates or ranges and (2) the classification of each job into a particular labor grade by deciding which already classified jobs the particular job most closely resembles. The systematic approach of the evaluation method is, in short, dispensed with—and so are the many subsidiary advantages of such an approach. By the same token, however, whatever deficiencies the management or union sees in evaluation are also bypassed. The procedure, a not too satisfactory compromise between evaluations and individual rates for each job, is not now common in industry and, for the reasons indicated in the discussion of evaluation, can probably be expected to become increasingly less so in the years ahead.

CONCESSIONARY BARGAINING

Organized labor officially marked its one-hundredth anniversary in 1981, but it was hardly a time for rejoicing. Starting in the summer of that year, the nation slid into the worst recession since the Great Depression. Unemployment soared from 7.2 percent in 1981 to the previously noted 10.8 percent in 1982, the highest level since 1940, and remained in double digits until well into 1983. And these were just the overall figures. Statistics for much of the blue-collar world, labor's strongest base of operations by far, were at least as gloomy.

Not since the 1930s, in fact, had labor–management contracts been negotiated under such adverse conditions. In a few individual industries—shoe manufacturing, in the 1950s when foreign competition began to flood the U.S. marketplace, and meatpacking, in the 1950s and 1960s when nonunion packing in the South endangered many unionized northern packers—the unions involved had been forced by economic adversity to give back some of their previously gotten wages and benefits. And in previous post–World War II recessions, the pace of wage increases and benefit gains had, of course, slowed. Wholesale concessions granted employers at the bargaining table, however, had not been given in any significant way. Now, they were.

In an effort to save jobs, unions made concessions on wages as they never had before and forfeited benefits that had been enjoyed for as long as 40 years. At times, union leaders were put in the awkward position of urging members to accept the lower standards of employment, and frequently these concessions were negotiated before the expiration date of contracts.

No one seemed to be immune. Concessions in automobiles and steel got the most publicity, but several thousand other negotiations resulted in either a pay freeze or a reduction. The mighty Teamsters agreed to freeze the hourly pay of their more than 200,000 over-the-road truck drivers at $13.30 for 38 months and to use all cost-of-living adjustments scheduled to be made during this period to finance health care. They later granted further economic concessions to particularly marginal employers. In the hard-pressed meat packing industry, the United Food and Commercial Workers allowed weaker companies to reduce pay and benefits by up to $4 per hour—in some cases thereby chopping compensation levels by 40 percent. At Continental Airlines, pilots and flight attendants accepted wages that were a whopping 45 percent below previous levels, although only after the carrier had filed for bankruptcy and dismissed 12,000 of its workers (prior to rehiring 4,200 of them) and after the unions had gone out on an unsuccessful strike.

Even when employees got *more* pay, moreover, it frequently was anything but liberal. Lump-sum payments—often in the neighborhood of a modest $500—were the order of the day, generally granted the workforce at the time the new contract went into effect. Since these payments were not included in the basic wage rate, they did not increase costs affected by the latter, such as overtime, holiday and vacation pay, and pensions.

At least, with the ending of the recession in late 1983, this remarkable period of labor concessions could be expected finally to be over. Employers who were once again making money (in cases such as the automobile industry, quite sizable amounts of it) could no longer credibly ask further sacrifices of their workers.

But many employers—not all of them by any means running in the red—still felt the need for concessions from their unions to survive amid accelerating foreign imports and nonunion competition. And, with the threat of job losses still a very meaningful one, they continued to negotiate concessions—sometimes, as at Eastern Airlines, with contingent compensation such as stock ownership plans and/or some guaranteed union input into corporate business decisions (both of which topics will be dealt with in Chapter 9). Pay freezes and reductions went on in the food, trucking, airlines, and electrical products industries, in particular. Years after the general recession, some employers were still demanding concessions, and at times unions capitulated. In 1988, at its Indianapolis engine plant, Navistar negotiated the equivalent of a $3 per hour wage cut with the UAW. In 1989, the independent union of flight attendants agreed to a $33 million wage cut with Pan American World Airways, although the concessions were not sufficient to keep this venerable carrier flying. It went out of business two years later.

And the appearance of a new recession in the early 1990s combined with the global competitive realities to keep most union wage gains unexciting. The recession had become history by the middle years of the decade, but the global realities only accelerated. The all-industries median and weighted average deferred wage increases negotiated for 1999 were a not very impressive 3.0 percent and 2.9 percent, and the figures for 2000—at 3.0 percent and 3.0 percent, respectively— were hardly better.[9] Essentially, these percentages were about the same as they had been in each year over the entire past decade, a fact that was of at least as much concern to the labor movement as the modest increases themselves. (Exhibits 7-3 and 7-4, both typical

EXHIBIT 7-3

SOURCE: Carol/Simpson Productions.

labor publication cartoons published in the early 1990s, show labor's frustration with this state of affairs.)

The median weekly earnings of unionized workers across all industries continued to be well ahead of those of their nonunion counterparts, as Chapter 1 has pointed out, but the gap was narrowing. And it had continued to narrow when a healthy economy returned to lead America into the twenty-first century. For all of its

EXHIBIT 7-4

SOURCE: AFL-CIO News.

past conquests and future potential, organized labor generally could boast of little in the way of wage bargaining victories in the two decades following its centennial anniversary.

TWO-TIER WAGE SYSTEMS

Concessionary bargaining obviously (unless everyone in the industry has made concessions) violates the deeply rooted union principle of equal pay for equal work. Employees who perform the same jobs as others working elsewhere now get less (or more) pay than those others. But at least the violation of the principle is an indirect and relatively subtle one. Being out of sight, the better-paid workers of competitors in other places are generally out of mind—if, indeed, the latter's now-favored position is even recognized by those who have made concessions. Under any conditions, there can be no direct jealousies on the part of the have-nots: Their own immediate colleagues are paid no more than they are.

In the case of another development of the recent past, "equal pay for equal work" is frontally assaulted. Under the **two-tier wage system**, workers hired after the labor agreement is signed get pay rates that are below, and sometimes well below, those in the same workforce whose dates of hire took place under a previous contract. Thus, newly hired pilots at American Airlines, which in the mid-1980s had a two-tier system in place and estimated that it was saving a rather handsome $100 million annually from it, could in those days expect to be paid at a rate 50 percent less than pilots whose hiring predated 1983, when two-tiering was sanctioned by a new contract. And, under the language of that contract, they would never have an opportunity to catch up with the more-favored pilots. They had been penalized as unborn employees to protect those who were already present (and who were, not coincidentally, voting union members) when the negotiations were carried on.

American Airlines hardly stood alone then, either. By the mid-1980s, the two-tier system had become increasingly important in wage negotiations. And, whereas such arrangements were included in less than 4 percent of all new contracts in 1980, the number soared to 9 percent by 1987 and probably covered over 1 million workers.[10] By 1997, a hefty 38 percent of agreements provided this kind of arrangement.[11] Nor was two-tiering engineered by only employers who were relatively poverty-stricken. Such comparatively well-off organizations as Boeing, United Parcel Service, Giant Food, Safeway Stores, Dow Chemical, the U.S. Postal Service, Alcoa, and General Dynamics also implemented it in this period.

But if the two-tier system can strengthen an employer's competitive situation and income statement, it can also cause problems in the form of employee unhappiness and, ultimately, worker retention and recruitment. The system has an obvious unfairness to it that only a candidate for sainthood among the newly hired workers could be expected to ignore. And, as employees came aboard at the lower rate, they almost inevitably, and rather quickly, became discontented. The package sorter for UPS who could expect $9.18 an hour when the person working next to him got $14.01 could be excused for studying the help-wanted ads at his first lunch hour. And many new hires would undoubtedly empathize with the supermarket clerk whose $7.01 wage rate allowed her barely 60 percent of the earnings of many of her colleagues and who asserted with some finality, "Sure, I knew what this work paid when I accepted it. What I didn't realize was just how inequitable it was. Just as soon as I find something else, I'm gone."

Nor has the system necessarily pleased members of the upper-wage tier. They have often worried that because of their higher rates their employers now have a logical reason to get rid of them—or, at the least, to allow them fewer hours of work per week than the newer hires.

Quite a few employers have also become disenchanted with the system, primarily because of lower employee morale, increased labor turnover, reduced labor productivity, and poor quality of workmanship. When the U.S. Navy complained about sloppy work done by its employees, Hughes Aircraft abolished its two-tier scale. So did General Dynamics, LTV Corporation, and the U.S. Postal Service. Even as early as 1987, American Airlines agreed with its pilots union to merge by stages the pay scales of those newly hired with the scales of senior pilots, and in 1988 it completed the cycle by merging the pay scales for its flight attendants. In 1999, Delta Air Lines readily agreed to eliminate an unpopular "B-scale system," which for some years had paid new pilots less than senior ones who did the same work

But the tiered compensation, such reactions as these notwithstanding, is still very much alive. Twenty-nine percent of all agreements still stipulate the lower wage rates for newly hired workers—even though this is, of course, down from the 38 percent of 1997 and the 35 percent of 1998, and it is also true that under most of these contracts the rates for the new employees will at some point catch up to the rates of their senior colleagues. Such visible groups as the Northwest Airlines pilots and Lockheed machinists have accepted two-tier arrangements relatively recently. In a lesser variation of two-tiering, new UAW workers at automobile plants continue to begin at 85 percent of full wages and advance to 100 percent only after 18 months. And 11 percent of surveyed managements without the system in their current agreements reported in 1999 that they hoped to implement a two-tier plan in their next set of union negotiations.[12]

For all of its obvious negatives, the alternative to two-tiering in many situations is no work at all—a fact that accounts for both the rise of this phenomenon and, in a world of job insecurity, its persistence.

SOME CONCLUDING THOUGHTS

As this chapter has indicated, wage issues pose very difficult collective bargaining problems, and the resultant complications make wage controversies a major cause of strikes. But the fact remains that such strikes take place in only a comparatively few instances. Although the stakes can be very high and the problems formidable, employers and unions in the vast majority of cases ultimately find a peaceful solution in the wage area as in other areas of bargaining.

Some of the settlements, admittedly, may not be the kind that would be advocated by economists, and some clearly fail to adjust the issues in a way that reflects equity and fairness. But the parties most often do resolve their wage disputes in a manner that proves generally satisfactory to all concerned.

It should be remembered that these wage problems are not resolved in an antiseptic economic laboratory where wage models may be constructed. If the settlements do, at times, offend the economic purist, it must be appreciated that these issues are dealt with in the practical day-to-day world, where pressures, motives, and attitudes cannot be isolated from negotiations. Given such realities, it is to the credit of both parties that mutual accommodation has become increasingly visible.

DISCUSSION QUESTIONS

1. Both industry A and industry B are extensively organized by conscientious and honestly run labor unions. Still, since 1968, the wages within industry A have risen at about three times the rate of those in industry B. How might you account for the difference in the wage situation between these two industries?

2. "Even though the actual wage rate that will be negotiated in a particular negotiation is not determinable, it is certain that the set of arguments that union and management representatives will use to support their respective positions will not change from negotiation to negotiation." To what extent, if any, do you agree with this statement?

3. Compare the methods available for the adjustment of wages during the effective period of a labor agreement, and defend what you would judge to be the most desirable arrangement.

4. "From the employer's point of view, it is inherently inequitable—the laws notwithstanding—to require the payment of equal wages to women and to men for performing the same job." Construct the strongest case that you can in support of this statement, and then balance your case with the most convincing opposing arguments that you can muster.

5. Recognizing the present-day circumstances in which you reply to this question, what do you believe to be the most important wage determinant in collective bargaining? Why?

6. What possible problems might confront management and unions in the negotiation and administration of contractual language dealing with overtime?

MINICASES

 Dispensation

The Marsh Company, a 90-year-old Akron clothing maker best known for its golf shirts and men's underwear, is genuinely convinced that unless it can cut its labor costs appreciably, it will soon be on the brink of extinction. Although the union with which it has dealt for many years has prided itself on enforcing uniform industrywide contractual terms (in separate contracts for each company), relations between the parties have been good in recent years. Accordingly, Personnel Vice President Lillian Rosenblatt believes that the union could be amenable to some holding of the line on employee benefits for the first two years of the new three-year contract for which bargaining is scheduled to begin in four weeks, and perhaps even a temporary wage freeze.

If such dispensation is not achieved in the bargaining, Rosenblatt personally has no doubts but that Marsh will have to close its doors within a year, thereby terminating the employment of its 295 workers. All but 44 of these employees are union members and most of them are relative old-timers since the workforce has an average age of 43. She also recognizes, however, that if the union grants concessions to Marsh, other companies in this currently depressed industry would immediately pursue the labor organization for similar downward revisions in their own contracts. The latter consequence is something that the union clearly would not welcome and might not be politically able to sustain in any event.

If you were Vice President Rosenblatt, how would you deal with this subject of contractual dispensation?

#2 An Employee Refusal to Work Overtime

The labor agreement stipulates that "changes in the work schedule" must be "mutually agreeable to both the company and the union." Gryzmisk, who has refused to work six hours of overtime as he was requested to do by his supervisor, is given a one-day suspension for his action.

The union supports Gryzmisk all the way to arbitration on the grounds that the relevant overtime constituted a "change in the work schedule" that it had not approved. The management argues before the arbitrator that the six hours in no way could be considered a change that needed union acceptance since it was for a "limited and specified" duration.

As the arbitrator in this case, what would you have decided?

NOTES

[1]Data furnished by the Bureau of Labor Statistics, U.S. Department of Labor.

[2]Recognition of the difference between firms and industries should also be taken into account when the *non-money* items of collective bargaining are negotiated. A seniority system, for example, that is suitable for one employer–union relationship may not fit the needs of the employer and employees of another plant. Union security formulas, checkoff arrangements, managerial prerogative systems, grievance procedures, discharge and disciplinary arrangements, and the character of the union obligations should be geared fundamentally to the particular collective bargaining relationship. Management and union representatives are at times astonished to learn of the contractual arrangement of another employer–union relationship. The fact is, however, that such a formula can frequently be explained logically in terms of the environment of that firm.

[3]*Wall Street Journal*, May 25, 1995, p. B4.

[4]Bureau of National Affairs, *1999 Source Book on Collective Bargaining* (Washington, DC: Bureau of National Affairs, 1999), p. 29.

[5]*Business Week*, April 11, 1983, p. 28.

[6]*Hooker Chemical Corporation,* 50 LA 1091.

[7]*Safeway Stores Inc.*, 45 LA 1163.

[8]Summer H. Slichter, James J. Healy, and E. Robert Livernash, *The Impact of Collective Bargaining on Management* (Washington, DC: Brookings Institution, 1960), pp. 563–64.

[9]Bureau of National Affairs, *1999 Source Book on Collective Bargaining*, p. 190.

[10]*Wall Street Journal*, April 18, 1989, p. 1.

[11]Bureau of National Affairs, op cit, *1999 Source Book on Collective Bargaining*, p. 33.

[12]Ibid., pp. 33–34.

SELECTED REFERENCES

Baker, Dean, ed. *Getting Prices Right: The Debate over the Consumer Price Index*. Armonk, NY: M. E. Sharpe, 1998.

Blinder, Alan S., ed. *Paying for Productivity: A Look at the Evidence*. Washington, DC: Brookings Institution, 1990.

Booth, Alison L. *The Economics of the Trade Union*. Cambridge, United Kingdom: Cambridge University Press, 1995.

Card, David, and Alan B. Krueger. *Myth and Measurement: The New Economics of the Minimum Wage*. Princeton, NJ: Princeton University Press, 1995.

Dunlop, John T. *Wage Determination under Trade Unions*. New York: Macmillan, 1944.

Ehrenberg, Ronald C., and Robert S. Smith. *Modern Labor Economics: Theory and Public Policy*, 5th ed. New York: Harper Collins, 1994.

Filer, Randall K., Daniel S. Hamermesh, and Albert Rees. *The Economics of Work and Pay*, 6th ed. New York: Harper Collins, 1996.

Goldin, Claudia. *Understanding the Gender Gap: An Economic History of American Women.* New York: Oxford University Press, 1990.

Gottlieb, Benjamin H., E. Kevin Kelloway, and Elizabeth Barham. *Flexible Work Arrangements.* New York: Wiley, 1998.

Hill, M. Anne, and Mark R. Killingsworth, eds. *Comparable Worth: Analyses and Evidence.* Ithaca, NY: ILR Press, Cornell University, 1989.

Hirsch, Barry T. *Labor Unions and the Economic Performance of Firms.* Kalamazoo, MI: W. E. Upjohn Institute, 1991.

Lawler, Edward E. *Pay and Organization Development.* Reading, MA: Addison-Wesley, 1981.

Lewis, H. G. *Union Relative Wage Effects: A Survey.* Chicago: University of Chicago Press, 1986.

Milkovich, George T., and Jerry M. Newman. *Compensation.* Plano, TX: Business Publications, 1984.

Mitchell, Daniel J. B. *Unions, Wages and Inflation.* Washington, DC: Brookings Institution, 1980.

Owen, John D. *Working Hours.* Lexington, MA: Lexington Books, 1979.

Roediger, David R., and Philip S. Foner. *Our Own Time.* Westport, CT: Greenwood, 1989.

Ross, Arthur M. *Trade Union Wage Policies.* Berkeley: University of California Press, 1948.

Sweeney, John J. *America Needs a Raise.* Boston: Houghton Mifflin, 1996.

Rees, Albert. *The Economics of Trade Unions*, 2nd rev. ed. Chicago: University of Chicago Press, 1977.

Reynolds, Lloyd G., Stanley H. Masters, and Colletta H. Moser. *Economics of Labor.* Englewood Cliffs, NJ: Prentice Hall, 1987.

Silverstein, Pam, and Jozetta H. Srb. *Flextime: Where, When, and How?* Ithaca, NY: ILR Press, Cornell University, 1979.

Stigler, George J. *The Theory of Price.* New York: Macmillan, 1966.

Mandatory Overtime: The Case of the Periodic Inventory

Cast of Characters

Bolt	Employee who filed class action grievance
Winner	General Manager
Willis	Employee Relations Manager
New	Another Employee

*Y*ou are the arbitrator in this case. In November 1996, the company required production workers to work overtime to conduct an inventory. For 31 years, the company never compelled overtime for this purpose. A sufficient number of employees always volunteered for the job. This time, the company forced overtime because an insufficient number of employees volunteered. Another fact of significance is that the company frequently compelled overtime for production work. The union did not file grievances for that kind of forced overtime.

Your job is to apply Section 18 of the Labor Agreement to the facts of the case. Be sure that you understand the facts and contractual provisions before attempting to decide the case. Also, make a list of the major arguments of both sides, keeping them firmly in mind before deciding the dispute. Complete knowledge of the facts, contractual language, and the parties' arguments are indispensable in deciding any kind of case. Although arbitrations fall within certain "pigeonholes," such as discipline, overtime, seniority, management and union rights, holiday or vacation pay, each case has its own particular set of facts and contractual language.

In the final analysis, therefore, your task as arbitrator is to apply Section 18 to the circumstances of this case. Whatever decision you make, be prepared to defend it with clear and logical reasoning, rooted to the facts and contractual language. Good luck!

INTRODUCTION

The dispute surfaced when the Company forced production employees to conduct an inventory on Saturday, November 21, 1996. Some employees refused to work the overtime day and received a Point under the Employer's Attendance Program. Accumulation of Points results in progressive discipline.

Kay Bolt filed Grievance Number 96-45, a class action complaint, protesting the Employer's action and stating "Company is in violation of Section 18, but not limited to." The grievance requests that affected employees "be made whole." As a remedy:

> The Union asks the arbitrator to declare that overtime for the annual inventory shall not be mandatory, and, that the Company expunge any points

given under the attendance program from all employees covered by the class action grievance.

The Company denied the grievance in all steps of the Grievance Procedure. As a result, the Parties convened this arbitration for determination of the dispute.

LABOR AGREEMENT

SECTION 18—RESPONSIBILITIES

(a) The parties recognize that the operation of the plant and the direction of the work force therein is the sole responsibility of the Company. Such responsibility includes among other things, the full right to assign work, to discharge, discipline, or suspend for just cause, and the right to hire, transfer, promote, demote, or lay off employees because of lack of work or for other legitimate reason, but not in violation of the provisions of this contract.

(b) The Union agrees that each employee they represent will do all work assigned to him/her to the best of his/her ability and will cooperate with the Management to the fullest extent possible to improve quality and quantity of production, utilization of manpower, safety, housekeeping, and elimination of waste.

(c) The parties recognize that operations in the plant must be scheduled to meet customer requirements.

The parties also recognize the basic obligations of employees to work over time to meet such customer requirements. No employee will be required to work more than 12 hours per tour while working on the continuous run mode.

It is understood that the employees regularly assigned to the machines or operations required to meet production schedules will be assigned the required overtime work, where operating conditions permit. When the assigned employee declines the overtime work for just and sufficient reason, the overtime work shall be assigned to other qualified employees on a rotation basis.

•••

ISSUE

Under the circumstances of this case, did the Company violate Section 18 or any other material provision of the Labor Agreement? If it did, what should the remedy be?

BACKGROUND

Character of Business

Located in Terre Haute, Indiana, the Company produces folding cartons. It manufactures the product for specific customers. In this respect, Michael Winner, General Manager, testified:

Q: Is there any piece of product in your plant that is not dedicated to a specific customer?
A: No, sir.
Q: Is every unit of every order dedicated to a specific customer?
A: Yes. Every product that we manufacture is built specifically to an individual customer application.

•••

Q: So you make no generic products?

A: That's correct.

Q: Nothing that's stacked on shelves and waiting for a customer to call?

A: That's correct. We manufacture only to specific customer purchase orders.

Q: So, every piece of inventory is headed for shipment to a customer?

A: Every piece, that's correct.

Q: Okay.

A: Finished goods, inventory, and every piece of raw material with the exception of some supplies likewise is dedicated to a specific customer application.

In regard to the nature of the Employer's business, Employee Relations Manager Willis also said that it manufactures for specific customers, and that each piece of material inventoried is designed for a specific customer. Thus:

Q: And you agree with the testimony of Mr. Winner that every piece of inventory, or every piece of product that is inventoried is predesignated for a particular customer?

A: Yes.

Q: Nothing is generic?

A: No.

Q: So, does each piece of product inventoried match a customer requirement?

A: Yes.

Physical Periodic Inventory

At least once a year, the Company conducts a physical periodic inventory. Winner explained the purpose of the inventory:

The purpose of the inventory is to convert, confirm the quantity and the value of materials that we have both in finished goods, also in work in process in raw materials.

Almost all such inventories occur on Saturday to minimize interference with production. Inventories are conducted by "pairs," consisting of one (1) bargaining unit employee and one (1) salaried employee. In the inventory of October 28, 1992, there were twelve (12) pairs, one (1) salaried person, and one (1) bargaining unit employee. For the one conducted on July 21, 1993, there were twelve (12) pairs, but one (1) was composed of two (2) salaried persons. Additional inventories were carried out on October 28, 1993, and June 23, 1994. Invariably each pair was staffed with at least one (1) bargaining unit employee and one (1) salaried employee.

November 21, 1996, Periodic Inventory

Previously, sufficient production employees volunteered for inventory duty. No one was mandated to work for that purpose. Since inventories were always held on a weekend day, almost always on Saturday, the employee received the appropriate overtime rate of pay.

Kenneth New, employed by the Company since 1967, testified on the matter this way:

Q: Since 1967, have you been aware of the company conducting periodic inventories?

A: Yes.

Q: Have you ever known, in the years that you have been in the plant, for employees to be forced through mandatory overtime to perform that inventory?

A: Just the last few years.

Q: Since this grievance?

A: Yes.

And:

Q: So, so by your reference, the last six or seven years, at least four or five years before the 1996 inventory, the company has, in your words, pushed mandatory overtime?

A: Yes. Not, not on the . . .

Q: Not on inventory.

A: Okay.

In their Stipulation, the Parties agreed:

Number Six: The November 21, 1996, inventory date is quite possibly the first time that inventory work has been done on a mandatory overtime basis. Six A: On prior occasions, enough volunteers were secured to staff inventory needs.

On November 18, the Company posted the following notice:

We need volunteers to help with the inventory on Sat. 11/21. We need a total of 25 workers to work either one of two shifts, 1st shift 7 AM–3 PM, 2nd shift 11 PM–7 AM. Rolls will be served 7 AM with pizza being served at 11:30 AM and 5:00 PM. Please sign up below and list your shift preference. If we do not have 25 volunteers then the 25 least senior employees will be required to work.

As it turned out, six (6) employees volunteered to conduct the inventory. The other employees were mandated to work. As said, this was the first time in thirty-one (31) years that the Company forced employees to participate in the inventory.

Contract Negotiations

During the negotiations that resulted in the 1986 Labor Agreement, the Union proposed to change the language of Section 18 to read:

Overtime shall be worked when necessary, but refusal of any employee to work overtime shall not be a breach of this contract or discriminated against for refusal to work overtime.

The Employer refused to agree to the change, and the Union removed it from the bargaining table.

In the negotiations that resulted in the 1991 contract, the Union proposed to add to Section 18 the following:

(d)(new) Overtime shall be worked when necessary, but the refusal of any employee to work overtime shall not be a breach of this contract nor shall any employee be disciplined or discriminated against for refusal to work overtime. It is understood that the employees regularly assigned to the machines or operations required to meet production schedules will be assigned the required overtime work.

The Employer refused to agree to the Union's proposal, and the Union dropped it. Once again, the Union attempted to change the language of Section 18 during the 1994 negotiations. It proposed:

> Parag. C *Change* Overtime shall be permitted when necessary, but the refusal of any employee to work overtime shall not be deemed a breach of contract, nor shall any employee be disciplined or discriminated against for refusal to work overtime unless such refusal is continual and habitual at which time management may reassign such individual to equipment that normally does not require as much overtime.

Again the Company refused, and the proposal was withdrawn by the Union on February 15, 1994. Had the Union prevailed, *all mandatory overtime, whether for production, inventory, or maintenance, would have been prohibited.*

In the Employer's posthearing brief, it states that it rejected a Union proposal made during the 1997 contract negotiations to change the language of Section 18, which would make all overtime voluntary. (Company Posthearing Brief, p. 8) No consideration will be given to this item because it was not disclosed during the arbitration hearing. Posthearing briefs are limited to the facts, documents, and circumstances revealed during the hearing.

POSITIONS OF THE PARTIES

Both Parties filed comprehensive posthearing briefs to support their respective positions. According to the Union:

> The Company has no right to force overtime, except in situations where the employee may be required to work on the machine or in operations required to meet production schedules and customer requirements. It has been the past practice of the Company for at least thirty-one years to require overtime, for taking the annual inventory, on a voluntary basis. The Union's position is supported, both by the contract language and by the well established past practice of the parties. (Union Posthearing Brief, p. 9)

The Union argues that mandatory overtime for production purposes has been frequent in the plant, but not for periodic inventories. It states:

> Overlaying this entire situation is the past practice of the parties. It is undisputed that the Company, in thirty-one years, has never forced overtime for inventory until the events which gave rise to this grievance.

Referring to Section 18, the Union concedes that employees may be forced "to work overtime to meet such customer requirements." On this basis, the mandatory overtime for the November 21 inventory was "probably required for accounting purposes, and not required to meet customer requirements." Therefore, claims the Union, the grievance should be granted on those grounds.

Again with reference to Section 18, the Union emphasizes that it states, "Employees regularly assigned to the machines or operations required to meet production schedules will be assigned the required overtime work." According to the Union, such language is an additional factor supporting its position. It means that mandatory overtime may be assigned only to employees assigned to production work. Since the inventory was not assigned to meet production schedules, the Company violated Section 18(c).

To support its position, the Employer states:

When there is no evidence of bad faith, an employer has the right to utilize its contractual prerogatives. Key to the near unanimity of arbitral authority on this point is the pragmatic recognition that efficient use of its employees is the core of the managerial function. Without this right, an employer's ability to conduct its enterprise would be so seriously impaired as to cause flirtation with economic disaster for the enterprise and an attendant lack of job security for its employees. This arbitrator should rule that these parties could not have reasonably intended for grievants to be able to refuse overtime in this case. *By this arbitration, the Union is trying to achieve what it tried and failed to achieve during 1986, 1991, 1994, and 1997 negotiations. This grievance effort should be summarily rejected.* (Emphasis in original) (Company Posthearing Brief, pp. 34–35)

Contrary to the Union, the Company contends that the periodic inventory is undertaken to meet customer requirements. It also stresses that Section 18(a) authorizes the Company to "direct the workforce" and that it has the "full right to assign work." In its judgment, *work* refers not only to production work but to all work including inventory work.

Economic Supplements under

Collective Bargaining

$\mathcal{T}$he incorporation of supplementary economic benefits—from paid vacations to pension plans—in collective bargaining contracts is widespread. Although they have stabilized in their expense to employers in the past few years after hitting a peak of $14,807 per employee in 1995, such benefits increased dramatically in the three decades prior to 1995, both in their value to workers and in their variety, and are widely expected to resume their upward climb in the near future.[1] And because, even with stabilization, these supplements to the basic wage rate are now on the average equivalent to over 41 percent of payroll, it is understandable that some managers express hostility when the once accepted designation *fringe benefits* is used to describe this area. Nor does the adjective seem particularly applicable when it is realized that such benefits now cost employers more than $500 billion annually. At these levels, they are anything but "fringe." Habits are not easily broken, however, and *fringe* will most likely persist indefinitely as a widely used term.

Many of the benefits are not new. In fact, some of them were introduced by employers on a unilateral basis before the advent of unionism. However, unions have been a major force behind the mushrooming of this form of compensation, and, due in no small measure to pressure from labor, many benefits have found their way into the world of work with increasing regularity.

Health benefits alone now average 11 percent of payroll, followed by paid time off (10.5 percent), legally required benefits such as Social Security, unemployment compensation, and workers' compensation (almost 9 percent), retirement and savings plans (close to 7 percent), rest and lunch periods (2 percent), miscellaneous benefits (just under 2 percent), and life insurance (about 0.5 percent). In terms of cents per payroll hour, this comes out to roughly $7.25; in annual dollars per employee, the mean or average payment is now slightly below its peak figure of $14,807, but still a not insignificant $14,500.[2]

Beyond the widespread kinds of benefits cited above, many labor agreements contain special benefits, ones that are either unique or at least not widely prevailing in the working world. Resort hotels in Hawaii grant free use of their golf courses to their International Longshoremen's and Warehousemen's Union members. Clerks at a West Coast supermarket chain can receive almost unlimited use of free psychiatric services and so, too, under certain conditions, can every member of their families. A small Middle Atlantic health care facility grants paid paternity leave to members of the bargaining unit, some 15 percent of all contracts allow paid time off for voting, and a handful of agreements give paid time off to conduct union business.

Some employers provide workers with help in filling out their income tax returns; others emphasize tuition subsidization for college-attending children of employees. Some unionists—Steelworkers conspicuously among them—are eligible for comprehensive alcohol- and drug-addiction rehabilitation, going well beyond the token benefits offered in many other employment settings. Day care for employee children has become more common as a contractually granted benefit: By 2000, about 20 percent of all unionized workers were entitled to some variation of it. Many teachers can receive additional compensation for helping out in extracurricular activities.

Prepaid group legal plans, too, have taken root in recent years, although only about one in 20 contracts has as yet provided for them. Hundreds of these arrangements now offer free routine services such as uncontested divorces, wills, title transfers, and help with landlord–tenant problems, and some even provide free counsel for (limited) criminal offenses. It is possible that such a benefit will burgeon in the years ahead. In the recent past, the UAW has implemented legal services plans with the automobile manufacturers, and UAW activities have, of course, often proven influential in generating trends. Not long ago another potential shot in the arm was provided when the American Telephone and Telegraph Company in new contracts with its 110,000 Communication Workers and Electrical Workers agreed to provide generous legal services at reduced rates at qualified law firms. Many benefit trend watchers predict that such plans, which generally cost employers only several cents an hour per worker, will become as commonplace as health insurance and pensions before many more years have elapsed. On the other hand, even a free will and a bargain-rate criminal defense may prove to have limited appeal as compared with, for example, more money in the pay envelope. And, in any event, this chapter focuses on the more currently widespread and thus presently costly economic supplements.

PENSION AND RETIREMENT PLANS

Private pensions began to be a labor relations issue of some consequence in the late 1940s. A definite boost was given such plans by the U.S. Supreme Court's 1949 *Inland Steel* decision that employers could not refuse to bargain with their unions over this issue.[3] Managers still did not have to grant such employee benefits, but they could no longer legally dismiss union demands for them out of hand.

Other factors, particularly in more recent years, have also contributed to the growth of the pension plans. One of them is the modest level of benefits provided by the Social Security System. Another is the population's increased longevity and a commensurate lengthening of the number of postretirement years. Still a third, it is generally agreed, is the spread of union-spawned seniority and related provisions in labor contracts, as well as the illegalizing of compulsory retirement for most jobs, making it all but impossible to terminate employment for older bargaining unit members *except* by pension.

In addition, there has been a growing managerial awareness—on the part of nonunion employers as well as unionized ones—of an organizational obligation to employees after their retirement. The typical present-day employer is willing to consider pensions a part of normal business costs, something to be charged against revenues in much the same way that insurance of plant and machinery is so charged.

Not that there is unanimity on details.

Ninety-four percent of current labor contracts provide for some pension program, but 70 percent of these have a **defined benefit pension plan**, through which fixed, periodic payments (most often, so much per month per year of credited service) are made to retirees, and about one-third of the agreements stipulate **defined contributions**, through which specified contributions are deposited to an individual account for each participant. One out of five contracts offers both types of plan, with employees generally restricted to the one of their choice, although a few of them let covered workers participate in both.[4] Over the past two decades, there has been a trend away from defined benefit plans, in which the employer bears all of the investment risks and retirees receive checks for the rest of their lives, to defined contribution plans, in which investment risks are borne by workers and there are no guaranteed fixed amounts for life.

There are other causes of variation. Some managers insist that employees help pay for their pensions by making regular contributions to the pension fund during their working years. There are, understandably, wide differences of opinion among executives as to appropriate payment levels for pension plans. Some employers argue that their lack of financial resources rules out the establishment of any pension plan even though they would otherwise be happy to have one. Many smaller employers (in particular) have also cited the long-term character and unknown aspects of pension costs as justification for strengthening other fringe benefits in lieu of pensions. And most, but not quite all, managements have never even remotely thought of extending pension privileges to the part-time workforce.

All of these facts notwithstanding, the moral imperative of providing some kind of private pension to the retired full-time employee if at all possible is no longer seriously questioned by any responsible management at the labor relations bargaining table.

From a modest beginning in 1946, pension plans in American industry have grown phenomenally. Roughly 10 million employees were covered by the end of the 1940s, but this figure had doubled to 20 million by 1960, and the most recent Bureau of Labor Statistics information shows some 33 million wage and salary workers, almost half of them in the ranks of unions, currently encompassed by private pensions.

Other growth-related figures are at least as impressive. In 1970, only 30 percent of couples aged 65 to 69 received a private pension, but by 2004, 88 percent will. By 1990, pension funds were holding a staggering $2.5 trillion in assets—26 percent of the equity and 15 percent of the taxable bonds in the United States—and on a per capita basis this equated to some $8,000 for every person in the nation.[5] By the beginning of the 1990s, retirees were annually receiving from these private plans $220 billion, or half again as much as the $148 billion that the Social Security program was then paying out each year.[6]

On the other hand, some of these pension figures can be somewhat misleading. The considerable inflation of some relatively recent years has at times made gains more apparent than real: Average pensions increased 20.6 percent between 1974 and 1978, for example, but the consumer price index rose 23 percent in this period, and the real benefits, therefore, actually dipped a bit.[7]

Retirees did not fare quite as badly in the 1980s and 1990s, since inflation was relatively modest in those years. But even now the typical private pension recipient is hardly being overwhelmed with riches. In 1999, the average retiree received just over $6,500 per year from his or her pension, and even considering that most but far from all pensioners also receive a Social Security benefit this still does not add up to an opulent standard of living.

Many pension fund students—including most union pension negotiators—have urged that the payout amounts at least be indexed to changes in the consumer price index (as Social Security benefits have been since 1975), but their urgings have largely gone unheeded. Cost-of-living adjustments were found in only two of 202 pension plans surveyed in a recent year by the Bureau of National Affairs, and in only 11 of these plans were benefits in any way increased for retirees.[8]

❖ Major Pension Features

◆ **Voluntary Retirement** Until national legislation banning mandatory retirement before age 70 went into effect in 1979, to be followed by later legislation making mandatory retirement at any age (except for law enforcement officers, airline pilots, and top executives with yearly pension benefits of at least $44,000) illegal, most plans set the required age for retirement at 65. The changes were not expected to make much practical difference, however, since as a general statement the heavy preponderance of employees have not chosen to work beyond their early sixties if allowed even minimally acceptable pensions prior to that. Certainly, this is the present belief of the U.S. Department of Labor, which has estimated that only about 200,000 more people annually will continue working as a result of the legal change.

The Labor Department was possibly aware in making this estimate of such relevant situations as that at the Northrop Corporation, where each year only about one in 50 employees has chosen to stay on beyond age 65, and that at Chicago's Bankers Life and Casualty Company, which has had voluntary retirement for over four decades but where only 3.5 percent of the 3,900 home-office employees are over 65. The story is even more graphic at Motorola: Of its roughly 73,000 full-time U.S. employees, only 283 are over 65.

Nor have many unions—particularly in manufacturing (where the size of recent-year unemployment figures has been of significant influence) done anything to discourage voluntary early retirement. In fact, labor organizations have increasingly sought to open up further job opportunities in the face of technological change and changing market demands even before age 65, and some provision for this benefit is now made under the pension stipulation of almost every contract.

Almost two-thirds of the labor–management relationships have embraced 55 years as the age requirement for early retirement, with 60, 50, and 62, respectively, being the next most frequently stipulated ages. And about nine out of 10 contracts also mandate a service requirement, with well over half of these calling for 10 years in the employer's service, followed by five years and 15 years (16 percent of the agreements stipulate each of these) and 20 years (10 percent).[9] Typically, retirement benefits are proportionately reduced for every year that the employee is under age 65.

Some arrangements are even more liberal from the employee viewpoint. The UAW has for some years now prided itself on a "30 and out" policy in the automobile industry, whereby workers can retire as early as age 47, with relatively generous monthly pensions that are identical to those received by employees who retire at any age, subject only to minimum service requirements having been met. In a typical year, approximately 70 percent of these UAW members do choose retirement as soon as they can gain it, and the average retirement age at General Motors is a not very ancient 58.

Under the steel industry arrangement, there is a variant of "30 and out," but the Steelworker approach has been to encourage at least skilled workers (always at a premium) to stay on at a minimum until age 62, and those who choose to retire before that age receive reduced benefits in return for their decision. The steel industry benefit reduction system for voluntary early retirement is more common than the automobile situation. But contracts in the clothing, maritime, and mining industries—to name only three of a fast-growing number—have adopted the latter arrangement. If workers in these industries meet most often 30 years of service (and invariably at least 20), they have nothing to gain in the way of pension size by staying on (although, again, soaring prices could always be a greater dissuader to those otherwise tempted to leave the payroll).

Under plans that provide for pension benefits to workers who have been permanently disabled and who have not reached the normal retirement age, it is also usually required that such workers have a specified number of years of service with the employer to be eligible for such benefits. Under many of these contracts, 10 to 15 years of service is required before an employee may expect to draw pension benefits because of permanent disability.

◆ The Financing of Pensions The question of who is to finance the pension plans—the employer alone or the employer and the employee jointly—has been an important issue ever since collectively bargained pensions attained prominence, and it continues to pose problems at the bargaining table. At the present time, in about nine out of ten plans, employers finance the entire cost of retirement benefits (and the plans involved are, therefore, called **noncontributory**, in recognition of the lack of expense to the employee); the remainder are financed jointly (and, thus. on a **contributory** basis). Jointly financed plans remain common in some manufacturing industries (notably textiles, petroleum, and chemicals), as well as in finance and teaching.

Arguments can be, and are, erected in favor of either position. In favor of non-contributory plans, it is frequently contended that (1) the average employee cannot afford to contribute; (2) the employee is already making a contribution to another retirement program, that of Social Security, and enough is enough; (3) the employer should exclusively bear the costs of pensions because these are no less important than depreciation expenses for machinery and plant; (4) the return to the management from the plan in terms of lower labor turnover rates (the pension acting as an inducement to stay) and increased efficiency justifies the cost; and (5) employers can charge their pension plan contributions against taxes, whereas employees cannot.

On the other, or procontributory plan, side of the ledger, proponents claim that (1) since there is a definite limit to the economic obligations that employers can assume at a given time, employee contributions ensure better pensions; (2) employees will appreciate plans to which they contribute, as they might not appreciate the noncontributory arrangement and, hence, the contributory plan is psychologically better for the organization in terms of heightened morale and loyalty; and (3) when workers contribute, they have a stronger claim to their pensions as a matter of right.

Most employees and their unions, having heard both sets of arguments, have preferred the noncontributory plan.

Whether the plan is contributory or noncontributory, of course, it must be financed so that the benefits that have been promised upon retirement are indeed available at that point. If the money is simply not there, or if the employer is unwilling for whatever reason to make the counted-upon disbursement, it is of small consolation to the retiree that the plan was a noncontributory one. The same statement, needless to say, applies if the employer vanishes from the scene by virtue of going out of business.

◆ Funding and Vesting *Funded pension plans*—those in which pensions are paid from separated funds, isolated from the general assets of the firm and earmarked specifically for retirees—ensure that the benefits are in fact guaranteed. *Unfunded* plans depend strictly on employer ability and willingness to comply with the pension plan provisions by making pension payments out of current funds. As such, the latter can offer no assurances at all.

Vesting refers to the right of workers to take their credited pension entitlements with them should their employment terminate before they reach the stipulated retirement age. The member of the organization's labor force who is permanently laid off or who quits without possessing a nonforfeitable vesting right is obviously no better off than the employee who has stayed all the way to stipulated retirement only to find that lack of appropriate funding has made the pension a cruel hoax.

As pensions spread in the 1950s and 1960s, improvements in both of these areas took place. Only 7 percent of all workers covered by private pension systems belonged to unfunded plans even as early as 1960, and even fewer did a decade later. As for vesting, where only 25 percent of the plans studied by the Department of Labor in 1952 allowed it, 67 percent of those surveyed 11 years later did so, however much the vesting privilege remained qualified, and by common estimate the figure greatly exceeded 80 percent by the 1970s.[10]

♦ **The Advent of ERISA**   A blatant amount of abuse with respect to private pension plans had nonetheless also developed by the 1970s. Many employees who had counted on a pension simply, if tragically, did not receive the benefit. Hearings held by the Senate Labor Committee at this time disclosed that in some cases funded pension plans had been plundered or misused by their administrators. Another abuse involved the discharge or permanent layoff of employees just before they would (having qualified under age and service requirements) have been entitled to vesting. Situations such as these were unfortunately widespread.

Even more often, however, neither plunder nor specific immorality was involved, but rather the simple inability of the employer to pay. Such a case was that of the Studebaker Corporation, which permanently stopped its operations in the United States in 1964 and because it had never had a funded plan was unable to offer its many terminated employees the pension benefits established in the Studebaker collective bargaining contracts. As one source could quite justifiably say about the general situation, "In all too many cases, the pension promise shrinks to this: 'If you remain in good health and stay with the same company until you are 65 years old, and if the company is still in business, and if your department has not been abolished, and if you haven't been laid off for too long a period, and if there is enough money in the [pension] fund, and if that money has been prudently managed, you will get a pension.'"[11]

There were too many contingencies in all of this for Congress to ignore, given the importance of the subject to so many, and in 1974 it enacted a major piece of legislation, the **Employee Retirement Income Security Act (ERISA)**, that was designed to deal with the obstacles to pension payment.

To deal with the abuse involving the age and service requirements, ERISA provides for vesting of pension benefits. The employer has two options to protect its employees: either 100 percent vesting after five years of service or 100 percent vesting after seven years of service. Under the latter, 20 percent is vested after three years and 20 percent additional in each of the next four years.

So that funds will be available upon employees' retirement, the law requires that all newly adopted pension plans be fully funded to pay the benefits due retired employees. For those plans in existence before the law became effective, employers have the obligation to fund for past service obligations over a specified period of time. To ensure further that employees receive the pension benefits upon retirement, the 1974 law established the Pension Benefit Guaranty Corporation (PBGC), a government agency that in the late 1990s was guaranteeing pensions up to a maximum of $27,000 per year should an employer go out of business or terminate the plan. Other ERISA safeguards involve the placing of a fiduciary responsibility on pension plan administrators, annual reporting and disclosure requirements, and the right of each employee each year to receive information about his or her vesting and accumulated benefit status.

To raise the necessary funds to provide the guarantee, employers were initially required to pay $1 per worker annually, and this amount has steadily risen through the years, although special congressional authorization has been needed each time, to a current maximum of $72 per participant.

The increases have been necessary. By the 1990s, the PBGC was operating at a gigantic deficit. The bankruptcy of firms in the basic steel industry had left it holding the bag for more than $2.5 billion by the end of the 1980s, and it had had to assume an additional $1.2 billion burden in 1992 just from the two bankruptcies of Pan American and Eastern Airlines alone. At the time of this writing, while the PBGC had $8 billion in assets, it was not only paying out $750 million annually in benefits for those of the 66,000 PBGC-insured plans that had failed but—of even more concern to it—was also estimating that some 16,000 of those plans were underfunded to the magnitude of some $53 billion and that this latter total was growing appreciably each year. And the PBGC was guaranteeing, in accordance with its mandate under ERISA, only defined benefit plans—not the defined contribution plans now stipulated, as noted, in one-third of all labor–management contracts.

Bills had been introduced in Congress that would significantly raise the insurance premiums paid by the underfunded plans, force thousands of employers with healthy plans also to boost their pension contributions more than had been the case in the past, protect defined contribution plans, and give the PBGC a larger say in mergers and asset sales affecting pension plans: "We're not going to stand by while people continue to break promises," the angry PBGC executive director had declared.[12] But actual implementation of such harsh medicine as the PBGC's congressional allies were prescribing still seemed some distance away.

Of course, it is unthinkable that Congress would break faith with the retired citizens of the nation. In the final analysis, as it did with the savings and loan industry, the federal government would have to make good on the pensions.

ERISA may not have deserved the description given it by one of its sponsors, Senator Jacob K. Javits of New York, when it was enacted. He called it "the greatest development in the life of the American worker since Social Security." Other developments, including many of the ones directly involving labor–management relations and thus outlined in earlier portions of this book, might strike the student as having been even greater. It is difficult to arbitrate in these matters of taste. It is safe to say, however, that the law has already gone a long way toward protecting employee interests. A staggering $250 billion in assets are now covered by ERISA. The scandal-ridden $8.2 billion Central States Pension Fund of the International Brotherhood of Teamsters has been fully cleaned up, and more improvements will undoubtedly come. Even without the new legislation being sought, the PBGC has been able to force some of the more notoriously underfunded plans to come up with more funding—most notably, the General Motors plan, which had an almost unbelievable underfunding total of $20.18 billion in 1993 and under PBGC prodding put an additional $4 billion in cash into its plan. The federal standards, moreover, have certainly given pension fund trustees a better sense of what their responsibilities are, and the vesting and guarantee features of ERISA have also worked in no small measure in favor of workers.

The impact of the law has, it is true, increased the cost of pension programs and thus in some cases led to smaller benefits. A smaller but guaranteed pension, however, is better than no pension at all for an employee who has devoted all or most of a working life to an employer.

TAX-DEFERRED RETIREMENT SAVINGS PLANS

Roughly two-thirds of all bargaining agreements provide 401(k) or other **tax-deferred retirement savings plans** through which employees can get tax breaks by contributing their own money to their own accounts, but even here the cost to the employer can be appreciable. Almost 70 percent of all managements match at least some portion of the employee contributions, with a 50 percent match being quite common and 25 percent matchings constituting the typical minimum for employers who put any of their money at all into this kind of benefit. Generally, there are contribution limits that run from 1 percent to 6 percent of the bargaining unit member's salary. A small petroleum company in the Southwest very possibly deserves an award for "Most Generous Employer" in this activity: It matches 200 percent of worker contributions, up to 3 percent of salary.[13]

Typically, such plans are offered along with the defined benefit and contribution plan programs. According to the Bureau of National Affairs, almost 90 percent of companies with tax-deferred retirement savings plans in 1999 also offered defined benefit pension plans, as 52 percent of them did, defined contribution plans (17 percent), or both (19 percent). But smaller employers were less likely than their larger counterparts to match employee contributions. Only 62 percent of labor contracts covering fewer than 1,000 workers engaged in any matching, while 84 percent of agreements covering 1,000 or more people did so.[14]

There has been a slight trend over the past few years for managements in both large and small organizations to grant higher matching percentages on retirement savings contributions in return for union concessions on other parts of the economic package, such as wages.

VACATIONS WITH PAY

Vacations with pay for wage earners also constitute a comparatively new development in American history. A scant six decades ago, very few workers covered by collective bargaining contracts received pay during vacation periods, and, at that time, other employees were permitted time off only if they were willing to sacrifice pay. Today the employer not furnishing this type of pay for time not worked is in a definite minority: 93 percent of all present-day labor agreements provide for paid vacations.

In addition to the influence of World War II and Korean War wage controls (which generally did not deal with fringes and implicitly allowed such benefits to be given in lieu of wage hikes) in spearheading the spread of paid vacations and also of paid holidays, a growing recognition by employers, employees, and unions of the benefits of such a policy (in terms of worker health, personal development, and productivity) has contributed to the growth. And as job security considerations have become more important in the recent past, employee representatives have also seen in vacations (as they have in holidays) a way to preserve existing jobs. This has been especially true in such troubled industries as automobiles, steel, and rubber, and it has in fact been in these sectors that vacations, the most expensive of all payments for time not worked, have received particular priority in the bargaining. Once liberalized there, they have gone on to exert pressures (by their very visibility in these major industries) on other unions, and on nonunion employers who would be just as happy remaining nonunion, to expand them where *they* operate.

One eye-catching vacation experiment, however, has not spread very far. In 1962, the Steelworkers and metal can manufacturers negotiated a **sabbatical paid vacation** of 13 weeks' duration, allowed all employees with 15 or more years of service every five years, and the following year the basic steel industry incorporated essentially the same agreement for the senior half of its workforce. After almost four decades, the concept had had no other takers, perhaps because its lavishness in terms of both leisure time and cost to the employer had made it too much of a good thing (and it is now no more—a victim of the bargaining concessions of the 1980s— even in steel). Its very creation, however, says something about vacation appeal.

Paid vacations have also undergone steady liberalization as a worker benefit. In recent years, an annual five-week vacation (normally requiring 20 years of service or more) has been bargained by the parties in almost two-thirds of all labor relationships, even though 30 years ago it was virtually nonexistent. Six-week vacations for employees with high seniority are, in fact, now beginning to emerge as a vacation entitlement of some visibility (almost one-quarter of all contracts now provide for them, typically calling for either 25 or 30 years on the payroll), and there are even seven-week vacations at American Metal Climax, Rockwell International, Boise Cascade, and in the rubber industry (among other places). Four-week vacations (usually after at least 15 years) are today included in 90 percent of all agreements, or more than triple the 1960 frequency. Of more significance to shorter-term workers is the three-week vacation, provided for in over 95 percent of contracts (as against 78 percent in 1960) and most frequently requiring six to nine years of service (where 15 years was the modal prerequisite a very few years ago). Virtually all employees, moreover, can count on a two-week vacation after building up five years of seniority, and contracts increasingly allow this length of time off after only one or two years of service. The only stagnation that has occurred is, in fact, in the one-week vacation area: One year of service has entitled most employees to a single week of vacation with pay for well over a decade now, and the next frontier relating to the one-week vacation will probably be either its total abolition in favor of the two-week vacation after one year—an arrangement that is even now granted by about 35 percent of all agreements—or its being offered strictly as a reward for six months of credited service, as almost 30 percent of all employers now stipulate.

In qualifying for vacations, most labor agreements require that an employee must have worked a certain number of hours, days, or months prior to the vacation period, and failure of the employee to comply with such stipulations results in the forfeiture of the vacation benefits. The rate of pay to which the employee is entitled during a vacation is ordinarily computed on the basis of the regular hourly rate, although in a comparatively small number of agreements vacation benefits are calculated on the basis of average hourly earnings over a certain period of time preceding the vacation, and, in some agreements, vacation pay is calculated as a specified percentage of annual earnings; usually this latter figure amounts to between 2.0 and 2.5 percent of the annual earnings.

A problem arises involving the payment of workers who work during their vacation periods. In some contracts, the employees have the option of taking the vacation to which they are entitled or of working during this period. Other labor agreements allow the employer the option of giving pay *instead* of vacations if production requirements make it necessary to schedule the worker during the vacation period. No less than in the case of the sabbaticals, when employees work during their vacation periods either upon their own or the employer's option, the principles upon which paid vacations are based (health, productivity, and so on) are, of course, violated. In any event, in most labor agreements, employees under these circumstances are given their vacation pay plus the regular wages they earn. In a few cases, particularly when the employer schedules work during a vacation period, the wage earned by the employee working during a vacation period is calculated at either time and a half or double the regular rate. Such earnings are in addition to the employee's vacation pay.

In a majority of contracts, management has the ultimate authority to schedule the vacation period. Under an increasingly large number of agreements, however, the employer is required to take into consideration seniority and employee desires. A fairly sizable number of labor agreements permit management to schedule vacations during plant shutdowns.

Another vacation issue involves the status of employees who—through discharge, retirement, voluntary quit, permanent layoff, or death—are separated from the payroll before their vacation period. When the contract is either silent or unclear on this contingency, and when a convincing past practice between the parties on the matter cannot be established, arbitrators have generally held that employees who otherwise meet the vacation pay requirements (or, in the case of death, their estates) are to be awarded the pay. (Exhibit 8-1, drawn from one current and fairly typical labor agreement, is explicit on some but not all of these situations.) Vacation pay, they have pointed out, is an earned right.

Still another question that can arise when the union and management have not unequivocally dealt with it in their agreement and there is no helpful past practice on the point focuses on whether or not workers' incentive payments should be included in the vacation pay that they receive. Arbitrators have usually ruled that such payments should be included, certainly if vacation pay is based on current hourly earnings. And yet another issue—again, in the absence of both clear-cut contractual language and persuasive past practice—can involve whether a new labor agreement that increases pay rates and takes effect before a worker goes on vacation should determine the vacation pay or if the older (and lesser) rate should be used. Here some arbitrators have held that the rate prevailing at the time of the vacation should be used, but others have worked out compromises, usually by prorating both rates.

HOLIDAYS WITH PAY

Similar to paid vacations, paid holidays for production workers were not a common practice before the middle of the twentieth century. At present nearly all labor agreements incorporate some formula for paid holidays, with some construction contracts being the only conspicuous exceptions at this point.

The median number of such holidays granted in 2000 was 11, and almost no unionized employee could expect fewer than six (although workers in a class with the Bath Iron Works's 4,500 shipbuilders, who received 35 holidays, or almost three for each month, were not in great supply). There was almost universal agreement among the contracts on at least four of these specific holidays: More than 98 percent allowed paid time off for Independence Day, Labor Day, Thanksgiving, and Christmas. And well over 96 percent of all contracts paid for holidays on New Year's Day and Memorial Day. Wider variation takes place where more than six holidays are sanctioned, but half-days before Thanksgiving, Christmas, and New Year's Day are frequently specified, and in an increasing number of cases some holidays are

EXHIBIT 8-1

ARTICLE 7. VACATIONS

Section I. Eligibility

(1) After one (1) year of continuous service, an employee shall be eligible for vacation benefits as follows:

Service	Time	Vacation Pay at Rates According to Section 2
1 year	2 weeks	80 hours
7 years	3 weeks	120 hours
15 years	4 weeks	160 hours
20 years	5 weeks	200 hours

(2) The employee with the greatest seniority in the vacation scheduling group shall have first preferences in selection of his vacation. Vacation quotas will be applied by classification, unit or division, and across shifts.

Section 2. Vacation Year

(1) The vacation year begins on the anniversary date of employment. Each employee becomes eligible for the revised vacation schedule in his next anniversary date. Vacations must be taken during the year. They are not cumulative

(2) If an employee is ill during his scheduled vacation period and the illness extends beyond his anniversary date, the employee has the option—upon notification to his supervisor, of either being paid for unused vacation or taking this unused vacation prior to returning to work.

Section 3. Emergency Cancellations

(1) In case of an emergency the Company may, at its option, require any or all employees to work in lieu of receiving a vacation from work, and in such event an employee shall receive two (2) times his normal base rate for time actually worked. Wherever possible, reasonable advance notice of an emergency will be given to the employee and a Union officer. It is clearly understood any employee who worked the emergency time shall not be required to work any other emergency work that may occur within their anniversary period and shall have the right to vacation selection by seniority preference or elect to take vacation pay in lieu of time off.

(2) In the event an employee must work due to the emergency, the Company shall reimburse the employee for provable losses of deposits, license fees, and reservations.

(3) In the event a cancellation exceeds the anniversary date, an employee will have an additional sixty (60) days in which to take vacation. In any case an employee must take all vacations or forfeit the remainder.

Section 4. Vacations during Planned Shutdowns

(1) It is the Company intent to schedule planned maintenance shutdowns during the summer months whenever feasible in order to provide employees an opportunity to schedule summer vacations. The company shall post its intended shutdown schedule on or before March 1.

(2) Employees, in affected units, who do not schedule vacations for the shutdowns shall be assigned according to the temporary transfer language.

(3) These provisions shall not be construed to limit the Company's right to schedule planned maintenance shutdowns at any other time.

EXHIBIT 8-1
(continued)

Section 5. Approval

(1) All vacations must be scheduled in increments of one full week except that employees with at least three weeks' vacation eligibility may schedule up to one week of their vacation in one-, two-, or three-day increments with advance approval.

(2) A vacation scheduling list will be posted on or about January 15 of each year. Final vacations will be awarded according to plantwide seniority within the vacation selection group on March 31. The vacation scheduling period shall cover the full payroll weeks beginning in April through year end. The Company will schedule vacations in the first quarter on a first-come, first-served basis. The vacation quota shall not be less than 10 percent.

(3) All requests for one-day vacations must be made in writing to the immediate supervisor at least 48 hours in advance and not more than thirty (30) days in advance. The request will be honored providing that the operation in any work area is not seriously affected.

(4) If an employee is absent due to an emergency beyond his control, he may request on his first day back, vacation time for the absence using only those single day vacation days allotted to him. All answers to emergency vacation requests will be made by the end of the Division Manager's second scheduled shift following the day the request is made. (Failure to comply on a timely basis will result in automatic approval.)

Section 6. Vacation Pay upon Retirement or Termination

Upon retirement or termination, employees will be paid for vacation earned during the period worked beyond their anniversary date in accordance with the following formula—calendar days between anniversary and retirement date divided by 365 days multiplied by normal vacation benefits and defined in Article 7 of the present Agreement.

Section 7. Vacation Pay upon Death

The estate of a deceased employee will be paid for all vacation earned during the period worked beyond his anniversary date in accordance with the following formula—calendar days between anniversary and date of death divided by 365 days multiplied by normal vacation benefits as defined in Article 7 of the present Agreement.

---

oriented on an individual basis, such as the employee's birthday, the date on which the employee joined the union (in some Transport Worker contracts, among others), and personal days off. Under this latter agreement, the employer by definition is not penalized with whatever inefficiencies may result from a complete shutdown, and this is probably the major reason why it has become increasingly popular: Over 50 percent of all contracts now sanction such an arrangement, up from just under 40 percent as recently as 1980.

Many agreements also recognize any of a variety of state and local holidays, ranging from Patriot's Day in Massachusetts to Mardi Gras in parts of the South. Company—and even union—picnics are declared occasions for paid holidays in a somewhat smaller number of contracts. (The Electrical Workers [IUE] at the Newport, Tennessee, plant of Electro-Voice, Inc., may be unique, however; a few years ago they won as a new paid holiday February 2, Groundhog Day.)

Sometimes employees may have one or two more or less holidays in one year of their labor contract than in another due to the vagaries of the calendar. The current four-year DaimlerChrylers–UAW agreement, for example, grants 67 paid holidays between 1999 and 2003, but because the days between Christmas and New Year's in some of these years encompass one or more weekend days and because there are

CHAPTER 8 ECONOMIC SUPPLEMENTS UNDER COLLECTIVE BARGAINING

federal election days in 2000 and 2002 but not in the other years, the holiday schedules are not symmetrical.

In addition to the trend toward the personal holiday, there has been a steady
movement toward three-day weekends. The latter owes its genesis to Congress,
which in 1968 enacted a Monday Holidays Law, shifting the observance of four holidays (President's Day, the third Monday in February; Memorial Day; Columbus
Day; and Veterans Day) to Mondays for employees of the federal government. No
other employers are bound by the Monday Holidays Law, but there has been a
decided tendency for them to follow Congress's lead, frequently in accommodation
of union demands. Martin Luther King, Jr. Day, observed always on a January
Monday, has in recent years allowed yet one more long weekend for many (an estimated 18 percent of all unionists by the late 1990s, rising from about 9 percent in
1989). Such other weekend lengtheners as a full day after Thanksgiving, the Friday
before or the Tuesday after a Monday Holidays Law holiday, Good Friday, and even
Easter Monday have also become increasingly popular.

A definite shot in the arm to the spread of paid holidays was also effected in
1976, by the so-often-influential UAW. Alarmed by declining employment for automobile workers and buoyed on by its own estimate that production in 1990 would
be almost 50 percent higher than in 1976 but that only 5 percent more workers
would be needed to yield this higher output ("How long," asked the UAW president, "can we go on providing higher and higher benefits for fewer and fewer workers?"),[15] the union negotiated seven "personal paid holidays" in addition to 13
existing regular holidays. By this action, which was obviously geared fully to job
security and not directed a whit toward increased leisure time per se, the UAW
claimed to have created 11,000 new jobs just at General Motors alone. It expected
that in future bargaining (not only its own but, by a process of coercive comparison,
the bargaining of other unions) such acts of creation would be expanded, and to
some extent they have been.

Most labor agreements place certain obligations upon employees who desire to
qualify for paid holidays, with the common objective in this respect being that of
minimizing absenteeism. The most frequently mentioned such requirement is that an
employee must work the last scheduled day before and the first scheduled day after
a holiday. The obligation is waived when the employee does not work on the day
before or after the holiday because of illness, authorized leave of absence, jury duty,
death in the family, or some other justifiable reason. Under some collective bargaining relationships, illness must be proved by a doctor's certificate, by nurse visitation,
or by some other device.

Production requirements and emergency situations at times require that
employees work on holidays, and such circumstances raise the problem of rates of
pay for work on these days. About three-quarters of all labor agreements provide
for double time for work on holidays, and a small number of contracts now call for
triple time. In the continuous operation industries, such as the hotel, restaurant, and
transportation sectors, labor agreements frequently substitute another full day off
with pay for a holiday on which an employee worked.

An additional problem involves payment for holiday time when the holiday falls
on a day on which the employee would not ordinarily work. For example, if an
organization's workforce does not normally work on Saturdays and if in a particular year July 4 (a paid holiday under the collective bargaining agreement) falls on a
Saturday, the question arises as to whether employees are entitled to holiday pay.
Another aspect of the same general problem involves a paid holiday falling during

an employee's vacation period. Some unions claim that pay for holidays constitutes a kind of vested benefit to employees, regardless of the calendar week on which the holiday occurs. Thus, if the holiday falls on a regular nonworkday, some unions ask that another day be designated as the holiday or that the employee be given a day's wages; or if the holiday falls during an employee's vacation period, that the employee receive another day's paid vacation or wages for the holiday. The opposing view holds that payment for holidays falling on a day on which employees do not regularly work violates the basic principle underlying paid holidays, which is protection of employees from loss of wages. Many labor agreements reflect the thinking of the labor unions on this issue and designate, for example, another day off with pay if a holiday falls on a nonworkday. But a large number of labor agreements do not treat the problem one way or the other, and frequently because of the nature of the language establishing holidays with pay, controversies in this respect—as in the case of vacation pay—are settled in arbitration.

NEGOTIATED HEALTH INSURANCE PLANS

Private employers now provide health coverage to two out of every three Americans, and it doesn't come cheaply. The average cost for employers per employee (both union and nonunion) is now just under $4,000 and this figure marks a dramatic jump from 1984, when it was only $1,453, and 1988, when the statistic was $2,555.[16] Health plans have, in fact, now passed pensions as the most expensive single employee benefit: They currently cost an estimated 11 percent of total payroll, as noted earlier, more than the approximately 10.5 percent of payroll consumed by paid time off.

In collective bargaining agreements, all of the following are generally covered: life insurance or death benefits; accidental death and dismemberment benefits; accident and sickness expense defrayal; and either cash or services to cover hospital, surgical, maternity, and medical care. The boundaries of the package have been extended to major medical insurance (often defraying all such expenses up to 80 percent of their total) and, more recently, to dental insurance and psychiatric benefits.

These economic supplements gradually spread for a variety of reasons. Insurance programs were also a major fringe issue in the period of wage control during World War II and the Korean War, although to a far smaller extent than were vacations and holidays. Increasingly, both employers and unions have recognized that few of their workers are remotely prepared to handle the rapidly rising health costs on their own. The Internal Revenue Service has also provided some spur by permitting employers to deduct most such payments as business expenses for tax purposes. Group insurance allows purchasing economies not available to individuals. And the fact that the Social Security program has not provided protection for most risks covered by these insurance plans has made the private insurance system a widely sought one.

Today's typical bargained health and welfare package is of no small dimensions. There is a strong likelihood that it includes life insurance for an amount approximating at least one half of the employee's annual salary; disability and sickness benefits of at least $250 weekly for at least six months; semiprivate hospital room and hospital board for as long as 90 days, together with such add-ons as drugs and medicines, X-ray examinations, and operating-room expenses (under either Blue Cross or a private insurance company plan); surgical expenses up to a $25,000 maximum for contingencies not covered by workers' compensation legislation; and coverage for the employee's dependents as well as himself or herself for all or most of these benefits. And, as in the cases of pensions, vacations, and holidays, these emoluments are continuing their own process of liberalization, with discernible trends in recent years involving an increase in the amount and duration of the benefits; extension of the benefits to retired workers, as well as to those dependents not yet covered; defrayal of the expenses of at least some medically related drugs; added protection for catastrophic illnesses and accidents, and the broadening of dental and mental health benefits. They have come a long way since the 1950s and 1960s, when only catastrophic illnesses were covered (assuming, of course, that there was health care expense defrayal at all) and even then only a small portion of the total cost—$30 to $40 per day was a common payment—was picked up by the employee plan. *(Case 4 centers on employer-financed sick pay.)*

Until recent years, there was a commensurately strong trend toward exclusive employer financing of the health benefit package. Twenty-one percent of all unionized employers footed the entire bill in 1949; roughly 40 percent did so in 1956; an estimated 53 percent paid the full cost in 1984.[17] *(Case 5 involves an unusual problem relating to a group life insurance program.)*

But as these health care costs for managements skyrocketed in the 1980s—by the middle years of that decade they were rising at almost twice the rate of inflation and added up to more than $85 billion on an annual basis—employers, for the first time, were pressing unions to help them contain such major expenses through collective bargaining.

Two particularly significant milestones in this regard were implemented in 1985. At General Motors, whose health-benefit expenditures had almost quadrupled in the past decade (and in whose health plan roughly 1 percent of the U.S. population, counting retirees and dependents, was enrolled), the UAW agreed to help pare $220 million annually from GM's $2.2 billion health care bill without penalizing employees at all. Under an "Informed Choice Plan," employees can now select one of three options, each of them less costly to General Motors (which continues to pay essentially all of the health bill) than the pre-1985 programs. They can opt to use a health maintenance organization, or HMO, providing specified services—hospitalization included—for a predetermined amount. They can choose, instead, to deal with a preferred provider organization, which charges for each service provided but at a discount or otherwise favorable rate to GM. Or they can elect to continue receiving their traditional insurance coverage but now with the requirement of preauthorization from an independent review group before certain specified treatments.

And in another widely publicized action, the joint labor–management Teamsters Central States Welfare Fund contracted with Voluntary Hospitals of America, Inc., for discounts through a preferred provider relationship geared to slicing a similar 10 percent from the fund's $350 million medical bill. As the fund's executive director quite justifiably commented as these negotiations were concluded, "These dollars will be available for wages and other things if we don't utilize them for health."[18]

Nearly two decades later, labor's bargaining table support for such measures as these and related health-cost containment ones (mandatory second surgical opinions, for example) is anything but a rarity. In addition to the Automobile Workers and the Teamsters, whose original actions have now been duplicated in many other negotiations of these two unions, the Communications Workers, Mine Workers, and Rubber Workers have been particularly receptive to accepting such cost-containment measures. Numerous other labor organizations have also moved in this direction, recognizing that in these actions the burden falls fully on the health care providers and not on bargaining unit members themselves (whose actual benefits are rarely reduced in the process and often, indeed, even expand). As *The New York Times* has observed in analyzing this development, "many unions seem to be discovering a self-interest in joint (union–management) approaches to the broader question of bringing the system under control."[19]

By 1999, some three-quarters of all employees were enrolling in the plans, and unionists were participating in the changeover at least as much as were nonunionists.

Health care cost containment for employers was also now being achieved in no small way by a dramatic reversal of the trend toward exclusive management financing of the package. The percentage of comprehensive plans requiring workers to share premium costs rose from 28 percent in 1989 to 93 percent 10 years later, and it continues to rise. Most such plans under labor contracts now call for some combination of deductibles, copayments, and premium contributions: 85 percent of 1999 contracts imposed copayments for medical services, up from 78 percent only one year earlier. Deductible requirements (now in 77 percent of all agreements) and stipulations that employees have to pay some of the health insurance premiums (in 65 percent) have also gone up appreciably in the recent past.[20]

In many of these cases some of the employer costs have, of course, simply been shifted to the workforce, and unionized workers have not been nearly as amenable to the management bargaining table requests for copayments and deductibles. Recent bitter strikes—most notably in the telephone industry against three regional Baby Bell telephone companies (where picket signs declared "Cutting Our Health Benefits Is Sick") and in the bituminous coal industry against the Pittston Coal Group—have, in fact, stemmed almost exclusively from this emotional issue.

Nor did it seem likely that the management cost-containment measures would end there. On the eve of the bargaining for the year 2000, not one of 147 employers responding to a Bureau of National Affairs survey planned to offer to soften any of their initiatives. And 19 percent of these employers announced that they would propose such new measures as a requirement that workers choose outpatient surgery whenever that alternative to hospitalization was feasible, the prohibition or restriction of reimbursement for brand-name prescription drugs (which 71 percent of all contracts contained even in 1999), and the establishment of wellness programs.[21]

Managers defended these moves as having been dictated not by avarice but by necessity. The savings realized by their current cost-containment efforts had, many of them believed, hit diminishing returns, and insurance companies were rapidly raising rates for the coverage that they offered. Unionists tended to disagree, pointing out that they were all for new and more imaginative ways to stabilize costs, so long as these ways didn't constitute merely another round of cost-shifting.

DISMISSAL PAY

Unlike all the wage supplements discussed previously, **dismissal, or severance, pay,** is still not a common product of collective bargaining. According to Bureau of Labor Statistics information, only about 39 percent of all contracts provide such a benefit at the present time, and this figure represents a very modest rate of growth over the past two decades: In the late 1970s, the statistic was about 30 percent. On an industrywide basis, the practice remains largely confined to contracts negotiated by the Steelworkers, Auto Workers, Communications Workers, Needletrades Union, and Electrical Workers—although many sectors of the newspaper and railroad industries also have such plans.

Dismissal pay provisions normally limit payments to workers displaced because of technological change, plant merger, permanent curtailment of the company's operations, permanent disability, or retirement before the employee is entitled to a pension. Workers discharged for cause and employees who refuse another job with the employer usually forfeit dismissal pay rights, as do workers who voluntarily quit a job.

The amount of payment provided for in dismissal pay arrangements varies directly with the length of service of the employee. The longer the service, the greater the amount of money. Ordinarily, a top limit is placed upon the amount that an employee can receive. Although labor agreements vary in respect to the payment formula, as a general rule low-service workers receive one week's wages for each year of service prior to dismissal, with higher than proportional allowances for high-service employees (up to 60 weeks' pay, for example, for 15 or more years of service and as high as 105 weeks' pay for workers with 25 or more years).

A problem involving dismissal pay occurs when an employee is subsequently rehired by the employer. There is little uniformity in collective bargaining contracts relative to the handling of this problem. Actually, a large number of labor agreements that provide for dismissal pay are silent on whether employees must make restitution to the employer upon being rehired or whether they may keep the money paid to them when their employment was originally terminated. Some agreements, however, specifically provide that such employees must return the money; for example, one telephone industry collective bargaining contract stipulates that such employees must repay to the company any termination payment, either in a lump sum or through payroll deduction at a rate of not less than 10 percent each payroll period until the full amount is paid. Balancing this employer tight-fistedness are the almost one-third of all contracts that explicitly waive the repayment of severance pay for those rehired and many others that remove the repayment obligation after a designated period of time.

Since the dismissal provision is designed to cushion the effects of employment termination through technological change, merger, and cessation of business (as well as through involuntary retirement due to personal health misfortunes), it is logical to conclude that this benefit, too, will spread in the years ahead despite its far from staggering growth in the recent past.

REPORTING PAY

Under the provisions of over 80 percent of the collective bargaining contracts currently in force, employees who are scheduled to work, and who do not have instructions from the employer *not* to report to their jobs, are guaranteed a certain amount of work for that day or compensation instead of work. Issues involved in the negotiation of **reporting pay** arrangements are the amount of the guarantee and the rate of compensation, the amount of notice required for the employer to avoid guaranteed payment, the conditions relieving the employer of the obligation to award reporting pay, and the conditions under which such pay must be forfeited by employees.

Labor agreements establish a variety of formulas for the calculation of the amount of the guarantee. Reporting pay ranges from a stingy one-hour guarantee to a full day. About 65 percent of labor contracts dealing with this issue provide for four hours' pay; approximately 15 percent call for eight hours' pay. These rates are calculated on a straight-time basis. However, under circumstances where workers are called back to work by management outside of regularly scheduled hours, such employees are frequently compensated at premium rates, ordinarily at time and one half the regular rate. Such reimbursement, known as call-in pay, might be awarded a worker, if, for example, the worker is called back to work before having been off for 16 hours. Thus, if the employee regularly works the first shift and is called back under some emergency condition to work the third shift, the labor agreement might require that there be payment at premium rates. In the event that the employee reports for such work only to find that the employer no longer has need for his services, the employee will still be entitled to a certain number of guaranteed hours of pay calculated at premium rates.

In most agreements providing for reporting pay, the management is relieved of the obligation to guarantee work or to make a cash payment to employees when the employer notifies employees not to report to work. Contracts frequently provide that such notice must be given employees before the end of the workers' previous shift, although in some cases the employer may be freed from the obligation by giving notice a certain number of hours before employees are scheduled to work. Eight hours' notice is provided in many labor contracts.

In addition, employers do not have to give reporting pay when failure to provide work is due to causes beyond the control of the management. Thus, when work is not available because of fires, strikes, power failures, or "acts of God," in most contracts either employers are not obligated to award reporting pay or the amount of the pay is substantially reduced. Of course, there are many questions of interpretation involved in this situation. For example, does power failure resulting from faulty maintenance relieve the employer of the obligation? As in so many previous cases, such questions are resolved through the grievance procedure and at times through arbitration.

Thus, one arbitrator awarded the grievants reporting pay under a contract providing for such pay for employees who reported to work but found none available unless "the plant delay results from causes beyond the control of the company." The collapse of a flue had required the shutting down of a furnace used in the production process. The union pointed out that the flue had not been inspected for three years and argued—convincingly to the arbitrator—that adequate inspection would have prevented the collapse and that the occurrence had consequently been very much within the management's control. In another situation, however, an arbitrator ruled that the employer did not have to give reporting pay to employees who had not been able to work because the plant had been closed due to icy roads caused by freezing rain. Even though the workers had navigated the roads without problems and, in fact, had not even seen any accidents on their various routes, freezing rain was clearly an "act of God" exempting the employer from having to pay, in the arbitrator's opinion; to expect the management to do something about it, the arbitrator in essence declared, was expecting too much.[22]

Under certain other circumstances, employees forfeit reporting pay. If employees, for example, fail to keep management notified of change of address, reporting pay is forfeited under many labor agreements. Other forfeitures might result if employees refuse to accept work other than their own jobs, leave the workplace before notice is given to other employees not to report to work, or fail to report to work even though no work is available.

SUPPLEMENTARY UNEMPLOYMENT BENEFIT PLANS

The **supplementary unemployment benefit (SUB)** plan attracted national attention in the mid-1950s, when both the nation's automobile makers and its basic steel companies negotiated such plans with their unionized workers. Essentially, SUB arrangements constitute a compromise between the "guaranteed annual wage" demanded by many unions in the late 1940s and early 1950s and a continuing management unwillingness to grant such relatively complete job security as the guaranteed wage designation would indicate. The plans are geared primarily to two goals: (1) supplementing the unemployment benefits of the various state unemployment insurance systems and (2) allowing further income to still-unemployed workers after state payments have been exhausted. They also seek to minimize or even eliminate the income difference between the salaried employee and the hourly-rate worker, who is more apt to be laid off when business declines than the payroll member who is paid by the month or year. And they implicitly recognize at least one weakness in the state systems: Since the states started paying benefits in the late 1930s, the average ratio of these benefits to average wage levels of employees when working has steadily dropped from approximately 40 percent then to somewhat less than 35 percent today. Today, Hawaii has the most liberal ratio, 46 percent, while Louisiana, with a meager 27 percent, comes in at the bottom of the states.

Half of all manufacturing workers in the United States now have some kind of SUB plan. Almost total coverage has been achieved in the rubber and plastics industries, where 95 percent of the workers have such a benefit. In second place are automobile and aerospace employees, some 82 percent of whom are covered. Other industries now granting significant SUB protection are "primary metals" (steel and aluminum, in particular), where the coverage statistic is 70 percent, and apparel, 61 percent of whose employees have an SUB arrangement. In all of these heavily unionized sectors—as well as in the glass, farm equipment, electrical, can, bakery, chemical and retailing, printing and publishing, petroleum, and maritime industries, where significant but lesser proportions are covered—there are some major elements of similarity.

All SUB plans, for example, require that employees have a certain amount of service with the company before they are eligible to draw benefits; the seniority period varies among the different plans—with a one-year requirement in the basic auto and can contracts contrasting with a five-year prerequisite (the most extreme) in a few contracts negotiated by the Oil, Chemical, and Atomic Workers Union. In addition to seniority stipulations, virtually all plans require that the unemployed worker be willing and able to work. The test in this latter connection is, most often, the registration for work by the unemployed worker with a state unemployment service office. Beyond this, the plans invariably limit benefits to workers who are unemployed because of layoff resulting from a reduction in the work force by the company. Workers who are out of work because of discipline, strikes, or "acts of God" cannot draw benefits. Nor can workers do so whose curtailment of employment is attributable to government regulation or to public controls over the amount or nature of materials or products that the company uses or sells.

Under the most prevalent type of SUB agreement, all employees start to acquire credit units at the rate of one-half unit for each week in which they work. When they complete enough service to qualify for the benefits (the one to five years cited in the preceding paragraph), they are officially credited with these units, which they can then trade off for SUB pay when unemployed up to a maximum unemployment duration. Most plans now have set this maximum at 52 weeks and, consequently, an automobile or steel industry worker with two years of continuous employment has achieved the maximum amount of SUB coverage. Under about half the current plans, however, the ratio of credit units to weeks of benefit can be increased when the SUB fund falls below a certain level, thereby shortening the duration of benefits. Another common variation is to adjust the ratio in such a way that laid-off workers with long service are protected for a proportionately longer length of time than are shorter-service employees.

Almost universally, employees are entitled to draw benefits only up to the amount of credits that they have established and can receive no benefits—no matter how large the amount of their credits—during the first week of unemployment, a stipulation that is consistent with the one-week waiting period under most state unemployment insurance plans. In addition, credit units are canceled in the event of a willful misrepresentation of facts in connection with the employee's application for either state or SUB income.

Benefit formulas under most layoffs currently set a normal level of payments at 60 to 65 percent of take-home pay (gross pay minus taxes) for all eligible employees. This level comprises payments from both the negotiated benefit plan and the state system. If, for example, a worker whose normal take-home amount is $530 is laid off, a plan calling for 65 percent of his take-home pay allows him $345. And if the worker's state unemployment compensation totals $180 weekly, the SUB plan would then pay him the weekly sum of $165 to make up the difference. There is some debate even among the most rabid advocates of SUB plans as to whether the level should be pushed much beyond this 65 percent figure, for even at this percentage several plans have experienced the ironic situation of workers' preferring total layoff to work. Under UAW contracts in the automobile industry, workers with the minimal years of seniority now actually receive 95 percent of their after-tax wages while on layoff (minus $12.50 for such work-related expenses as transportation, work clothing, and lunches) for up to 52 weeks—and they almost invariably prefer such a well-remunerated enforced leisure period to their normal work assignments! The same preference for layoff has been amply in evidence in steel, where in recent years senior workers have been guaranteed SUB payments of up to $450 per week for two full years—and after that either a job at another plant or a pension.

To establish the fund for the payment of supplementary unemployment benefits, most plans require that the employer—who invariably exclusively finances all SUB plans—contribute a certain amount of money per work hour. Many agreements call for a cash contribution of $.20 per hour, although several go as low as $.05 and about the same number require $.30 or more. The payment into this fund most often represents the *maximum* liability of the company, however. Typically, a maximum size of the fund is defined, and company contributions for any one contractual period stop completely when this limit is reached and maintained; the objectives, aside from relieving the companies of too rigorous payments, are to prevent too large an accumulation of fund money and to encourage the companies to stabilize their employment levels. On the other hand, when fund finances fall below the stipulated amount, because of SUB-financed payments, the employer must resume payments at the rate required by the plan. In addition, many SUB plans—including most of those negotiated by the Steelworkers—require a further company liability: When the SUB fund reaches the "maximum" level, companies continue to make contributions—first to a Savings and Vacation Plan (to keep its benefits fully current) and then once again to the SUB fund—until approximately $450 per employee is accumulated. Only at this point do company contributions cease.

There seems to be little question that SUB plans not only warded off individual hardship but also maintained a good deal of consumer purchasing power in the United States during the several general recessions of the past three decades. Without them, the bleak economies of countless cities and states with a heavy dependence on automobile, steel, rubber, and other mass-production factory employment would undoubtedly have been even bleaker.

But it is also true that such plans are quite vulnerable to long-term plant closings and mass layoffs and that in several SUB industries marked by such circumstances in the 1974–1975, 1981–1983, and 1991–1992 recessions, the SUB money simply ran out. Hundreds of thousands of automobile and steel workers in particular found themselves receiving only state unemployment compensation when their employers' funds were depleted amid mammoth and long-lasting unemployment. And many of these workers, ultimately exhausting their state entitlements as well, wound up on welfare rolls.

This outcome should have come as no surprise. SUB was never designed to cope with anything but normal, short-term plant closings and recessions that were relatively mild in their impact. And if the monies had been a major consolation both in lesser post-1955 recessions and in the early stages of the more major ones, it was inevitable that sooner or later the horrendous layoff statistics of the latter would cause the SUB wells to run dry. Although constantly liberalized and always replenished when good times returned, there was no way that such benefits by themselves could offer sufficient protection against large-scale and enduring unemployment, even when incurred by such historically opulent organizations as General Motors and USX (to say nothing of their less affluent competitors). As a valuable (and expensive) segment of the overall employee benefit package, SUB would undoubtedly be of help to the *short-term unemployed* in at least the cyclical industries where it had—not by accident—been established, and perhaps in others where it might be implemented in the years ahead. To claim that it could do anything more, however, would be both unfair to the parties who had negotiated it and cruelly misleading to the employees covered by it.

At any rate, outside of the manufacturing sector, the growth of SUB plans has been far from impressive. Most craft unions continue to greet such a device with total apathy, preferring to substitute other economic improvements for its introduction. And seniority protection appears to have thus far satisfied workers in many noncraft industries sufficiently so that SUB has not become a major union demand there. But the continuing hold of SUB upon the several major industries in which it was originally negotiated, and the constant improvement of SUB allowances there, remain facts that cannot be ignored, either in assessing the creativity of the collective bargaining process or in judging the potential impact of this "guaranteed annual wage" compromise should the employment instabilities that have always characterized most industries in which SUB has now been implemented spread to other parts of the economy. If SUB extensions have not been impressive in total, SUB today does exist in sectors where it is needed—namely, those where job insecurity is the greatest.

SOME CONCLUDING THOUGHTS

Whether SUB will ultimately achieve the universality of pension plans, health insurance, paid vacations, and paid holidays (and such various other widespread but considerably lesser benefits as paid time off for obligations stemming from death in the family and for jury duty) remains an open question, but even in the case of SUB a broader issue does not. It appears to be all but axiomatic to collective bargaining that *any* benefit, once implemented by the parties, becomes subject through the years to a process of continuous liberalization from the workers' viewpoint. Even supplementary unemployment benefits have undergone this process in the years since 1955, when the automobile industry's maximum of $30 weekly for no more than 26 weeks was considered generous.

Many of these benefits continue to allow the same cost advantages to the parties, in terms of both group insurance savings and tax minimization, that they did at the time of their various inceptions. Generally tight labor markets have further led employers to amass attractive benefit packages, to be placed in the front window as recruitment devices. And considerations of worker retention, productivity, and pure pride have also undoubtedly stirred both managers and union leaders in their bargaining on these economic supplements. As the new worker needs and wants in the benefit area have become active, the collective bargaining parties have clearly responded to the challenge.

However, neither for the bargaining parties nor for the nation as a whole is this situation an unmixed blessing. Increasing caution from both managements and unions will, in fact, be required as the liberalization process continues, and at least six warnings appear warranted.

In the first place, many improvements in the benefit portfolio automatically present potentially troublesome sources of union grievances that would otherwise be absent. Increasing latitude for employee choice of vacation time, by the incorporation of a "seniority shall govern, so far as possible, in the selection of the vacation period" contractual clause, for example, carries far more potential for controversy than a clear-cut statement reserving vacation scheduling strictly for management discretion. As a second example in this area, with two weeks being the maximum vacation allowance, there is usually no question of carryover credit from year to year; workers are not confronted with "too much of a good thing" and normally do not seek to bank unwanted vacation time until it may be worth more to them. Under a more liberal allowance, however, the question does arise, as many employers and unions can testify, and policies must be both established and consistently adhered to if problems on this score are to be averted.

The list of such newly created grievance possibilities could be extended considerably to virtually all the benefit sectors. Who qualifies as a dependent under an expanded health insurance plan that now accommodates such individuals? What religious credentials must be established to authorize paid time off "as conscience may dictate" on Good Friday or Yom Kippur? Is a suddenly decreed national day of mourning an "act of God," relieving the management of an obligation to grant reporting pay, or do its circumstances compel the employer to pay such amounts? How many hours or weeks of work—and under what conditions—constitute a year, for purposes of calculating pension entitlement within a system granting a flat monthly payment "per year of service?" In a less generous age, these and obviously a myriad of similar questions were automatically excluded.

Second, even on the now rare occasions upon which the benefits are not formally liberalized, many of them automatically become more costly simply because wages have been increased. All wage-related benefits fall into this category, and a $.75 per hour wage increase will thus inevitably elevate total employment costs by considerably more than this face amount because of the simultaneous rise in the worth of each holiday, vacation period, and any other allowance pegged to the basic wage rate. This industrial relations truism would hardly be worth citing were it not so often ignored in union–management bargaining rooms, in favor of accommodating only wage increases to increases in productivity (for example) rather than wage increases plus wage-related benefit increases. The degree of danger in overlooking these inflationary ramifications, moreover, obviously rises with the increasing value of the benefit itself.

In the third place, one suspects that managements have—at least at times—generated *negative* employee motivation by implementing benefits without either participation or approval of work force representatives in the process. The day of company paternalism, fortunately, now lies far in the past for the large mainstream of American industry. But the arousal of employee ego involvement is all the more imperative in today's sophisticated industrial world. Describing a deep and enthusiastic interest in unionization on the part of employees at a large Pittsburgh plant "that was well known as having excellent wages and working conditions, and supposedly had almost perfect employee relationships," Leland Hazard once memorably quoted the following remarks of "one attractive girl" to explain the general sentiment:

> It's about time something like this happened. We have got to stand on our own feet. They do everything for you but provide a husband, and I even know girls who they got a husband for. And them what ain't got time to get pregnant, they get foster kids for [23]

To an objective observer, such biting of the hand that has been feeding may seem quite unfair, but such employee reaction to benefits is, nonetheless, a frequently encountered fact of life.

Related to this question of negative motivation, but isolable as a fourth potential problem, must stand the very real alternative possibility of *no* employee motivation whatsoever. Not being masochistic as a class, employers logically expect some benefits from their expenditures in the wage supplement area—particularly more satisfactory worker retention figures, an improved recruitment performance, and, above all, generally increased employee productivity. Without such returns on the benefit investment, managements would be engaging in clear-cut wastage.

One can readily locate situations in which employee benefits have obviously achieved at least some of the desired results. Particularly in those areas where benefit entitlement expands with increasing seniority (pensions and vacations, for example), greater worker retention has undoubtedly often been fostered. Yet there is to this moment no convincing proof that benefits have significantly affected employee motivation on any large-scale basis in American industry. There is a critical need for much more research into this subject by employers and other interested parties than has thus far been conducted, for the possibility that industry may be undergoing an ever-increasing expense that may be returning very little in the way of concrete worker performance cannot as yet be safely dismissed.

Fifth, it is possible that overall employment has suffered—and conceivably will continue to suffer—from the continuation of benefit expansion of the type described in this chapter. As in the preceding case, the evidence thus far is not fully conclusive. But the increasing cost pressures involved appear to have combined with related factors to push in this direction. New employees must receive the full panoply of benefits that present employees already have: It is a lot cheaper, many employers believe, to work existing employees harder by tightening up on managerial controls and even by asking for (and paying for) overtime than to add new members to the pay-roll. When extra hired hands are needed, they can always be procured from temporary help agencies (and, indeed, the large growth in benefits is generally conceded to be the foremost reason for the flourishing of these "temps," who collectively constitute America's fastest-growing single industry): Workers sent over by the temporary agencies do not get the benefits.

Finally, unlike wage increases (which can often be at least partially negated by such mechanisms as job reevaluation and incentive rate implementation or modification), the benefit package has a strong tendency to remain a permanent part of the landscape. Except in extreme cases of employer financial crisis, it is quite immune from disintegration. And if any significant positive effect of benefits on employee motivation thus far remains to be proven, the annals of industrial history are replete with examples of managements that have encountered surprisingly intense worker resistance in attempting to dismantle even such relatively minor portions of their benefit packages as physical fitness programs or banking facilities. Downward revisions of the leisure time, health, and pension offerings remain several miles beyond the realm of the conceivable. In short, once the parties introduce a benefit, they can expect to be wedded to it for life, with the only important questions focusing on the timing and degrees of the subsequent benefit liberalizations.

For all the reservations expressed in the preceding paragraphs, employee benefits hardly warrant an evaluation similar to that given by the old railroad baron James Hill to the passenger train ("like the male teat, neither useful nor ornamental"). They do provide considerable security at minimal cost to the covered employees (whether or not the latter explicitly desire such protection in lieu of other forms of compensation), at least at times abet the employer's recruitment and retention efforts in a tight labor market, and minimize the tax burdens of both employer and worker. If there is room for doubt that they also allow the employer any significant return in the form of worker morale and productivity, these other reasons alone are probably sufficient to justify their dramatic spread.

And because the benefit package has become so relatively standardized among employers in this time interval, too, the wage supplements probably also perform a further (if less constructive) function for managers and the unions with which they deal. Their presence in anything approaching the typical dimensions prevents invidious comparisons by both current and potential employees in evaluating the desirability of the organization as an employer. The extent of worker knowledge of specific benefits may fall far short of perfection, but at the present time, because management pattern-following has been so prevalent in this area, the absence of 10 or 11 paid holidays, a three-week paid vacation after no more than 10 years of service, significant medical coverage for all members of the family, satisfactory pensions, and really any of the various parts of the generally conspicuous benefit portfolio are often grounds for workers' dissatisfaction.

Thus, it can be predicted quite fearlessly that the years ahead will see a continuation of the benefit growth. As indicated, it appears to be all but axiomatic to industrial relations that any benefit, once implemented, through the years becomes subject to a process of continuous liberalization from the worker's viewpoint. And, while variety in these economic supplements has now become increasingly difficult to achieve, there is little doubt that new ones (perhaps more emphatically in the areas of income stabilization and employment relief) will join the already crowded ranks.

Possibly, however, increasing awareness on the part of benefit implementors as to the various problem areas outlined here will result in some slowing down of the liberalization process and restrain the introduction of new types of benefits until thorough investigation—tailored to the needs of individual managements and unions—has taken place. At the very least, the future demands considerably more research into these areas than has thus far been carried out. And such an omission seems particularly blatant when one realizes that there remain few other aspects of industrial relations that have not been subjected to searching scrutiny. But one must be a pessimist on these scores: Thus far, both the research and any kind of meaningful benefit deceleration have been notably absent.

DISCUSSION QUESTIONS

1. "If there had been no labor unions in this country in the past 30 years or so, the growth of employee benefits would perhaps have been only a small fraction of what it has actually been." Discuss.
2. "It is not the business of the government to protect employee pension interests. ERISA is a classic example of unjustified governmental intervention in private employer–employee matters." Comment fully.
3. "Vacations and holidays are far more important for what they do in the way of job security than for what they do in the area of leisure time." Does this statement seem valid to you? Why or why not?
4. Which set of arguments as expressed in this chapter's section on pensions carries more weight with you: the case *for* contributory plans or the case *against* them?
5. "SUB plans of the type negotiated in the automobile and steel sectors are wholly undesirable. They discourage employees in the incentive to work, replace state unemployment compensation systems, discriminate against the worker not represented by a union, place an undetermined but intolerable burden on management, are financially unsound, and can actually cause permanent unemployment among some workers." In the light of your understanding of the character of these SUB plans, evaluate this statement.

MINICASES

 The Case of Henry Jennings

After Henry R. Jennings, a stockroom employee who only last week celebrated the tenth anniversary of his coming to the Kruger Corporation, hits his supervisor, he is discharged and, having spent his fury in the single blow, he accepts this consequence with understanding.

"I don't know what got into me, Mr. Reilly," he tells the divisional labor relations manager. "But I deserve to be fired and I accept my punishment like a man. Just tell me where I should go to collect my four weeks' vacation pay, though. I'm due it because the collective bargaining agreement here says that 'the standard annual vacation allowance for 10 years and more of continuous active employment is four weeks (20 business days) of vacation.' I don't deserve a recommendation from the company after what I've done, but I am entitled to my vacation money."

Assuming that his reading of the relevant language is accurate and that there is nothing else in writing concerning vacation pay, is he entitled to what he is requesting, or is he not?

 ## The Case of Timmy Aldrich

Exactly one year ago this week, Timothy ("Timmy") Aldrich was hired by the Smedley Bottled Gas Company to come in each Friday afternoon at 2 P.M., following his day of classes as a senior at Andover High School, and spend two hours sweeping out the back rooms of the employer's warehouse.

He now asks Human Resources Vice President Louise Perlmutter where he should go to get his two weeks' vacation pay, for he has decided—he says—to take his paid vacation over the next fortnight. Informed that he is entitled to no vacation at all, much less a paid one, he becomes irate and produces a copy of the labor agreement. From the latter, he reads aloud a provision that says, "All employees shall be entitled to two full weeks of paid vacation after one year of employment." Informed that the language is not applicable to him, he replies, "It says all employees. What do you think I am, the company mascot?"

Would you give Timmy the two weeks' pay?

NOTES

[1]Bureau of National Affairs, *1995 Source Book on Collective Bargaining* (Washington, DC: Bureau of National Affairs, 1995), p. 153.

[2]Except as noted, all statistics in this chapter are based on data furnished by the Bureau of Labor Statistics, U.S. Department of Labor.

[3]*Inland Steel Co. v. United Steelworkers of America*, 336 U.S. 960 (1949).

[4]Bureau of National Affairs, *1999 Source Book on Collective Bargaining* (Washington, DC: Bureau of National Affairs, 1999), pp. 43–44.

[5]*Wall Street Journal*, May 15, 1990, p. A1.

[6]*Wall Street Journal*, January 16, 1990, p. A1.

[7]*Monthly Labor Review*, 102, No. 4 (April 1979), p. 32.

[8]Bureau of National Affairs, *Basic Patterns in Union Contracts*, 14th ed. (Washington, DC: Bureau of National Affairs, 1995), p. 28.

[9]Ibid., p. 29.

[10]*Monthly Labor Review* (September 1964), p. 1014.

[11]James H. Schulz and Guy Carrin, *Pension Aspects of the Economics of Aging: Present and Future Roles of Private Pensions* (Washington, DC: United States Senate Special Committee on Aging, 1970), p. 39.

[12]*Business Week*, September 19, 1994, p. 91.

[13]Bureau of National Affairs, *1999 Source Book on Collective Bargaining* (Washington, DC: Bureau of National Affairs, 1999), p. 45.

[14]Ibid.

[15]*Business Week*, October 25, 1976, p. 116.

[16]*Wall Street Journal*, August 11, 1989, p. B1.

[17]*Time*, September 11, 1989, p. 54.

[18]*The New York Times*, July 9, 1985, p. D2.

[19]Ibid.

[20]Bureau of National Affairs, *1999 Source Book on Collective Bargaining* (Washington, DC: Bureau of National Affairs, 1999), p. 39

[21]Ibid., pp. 41–42.

[22]Bureau of National Affairs, *Grievance Guide*, 8th ed. (Washington, DC: Bureau of National Affairs, 1992), pp. 442–43.

[23]Leland Hazard, "Unionism: Past and Future," *Harvard Business Review* (March–April 1958).

SELECTED REFERENCES

Allen, Everett T., Jr., et al. *Pension Planning*. Homewood, IL: Richard D. Irwin, 1984.

Beam, Burton T., Jr., and John J. McFadden. *Employee Benefits*, 5th ed. New York: Dearborn Financial Publishing, 1998.

Bernstein, Irving. *A Caring Society: The New Deal, the Worker, and the Great Depression*. Boston: Houghton Mifflin, 1985.

Crane, F. G. *Insurance Principles and Practice*, 2nd ed. New York: John Wiley, 1984.

DeCenzo, David A., and Stephen J. Holoviak. *Employee Benefits*. Englewood Cliffs, NJ: Prentice Hall, 1989.

Doeringer, Peter B., ed. *Bridges to Retirement: Older Workers in a Changing Labor Market*. Ithaca, NY: ILR Press, Cornell University, 1990.

Employee Benefit Research Institute. *Fundamentals of Employee Benefit Programs*, 5th ed. Washington, DC: Employee Benefit Research Institute, 1996.

Griffes, Ernest J. E. *Employee Benefit Programs*, 2nd ed. Homewood, IL: Dow Jones-Irwin, 1990.

Ippolito, Richard A. *Pensions, Economics and Public Policy*. Homewood IL: Dow Jones-Irwin, 1986.

Krajcinovic, Ivana. *From Company Doctors to Managed Care: The United Mine Workers' Noble Experiment*. Ithaca, NY: ILR Press, Cornell University, 1997.

MacDonald, Jeffrey A., and Anne Bingham. *Pension Handbook for Union Negotiators*. Washington, DC: Bureau of National Affairs, 1986.

McCaffery, Robert M. *Employee Benefit Programs: A Total Compensation Perspective*. Boston: PWS-Kent, 1988.

Prentice Hall Editorial Staff. *Employee Benefit Plans Under ERISA: Federal Regulations*. Englewood Cliffs, NJ: Prentice Hall, 1985.

Rifkin, Jeremy, and Randy Barber. *The North Will Rise Again: Pensions, Politics and Power in the 1980s*. Boston: Beacon Press, 1980.

Rosenbloom, Jerry S., ed. *The Handbook of Employee Benefits: Design, Funding, and Administration*, 4th ed. Chicago: Irwin Professional Publishing, 1996.

CASE 4

Sick Pay: The Case of the Union Meeting Attendance

Cast of Characters

Lewis	Grievant
Mills	Grievant
Gant	Grievant
Camel	Union Officer
Moore	Jail Superintendent

*Y*ou are the arbitrator in this case. It involves payment to employees who are sick or injured and are unable to work. The compensation is usually called sick or disability pay.

In the typical contractual provision, as demonstrated by the case at hand, employees build up sick pay benefits by working, usually one day per month for each month of service. The amount received would be the same as if the employee had actually been working.

One of the most important, if not the most important, problem in the administration of sick pay provisions constitutes abuse by employees. It is difficult to find data demonstrating the extent of abuse, but it is safe to say that it could be considerable. Since employers pay the benefit out of current revenue, they have a financial motive to curb abuse. In the case at hand, the employer denied sick pay because the employees attended a union meeting on a day for which they claimed payment because of their alleged illnesses.

Abuse comes in a variety of forms, from deliberately faking illness or injury to lesser forms of abuse, such as delaying return to work. For example, in one arbitration case, the employer submitted sufficient evidence to demonstrate that a female employee had delayed her return to work for a few days because she wanted the extra time for spring cleaning of her home. Part of the evidence was the report of an investigator who made a surprise visit to the employee's home. In extreme cases of abuse, the employer will not only deny the benefit but will also discipline the employee, at times with discharge.

In this case, your task is to apply Article XII, Section 17.7, to the circumstances of the case. One Employer argument was that by attending the Union meeting the employees delayed their return to work. A Union contention was that the employees' shift ended at 2:30 P.M., while attendance at the meeting started at 6:30 P.M. On this basis, the Union argued that the Employer had no business interfering with the personal life of its employees. In your quest for a sound decision, you must evaluate each party's argument.

346

CIRCUMSTANCES OF DISPUTE

Attendance at Union Meeting

This case involves denial of sick leave pay to Jail Officers Andy Lewis, Charles Mills, and Clarence Gant because they attended a union meeting on the day for which they claimed such compensation. When the circumstances of this case arose they were assigned to the first shift at the Monroe County Jail, 5:30 A.M. to 2:30 P.M. Before their Monday, January 12, 1991, shift each called the jail stating that he would not report on that shift because of illness.

Lewis called Sunday night, January 11, at 8 P.M., stating that he would not report because he had influenza. On Sunday night at 9:30 P.M. Mills's wife called stating that he would not report for the Monday shift. According to Mills, he had influenza and a sore throat and could not talk. Gant called in sick at about 3 A.M. Monday, January 12. He testified that he had a swollen left leg, a complication from his diabetic condition.

The grievants did not work their tours of duty on Monday, January 12. None went to a physician for treatment of his condition. Despite their claims of illness, the Jail Officers attended a Union meeting, which started that evening at 6:30 P.M. It was held in a back room of the Brass Rail, a bar and grill. According to the grievants, it was a "very important and critical" meeting dealing with shift preference. Union officers had announced the agenda before the session, encouraging all members to attend. In the case of Gant, Sergeant Camel, a union officer, called him on the morning of January 12 to tell him about the importance of the meeting and to ask him to attend if at all possible. Each grievant testified that his illness had improved toward the evening, permitting attendance at the meeting.

Approximately 35 members attended the Union meeting. It lasted between 30 and 45 minutes. At the session, the grievants were seated and raised their hands to vote on the issues involved. Each testified that he went directly home after the meeting and to bed.

On Tuesday, January 13, Lewis and Gant reported for duty and worked the entire shift. Mills did not work Tuesday, testifying that his regular days off were Tuesday and Wednesday in the workweek.

Meetings with Moore

At the time of the events of this case John Moore served as Jail Superintendent, having been promoted to the position in January 1991. Previously he was the Deputy Jail Superintendent. On January 19, he sent each employee a letter dealing with the circumstances of January 12, stating:

> It has come to my attention that on Monday, January 12, 1991 (a regularly scheduled work day for you) you reported that you were sick and then did not work. Additionally I was informed that you attended a meeting at the "Brass Rail" later that same day.
>
> If these circumstances are accurate it appears you may have misused the sick leave policy. I am notifying you in accordance with the agreement and practice at Local 2661 of the Jail Officer's Union. I am also soliciting a response from you for the facts in this case before I proceed.

Subsequently Gant and Lewis responded in writing to Moore's letter of January 19. Mills did not respond, claiming that he did not receive the Jail Superintendent's letter. Moore testified that he either gave Mills the letter or paraphrased its terms in the meeting he had with him on January 26.

On January 22, Moore met with Lewis, who was accompanied by a Union representative. Lewis testified that Moore had told him:

> If I was ill and felt better, I should have reported to duty on January 12 and worked the eight-hour day.*

On January 26, Moore met with Mills, who testified that the Jail Superintendent told him that this was a disciplinary meeting and that I "abused sick time and should have worked January 12." A Union representative was not present at that session. Moore denied that he told Mills the meeting was for disciplinary purposes.

On January 16, Moore met with Gant, who did not have Union representation. Gant related the events of the session this way: Moore told him that he had information that the grievants had attended the Union meeting on January 12. Gant said that his left leg was swollen and painful that day. The condition eased somewhat that evening, and he attended the Union meeting because the issue was crucial. Gant offered to unwrap his leg to show it to the Jail Superintendent. Moore declared that would not be necessary because he [Moore] was familiar with complications resulting from diabetes and did not doubt that Gant's leg caused him considerable discomfort.

Employer Action and Grievance

In letters dated January 26 Moore notified each employee that the Employer had

> added 8 hours of sick time to your accumulated sick time and deducted 8 hours pay.

Each employee was not paid sick leave pay for January 12. Thus, in protest, the Union filed Grievance Number 91-G-9, which stated:

> The union has just become aware the rights of Andy Lewis, Skip Gant, Chuck Mills, and Local 2661 have been violated under section 12 and section 17.7 of the contract. A work day in the contract under section 12.1 is defined as 8–1/2 consecutive hours. It is not 9 hours or anything more but 8–1/2. Under section 17.7 an employee is eligible to use accumulated paid sick time as income protection when he or she is unable to work on a scheduled work day because of personal illness or injury, or a medical appointment. A jail officer is not on 24 hour call and what an employee does on his off time is not the concern of the employer. The union demands the violations cease immediately and that the Grievants be made whole.

Failing to settle the dispute in the Grievance Procedure, the parties convened this arbitration for its determination.

LABOR AGREEMENT

ARTICLE XII—WORK SCHEDULE

Section 12.1

A regular five day work week shall consist of five (5) days of 8–1/2 consecutive hours each which include a roll call period and an unpaid lunch period of thirty minutes per day.

---

*In Lewis's letter to Moore dated January 20, Lewis stated: "At approximately 1600 hours I felt well enough to attend a Union meeting lasting 45 minutes."

Section 17.7 Sick Time Income Protection

Permanent employees accumulate paid sick days at the rate of one (1) day per month for each month of service. An employee is eligible to use accumulated paid sick time as income protection when he is unable to work on a scheduled work day because of personal illness or injury, or a medical appointment.

ISSUE

Under the circumstances of this case, did the employer violate Section 17.7 of the Labor Agreement? If so, what should the remedy be?

POSITIONS OF THE PARTIES

On its behalf, the Employer argues:

> The proper administration of the sick time income provision is a responsibility of the employer. Management has a legitimate concern in preventing abuse or misuse of this provision. In this case, the employer faced a situation wherein three officers of the same shift called in sick. Then all three officers allegedly recovered during the day sufficiently so that they could drive to and from a meeting place, and participate in a meeting. Faced with such facts, a prudent manager would and did conclude that they were ineligible for sick time income protection. (Employer Posthearing Brief, p. 3)

And:

> If an employee is so ill that he is unable to work, then, according to Section 17.7, he should be able to use accumulated sick leave time. However, an employee that is ill has the responsibility to take the steps necessary to recover in a timely fashion. One such important step is to refrain from other activities. Simply stated, if a person is ill, he should remain home and take care of himself. Obviously, necessary trips to the Doctor, the Hospital or the Pharmacy are exceptions. (Employer Posthearing Brief, p. 2)

In addition, argues the Employer, the grievants violated the Twenty-four-Hour Rule by leaving their homes during the day for which they requested sick pay. As Jail Superintendent Moore said in a letter to one of the grievants:

> It is my understanding it is not unreasonable for an employer to expect employees exercising the use of sick time to refrain from personal activities away from home for the *entire* day in which sick time is taken unless the activities are medical ones related to the illness or of an emergency nature. (Emphasis supplied)

On its part, the Union contends that the Employer violated Section 17.7 of the contract, and the grievance should be granted. Among the Union's contentions are these: On January 12, the three (3) grievants were ill, and the Employer presented no objective evidence proving that they were not sick; attendance at the Union meeting was important to all officers, and "their attendance did not delay their return to work"; when they attended the meeting, they were off duty, "the shift ending at 2:30 P.M."; what employees do on their off-duty time is not the business of the Employer. "Free time belongs to the employee, and the Jail should respect that right. In this nation, we have gone far beyond the era of paternalism when employers control the personal lives of the employees."

Finally, the Union argues that the so-called Twenty-four-Hour Rule has no contractual basis and that the Union never agreed to it.

Life Insurance: The Case of the Life-Support System

C A S E

5

Cast of Characters

Dills	Deceased Employee
Mrs. Dills	His Widow
White	Manager of Insurance Benefits
Paul	Director of Industrial Relations
Johns	Union President
Sykes	Union Committeeman

*C*oincidentally, this case arose in the midst of a heated public debate concerning the use of a life-support system to prevent death. Although the arbitrator did not deal directly with that problem, as you will see, the use of a life-support system was a feature of the dispute. The employee, who subsequently died as a result of injuries sustained in an automobile accident, was kept alive for a time by the use of a life-support system. Under the company's insurance policy, double indemnity (twice the amount for natural death) for loss of life resulting from an accident is paid provided that the employee dies within 90 days following the accident.

In this case, the employee died after the 90-day period, and the employer refused to award the widow of the employee the double indemnity benefit. On behalf of the widow, the union carried the case to arbitration, requesting that the arbitrator direct double indemnity despite the 90-day rule.

GRIEVANCE AND LABOR AGREEMENT

Involved in this case is the determination of when an employee's loss of life occurred resulting from an accident for purposes of insurance. On the grounds that his loss of life occurred after the allowable time limits expired for double indemnity under its insurance program, the Company refused to pay the beneficiary of Dills the sum of $9,000. In protest, Dills's widow and the Union filed Grievance Number 27046, dated June 27, 1975, which states:

ART. XIX, PAR. 98

Every employee upon acquiring seniority with the Company will receive a life insurance policy of $9,000 plus A D and D,* provided that the employee remains in active employment. The full premium will be paid by the Company. On 6/2/75

---

*"A D and D" means accidental death and dismemberment.

Dills died from injuries received in an accident. Company refuses to pay accidental death benefit.

As a remedy, the Union requests that the Company pay "Mrs. Dills all monies due."

ISSUE

The basic question to be determined in this dispute is framed as follows: Under the circumstances of this case, did the Company violate Article XIX, Paragraph 98 of the Labor Agreement? If so, what should the remedy be?

BACKGROUND

Death of Dills

Dills was hired by the Company on December 4, 1956. He was assigned as an Inspector in Plant 2 on the second shift. He also served as a Union Steward.

On February 5, 1975, Dills was involved in an automobile accident. He was taken to a hospital, and he eventually died 117 days after the accident. In his death certificate, the cause of death resulted from:

Internal injuries with fractured left ribs, left hemathorax, and ruptured spleen—2-vehicle accident.

While in the hospital, Dills underwent four (4) operations, the last of which took place on April 25, 1975. After the second operation, Dills was placed on a life support system. This system consisted of a respirator to facilitate breathing and to keep his lungs free from fluid; a heart monitor; intravenous feeding, and blood transfusions. For one (1) week, the life-supporting system was removed, but after this week his condition dictated the resumption of the life-support system.

On April 28, 1975, three (3) days following his last operation, Mrs. Dills testified, the attending doctor told her:

He will die. He is a terminal case. Only the life-support system is keeping him alive.

Dills became progressively worse, and despite the life-support system, he died on June 2, 1975.

Ninety-Day Limit

Hoosier Life and Casualty carries the insurance for the Company. Under the accidental death and dismemberment (A D and D) feature of the insurance program, it is stated:

If an employee suffers a nonoccupational bodily injury caused by an accident and as a direct result of such injury and, to the exclusion of all other causes, *sustains within no more than ninety days* after the date of the accident which causes such injury *any of the losses listed* in the Table of Benefits in this section, then, provided:

A. the injury occurs while insurance is in force for the employee under this Title: and

B. the loss resulting from the injury is not excluded from coverage in accordance with Section 2 of this Title:

the Insurance Company shall, subject to the terms of this policy, pay a benefit in the amount provided for such loss in said Table of Benefits but in no case shall more than the Principal Sum be paid for all losses sustained by an employee through any one accident.

Along with the entire insurance program, the A D and D feature, including the 90-day limit, was made known to the employees in a booklet distributed to them. As indicated below, the Union was also aware of the 90-day feature governing A D and D benefits.

Following Dills's death, Mrs. Dills was paid the $9,000 life insurance death benefit. Through the Union, the widow also claimed that she was entitled to an additional $9,000 because her husband's death resulted from an accident. White, Manager of Insurance Benefits, submitted the claim, but it was denied by the Insurance Carrier. Mrs. Dills testified that the carrier denied the claim because Dills's death occurred more than 90 days following the automobile accident.

This arbitration was convened because the Union contends that an additional $9,000 should be paid to Dills's beneficiary on the grounds that his death resulted from an accident. Its chief argument is that the 90-day limitation contained in the insurance policy has no standing under the Labor Agreement since the Labor Agreement, including Paragraph 98, was negotiated between the Union and the Company and not between the Union and the Insurance Carrier. In other words, the Union argument is that the 90-day stricture, relied upon by the Company to deny the accidental death benefit, does not control this dispute because there is no such limitation in Paragraph 98.

NEGOTIATIONS OF 1974 LABOR AGREEMENT

In January 1974, the Parties were in the negotiations that eventually resulted in the adoption of the current Labor Agreement. On January 9, the Union presented the following proposal to the Company:

> Under A D & D it is proposed that if medical treatment begins prior to the ninety (90)-day period for the injury incurred, that it would not waive the right of collection of the principal sums listed, if loss occurs after the ninety (90)-day period. Also refer to proposal #29. (Anywhere 90-day appears—rewrite.)

On April 24, 1974, while discussing the 90-day limitation in question, the following exchange took place between Paul, Director of Industrial Relations; Johns, Union President; and Sykes, Union Committeeman:

Paul: All through here, Charlie, I have forgotten how many references you people made to—90 days. I would say there was something like 8 to 10 places. Just guessing off the top of my head. Talking about the 90 days on A D & D and that type of thing. I went over this in quite some detail with the guys in Insurance. This is pretty much standard language. In almost all your insurance policies.

Johns: It might be standard language. But it looks like if somebody was to die and they need 90 days afterward or the fact they was to have to take an arm off, or something like that. It all has to be done within 90 days or they don't get it.

Paul: That's right—that's exactly true. If you had 120 days, it would be the same damn problem.

Sykes: No, Marv. You take now—say a man has got his arm all messed up and hell, they're operating on it and operating on it, trying to save that arm. Now you're putting a burden on that man there, saying it gets up to 89 days and say, "Hell, hack it off." If he's got any chance at all you know they're gonna keep working on that arm. It may be . . .

Paul: I think you're going for outside choices. I can't recall, in my brief tenure here, that we've had that happen.

Sykes: We had it on a guy's eye. It came up, and he thought they were going to take it out. I don't know right now how he stands. But it was going over 90 days and they were talking about taking it out after 90 days.

Paul: But, really, this thing . . .

Johns: We've got two of them. Page is about to lose his eye—about 120 days after—from a nail. Then also Goodwine, he got carbide in his eye and they had several operations on it and there's a chance he might lose it.

Paul: This is pretty much standard. This 90-day thing is all the way through your entire program.

Johns: Well, what we're saying here is, if treatment starts before the 90 days period . . .

Paul: I know what you're saying. But we've talked about it quite a lot and the consensus is that you got to stay with something so you might as well stay with the standard clause, which we've got and which is preferable among everybody else.

In any event, the Company did not agree to the Union's proposal as cited above. It rejected the Union demand that the 90-day limitation would not count if the loss of life, sight, or limbs occurred after that time period provided that medical treatment started within the 90-day period. On June 19, 1974, the current Labor Agreement became effective, and contained Paragraph 98 as cited earlier. This provision appeared in the previous Labor Agreement in its current form except that the life insurance benefit was raised to $9,000 from $7,500. In addition, the Company continued to use the same Insurance Carrier, and the policy contained the 90-day limitation for loss of life, sight, or limbs resulting from an accident.

ANALYSIS OF THE EVIDENCE

Union Position: Paragraph 98 Controls Dispute

According to the Union, Paragraph 98 establishes the merits of the claim in an unambiguous manner. It urges further that the 90-day limitation contained in the insurance policy is solely between the Company and the Insurance Carrier and may not be used to apply Paragraph 98. It argues:

We contend that the insurance contract is not incorporated in Paragraph 98. Any provision of the insurance policy is not binding upon the Union. It may not be used to undermine the unambiguous language of Paragraph 98. The Labor Agreement is determinative and not the insurance policy which is a contract between the Company and the Insurance Carrier. Paragraph 98 says the Company shall pay the benefit. There is no ambiguity in Paragraph 98. It is clear. It says the Company will pay the benefit. It does not say the Insurance Carrier will pay the benefit.

As a matter of fact, the Union, with vigor, argues that the Arbitrator should base his decision strictly on the language of Paragraph 98. It says that evidence submitted by the Company is not material and should not be given any weight. Included in this category are the 1974 negotiations that resulted in the instant Labor Agreement, previous administration of the A D and D program,* and the booklet distributed to employees explaining the insurance program. To buttress its position, the Union refers to an arbitration decision, dated December 15, 1972, involving the Parties, rendered by Arbitrator Kess. In that case, the issue involved the application of that portion of the Labor Agreement (not Paragraph 98) that deals with weekly benefits for employees who are absent from work because of accident or illness. While granting the grievance, Arbitrator Kess observed that the controlling contractual language was "clear and unambiguous." In addition, he relied on the Union argument that the insurance policy between the Company and the Insurance Carrier was not incorporated in that area of the Labor Agreement involved in this case.

Character of Paragraph 98

It is self-evident, of course, that Paragraph 98 is an agreement reached solely by the Parties. As the Union says, the Insurance Carrier and the policy under which benefits are paid are not expressly mentioned in the provision. To this extent, the Union agreement has merit—the Company and the Union reached the agreement contained in Paragraph 98, and this agreement is solely between them and not between the Union and the Insurance Carrier. Thus, the Union is on sound ground when it argues that Paragraph 98 should govern the dispute. If there is a conflict between the language of the provision and the contract executed by the Company and the Insurance Carrier, any such conflict should be resolved in favor of the language contained in Paragraph 98.

On the other hand, the Union argument breaks down because Paragraph 98 is not written in unambiguous terms as it relates to the dispute at hand. The provision is clear to the extent that each employee acquiring seniority will be covered by a $9,000 life insurance policy. It also is clear that the Company will pay the premium. However, what about benefits for accidental death and dismemberment? Paragraph 98 says that each employee will be covered by a life insurance policy "plus A D and D." It does not specify the amount of any such benefit, and it does not spell out the circumstances under which such a benefit will be paid. In addition, the provision is silent as to when loss of life, limbs, or sight must occur following an accident for the benefit to be paid.

Union Counsel argues that Paragraph 98 does not say that loss of life must occur within ninety days of an accident for the accident death benefit (double indemnity) to be paid. This is true. However, it is equally true that Paragraph 98 does not specify that such a benefit will be paid regardless of when loss of life occurs following an accident.

---

*The Company submitted two instances demonstrating that 50 percent of the principal sum was paid to two (2) employees who each lost the sight of one eye. It points out that this benefit was paid under the insurance policy, and stresses further that Paragraph 98 does not provide for a specific amount of benefit for accidental death, dismemberment, or loss of sight. Hence, the Company argues that the insurance policy is incorporated into Paragraph 98.

In short, for purposes of this case, Paragraph 98 is ambiguous and unclear. Indeed, for the Union position to prevail solely on the basis of contractual language, Paragraph 98 would have to say unambiguously and unequivocally that the accidental death benefit shall be paid "regardless of when death occurs following an accident." It obviously does not say that, and Paragraph 98 by reasonable inference simply cannot be held to mean what the Union would like it to mean. Thus, the position of the Union may not prevail solely on the basis of the language of Paragraph 98. As to the material issue involved in this dispute—when loss of life must occur following an accident for accidental death benefit eligibility—the provision is obviously not clear at all. For this reason, the Kess decision does not stand as a valid precedent. Not only did the dispute arbitrated by Kess arise under a different provision of the Labor Agreement, but, what is equally important, Kess held that the controlling language in his case was clear and unambiguous. In this case, it is incontrovertible that Paragraph 98 is not written in unambiguous terms as it relates to the instant dispute. To hold that the language is clear beyond reasonable doubt as to the material issue would be a masterpiece of error.

Union Recognition of Ninety-Day Limit

It would likewise be a most grievous error for the Arbitrator to find that the Union and the employees are not bound by the 90-day limit contained in the policy in effect between the Company and the Insurance Carrier. True, the Insurance Carrier is not a party to Paragraph 98. As mentioned earlier, Paragraph 98 is a contractual provision negotiated by the Parties. It was not negotiated between the Union and the Insurance Carrier.

Despite these considerations, *the evidence is incontrovertible that the Union recognized that the 90-day limit contained in the insurance policy is incorporated into Paragraph 98.* The best evidence for this conclusion is the fact that the Union attempted unsuccessfully to broaden the 90-day limit. In his argument, Union Counsel says that the negotiations do not count and should not be given any weight. He argues that under the *parol-evidence* rule what was proposed, discussed, and rejected in negotiations should not prejudice the Union's position. Such an argument would have merit if Paragraph 98 were written in clear-cut and unambiguous terms as it relates to the material issue in this case. Under these circumstances, the events of the 1974 negotiations would not count and would not prejudice the Union's case. Under the parol-evidence rule, what was proposed, discussed, and rejected may not properly be held to vary *unambiguous* contractual language. As abundantly demonstrated, however, Paragraph 98 is ambiguous as it relates to the circumstances of this dispute.

Since it is ambiguous and uncertain, the events of the 1974 negotiations are squarely material to the application of Paragraph 98. In those negotiations the Union endeavored to change the 90-day limit. It demanded that the 90-day limit not apply if medical treatment were obtained within the 90-day period. That is, if medical treatment were administered to an employee within the 90-day period, the employee would be eligible for A D and D benefits regardless of when loss of life, limbs, or sight would occur. Indeed, if the Union really believed that the 90-day limit did not apply to Paragraph 98, why in the world did it make such a proposal? Common sense alone tells us that the Union made this proposal because it recognized that A D and D benefits are not paid when loss of life, limbs, or sight occurs after 90 days following an accident. In short, the Union was fully aware of the limit.

The Company rejected the Union's demand, and Paragraph 98 remains in the current Labor Agreement as it appeared in previous contracts except for the increase of the principal benefit.

That the Union knew what the 90-day limit was all about is made crystal clear in the exchange between the Company and Union representatives in the 1974 negotiations. This entire exchange was cited earlier in this Opinion. In any event recall the following:

> **Johns:** But it looks like if somebody was to die and they need 90 days afterward or the fact that if they was to have to take an arm off, or something like that. It all has to be done within 90 days or they don't get it.
>
> **Paul:** *That's right—that's exactly true.* (Emphasis added)

In other words, the 90-day limit is a part of Paragraph 98. The Union knew it and tried without success to change it. Union Counsel cautions the Arbitrator that he would commit the cardinal sin of arbitrators if he were to read the 90-day limit into the provision. To the contrary, the conduct of the Union in the 1974 negotiations proves conclusively that it recognized the 90-day limit. *That is why it tried to remove the stricture in the 1974 negotiations.* The Arbitrator does not inject into Paragraph 98 the 90-day limit. It was there before the Arbitrator was called upon to decide this dispute. He does not read into the provision a restriction that was not previously recognized by the Union.

In light of these observations, the Arbitrator finds that Paragraph 98 contains the 90-day limit, which is in the insurance policy. Though not expressly mentioned in the provision, one would have to shut one's eyes to the clearest and most incontrovertible evidence that the Union was fully aware that the 90-day limit is incorporated into the provision.

In short, the Arbitrator regards Paragraph 98 as if it expressly contained the stricture found in the insurance policy. The limitation on the payment of accidental death benefits is this: *Loss of life caused by accident must occur within 90 days after the date of accident.*

Meaning of "Loss of Life" under Paragraph 98

It should logically follow, therefore, that the grievance should be denied. Dills's accident occurred on February 5, 1975, and he did not die until 117 days later. His death certificate was executed on June 2, 1975. Though his loss of life was caused by an accident, he died beyond the 90-day limit. Understandably, the Company argues:

> The Union has failed to prove that the Company violated the contract by not paying an additional $9,000 to the widow of employee Dills.
>
> The Union acknowledged, by virtue of their proposal submitted to the Company during the negotiations that they recognized the 90-day limitation in A D & D and wished to broaden this limitation . . .
>
> It is very evident and clear that the Union is attempting to obtain in this arbitration proceeding what it could not obtain at the bargaining table of negotiations in the formulation of this labor agreement.

In other words, since the Union failed to broaden the 90-day limit, and since Dills died after the 90-day limit, the Company requests that the grievance should be denied.

Without question, Dills died on June 2, 1975. The death certificate was executed on that date. It was not, of course, executed within the 90-day limit. On these grounds, the grievance should have no standing under Paragraph 98. The fact that the Insurance Carrier denied the claim is additional proof that for purposes of Paragraph 98 Dills died after the 90-day limit.

What is involved here, however, is the construction of the term *loss of life* as contained in the A D and D feature of the insurance program. It says that in the "event of loss of life" the benefit will be the principal sum of the life insurance policy. At the risk of inviting understandable censure by the Company, the Arbitrator construes Dills's "loss of life" for purposes of Paragraph 98 as of April 28, 1975, which was within the 90-day period. On this date, the uncontested evidence demonstrates that the medical authorities said that Dills had no chance to live. Uncontested evidence demonstrates that "life" was prolonged beyond that date by a life-support system. For all practical purposes, Dills's life expired as a human being on April 28. If the life-support system of Dills had been taken away, he would have officially died before the 90-day period expired. Only by the use of the life-support system did he linger until June 2, 1975.

For purposes of Paragraph 98, "life" means more than being maintained as a vegetable by a life-support system. "Life" means that the person can function as a human being and has a reasonable chance for recovery. We should not believe in miracles, and no miracle occurred in this case. Medical authority said that Dills had absolutely no chance to recover, and he did die as predicted. Only by the use of a life-support system did he technically "live" until after the 90 days had expired. In other words, the Company places an unrealistic construction on the term *life* under the circumstances of this case. For all realistic purposes, Dills for purposes of Paragraph 98 lost his life as of April 28, 1975. For these reasons, the Arbitrator shall grant the grievance.

CONCLUSIONS

Having reached this conclusion under the circumstances of this case, the Arbitrator cautions all concerned not to read too much into his decision. He does not write into Paragraph 98 the proposal that the Union unsuccessfully attempted to advance in the 1974 contract negotiations. The 90-day limit still applies for purposes of Paragraph 98. That is, loss of life, sight, or limbs must occur within 90 days following an accident. Nothing in this decision is intended to undermine the integrity of the 90-day limit.

Put succinctly, the Arbitrator grants this grievance solely and exclusively because of the particular circumstances of this case: Dills effectively and realistically lost his life within the 90-day period. He was maintained beyond this time by a life-support system. Beyond this, the Arbitrator establishes no precedent and makes no exception to the 90-day limit. As a result of the narrow set of facts under which the Arbitrator has applied Paragraph 98 in this particular case, the Union, of course, does not gain in arbitration what it failed to achieve in contract negotiations. What is at stake in this case is exclusively the Arbitrator's construction of "loss of life" under its particular facts and circumstances. This is the full and only extent of the Arbitrator's decision to grant the grievance.

If the Union believes that the 90-day limit is unfair and unrealistic, it must change it in collective bargaining and not in arbitration. Nothing the Arbitrator has said in this case removes the 90-day limit for the purpose of the application of

Paragraph 98. All that the Arbitrator has said in this case is that for purposes of Paragraph 98 Dills lost his life effective on April 28, 1975. On that date, the 90-day limit had not expired.

Questions

1. Why did the arbitrator find that the 90-day rule is incorporated into Paragraph 98 though it does not appear in the express language of the provision?
2. Was the arbitrator's decision to award the widow double indemnity consistent with his finding that the 90-day rule was incorporated into Paragraph 98? Defend your position with cogent arguments.
3. Assume that an employee injures his hand, and after 90 days the hand is amputated. To what extent would the arbitrator's decision in this case stand as a valid precedent for the employee's claim that he should be indemnified for the loss of the hand?
4. Why did the arbitrator hold that the employee lost his life within 90 days for insurance purposes following the accident even though he died on the 117th day?

Institutional Issues under

Collective Bargaining

*L*abor contracts contain a variety of issues that do not fall into the general category of wages or economic supplements. They deal with the rights and duties of the employer, the union, and the employees themselves. Some of them—such as seniority and discharge—directly serve to protect the job rights of workers and might be most appropriately thought of as "administrative" concerns. These will be treated in such a manner in Chapter 10.

Other subjects, however, tend to supply the institutional needs of either the labor organization or the particular management—through "compulsory union membership" clauses, for example, or by provisions explicitly allowing the management the right to make decisions for the direction of the labor force and the operation of the plant. These matters will be dealt with in the paragraphs that follow in this chapter.

This institutional dimension of collective bargaining can on occasion give the negotiators considerably more trouble than do the wage or benefit issues. It is, for example, at times infinitely easier to compromise and settle a health care controversy than to resolve a heated difference of opinion as to whether a worker should be compelled to join a union as a condition of employment. For all the thorniness of many wage and benefit issues, some of the longest and most bitter individual strikes have had as their source conflicts dealing with the institutional issues of collective bargaining.

UNION MEMBERSHIP AS A CONDITION OF EMPLOYMENT

Prior to the passage of the Wagner Act in 1935, there was essentially only one way in which a union could get itself recognized by an unsympathetic management: through the use of raw economic strength. If the labor organization succeeded in pulling all or a significant part of the employees out on strike, or in having its membership boycott the production or services of the employer in the marketplace, it stood a good chance of forcing the employer to come to terms. Lacking such economic strength, however, the union had no recourse—even if all the organization's workers wanted to join it—in the face of management opposition to its presence.

The 1935 legislation, as we know, greatly improved the lot of the union in this regard. It provided for a secret-ballot election by the employees, should the employer express doubt as to the union's majority status. It also gave the union the exclusive right to bargain for all workers in the designated bargaining unit, should the election prove that it did indeed have majority support. As Chapter 3 has indicated, these new ground rules for union recognition continue to this day.

Legally fostered recognition has not been synonymous with any assured status for the union as an institution, however. In fact, in the many years since the Wagner Act, unions have still been able to find three grounds for insecurity. For one, the law has given the recognized labor organization no guarantee that it could not be dislodged by a rival union at some later date. For a second, there have still been many communication avenues open to antagonistic employers who choose to make known to their employees their antiunion feelings in an attempt to rid themselves of certified unions after a designated interval following the signing of the initial contract. And for a third, the government has not granted recognized unions protection against **free riders**—employees who choose to remain outside the union and thus gain the benefits of unionism without in any way helping to pay for those benefits.

Under the law, the union clearly has not only the right but also the *obligation* to represent all employees in the bargaining unit, regardless of their membership or nonmembership in the union. Unions have particularly feared that the free-rider attitude could become contagious, resulting in the loss through a subsequent election (in which nonmembers as well as members can vote) of their majority status and thus of their representation rights.

Consequently, organized labor has turned to its own bargaining table efforts in an attempt to gain a further measure of institutional security. By and large, such attempts have been successful. Today, about 82 percent of all contracts contain some kind of "union security" provision.[1]

FORMS OF UNION SECURITY

Such provisions, which are frequently also referred to as "compulsory union membership" devices, essentially are three in number: the closed shop, the union shop, and the maintenance-of-membership arrangement. Brief reference has already been made to each. A common denominator to all is that in one way or another membership in the union is made a condition of employment for at least some workers. They differ, however, in the timing for the requirement of union membership and in the degree of freedom of choice allowed the worker in the decision about joining the labor organization.

The closed shop and union shop are dissimilar in that, under the former, the worker must belong to the union *before* obtaining a job, whereas the latter requires union membership within a certain time period *after* the worker is hired. Under a maintenance-of-membership arrangement, the worker is free to elect whether or not to join the union. The worker who does join, however, must maintain membership in the union for the duration of the contract period or else forfeit the job.

These forms of compulsory union membership can also be viewed as differing with respect to the freedom of the employer to hire workers. Under the closed shop, the employer must hire only union members. This constraint allows the union in effect to serve as the employment agency in most situations and to refer workers to the employer upon request. Under union shop and maintenance-of-membership arrangements, the employer has free access to the labor market. The employer may hire whomever it wants, and the union security provision becomes operative only after the worker is employed.

A final significant feature of union security is that it has received considerable attention from both Congress and the state legislatures. The laws these bodies have enacted must be taken into account at the bargaining table, and union security provisions that disregard these relevant public fiats do so only at a definite risk.

The **closed shop**, obviously the most advantageous arrangement from labor's point of view, appeared in 33 percent of the nation's agreements in 1946. Prohibited for interstate commerce by the Taft-Hartley Act of 1947, it visibly decreased in its frequency in the years thereafter, and less than 5 percent of all contracts today contain such a provision. Many of these are in intrastate commerce, of course, but some are in the construction industry on an interstate basis. Much of the latter sector refused, rather bluntly, to abide by the Taft-Hartley stricture and in fact openly flouted it until 1959, when the Landrum-Griffin Act recognized the special characteristics of that sector and officially allowed it a stronger form of union security that approximates the closed shop.

With the decrease in usage of the closed shop, the **union shop** became the most widespread form of union membership employment condition. After being part of only 17 percent of all contracts in 1946, it appeared in about 64 percent of all labor agreements in 1959, and the figure is at about the 73 percent level today.

The **maintenance-of-membership** arrangement, originating in the abnormal labor market days of World War II, is still fully legal but is utilized relatively infrequently. After appearing in about one-quarter of all contracts in 1946, it steadily lost ground thereafter, and only about 4 percent of all contracts now make provision for it. Much of the loss has undoubtedly been absorbed by the gains of the union shop, which maintenance-of-membership employers, having already taken this step toward accommodating the union, have rarely resisted very adamantly. (But some of *this* loss, in turn, is not entirely real: Some arrangements have adopted the name of "union shop" but been modified in practice to equate or nearly equate to maintenance-of-membership. There is sometimes a danger in taking things at face value.)

Two other brands of union security, neither at all common, constitute compromises between the union's goal of greatest possible security and the management's reluctance to grant such institutional status. Under the **agency shop**, nonunion members of the bargaining unit must make a regular financial contribution—usually the equivalent of the union dues—to the labor organization, but no one is compelled to join the union. The money is, in fact, at times donated to recognized charitable organizations. Nonetheless, the incentive for a worker to remain in the free-rider class is clearly reduced in this situation, and the union thus gains some measure of protection. The **preferential shop** gives union members preference in hiring but allows the employment of nonunionists, and its value seems to depend on how the parties construe the word *preference*.

Although the straight union shop appears to be the most popular form of union security, some employers and unions have negotiated variations of this species of compulsory union membership. Under some contracts, employees who are not union members when the union shop agreement becomes effective are not required to join the union. Some agreements exempt employees with comparatively long service with the organization. Under other contracts, old employees (only) are permitted to withdraw from the union at the expiration of the agreement without forfeiting their jobs. Under this arrangement, a so-called escape period of about 15 days is included in the labor contract. If an employee does not terminate union membership within the escape period, he or she must maintain membership under the new arrangement. Newly hired workers, however, are required to join the union.

Whether the straight union shop or modifications of it are negotiated, Taft-Hartley forbids an arrangement that compels a worker to join a union as a condition of employment unless 30 days have elapsed from the effective date of the contract or the beginning of employment, whichever is later. In administering this section of the law, the National Labor Relations Board has held that the 30-day grace period does not apply to employees who are already members of the union. However, it interprets the provision literally for workers who are not union members on the effective date of the contract or who are subsequently employed. Thus, in one case, a union shop arrangement was declared unlawful because it required workers to join the union 29 days following the beginning of employment. Another union security arrangement was held to be illegal because it compelled employees to join the union if they had been on the company's payroll 30 or more days; in invalidating this agreement, the board ruled that it violated the law because it did not accord employees subject to its coverage the legal 30-day grace period for becoming union members *after the effective date* of the contract.

Where some negotiators have adopted variations of the straight union shop, others have devised a number of alternatives to the maintenance-of-membership arrangement. Only at the termination of the agreement are employees under most maintenance-of-membership arrangements permitted to withdraw from the union without forfeiting their jobs, and usually only a 15-day period is provided at the end of the contract period, during which time the employee may terminate union membership. But many agreements have a considerably less liberal period of withdrawal, from the worker's viewpoint, and some contracts allow more than 15 days. If an employee fails to withdraw during this "escape" time, the worker must almost invariably remain in the union for the duration of the new collective bargaining agreement.

Under some labor agreements, maintenance-of-membership arrangements also provide for an escape period after the *signing* of the agreement, to permit withdrawals of existing members from the union. Other agreements do not afford this opportunity to current members of the union but restrict the principle of voluntary withdrawal to newly hired workers.

These modifications are fully consistent with the law in all but the 21 "right-to-work" states, which ban any form of compulsory union membership, but certain other arrangements are not. Reference has already been made to the terms of Taft-Hartley under which an employee cannot lawfully be discharged from a job because of loss of union membership unless the employee loses the membership because of nonpayment of dues or initiation fees. In spite of the existence of an arrangement requiring union membership as a condition of employment, expulsion from a union for any reason other than nonpayment of dues or initiation fees *cannot* result in loss of employment. The National Labor Relations Board will order the reinstatement of an employee to his or her former job with back pay where this feature of the law is violated. Depending on the circumstances of a particular case, the board will require the employer or the union, or both, to pay back wages to such an employee.

The board has, in fact, applied a literal interpretation to this feature of Taft-Hartley. In one case the board held that a worker actually does not have to join a union even though a union shop arrangement may be in existence.[2] The employee's only obligation under the law is the willingness to tender the dues and initiation fees required by the union. In this case, three workers were willing to pay their union dues and initiation fees but they refused to assume any other union-related obligations, or even to attend the union meeting at which they would be voted upon and accepted. As a result, the union had secured the discharge of these workers under the terms of the union security arrangement included in the labor agreement. The board held that the discharge of workers under such circumstances violated the Taft-Hartley law, ruled that both the union and the company engaged in unfair labor practices, and ordered the workers reinstated in their jobs with full back pay.

❖ Right-to-Work Laws

The right-to-work laws themselves, of course, serve as formidable obstacles to union security arrangements in the primarily southern and western states in which they remain on the books. The labor movement in these states does not have much political muscle because union membership there is very low. On the other hand, not only has the effect of the right-to-work laws on labor relations in these states been highly debatable, but twice in the post Taft-Hartley years, U.S. Congress has come relatively close to repealing the relevant Taft-Hartley section permitting the enactment of such state laws (**Section 14b**): In 1965–1966, a repeal measure passed the House by a 20-vote margin and, although a filibuster in the Senate prevented the bill from being voted upon there, the AFL-CIO claimed that 56 Senate votes, or five more than the majority needed, would have been registered in favor of repeal had there *been* a vote. In 1977, too, the AFL-CIO was quite certain that a newly elected liberal Democratic Congress would rescind Section 14b, although this time labor's efforts were—to the surprise of many observers—tabled by both branches. And although there was at the time of this writing little likelihood that the repeal efforts would soon be resumed on Capitol Hill, it was a safe bet that ultimately they would be.

Were Congress to remove Section 14b, this action would nullify all right-to-work laws as far as these laws apply to interstate commerce, because of the **federal preemption doctrine**, which forbids states to pass laws in conflict with a federal statute. And in that event the right-to-work laws existing in Alabama, Arizona, Arkansas, Florida, Georgia, Idaho, Iowa, Kansas, Louisiana, Mississippi, Nebraska, Nevada, North Carolina, North Dakota, South Carolina, South Dakota, Tennessee, Texas, Utah, Virginia, and Wyoming would have application only in the area of intrastate commerce. They would cease to have any effect on firms engaged in interstate dealings. (Exhibit 9-1 shows all of the 21 states currently involved, and also the tendency of these states to be in the Southeast, the Southwest, and the Plains areas of the country.)

EXHIBIT 9-1

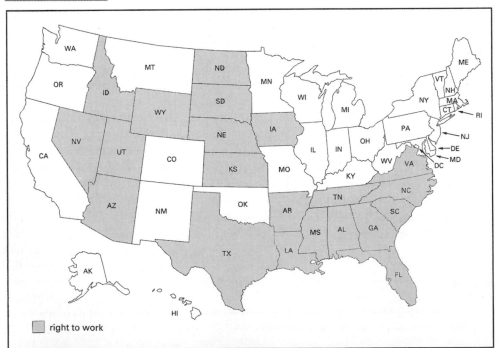

 right to work

SOURCE: Michael R. Carroll, Norbert F. Elbert, and Robert D. Hatfield, *Human Resource Management*, 5th ed. (Englewood Cliffs, NJ: Prentice Hall, 1995), p. 646.

In the other direction, there was also a strong chance as this edition approached publication that several states would be battlegrounds for new right-to-work laws. Until 1986, when Idaho became the twenty-first right-to-work state, no state had passed such a law since 1976, when Louisiana did so. But many right-to-work advocates were optimistic about near-term prospects for antiunion shop legislation in New Mexico, Oklahoma, and Montana. And there was even an outside chance as this was being written that Pennsylvania, Illinois, Michigan, Ohio, and Wisconsin— states whose unionized percentages of the workforce were greater than the national average—would have right-to-work laws on *their* books within a matter of an election year or so. If any of them in fact did, new ground would be broken in the sense of a northern industrial state's joining the right-to-work states' roster: Indiana, which can fairly also be called a northern industrial state, did have such legislation between 1957 and 1965 but repealed it in the latter year, the only state ever to throw out a right-to-work law after installing it. New Hampshire, certainly northern and increasingly industrial, was viewed by many observers in the 1990s as another potential groundbreaker, but right-to-work advocates in the Granite State suffered defeat in both of these years when their legislative efforts twice fell short of passage in the New Hampshire House of Representatives. They also, nonetheless, remained optimistic about the future.

Nor were the forces seeking these new right-to-work laws exactly poverty-stricken. The National Right to Work Committee, based in Fairfax, Virginia, by some estimates now receives $10 million in annual contributions (and sends out approximately 25 million letters to and on behalf of its 1.7 million individual and institutional members). Some of the money goes to such relatively broader projects as attacks on public-sector unionism and investigations into what the organization sees as the spread of prounion materials into public schools, and the committee recently pushed hard if unsuccessfully for a congressional bill that would make the committing of violence on picket lines punishable by up to 20 years in prison and a $10,000 fine. But most of the group's money is directed to the key item on the committee's agenda, the advance of the right-to-work movement itself.

Regardless of the fate of right-to-work legislation, however, it seems very likely that the question of whether union security provisions should be negotiated in labor agreements will remain a controversial one for some time to come—among the general public and some direct parties to collective bargaining if not among the large segment of unionized industry that has already granted such union security.

This controversy actually contains three major elements: morality, labor relations stability, and power. Whether it is *morally* right to force an employee to join a union in order to be able to work is not an easy issue to resolve. Unions and supporters of unionism often argue that it is not "fair" to permit an employee to benefit from collective bargaining without paying dues, given the fact that the union must under the law represent all workers in the bargaining unit. And the argument is not without logic. Improvements obtained in collective bargaining *do* benefit nonunion members as well as union-member employees, and the union *is* compelled by law to represent nonunion bargaining unit employees, even in the grievance procedure, in the same fashion that it represents union members. Against this argument stands the equally plausible one that employees should not be forced to join a union in order to work. Such compulsion seems to many people to be undemocratic, immoral, and unjust. Almost everyone, however, has different ideas on what is morally correct in this controversy. Even the clergy has been drawn into the fight, and its members have exhibited the same lack of unanimity in their opinions as have other people. And if these stewards of God are not certain what is morally correct, how can two college professors writing a textbook make a judgment that will once and for all resolve the moral issue?

Congress itself, however, has now made a judgment as to what employees should appropriately do when they have bona fide religious beliefs against joining labor organizations or financially supporting them. In a 1980 amendment to Taft-Hartley, it decreed that such workers need not violate those beliefs. Instead, in something of a variation of the agency shop, they must make a contribution equal to the amount of the dues to a nonlabor, nonreligious charity. The amendment also provides that if the religious objector requests a labor organization to handle a grievance on his or her behalf, the union may charge the employee a "reasonable" amount for such servicing.

Some observers claim that union security is the key to *stability in labor relations*. They argue that a union that operates under a union-shop arrangement will be more responsible and judicious in the handling of grievances and in other day-to-day relations with its employers because of its guaranteed status. And, again, there is some strength to this argument. At times, conflict between union members and nonunion employees does hamper effective organizational operation, and on this basis some employers may welcome an arrangement that forces all employees to join the union, as a way of precluding such conflicts. Moreover, unions can also claim that in the absence of a union security provision, the union officers must spend considerable time in organizing the unorganized and keeping the organized content so that they will not drop out of the union. Proponents of this position justifiably declare that if union officers are relieved from this organizational chore, they can spend their time in more constructive ways, which will be beneficial not only to the employees but also to the employer.

On the other hand, other debaters point out with equal justification that unions that do enjoy a union security arrangement sometimes use this extra time to find new ways to harass the employer. The solution to this particular controversy appears to an outsider to depend upon the character of the union involved and upon its relationship with the employer. Clearly, no one would blame an employer for resisting the granting of the union shop to a union that had traditionally made outrageous demands at the bargaining table, continually pressed grievances that had no merit, and, in short, sought to harass management at every turn.

At times, finally, employers and unions themselves argue along morality and labor relations lines to conceal a different purpose—their respective desires for *power* in the bargaining relationship. It is self-evident that the union does have more comparative influence in the negotiation of labor agreements and in its day-to-day relationship with the employer when it operates under a union shop. And, by the same token, the employer has more comparative influence when employees need not join the union to work and may terminate their membership at any time. Or, in short, the parties may speak in terms of morality merely as a smoke screen to conceal an equally logical but less euphemistic power issue.

But *power* still remains a rather nebulous term. The old saying that in poker a Smith and Wesson beats four aces is certainly true and lucidly pinpoints exactly where the power lies, and why. However, as a general statement, depending on the assumptions one makes, a union could have infinitely more power than a management, and the reverse would be true under a different set of assumptions and circumstances. Given this elusiveness, as well as the unhappy connotations often placed on the word, it is perhaps not surprising that the verbal controversy over union security continues to be waged along the other lines described as well as those of power.

THE CHECKOFF

Checkoff arrangements are included in the large majority of collective bargaining contracts. This dues-collection method, whereby the employer agrees to deduct from the employee's pay monthly union dues (and in some cases also initiation fees, fines, and special assessments) for transmittal to the union, has obvious advantages for labor organizations, not only in terms of time and money savings but also because it further strengthens the union's institutional status. For the same reasons, many managers are not enthusiastic about the checkoff, although some have preferred it to the constant visits of union dues-collectors to the workplace. Once willing to grant the union shop, however, employers have rarely made a major bargaining issue of the checkoff per se. And the growth of this mechanism has been remarkably consistent with that of the union security measure: Where in 1946 about 40 percent of all labor agreements provided for the checkoff system of dues collection, this figure is, as we know, somewhat over 95 percent today.

Taft-Hartley, as was also pointed out earlier, regulates the checkoff as well as union security; under the law, the checkoff is lawful only on written authorization of the individual employee. And the employee's written authorization may be irrevocable for only one year or for the duration of the contract, whichever is shorter.

Checkoff provisions frequently deal with matters other than the specification of items that the management agrees to deduct. Some arrangements specify a maximum deduction that the employer will check off in any one month, require each employee to sign a new authorization card in the event that dues are increased, indemnify the management against any liability for action taken in reliance upon authorization cards submitted by the union, require the union to reimburse the employer for any illegal deductions, and provide that the union share in the expense of collecting dues through the checkoff method. Not all these items, of course, appear in each and every checkoff arrangement; many labor agreements, however, contain one or more of them.

The checkoff is an important issue of collective bargaining, but understandably it does not normally constitute a crucial point of controversy between employers and unions. It does not contain the features of conflicting philosophy that are involved in the union security problem, falls far short of other problems of collective bargaining as a vexatious issue, and has rarely by itself become a major strike issue, since the stakes are not that high. As a matter of fact, even though the checkoff serves the institutional needs of the union, employers often find some gain from the incorporation of the device in the agreement. This would be particularly true where the labor contract contains a union security arrangement. Not only does the checkoff eliminate the previously noted need of dues collection on the employer's premises, with the attendant impact upon orderly operations, but it also avoids the need of starting the discharge process for employees who are negligent in the payment of dues. Frequently, without a checkoff, an employee who must belong to a union as a condition of employment will delay paying dues, and the employer and union are both faced with the task of instituting the discharge process, which is most commonly suspended when the employee, faced with loss of employment, pays the owed dues at the last possible minute. The checkoff eliminates the need for this wasted and time-consuming effort on the part of busy employer and union representatives.

Even when the union shop is not in effect, moreover, the checkoff need not necessarily be given permanent status. The employee is obligated to pay dues for one year only, and if he or she desires to stop the checkoff it is possible to do so during the escape period. But under any circumstances, if the management believes that the union with which it deals is so irresponsible as not to deserve the checkoff, it need not agree to it as part of the renegotiated contract, and the mechanism is, consequently, also revocable from the employer's point of view.

UNION OBLIGATIONS

The typical collective bargaining contract contains one or more provisions (such as those listed in Exhibit 9-2, drawn from a current contract between the Oil, Chemical and Atomic Workers and a medium-sized chemical company) that establish certain obligations on the part of the labor organization. By far the most important of these obligations involves the pledge of a union that it will not strike during the life of the labor agreement. Most employers will, in fact, refuse to sign a collec-

---

EXHIBIT 9-2

<table>
<tr><td colspan="1" align="center">**ARTICLE 2**</td></tr>
</table>

Section 3. No Strike—No Lockout

(1) During the life of this Agreement there shall be no strike, work stoppage, slowdown, nor any other interruption of work by the Union or its members, and there shall be no lockout by the Company. In the event of a violation of this provision, either party to the Agreement may seek relief under the Grievance and Arbitration provisions of the Agreement or may pursue his remedy before the court or the Labor Board, as the case may be.

(2) As an alternative, either party, in the event of an alleged or asserted breach of the no strike—no lockout clause, may institute expedited arbitration by telegram to the Federal Mediation and Conciliation Service and request that the FMCS designate an Arbitrator as quickly as possible. The Arbitrator shall hold the hearing as promptly as possible, notice to be served on any officer of the Company and on the President, Vice President or Secretary-Treasurer of the Union (any one of the three officers of the Union). The Arbitrator shall set the date, time and place of hearing and shall issue his award orally as soon after the completion of the hearing as possible.

(3) Individual employees or groups of employees who adopt methods other than those provided in the grievance procedure for the settlement of their grievances shall be subject to disciplinary action, including discharge. Any disciplinary action taken by the Company under this clause shall be subject to review under the grievance procedure.

(4) Should any dispute arise between the Company and the Union, or between the Company and any employee or employees, the Union will cooperate to prevent and/or terminate a work stoppage or suspension of work or a slowdown on the part of the employees on account of such dispute. A violation of this paragraph by any employee or group of employees will give the Company the right to administer discipline including discharge. In administering discipline, including discharge, the Company shall have the right to distinguish between those instigating or leading the work stoppage or suspension of work or slowdown and those who simply participate therein. Any disciplinary action taken by the Company under this clause shall be subject to review under the grievance procedure.

tive bargaining contract unless the union agrees that it will not interrupt operations during the effective contractual period.

The incorporation of a **no-strike clause** in a labor agreement means that all disputes relating to the interpretation and the application of a labor agreement are to be resolved through the grievance and arbitration procedure in an orderly and peaceful manner and not through industrial warfare. The pledge of the union not to strike during the contract period stabilizes industrial relations and thereby protects the interests of the employer, the union, and the employees. Indeed, a chief advantage that employers obtain from the collective bargaining process is the assurance that the organization will operate free from strikes or other forms of interruption (slowdowns, for example) during the period of the agreement.

Managements and unions have negotiated two major forms of no-strike provisions. Under one category, there is an *absolute and unconditional* surrender on the part of the union of its right to strike or otherwise to interfere with operations during the life of the labor agreement. The union agrees that it will not strike for any purpose or under any circumstances. Employers, of course, obtain maximum security against strikes from this provision.

Under the second major form, the union can use the strike only under certain *limited* circumstances. For example, in the automobile industry the union may strike against company-imposed production standards. Such strikes may not take place, however, before all attempts are made in the grievance procedure to negotiate production standard complaints. Other collective bargaining contracts provide that unions can strike for any purpose during the contract period but only after the entire grievance procedure has been exhausted, when the employer refuses to abide by an arbitrator's decision, or when a deadlock occurs during a wage-reopening negotiation. The union cannot strike under any other conditions for the length of the contract.

In the vast majority of cases, labor organizations fulfill their no-strike obligations just as most unionized employers fulfill all their contractually delineated responsibilities. However, in the event that violations do take place, employers have available to them a series of remedies. In the first place, under the terms of Taft-Hartley, they can sue unions for violations of collective bargaining contracts in the U.S. district courts. And, although judgments obtained in such court proceedings may be assessed only against the labor organization and not against individual union members, additional remedies are provided for in many collective bargaining contracts. Under some of them, strikes called by a labor union in violation of a no-strike pledge terminate the entire collective bargaining contract. In others, the checkoff and any agreement requiring membership as a condition of employment are suspended.

In addition, the employer may elect to seek penalties against the instigators and the active participants, or either group, in such a strike. Many contracts clearly provide that employees actively participating in a strike during the life of a collective bargaining contract are subject to discharge, suspension, loss of seniority rights, or termination of other benefits under the contract, including vacation and holiday pay. The right of an employer to discharge workers participating in such strikes has been upheld by the Supreme Court.

And arbitrators will usually sustain the right of employers to discharge or otherwise discipline workers who instigate or actively participate in an unlawful strike or slowdown. Such decisions are based on the principle that the inclusion of a no-strike clause in a labor agreement serves as the device to stabilize labor relations during the contract period and as a pledge to resolve all disputes arising under the contract through the grievance procedure.

In 1970, the Supreme Court provided employers with a powerful legal weapon to deal with strikes that violate a no-strike clause. The high court, in *Boys Markets* v. *Retail Clerks*,[3] held that, when a contract incorporates a no-strike agreement and an arbitration procedure, a federal court may issue an injunction to terminate the strike. This decision permits employers to go into court to force employees back to work when a labor agreement contains these features. The idea behind the decision is that the grievance procedure and arbitration should be used to settle disputes that arise during the course of a collective bargaining contract.

❖ Wildcat Strikes

At times, however, strikes and other interruptions that are not authorized by the labor organization do occur. These work stoppages, commonly known as **wildcat strikes,** are instigated by a group of workers, sometimes including union officers, without the sanction of the labor union. Under many labor agreements, the employer has the right to discharge such employees or to penalize them otherwise for such activities. At times in the past employers imposed a stiffer penalty on local union officers, including stewards and grievance committee persons, than on rank-and-file employees who committed the same offense. Disparate discipline was justified, they thought, because union officials had a greater obligation to comply and enforce the no-strike clause. In a 1983 case, however, the U.S. Supreme Court held that employers may not impose more severe discipline on union officials who commit the same offense as rank-and-file employees.[4] If both, for example, instigate a wildcat strike, engage in picketing, or encourage other employees to join the strike, an employer may not discharge the union officials while only suspending the rank-and-file employees. Should a management desire to penalize union officials more severely, it must negotiate a contract provision that specifically authorizes disparate treatment by placing special obligations on the officials. It is not likely, however, that many unions would agree to such a contractual provision.

A special problem has been created by Taft-Hartley in reference to wildcat strikes. Under this law, a labor union is responsible for the action of agents even though the union does not authorize or ratify such conduct.[5] Thus, an employer may sue a union because of a wildcat strike even though the union does not in any way condone the stoppage. As a result of this state of affairs, unions and employers have negotiated the so-called nonsuability clauses which were mentioned in Chapter 3. Under these arrangements, the management agrees that it will not sue a labor union because of wildcat strikes, provided that the union fulfills its obligation to terminate the work stoppage. Frequently, the labor contract specifies exactly what the union must do in order to free itself from the possibility of damage suits. Thus, in some contracts containing nonsuability clauses, the union agrees to announce orally and in writing that it disavows the strike, to order the workers back to their jobs, and to refuse any form of strike relief to the participants in such work stoppages.

❖ Other Strike Considerations

Other features of some contracts also deal with strike situations. Under many labor agreements, the union agrees that it will protect the employer's property during strikes. To accomplish this objective, the union typically promises to cooperate with the management in the orderly cessation of operations and the shutting down of machinery. In addition, some unions agree to facilitate the proper maintenance of machinery during strikes even if achieving this objective requires the employment of certain bargaining unit maintenance personnel during the strike. Nor is it uncommon for unions to agree in the labor contract that management and supervisory personnel entering and leaving the premises in a strike situation will not be interfered with by the labor organization.

❖ Other Union Obligations and Constraints

Many contracts place other obligations upon unions, not relating to strikes and slowdowns. Under some agreements, for example, the union obligates itself not to conduct on the employer's time or property *any* union activities that will interfere with efficient operations. The outstanding exception to this rule, however, involves the handling of grievances: Meetings of union and employer representatives that deal directly with grievance administration are usually conducted on employer time. Some agreements also permit union officials to collect dues on employer property where the checkoff is not in existence. Another exception found in many contracts involves the permission given to employees and union officers to discuss union business or to solicit union membership during lunch and rest periods.

Another frequently encountered limitation of union activity on the employer's property involves restrictions of visits by representatives of the international union with which the local is affiliated. Still another denies unions permission to post notices on the premises or to use employer bulletin boards without the permission of the employer. Where the union is allowed to use bulletin boards, many labor contracts specify the character of notices that the union may post; notices are permitted, for example, only when they pertain to union meetings and social affairs, union appointments and elections, reports of union committees, and rulings of the international union. Specifically prohibited on many occasions are notices that are controversial, propagandist, or political in nature.

MANAGERIAL PREROGATIVES

Once upon a time, a vice president for industrial relations of a large corporation was bargaining against a strike deadline with only hours to spare and making no progress whatsoever. The parties remained poles apart, and the executive—not an especially calm person to start with—was approaching the condition of a nervous wreck.

Suddenly, a messenger informed him that his wife, nine months pregnant, had been taken to the hospital, and the union (which had not to that point shown itself to be particularly accommodating) in no way argued with his suggestion that he make a quick trip to see her. At his wife's bedside, a strange contrast could be seen: The baby had not yet arrived, and his wife, though in considerable pain, was amazingly calm and composed; he, however, was more of a nervous wreck than ever.

The industrial relations man asked the nurse to explain his wife's commendable placidity and was told, "It must be that wonderful new tranquilizer that she's been given: Twilight Zone." The executive said, "Great! Great! Give me some, too! Give me some, too!" The nurse responded, "I'm sorry, sir, but that's only for labor." And the executive replied, "My God! Is there nothing left for management?"

That collective bargaining is in many ways synonymous with limitations on managerial authority is an observation that was offered on the earliest pages of this book. A fundamental characteristic of the process is restriction on the power of the management to make decisions in the area of employer–employee relations, and much of the controversy about collective bargaining grows out of this factor. On the one hand, the labor union seeks to limit the authority of management to make decisions when it believes that such restrictions will serve the interests of its members or will tend to satisfy the institutional needs of the union itself. On the other hand, the responsibility for efficiency in operation of the enterprise rests with management. The reason for the existence of management, in fact, is the overall administration of the business, and executives attempt to retain free from limitations those functions that they believe are indispensable to this end.

The problem is, moreover, hardly disposed of simply because most union leaders assert—and normally, in good faith—that they have no intention of interfering with the "proper functions of management." Years of witnessing official union interest expand from the historical wages and hours context into such newer areas as those outlined in this portion of the book have understandably led managers to conclude that what is "proper" for the union depends on the situation and the values of the union membership.

Nor do employers find much consolation in the fact that the managerial decision-making process is already limited and modified by such economic forces as labor market conditions, by such laws as those pertaining to minimum wages and discrimination, and by the employee-oriented spirit of our society. If unionism is not by any means the only restriction on employer freedom of action in the personnel sphere, it is nonetheless a highly important one for managements whose employees live under a union contract.

Beyond this, finally, the controversy is hardly confined to the personnel area, for managers can point to numerous (although proportionately infrequent) instances of strong union interest in such relatively removed fields as finance, plant location, pricing, and other "proper" management functions. In recent years, for example, some railroad unions have constantly blamed their employers' high degree of bonded indebtedness for depriving railroad workers of "adequate" wage increases; legal representatives of the Ladies' Garment Workers as well as those of several other unions have become familiar faces in courtrooms, to protest plant relocations of their union's employers; and the United Automobile Workers' interest in the pricing of cars is now all but taken for granted in automobile industry bargaining rooms (although the UAW's freely offered advice on this subject has yet to be accepted by the automobile manufacturers). Given the present state of the government's "legal duty to bargain" provisions, as Chapter 3 has indicated, no one can assert with complete confidence that such examples will not multiply in the years ahead.

In many ways, in fact, ramifications of the subject extend far beyond the two parties to collective bargaining. There is justification for arguing that the "managerial rights" issue really pivots upon the broader question of what the appropriate function of labor unions in the life of our nation should be.

Managements have frequently translated their own thoughts on the subject into concrete action. Approximately 80 percent of all labor agreements today contain clauses that explicitly recognize certain stipulated types of decisions as being "vested exclusively in the management." Such clauses are commonly called **"management prerogative," "management rights,"** or (more appropriately, to many managers) **"management security"** clauses.

Fairly typical of management prerogative provisions is the following, culled from the current agreement of a large midwestern durable goods manufacturer:

> Subject to the provisions of this agreement, the management of the business and of the plants and the direction of the working forces, including but not limited to the right to direct, plan, and control plant operations and to establish and to change work schedules, to hire, promote, demote, transfer, suspend, discipline, or discharge employees for cause or to relieve from duty employees because of lack of work or for other legitimate reasons, to introduce new and improved methods or facilities, to determine the products to be handled, produced, or manufactured, to determine the schedules of production and the methods, processes, and the means of production, to make shop rules and regulations not inconsistent with this agreement and to manage the plants in the traditional manner, is vested exclusively in the Company. Nothing in this agreement shall be deemed to limit the Company in any way in the exercise of the regular and customary functions of management.

Some rights clauses, by way of contrast, limit themselves to short, general statements. These are much more readable than the one above, but considerably less specific—for example, "the right to manage the plant and to direct the work forces and operations of the plant, subject to the limitations of this Agreement, is exclusively vested in, and retained by, the Company." On the other hand, the management rights clause cited is itself a model of brevity when compared with that of at least one of its counterparts: The current agreement between the Kuhlman Electric Company of Detroit and the UAW contains one that consumes over a dozen pages; it is, as one observer commented when it was originally inserted in a prior contract, a "likely candidate for the *Guinness Book of Records*.[6]

No matter which way management injects such clauses into the contract, however, two industrial relations truisms must also be appreciated: (1) The power of the rights clause is always subject to qualification by the wording of every other clause in the labor agreement; and (2) consistent administrative practices on the part of the management must implement the rights clause if it is to stand up before an arbitrator.

❖ The Residual Theory of Management Rights

According to one point of view, moreover, the inclusion of such a clause in a labor agreement is unnecessary, and, of course, a sizable minority of the agreements does not make any reference to managerial rights. This practice of omission is often based on the belief that the employer retains all rights of management that are not relinquished, modified, or eliminated by the contract. In the absence of collective bargaining, according to this view, the management has the power to make any decision in the area of labor relations that it desires (subject to considerations of law, the marketplace, and so on). This right is based on the simple fact that the employer is the owner of the business. For example, the employer's right to promote, demote, lay off, make overtime assignments, and rehire may be limited by the seniority provisions of the collective bargaining contract. Or the contract may stipulate that layoffs be based on a certain formula. However, to the extent that such a formula does not limit the right of the employer to lay off, it follows that management may exercise this function on a unilateral basis. *(Cases 6 and 7 deal with management rights.)*

This concept of management prerogatives is sometimes called the ***residual theory* of management rights**. That is, all rights reside in management except those that are limited by the labor agreement or conditioned by a past practice. Where a management embraces the residual theory, it most commonly takes a stiff attitude at the bargaining table relative to union demands that would tend to further limit rights of management. It views the collective bargaining process as a tug of war between the management and the union—management resisting further invasions by the union into the citadel of management rights, which are to be protected at all costs as a matter of principle.

Such employers are not particularly concerned with the merits of a union demand; *any* demand that would impose additional limitations on management must be resisted. For example, such a management, regardless of the merits of a particular claim, would typically resist the incorporation of working rules into the labor agreement—rules dealing with such topics as payment to employees for work not actually performed, limitations on technological change or other innovations in the operation of the business, the amount of production an employee must turn out to hold a job, and how many workers are required to perform a job. One can also safely predict that a residualist management would strongly resist any demand that would limit its right to move an operation from one plant to another, shut down one plant of a multiple-plant operation, subcontract work, or compel employees to work overtime. In addition, such a management would quite probably try aggressively, when the occasion seemed appropriate, to regain rights that it had previously relinquished.

Today, in fact, many employers are striving to reclaim the right to make unilateral determinations of working rules. Many recent strikes in a host of sectors as diverse as the airlines, television, and teaching have been waged because managements desired to erase from the bargaining relationship working rules to which they had agreed in previous years. It is understandable why labor organizations resist these attempts of management: With the elimination of working rules, employees could more easily be laid off, for example. Since new technology and changing market demands constitute in many relationships constant threats to job security, it is no mystery why some unions would rather strike than concede on this point.

❖ The Trusteeship Theory of Management Rights

The opposing view of the theory of residual rights is based on the idea that management has responsibilities other than to the maximization of managerial authority. It proceeds from the proposition that management is the "trustee" of the interests of employees, the union, and society, as well as of the interests of the business, the stockholders, and the management hierarchy. Under the *trusteeship theory*, a management would invariably be willing to discuss and negotiate a union demand on the merits of the case rather than reject it out of hand because it would impose additional limitations on organizational operations. Such an employer would not necessarily agree to additional limitations but would be completely amenable to discussing, consulting, and ultimately negotiating with the union on any demand that the latter might bring up at a collective bargaining session. The trusteeship management does not take the position that the line separating management rights from that of negotiable issues is fixed and not subject to change. Rather, it attempts to balance the rights of all concerned with the goal of arriving at a solution that would be most mutually satisfactory. As such, the trusteeship and residual theories are poles apart in terms of management's attitude at the bargaining table and even in the day-to-day relationship between the employer and the union.

There is no "divine right" concept of management in the trusteeship theory, a statement that cannot be made for the residualist camp. No better summary of the differences between the two theories on this score has ever been made than that offered many years ago by the then–general counsel of the United Steelworkers of America:

> Too many spokesmen for management assume that labor's rights are not steeped in past practice or tradition but are limited strictly to those specified in a contract; while management's rights are all-inclusive except as specifically taken away by a specific clause in a labor agreement. Labor always had many inherent rights, such as the right to strike; the right to organize despite interference from management, police powers, and even courts; the right to a fair share of the company's income even though this right was often denied; the right to safe, healthful working conditions with adequate opportunity for rest. Collective bargaining does not establish some hitherto nonexisting rights; it provides the power to enforce rights of labor which the labor movement was dedicated to long before the institution of arbitration had become so widely practiced in labor relations.[7]

It is impossible to determine how many employers follow the residual theory of management rights and how many follow the trusteeship theory. Crosscurrents are clearly at work: the previously mentioned management attempt to regain work-rule flexibility and the equally visible trend to more employee-centered management that was described in Chapter 1. Trusteeship managements, however, from all of the evidence definitely do remain in the distinct minority. Moreover, there is no universal truth as to which would be a better policy for management to follow or whether some compromise between the two might form the optimum arrangement. The answer to this problem must be determined by each employer in light of the particular labor relations environment.

CODETERMINATION AND UNIONS IN THE BOARDROOM

The concept of workers' *directly* playing a major role in corporate decision making by means of board of director membership, or **codetermination** as it is generally called, has never taken root in the United States. At least to date, American labor leadership has preferred to oppose rather than to join in any kind of partnership with management, and the official AFL-CIO position has been one of not desiring "to blur in any way the distinctions between the respective roles of management and labor in the plant." Managers act; unions react.

Yet in other countries codetermination has become a reality, most notably in Germany, where in 1946 the occupying British administrators in the Ruhr Valley introduced the idea to the West German steel industry as something of a compromise between nationalization and free enterprise. It was extended to the coal industry in that country in 1951 and—in the face of concerted union pressure magnified by the threat of a general strike—to larger companies in all German industries one year later.

Even in Germany employees have not received literal codetermination powers in the typical situation. Only in steel and coal, the original frontiers, have stockholders and workers controlled an identical number of directors; in all other sectors workers were legally allowed only a one-third representation on corporate boards until 1976, and they still, under a complicated formula, lack fully equal representation in practice. But after more than five decades even executives in Germany seem to be wholly adjusted to the concept. They are, indeed, cooperating—as are their unions—in helping other European countries (Sweden and Denmark most notably) experiment with it, being in the main convinced that Germany's economic prosperity and generally peaceful labor relations owe something to the idea.

Why codetermination has nonetheless been as welcome to U.S. business managers as a drunkard at an Alcoholics Anonymous meeting, and not of much interest to American unionists either, can undoubtedly be explained along several lines. Western European workers, as a general rule, have historically lacked the prospects for upward mobility that their American counterparts have had and thus have had greater incentive to improve their present working environments, because they feel more tied to these. And in the United States, the values of private enterprise, property rights, and individualism have been developed to a degree absolutely unknown in other lands. Against this backdrop, codetermination seems dangerously socialistic. Nor can the general resistance of U.S. employers throughout labor history to unionizing efforts be completely overlooked as an explanation. On such adversarial initial relationships are adversarial later relationships often built.

Yet even in the United States the situation may finally be changing. In 1980, the Chrysler Corporation gave the then—UAW president Douglas A. Fraser one of the 18 seats on its board of directors. And the impressive performance that he registered in the several years following this milestone, the first instance of a major American corporation's electing a union leader to such a position, had led at least some observers to predict that the future would see more such union directors.

Chrysler had not offered Fraser, despite his universal reputation as a man of considerable intellect and unimpeachable character, this seat with any notable enthusiasm. It had done so quite reluctantly, in fact, as part of the price that it had to pay to win from the UAW economic concessions vital to its survival. And even within Chrysler's managerial hierarchy itself, many people had undoubtedly shared the sentiments of General Motors Chairman Thomas A. Murphy that the move would make "as much sense as having a member of GM's management sitting on the board of an international union."[8] Nor did Fraser's acceptance of the directorship, his considerable popularity within the union notwithstanding, occur without a good deal of negative comment from his own constituents: The word *sell-out* received particularly frequent mention from the UAW rank and file. Some other critics—among them, law professors—feared that a conflict of interest on Fraser's part was unavoidable, since the interests of the shareholders and those of the union would inevitably operate, at times, in opposing directions.

Within months of the UAW leader's advent to the board, however, all of these sentiments appeared to have been groundless. Chrysler itself could muster nothing but praise for Fraser's contributions, especially his ability to ask pointed, well-informed questions: "He has," corporation Chairman Lee Iacocca could assert, "stimulated our board to think."[9] Another company insider declared that "Doug [can] speak with credibility to the workers because, as a director, he [has] seen the detailed financial data."[10] And there was general agreement among all who saw Fraser in action that the UAW leader, who temporarily suspended his participation in the board meetings when UAW members in Canada struck Chrysler in late 1982, had been flawless in avoiding not only any conflict of interest but even the appearance of such conflict.

By his own admission, Fraser's chief objective in accepting the board seat had been to incorporate worker thinking into managerial decision making. ("I can't represent my members if I'm always reacting to management decisions," he had said, "... we can bring an important resource to the board. People in the plants will tell me things they won't tell management").[11] When he retired four years later, to be succeeded on the board by his successor as UAW president—Owen W. Bieber—his board tenure as judged by this standard had clearly been a successful one. Iacocca had in fact come to have so much respect for Fraser that despite the latter's retirement from the union, the Chrysler chief executive reportedly tried, without success, to keep him on as a director instead of Bieber.

And to some extent, the favorable precedent set by Fraser had generated interest in duplicating such union participation elsewhere. By the time of this writing the now-defunct Pan American World Airways and Eastern Airlines (where, as noted earlier, not one but four board of director seats were filled by union nominees), Trans World Airlines, USX, Inland Steel, LTV, Northwest Airlines, Weirton Steel, and even the giant UAL Corporation (the parent company of United Airlines) had followed Chrysler's lead in electing union-proposed directors. Almost every major aluminum company had done so, most of them in response to union demands in the later 1990s. So, too, had a variety of smaller trucking, steel, and food industry employers. Companies in other industries—rubber and communications, most notably—were seriously studying the board membership idea and appeared on the verge of implementing it. Most of these companies had, moreover, also accompanied their bestowal of board membership with a transfer of stock ownership into bargaining unit member hands (discussed in the next section).

But most American companies, nonetheless, remain adamantly opposed to such union activities. "The pure and simple notion of opening the books and being a member of the board is a cure for which there is no known illness," one not atypical company negotiator has said.[12] And many managers also continue to advance the argument, presumably in all sincerity, that having a unionist on the board would expose the corporation to lawsuits for conflict of interest, Fraser's performance notwithstanding. Moreover, it is not irrelevant that virtually every employer that has granted unions the greater privileges has been, as Chrysler, confronted with significant financial problems at the time of the offering and has sought some kind of union pay concession in return. Nor does any reputable authority in the field see anything that remotely resembles full German-style codetermination in the United States as being closer than several million light-years away.

Nor, ironically, has Chrysler itself been steadily wedded to the concept of having a U.S. labor leader sit on its board in the years since 1980. In 1991, the automobile company cut its number of directors from 18 to 13 by not renominating Bieber and four others. The company defended its move as part of its then-current $3 billion cost-cutting campaign, although detached observers (who realized that the most that would be saved in annual directors' fees and expenses was a relatively modest $150,000) thought that the action was an unnecessarily gratuitous insult to a unionist who simply hadn't measured up to the high Fraser standard. (Bieber at least began a new tradition: After he retired in 1995 as UAW president, Chrysler's interest in *his* successor, the tough-talking Stephen P. Yokich, as a member of the board was equally invisible.)

And although, in 1998, the UAW finally was allowed to return to the board, the employer was no longer officially Chrysler. It had become DaimlerChrysler through a merger that year between the German automotive giant Daimler-Benz and itself, and the American union hardly came away with massive clout on the new 20-seat board: German labor got, as it was entitled to do under existing legislation in Germany, 10 board seats and even the single UAW seat was due exclusively to an agreement by the German metalworker union IG Metall to give up one of *its* allotted seats, and not to any particular desire for the arrangement on the part of the American component of the new management.

Yet some thoughtful students of the subject were in the last years of the twentieth century starting to believe that the concept of unionists in the boardroom would spread. They pointed, of course, to the U. S. managements that *had* accepted unionists in the years following the landmark Fraser appointment. Some also saw such moves as logical trade-offs for financially troubled corporations (as a way of gaining greater economic cooperation from the unions involved), as a means of broadening corporate social responsibility not unlike the appointment of women and minorities to boards, and as a method of getting unions to more fully appreciate employer problems and need for profitability.

It seems safe to say, under any conditions, that whether or not the Fraser precedent ever becomes a normal part of American corporate governance, the topic can never again really be ignored.

EMPLOYEE STOCK OWNERSHIP PLANS

Employee stock ownership plans, or ESOPs, have their share of enthusiastic supporters. Such supporters did not, however, until very recent years, include union leaders. Until the mid-1970s, organized labor was generally against the concept, but by the 1990s many unions were actively participating in ESOPs.

Labor's historical antagonism to employee ownership tended to be based on two considerations. First, many past plans—most notably in the paternalistic era of the 1920s—had a definitely antilabor purpose. If the worker could be given more reason to identify with the management, it was reasoned by plan advocates, there would be less need to identify with management's bargaining table adversary.

Second, labor was—and is—well aware that a major decline in the price of the company stock would carry with it obvious penalties for the participating employee. Such major declines did, of course, occur on a wholesale basis in the 1930s (as did, even worse, bankruptcies) and presumably could be expected to occur again. Postdepression employee stock ownership plans were, therefore, in union eyes something like lexicographer Samuel Johnson's description of a second marriage, the triumph of hope over experience.

Such misgivings continue to be nursed by unions. But increasingly since the mid-1970s they have been outweighed, at least for many labor leaders, by another consideration: Many hard-pressed employers have simply been unwilling to allow further increases in fixed payroll expenses and have refused to consider anything but compensation that is tied to the firm's economic performance. Labor has, in short, embraced ESOPs because it has had little choice.

Board representation—costless to the employer economically, if not philosophically—has usually been accompanied by such stock ownership. And, in fact, most companies cited in the previous section have, as noted, granted both. Employees currently own 55 percent of the stock at UAL Corporation, 45 percent at TWA, about 37.5 percent at Northwest Airlines, and some 15 percent at the U.S. operations of DaimlerChrysler. At Weirton Steel, they own literally all of the company, the

8,000 workers there having been forced in 1984 by Weirton's then-parent National Steel either to buy it or let it die a natural death. ("We had to buy the mill. It was either that or nothing," in the words of one mill worker.)[13]

But board representation is hardly an inseparable part of an ESOP, and many more unionized employers—in steel, autos, rubber, glass, trucking, the airlines, and food—have granted only the latter than have given both kinds of concession to their unions. As of mid-1999, some 11,000 companies—many of them unionized—had placed a meaningful percentage of their stock shares in the hands of their employees, but only a relative handful had allowed employee representatives on their boards. Typical of a large ESOP organization is Avis, whose 13,500 employees bought the company in 1987 for $1.75 billion but have yet to acquire either board seats or voting rights.

Actually, many employers have seen a variety of advantages for themselves in the ESOP beyond the reduction of wage pressures and often have needed very little if any prodding before installing it. Under the Employee Retirement Income Security Act of 1974 and the 1975 enactment of a further congressional sweetener, significant tax benefits are allowed employers who implement ESOPs. And the plans can help capital-intensive companies raise vast amounts of money cheaply: Even if the provisions of the ESOP let workers buy their shares at some kind of discount, a not uncommon situation, the monies involved are still usually far less than managements would have to pay a bank or, in the case of floating debt issues, less than the underwriting costs. Moreover, as the median age of employees rises markedly, the cost of pension plans is bound to climb and ESOPs become a relatively more desirable way for organizations to help their employees develop some kind of supplemental savings plan.

In an era of corporate takeovers, ESOPs can also both finance takeover attempts and frustrate them, depending upon which goal is embraced: Investors trying to take over can decrease their costs of borrowing if part of the stock is reserved for employees; but raiders can also be thwarted by using the ESOP device to put a portion of the company into presumably friendly hands. Nor can management's long-held belief that when workers have an ownership interest they may well have an incentive to put forth extra effort be ignored in explaining why companies have warmed to the ESOP concept. Unionized employees—as well as nonunion workers—have not necessarily had their stock forced upon them, but unions that have indicated a willingness to accept an ESOP in lieu of a wage improvement have generally found a ready audience on the other side of the bargaining table. A good deal of the notable growth in ESOPs since 1975—from a mere 200 plans then to the above-noted total of 11,000 by 1999, with the over 10 million participating workers typically owning from 15 to 35 percent of the company's stock—has been due to the concessionary bargaining of unions in this area and management's favorable response as far as employee stock ownership has been concerned.

As in the case of union board membership, fears of a potential conflict of interest have accompanied the growth of labor–management ESOPs. "Some observers and many international labor officials worry," as one expert has pointed out, "that worker [representatives] may be co-opted, getting caught up in the predominant interest to make company profits rather than fight for individual worker rights." He sees, with or without board representation, "a dangerous potential for stock ownership . . . to lead to a type of in-house unionism, in which there is the appearance of a . . . battle, when in reality, labor representatives are simply going through the motions of conflict for political reasons."[14]

Against this consideration, however, can be stacked the very real fact that the new arrangement has already shown that it can improve the level of corporate efficiency. At one leading airline, for example, within a year of the ESOP's implementation, the productivity of that carrier's mechanics was increasing at an annual rate of 5 percent. ("There is a tremendous dynamic for employees to run a better company and provide the best service," the union president involved could comment with obvious pride, "because they're owners now.") Similar performances have been registered in parts of the steel, trucking and food industries, while Avis seems to be trying even harder with its ESOP to overtake first-place Hertz in market share and has recorded considerably higher profit-sales ratios than its arch competitor in most of the years since it sold the company to the workers.

On the other hand, major worker ownership has yet to rescue Rath, which continues to have as many financial problems as ever, or a host of other poverty-stricken ESOP workplaces. New Jersey's Hyatt Clark Industries, a ball-bearing maker that its workers bought from General Motors in 1981 in a buy-or-die situation, died six years later, its widely heralded ESOP notwithstanding. Nor at the time of this writing did workers at the large brokerage firm Thomson McKinnon (where 77 percent of the shares are owned through ESOPs), retailer Carter Hawley Hale (about 45 percent employee owned), or Burlington Industries (49 percent until a controversial public offering by the North Carolina company diluted this employee portion to 3 percent not long ago) have much optimism that their barely solvent firms would ultimately return to them any of the nonfunded, uninsured ESOP monies on which they had once counted for their retirements. And at Weirton Steel, in the many years since the employees bought 100 percent of that operation, notwithstanding a series of sizable wage and job cuts, the company has almost continually been in a precarious financial situation.

For that matter, even in the once-happy Avis and UAL organizations, all was not sweetness and light at the time of this writing, either. Avis workers, one-third of them represented by the Teamsters, had been quite outspoken in complaining about their lack of board seats and voting rights, something to which they thought that their 100 percent membership entitled them. And at United Airlines the 55 percent that the employees bought in 1994 by paying a staggering $4.9 billion in concessions was now scheduled to end and the workers were reluctant to make any more concessions to renew the arrangement: Enough, they thought, was enough.

Again, as in the case of unions in the boardroom, it could be said with certainty only that the ESOP even in its relative infancy as a labor relations topic was something that the parties could never again entirely overlook.

QUALITY OF WORK LIFE PROGRAMS

Still something else that may be changing in labor–management relationships is the historic unwillingness of both parties to allow joint worker and management problem solving of workplace problems. An increasing number of unions, either on their own initiative or on the employer's, have become involved in so-called **quality of work life** (QWL) activities, denoting a movement whose title has no fully acceptable simple definition but basically connotes direct participation by workers in day-to-day decision making on the job. Most often, employees get a voice in work scheduling, quality control, compensation, a determination of the job environment itself, and/or other significant working factors. The goal is a twofold one: increased productivity and improved union–management relations.

It is impossible to know how many organizations currently have such programs, since not only is there no formalized record keeping but many QWL programs go by some other name—"employee involvement," "jointness," or "worker participation," for example. The list of unionized users even now, a mere two decades after the first major implementation, is nonetheless impressive. All of the nation's automobile manufacturers have a QWL program, most notably General Motors, which has one in each of 66 plants, and Ford, where thousands of worker–management teams at 86 of that company's 91 locations meet every week to attack production and quality problems; Westinghouse has worker–management "quality circles," small groups that meet regularly to discuss product quality improvement, in 50 facilities (63 such groups are in its Baltimore defense complex alone); the major steelmakers have a variety of "labor–management participation committees"; and every Bell System company is experimenting with QWL principles. Programs have also been installed in coal mining and retail food.

General Electric, which for years resisted the concept, rapidly implemented it in the last years of the 1980s, and an estimated 40 percent of the unionized GE workforce was included in QWL arrangements by the late 1990s. The list of unionized employers with QWL efforts very much in place now also includes, among literally hundreds of others, Boeing, Caterpillar, the U.S. Postal Service, the Philadelphia Zoo, the New York City Sanitation Department, and Levi Strauss.

Many nonunion organizations have had such worker involvement efforts for years, often with the thought that such projects might help preserve nonunion status by improving employee morale. But unions have almost unanimously opposed the idea, partly because of fear that membership loyalty to the labor organization might be weakened by closer exposure to management and partly because of a suspicion (often fully justified) that the concept (as in the case of ESOPs) constituted a direct effort on the employer's part to pave the way for ultimate nonunion status. ("You've got to put up or shut up," one union chief executive told a group of major industrial leaders a while ago on this subject. "You can't ask unions to walk hand in hand into the unknown land of worker participation while going full speed ahead with union-bashing antilabor programs. There has to be a greater acceptance of unions in this country. I want very much to cooperate in consensus-building and problem-solving, but management can't expect cooperation when the hand it puts around my shoulder has a knife in it."[15]) Many unions still take a dim view of worker participation. (Exhibits 9-3 and 9-4, illustratively, constitute something less than a resounding endorsement on the part of the United Mine Workers.) And such developments as the NLRB's 1992 *Electromation* ruling (the board decision, discussed in Chapter 3, that a nonunion company's "action committees" composed of both rank-and-file employees and managers were illegal employer-dominated labor organizations established to keep genuine unions out) have reinforced some further fears on the part of some unions regarding management motives.

Why, then, the new collaboration? One reason has certainly been the same factor that has generated offers of board membership and ESOPs to unionists: economic adversity. Most, if not all, of the unionized organizations have suffered financial hardship, and jobs have definitely been at stake. Employees recognize that if they can improve quality and productivity, their employers will be healthier and they will consequently be able to retain their jobs as might not otherwise be the case. Another reason for the collaboration seems to be an increasing awareness on the

EXHIBIT 9-3

SOURCE: *United Mine Workers Journal*, July 1990, p. 6.

'COOPERATE OR ELSE'
How To Avoid Management Traps

It goes by many names—"worker participation," "labor-management cooperation," "quality of work life circles"—but no matter what it's called, UMWA members should proceed with caution if your employer tries to implement one of these programs.

If your company tries to implement, or approaches your local union about negotiating, a so-called cooperative agreement you should *immediately* contact your UMWA regional director. The four UMWA regional directors have been trained to distinguish legitimate efforts to improve labor-management relations from attempts to circumvent the union structure.

✔ **Watch out** if management attempts to impose a "cooperative" program without first negotiating with the union. It's not cooperation when when one side has no say-so in the formulation or implementation of the program.

✔ **Watch out** if management attempts to cut the union out of the process by using a cooperative program to subvert or go around contractual provisions. "Cooperative" efforts which require workers to go without things like job classifications and seniority rights undercut the reason our union fights for a contract in the first place.

✔ **Watch out** if the company attempts to get the union leadership to endorse questionable business decisions. If those decisions later turn out to be bad, management can then blame the union.

✔ **Watch out** if management's only goal seems to be to increase production. A truly cooperative effort means that *both* sides get something they want: if the union helps management increase production or meet other company goals, then the company should give the workers, through the union, more control over the day-to-day conditions that affect the quality of workers' time on the job.

No two cooperative programs are alike, but those that are in the best interest of the union and the company, such as the union's EESP agreement with Island Creek Coal

Co.*, share several characteristics:

● Top-level management must be involved. Otherwise, middle and lower management, down to the mine level, may make agreements with the union that the ultimate decision makers in upper management can later abandon, claiming "miscommunication" with lower-level managers.

● The company must recognize the union leadership as the representative of the workers. "Cooperative" efforts that minimize the role of local

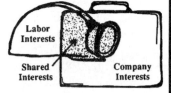

Labor Interests
Shared Interests
Company Interests

union leadership are usually nothing more than elaborate union-busting techniques designed to get workers to believe they don't need a union to solve problems on the job.

● The union leadership must have a co-equal role in formulating and implementing the program. Cooperation is a two-way street, and any program that allows management to independently decide and change the rules is not about cooperation.

● Both parties must be committed to making the program work. Efforts continually plagued by "miscommunications" and "misunderstandings" between upper management (the policy makers) and middle and lower management (the implementers) or by agreements between upper-level management and the union that somehow never get implemented may be signals that the company is not serious about making the program work.

● There should be regular progress meetings to evaluate the program and a mechanism to deter management from ignoring the parts of the program that benefit workers or from unilaterally ending the program.

* Note: A future issue of the *Journal* will examine the Employment and Economic Security Pact (EESP) begun by the UMWA and the Island Creek Coal Co. in 1987

---

part of unions (and managements) of a trend toward a dehumanization of work in many situations: Kahil Gibran may have called work "love made visible" and the Benedictines may say that "to work is to pray," but most people have always been less than enthusiastic about their own jobs, and in recent years the level of discontent amid new technology and an ever-lessened worker control over the working

EXHIBIT 9-4

SOURCE: *United Mine Workers Journal*, July 1990, p. 7.

environment appear to have grown appreciably. Many unions have been willing to explore new solutions in the face of this development.

❖ Saturn's Ambitious QWL Program

A QWL landmark of sorts was reached in late 1990 when the world's largest industrial company, General Motors, opened a new $5 billion automobile plant 35 miles south of Nashville in the town of Spring Hill, Tennessee. Designed to produce an entirely new small car, Saturn, in GM's first new car-making division since the company acquired Chevrolet in 1918, the facility was conceived with the idea of enlisting the United Automobile Workers as a virtually equal partner with management and in so doing to narrow the existing $2,000 per car cost advantage enjoyed by the Japanese on their smaller cars. Over the previous decade, this advantage had been a major factor in decreasing GM's share of the U.S. market from 46 percent to a frightening 32 percent.

Spring Hill opened with UAW representatives on all planning and operating committees from the shop floor to the top management of this wholly owned GM subsidiary. The unionists had been granted a major role in these committees, which make decisions on such matters as deciding on the suppliers of parts and equipment as well as on more orthodox labor–management issues. And the workers could in fact block a potential decision, although not indefinitely ("In the event an alternative solution is not found," in the words of the GM-UAW agreement at Saturn, "the blocking party must reevaluate [its] position in the context of the philosophy and mission").

In addition, all 4,500 Saturn production employees had been assigned to work teams of six to 15 UAW members and permitted to make all of their decisions—including work and vacation scheduling and the controlling of variable costs—without the presence of any supervisor in an attempt to substitute peer pressure and work pride for the traditional management methods that in recent years had seemed not to serve GM so well. Teams of workers were even charged with doing the hiring in an attempt to ensure that only those who could accept the new autonomy on a day-to-day basis would be included in the new arrangement. All workers were to get virtually total protection against layoffs and annual salaries instead of hourly pay.

As the dean of MIT's Sloan School of Management said in examining all of this,

> If Saturn is successful it will prove that it's possible to junk the old bureaucracies, change the corporate culture, change the adversarial relationship between union and management, and put it all back together right. If they succeed, it will be a big positive for America. If not, it will be a huge downer.[16]

The Saturn venture got off to a slow start. Bugs in the form of faulty seat backs that could flip over without warning and bad engine coolants forced the management to back off from its initial daily production goal of 900 cars to a more realistic 700. And another key innovation at Spring Hill—the tying of 20 percent of pay to the achievement of the original productivity and quality goals and the payment of a bonus if these objectives were exceeded—was accordingly, at the union's request, delayed. But even amid the inauspicious beginning, great expectations on the part of both labor and management continued, and the parties indeed pointed to the mutually agreed upon pay basis adjustment as an example of teamwork and goodwill.

By the mid-1990s, the experiment was paying off handsomely. Daily production had for some time been at the plant capacity level of 1,133 cars, and the Saturn—now one of the fastest-selling subcompacts in the industry—was generally regarded as one of the highest-quality American cars, with defect rates at the low levels of the best Japanese automobiles. Absenteeism was averaging barely 2.5 percent (in contrast to four and five times that percentage at other GM plants). With their now-restored bonus arrangement, the unionized workers were earning close to $50,000 annually, with about $10,000 of this amount coming from the bonuses. Overall, the now-7,000 Saturn employees, although averaging some 12 percent less in salary than GM's other workers, were making about $4,000 more than their counterparts elsewhere in the organization as the productivity and quality goals were exceeded. GM was freely capitalizing on all of this with an advertising theme of "not just another car company" and a focus in its marketing campaigns on happy employees working cooperatively with management to build outstanding vehicles. And visitors from other corporations all over the world were flocking to Spring Hill to study the operation with thoughts of implementing its essential ingredients into their own businesses.

But problems were also arising in these years. To meet the large market demands, the plant had gone on a 50-hour (and sometimes longer) workweek, and this was taking its toll on employee morale. New hires, often GM workers laid off at other GM installations across the country, were frequently less enthusiastic about the Saturn employee participation framework than the hand-picked original workers had been. The newcomers also tended to view with unconcealed misgivings the UAW's close relationship with the Spring Hill management.

Amid Saturn's huge prosperity, these challenges could probably have been surmounted by the company. But in the late 1990s a different kind of development, one that was far more frustrating on all fronts, arose: The market for all small cars, Saturns included, began to slump, falling 10 percent in 1997 and close to 20 percent in each of the next two years. The Saturn bonuses inevitably dropped as the management cut shifts as part of the reductions in production, and as the times turned bad the workers also, increasingly, complained that the company was now freezing them out of major decisions. The UAW leader at Saturn announced in mid-1998 that "GM management isn't working with us anymore. They make decisions on things such as [subcontracting] without our input. There's no partnership here."[17] The union was especially upset by a GM decision that it claimed had been made unilaterally to build a midsized Saturn in an existing GM factory in Wilmington, Delaware, instead of at Spring Hill.

In their 1999 election, the Spring Hill unionists voted out all of the local leaders who had supported the cooperative experiment with management over the past nine years and replaced them with union officials who advocated a more traditional union–management relationship. At the time of this writing, the cooperative experiment was still alive because two-thirds of the workers had also voted (in a separate vote, one year previously) to retain the arrangement. But given the radical change in union leadership, the future of the Saturn experiment was anything but assured.

Even if Saturn's ambitious QWL program does survive, moreover, the possibility that the *overall* growth of QWL may reflect nothing more than a fad cannot be dismissed. It is reasonable to expect that if no satisfactory rewards for both managements and unions can be attributed to QWL, the latter's tenure on the collective bargaining landscape may be short-lived. To date, even allowing for economic hard times that cannot be expected to continue indefinitely, the returns in many workplaces have not been particularly impressive, indeed, in terms of documented major improvements in either morale or productivity. And it must be recognized again (as it was in Chapter 1) that the United States has never been a particularly fruitful territory for the genuine union–management cooperation that QWL obviously requires if it hopes to survive.

John F. Kennedy frequently declared to proud parents who presented him with their new baby for what was at least for them a memorable moment, "It looks like a nice baby. We'll know more later." The same statement can perhaps be made on behalf of quality of work life programs.

SOME CONCLUDING THOUGHTS

If unions and management are viewed as institutions, as distinct from the individuals whom they represent, the issues considered in this chapter take on special meaning. Institutions can survive long after individuals have perished, and in a real sense the problems of union security, union obligations, and management rights are related to the *survival* of the bargaining institutions. Union security measures preserve the union per se (although in so doing they may also allow it to do a better job for its members). Similarly, to survive and function as an effective institution, management must be concerned with its prerogatives to operate the business efficiently. It must also be concerned with union obligations as these might affect its continued effectiveness.

In principle, therefore, the devices of collective bargaining that feed the institutional needs of the union and the firm are cut from the same cloth. They are designed to assure the long-run interests of the two organizations. The objectives of unions and employers are quite different, but to carry out their respective functions both need security of operation. Business operates to make a profit and thus must be defended against encroachments of organized labor that might unreasonably interfere with its efficiency as a dynamic organization in the society. Its insistence on management prerogatives stands as a bulwark of defense in this objective.

But unions also justify themselves as institutions on the American scene in their attempting to protect and advance the welfare of their members, and union security arrangements are an important avenue toward the realization of this objective. Although there may be philosophical objections to compulsory union membership, there cannot be any question that union security arrangements serve the long-run survival needs of organized labor.

Over the years, employers and unions have been relatively successful in reconciling these fundamental objectives however much the verbal controversies continue to rage (and however foreign to both of their philosophies the idea of full "codetermination" may be). Businesses that have engaged in collective bargaining relationships have by and large not only been able to survive but often have flourished. Many of the most influential and prosperous firms in this country (the automobile companies and the airlines, at least in normal years, come immediately to mind) have, as we know, been highly unionized for years. Likewise, organized labor not only has survived but has grown appreciably in strength over time, the contemporary unexciting performance of union membership totals being accountable chiefly by causes other than management destruction. Although the objectives of the two institutions are quite different, and although occasional major impasses are reached in the bargaining on these issues, sufficient protection for both organizations has been provided in the vast majority of unionized industry.

DISCUSSION QUESTIONS

1. Arguing in favor of right-to-work laws, a publication of the National Association of Manufacturers has expressed the view that "no argument for compulsory unionism—however persuasive—can possibly justify invasion of the right of individual choice." Do you agree or disagree? Why?

2. "From the viewpoint of providing maximum justice to all concerned, the agency shop constitutes the optimum union security arrangement." To what extent, if any, do you agree with this statement?

3. "Good unions don't need compulsory unionism. Bad unions don't deserve compulsory unionism." Comment.

4. Evaluate the opinion of a former Steelworker Union president that "nothing could be worse than to have . . . management appease the union, and nothing could be worse than to have the union appease management." Relate your remarks to the areas of management rights and union security.

MINICASES

 #1 A Question of Freedom

"I can see arguments both for and against right-to-work laws," says a fellow student in your class. "But there is one overriding reason why I'm on balance against these laws. And it involves the question of freedom.

"Specifically, it relates to freedom of contract, a basic and critical right in this land of free enterprise and individualism in which we live. A union shop can come about in only one way: The union—for whatever reason—has asked for such an arrangement in its collective bargaining with the management, and the management—again, on whatever it considers to be good grounds—has agreed to grant the union shop. This being the case, what right does the government have to intrude and tell the two parties, 'That's too bad—you still can't have it'?"

How would you respond?

#2 An Original Proposal

MEMORANDUM TO: John T. Kelly, Chairman of the Board, Fenwick Chemical Corporation
FROM: Joyce M. Walters, Senior Vice President for Labor Relations
SUBJECT: Proposed Appointment of Four Union Leaders to Fenwick Board of Directors

I'm not saying that it would solve all our problems, but I'd like to know what we'd lose by giving four of the 20 seats on our board of directors to officer nominees of the Chemical Workers Union.

By my calculations, we're talking about only one-fifth of the board membership, so there's no way that board decisions could actually result from just union desires even if all four union people were united on something. And since the union has been yelling for years for just one seat, imagine how pleased it would be with four. We'd save a bundle in the wages and benefits that the Chemical Workers wouldn't demand in the face of our magnanimity. Maybe one or two of the union people would make real contributions to board deliberations at least once in a while. And can you imagine a union's voting to strike under these conditions?

I know that almost no U.S. company has even one such director, but with our currently depressed earnings and gloomy near-term financial outlook, we've got to do something. The race these days is won by those who are imaginative.

How much of a point, if any, does Walters have?

NOTES

[1]All statistics in this section are based on information furnished by the Bureau of Labor Statistics, U.S. Department of Labor.
[2]*Union Starch & Refining Co.*, 87 NLRB 779 (1949).

[3]398 U.S. 235 (1970).

[4]*Metropolitan Edison Co. v. NLRB*, Case No. 81-1664, April 4, 1983.

[5]Section 301(e) states: "For purposes of this section, in determining whether any person is acting as an 'agent' of another person as to make such other person responsible for his acts, the question of whether the specific acts performed were actually authorized or subsequently ratified shall not be controlling."

[6]*The New York Times*, December 12, 1976, p. F13.

[7]"Management's Reserved Rights under Collective Bargaining," *Monthly Labor Review*, 79, no. 10 (October 1956), p. 1172.

[8]*Time*, May 19, 1980, p. 78.

[9]*Wall Street Journal*, March 12, 1981, p. 33.

[10]Ibid.

[11]*Business Week*, November 22, 1982, p. 30.

[12]*Business Week*, February 1, 1982, p. 17.

[13]*Wall Street Journal,* September 17, 1985, p. 1.

[14]Warner Woodworth, "Promethean Industrial Relations: Labor, ESOPs, and the Boardroom," in *Proceedings of the 1985 Spring Meeting, Industrial Relations Research Association, April 18–19, 1985* (Washington, DC: Industrial Relations Research Association, 1985), p. 623.

[15]A. H. Raskin, "Frustrated and Wary, Labor Marks Its Day," *The New York Times*, September 5, 1982, p. F6.

[16]*Time*, October 29, 1990, p. 74.

[17]*Wall Street Journal*, July 20, 1998, p. A4.

SELECTED REFERENCES

Barra, Ralph. *Putting Quality Circles to Work*. New York: McGraw-Hill, 1983.

Blasi, Joseph R. *Employee Ownership: Revolution or Ripoff?* New York: Harper Business, 1988.

Bluestone, Barry, and Irving Bluestone. *Negotiating the Future*. New York: Basic Books, 1992.

Bourdon, Clinton C., and Raymond E. Levitt. *Union and Open-Shop Construction*. Lexington, MA: Heath, 1980.

Cooke, William N. *Labor–Management Cooperation*. Kalamazoo, MI: Upjohn Institute, 1990.

Graham-Moore, Brian, and Timothy L. Ross, eds. *Gainsharing and Employee Involvement*. Washington, DC: Bureau of National Affairs, 1995.

Harris, Howell John. *The Right to Manage*. Madison: University of Wisconsin Press, 1982.

Heckscher, Charles. *The New Unionism: Employee Involvement in the Changing Corporation*. New York: Basic Books, 1988.

Hill, Marvin F., Jr., and Anthony V. Sinicropi. *Management Rights: A Legal and Arbitral Analysis*. Washington, DC: Bureau of National Affairs, 1986.

Kochan, Thomas A., and Paul Osterman. *The Mutual Gains Enterprise*. Boston: Harvard Business School Press, 1994.

Rosen, Corey, and Karen M. Young, eds. *Understanding Employee Ownership*. Ithaca, NY: ILR Press, Cornell University, 1991.

Rosenthal, Edward Cohen, and Cynthia Burton. *Mutual Gains: A Guide to Union–Management Cooperation*, 2nd ed., rev. Ithaca, NY: ILR Press, Cornell University, 1993.

Rothschild, Joyce, and J. Allen Whitt. *The Cooperative Workplace*. Cambridge: Cambridge University Press, 1986.

Russell, Raymond, *Sharing Ownership in the Workplace*. Albany: State University of New York Press, 1985.

Thelen, Kathleen A. *Union of Parts: Labor Politics in Postwar Germany*. Ithaca, NY: Cornell University Press, 1991.

Whyte, William Foote, et al. *Worker Participation and Ownership*. Ithaca, NY: ILR Press, Cornell University, 1983.

Management Rights

Critical in arbitration are cases in which a union challenges the right of an employer to manage the plant. To promote efficiency, employers constantly introduce new methods, adopt technological improvements, and make more effective use of the labor force. In the typical labor agreement, a management prerogative clause guarantees the employer the sole right to adopt measures calculated to ensure efficient operation. Disputes arise, however, when a union claims that the exercise of such a management right violates terms and conditions of employment specified in the labor agreement. In general, the rule is that an employer may make any decision in the operation of the plant or in the direction of the labor force unless such decision violates provisions of the collective bargaining contract. In such cases, the arbitrator's responsibility is to determine whether a violation has occurred. The arbitrator reviews the material provisions of the labor agreement and the relevant evidence in light of the employer's action. In the event that a violation is found, the arbitrator will restore the status quo and also award back pay if the latter issue is involved in the dispute. On the other hand, should it be determined that no violation has occurred, a grievance protesting the right of the employer to manage the plant and direct the labor force will be denied.

Case 6 is quite interesting. It involves the distribution of complimentary tickets to varsity junior-senior high school football and basketball games. The school is located in a small town in the northwestern section of Indiana. The community supports the school's athletic programs, particularly basketball, with fervor and enthusiasm.

The case attracted considerable interest. With the mutual consent of the parties, the hearing was attended by a local newspaper reporter. When the decision came down, sections of it, including the ruling, were published in the local newspaper.

The case involves not only the Master Contract but also the Indiana Teachers' Law, enacted by the Indiana General Assembly in 1973. The union asserted that the school had violated the Master Contract and Public Law 217, as the legislation is commonly called; the employer asserted that it had not violated either of them.

In large measure, the basic facts of the case are not in dispute. Before the school year 1992–1993, complimentary tickets were given only to coaches. When the teachers' association complained, the new policy provided for one free ticket to all members of the faculty. The policy remained the same for the next school year, 1993–1994.

The case was generated when the employer unilaterally changed the ticket policy for the 1994–1995 school year. It did not consult, discuss, or bargain with the association before the current policy went into effect. Under the policy, certain persons, including high school coaches, received free tickets for themselves, their spouses, and their families. Other persons, including school board members and junior high school coaches, received free tickets for themselves and their spouses but not their families. In the third category were elementary principals, elementary coaches, and junior high school teachers. They received complimentary tickets only for themselves and not for their spouses and families.

When the Grievance Procedure did not result in a settlement, the issue was advanced to arbitration. Neither in the Master Contract nor in Public Law 217 is there a specific mention about athletic tickets. Nonetheless, the arbitrator held that the employer had violated Public Law 217 and the Master Contract. As you read the case, determine whether the arbitrator used sound reasoning for his decision.

You are the arbitrator in Case 7. It involves the union's claim that the company, a large grain producer, did not assign a second helper when Bean Plant 1 and Bean Plant 3 operated on the second shift. Originally, two helpers were scheduled to work the shift. One helper, however, called in the early afternoon to report off work because he had to take his wife to the hospital.

What complicated matters is that the first-shift supervisor, a supervisor-trainee, asked the two first-shift helpers to stay over and fill the vacancy on the second shift. Both refused the assignment. When the regular second-shift supervisor arrived on the scene, he refused to assign another helper to the second shift. That was the event that caused the dispute and the eventual arbitration.

Section 2 is a typical management rights clause providing a wide variety of employer rights. Like the usual management rights provision, Section 2 says that, in the exercise of its rights, the employer may not violate any provision of the contract. Nothing in the contract, standing by itself, limits the employer's rights, including the right to direct the working force and "to determine how many men it will employ or retain."

Before this dispute occurred, the company and union had agreed to an "Operator and Helper Scheduling" system called, for convenience, the "Schedule." It establishes the circumstances under which the employer must assign a helper(s) to the operators of the bean plant's equipment. Among the problems you will be required to determine in this case is whether the Schedule is part of the Labor Agreement. If it is not, you will be compelled to decide the case on the basis of Section 2, the Management Rights provision. If the Schedule is part of the contract, your job will be to determine whether the company was obligated to assign a second helper to the bean plant. Understand the Schedule fully before you make your decision. In this connection, there is a question of credibility of a union witness. If you believe the witness, who claimed that the parties agreed to a second helper when Bean Plants 1 and 3 operated, your decision would appear to be self-evident. If you do not, the decision will be based upon the Schedule, taking into account Section 2, the Management Rights provision.

Management Rights: The Case of the Complimentary Tickets

Cast of Characters

Pell	School Superintendent
Lewis	Association President
Bullitt	School Principal
Ott	Former Athletic Director
Franco	Current Athletic Director
Cain	School Attorney
Katz	School Board President
Fouk	Association Vice President

GRIEVANCE

*W*hen the Employer unilaterally changed a policy dealing with complimentary tickets to athletic events, the North Miami Education Association filed Grievance Number 5, dated September 16, 1995, which states:

> In the fall of 1995, the administration of the Junior-Senior High School unilaterally adopted a policy on tickets which conferred fringe benefits on some members of the bargaining unit, while excluding others, without bargaining with the exclusive representative in violation of the Master Contract and Public Law 217. This change in working conditions was made without even prior discussion of the exclusive representative.

On September 24, 1995, Larry Pell, School Superintendent, denied the grievance, stating:

> Public Law 217 and the Master Contract are not applicable inasmuch as ticket policy is not covered under Public Law 217, nor the Master Contract. Administration of the ticket sales and distribution are under the authority of the Athletic Department and not covered by Public Law 217 or within the context of the Master Contract, and further, said policy related thereto is not wage-related fringe benefits.

Failing to settle the dispute in the Grievance Procedure, the Parties convened this arbitration for its determination.

MASTER CONTRACT

ARTICLE I. RECOGNITION AND BOARD RIGHTS

A. *Recognition.* The Board recognizes the North Miami Education Association (hereinafter, the Association) as the sole exclusive bargaining representative for all licensed contractual employees of the Board with respect to salaries and other conditions of employment, except employees in the following classifications: Superintendent, Principal, Assistant Principal, Guidance Counselors, and Head Football and Basketball Coaches. This recognition shall continue until successfully challenged by members of the Negotiating Unit under provisions of Indiana Public Law 217, and the rules and regulations of the Indiana Education Employment Relations Board. The term "teacher," when hereinafter used, shall refer to every employee in the above defined Association.

ARTICLE XV. EFFECT OF AGREEMENT

A. The provisions of this Agreement, when ratified by the Board and the Association, shall be incorporated into and be considered a part of the policies of the Board as of the execution of this Agreement. The application of all terms and conditions of employment shall be exercised in conformity with the provisions of this Agreement, all state and national laws and regulations, other appropriate Board policies and procedures, and in a manner which is not arbitrary, capricious, or discriminatory.

•••

D. Any individual contract or agreement between the Board and any individual teacher shall be expressly subject to the terms and conditions of this Agreement or successor Agreement.

PUBLIC LAW 217

A school employer shall bargain collectively with the exclusive representative on the following: salary, wages, hours, and salary and wage-related fringe benefits. A contract may also contain a grievance procedure culminating in final and binding arbitration of unresolved grievances, but such binding arbitration shall have no power to amend, add to, subtract from or supplement provisions of the contract.*

A school employer shall discuss with the exclusive representative of certificated employees, . . . the following matters: working conditions, other than those provided in Section 4; curriculum development and revision; textbook selection; teaching methods; selection, assignment or promotion of personnel; student discipline; expulsion or supervision of students; pupil-teacher ratio; class size or budget appropriations. . . .**

It is an unfair labor practice for a school employer to refuse to bargain collectively or discuss with an exclusive representative as required by any provisions of this chapter.***

---

*Section 4.
**Section 5.
***Section 7(a)(5).

ISSUE

Under the circumstances of this case, did the Employer violate the material provisions of Public Law 217 or the Master Contract? If so, what should the remedy be?

CIRCUMSTANCES OF DISPUTE

Previous Athletic Ticket Policy

At the crux of this dispute is the Employer policy of distributing free tickets to faculty members for athletic events. Before school year 1992–1993 the faculty as a group did not receive free tickets, the Employer limiting the benefit to coaches of athletic teams. Michael Lewis, Association President, discussed the issue with Steven Bullitt, Principal of North Miami Junior-Senior High School. Lewis testified that he told the Principal that it is not appropriate to issue complimentary tickets to some teachers because of their status as coaches. As a result of this discussion, for the school year 1992–1993 the Employer on April 22, 1992, announced the following policy:

> The following is the Athletic Department's policy on admission to Varsity Ball Games for the 1992–1993 school year. (Varsity Boys Basketball and Football)
>
> Teachers at North Miami High School (Coaches included)—One (1) free pass for all varsity football/basketball contests.

It was signed by Bullitt and Mike Ott, the then Athletic Director. Lewis said that the policy was satisfactory to the Association because all teachers received the same benefit. Alan Franco replaced Ott as Athletic Director for the school year 1993–1994. On August 27, 1993, he put into effect the same ticket policy as prevailed for the previous school year. (Joint Exhibit 5) Before doing so, Franco discussed the matter with Bullitt. After receiving approval from the Principal, Franco testified,

> I went to Lewis and asked if he had a problem with the policy. He said he did not.

Lewis said:

> Franco asked me if the policy reflected my understanding with the School Administration. I replied it did.

Negotiation of 1994–1995 Contract

On May 14, 1995, the Association proposed the following while the Parties were negotiating the current Master Contract:

> Teachers and families invited as guests to all school functions.

In the negotiations, Lewis served as chief spokesperson for the Association, and George Cain, Attorney at Law, served in the same capacity for the Employer. Both sides recognized the Association's proposal to include free tickets to athletic events. According to Lewis, Cain, who did not appear at the arbitration, asserted that the School Board had no authority over the ticket policy for athletic events, stating that the School's Athletic Department had full power over that matter. Sherman Katz, School Board President, who attended the negotiations, testified that Cain said no to many Association proposals, including its athletic ticket event proposal. He also declared that Cain stated that not only was the athletic ticket policy not within the control of the School Board, but also, "We did not want to get involved with that policy."

Lewis testified that he told the School Board that it had the power to instruct the Athletic Director what to do about ticket policy. He also said that neither the Employer nor the Association stated that the ticket policy for athletic events was not negotiable. Bernard Fouk, Association Vice President, who participated in the negotiations, also declared that neither side stated that the ticket policy was not negotiable. With respect to this issue, Katz testified:

> We never thought the ticket policy to be nonnegotiable. We did not wish to negotiate on that issue.

In addition, he said:

> The School Board has the power to tell the Athletic Director what to do if we wanted to exercise our power.

In any event, the Association dropped the proposal in question, and athletic ticket policy is not expressly contained in the Master Contract. Association witnesses testified that the issue had been withdrawn not because they believed it to be nonnegotiable but because, said Lewis, they were

> at the later stages of the negotiations to get a contract. It was part of the negotiations. If they said it was not negotiable, we would not have removed it from the bargaining table.

Current Athletic Ticket Policy

In August or September, 1994, Franco put into effect the athletic ticket policy for the 1994–1995 school year. He did this without bargaining or discussing the issue with the Association. In this respect, he testified:

> I did not contact the Association because it did not seem to me that it was important to do so. I felt no need to contact the Association. I manage the ticket policy. It is part of my responsibility as Athletic Director.

Franco also testified that neither he nor the Principal requested permission from the School Board to put the policy into effect. Katz declared:

> The School Board did not write the ticket policy, and we were not asked to approve it.

As prepared by Franco and approved by the School Principal, the current policy provides:

> Because of expanded athletic programs with ever increasing numbers of people involved, and a constant financial fight for the program's existence, it is necessary that a written "Ticket Policy" be published at this time.

> I. The following people shall receive *"All Sports Tickets"* for themselves, their spouse and family for all Jr.-Sr. High Athletic Events.
>
>   1. Superintendent
>   2. High School Principal
>   3. High School Assistant Principal
>   4. Athletic Director
>   5. High School Coaches

II. The people listed below shall receive *"All Sports Tickets"* for themselves and their spouse *only* for all Jr.-Sr. High Athletic Events.

1. Present School Board Members
2. Jr. High Coaches
3. High School Band Director
4. Pep Club Sponsor
5. Cheerleader Sponsor

III. The people listed below shall receive *"All Sports Tickets"* for themselves *only* for all Jr.-Sr. High Athletic Events.

1. Elementary Principals
2. Elementary Coaches
3. H.S./J.H. Teachers only

IV. Any Elem. or H.S. Faculty or staff member *volunteering* for 3 or more times to take tickets during the year will receive family passes for J.H. and H.S. events for all sports. See Mr. Franco for assignments and tickets. (Emphasis in original)

During the arbitration, the Association stated that it did not object to family passes for teachers or staff who volunteer their services at athletic events. In addition, the Association recognizes that the Head Football and Basketball Coaches are not included in the bargaining unit as established by Section 1, Paragraph A of the Master Agreement. Thus, the Association states:

> The Association contends the corporation was within its legal and contractual rights only in conferring unnegotiated fringe benefits of this nature to coaching positions outside the bargaining unit, i.e., head football coach and basketball coach as set forth in contract Section 1, paragraph A. (Association Posthearing Brief, p. 4)

Other Coaches, included in the bargaining unit, receive benefits not available under the previous policy. As a result of the new policy, high school coaches receive free all sports tickets for the coach, spouse, and family. Coaches assigned to the junior high school receive without charge the same kind of ticket for the coach and spouse. Faculty members other than coaches continue to receive free or complimentary tickets that do not apply to the spouse or family.

Funding of Athletic Program

Athletic Director Franco testified that the financial arrangements for the school's athletic program are controlled exclusively by the Athletic Department. The sports program is financed by funds generated from the sale of tickets and fund raisers. Equally, disbursement of funds is the exclusive prerogative of the Athletic Department. He also said:

> I do not ask the School Board for authority to raise or spend funds.

Like Franco, Katz declared that the School Board is not involved in the collection or disbursement of funds for the school's athletic program. These financial transactions fall within the exclusive control of the Principal and the Athletic Department. Though the School Board receives an annual accounting of Athletic Department receipts and expenditures, it does not intervene in financial matters of the athletic program.

POSITIONS OF THE PARTIES

Whereas the Association requests that the grievance be granted, the Employer asserts that it should be denied. Both Parties filed posthearing briefs, and arguments contained in them will be referenced in the following portion of this decision to the extent necessary and appropriate for purposes of this case.

EVALUATION OF THE EVIDENCE

Application of Public Law 217: Mandatory
Issues of Collective Bargaining

To test the merits of the grievance, we must determine whether the Employer violated material provisions of Public Law 217 and/or the Master Contract. With respect to the first issue, no dispute exists that the Employer put into effect the current athletic ticket policy without bargaining or discussing the matter with the Association. In the Employer's view, however, no violation of the statute occurred because ticket policy is not covered by Public Law 217. In this respect, it argues:

> Public Law 217 in the State of Indiana does not provide that ticket policy is a negotiable or even a discussable item under Public Law 217. (Employer Posthearing Brief, p. 1)

Section 4 of Public Law 217 states:

> A school employer shall bargain collectively with the exclusive representative on the following: salary, wages, hours, and salary and wage-related fringe benefits.

According to the Association, athletic ticket policy is a salary or wage-related fringe benefit, asserting on this basis that the Employer violated the statute when it changed the policy without prior bargaining with it. Thus:

> First, the policy constitutes unilateral action by the employer upon a mandatory subject of bargaining, having bypassed the exclusive representative and refusing to negotiate said policy at the bargaining table. (Association Posthearing Brief, p. 2)

And:

> There can be no question that a policy that permits free admission to athletic events to some employees, as opposed to out-of-pocket expense to attend said event, is a salary or wage-related fringe benefit. The school corporation presented no evidence to the contrary. (Association Posthearing Brief, p. 4)

To qualify as a fringe benefit under Section 4 of Public Law 217, the benefit must be directly related to or based on teachers' salaries. Under this standard, the Association argument does not have merit. It does not have merit because athletic tickets are not related to or based upon salary. Teacher salary has absolutely nothing to do with athletic tickets. Contrast athletic tickets with salary-related fringe benefits, such as sick leave, sabbaticals, and personal leave days. The amount of compensation teachers receive for these fringe benefits is directly related to or based upon salaries. Since athletic ticket policy is not a salary-related fringe benefit, the Employer did not violate Section 4 of Public Law 217 when it changed the policy without prior bargaining with the Association. In short, athletic ticket policy is not a mandatory issue of collective bargaining under the terms of the statute.

Discussable Issues: Funding of Athletic Program

In contrast to federal labor relations law and other public-sector state statutes, under Indiana Public Law 217, a school employer commits an unfair labor practice should it refuse to discuss certain issues with the teachers' representative. Section 5 provides that a school employer must discuss

> the following matters: working conditions other than those provided in Section 4; . . .

With vigor, the Employer argues that athletic ticket policy is not a discussable issue covered by the Indiana statute. Since it is not, the Employer may unilaterally put policy into effect or change it without prior discussion with the Association. To support this position, the Employer stresses that the Athletic Department has full authority to raise and spend funds for the School's athletic program. In these financial matters, the School Board plays no role whatsoever. Neither does it appropriate money to run the program or control expenditures. Given the character of the funding system, athletic ticket policy is not a discussable issue.

In this respect, the Employer argues:

> The North Miami Education Association has attempted to imply that the Athletic Director by being an employee of the School Corporation creates the authority and management of the athletic program by the School Board. The evidence is quite clear from the testimony presented that the School Board has not attempted to intercede in the management facilities of the ticket distribution, nor have they involved themselves in the raising of athletic funds nor the expenditures thereunder, leaving this totally to the discretion of the Athletic Department under the direction of the Athletic Director. (Employer Posthearing Brief, p. 2)

With full deference to the Employer and Counsel, this argument does not have merit. Nothing in Public Law 217 states that an issue is not discussable or bargainable for that matter just because a school's extracurricular function is funded by sources other than School Board appropriations. If the Indiana General Assembly intended that condition, it would have achieved that objective by adopting precise exclusionary language. To believe that the General Assembly was not aware that some extracurricular functions are financed in whole or in part by outside funds would degrade its intelligence.

In addition, a Hearing Examiner of the Indiana Education Employment Relations Board (IEERB), the enforcement agency of Public Law 217, rejected the Employer's position herein considered.* A teacher sponsoring the production of the school yearbook had traditionally been paid from the profits of yearbook sales. The school employer refused to bargain regarding the compensation of the sponsor. Finding that the school employer violated Public Law 217, the Hearing Examiner stated:

> The Respondent's position . . . appeared to be that, since the junior high yearbook sponsor is not paid by the Respondent, but receives the profit from the sale of the yearbooks as compensation for that position, then there is no need to bargain the compensation for it. Section 4 of the Act does not distinguish

---

*HER, Case U-76-60-315 (Avon), 77 IEERB 405.

the source of money paid for extra-curricular duties required in bargaining on "salary [etc.]" . . . Therefore . . . the evidence supports a finding of a violation by the Respondent of its duty to bargain under Section 7(a)(5) of the Act.

True, the case dealt with teacher compensation, and not athletic ticket policy. Nonetheless, the same principle applies in the sense that the independent source of athletic program funds does not per se exclude the issue as discussable under Section 5 of Public Law 217. The Employer has not cited an IEERB or court decision supporting its position that issues arising from a school extracurricular function are excluded from the scope of the statute just because the function is funded by sources other than state or local appropriations.

Nothing that occurred in the negotiations resulting in the current Master Contract waived the Association's right under Public Law 217 to discuss the athletic ticket policy in question. It attempted but failed to secure a much more comprehensive ticket benefit compared with the one then in existence. Its failure may not properly be translated to the Association's abandonment of its statutory rights. As the record clearly shows, it did not withdraw the proposal on the grounds that it was not a bargainable or discussable issue under Public Law 217.

Working Conditions under Public Law 217

Despite the preceding observations, the grievance would not have merit if it is held that athletic ticket policy does not constitute a working condition under Section 5 of Public Law 217. School employers are required only to discuss matters relating to working conditions. They have no obligation to discuss issues that are not working conditions.

That athletic ticket policy constitutes a working condition, and, hence, is discussable under the Indiana statute, is best manifested by the events that generated the policy for the school year 1992–1993. Recall that the Association President discussed the issue with the School Principal. That policy was not made effective until such discussions were held. Indeed, Bullitt did not testify in the arbitration. Lewis's declarations in this respect stand unchallenged and uncontradicted. If the Employer really believed that athletic ticket policy is not a working condition under Public Law 217, it would follow that Bullitt would not have discussed the issue with the Association. Instead of that, the record clearly shows that the policy was drafted and put into effect only after the discussion took place. Indeed, it is far too late in the game for the Employer to contend that athletic ticket policy is not a working condition, not a discussable item, under Section 5 of Public Law 217. Its own action makes such an argument unacceptable and totally without merit.

Aside from the preceding, athletic ticket policy inherently is a working condition for purposes of the Statute. It regulates attendance at an important school activity. As no other extracurricular function, the athletic program serves as a magnet and focal point for students, alumni, faculty, and the general public. Where, as here, the school employer treats the faculty differently for purposes of complimentary admission to athletic events, the net result is a divided faculty adversely affecting teacher morale. Feelings of resentment, discrimination, and favoritism tend to reduce loyalty and dedication to a school. Clearly, a purpose of Public Law 217 is to provide equal treatment for faculty members covered by a collective bargaining contract. To argue that the athletic ticket policy is not a working condition totally ignores adverse results generated by a policy that provides substantial benefits to some faculty members not enjoyed by all.

Public Law 217: Conclusions

For the reasons expressed, the Employer violated Public Law 217 under the circumstances of this case. Though not a mandatory issue of collective bargaining, athletic ticket policy, a working condition, falls within the scope of Section 5 of the Statute even though the athletic program is funded by sources other than School Board appropriations.

Under the terms of the Statute, the Employer was required to discuss the issue with the Association prior to changing the athletic ticket policy in question. Since it did not, and instead unilaterally implemented the change, the Employer engaged in an unfair labor practice under the terms of the Indiana Statute.

Application of Master Contract

Not only did the Employer violate Public Law 217, but it also violated the Master Contract under the circumstances of this case. To defend its position that a contractual violation did not take place, the Employer correctly points out that the athletic ticket policy does not appear in the Master Contract. Since it is not mentioned, the Employer has the unilateral right to change the policy at its discretion. In this respect, the Employer asserts:

> The Master Contract (Exhibits 1 and 1-A) does not mention, and the North Miami Education Association fails to identify under any specific paragraph, where the issue of ticket policy is under the Contract as submitted and admitted to evidence herein. The answer of the Board was previously, and still is, that Public Law 217 and the Master Contract are not applicable in as much as the ticket policy is not covered thereunder. (Employer Posthearing Brief, p. 1)

And:

> It is the position of the North Miami Community School Board of School Trustees that said policy is not covered by the contractual provisions between the School Board and the teachers association, nor covered by state law, in that it is an athletic policy totally separate and autonomous of the School Corporation. (Employer Posthearing Brief, p. 4)

With full respect, the Employer's argument does not square with accepted principles of contract construction. To be binding, a working condition need not appear in a labor agreement as long as it constitutes a recognized past practice. Perhaps Arbitrator Arthur Jacobs put it best when he stated:

> A union–management contract is far more than words on paper. It is also all the oral understandings, interpretations and mutually acceptable habits of action which have grown up around it over the course of time. Stable and peaceful relations between the parties depend upon the development of a mutually satisfactory superstructure of understanding which gives operating significance and practicality to the purely legal wording of the written contract. Peaceful relations depend, further, upon both parties faithfully living up to their mutual commitments as embodied not only in the actual contract itself but also in the modes of action which have become an integral part of it. (*Cola-Cola Bottling Co.*, 9 LA 197, 198)*

---

*See also *Alpena Gen. Hosp.*, 50 LA 48, 51 (Jones); *Metal Specialty Co.*, 39 LA 1265, 1269 (Volz); *Esso Standard Oil*, 16 LA 73, 74 (McCoy); *Phillips Petroleum*, 24 LA 191, 194 (Merrill).

Indeed, the U.S. Supreme Court supported the proposition when it said:

> The collective bargaining agreement states the rights and duties of the parties. It is more than a contract; it is a generalized code to govern a myriad of cases which the draftsmen cannot wholly anticipate. . . . The collective agreement covers the whole employment relationship. (*United Steelworkers* v. *Warrior & Gulf Navigation Co.*, 80 S. Ct. 1347, 1351–1352 (1960))

In the case at hand, an athletic ticket policy practice started in the 1992–1993 school year. Under that practice, teachers, including coaches, received one complimentary ticket for varsity football and basketball games. The practice continued through the next academic year. This working condition constitutes a practice binding on the Employer and the Association under the applicable standards governing the issue. These standards were articulated by the Elkouris this way:

> In the absence of a written agreement, "past practice," to be binding on both Parties, must be (1) unequivocal; (2) clearly enunciated and acted upon; (3) readily ascertainable over a reasonable period of time as a fixed and established practice accepted by both Parties.*

Clearly, this case meets the standards for a binding past practice. After the discussion between the School Principal and Association President, the athletic ticket policy appeared in a written document distributed to all teachers. Thus, the practice was "unequivocal, clearly enunciated and acted upon." Since the practice was in effect for two years, it was "readily ascertainable over a reasonable period of time as a fixed and established practice." Obviously, the practice was "accepted by both Parties" given the undisputed evidence that the ticket policy was discussed and approved by the Employer and Association.

Master Contract Conclusions

It follows, therefore, that the Employer violated the Master Contract under the circumstances of this case. It violated Section 1, Paragraph A, the Recognition provision, when it abandoned the practice without prior discussion with the Association. By that conduct, establishing in place of the practice a policy conferring special ticket benefits for a portion of the faculty, the Employer violated Section XV, Paragraph A because it exercised its authority in an arbitrary, capricious, and discriminatory manner. Since the working condition embraced by the practice constituted a term and condition of employment, the Employer in effect entered into individual agreements with those faculty members who received without charge athletic tickets for their families and spouses in violation of Section XV, Paragraph D of the Master Contract.

Remedy for Violation

For the reasons expressed in this decision, the Employer violated the material provisions of Public Law 217 and the Master Contract. To remedy the violation, the Employer shall be directed to rescind the athletic ticket policy that it wrongfully established for the school year 1995–1996 and restore the policy established on April 22, 1992, submitted in the arbitration as Joint Exhibit 4.

---

*Frank Elkouri and Edna Elkouri, *How Arbitration Works*, 4th ed. (Washington, D.C.: Bureau of National Affairs, 1985), p. 439.

AWARD OF ARBITRATOR

1. Grievance Number 5, dated September 16, 1995, filed by the North Miami Education Association, is granted on the grounds that under the circumstances of this case the Employer violated the material provisions of Indiana Public Law 217 and the Master Contract.
2. Upon receipt of this Award, the Employer is directed to rescind the Athletic Ticket Policy effective for the school year 1995–1996 and restore the policy established on April 22, 1992.

Questions

1. Even though the Master Contract does not mention athletic ticket policy, the arbitrator still held that the employer had violated the Master Contract. What reasoning did he use to find the violation?
2. Explain how the arbitrator reached the finding that athletic ticket policy constituted a "working condition" under Public Law 217.
3. Indicate the circumstances in which an event amounts to a past practice for contractual interpretation and application purposes.
4. Why did the arbitrator hold that the funding of the athletic program did not support the employer's position?

Management Rights: The Case of Filling a Vacancy

Cast of Characters

Clear	Grievant
Engel	Employee
Newton	Supervisor
Hall	Supervisor
Tell	Union Representative
Iron	Bean Plant Manager

GRIEVANCE AND LABOR AGREEMENT

*O*n September 17, 1995, Donald Clear filed Grievance Number 96, which stated:

> Violation of Article IV, Section 12, Para. 115. Company failed to make every effort to secure help to properly man shift when employees are absent in classification where help is needed. Employee requesting 8 hours pay at $1\frac{1}{2}$ rate for Sept. 17, 1995, on 3–11 shift.

Material to the dispute are the following provisions of the Labor Agreement:

ARTICLE I

Section 2 (Paragraph 4)

The operation of the plant and the direction of the working force employed therein including the right to hire, promote, demote, suspend, lay off, transfer, discharge, or discipline for cause, and the right to determine how many men it will employ or retain, as well as to maintain discipline and efficiency, are invested exclusively with the Company subject to the provisions of this agreement.

ARTICLE IV

Section 12 (Paragraph 115)

In pertinent part, this provision states:

   The Company agrees to make every effort to secure help to properly man shifts when employees are absent or a vacancy exists in a classification where help is needed.

BASIC QUESTION

The basic question to be determined in this arbitration is framed as follows: Under the circumstances of this case, did the Company violate Paragraph 115 of the Labor Agreement? If so, what should the remedy be?

BACKGROUND

On September 17, 1995, one Operator and two Helpers were scheduled in the Bean Plant for the second shift. At about 1:40 P.M., one of the Helpers, Steve Engel, reported off work because he had to take his wife to the hospital. Les Newton, a first-shift Supervisor, took the call. Newton was hired in August 1995, and was assigned as a Supervisor-Trainee. Advised that Engel would not report to work, he asked both first-shift Helpers to fill the vacancy, but each refused.

Robert Hall, second-shift Supervisor, reported at about 2:45 P.M. He observed that the following equipment was scheduled to operate on the second shift:

No. 1 Plant

No. 3 Plant (on the Mill side of the Bean Plant. It was not to operate on the Extraction side)

20–0 system

On the other hand, the additional equipment in the Bean Plant was not scheduled to operate on the second shift. This included Plants No. 2 and 4, the Griffith System, and the Grit Recovery System.

Hall refused to fill the Helper vacancy on the second shift. He testified:

Because less than 50 percent of the Bean Plant equipment was running, there was no need to fill the vacancy. There were two men there (one Operator and one Helper) and there was no need for the second Helper.

He also testified that had Engel reported to work, he would not have been assigned as a Helper but would have performed miscellaneous cleanup work. Hall further said that the Operator and the Helper who manned the second shift were not required to perform more work than they normally carry out. He said:

The absence of the second Helper did not place an unreasonable burden on them.

Clear was assigned as a Helper on the third shift. He filed his grievance because he believed that the Company should have called him to fill the second-shift vacancy on an overtime basis.

On November 8, 1993, the Company and Union agreed to a document styled "Operator and Helper Scheduling," hereinafter called the "Schedule," for the Bean Plant. Union Representative Fred Tell testified:

When Marvin Iron returned to the Bean Plant,* a Steward and I told him this is the way we have been doing it. The document was agreeable to all concerned. In the past, we settled grievances on the basis of the Schedule.

---

*Iron returned as Bean Plant Manager in June 1993. Subsequently, he was appointed the Plant Manager of all Company operations.

With respect to the Schedule, Iron testified:

So I sat down with the Union people and developed the Schedule guidelines.

The Schedule states:

I. #1 Plant plus any other system operating
   One Operator and One Helper in Extraction and Mill
II. #1 Plant, #2 Plant plus any other system operating
   One Operator and Two Helpers in Extraction and Mill
III. #1 Plant *only* with 20/0 and/or Griffith
   One Operator & One Helper in Mill
   Operator only in Extraction
IV. #2 Plant only with 20/0 and/or Griffith
   One Operator & One Helper in Mill
   Operator only in Extraction
V. #2 Plant and #4 Plant Operating with #4 Plant Grit Recovery System
   Operating
   One Operator and One Helper in Extraction and Mill
VI. #2 Plant and #4 Plant Operating with #4 Plant product going directly to
   Hominy Feed
   One Operator and One Helper in Extraction
   Operator Only in Mill
VII. #2 Plant, #4 Plant and/or 20/0 and Griffith systems operating
   One Operator and One Helper in Mill and Extraction
VIII. With certain schedules and operating conditions, the plant operation
   would not require the complete services of two men (i.e., Operator and
   Helper). Under these conditions, the Helper would be assigned work such
   as cleaning tanks, changing screens, dust collector work, etc. An example
   would be #2 Plant running along with the 20/0 system. In this case the
   Mill Operator would have the operating responsibilities of #2 Plant with
   the Helper assisting on the 20/0 system. The Helper would be assigned
   other work such as sifter repairs, hammer mill work, etc.

Plant No. 3 is not mentioned in the Schedule. To explain this omission, Tell testified:

No. 3 is not in the Schedule because No. 3 was not in production at the time it was agreed to. When it went into operation, we grieved that there should be an additional Operator in the Bean Plant. The Company said no. But it was agreed that one additional Helper would be assigned when No. 1 and 3 Plants were operating. This was our understanding.

On his part, Iron testified that Plant No. 3 went into operation in 1991. He said:

When the Schedule was negotiated, No. 3 was in operation, being the day of TVP (hamburger helper). No. 3 is not in the Schedule because No. 3 is an extension of Plant No. 1. It was not necessary to put No. 3 into the Schedule. No. 3 cannot operate unless Plant No. 1 operates. But No. 1 can operate without No. 3.

Iron also testified that he did not recall any additional negotiations about Plant No. 3 as far as adding another Helper was concerned.

Engel testified (contrary to Tell) as to when Plant No. 3 went into operation. He said:

Plant No. 3 went into full operation in early 1993. It was not in full operation in 1991. I can't say that it was in full operation when the Schedule was drawn up.

POSITIONS OF THE PARTIES

The position of the Union is that the grievance should be granted, and the Company requests that it be denied.

CHAPTER

10

Administrative Issues under
Collective Bargaining

$\mathscr{P}$rovisions relating to seniority, discipline, health and safety, subcontracting, and the various other administrative areas of the labor relationship, as in the case of institutional provisions, have the common characteristic of falling into the noneconomic classification of collective bargaining. But they are hardly of minor importance.

A seniority clause, for example, can have a vital impact upon the efficient operation of the productive process. And the protection afforded an employee as a result of a discharge clause can be of much greater importance than any of the rights enjoyed as a result of the negotiation of wage rates or benefits. It matters little to the worker who has been discharged for an obviously unfair reason that the wages called for by the labor contract are very generous.

Moreover, nowadays, technological change is of overriding importance in many labor relationships, dwarfing even the subject of wage issues in such instances. Literally thousands of jobs are being eliminated by such change each week in the economy, and it is a rare union that does not see the development, now actually accelerating, as a formidable one from the viewpoint of job security. This volume has already dealt with union economic demands that are rooted at least partially in this problem: early retirement, severance pay, and SUB plans, among others. As we shall see, many administrative issues also flow from workers' fears that amid rampant technological innovation their jobs are very vulnerable.

In short, as important as the negotiation of economic issues may be, one cannot ignore these nonwage administrative issues of collective bargaining. The two are interwoven, and to ignore or slight either—just as to overlook the institutional area of the contract—would represent a distortion of present-day labor relations in the United States.

SENIORITY

The principle of **seniority**, under which the employee with the greater length of organizational or organizational subunit service receives increased job security and improved working conditions (and, commonly, greater entitlement to employee benefits), is not a new one. Over a thousand years ago promotion in the Chinese civil service was governed by time in grade, and two centuries ago seniority was rigorously applied in the Prussian bureaucracy to determine personnel advancement as the only alternative to the corruption that was almost a national pastime of the period. And, while in the British civil service in the mid-nineteenth century promotion was theoretically to be based on "merit," in practice seniority was the dominant factor—again, as an antidote to favoritism by decision makers.[1] In the United States, the armed forces have emphasized it from the days of Andrew Jackson, and the railroads and printing trades have stressed it for over a century.

For at least three reasons, however, seniority has received increasing stress in labor contracts over the past few decades.

In the first place, both management and employee representatives have become convinced that there is a certain amount of justice to the arrangement, especially in times of work contraction or recall opportunities after layoffs.

Second, the application of seniority is an objective one, calculated to avoid arbitrariness in the selection of personnel for particular jobs and, consequently, less irksome for labor negotiators to deal with than an alternative criteria such as ability. Who is the most *able* man or woman among the several seeking a given promotion (or, for that matter, the most valuable player in the National Football League or the best member of the United States Senate) can generally not be determined with anything approaching precision; the most *senior* person can be pinpointed with absolutely no room for argument, simply by getting out the personnel records and taking a look.

Third, many employee benefit programs that have mushroomed in these years have been geared almost exclusively to seniority—often to make them more acceptable to the managements by restricting the number of employees entitled to the benefits. It is inconceivable, for example, that almost one-quarter of all labor contracts would provide—as they now do—six weeks of paid vacation, were it not for the fact that these contracts also call for a significant number of years of service (most often, 30 and rarely less than 25 years) in order for employees to get such a benefit. Similarly, some 90 percent of all disability pension provisions (which are themselves contained in almost 90 percent of all labor agreements) contain a years-of-service requirement, generally 10 or 15 years.[2]

It is also an industrial relations truism that if management doesn't want to reward on the basis of seniority, because in most cases rewarding on the basis of ability *is* the only realistic alternative, it must make sure that the four basic tools of performance evaluation are not only in place but relatively error free. These are (1) employee records, (2) job descriptions, (3) merit rating plans, and (4) supervisory rating competency. To withstand challenge in the grievance procedure and in arbitration, the records and the descriptions must be accurate, up-to-date, and comprehensive, the merit rating plans must be entirely defensible, and the supervisory rating ability must be beyond question. Together, all of this forms a tall order for employers—one which is obviously needed where differential ability is meaningful but is hardly necessary in many bargaining unit situations. Seniority can be a far less onerous substitute.

These days, most labor agreements provide for seniority to play a major role in such areas as layoffs, recalls after layoffs, work assignments, transfers, and shift preferences. In addition to the almost 50 percent of all pensions that grant so much per month per year of credited service and to vacation entitlements (which are invariably based on length of service), such benefits as severance pay and sick leave are normally based on seniority. Even in the case of promotions, seniority is most often of some importance, although here considerations of ability and (at times) physical fitness are usually more important. Thus, among other things, the application of the seniority principle relates to both employee job security and employee economic well-being, and by the same token it limits the freedom of the management to direct the labor force and to maximize profits. A seniority structure that approaches the ideal would be one that protects the members of the workforce while not placing unreasonable restrictions on management's right to manage.

Many decisions must be made concerning the length of service criterion in collective bargaining beyond the crucial determination of the parts of the employment relationship that should be influenced at all by seniority. What should be the organizational units in which workers acquire and apply seniority credits? Under what circumstances may employees lose seniority? How about the seniority status of employees who transfer from one part of the bargaining unit to another or who leave the bargaining unit altogether? What, if any, exceptions to the seniority system should there be?

❖ Units for Seniority

There are three major systems relating to the unit in which an employee acquires and applies seniority credits: employerwide, departmental or occupational, and a combined employer and departmental seniority system. Under an *employerwide seniority system*, the seniority status of each employee equals that person's total service with the firm. Thus, transfers from job to job within the establishment or transfers from one department to another have no effect on an employee's seniority standing. Subject to other features of the seniority structure, an employee under the employerwide system will apply his or her seniority for purposes covered by the seniority system on a strictly organizationwide basis. In actual practice, this system is not used in situations in which it would be necessary for an employee to undergo a considerable training period when the employee takes a new job to replace a worker with less seniority. It is practicable only for payrolls in which the jobs are more or less interchangeable. An employerwide system obviously gives the greatest protection to employees with the longest length of service. On the other hand, depending on the other features of the seniority structure, it could serve as a deterrent to the efficiency and productivity of the organization.

Under *departmental* or *occupational seniority systems*, separate seniority lists are established for each department or occupational grouping in the organization. If such a system does not have any qualifications or limitations, employees can apply seniority credits only within their own department or occupation. Such a system facilitates administration in large organizations employing a considerable number of workers. It minimizes the opportunity for large-scale displacement of workers from their jobs in the event of layoffs or discontinuation of particular jobs because of technological innovations or because of permanent changes in the market for products. On the other hand, if layoffs in one department become necessary, or if certain jobs in such a department are permanently discontinued while other departments are not affected, a state of affairs could develop in which employees with long service in an organization would find themselves out of a job while employees with less seniority were working full time. In addition, under a strict departmental seniority structure, transfers between departments tend to be discouraged because a transfer could result in complete loss of accumulated seniority.

As a result of the problems arising from a strict employerwide seniority system, many managements and unions have negotiated a number of plans combining these two types of seniority structures. Under a combination system, seniority may be applied in one unit for certain purposes and in another unit for other purposes. Thus, seniority might be applied on an employerwide basis for purposes of layoffs, and departmentwide seniority may be used as the basis of promotion. A variation of this system is to permit employees to *apply* their seniority only within the department in which they are working but to *compute* such seniority on the basis of total service with the employer. In addition, although the general application of seniority is limited to a departmental basis, employees laid off in a particular department may claim work in a general labor pool in which the jobs are relatively unskilled and in which newly hired employees start out before being promoted to other departments. At times, a distinction is drawn between temporary layoffs resulting from lack of business or material shortages and permanent layoffs resulting from changes in technology or permanent changes in the products manufactured. Under the former situation, seniority may be applied only on a departmental basis, or seniority might not govern at all (as in the automobile industry), whereas under the latter circumstances, employees have the opportunity to apply their seniority on an employerwide basis. Other variations of the combination system are used within industry as determined by the circumstances of a particular employer.

❖ Limitations on Seniority

Regardless of the type of system under which seniority credits are accumulated and applied, many collective bargaining agreements place certain limitations on length of service as a factor in connection with layoffs. In some cases, seniority systems provide for the retention of more-senior employees only when they are qualified to perform the jobs that are available. In considerably fewer labor agreements, a senior employee will be retained in the event of layoffs only when the employee is able to perform an available job "as well as" other employees eligible for layoff.

Although a large number of labor agreements permit employees scheduled for layoff to displace less-senior employees, limitations on the chain of displacement or **bumping** process are also included in many labor agreements. Employers, unions, employees, and students of labor relations recognize the inherent disadvantages of seniority structures that permit unlimited bumping. Bumping could result in serious obstacles to efficiency and productivity to the detriment of all concerned, could cause extreme uncertainty and confusion to workers who might be required to take a number of different jobs as a result of a single layoff, and could result in serious internal political problems for the labor organization.

For these reasons, many labor agreements allow an employee to displace a less-senior worker in the event of a layoff only when the former employee has a minimum amount of service with the employer. Other contracts circumscribe the bumping process by limiting the opportunity of a senior employee to displace a junior worker to jobs that the employee with longer service has already held. Under other seniority systems, the area into which the employee may bump is itself limited: It may be stipulated that employees can bump only on a departmental or divisional basis or can displace workers only with equal or lower labor grades. In addition, the objective of limiting the displacement process is achieved by permitting the displacement of only the *least*-senior employee in the bumping area and not of any other less-senior employees.

Most labor agreements provide for rehiring in reverse order of layoffs—the last employee laid off is the first rehired. In addition, laid-off employees are given preference over new workers for vacancies that arise anywhere in the place. However, such preferences given employees with longer service are frequently limited to the extent that the employee in question is competent to perform the available work. In this connection, the problem of the reemployment of laid-off workers becomes somewhat complicated when a straight departmental seniority system is used. In such a case, although a labor agreement might provide for the rehiring of workers in the reverse order of layoffs, operations might not resume in reverse order to the slack in production, and thus employees with shorter service might be recalled to work before employees with greater seniority. To avoid such a state of affairs, some labor contracts provide the older employee in terms of service with the opportunity of returning to work first, provided that the person has the ability to carry out the duties of the available job.

Length of service as a factor in promotion is, as noted, of less importance than it is in layoffs and rehiring, and in only a relative handful of labor agreements is length of service the sole factor in making promotions. The incidence is low because all parties to collective bargaining realize that a hospital custodian, for example, in spite of many years of service in this position, is not qualified to be promoted to, say, a nurse's job. But if such a criterion is rarely the sole factor in the assignment of workers to higher-rated jobs, the vast majority of labor agreements now require that seniority along with other factors be given *consideration*. In many contracts, seniority governs promotions when the senior employee is "qualified" to fill the position in question. Under others, seniority becomes the determining criterion in promotions when the senior employee has ability for the job in question "equal to that" of all other employees who may desire the better job. Under the latter seniority structure, length of service is thus of secondary importance to the ability factor.

In practice, management makes the decision about which worker among those bidding for the job gets the promotion. And, in the heavy majority of cases, this decision of the employer is satisfactory to all concerned, usually because the senior employee *is* best qualified for the job in question or because the employer is completely willing to give preference to the senior employee when ability differences among employees are not readily discernible. Even when management believes that the senior worker is not up to the level of competence of others who seek a promotion, moreover, it may choose to avoid the administrative arduousness referred to earlier by allowing the senior person to advance. Abraham Lincoln once observed that whenever he put someone on the federal payroll he created several enemies and an ingrate, the question of who is most senior is not open to any dispute at all because, as noted, it is a statement of absolute fact (although an occasional ingrate may still emerge in the process).

At times, however, employers do pass over senior employees in favor of those with shorter service in making a promotion, and unions do protest such actions through the grievance procedure—arguing that the bypassed worker is "qualified" (if this is all that the labor agreement requires) or does have "equal" ability (if that is contractually stipulated) and therefore is entitled to the job. In the first of these two situations, the spurned employee's entry work record (including absenteeism, tardiness, and accidents, if any) is scrutinized; in the second, the comparative ability of one or more other bidders for the promotion is the issue involved and studied. Ordinarily, such disputes are jointly resolved on the basis of these considerations. At times, however, the parties are still in disagreement, and the matter is then most often referred to an impartial arbitrator, who will make the decision in the case. *(Case 8 deals with a seniority problem.)*

❖ Seniority in Transfers

Another seniority problem involves the seniority status of employees who transfer from one department to another. Although interdepartmental transfers do not create a seniority issue under a straight employerwide seniority system, to the extent that seniority is acquired or applied on a departmentwide basis, the problem of transfers does become important. Reference has been made to the fact that interdepartmental transfers are discouraged when employees lose all accumulated seniority upon entering a new department. Some contracts deal with this by allowing a transferred employee to retain seniority in the old department while starting at the bottom of the seniority scale in the new department; under these circumstances, such an employee would exercise seniority rights in the old department in the event that the employee were laid off from the new department. Some contracts even permit such an employee to further accumulate seniority for application in the old department in the event that he or she is laid off from the new department. Another approach to the problem permits the transferred employee to carry seniority acquired in the old department to the new department. This is a common practice where the job itself is transferred to a new department, where the job or the department itself is permanently abolished, or when two or more departments are merged.

Still another seniority problem arises under the circumstances of an employee's transferring entirely out of the bargaining unit. This issue is particularly related to the seniority status of workers who are selected by management to fill supervisory jobs. There are three major approaches. Under some contracts, a rank-and-file employee who takes a supervisory job simply loses accumulated seniority. If for some reason the supervisory job is terminated and the employee desires to return to a job covered by the collective bargaining contract, he or she is treated as a new employee for purposes of seniority. Another method is to permit such an employee when serving as a supervisor to retain all seniority credits earned earlier. Under this approach, if the employee transfers back to the bargaining unit, the employee returns with the same number of seniority credits as before the transfer. Finally, under some contracts, an employee taking a supervisor's job accumulates seniority in the bargaining unit while serving as a supervisor. If the employee returns to the bargaining unit, that worker comes back not only with the seniority credits acquired before taking the supervisory job but also with seniority credits accumulated while serving as a member of management. Rank, at times, does have its privileges.

Obviously, seniority status is not a problem when management fills its supervisory posts by hiring people not presently employed in the place. On the other hand, the problem is a real one when the employer elects to fill such jobs from the rank and file. It is understandable that a worker with long seniority in the bargaining unit would hesitate to take a first-line supervisory job if doing so would forfeit accumulated seniority. In recognition of this situation, many employers and unions have agreed that workers promoted from the bargaining unit to supervisors' jobs may at least retain the seniority they accumulated while covered by the labor agreement. Whatever approach unions and managements take to this problem, it would generally be desirable to spell out the method in the labor agreement. Confusion, uncertainty, and controversy could arise when the contract is silent on this issue.

At times seniority may be used as the basis of a transfer to a job within the same wage classification. Such an opportunity may be used by an employee who desires to move to a different shift, for instance from the night to the day shift. Or if the employee and the supervisor cannot get along, the employee may exercise transfer rights to a job in another area of the facility or to a different shift. Under these circumstances, the transfer would be beneficial to the management and the employee. Normally, however, there are restrictions on employee transfer rights. When the transfer is within the same wage classification but to another job, the employee must have qualifications to perform the work. Transfer provisions also do not ordinarily permit bumping. Before a transfer may occur, there must be a job vacancy. Recognizing that promiscuous transfers could be harmful to organizational efficiency, employers insist that the employees' right to transfer be limited. For example, some contracts require that an employee be within a job classification, often for six months or a year, before the employee may exercise transfer rights. In addition, when two or more employees desire to transfer to the same job, normally labor agreements will give preference to the senior employee provided that the senior bidder has qualifications relatively equal to those of a junior service employee.

❖ Exceptions to the Seniority System

Under many collective bargaining contracts there is provision for some exemptions from the normal operation of the seniority structure. One of these involves the issue of **superseniority** for union officers. Some managements and unions have agreed that designated union officers may have a preferred status in the event of layoffs. Such employees are protected in employment regardless of their length of service. They are entitled to such consideration strictly by virtue of the union office they hold, however, and lose their superseniority status when their term of office is terminated.

Preference is afforded union officers because their presence in the facility is necessary for the effective operation of the grievance procedure. On this basis, the National Labor Relations Board has held that only those union officers, such as stewards, who participate directly in the processing of grievances are entitled to superseniority status. Such a benefit for officers who do not perform on-the-job contract administration functions is not lawful, said the NLRB, because to grant them superseniority unjustifiably discriminates against employees for union-related reasons.

The test is whether a particular officer is involved in grievance processing and not status in the union. As a result, the board has held unlawful superseniority granted to a union treasurer, a recording secretary, and a sergeant-at-arms because their presence was not required for the day-to-day operation of the grievance procedure.

Beyond specifying the precise union officers who are entitled to protection against layoff, another issue concerns the bumping rights of employees protected under such an arrangement. Contracts are usually explicit as to just what job or jobs such employees are entitled to when they are scheduled for layoff. In addition, it is common practice to make clear the rate of pay that the employee will earn in the new job. Thus, if a worker protected by superseniority takes another job that pays a lower rate than his or her regular job to avoid layoff, the contract specifies whether that employee will get the rate of the job filled or the rate of the regular job. Obviously, when these problems are resolved in the labor agreement, there is less chance for controversy during the hectic atmosphere of a layoff itself.

Some labor agreements also permit management to retain in employment during periods of layoff a certain number of nonunion-officer employees regardless of their seniority status. Such employees are designated as "exceptional," "specially skilled," "indispensable," or "meritorious" in collective bargaining contracts. As in the case of superseniority, problems growing out of this exception to the seniority rule are normally resolved in the collective bargaining contract. Problems in this connection involve the number of employees falling into this category, the kind of jobs they must be holding to receive such preferential status, their bumping rights (if any), and the rate of pay they shall earn in the event that they are retained in employment in jobs other than their regular ones.

Another general exception to the normal operation of a seniority system involves newly hired workers. Under most labor agreements, such workers must first serve a probationary period before they are protected by the labor agreement. Such probationary periods are frequently specified as being from about 30 to 90 days, and during this period of time the new worker can be laid off, demoted, transferred, or otherwise assigned work without reference to the seniority structure at all. However, once such an employee serves out this probationary period, seniority under most labor agreements is calculated from the first day of hire by the employer.

Under the terms of many collective bargaining contracts, employers may lay off workers on a *temporary* basis without reference to the seniority structure. Such layoffs are for short periods of time and result from purely temporary factors, such as shortages of material and power failures. It is, of course, vital in this connection that the labor agreement define the temporary layoff. Some agreements define the term as any layoff for fewer than five or even ten working days. Other contracts, however, specify that the seniority structure must be followed for any layoff in excess of twenty-four hours.

Finally, virtually all seniority structures specify circumstances under which an employee loses seniority credits. All employees should fully understand the exact nature of these circumstances and the significance of losing seniority credits. Under the terms of most contracts, employees lose seniority if they are discharged, voluntarily quit, fail to notify the management within a certain time period (usually five working days) of an intention to return to work after the employer recalls employees following a layoff, or fail to return to work after an authorized leave of absence. They also generally are separated from their seniority if they neglect to report to work within a certain period of time (usually 90 working days) after discharge from military service or are laid off continuously for a long period of time, usually from about 24 to 48 months.

❖ An Overall Evaluation

However qualified it may be in particular situations, there can be no denying the current acceptability of the seniority criterion in regulating potential competition among employees for jobs and job status. The traditional arguments that seniority fosters laziness, rewards mediocrity, and crimps individual initiative are no longer automatically brought into play by managers to oppose this length-of-service criterion. And the on-balance benefits of seniority, both in improving employee morale and in minimizing administrative problems, are no longer seriously questioned by progressive managements, *if* length of service is limited by such other factors as ability when these are relevant. Although it is probably true that in general a seniority system tends to reduce the efficiency of operations to some extent, if care is taken to design a system for the needs of the particular organization, and if length of service is appropriately limited in its application, the net loss to efficiency is normally not very noticeable.

Beyond this, many would argue that efficiency, despite its obvious importance, should not be the only goal of American industry. The advantages of providing a measure of job security to employees, and thereby relieving them of the frustrations of discrimination and unfair treatment, cannot be easily quantified. But human values have become the increasing concern of modern management, and the judicious use of seniority clearly serves the human equation.

❖ Seniority versus Affirmative Action

Because seniority is such a major factor in layoffs—almost 50 percent of all contracts now use it as the exclusive criterion in such circumstances, with another 30 percent commanding that it be a determining layoff factor—it has generated considerable tension between white male workers and minority and female ones. Generally having been more recently hired, the two latter groups have also been, in accordance with seniority, the first to go when work forces are pared to accommodate hard times. Thus, amid declining economic conditions of both the mid-1970s and the early 1980s, for example, many workplaces within months became once again as white and as male as they had been years earlier.

Equal opportunity had, of course, finally come to minorities and females in the 1960s and 1970s. It had had many causes—among them, certainly, more progressive mores of society and more enlightened attitudes on the part of the new breed of industrial leader. But one factor had clearly been paramount: Title VII of the Civil Rights Act of 1964, with its ban on job discrimination by race, sex, color, religion, or national origin and its application to all corporations, state and local governments, labor organizations, and employment agencies having more than 15 employees. After this landmark legislation, blacks, women, and other minority group members had been hired and promoted, often in some abundance, into jobs for which even in an expanding economy they had generally been treated like wallflowers at an orgy.

To the Equal Employment Opportunity Commission, charged (together with the Justice Department) with enforcing Title VII and empowered to sue the title's violators, what employers should do in the face of the need for layoffs was clear: Give special protection to the newly recruited groups to compensate them for past discrimination. At least as clear, however, was the fact that union contracts commanded respect for the seniority principle and its "last in, first out" principle. And, all but universally, the second of these Hobson's choices was embraced by the management community as the economy sank to its lowest levels since the Great Depression of the 1930s in a 1975 tailspin that would be exceeded in its enormity only by the impact of the 1981–1983 recession.

As court dockets became clogged with consequent affirmative action versus seniority suits (with the EEOC lending its full weight to minorities and women, and the U.S. Department of Justice generally supporting seniority), most experts felt that seniority would ultimately triumph—at the U.S. Supreme Court level, where the issue would inevitably wind up. For one thing, the 1964 Civil Rights Act itself specifically approved "bona fide" seniority systems in layoffs (although it omitted any helpful interpretations as to what was bona fide). For another, the lower courts had already consistently upheld the seniority system, most notably in the case of *Jersey Central Power and Light Co.*, in which a U.S. appeals court judge ruled that Congress had not mandated such a sweeping remedy as that proposed by the EEOC and that only Congress could do so. And for a third, layoff by seniority was specifically sanctioned even on the occasion of the EEOC's most conspicuous victory: In 1973, by a consent decree, the American Telephone and Telegraph Company agreed to pay $51 million in back wages and raises.

In two complex 1977 decisions involving United Air Lines flight attendants and truck drivers employed by T.I.M.E.–D.C. Inc., the Supreme Court ruled that, although it might perpetuate the effects of past discrimination against women and minorities, an otherwise "neutral" seniority system did not violate the Civil Rights Act. But this was not to be the last judicial word on the subject. In 1979 the Court ruled on a major new "reverse discrimination" suit, brought by a white worker at a Kaiser Aluminum plant in Louisiana on the grounds that he had been discriminated against by being turned down for a company training program designed to increase the number of blacks in skilled craft jobs. The worker, Brian F. Weber, pointed out that he had been rejected even though two black workers who were accepted had less seniority. The case stemmed from a 1974 company–union agreement to establish a new skilled job program, open to blacks and whites on a 50-50 basis until blacks had achieved a 39 percent representation in such skilled jobs (39 percent because this equaled their current representation in the area workforce).

The Court decided against Weber. By a five to two majority, it declared that an employer could give preference to minorities (and women) in hiring and promoting for "traditionally segregated job categories" and that it didn't matter that the employer had never practiced discrimination. In so doing it greatly relieved Kaiser Aluminum (and, obviously, many other employers) of an understandable worry: Until this decision, the Civil Rights Act had appeared to allow remedial discrimination only if past discrimination had been proved, and if Kaiser, amid this circumstance, had admitted any such past discrimination it would have opened itself to all sorts of lawsuits from injured employees. The Court's *Weber* ruling extricated Kaiser, which perhaps for a while was starting to believe the old adage that no good deed goes unpunished, from this unenviable dilemma.

Yet the decision was decided on rather narrow grounds. As Justice William Brennan pointed out in writing the majority opinion, the only key was whether the Civil Rights Act forbade *voluntary* endeavors of the Kaiser variety. The decision that it did not was hardly tantamount to *requiring* employers to establish affirmative action programs.

❖ Supreme Court Decisions in the 1980s

In a series of decisions issued between 1984 and 1989, the U.S. Supreme Court continued to address the problem of affirmative action. In *Firefighters* v. *Stotts*, involving firefighters employed by the City of Memphis, the high court held that an affirmative action program may not be used to lay off senior white employees and retain junior black workers. The city had laid off senior white employees ahead of junior black employees to maintain a court-ordered balance between white and black firefighters, but the Supreme Court held that Title VII was violated by such preferential treatment afforded black employees. As in *T.I.M.E.–D.C.*, the high court held that the seniority system as it applies to layoffs was bona fide and not intended for discrimination against black employees.

In 1986, the high court again held that junior black employees could not be retained and senior white employees laid off in *Wygant* v. *Jackson Board of Education*. In Jackson, Michigan, the board of education had negotiated a labor agreement with the teachers' union stipulating that junior black teachers would be kept on while senior white teachers would be laid off. Such a system was negotiated to keep black teachers as "role models." By a five to four majority, the high court held that the white teachers were denied equal protection of the law and that the affirmative action program to maintain black teachers as role models could not alone justify laying off the senior white teachers.

The Court did not slam the door on all aspects of affirmative action. Even in the matter of layoffs, it hinted in *Wygant*, such special circumstances as a showing of blatant historical discrimination by the employer against minorities might even now justify the layoffs of white employees who were senior to minority employees and the retention of the minority group members. And in two later 1986 decisions—respectively involving black firefighters in Cleveland and sheet metal workers in New York—the judges continued this latter theme. The judiciary could, as Justice Brennan wrote for the majority in the latter case, properly order "race-conscious affirmative action [as] relief to dissipate the lingering effects of pervasive discrimination."

For women, moreover, the Court had even better news. In 1987, the justices ruled in *Johnson* v. *Transportation Agency* that the public transportation agency of Santa Clara County, California, had properly awarded a road dispatcher's job to Diane Joyce, even though she had scored two points less than a man (the plaintiff, Paul Johnson) on a performance test and Johnson had had more seniority than Joyce. Joyce had been found to be fully qualified in all respects by a supervisory panel. And the Court decreed that because there had been a "manifest [sexual] imbalance" in the workforce and such affirmative action would not by itself "unnecessarily trammel" the rights of other workers, the employer could voluntarily implement the affirmative action.

But a variety of 1989 decisions dispelled any real doubt as to where the Ronald Reagan appointees who now firmly fashioned the high court decisions stood on such matters. In *Lorance* v. *A.T. & T. Technologies*, the Court severely restricted the time period during which certain discriminatory practices involving a seniority system could be challenged. In *Price Waterhouse*, while declaring that employers must prove that their refusal to promote employees was based on legitimate business reasons, it lowered the burden of proof required in these situations to the weakest possible standard.

Warming to their work, the judges then reversed in *Wards Cove* v. *Atonio* an 18 year old precedent and ruled that plaintiffs, not employers, had the burden of proving whether a job requirement that was shown statistically to screen out minorities or women was a "business necessity." In further votes, the members of the highest judiciary decided that court-approved affirmative action settlements could be reopened to let white male employees file reverse discrimination lawsuits (*Martin* v. *Wilks*) and that an 1866 civil rights law was inapplicable to cases of racial harassment or other discrimination by an employer after a person was hired (in *Patterson* v. *McLean Credit Union*).

The Court, even before two additional conservative justices replaced liberal ones on it during George H. W. Bush's White House years, had drifted very much to the right. Without some kind of legislative intervention, it was obvious that both women and minorities would find it much harder to prevail in their attacks on alleged job discrimination than they had prior to the new wave of rulings.

❖ The Civil Rights Act of 1991 and a 1995 Supreme Court Ruling

Legislative intervention did, however, come about—during, in fact, an economic recession that was even more severe than the tailspins of the 1970s and 1980s. Strong actions by any of our three branches of government can generally be counted upon to produce reactions from others of them. And, while the **Civil Rights Act of 1991** is hardly in a class with the 1964 Civil Rights Act in its ambitiousness, it is notable for two major thrusts: (1) the effective countering of the several 1989 Supreme Court decisions and (2) the extension for the first time of punitive damages to victims of employment discrimination based on sex, race, or (under an amendment to the 1990 Americans with Disabilities Act) disability.

Now a plaintiff claiming that a seniority system is discriminatory could rely on the date that the system was adopted, the date that he or she became subject to the system, or the date that the person was allegedly injured by the system (reversing *Lorance*). The *Price Waterhouse*–required burden of proof was raised appreciably;

Wards Cove was negated by the actual shifting of the "business necessity" proof burden back to the employer; and the tenets of both *Martin* and *Patterson* vanished as though they had never been.

Nor could employers found guilty of intentional discrimination henceforth get off with the mere payments of compensatory damages (future economic losses, pain and suffering, mental anguish, inconvenience, and other nonpecuniary losses), as onerous as these might be. If the plaintiff could prove that the management acted in a discriminatory practice "with malice or with reckless indifference to the federally protected rights of an aggrieved individual," an additional price must be paid by the employer—up to $300,000 in punitive damages depending on the size of the organization.

The 1991 legislation is still very much on the books, but in the always-changing world of its subject matter another major action from the government was not long in coming, and once again it modified what had preceded it. In mid-1995, the Supreme Court continued its own *assault* on affirmative action by ruling in a five to four vote that Congress must meet a very tough legal standard to justify any hiring or contracting practice based on race.

The Court's decision was rendered in a case brought to it by Randy M. Pech, the white owner of Adarand Constructors, Inc., a Colorado company. He had submitted the low bid for subcontracting work but had lost the work to a company designated as disadvantaged because of its Hispanic ownership (the prime contractor was one of almost 200,000 federal contractors required under a 1965 Lyndon Johnson executive order to adopt an affirmative hiring plan). The Court did not strike down any particular program (including the prime contractor's), but said that any preferential program must be subject to "strict scrutiny" to distinguish between legitimate programs that redress real past discrimination and programs that "are in fact motivated by illegitimate notions of racial inferiority or simple racial politics."

Most observers thought that all of this—the 1991 legislation notwithstanding—was just one more nail in the coffin of affirmative action, at least as far as race was concerned. It seemed certain to generate a host of court challenges to existing governmental affirmative action programs and to add ammunition to the increasingly negative feelings of much of the American citizenry concerning the whole preferential system.

DISCHARGE AND DISCIPLINE

To the naked eye, in the absence of a collective bargaining agreement, the employer is relatively unfettered in applying discipline. Actions cannot be taken, to be sure, that conflict with federal, state, or local labor laws. The government has also, as we know, been anything but bashful in dealing with the subject of discrimination against individuals on a variety of grounds, and clearly the disciplinary efforts cannot run afoul of these constraints either. Except only for such considerations, however, the management is as free to deal disciplinarily with its payroll members as it chooses—even if it chooses to act quite arbitrarily, inconsistently, autocratically, and harshly. The employer can discipline for any reason or, indeed, for no reason at all.

The advent of the union changes all of this, in the sense that *specific standards* are now established for the discipline. In general, labor–management contracts state that employers may discipline only for "just cause" (or "just and proper cause" or "proper cause"), and even when they do not, such a stricture is assumed to be implied if there is no concrete language to the contrary. And the critical interpretation of just cause is accomplished through industrial practice and common sense, as well as (if need be) the grievance procedure and the arbitration process.

Every year, close to half of all the arbitration cases that are decided under either American Arbitration Association or Federal Mediation and Conciliation Service auspices involve discipline, most frequently discharge situations, and this is entirely understandable. The right of the employer to discipline is essential to operating a successful enterprise, but—as one arbitrator phrased it in ruling against a company in a discharge case:

> If the Company can discharge without cause, it can lay off without cause. It can recall, transfer or promote in violation of the seniority provisions simply by invoking its claimed right to discharge. Thus, to interpret the Agreement in accord with the claim of the Company would reduce to a nullity the fundamental provision of a labor–management agreement—the security of a worker in his job.[3]

In addition, the stigma of discharge would hardly make it easier for the former employee to find another job. Thus, discharges have even more serious consequences for workers than do permanent layoffs.

Although the majority of contracts contain only the previously noted general and simple statement that discharge can be made only for just cause, many labor agreements list one or more specific grounds for discharge: violation of employment rules, failure to meet work standards, incompetence, violation of the collective bargaining contract (including in this category the instigation of or participation in a strike or a slowdown in violation of the agreement), excessive absenteeism or tardiness, intoxication, dishonesty, insubordination, and fighting on the employer's property. Labor agreements that list specific causes for discharge normally also include a general statement that discharge may be made for "any other just or proper reason."

In addition, many contracts distinguish between causes for immediate discharge and offenses that require one or more warnings. Sabotage, stealing, drunkenness on the job, and loan-sharking are examples of infractions that would normally warrant discharge for a first offense. These are viewed as sufficiently serious so that no specific warning or previous disciplinary action is needed. A discharge for excessive absenteeism or tardiness, on the other hand, would need to be preceded by a certain number of warnings.

And in recognition of the fact that not all employee infractions are grave enough to warrant discharge at all, most contracts explicitly recognize lesser forms of permissible discipline, including oral and written reprimand, suspension without pay for varying lengths of time, demotion, and denial of vacation pay. Moreover, union and management representatives in the grievance procedure will often agree on a lesser measure of discipline even though the employer presumably has the grounds to discharge an employee for a particular offense. At times, the union and the employee in question will be willing to settle a case on these terms rather than risk taking the case to arbitration.

A very large number of collective bargaining contracts specify a distinct procedure for discharge cases (and many also do so for disciplinary layoffs, as Exhibit 10-1, culled from the current General Motors-UAW agreement, demonstrates). Many of them require notice to the employee and the union before the discharge takes place. Such notification is generally required to contain the specific reasons for the discharge. A hearing on the case is also provided for in many

EXHIBIT 10-1

DISCIPLINARY LAYOFFS AND DISCHARGES

(76) Any employee who has been disciplined by a suspension, layoff or discharge will be furnished a brief written statement advising him of his right to representation and describing the misconduct for which he has been suspended, laid off or discharged and, in the case of a layoff or discharge, the extent of the discipline. Thereafter, he may request the presence of the committeeman for his district to discuss the case privately with him in a suitable office designated by the Local Management, or other location by mutual agreement, before he is required to leave the plant. The committeeman will be called promptly without regard to the restrictions on his time as provided in Paragraphs (18) and (19a) of the Representation Section. Whether called or not, the committeeman will be advised in writing within one working day of 24 hours of the fact of written reprimand, suspension, layoff or discharge and will be given a copy of the statement given to the employee. After a suspension has been converted to a layoff or discharge, the committeeman will be notified in writing of the fact of layoff or discharge. The written statement furnished to the employee pursuant to the first sentence of this paragraph shall not limit Management's rights, including the right to rely on additional or supplemental information not contained in the statement to the employee.

(76a) When a suspension, layoff or discharge of an employee is contemplated, the employee, where circumstances permit, will be offered an interview to allow him to answer the charges involved in the situation for which such discipline is being considered before he is required to leave the plant. An employee who, for the purpose of being interviewed concerning discipline, is called to the plant, or removed from his work to the foreman's desk or to an office, or called to an office, may, if he so desires, request the presence of his District Committeeman to represent him during such interview.

(76b) The employee will be tendered a copy of any warning, reprimand, suspension or disciplinary layoff entered on his personnel record, within three days of the action taken. In imposing discipline on a current charge, Management will not take into account any prior infractions which occurred more than three years previously nor impose discipline on an employee for falsification of his employment application after a period of (18) months from his date of hire.

(77) It is important that complaints regarding unjust or discriminatory layoffs or discharges be handled promptly according to the Grievance Procedure. Grievances must be filed within three working days of the layoff or discharge. Within two working days after a grievance has been answered by higher supervision, pursuant to Paragraph 30 above, the specific charge will be discussed with designated representatives of local Plant Management, the Chairman of the Shop Committee, or his designated representative, and another member of the Shop Committee or the district committeeman who filed the grievance. If the grievance is not resolved, local Plant Management will review and render a decision on the case within three working days thereafter. In any event, local Plant Management will render a decision on the case within 10 working days from the date the grievance is filed. If a Notice of Unadjusted Grievance is not submitted by the Shop Committee within five (5) working days of a decision of the local Plant Management, the matter will be considered closed.

labor agreements, typically requiring the presence of not only the worker in question and an appropriate management official but also a representative of the labor organization. Frequently, collective bargaining agreements provide for a suspension period before the discharge becomes effective. The alleged advantage of this procedure is that it provides for an opportunity to cool tempers and offers a period of time for all parties to make a careful investigation and evaluation of the facts of the case.

Appeals of discharges are invariably taken through the regular grievance procedure because the appeal is looked upon as a grievance, and the stipulated courses of action must be respected. If, for example, the labor agreement provides that the employee or the union must appeal a discharge within a certain number of days, such appeal must be made during this period or the discharge may become permanent regardless of the merits of the case. Likewise, a management that neglects its obligation to give an answer to the appeal within the stipulated number of days may find that it has lost its right do discharge the worker regardless of the justice of the situation.

Frequently, labor agreements also provide that a discharge case has priority over all other cases in the grievance procedure. Some of them even waive the first steps of the grievance procedure and start a discharge case at the top levels of the procedure. In these arrangements, employers and unions recognize the fact that it is to the mutual advantage of all concerned to expedite. Workers want to know as quickly as possible whether or not they still have a job. The management also has an interest in the prompt settlement of a discharge case, because of the disciplinary implications involved and because labor agreements normally require that the employer award the employee loss of earnings when a discharge is withdrawn.

From the foregoing, it should be clear that under a collective bargaining relationship, the employer does not lose the right to discipline or discharge; it is, however, more difficult for management to exercise this function. There must be just cause, a specific procedure must be followed, and, of course, management must have the proof that an employee committed the offensive act.

❖ The Need for Proof

If a case does go to arbitration, in fact, the arbitrator will be particularly concerned with the quality of *proof* that management offers in the hearing. On many occasions, employers have lost discharge cases in arbitration because the evidence they have presented is not sufficient to prove the case for discharge. At times, the management's case against the employee has simply been poorly prepared; at other times, the management has not been able to assemble the proof despite the most conscientious of employer efforts. (One difficulty in this latter regard, as all arbitrators are well aware, is that employees dislike testifying against other employees.)

If the arbitrator did not demand convincing proof before sustaining discipline, however, the protection afforded employees by the labor agreement would be worthless. The same situation prevails in our civil life: Juries have freed criminals because the state has not proved its case. Such courses of action reflect one of the most cardinal features of our system of justice, the presumption that people are innocent until proven guilty, and this hallmark of our civil life plays no less a role in the American system of industrial relations. This situation has undoubtedly resulted in the reinstatement to their jobs with full back pay for employees who are in fact "guilty," but it is beyond argument that an employer bears the obligation to prove charges against employees it has displaced. In the absence of such an obligation, this most important benefit allowed employees under a collective bargaining contract, protection against arbitrary management treatment, is obviously negated. *(Cases 9 and 10 involve the discharge of employees. Case 10 is particularly called to your attention because of its strange circumstances.)*

Thus, an arbitrator in a case involving Greyhound Lines overruled the discharge of an employee who had been terminated for attempted arson. One night outside the employer's premises, a security guard had observed a man throwing what appeared to be a lighted object into a trash bin and had identified the thrower as the grievant. But at the hearing it was conclusively established that the guard had made his observation from a distance of roughly 100 yards and that the street on which the incident took place was poorly lit. This, reasoned the arbitrator, made the guard's testimony something less than convincing proof that the infraction—although by any standard a dischargeable offense—had been committed by the grievant.[4]

Conversely, even circumstantial evidence can constitute proof of wrongdoing, as it did in the case of a Max Factor & Co. employee who had been seen secreting company products on her person by a coworker, who then notified a plant guard. The guard in turn notified a supervisor, who directed the guard to recover the items from the employee. Even though the employee and the guard were alone when the goods were recovered, the stolen items were returned to the processing line and so disappeared as evidence, and the employee later denied the guard's testimony regarding the pilferage, the arbitrator decided that the employee's discharge by the company had been justified. He ruled that the testimonies of the coworker, the guard, and the supervisor added up to sufficient circumstantial evidence to prove the employee's guilt.[5]

Some arbitrators in deciding discipline cases demand extremely high standards of proof—"proof beyond a reasonable doubt" or even "proof beyond the shadow of a doubt." They see such cases as comparable to criminal (as opposed to civil) court proceedings, where such standards do control. They recognize that discharge is, as it has often been described, the "capital punishment" of the world of work and that even reprimands, suspensions, and other disciplinary penalties short of termination put workers on thinner ice as far as staving off discharge in the future. Most arbitrators, however, agree with veteran arbitrator Arnold M. Zack, who has pointed out that (unlike criminal court proceedings) discipline arbitrations "do not entail the potential of the death penalty, incarceration, or loss of freedom that drives the higher standards for criminal proceedings" and that the controlling standard in arbitration, by definition, "is really no more than the ability to convince the arbitrator."[6] Convincing proof, described by whatever terms in arbitration, is evidence that the arbitrator thinks is sufficient to support the position of the side bringing the charges.

❖ The Need for Meaningful Communication

Fully as important as the need for convincing proof is the necessity for the rules to be *clear* and *specifically communicated*, or employees simply cannot be held responsible for violating them. It is generally agreed that this stricture need not apply where the conduct involved is so obviously wrong on both moral and legal grounds that a specific rule is not needed: There is certainly no need, for example, to have an explicit rule banning employees from threatening supervision with a knife, and falsification of one's work records is—again—so clearly reprehensible that workers need not be given advance notice that this constitutes unacceptable behavior. On the other hand, it cannot be taken for granted by the employer that employees will always know what is expected of them, and most often specific communication is essential to sound discipline. It is better to saturate the landscape with such information than not to give enough.

Machinery for conveying behavioral expectations abounds in organizations. Employee handbooks, bulletin board postings, house organs, special memorandums from the management, and incorporation of the rules into the union contract are common avenues of communication. So, too, is oral publicity, by the personnel office (during orientation, for example) and also by supervision. Consistent enforcement of the rules, let it not be forgotten, lends another kind of visibility to them.

What is important, however, is not the exact methodology by which the rules are made known, but rather the fact that they *are* made known. No employee, when confronted with discipline, should be able to argue credibly that he or she did not realize that the conduct involved was forbidden or—for that matter—that *changes* in the rules or a managerial intention to apply an existing rule more strictly had not been brought to the attention of the work force.

❖ Mitigating Circumstances

Finally, in assessing penalties, the arbitrator will fully weigh *extenuating* or *mitigating circumstances*. Is it appropriate, for example, to discipline an employee, who, at the company Christmas party, gets drunk, throws the contents of a can of beer in the face of the industrial relations manager, and makes the air purple with obscene remarks in the process? One would certainly think so, but a case involving exactly this set of circumstances reached the arbitration stage a while ago, and the arbitrator overturned the 30-day suspension that the employee had been given for his behavior by the company and ordered that he be given full back pay as well. The decision was based primarily on the following considerations: (1) The man had worked for the company 33 years without a prior incident of insubordination; (2) the offense had been committed neither during working hours nor under plant disciplinary conditions, and the employee's conduct appeared to stem from his consuming too much alcohol rather than being connected to the employment relationship; and (3) although there had been prior incidents of drunken fights at the Christmas party, the company had continued to give out free and unlimited liquor and it consequently ran the risk of "predictable consequences."[7]

Mitigating circumstances—here, of course, three of them—completely changed the outcome from what might have been expected. Whether or not there is a labor arbitrator in the picture, a sound disciplinary policy commands nothing less than that these circumstances be carefully scrutinized when they exist.

Particularly when it is notably superior or glaringly inferior, a *past record*, for example, can make a large difference in evaluating the severity of a given offense. Even incidents that by themselves might hardly warrant much of a penalty at all, much less discharge, might generate a termination of employment under the most enlightened of disciplinary policies if they form a "last straw" in a long history of similar incidents. The alcoholic employee who has been warned on many occasions about his bad attendance record (as well as counseled about his underlying problem) and then is suspended for five days with the understanding that one more similar absence will cause his discharge and who then absents himself for the same drink-related reason may be said to illustrate this category. On the other side of the scales, a worker who might otherwise be terminated for a very serious offense—using abusive language in talking to a supervisor, let us say—could conceivably be given a lesser penalty in view of the worker's 11 years of superior performance (and absence of disciplinary infractions within it) in the service of the company.

In fact, *length of service*, in its own right, irrespective of its quality, can serve as a mitigating circumstance. Arbitrators have regularly accepted long service as something working in the disciplined employee's favor and so, too, in general have nonunion employers. Longevity itself presumably deserves some reward, but there are other considerations as well: *Losing* a great deal of seniority can impose a large—if not fully calculable—cost on an employee who does so. And when such a fate is suffered by a relative old-timer, the morale of the entire workforce can be impaired.

Still another kind of extenuating circumstance at times lies in the *behavior of management personnel* themselves. The employer is on very shaky ground in attempting to enforce a rule against solicitation by employees on company premises if it is known that supervisors regularly peddle merchandise within the building, and the employer deserves no better fate in administering an antiobesity rule if members of management tip the scales at significantly more than their allotted poundage. Employees can hardly be expected to observe rules that are so obviously ignored by their superiors.

SAFETY AND HEALTH OF EMPLOYEES

Despite significant progress over the decades, working for a living remains something less than the safest of all human endeavors. The statistics, understandably, vary widely industry by industry—with the mining of coal or packinghouse work, for example, being potentially more dangerous to worker safety and health than, say, the practicing of dermatology, by several light-years. But it is a common estimate on the part of experts that as many as 60,000 deaths (or far more than are caused by automobile accidents) occur every year as a result of occupational disease and that some 500,000 people annually develop a debilitating occupational illness. Another 10,000 deaths are caused each year by workplace accidents—about 30 each day.

Other figures relating to employee safety and health are similarly discomforting. In the opinion of many informed observers, roughly 25 percent of all workers are regularly exposed to major health and safety hazards. A job-related illness or injury is annually incurred by one out of every 11 workers in the United States, costing the nation an estimated $23 billion each year in the form of lost wages, medical expenses, insurance claims, and decreased productivity.[8] And it has been predicted that one out of every six working men presently 35 years of age will be disabled for at least six months before they reach age 65 and that one-tenth of those men will be permanently disabled.[9] (There are no comparable statistics available for working women.)

Given all of this information, few people would argue that employees do not have a real interest in the area of industrial safety and health. After all, it is the worker and the worker's family who suffer the most devastating consequences of neglect in this area. And, although most employers can sincerely claim that they, too, are deeply interested in safe and healthy working environments, such concern cannot restore to life a person killed on the job, or restore an employee's limbs, or succor an employee's family when an employment-caused accident or illness leads to a long-term disability. This consideration is, in fact, at the root of a longstanding policy of the National Labor Relations Board that safety and health demands of unions are mandatory subjects of collective bargaining. Employers must bargain on these issues even though working conditions are also subject to the many safety and health regulations imposed by federal and state statutes. Not surprisingly, then, most collective bargaining contracts contain explicit provisions relating to the safety and health area, although such provisions take one of two routes, depending upon the particular contract.

On the one hand, many contracts merely state in general terms that the management is required to take measures to protect the safety and health of employees. At times, the term *measures* is qualified by the word *reasonable*. When a contract contains such a broad and general statement, the problem of application and interpretation is obviously involved, and disagreements between the management and union in this regard are commonly resolved through the regular grievance procedure or by the operation of a special safety committee.

The second category of contracts provides a detailed and specific listing of safety and health measures that obligate the employer. Thus, many agreements stipulate that the latter must provide adequate heat, light, and ventilation; control drafts, noise, toxic fumes, dust, dirt, and grease; provide certain safety equipment, such as hoods, goggles, special shoes and boots, and other items of special clothing; and place guards and other safety devices on machines. In addition, under many contracts, the management must provide first-aid stations and keep a nurse on duty.

Many labor agreements impose obligations on employees and unions as well as on employers in the matter of safety. Such provisions recognize the fact that safety, despite the individual employee's crucial stake in it, is a joint problem requiring the cooperation of the management, employees, and union. Under many labor agreements, employees must obey safety rules and wear appropriate safety equipment, and employees who violate such rules are subject to discipline. In some labor agreements, the union assumes the obligation of educating its members in complying with safety rules and procedures of the plant. And some agreements, in the interest of safety, also establish a joint union–management safety committee. Many of these committees serve as advisory bodies on the general problem of safety and health; others, however, have the authority to establish and enforce safety and health rules, allowing the union a considerably more active role.

❖ The Occupational Safety and Health Act and Its Consequences to Date

A high point in the area of employment safety and health was reached in the last days of 1970 with the enactment of the **Occupational Safety and Health Act**, generally referred to (as is the federal agency primarily charged with administering it) as OSHA. Under it, the federal government assumed a significant role in this area for the first time in history, and individual states were allowed to share jurisdiction if their plans for doing so could meet with the approval of Washington. OSHA inspectors were granted authority to inspect for violations (without prior notice to the employer) at the nation's 5 million workplaces and to issue citations leading to possibly heavy fines and even, as a last resort, jail sentences.

The then—AFL-CIO president Meany applauded OSHA's enactment as "a long step down the road toward a safe and healthy workplace"; Richard M. Nixon, in signing it as President, referred to the act as "a landmark piece of legislation"; and the normally unemotional *Monthly Labor Review* passionately proclaimed it a "revolutionary program." Great expectations, in short, accompanied passage.

❖ Criticisms of OSHA

Yet disillusionment was quick to set in and, within a very few years, OSHA appeared to be all but friendless, its critics coming in almost equal numbers from the ranks of labor and management. By the end of the 1970s, the administrator of OSHA could sadly point out that the legislation had succeeded in alienating both sides. "Business and labor," she declared, "have criticized OSHA for nit-picking and the stringent enforcement of so-called nuisance standards. . . . Organized labor has complained that OSHA has been excruciatingly slow in adopting major health standards to protect large numbers of workers from widespread threats to their health."[10]

The complaints were justified. With fewer than 3,000 inspectors available to visit the 5 million places of work, the average employer could expect to see an OSHA agent roughly every 75 years. Yet when they did show up, these civil servants, as the administrator also pointed out, "were citing violations of regulations on everything from coat hooks to split toilet seats."[11] Moreover, OSHA's 325 pages of safety and health standards were so technical as to be unintelligible to the vast majority of employers without professional (and thus costly) help: In its first months alone, the agency had adopted almost 5,000 "consensus" safety standards. And the standards themselves were under any conditions expensive to satisfy, OSHA's noise-control demands alone potentially costing management anywhere from $13 billion to $31 billion (depending upon the final severity of these rules). OSHA, as one by no means atypical employer said of it at the end of its first decade, "is to a management what a knife is to a throat."

On the other hand, the agency's penalties for violations had averaged a not very punitive $25 each, with companies convicted of criminal violations being so rare as to be essentially invisible. And for all the "safety" standards, only three major "health" standards and a fourth one covering 14 carcinogenic substances had been promulgated by the 1980s.

And it was the latter trend—only—that continued after the inauguration of Ronald Reagan as the nation's chief executive in 1981. Budgetary cuts reduced the meager inspection staff by almost two-thirds, to a far more meager 1,100 within a year. Under a presidential executive order, health and safety standards and regulations were weakened by a requirement that benefits be weighed against costs. Three of every four manufacturing firms were exempted from routine safety inspections (in the interests of more governmental concentration on high-hazard manufacturing industries). And much emphasis was generally placed on voluntary employer compliance.

By 1985, the AFL-CIO was charging the Reagan administration with having "undertaken a systematic assault" upon OSHA. With minimal restraint, the federation's magazine commented, "Students of public administration may well rate the Reagan administration's emasculation of the Occupational Safety and Health Administration as its greatest bureaucratic coup."[12]

❖ A More Aggressive Approach

Stung by the criticism, the Reagan appointees at OSHA began to take a much harder line toward health and safety after 1985. In the next three years, the agency issued 20 new protective regulations, compared with 27 such rules in the previous 14 years, and by 1988 it was regularly making headlines by hitting some of the nation's largest employers with significant fines. In one week alone, the Chrysler Corporation was fined $1.57 million for violating OSHA rules, and the country's biggest meatpacker (IBP Inc.) was docked a hefty $2.59 million. Ford, General Dynamics, and Caterpillar were also the recipients of major financial penalties for failing to monitor the safety of their workplaces adequately.

After it took office in 1989, the George H. W. Bush administration continued the trend, vehemently denying that even amid its own budgetary constraints it would ever remotely retreat from safety and promising to finance OSHA better in the years ahead. It encouraged the agency to seek financing from Congress for another 179 inspectors, the first increase in the inspector contingent in a decade. In these early months of the Bush era, too, a more aggressive OSHA was busy promulgating the agency's first standard to protect on-the-job motor vehicle drivers, trying to raise the size of criminal fines for the most blatant job-site violations, and greatly expanding efforts to reduce carpal tunnel syndrome (involving arm, hand, and wrist injuries caused by repetitive motions).

Congress responded to the Bush desire for a more activist OSHA by authorizing a few more inspectors and greatly raising the level of fines. In the early 1990s, a record $10 million was levied against IMC Fertilizer after an explosion at a Louisiana nitroparaffin plant killed eight IMC workers and injured 120 more, and Citgo Petroleum had to pay $6 million in the aftermath of an explosion that killed six workers. Phillips Petroleum was socked with a $4 million fine and Arco Chemical with a $3.5 million one for their roles in similar tragedies. And the Bush OSHA broke new ground in restricting workplace smoking, developing new "ergonomics" requirements to cut down on the repetitive employee motions (particularly in the meatpacking and automobile industries), upgrading rules in the chemical processing sector, and working closely with such outside advocacy groups as the National Safe Workplace Institute.

❖ Some Mixed Results

OSHA continued to have money problems throughout the penny-pinching Bush years and also the similarly financially pressed Clinton era. In fact, the overall statistics were, if anything, less impressive by the late 1990s than two decades earlier. Responsible now for protecting the health of over 105 million workers, OSHA had 1,200 inspectors for nearly 3.6 million employers (there are now six times as many fish and game inspectors on the federal payroll than there are OSHA inspectors). At current levels inspectors could inspect workplaces once every 84 years and could conduct a surprise inspection of high-hazard workplaces only once every 25 years. For all of the large fines that OSHA had levied after 1985, the median penalty paid by an employer for a violation that caused the death or serious injury of a worker was still less than $500. And as of the eve of the new millennium, the Department of Justice had not only prosecuted fewer than 40 criminal OSHA cases but had jailed a grand total of three employers, none of them for more than six months (the maximum sentence sanctioned by the law).

A bitter charge made by one observer in the wake of a 1991 North Carolina poultry plant fire that killed 25 workers—"There's a USDA inspector in every poultry plant to protect consumers from getting a stomachache, but there's nobody protecting people from getting killed"[13]—could have been made with equal validity nine years later. (Exhibit 10-2 discusses the situation in more detail.)

Yet OSHA has continued—all of these problems notwithstanding—to have a significant and positive impact on employee health and safety. Despite the cutbacks, most of OSHA's formidable standards still govern, and their very presence has generated enormous expenditures on capital investments linked to this area. By some estimates, as much as $7 billion annually is being spent by managements for health and safety, representing a doubling of the annual rate of a decade ago, and there is no question that the employer community's willingness to correct hazards and improve such vital environmental ingredients as ventilation, noise levels, and machine safety is much greater now than it was before OSHA's passage.

Essentially all experts also agree that because of OSHA employers know far more about such dangerous substances as asbestos, vinyl chloride, cotton dust, and many other actual or probable carcinogens than they formerly did and that appropriate actions to protect workers from these have been taken. It is also a widely held belief among OSHA watchers that simply by pressing the issue of employee safety and health, OSHA has made employers much more aware of workplace dangers than they would otherwise have been.

❖ Labor Activities Regarding Safety and Health

From organized labor, the activity has been even more pronounced, as the next few exhibits in this chapter show. Ironically, the dissatisfaction with OSHA's enforcement has added impetus to labor's efforts, and literally hundreds of recent major contract innovations can be traced to this impetus.

Such innovations include the establishment in Oil, Chemical, and Atomic Worker–employer agreements of local joint health and safety committees with not only access to company data but also the right to arbitrate unresolved safety controversies. They encompass also the training of local UAW officials as full-time paid health and safety monitors in the automobile industry and a requirement won by the Steelworkers that when steel and aluminum industry workers are transferred out of dangerous jobs to lower-paying ones because of the hazards of continued exposure to toxic substances they must be paid at the higher rate.

The Rubber Workers have now won access to the lists of chemicals used by most rubber companies; the union also now has a program whereby rubber companies are required to contribute $.01 per hour worked for research (conducted by both Harvard and North Carolina) into potential health hazards. (Exhibit 10-3, pp. 430–31, illustrates typical language negotiated by the Oil, Chemical, and Atomic Workers in the chemical and petroleum industries, and Exhibit 10-4, p. 432, attests to the emphasis placed on safety and health protection by the Teamsters. The Flight Attendants have taken a particular interest in AIDS, explained in Exhibit 10-5, p. 433, and resulting in such activities as a confidential questionnaire sent to all members and included here as Exhibit 10-6, pp. 434–35. The Flight Attendants understandably have also directed some emphasis to such air safety problems as icing, as Exhibit 10-7, p. 436, illustrates.) And an ever-growing number of unions now makes ambitious use of the national Freedom of Information Act to obtain employer health and safety records, and in some cases thereupon to file complaints of their own with OSHA charging the management with violations of the law.

Many unions, possibly most, are still not much more active than they have been historically in the area of safety and health. Others do no more than the minimum required to prevent membership outbursts. But the momentum set in motion, first by the high hopes for OSHA and then by the fears of the act's inadequacies, shows no sign of abating. Most probably then, the years ahead should see even more activity and expenditure both at the bargaining table and (from all concerned groups) in lobbying efforts toward a goal that all but the most selfish segments of society can applaud: the minimization of occupational hazards in the American workplace.

EXHIBIT 10-3

ARTICLE 18. SAFETY AND HEALTH

1. The Company shall institute and maintain all reasonable and necessary precautions for safeguarding the health and safety of its employees, and all employees are expected to cooperate in the implementation thereof. Both the Company and the Union recognize their mutual obligations to assist in the prevention, correction and elimination of all unhealthy and unsafe working conditions and practices.

2. A Safety Committee, composed of three (3) Union members and the Union President and four (4) members of Management, one (1) of whom shall be chairman, shall be established. The Union shall have the right of selection of its members. The Committee shall meet at least once each month on a regularly scheduled basis for the purpose of jointly reviewing and discussing plant safety conditions and investigating accidents. In addition to Company established safety rules and procedures, the Safety Committee may develop and recommend the adoption of appropriate safety rules and procedures to improve and correct unsafe conditions. The Company further agrees to examine any recommendation with respect to safety and health, and to take such action as may be appropriate on recommendations which are submitted by a majority of the Safety Committee.

3. Written minutes shall be made at each Safety Committee meeting. These minutes shall be posted on the plant safety bulletin board. Union members shall be paid at the rate of their assigned jobs for time spent at Safety Committee meetings and other appropriate Safety Committee functions as approved by the Division Manager.

4. Representatives of the International Union may request a meeting or inspection with Company officials to review safety problems and procedures. Such requests shall be made to the Plant Manager or his designee who shall arrange for such meeting or inspection at a mutually agreeable time. No request for such meeting or inspection will be unjustifiably denied.

5. The Company will continue to furnish employees with gas masks, gloves, and goggles, and where needed, raincoats, coveralls, rubber pacs or shoes for sandblasting, and slush boots, and lenses and frames for prescription safety glasses. Maintenance employees shall be furnished necessary tools by the Company.

6. The Company agrees to provide medical examinations or health tests when the necessity, nature of and/or frequency of such medical examination or health test is appropriate for exposures and/or working conditions. The results of such examinations or tests will be made available to the employee and his personal physician. These tests will be provided at no cost to the employee.

For the purposes of applying the above provisions, the Company will provide annual physical examinations of all hourly employees. The following shall be the basic contents of the annual examinations. The contents of the examinations may be modified by addition or deletion in compliance with federal (OSHA) standards promulgated by the Secretary of Labor and/or recommended testing from an accredited medical group or association. The tests performed and the procedure used shall be determined solely by the company medical department. Special examinations or tests on a more frequent basis than annually will be made as required by specific exposures and industrial hygiene standards.

Annual Physical Exams

1. Chest X-Ray
2. Pulmonary Function
3. Audiometric Testing
4. Ortho-Rater Eye Test
5. Electrocardiogram
6. Urinalysis
7. Blood Tests

EXHIBIT 10-3

(continued)

8. Blood Pressure
9. Breast Exam (Females Only)
10. Hands-on Test by Doctor (Eyes-Ears-Nose-Throat-Reflexes-Skeletal-Muscle)
11. Follow-Up Discussion between Doctor and Employee

Blood Tests—Annual on All People Tested

Chen-Zyme Panel includes twenty-two (22) separate tests plus complete blood count (CBC) with differential for baseline data.

Special Blood Tests for Benzene Exposure People
CBC with differential
Reticulocyte count
Serum bilirubin (included in chen-zyme panel on annual exams)

Special blood tests for exposure to lead, asbestos and pesticides (research) will also be provided.

7. The Company will pay all costs of employee's eye examination when the examination results in a prescription for eyeglasses or a change in the employee's existing prescription.

8. The Medical Program and physical examination shall not be used as a basis for shifting of personnel between jobs and classifications except for valid medical reasons. Upon request of the employee, the employee's physician shall be provided with a duplicate report in writing of the plant physician's examination. The employee will be given a report of the conclusions of the findings of the physical examination except in special cases.

Any dispute arising out of the results of a physical examination shall be limited to the question of whether the physical condition constitutes a hazard to the health and safety of the employee and his fellow employees or to the Company assets and whether the employee is physically capable of performing the job.

9. The Union may designate one representative from among the active employees to accompany Federal or State safety inspectors while they conduct walk-around safety inspections within the plant. The designated employee shall be compensated at his regular straight time rate for the time lost from the job while accompanying the inspector in the walk-around inspection.

PRODUCTION STANDARDS AND STAFFING

Certainly one of the most important functions of management is that of determining the amount of output that an employee must turn out in a given period. So important is this area to management's objective of operating an efficient plant that employers at times suffer long strikes to maintain this right as a unilateral one.

It is easy to understand why employers have such a vital interest in production standards. To the degree that employees increase output, unit labor costs decline. With declining labor costs, employers make a larger profit, or else they can translate lower labor costs into lower prices for their products or services with the expectation of thereby increasing the total volume of sales and strengthening the financial position of the company.

And if employees produce more, the employer will have to hire commensurately fewer additional employees, or may even be in a position to lay off present employees on a temporary or permanent basis. With a smaller labor force, the management could also save on the number of people needed to supervise the work of its employees.

What's more, even when contractual commitments or past practices obligate the company to assign a certain minimum number of workers to a given operation at all times,

EXHIBIT 10-4

Teamster Safety and Health Committees:
First Line of Defense Against Hazards

A strong union safety and health committee helps Teamster members deal more effectively with management.

Here are some of the activities of a successful union committee:

1. Asking the membership about hazards they face and about injuries and illnesses that may be caused by working conditions.

2. Looking for hazards. Some committees have the right in their contract to make inspections. Otherwise, committees can piece together the information with the help of stewards and members from each department or work area.

3. Investigating accidents, near misses, and illnesses. What were the conditions that helped cause the problem? Overloading the worker? Poor equipment design? Lack of maintenance? Lack of training?

How could the job be designed with better safeguards so a normal human mistake cannot become an injury?

4. Keeping written records on surveys, inspections, grievances, tests for hazards conducted by the company, workers' compensation cases, sickness and accident claims, and government standards that apply.

5. Helping to negotiate safety protections into the contract. Contract language should spell out the employer's safety responsibilities and the safety committee's rights.

6. Filing grievances when management fails to fix hazards.

7. Using government rules and rights, including calling for an inspection by the Occupational Safety and Health Administration or the Department of Transportation when necessary.

8. Using company safety rules. Often, management needs to be pushed to live by its own rules even when production would be affected.

9. Getting help from the International Union. Local unions can get advice, information, and training through the International's Safety and Health Department.

10. Educating the membership. The committee can help local officers keep all workers informed by talking to them individually, having group meetings during breaks, passing out leaflets, and reporting at union meetings.

TEAMSTERS AND MANAGEMENT: DIFFERENT AGENDAS ON SAFETY

What makes a typical management program on safety and health?

✔ Focusing only on hazards that involve "worker error."

✔ Slogans like "Safety Starts With You" that deflect attention away from *management's* responsibility to prevent hazards.

✔ Contests that reward workers for not reporting accidents and illnesses.

What makes a Teamster safety and health program?

✔ Focusing on steps management can take to remove hazards, such as...

● Redesigning jobs so workers won't hurt their backs, wrists, or necks.
● Improving ventilation.
● Reducing noise and vibration.
● Preventing chemicals from entering the air.
● Reducing unsafe workloads.

✔ Involving workers in learning about hazards and supporting efforts to get unsafe conditions corrected.

✔ Using our rights under union contracts and federal, state, and local laws to insist on safe and healthy jobs.

UPS clerk Mary Augsback says a strong safety committee "gives me somewhere to go when I have a complaint or need information and support."

EXHIBIT 10-5

AIDS, Critical and Terminal Illnesses:

ASSOCIATION OF
FLIGHT ATTENDANTS, AFL-CIO

ACT

AIDS, CRITICAL AND TERMINAL
ILLNESS AWARENESS MONTH

Support From Flying Partners Can Make a Difference

Ironically, some of the key health and interpersonal problems confronting flight attendants today are an unexpected byproduct of past victories. Flight attendants successfully struggled to make the profession a career that could last until retirement. No longer do we have to quit by age 32, or leave the job if we marry or become pregnant. These gains have raised our stature as seasoned, mature professionals in the eyes of the public and management. That's the good news.

The bad news is that growing older is not easy. The flight attendant population is now affected by the illnesses that go with age, like hypertension and heart disease. We are also more likely to have flying partners who are fighting cancer or who are HIV-positive than we were when the average career length was two years.

We're a maturing work force, a diverse work force, and sensitivity toward those among us with serious illnesses has become vital to our unity and solidarity. In recognition of this, AFA's Board of Directors has established March, 1992 as time for us to begin increasing our awareness about AIDS, and Critical and Terminal illnesses (ACT); how they impact our flying partners who are living with them; and how to interact caringly and tactfully with ill co-workers.

Living With Life-Threatening Illness

Imagine this: You've been a flight attendant for a number of years. You enjoy your job and your personal life. You have a good relationship with your flying partners. In general, life seems to be treating you well. Then, during a medical checkup, your doctor notices something and orders some additional tests. You are diagnosed as having a potentially serious health problem: a lump in your breast, an irregular PAP smear, an HIV-positive result on a blood test, a spot on your lungs in a chest X-ray, a heart problem.

Immediately, your life has changed. For now, of course, you can go to work as usual, function normally, and you still look the same as before. "But how long will that last?" you ask yourself. Medication and medical procedures to fight the disease may, for a time, affect how you look. The unfortunate, all-too-persistent "glamor" image of flight attendants, which equates personal worth with physical attractiveness, is an added pressure if treatment affects your appearance. Although you can work, you worry about losing your job, and your health insurance, if the company finds out. You want your co-workers' support, but you're afraid if they find out, even though your illness is not contagious, they will shun you.

This scenario gives a small glimpse into part of what chronically ill flight attendants go through. It's a scenario our sisters and brothers living with chronic disease know all too well.

If a Flying Partner Has a Life-Threatening Illness

If you know a flying partner has a chronic illness, you may feel awkward about how to act toward her/him. Your reactions may be: • I don't know what to say to the person, • when I do say something, it sounds stupid, • it's depressing to be around her/him, • I'm afraid I may "catch" the illness, even though I know it's not contagious, or in the case of HIV disease, not contagious through casual contact, • I'm afraid I might have to do extra work on a trip, but I feel guilty about saying anything, • the person is a constant reminder of my own mortality and vulnerability.

January / March • 1992 FLIGHTLOG

SOURCE: *Flightlog*, January–March, 1992, p. 4 (Association of Flight Attendants, AFL-CIO).

EXHIBIT 10-6

Confidential Membership Survey
Concerning Life-Threatening Illnesses

ASSOCIATION OF
FLIGHT ATTENDANTS, AFL-CIO

ACT

AIDS, CRITICAL AND TERMINAL
ILLNESS AWARENESS MONTH

Dear Colleague,

The primary purpose of this questionnaire is to determine, on a totally confidential basis: • how many among us are living with a life-threatening illness, • how many among us are caring for someone in this situation, and • what services the union should consider providing to assist members in maintaining their livelihood.

We are seeking to assess the overall impact of critical health issues among our members in order to identify topics which might be addressed in union publications or other forums. Please take a few minutes to complete this survey and return it by May 1, 1992.

Thank you for your interest and concern.

In Solidarity,

Dee Maki, National President

1. Are you reluctant in any way to work with someone who has been diagnosed with:
   HIV/AIDS? Yes ❏ No ❏
   Other life threatening illness? Yes ❏ No ❏

2. When you are working with someone with a critical illness, what are your primary concerns? *(check all that apply)*
   ❏ I prefer to avoid interaction with her/him.
   ❏ I am concerned about the ill person's appearance.
   ❏ I never seem to know what to say to them.
   ❏ I find it depressing to be around people who are ill.
   ❏ I'm afraid I might get it.
   ❏ I'm concerned the person won't do her/his share.
   ❏ I worry I may have to perform emergency first aid.
   ❏ I worry whether they can perform their safety duties.
   ❏ I worry about their well being.
   ❏ Other_____

3. Is someone close to you suffering from a life-threatening illness?
   Yes ❏ No ❏
   If yes, does this illness affect your: Spouse/domestic partner ❏
   A family member ❏ Friend(s) ❏ Co-worker(s) ❏ ? *(check all that apply)*

4. Are you presently or have you been a care-giver for someone who is critically ill?
   Yes ❏ No ❏
   If yes, is this person your: Spouse/domestic partner ❏ Child ❏
   Parent ❏ Sibling ❏ Friend ❏ Other ❏ _____

5. Have you ever been diagnosed as having a life-threatening illness?
   Yes ❏ No ❏ (If no, go to question 10.)

6. What was the diagnosis? *(Please be specific)*_____

7. How recently was the diagnosis confirmed?_____

8. Are you currently receiving treatment for your illness?
   Yes ❏ No ❏
   If yes, what type of treatment(s)?_____
   If no, why not?_____

9. Have you communicated that you are suffering from a life-threatening illness to: Your partner ❏ Your family ❏ Your friends ❏ Your co-workers ❏
   The company you work for ❏ ? *(check all that apply)*

10. Have you utilized AFA's Employee Assistance Program (EAP) as a resource to help you cope with your illness or the illness of someone close to you?
    Yes ❏ No ❏ If no, why not?_____

11. If available, would you utilize a long-term, union-based support system focused on helping you deal with your illness, bereavement, or the care of someone close to you who is ill? Yes ❏ No ❏

over

EXHIBIT 10-6 (continued)

If yes, which of the following services would you utilize?

a. Support Groups *(Check all that apply)*
   ❑ Exclusively for AFA members with critical and terminal illness.
   ❑ Exclusively for AFA members who care for someone with a critical or terminal illness.
   ❑ Exclusively for AFA members who are coping with bereavement.

b. Buddy Network
   ❑ An AFA-member buddy who would volunteer to provide you with extra help and support during your illness.
   ❑ An AFA-member buddy who would volunteer to provide you with extra **help** and support during the time that you are caring for someone who is ill.

If no, why not?_____

Demographic Information   *(Please check those areas which apply to you)*

Female ❑   Male ❑   Lineholder ❑   Reserve ❑   Number of years as a flight attendant:_____
Carrier size: Major ❑   National ❑   Regional ❑
Married ❑   Permanent domestic partner ❑   Single ❑
Do you consider yourself: Heterosexual ❑   Homosexual ❑   Bisexual ❑

Please fold, staple, stamp and return completed surveys by May 1, 1992.

Place 29 Cent
Stamp Here
Post Office will
not deliver
unless stamped

AFA S<small>PECIAL</small> P<small>ROJECTS</small> C<small>OORDINATOR</small>
A<small>SSOCIATION OF</small> F<small>LIGHT</small> A<small>TTENDANTS</small>, AFL-CIO
1625 M<small>ASSACHUSETTS</small> A<small>VENUE</small>, NW
W<small>ASHINGTON</small>, DC 20036

S<small>OURCE</small>: *Flightlog*, January–March, 1992, p. 4 (Association of Flight Attendants, AFL-CIO).

significant economies can be realized by management if it is able to impose higher production standards upon this inflexible crew.

If the interest of management in production standards is understandable, however, it is no less understandable that employees and their union representatives have an equal interest in ensuring "reasonableness" and "fairness" in this phase of the firm's operation. Before the advent of unions, employers could require employees to

EXHIBIT 10-7

'WE CAN'T SIT ON OUR HANDS AND WAIT'

AFA DEMANDED GROUNDING OF ATRS, BACKED
FLIGHT ATTENDANTS' DECISIONS NOT TO FLY

PHOTO: SIMMONS MEC PRES DEBORA SUTOR ON NBC NIGHTLY NEWS

Pressure exerted by AFA, the Air Line Pilots Association and aviation safety organizations helped compel the Federal Aviation Administration (FAA) to take decisive action to protect passengers and airline crews by grounding ATR-42 and ATR-72 commuter aircraft from flying during icing conditions.

The FAA's action came nearly six weeks after an American Eagle Super ATR operated by Simmons (Flight 4184) crashed in Roselawn, Indiana, on Oct. 31 during a rainstorm.

Two AFA members — Amanda Holberg and Sandi Modaff — were among the 68 passengers and crew who were killed. There were no survivors.

Icing conditions, as defined by the FAA's Dec. 9 order, occur when moisture is present and outside temperatures are below 40 degrees Fahrenheit, or when such conditions are forecast.

AFA called on the president of American Eagle (Simmons) to voluntarily ground its ATR aircraft several weeks before the FAA took action. "We wanted any flight attendants who felt that they could not fly in these known icing conditions to be relieved from duty without loss of pay," Debora Sutor, AFA MEC President at Simmons, explained during an interview on *NBC Nightly News*.

In AFA's letter to Simmons President Peter Piper, the then-AFA National President Dee Maki asked the company to take three actions: ground the ATRs in known or reported icing conditions, establish procedures so that flight attendants have sufficient information to make decisions regarding the safety of a flight, and allow flight attendants expressing a desire not to fly on ATRs to be relieved from duty without a loss of pay.

The union also sent a similar letter to the president and CEO of Atlantic Southeast Airlines, which operates 12 ATR aircraft upon which AFA flight attendants work.

AFA's actions followed the National Transportation Safety Board's nearly unprecedented recommendation that the ATRs be grounded before tests on the aircraft were completed. The wording of the board's "Class 1, Urgent Action" recommendation to the FAA left little doubt about the agency's grave concern:

"Prohibit the intentional operation of ATR-42 and ATR-72 airplanes in known or reported icing conditions until the effect of upper wing surface ice on the flying qualities and aileron hinge moment characteristics are examined further as recommended in A-94-181 and it is determined that the airplanes exhibit satisfactory flight characteristics."

American Eagle took no action to ground the aircraft or respond to AFA's demands until after the FAA issued its order. The company stated, however, that it would not take disciplinary action against flight attendants who elected not to fly in icing conditions, but said that their refusal to fly would mean a permanent transfer to Texas to fly the company's Saab aircraft. AFA called such a response "unacceptable."

American Eagle's policy toward pilots who refused to fly ATRs out of safety concerns was different. American Eagle allowed two pilots who were concerned about icing to refuse to fly the same ATR. The aircraft stayed on the ground until the company found a replacement. Flight attendants on the flight were not given the same option.

"This puts flight attendants in the untenable position of not having control

> **'WE WANTED ANY FLIGHT ATTENDANTS WHO FELT THAT THEY COULD NOT FLY IN THESE KNOWN ICING CONDITIONS TO BE RELIEVED FROM DUTY WITHOUT LOSS OF PAY.'**

over their safety," AFA Air Safety and Health Director Chris Witkowski said during an interview on *ABC World News Tonight*.

"We can't sit on our hands and wait for the company to do something," he said.

AFA's safety director urged Secretary of Transportation Federico Peña to strongly resist the industry's ongoing efforts to rescind the FAA's decision to ground the ATRs during icing conditions.

Before FAA grounded the flights, AFA President Maki announced that AFA was "prepared to back up flight attendants' decisions to safeguard themselves if they feel their safety is compromised by dangerous weather conditions."

A total of 152 ATRs operated by US carriers were affected by the order, including 48 at Simmons and 12 at Atlantic Southeast.

As this issue went to press, AFA continued to monitor the situation.

SOURCE: *Flightlog*, Spring 1995, p. 6 (Association of Flight Attendants, AFL-CIO).

produce as much as management directed. Failure to meet these production standards could result in the summary dismissal of the employee. At times, employees suffered accidents, psychological problems, and a generally shortened work life in meeting the standards of the employer. And, although modern enlightened management does not normally impose production standards that employees cannot reasonably attain, unions and employees are nonetheless still vitally concerned with the amount of production that an employee must turn out in a given length of time because of the obvious ramifications for job opportunities and union membership.

There is no simple solution to the problem of how much an employee must produce to hold a job or to earn a given amount of pay. At times, the determination of a solution is purely subjective in character; a supervisor's individual judgment is the criterion adopted to resolve the problem. To this, unions argue that the judgment of employees or labor union officers is as good as that of the management representatives.

More sophisticated methods of determination are available, but these techniques, too, are hardly so perfect or "scientific" as to end the controversy. Such techniques fall under the general title of time and motion studies. That is, having been shown the most efficient method of performing a job, so-called average employees, who are presumably working at average rates of speed, are timed. From such a study, management claims that all employees should produce at least the average amount in a given period. Where incentive wage systems are in effect, as we know, the employee receives premium pay for output above the average. However, production standards are important even when employees are paid by the hour, since failure to produce the average amount could result in employee discipline of some sort—ranging from a reprimand to discharge, with intervening levels such as a suspension or a demotion to a lower-paying job. Unions are far from convinced that time and motion studies constitute the final word in the resolution of the production standards problem. They claim that the studies are far from scientific, since they still involve human judgment, and that employees who are timed are often far better than average, so that their rate of speed is consequently unrealistically fast.

With few exceptions (most notably in the garment industries), unions have pressed for an effective means of review of employer establishment of production standards, rather than toward seeking the right to establish such standards initially. Organized labor has generally believed that employee and union institutional interests are served as effectively, and without the administrative and political complexities of initial standard establishment, if there is a union opportunity for challenge of the management action, either through arbitration or by the exercise of the right to strike during the contractual period in the event of unresolved production standards disputes.

Some unions have historically preferred the right to strike to arbitration in this area. The United Automobile Workers has, for example, steadfastly refused to relinquish its right to strike over production standards disputes, and, although the UAW now agrees to arbitration on virtually all other phases of the labor agreement, it is adamant in its opposition to the arbitration of standards. The international neither distrusts arbitrators nor challenges their professional competency. Rather, it believes that a union cannot properly prepare and present a case in arbitration that can successfully challenge production standards. It contends that the problems are so complicated, the proofs so difficult to assemble, and the data so hard to present in satisfactory form that arbitration is not the proper forum for resolving production standards disputes. In essence, it claims that employers have an advantage in any arbitration dealing with production standards, and the union does not intend to turn to this process because it would jeopardize the interests of its members.

On the other hand, most unions have now agreed to the arbitration of production standards. Beyond reflecting the general acceptance of the arbitration process itself, this course of action has behind it a highly practical reason: Frequently, production standards are protested by only a small group of employees in the plant. For example, the employer may have changed the standards in one department (because of improved technology, equipment, or methods) but left unaltered at least temporarily the standards in all other departments. Without arbitration, the only way in which the affected employees could seek relief would be for the entire labor force to strike—at times, a politically inopportune weapon for the union to use, because the employees in the other departments are satisfied and do not care to sacrifice earnings just to help out employees in a single department. Arbitration avoids this situation, while still allowing a final and binding decision on the grievance of the protesting employees.

There is, however, probably no area of labor relations in which management and organized labor still stand any further apart than in production standards. Standards lie at the heart of the employer's activities and are vital to the basic interests of the employees and unions. To say that they should be established "fairly" and "reasonably" is to recognize only an unrealizable ideal, since in the give and take of day-to-day operations deep and bitter conflicts are still bound to arise. The stakes are very high, and, as long as management seeks efficiency and the union seeks to protect the welfare of its members, there exists no easy way out of the problem. Certainly nothing approaching a panacea for it has yet been discovered by the parties to collective bargaining.

TECHNOLOGICAL CHANGE

"I essentially hoped to shuffle off to a quiet demise," declared the then-head of the AFL-CIO a while ago, "without ever having learned what a computer is all about or the intricacies of microwave transmission or low-frequency transmission or cable TV and satellite TV and all of those things. But I am aware that a revolution is going on."[14]

An *unparalleled* revolution, he could have added. In both the factory and the office, technological change is affecting employment needs so greatly that it is now estimated that some 45 million existing jobs in the United States (more than 40 percent of all jobs, indeed) will be directly touched in the next decade.

❖ The Threat to Jobs

Not long ago, many observers thought that the industrial robot, characterized by mechanical arms connected to reprogrammable computers, might soon affect a significant percentage of these jobs all by itself. A 1981 study conducted at Carnegie-Mellon University concluded that contemporary robots had the technical ability to perform millions of factory jobs and that some time after 1990 it would be technically possible to replace *all* manufacturing workers in the automotive, electrical equipment machinery, and fabricated metals industries—some 7.9 million—with robots.[15] At about the same time, the General Electric Corporation launched an ambitious program that was ultimately expected to lead to the replacement of half of its 37,000 assembly-line employees with robots. And with robots seemingly getting cheaper all the time—their average unit price dropped 20 percent in 1988 from the previous year, for example, to about $40,000—it was not hard to find industrial analysts as recently as 1990 who expected as many as 100,000 robots (up from 25,000 in 1990) to be in use by the year 2000.

Today, such dramatic estimates have been shown to have been unrealistic. A combination of some amount of robot unreliability and a managerial inability to mesh robots smoothly with workers and other equipment has put to rest the once common thought that robots would soon surpass $10 billion in annual worldwide sales and revolutionize the world of work almost overnight: Depending on how *robot* is defined, worldwide sales are currently around $2 billion a year and seem to be holding at approximately that level.

Even at that, however, industrial robots that can efficiently paint, weld, seal, assemble, and package all kinds of products and make such service-sector contributions as delivering meals to patients in hospitals and polishing retail store floors are now increasingly in evidence, as is a commensurate fear on the part of workers and their unions that major job displacement will be the consequence.

The robot hardly stands alone, moreover, as a form of changing technology significantly affecting the work force. Examples abound to show the impact of other forms of **automation**—broadly defined as a system of automatic devices that integrate the entire productive process—as well. At the Port of New York Authority waterfront, where almost 90 percent of all general cargo now moves in containers, fewer than 9,000 workers handle the same volume of freight that 30,000 workers did two decades ago. In 1995, Kansas City Power & Light Co. began installing a small electronic device in each of its 420,000 meters, thereby becoming the first U.S. utility to use such automatic readers. This innovation has rapidly spread, and experts expect that within a very few years all of the nation's 35,000 human meter readers will be nothing more than a memory. In railroading, the automatic dispatching of freight cars has made the human dispatcher about as commonplace as the steam locomotive.

Job obsolescence has already been the fate, too, of thousands of workers in retail trade, as symbolized by one mail-order house in which a computer now handles over 100,000 tallies each day, keeping an automatic record of the 12,000 items sold by the employer in the process. And human beings handling telephone calls are no longer an expense that can be easily justified with massive automation an alternative: In 1956, there were 250,000 telephone operators in the country; by 1999, the number had dropped to 50,000 and was rapidly falling.

Nor has governmental employment been immune from automation's inroads. The 450 U.S. Treasury Department clerical employees who were some time ago replaced by a single computer that can accommodate the billions of checks issued by the federal government every year are far from unique among the casualties of technological change in that sector.

The computer itself has clearly permeated the industrial world with a domination that no one could have predicted even two decades ago. Its speed and complexity have been doubling every 18 months and are expected to continue this doubling every 18 months through 2012. By then, the density of its circuits will most probably have increased a thousand-fold. By the year 2019, at least one respected expert expects that a $1,000 PC will have the raw computing power of the human brain (about 100 billion neurons and 100 trillion connections); he also predicts that such a computer will have the power of a thousand human brains by 2030 and the power of no less than a *billion* human brains by 2050—with, by definition, an almost unimaginable potential for the elimination of jobs.[16]

Even sticking solely to what has actually happened so far, however, the job loss has been absolutely staggering. Even placing all governmental and private estimates at their rock-bottom minimums, it is likely that 10,000 jobs are being eliminated *each week* in this manner.

Not all of the jobs involved are, of course, unionized ones. Retail trade is, as we know, hardly a hotbed of organized labor, and (although the Treasury clerks in the preceding example happen to have been union members) clerical work, too, is clearly far more nonunionized than it is unionized. But the fact remains that the blue-collar worker in mass-production industry—automobiles, steel, electrical, and other bastions of collective bargaining—has been the most visible victim to date of the new era of rampant technological change. The robot and other computer-based automation have a natural affinity for these sectors and, whatever the future brings, job totals here have already suffered most notably.

In the typical automated radio manufacturing establishment, for example, only two employees produce 1,000 radios per day, where standard hand assembly called for a labor force of 200. Fewer than 20 glass-blowing machines have for some time produced almost all the glass light bulbs used in the United States and, still having time on their hands, all the glass tubes used in radio and television sets. New technology has already eliminated thousands of automobile industry jobs, with robots—costing a mere $6 hourly to operate and able to do the work of two $20 an hour human workers—ever more tempting given the financial problems of that sector. And in steel the inroads of technology have combined with foreign competition to cut the 500,000 production workers of 20 years ago down to only about one-third of that figure. The steel industry itself has in recent years come back from the brink of near extinction; but the sight of steam once again billowing from the smokestacks of USX and Bethlehem brings no joy whatsoever to the thousands of permanently displaced workers still living in steel towns who are not being allowed to participate in the resurgence.

For all of these labor-displacement and related skill-rating effects, there are clearly some offsetting advantages. The employer implementing the changes presumably benefits, as in steel, either by gaining a competitive edge or by closing a competitive gap. The increased productivity that is created raises national living standards immensely: The average family income in the United States, at constant dollars, is now expected—for example—to reach almost $40,000 annually by the year 2004, up from less than two-thirds of that figure in 1994. Jobs are invariably made safer, with materials handling and other relatively dangerous occupational aspects either considerably minimized or eliminated altogether. Product quality is frequently improved, since the automatic machine has little room for human error. And even an improved national defense can be said to have been generated, with modern warfare now so dependent upon the most advanced technology.

Most important, it can be argued with considerable justification that everyone, in the long run, benefits from scientific progress. There are infinitely more people working in the automobile production and servicing industries (even now) than there ever were blacksmiths, for example. And the number of employees associated with the telephone industry vastly exceeds the highest labor force totals ever achieved by the town-crier profession.

All these arguments, however, are of small consolation to the employee actually being displaced or threatened by technology. Just as logically, the employee can echo the irrefutable statement of Lord Keynes that "in the long run, we are all dead." And one can often balance the fact that technology has generally improved working conditions by pointing to undesirable features of the problem that have an impact upon the workers: greater isolation of employees on the job, with less chance to talk face to face with other workers and supervisors; a greater mental strain, particularly since mistakes can now be much more costly; the deterioration of social groups, since it requires considerably less teamwork to run the modern operation; and the fact that jobs in the automated plant (or office) are fast becoming much more alike, with less on-the-job variety also often the case, and attendant psychological and social implications stemming from this situation.

But most worrisome of all to the industrial worker is the threat of displacement, or at least of severe skill requirement downgrading, through *future* technological change. Almost every employee survey on the subject that has been taken in the past decade has shown that at least three-quarters of the respondents believe themselves to be so threatened by such change.

The fears appear to be well grounded. If technological change undeniably creates new jobs and even industries, the possibility remains that, at the present time, it is destroying more jobs than it creates. And however many of the displaced are ultimately reabsorbed into the employed labor force, the increasing skill requirements of an automated world leave little room for at least unskilled and semiskilled workers to join their ranks. Nor are the prospects for even *skilled* manual workers these days appreciably greater.

Thus, while by far the greatest organizational problem of unions involves the organization of the white-collar sector in the face of the automation-caused changing complexion of the workforce, within the current arena of collective bargaining organized labor—both as the blue-collar worker's representative and for its own institutional preservation—has inevitably been forced toward the promotion of *measures minimizing job hardship for blue-collar workers.*

❖ Union-Sought Avenues for Cushioning the Employment Impact of Technological Change

Accordingly, unions have in recent years pushed hard, and with much success, for several devices geared explicitly to cushioning the employment impact of technological change. Some of these—SUB, pension vesting, severance pay, extended vacation periods, extra holidays, and early retirement provisions—have already been discussed as "economic supplements" (see Chapter 8). They have frequently been negotiated to satisfy goals other than adjustment to automated change: A desire for greater leisure purely and simply sometimes motivates vacation and holiday demands, for example, and severance pay implementation or liberalization may be triggered by, say, a union wish to protect workers unable to work because of permanent disability. In addition to these devices, several that tend to be more directly related to technological change deserve attention.

1. *Advance Notice of Layoff or Shutdown.* Such advance notice, impracticable for management in the case of sudden cancellation of orders and various other contingencies, is far more feasible when technological change is involved, since many months may be required to prepare for the new equipment and processes. An increasing number of agreements now call for notice considerably in excess of the few days traditionally provided for in many contracts, with most of the liberalizations now providing for six to twelve months.

Managements independently have often agreed with the advisability of such liberalization—to maintain or improve community images, to dispel potentially damaging employee rumors, and, frequently, because of a desire to develop placement and training plans for displaced workers. Very often, in fact, the actual notice given by management exceeds that stipulated in the contract. There seems to be little doubt, however, that unions have been instrumental in inserting longer advance notice provisions in some contracts—as in portions of the meatpacking, electrical, and electronics industries—that might otherwise not have modified traditional practices. Such certainly appears to have been the case in recent General Electric and Westinghouse negotiations, in which the companies agreed to give six months' notice before shutting down product lines (and sixty days' notice before installing robots). Bargaining in the telephone industry has resulted in comparable contractual obligations for the employer, and for the same reason.

2. *Adoption of the* **Attrition Principle**. An agreement to reduce jobs solely by attrition—through, in other words, deaths, voluntary resignations, retirements, and similar events—by definition gives maximum job security to the present jobholder, although it does nothing to secure the union's long-run institutional interests. As a compromise, it has appealed to many employers as an equitable and not unduly rigorous measure. Managements have proved particularly amenable to this arrangement when the voluntary resignation rate is expected to be high, when a high percentage of workers is nearing retirement age, or when no major reduction of the labor force is anticipated in the first place (and the number of jobs made obsolete by automation is consequently small to begin with). In other cases, unions have been the major force behind introduction of the principle—usually, however, with some modifications more favorable to the union as an institution placed upon it. Thus, the current agreement between the Order of Railroad Telegraphers and the Southern Pacific Railroad places an upper limit of 2 percent upon the jobs that can be abolished for any reason in a given year. Good faith is obviously required in such cases, however: If employers later feel that the upper limit is too severe for them to live with, given a bleak economic climate or other adverse conditions, they could understandably be tempted to encourage additional workers to leave by implementing unreasonable working conditions or otherwise lowering the employee satisfaction level in violation of the spirit of the agreement.

In recent years, many railroad workers have received the protection of the attrition principle, as have newspaper printers, printing-press workers, and postal service employees, among others.

3. *Retraining*. An expanding but unknown number of bargaining relationships now provides opportunities for displaced employees to retrain for another job in the same plant or another plant of the same company. The same protection is also increasingly being extended to employees for whom changes in equipment or operating methods make it mandatory to retrain in order to hold their current jobs. Often, such retraining opportunity, which is most commonly offered at company expense, is limited to workers who meet certain seniority specifications. General Electric workers, for example, must have at least three years of continuous service in order to qualify. At other times, preference but not a promise for retraining is granted senior workers, as in one Machinist union contract that provides that such employees "shall be given preference for training on new equipment, provided they have the capabilities required."

Where such provisions have significantly mitigated displacement, not unexpectedly, they have been implemented by companies whose operations have been expanding in areas other than those causing the initial displacement. "Retraining for *what?*" is a pertinent question when such expansion is not in evidence or at least is not highly likely. Lack of employee self-confidence or lack of worker interest sufficient to meet the new skill requirements have also been known to make the retraining opportunity an essentially valueless one for employees permitted to utilize it. The 52-year-old with a quarter-century's experience as a blast furnace operative and the grizzled veteran of two decades on the automobile assembly line often have little optimism that they can successfully be retrained for jobs in the sales, health, clerical, and other fields where positions *are* being created. And they frequently have no great amount of interest in finding out in any event. Thus, for example, when General Motors and the UAW cooperated a few years ago in a venture to train laid-off employees at two California automobile facilities for jobs in data processing (as well as aerospace), there were few takers: Only 1,522 of the 5,400 eligible workers signed up; many of the others thought that they might be rehired when GM and Toyota jointly began building new cars in the area and preferred to take their chances in this direction.

Nor can the U.S. government, it would seem, realistically be expected to do much to help the retraining efforts. Even the $3.5 billion Job Training Partnership Act, which took effect in late 1983 and was expected to train some 100,000 displaced workers (in addition to 1 million disadvantaged teenagers and adults), was widely perceived as a very modest effort in view of the numbers of people covered, the fact that only 70 percent of the monies would actually go for training, and—again—the immobility, real or imagined, of those displaced.

It appeared that retraining for positions outside the employer's operations, however appealing its theory, would remain in practice anything but a powerful answer to the job losses caused by technological change.

4. *Restrictions on Subcontracting.* Subcontracting, the term that stands for arrangements made by an employer (for reasons such as cost, quality, or speed of delivery) to have some portion of its work performed by employees of another organization, can obviously have major work-opportunity ramifications for the first organization's employees. There is probably no completely integrated employer in the nation, and some measure of subcontracting (or privatization, as the practice is more often known in the public sector, in recognition of the subcontracting of public services to private industry) has always been accepted by all unions as an economic necessity. But when the union can argue that union–member employees could have performed the subcontracted work, or that such work was previously done by bargaining unit employees, it can be counted on to do so. And when disputes do arise over this issue, they are often of major dimensions. In the face of automation-caused job insecurity, there has been an observable recent trend toward union control over many types of subcontracting; the battle has tended to move from open interunion competition to the union–management bargaining table.

So thorny is the subcontracting problem that almost half of all major contracts still make no direct reference to it in a special contractual section (such as the one depicted in Exhibit 10-8). But an increasing number of contracts are incorporating into various of their *other* sections (ranging from union recognition clauses to seniority articles) or in separate "memoranda of understanding" certain limitations on the procedure.

The limitations are of several kinds: (1) agreements that subcontractors will be used only on special occasions (for example, "where specialized equipment not

EXHIBIT 10-8

ARTICLE 19. SUBCONTRACTING

Section I. General

1. Whenever a contractor or subcontractor performs work on Company premises which would ordinarily be performed by employees covered by this Agreement, the Company will include a provision in the applicable contract requiring the contractor to pay (1) not less than the rates of pay provided for in this Agreement for the same character of work, and (2) one and one-half ($1\frac{1}{2}$) times the employees' regular rate of pay for hours worked in excess of forty (40) hours per week.

Section 2. Maintenance Subcontracting

1. Whenever the Company contemplates contracting out any type of work normally performed by maintenance employees it shall inform the President, Chairman of the Grievance Committee and the affected Shop Steward of its intentions prior to making a decision to award the contract.

2. It is further agreed that the Union retains the right to examine any existing or new subcontracting agreement for the purposes of checking wage scales and the specific work contracted.

3. The Company shall not subcontract the work of any maintenance employee when the total number of maintenance employees falls below:

a. 22 percent of the total active permanent workforce (excluding short-term disability, LTD, laid-off employees, and summer employees). For example, if the total hourly active workforce is 160, then the Company may not subcontract if the maintenance force falls below 35 (22 percent of 160). The maintenance force shall be counted in the same manner as the permanent workforce.

b. For the purposes of this paragraph Maintenance employees shall exclude Store-house Clerks and Salvage Section.

4. The Company will provide the Union quarterly reports summarizing subcontracting performed in the prior three (3) months plus a three month projection of anticipated major subcontracting projects, including a review of total workload.

5. The Company further agrees:

a. The purchase requisition will require designation of whether outside repairs or construction services will be required.

b. Contractors will not perform a significant amount of work outside the original scope of a job unless an additional subcontract notification is submitted.

c. The Company will submit a list of service contracts to the Union by January 31 of each year.

d. The Company will notify the Union as soon as practicable of any outside vendors called in for trouble-shooting that are not on service contracts.

available on company premises is required" or "where peculiar skills are needed"); (2) no-layoff guarantees to current employees (as in "no Employee of any craft, which craft is being utilized by an Outside Contractor, shall be laid off as long as the Outside Contractor is in the plant doing work that Employees in such craft are able to do"); (3) provisions giving the union veto power over any or all subcontracting; and (4) requirements that the management prove to the union that time, expense, or facility considerations prevent it from allowing current employees to perform the work.

Subcontracting has for some time been an area of large controversy in collective bargaining (as Exhibit 10-9 illustrates), and, in a time of widespread worries over jobs, concern about it can realistically be expected to increase. It seems a safe prediction, indeed, that management will fight even more vigorously to preserve its work assignment ability as foreign competition and cost pressures intensify. It appears no less a certainty that organized labor will continue to push for limitations on the employer's subcontracting flexibility (and sometimes to resort to indirect avenues such as advertising campaigns, as one major affiliate of the American Federation of State, County, and Municipal Employees did not long ago in pushing for limitations on the growing use of private firms to perform public services in

EXHIBIT 10-9

SOURCE: *Public Employee* magazine, November 1985, front cover.

CONTINUED ON PAGE 12

Exhibit 10-10). Only when more adequate solutions to the problems of technological change are formulated can one expect the conflict in this area to abate. (AFSCME itself regularly devotes much space in its primary publication to this issue, as Exhibit 10-11, pp. 448–451,—drawn from a 1999 issue of that journal, *Public Employee*—illustrates. The union here minces no words in lambasting the nation's largest private prison operator.)

5. *Other Measures.* Unions have also unilaterally attempted to minimize the administrative, institutional, and other problems of technological change through increasingly successful, if still limited, bargaining table campaigns for (1) shorter workweeks, often with a prohibition against overtime work when qualified workers are on layoff or where the overtime would result in layoffs; (2) the requirement of

GIVE PRIVATEERS THE HOOK!

Privatizing public services is not a simple matter. Any radical change in the way things are done includes dangers — so there are important questions that you should ask before you allow any of your services to be privatized. For example:

What happens if the private company won't take total responsibility for all services?

What happens when a private company goes broke?

When a private company hires inadequately trained or inexperienced workers, what happens to the quality of services?

Here's one answer. In a million dollar failed experiment in Florida, one county's jails were privatized, and experienced guards were replaced with untrained personnel. One prisoner escaped twice in one day, and an employee helped another prisoner escape. As the county took back supervision of the jails, a commissioner said he would never go for privatization again.

The ultimate question: What is really the best way to serve the public?

Capitalize on the experience that's already in place.

No one has more experience than CSEA members – in protecting our neighborhoods and our environment, maintaining our parks and roads, nurturing our children and our elderly, caring for our sick and mentally ill.

Keep that experience. Join CSEA in the drive to keep public services public. For a free copy of *"265,014 Reasons Why New York Shouldn't Be Plundered"*, call toll-free: **1-800-836-CSEA.**

CIVIL SERVICE EMPLOYEES ASSOCIATION
Local 1000, AFSCME, AFL-CIO
Joe McDermott, President

joint labor–management consultation prior to the introduction of any automated change; (3) the overhauling of wage structures with job upgrading to reflect the "increased responsibility" of automated factory jobs; and (4) special job and wage provisions for downgraded workers, to minimize income losses suffered by such workers, or to offset them entirely. In addition, unions have in some cases sought to facilitate new employment through the development of their own training, placement, and referral services. And, perhaps more visibly, they have often waged highly ambitious political lobbying campaigns (both on the international and AFL-CIO levels) for a vast array of employment-generating public works programs; far-reaching tax programs and expanded Social Security benefits (to increase consumer purchasing power and lessen the burden on those most likely to be displaced); and federal and state training programs.

As judged by short-run goals—the insertion of the various contract provisions within labor agreements and, in the latter case, the enactment of the lobbied-for legislation—unions have achieved a considerable measure of triumph (if less in the relatively miserly governmental years of the recent past than earlier). And the fact that they have frequently been aided in such campaigns by increasingly social-minded employers in no way detracts from this success. Although union aggressiveness and creativity have varied widely, there can be no denying that many unions have considerably alleviated the burdens of technological change for many workers.

Yet neither singly nor in combination have these measures, or the host of other automation-adjustment methods cited earlier, provided anything approaching a full solution for the basic problems with which they deal. The displacement and displacement threats continue as the march of technology continues to prove that it is both a blessing and a curse for society. A case can be made that a vicious circle is involved: Virtually all these measures increase labor costs for the managements concerned, giving the employer even further motivation for automating, and often thus causing the represented employees to lose jobs all the more rapidly.

There appears to be rather general agreement among all segments of our society on at least three relevant points, however. First, most of us concede that technological change is a product of society. It is not caused only by individuals, single firms, or groups of firms, but rather is an expression of our cultural heritage, our educational system, and our group dynamics. As such, unlike other problems affecting collective bargaining, it requires not only a private (labor–management) solution but a supplementary public (government) one. Second, we are essentially in agreement that no single group should bear the entire burden but that we should all bear it by making sure that the benefits of the increased productivity allowed by technology are shared by all. Without such a philosophical basis, automation and other such changes would mean that some would make spectacular gains, and others would shoulder the full burden. We do not want automation to divide the nation into "haves" and "have-nots." Third, we share general unanimity that this is a time for daring innovation in social dynamics and social engineering and that, although the problem is great, we fortunately have within our capacity the power to deal with the issues within a system of free enterprise. Since old methods will not work, we must innovate and pioneer.

The increasing attention being given to the consequences of technology at the bargaining table (and by the bargaining parties in the public arena) can thus be viewed as recognition of a great but not necessarily insurmountable challenge.

EXHIBIT 10-11

PRISON PRIVATIZATION

YOUNGSTOWN: Will Justice Be Served?

Prison privatization debate heats up after CCA disasters.

YOUNGSTOWN, OHIO

The Corrections Corporation of America (CCA) is on the run, trying to escape hellish publicity about escapes of dangerous criminals from its prisons, charges of inmate neglect, sky-high turnover among disgruntled employees, and the loudly vocalized distrust of public officials.

The Northeast Ohio Correctional Center in Youngstown is the first private prison in Ohio and holds 1,700 prisoners.

AP/Wide World Photos

SOURCE: *Public Employee*, January–February 1999, pp. 12–15.

EXHIBIT 10-11 (continued)

As a growing company and the nation's largest private prison operator — larger than all but four state prison systems — negative publicity is hitting CCA where it hurts. The company's earnings per share for the year, as of Nov. 1, were down 49 percent from the year before. Prospects for the coming year aren't too rosy either, as government officials rethink prison privatization and projects with CCA, in particular.

CCA troubles didn't start in July with the escape of six prisoners from the Northeast Ohio Correctional Center here. But the circumstances surrounding that break and CCA's response turned prison privatization into a national story, with CCA starring as the villain. NBC's "Dateline" has aired an exposé of CCA's dismal performance and CBS's "60 Minutes" is expected to do the same soon.

The script isn't what CCA or Ohio officials envisioned when the Youngstown prison project was planned. It was a sweet deal in the making: For $1, CCA could have 101 acres of land on which to build and then operate a prison, plus a 75 percent tax abatement for seven years. In return, Ohio would get its first private prison and Youngstown, with its suffering, steel-dependent economy, would get 450 desperately needed jobs.

But less than two years after his predecessor made that deal, Youngstown Mayor George McKelvey warns other officials, "You better be damned careful that you know what you're doing, that you have corrections experts on your side negotiating any development agreement for a prison." He claims CCA is "the most deceitful, dishonest corporation I have ever dealt with."

THE BREAK. It was broad daylight when six men, including four convicted killers, cut through a prison yard fence at the Northeast Ohio Correctional Center in Youngstown in late July. The prisoners, all transferred from Washington, D.C., cut through two chain-link fences and climbed over ground-level razor wire to escape. The break went undetected by prison officials for at least a half-hour before it was reported by an inmate. A month later, all six were back behind bars, but local officials were furious.

The prison escape "is the straw that broke the camel's back," claims Mayor McKelvey, noting the string of serious

"You'd better be damned careful that you know what you're doing..."

Youngstown Mayor McKelvey

problems at the 1,700-bed prison, including at least 13 stabbings, two of them fatal, since the facility opened in May 1997. By comparison, according to the Ohio Department of Rehabilitation and Corrections, all other state prisons, with 49,000 inmates combined, reported just 12 assaults with deadly weapons and no murders in 1997.

As circumstances of the break emerged, some alarming information came to light. CCA had allowed its prisoners to wear street clothes, which obvi-

ously disguises escapees. Also facilitating their escape were several serious security lapses: malfunctioning motion detectors and fence alarms; poor staff training; and limited patrols in the prison yard. Already poor relations with local law enforcement officials were made worse with the apparent two-hour delay in CCA's reporting the escape to local authorities. Perhaps the worst news of all for Youngstown officials, however, was the realization that violent prisoners remained at the medium-security prison; just two days before the break, CCA told a federal judge that all violent prisoners had been removed.

So outraged was Ohio Gov. George Voinovich (R) that he asked his attorney general to research ways that he could shut down the prison. AFSCME Pres. Gerald W. McEntee issued a statement supporting the governor's efforts, saying, "The prison break is the latest link in

a chain of disturbing events that provide hard evidence of CCA's inability to run a prison professionally and safely."

NO ISOLATED INCIDENT. CCA's problems with inmate classification came to light with the string of assaults at the prison. After inmates filed a class-action suit against CCA, a court directed the prison company to transfer all violent inmates. Approximately 300 inmates were transferred to other facilities over the coming months, sometimes with disastrous consequences.

Several of the inmates were moved to a CCA prison in Torrance, N.M., where, shortly after arrival, they attacked five staff persons. A week later, a gang of inmates attacked other inmates at the same New Mexico prison. State "response teams" were sent to quell the disturbance.

CO Jim Hobbs monitors privatization for OCSEA Chapter 0250. "CCA is trying to convince people that the Youngstown situation is an anomaly. It's not."

Two other Youngstown inmates were transferred to a CCA prison in Tennessee, despite a federal judge's directive to separate them. Once in Tennessee, one inmate stabbed the other to death. A consultant hired by CCA to evaluate the Youngstown prison's inmate classification system, called the failure to separate the inmates "a complete breakdown in security."

It's not only Youngstown inmates who've caused CCA problems, though:

- A two-man 1996 prison break in Houston alerted officials to the fact that a CCA facility that was supposed to hold only illegal immigrants was also holding 200 sex offenders from Oregon. "The unit was in no way designed for individuals with a violent criminal history," reports Allan Polunsky, head of the Texas Board of Criminal Justice.

EXHIBIT 10-11 (continued)

- South Carolina refused to renew a contract with CCA for running a juvenile detention facility after reports that boys were being mistreated there. Observers claimed that as many as 18 boys were held in a one-person cell, with only cups to serve as toilets.

- In September, a convicted rapist escaped from a Whiteville, Tenn., facility run by CCA.

- At another Whiteville prison, CO Jerry Reeves, on the job for just six weeks, was severely beaten by inmates. He was alone at the time, with no way of contacting help outside the recreation area.

- A prisoner at a CCA-owned facility in Mason, Tenn., stabbed a fellow inmate to death in late August.

- And in mid-October, four inmates, including two murderers, a rapist and an armed robber, escaped from the CCA-operated prison in Clifton, Tenn. Attacks at this prison in 1997 were 28 percent higher than in Tennessee state prisons overall, state officials report. Furthermore, the circumstances of the recent escape are eerily like those at Youngstown. Again, inmates cut through fence. Again, there were inadequate patrols of the prison yard. Again, inmates had to alert prison officials to the break, which led to significant delays in the notification of local law enforcement agencies.

Is CCA cutting corners on safety? It looks like it, but CCA keeps throwing up smoke screens to investigators. Members of the Correctional Institution Inspection Committee of the Ohio legislature and their two guests — corrections experts from the Ohio Civil Service Employees Association (OCSEA)/AFSCME Local 11 — were kept waiting for four hours when they went unannounced to the prison last April for an inspection. CCA called the delay a "misunderstand-

ing," apparently forgetting that Ohio law stipulates the state's rights to visit prisons without notice.

In the "Dateline" exposé on CCA, a group of former Youngstown prison COs all testified that saving money was foremost at the facility — a much greater priority than safety. According to reports, up until the prison break, CCA posted its daily stock market price on a sign outside of the Youngstown facility.

COs were encouraged to cut costs any way they could, even to hold back on

---

In Ohio, comparable costs per inmate are $37.86 at a public prison vs. $53.50 at CCA's Youngstown prison.

---

toilet paper for inmates. "I wouldn't treat a dog the way they treat prisoners there," one former CO told "Dateline."

Another former CO said that the July escape occurred at a shift change, a time when inmates knew the prison would be understaffed. COs routinely were encouraged to leave for the day even before someone came to replace them, so that there was no chance overtime would accrue.

The beating of CO Jerry Reeves in Tennessee represents highly disturbing staffing problems, according to Jim Hobbs, a CO with the Ohio Department of Rehabilitation and Corrections and chief steward of OCSEA Chapter 0250. Hobbs says in his prison, the Allen

Correctional Institute in Lima, Ohio, a CO never would have been left with prisoners alone or without communications equipment to signal help. But CCA claims no staffing violations occurred at the time Reeves was beaten.

"CCA shifts blame from themselves to almost anyone," says Hobbs, who monitors prison privatization for his local. Hobbs notes that a CO supervisor has been fired at the Clinton, Tenn., prison for the recent escapes there. "It especially amazes me that this company will blame an officer for a faulty piece of equipment," he says, referring to the Youngstown escape. CCA officials claim that a misaligned motion detector knocked out during an electrical storm went undetected for several weeks, and that COs were responsible not only for its detection, but also its repair. "Maintenance crews — not COs — are responsible for security technologies at prisons," says Hobbs.

FALLOUT. Will CCA be held accountable for the mounting deaths and injuries at its prisons, as well as the threats to public safety posed by the escapes?

Several families of inmates killed in CCA prison incidents described above have filed lawsuits against CCA for failing to protect the prisoners. Another lawsuit has been filed by the mother of an inmate at the Clifton, Tenn., prison who died from complications caused by sickle cell anemia after being denied medical treatment by CCA officials.

The U.S. Department of Justice conducted a three-month investigation of the Youngstown incident, the results of

Allen Zak

EXHIBIT 10-11

(continued)

which were unavailable as *Public Employee* went to press.

However, a bipartisan, prison-oversight committee of the Ohio legislature had concluded its investigation and, in October, released recommendations for legislative action. The committee's findings are a strong condemnation of events leading to CCA's construction and operation of the Youngstown prison. Recommendations include eliminating tax incentives for private prison operators in the state; requiring annual audits

---

"The unit was in no way designed for individuals with a violent criminal history."

Allan Polunsky, Texas Board of Criminal Justice

---

of private prisons to be paid for by prison operators; prohibiting out-of-state prisoners who are classified as maximum security or who have committed violent crimes while incarcerated; requiring immediate notification of local authorities when escapes occur; and banning prisoners from wearing street clothes.

In Tennessee, home to Nashville-based CCA, a once highly favorable prison-privatization environment has soured. Earlier this year, Republican Gov. Don Sundquist announced his support for privatizing the entire state prison system. He backed away from that position recently, saying that there are too many unanswered questions about how much money private prisons will really save.

A U.S. General Accounting Office cost analysis of private prisons in Tennessee, which is considered to be the best such analysis to date, revealed private prisons there are more costly to operate than public prisons. Figures from Ohio show the average daily cost per inmate at a publicly run medium-security prison is $37.86 per day, while CCA in Youngstown is charging $53.50 per inmate per day.

MISUNDERSTOOD. Do the frightening incidents, the lawsuits, the financial struggles today mean an end to private prisons or a crippling of CCA? Unlikely. The drive to privatize prisons stems from cost-cutting efforts, and observers believe that states considering privatization most likely will give it a try of their own.

Besides, as Jim Hobbs charges, CCA has managed to confuse the public with deceptions concerning their safety practices and cost savings.

To ensure that the private-prison debate remains fuzzy — and to divert attention from its flaws — CCA recently announced a giant public relations campaign, whose message will include the line, "Quietly going about the business of public safety." In print and television ads now being tested in Tennessee, the campaign emphasizes public safety, cost savings, staff professionalism and accountability. One report on the campaign notes that CCA wants the public to know "it's not a bad company, just misunderstood."

Hobbs intends to continue his fight to expose CCA and the misconceptions about private prisons in general. In addition to educating his local's members, Hobbs, with OCSEA support, orchestrated a media blitz in Lima, going to radio, TV and print media to discuss the prison privatization issue. Hobbs also has worked with a local legislator, who introduced legislation to stop the already approved construction of two more private prisons in the state, as well as any future private prison construction.

Hobbs believes the fight against privatization must focus heavily on public education and the lessons learned at Youngstown, where anger still simmers today.

"They [CCA] will be sorry that they did this to Youngstown," Mayor McKelvey told "Dateline." "I can assure you they will be sorry."

By Catherine Barnett Alexander

PUBLIC EMPLOYEE

PLANT CLOSINGS

If, as noted earlier, there has been something of a trend to liberal advance notice on the employer's part in the case of both layoffs and the closing of some product lines stemming from technological change, few labor–management contracts require much advance notice when an entire plant is to be permanently closed. According to the Bureau of Labor Statistics, less than one-quarter of all agreements contain such a provision. Even these, moreover, usually call for little more than a month or so in the way of notification.

Managements have some very rational reasons for wanting to keep their shutdown intentions confidential. Employees who realize that even with the best performance on their part they will lose their jobs might well engage in excess absenteeism, tardiness and even, at the extreme, vandalism (presumably in an attempt to get even). Customers, concerned about future replacement parts, could take their business elsewhere. Bankers might prove unwilling to extend further credit. Stock market considerations, too, may dictate playing it close to the vest when a shutdown is contemplated. Historically, most of organized labor could be said not only to have understood all of this but to have been relatively sympathetic to these managerial considerations.

Yet, as plant closings have accelerated in the past two decades—especially in such hard-pressed older industries as automobiles, rubber, steel and meatpacking—unions have changed their attitude. They have become quite active in attempting to block the closings, especially when they have viewed the latter as mere vehicles for switching jobs to plants with lower wages in the middle of union contracts, as has in fact often been the case.

Initially, labor turned to the courts. It challenged management closing actions there on the grounds that under Section 8(d) of Taft-Hartley neither party can force the other to modify an existing contract before it expires. But, while it won two major federal appeals court rulings on the subject, in 1979 and 1982, these decisions were both reversed in 1984 by a new conservative majority on the National Labor Relations Board. In cases involving respectively the Illinois Coil Spring Company and the United Technologies Corporation, the labor board held that employers need not bargain over the transfer of work unless a labor contract required them to do so. Moreover, said the board, there was no need to bargain at all if the plant move was due to factors other than cutting labor costs.

Lobbying hard for protective legislation on the subject in the face of such board unfriendliness, unions were finally rewarded four years later when Congress enacted a significant plant closing law. Under the provisions of the **Worker Adjustment and Retraining Notification Act of 1988** (known, appropriately enough, as WARN), companies with 100 or more full-time employees must give their workers and communities at least 60 days' notice of shutdowns and major layoffs when

- a plant closing would cost 50 or more full-time employees at a single site their jobs;
- a layoff is planned of six months or longer that would affect at least 50 workers who constitute at least one-third of the workforce;
- a six-month or longer layoff is planned of 500 or more workers even if these constitute less than one-third of the workforce.

Employers who violate the law, which became effective in February 1989, cannot expect to get off easily. They are liable for one day's pay plus the cost of employment benefits for each day that notice is not given to each worker. They also owe the local community up to $500 a day for each day that the required notice is not forthcoming, with a limit of $30,000. Notification to the local government gives the latter a chance to persuade the firm not to shut down.

Some loopholes are included in the law, and these have made it to some extent less effective. Plant closings or layoffs resulting from business activities that cannot be "reasonably foreseen," including natural disasters, are exempt from the notice requirement. Also exempted are "faltering companies" that have reasonable grounds for believing that a notice of closing would prevent them from obtaining capital that they need to stay in business. And of the total U.S. labor force only about 49 percent of employees are covered because of the limitation of WARN to companies with at least 100 employees. For those workers who are excluded, unions have quite predictably since 1988 pushed once again for notification requirements at the bargaining table.

But even with its limitations, the plant closing measure by any standard constitutes a giant step in the direction of protecting both worker and public interests. It avoids psychological trauma to workers who report to work only to find padlocked doors and suddenly abolished jobs. Notified of a shutdown, employees have the opportunity to seek other employment and training for new jobs. And cities and states can, with notification, try to locate ways of keeping the firm in business, presumably to the benefit of all concerned.

Ten years after the law's implementation, there was agreement in both management and labor union quarters that employers were generally complying with WARN. A Chicago-based watchdog Federation for Industrial Retention and Renewal, a grassroots group interested in economic dislocation, was annually announcing a "Plant Closing Dirty Dozen," and these allegedly extreme examples of irresponsible plant and community abandonment according to the federation had by 1999 included such major employers as General Motors, McDonnell Douglas, Scripps Howard, Reynolds Metals, Stroehmann Bakeries, and Zenith, as well as scores of less visible managements. But fewer than 50 lawsuits alleging violations had been filed, and even in most of *those* situations it appeared that some confusion as to the exact requirements of the law rather than a direct employer intent to evade had been the trigger.

In fact, overcompliance (on the part of managers who were not subject to WARN but who thought that they were) seemed to be far more common than undercompliance. Nor did employers appear to be finding the requirements of the new law particularly burdensome: WARN had been described by one qualified observer, in the context of causing trouble to business, as a "nonevent."[17] And most other experts seemed to share this opinion. If it was accurate, major progress in worker rights had been achieved at little or no cost to managements.

SOME CONCLUDING THOUGHTS

The mutual accommodations to the hard issues of collective bargaining that the parties have displayed in regard to wages, employee benefits, and institutional issues are no less in evidence when one inspects the current status of the administrative issues in our labor relations system. Management has increasingly recognized the job-protection and working-condition problems of the industrial employee and has made important concessions in these areas. At the same time there has been reciprocal recognition on the part of unions that the protection of the employee cannot be at the expense of the destruction of the business firm. The axiom that employees cannot receive any protection from a business that has ceased to exist appears to have been fully appreciated by all but the extreme recalcitrants of the labor movement, and workable compromises have usually been possible with respect to the areas of seniority, discipline, and most of the various other dimensions discussed in this chapter no less than in the case of previous topics.

Clearly, there is considerable room for future progress, and, on occasion, the conflicts between the parties on the administrative issues can be very serious. Production standards and subcontracting remain highly visible sticking points. And strikes do, of course, at times result. There should be no illusion that the sensitive matters of collective bargaining are adjusted without painful struggle. Even standing alone, however, this chapter demonstrates rather irrefutably that managers and unionized employee representatives have increasingly recognized each other's positions. It offers additional evidence of the growing maturity of the American labor relations system, a theme that in one way or another has marked so much of this book.

DISCUSSION QUESTIONS

1. It has generally been agreed that the increased use of the seniority concept in industrial relations has lessened the degree of mobility among workers. What can be said (a) for and (b) against such a consequence?
2. "The typical labor agreement's disciplinary procedures contain as many potential advantages for management as they do for unions and workers." Comment.
3. It has been observed that "management's perception of technological change is producing an offensive strategy; the union's perception is in general producing a defensive strategy." Confining your opinion to automated changes, do you agree?
4. The several devices noted in the Technological Change section of this chapter constitute the major existing avenues for minimizing employee resistance to such change. Can you suggest other measures that might be utilized in an attempt to realize this goal?

MINICASES

#1 The Dangerous Knife

The Northwest Electronics Corporation has a rule against the possession of dangerous knives on company property, and over the years it has disciplined (generally by discharging) more than a few of its approximately 5,000 employees for having violated it. In all such cases until now, however, the knife was visible (more than once because it was being brandished).

Recently, plant security guard Ralph Von Strasser, suspecting the possession of a knife by a female worker, unilaterally entered and searched her locker and her purse and discovered that his suspicions were in fact warranted since the dangerous knife was in the purse. As the woman made ready to leave the premises by the front gate at quitting time that afternoon, she was escorted to the security office and asked to empty her purse. She was not informed why this request was being made. Refusing to honor it, she took her purse and went out the gate.

She was informed when she showed up for work on the following morning that she had been discharged for "refusing to obey the legitimate order of a plant security officer." The case wound up in arbitration.

Had you been the arbitrator here, would you have sustained the discharge, and why or why not?

#2 Vocal Criticism by an Employee

A woman who owned 49 percent of a company's common stock became ill and had her son, who happened to work for the company as a stock boy, represent her at the company's annual meeting.

During the meeting, the son expressed several strong criticisms not only of management policies but also of three of the firm's top executives. Subsequently, the management discharged the son, contending that his "attitude toward work had changed considerably" and that he had begun to act "more like a manager than an employee."

Stalemated in the grievance procedure, the case went to an arbitrator. At the hearing, the union admitted that the son-employee had been "vocal in his criticism" and that he had "challenged the competence" of the various managers. But the union sought to have the discharge reversed on the grounds that the son had registered "complaints and criticism not as an employee but as a representative of his mother."

Did the son's actions at the meeting constitute in your opinion proper grounds for discharge?

NOTES

[1]Carl Gersuny, "Origins of Seniority Provisions in Collective Bargaining," in *Proceedings of the 1982 Spring Meeting, Industrial Relations Research Association, April 28–30, 1982* (Washington, DC: Industrial Relations Research Association, 1982), p. 520.

[2]*Basic Patterns in Union Contracts*, 14th ed. (Washington, DC: Bureau of National Affairs, 1995), p. 28.

[3]*Atwater Mfg. Co.*, 13 LA 747.749, as quoted in Frank Elkouri and Edna A. Elkouri, *How Arbitration Works*, 3rd ed. (Washington, DC: Bureau of National Affairs, 1973), p. 611.

[4]*Grievance Guide*, 8th ed. (Washington, DC: Bureau of National Affairs, 1992), p. 59. A second guard, who claimed to have seen "someone walking along a street just 35 feet from the bin" shortly after the first guard had called for assistance, also testified in this case, but his comments were even less persuasive with the arbitrator.

[5]Ibid., p. 65.

[6]Arnold M. Zack, *A Handbook for Grievance Arbitration* (New York: Lexington, 1992), p. 174.

[7]*Grievance Guide*, p. 49.

[8]*The New York Times*, September 20, 1989, p. 19.

[9]Joseph F. Follmann, Jr., *The Economics of Industrial Health* (New York: Amacom, 1978), p. 75.

[10]Eula Bingham, "The New Look at OSHA: Vital Changes," in *Proceedings of the 1978 Annual Spring Meeting, Industrial Relations Research Association, May 11–13, 1978* (Washington, DC: Industrial Relations Research Association, 1978), p. 488.

[11]Ibid.

[12]*American Federationist*, April–June 1982, p. 16.

[13]*Time*, September 16, 1991, p. 28.

[14]*The New York Times*, November 15, 1981, p. E3.

[15]Sar A. Levitan and Clifford M. Johnson, "The Future of Work: Does It Belong to Us or to the Robot?" *Monthly Labor Review*, September 1982, p. 11.

[16]*Business Week*, August 30, 1999, p. 120. The expert is Raymond C. Kurzweil, founder of Kurzweil Technologies, Inc.

[17]T. S. Lough, "WARN: The Rights, Duties, and Obligations of Employers, Employees, and Unions," *Labor Law Journal*, May 1991, p. 294.

SELECTED REFERENCES

Addison, John, ed. *Job Displacement: Consequences and Implications for Policy*. Detroit: Wayne State University Press, 1991.

Bell, Derrick, *Race, Racism and the Law*, 3rd ed. Boston: Little, Brown, 1992.

Belohlav, J. A. *The Art of Disciplining Your Employees*. Englewood Cliffs, NJ: Prentice Hall, 1985.

Bourdon, Clinton C., and Raymond E. Levitt. *Union and Open-Shop Construction*. Lexington, MA: Heath, 1980.

Cappelli, Peter. *Change at Work*. New York and London: Oxford University Press, 1997.

Clark, Claudia. *Radium Girls: Women and Industrial Health Reform*. Chapel Hill and London: University of North Carolina Press, 1997.

Curran, Daniel J. *Dead Laws for Dead Men: The Politics of Federal Coal Mine Health and Safety Legislation*. Pittsburgh: University of Pittsburgh Press, 1993.

Davis, Steven J., John C. Haltiwanger, and Scott Schuh. *Job Creation and Destruction*. Cambridge, MA: MIT Press, 1996.

Denenberg, Tia Schneider, and R. V. Denenberg. *Alcohol and Drugs: Issues in the Workplace*. Washington, DC: Bureau of National Affairs, 1984.

Donovan, Ronald, and Marsha J. Orr. *Subcontracting in the Public Sector: The New York State Experience*. Ithaca, NY: New York State School of Industrial and Labor Relations, 1982.

Fiscus, Ronald J. *The Constitutional Logic of Affirmative Action*. Durham, NC: Duke University Press, 1992.

Gersuny, Carl. *Punishment and Redress in a Modern Factory*. Lexington, MA: Heath, 1973.

Hannigan, Thomas A. *Managing Tomorrow's High-Performance Unions*. Westport, CT: Quorum, 1998.

Hume, A. Britton. *Death and the Mines*. New York: Grossman, 1971.

Katz, Harry C. *Shifting Gears: Changing Labor Relations in the U.S. Automobile Industry*. Cambridge, MA: MIT Press, 1985.

Koven, Adolph M., and Susan L. Smith. *Alcohol-Related Misconduct*. Dubuque, IA: Kendall/Hunt, 1984.

Lofgren, Don J. *Dangerous Premises: An Insider's View of OSHA Enforcement*. Ithaca, NY: ILR Press, Cornell University, 1989.

Nelkin, Dorothy, and Michael S. Brown. *Workers at Risk: Voices from the Workplace*. Chicago: University of Chicago Press, 1984.

Noble, Charles. *Liberalism at Work: The Rise and Fall of OSHA*. Philadelphia: Temple University Press, 1986.

Quick, James C., and Jonathan D. Quick, *Organizational Stress and Preventive Management*. New York: McGraw-Hill, 1984.

Redeker, James R. *Employee Discipline: Policies and Practices*. Washington, DC: Bureau of National Affairs, 1989.

Rhodes, S. R., and R. M. Steers. *Managing Employee Absenteeism*. Reading, MA: Addison-Wesley, 1990.

Robinson, James C. *Toil and Toxics*. Berkeley: University of California Press, 1991.

Sellers, Christopher C. *Hazards of the Job: From Industrial Disease to Environmental Health Science*. Chapel Hill and London: University of North Carolina Press, 1997.

Westin, Alan F., and Alfred G. Feliu. *Resolving Employment Disputes Without Litigation*. Washington, DC: Bureau of National Affairs, 1988.

Zuboff, Shoshana, *In the Age of the Smart Machine*. New York: Basic Books, 1988.

CASE 8

Seniority: The Case of the Temporary Assignments

Cast of Characters

Yeng, Will,	
Soho	Grievants
Black, Black,	
Black	Hired by Company on Temporary Basis
Bolo	Superintendent
Abbot	Vice President Field Operations
Mills	Company Secretary

*Y*ou are the arbitrator in this case. Involved are the construction site of the United Mine Workers of America (UMWA) and an Employer, Best Construction, engaged in the mine construction industry. After fire destroyed about 50 percent of the Randolph Preparation Plant and seriously damaged the other part, Reliable Coal Company, owner of the plant, selected Best Construction to repair the facility.

December 20 is a significant date in this case. On Friday, December 17, 1997, Reliable Coal advised Abbot, Best Construction's Vice President Field Operations, that he would be required to have certified electricians at the site on Monday, December 20. In other words, if the Employer wanted the business, it would have to secure certified electricians and have them report on December 20. If it could not do that, Reliable Coal would contact another mine construction firm. To get the job, Abbot promised to have the electricians at the preparation plant at 8 A.M., December 20.

Critical to your decision is the proper application of Article XVI, Section (j), the Temporary Assignment provision. Under Article XVI, seniority is of paramount importance in many areas of employment, such as layoffs, recalls, job bidding, and staffing of projects. Under the Temporary Assignment provision, however, the Employer may ask any employee, *regardless of seniority*, to work temporarily on a project, but not for more than 60 days.

There is no question that the project in question was covered by the UMWA contract. The Blacks accepted the assignment and ceased the temporary assignment when they successfully bid on permanent vacancies in Best Construction on January 19, 1998. Thus, the temporary assignment did not exceed the contractual limit of 60 days. The Union did not file a grievance protesting the Blacks' successful bid for permanent jobs.

INTRODUCTION

The case surfaced when the Company temporarily assigned three (3) employees junior in service to other employees to work at the Randolph Preparation Plant, Marion, Illinois, owned by the Reliable Coal Company.

In protest, Roger Yeng, Russell Will, and David Soho filed Grievances Number 98-4, 98-2, and 98-1, respectively. All grievances were submitted in January 1998. Each grievance claims that the Employer bypassed employees on the Company Panel* and instead hired on temporary assignment junior service employees to perform the work. Yeng was the only Grievant who testified in the arbitration. Hired to carry out the work were Ronnie Black, Dallas Black, and George Black.

By stipulation, the Parties agreed that Will and Soho are senior in service to Ronnie and Dallas Black, and Yeng was senior to George Black.

On January 11, 1998, the Grievance Committee supported the grievances, saying "the grievances are valid. Seniority and recall rights of Grievants were violated by Company action. Grievants are entitled to restitution."

On the same day, Raymond Bolo, Superintendent of the project, denied the grievances, stating:

> Grievance denied pursuant to the National Coal Mine Agreement of 1995 Article XVI and/or any other Article or Section thereof which may apply.

Having failed to settle the dispute in the Grievance Procedure, the Parties convened this arbitration for its determination.

NATIONAL COAL MINE CONSTRUCTION AGREEMENT OF 1995 (EFFECTIVE OCTOBER 1, 1995)

ARTICLE III—MANAGEMENT

This agreement is not intended to interfere with, abridge or limit the Employer's right to manage its construction operations. It is agreed that the management of said operations, including the direction and scheduling of the work force, the right to hire and discharge, the right to make reasonable rules of conduct, the direction, management and control of business, and other functions and responsibilities which heretofore have been vested in the management, are and shall remain vested exclusively in the Employer provided these rights are not in conflict with any of the provisions of this Agreement.

ARTICLE XVI—SENIORITY

Section (j) Temporary Assignment

The Employer may ask any employee, regardless of his seniority, to work temporarily at a project covered by a UMWA Agreement, but the employee shall have the right to refuse the assignment. When an employee works temporarily at another project, he shall not forfeit any rights at the project site where he is regularly employed and, upon completion of the temporary assignment, his employment rights at his regular project site shall be the same as if he never left. No

---

*In the coal industry, laid off employees are placed on the so-called Company Panel. These employees have priority for recall to work and must be rehired by seniority before the Company employs any other employee.

employee shall be penalized for refusing to accept a temporary assignment. Assignments which last sixty (60) work days or less shall be deemed temporary for purposes of this section.

ISSUE

Under the circumstances of this case, did the Employer violate Article XVI, Section (j) of the National Agreement? If so, what should the remedy be?

BACKGROUND

Damage at Randolph Preparation Plant

A major fire took place at the Randolph Preparation Plant, Reliable Coal Company, resulting in the total destruction of one-half (1/2) of the facility, and the other half (1/2) was severely damaged. The Employer's pictures of the damage reveal massive destruction of conduits, wires, and accessory equipment. During the week of December 14, 1997, Reliable Coal Company contacted Frank Abbot, Vice President Field Operations, Best Construction, concerning the damage to the preparation plant. In a meeting held there, Abbot and a Reliable representative toured the facility, discussed personnel requirements to repair the damage, and made preliminary estimates of the cost of the project. Abbot returned to Clarksburg, headquarters for the Employer, prepared cost estimates, and contacted Reliable.

According to Abbot, Reliable told him the Employer was required to have certified electricians at the preparation plant Monday, December 20. He testified:

> I was told by Reliable that it was essential that we furnish certified electricians at the site by Monday, December 20. Reliable asked me if we could have people on the job at that time. I said yes.

Blacks Hired

On Friday, December 17, Abbot testified, he intended to have qualified men at the site on the following Monday. He decided to hire the Blacks and three (3) electrical helpers. At that time, the Blacks were working on a Company project in Alabama. Abbot called the superintendent at the Alabama site, telling him what he wanted to do. The superintendent was reluctant "to let them go because they were his key people," said Abbot. Nonetheless Abbot prevailed, and the Alabama superintendent told him that the Blacks would be home the weekend of December 17. They live near the Randolph Preparation Plant, about thirty (30) minutes away.

The Employer contacted the Blacks by telephone, hired them, and instructed them to report to the project Monday, December 20. All three (3) are certified electricians for high voltage, surface, and underground. Ronnie Black was hired at "A" Grade, Dallas Black at "B" Grade, and George Black at "C" Grade. As instructed, the Blacks reported for duty on Monday, December 20.

Blacks' Duties

As to the duties the Blacks performed during the week of December 20, Abbot testified, they tested circuits, handled some "hot" wires, tore out the conduits damaged by the fire, installed temporary lights, helped set up the site, and "got into the equipment to make damage estimates."

The Blacks did not actually make estimates of the damage, but their work, particularly the last duty mentioned, was necessary to determine the costs of the repairs, said Abbot. Raymond Bolo, Superintendent of the project, sent in damage data to Clarksburg, where the actual money figures were established for Reliable.

When the Grievants were hired for the project, Grievant Yeng said, a fellow employee told him the kind of work the Blacks performed during the week of December 20. In this respect, Yeng testified:

> I was told they [Blacks] leveled trailers, tore out damaged conduits and wire, and cleaned up.

Grievants Recalled

By certified mail and telephone, the Grievants were notified to report to the Randolph project at 8 A.M. on Monday, December 27. Yeng testified he was called on Thursday, December 23, by Glenn Mills, Company Secretary, to report Monday morning. The Grievant also declared that the certified letter, dated December 23, was not received by him until December 29. However, responding to the phone call, Yeng reported on December 27 for work.

Like Yeng, Grievants Will and Soho reported at the project on December 27. Will and Soho are certified electricians, but Yeng is not. Will was recalled at the A Grade, Soho at the C Grade, and Yeng at the C Grade. The three (3) Grievants live within one (1) hour's drive from the Randolph Preparation Plant.

Jobs Posted

By January 19, 1998, said Abbot, the Company Panel was exhausted. As a result, the Employer posted permanent job vacancies for electrician jobs, four (4) vacancies for Class A; five (5) for Class B; and eight (8) for Class C.

David Soho and Ronnie Black were selected to fill two (2) of the three (3) Class A vacancies. Dallas Black was picked to fill one (1) of the Class B vacancies. George Black was chosen to fill one (1) of the Class C vacancies.

In regard to the Blacks, Abbot said that they were selected under Article XVI, Section (g), which gives preference to employees bidding to their home districts. Until they were transferred to the project in question, they were working in the Alabama District. District 12, however, is their home district, and they exercised their right to return to their home district. No grievance was filed to protest the Blacks' successful bids for permanent jobs at the Randolph Preparation Plant project.

POSITIONS OF THE PARTIES

The Company argues that Section (e) of Article XVI supports its position that the grievance should be denied. This provision establishes how employees are to be recalled to work from the Employer's panel. It states that notice of recall or confirmation of notice of recall should be made to the employee's last known address by certified mail, registered mail, telegram, or mailgram. It contends that these modes of communication are too slow, emphasizing it had to have certified electricians at the preparation plant on Monday, December 20.

In this respect, the Employer cited testimony offered by Abbot, who said:

> We used the temporary assignment clause to staff the jobs on Monday, December 20. If we went to the Company panel to recall the Grievants by certified or registered mail, they would not have been required to report to work immediately upon receipt of the letter. Employees have a reasonable amount of time to report to work, normally five (5) days.

In other words, had the Company used the modes of communication spelled out in the contract, they would be too slow and would jeopardize its business with Reliable Coal Company. In this respect, it asserts:

> The purpose of the temporary assignment provision is to allow an employer to efficiently use the skills of the employees in his work force and to quickly respond to emergency situations. Both of these elements were present in this case. Not only was it necessary for the company to put experienced employees on the site to cope with "hot" wire situations, it was necessary to get them there with very little prior notice. Ronnie, Dallas, and George Black were qualified to do the work that had to be done to get the Reliable project started, and they were available to begin immediately. The company knew they were available because they were working at its project in Alabama. It did not have to worry that they might have other commitments that would keep them from reporting on Monday morning.

In addition, the Company asserts, Article III—Management—authorizes its action in this case. It stresses that under the provision, the Employer has the right to direct the work force, control the business, and carry out the functions of management.

Finally, in its brief, Best Construction claims that if the Union wins this case, the Arbitrator would in effect erase Section (j) from the contract.

Not so, claims the Union, and the grievances should be granted. Its major argument is that since the Employer contacted the Blacks by telephone, it could have done the same with the Grievants. It highlights testimony of Abbot, who said:

> We could have called, but it would take time that we did not have. So I could not take the chance of not having people at the site on Monday, December 20.

According to the Union, the Company may not receive a favorable decision under the Management provision because what it did conflicted with a provision of the contract, Article XVI, Section (j).

Employee Discipline

The next two cases, the last ones in this book, deal with employee discipline. No issue in labor relations exceeds the importance of this area to all concerned. As a matter of fact, almost 50 percent of all arbitration cases concern discipline, and most involve discharge. To the employee, needless to say, the job is his or her most important asset. Take away the job, and the employee and family life collapse with tragic consequences. It is no wonder that unions elect to arbitrate discharge cases even when considerable doubt exists as to their merits. But to the employer, discipline under proper circumstances is necessary to maintain an efficient labor force. Failure to enforce rules of conduct could result in chaos within the firm.

You are the arbitrator in Case 9. In disputes involving employee discipline, the employer bears the burden of proof. The employee does not have the responsibility to prove that he or she did not commit the offense that resulted in discipline. Instead, the employer must present clear, convincing, and sufficient evidence to prove that the employee is guilty of the offense.

In discipline cases, the employer may present either one or both of two types of evidence: direct and circumstantial. Direct evidence means that a person(s) actually observed the disciplined employee commit the offense. In contrast, circumstantial evidence is related to a chain of events that proves that the employee engaged in the conduct that resulted in the discipline. Circumstantial evidence, however, would not normally stand if the defense presents a theory consistent with the facts reasonably indicating that another person may have committed the offense.

In Case 9, the company discharged an employee for leaving the plant early. Determine whether the employer used direct or circumstantial evidence to prove its case.

In addition, in cases of discipline, credibility of witnesses frequently becomes a problem. As you will learn, the discharged employee and plant superintendent clashed on the vital issue of the case. So, whom do you believe?

In short, your problem is to determine, on the basis of the record, whether the company presented sufficient, clear, and convincing evidence proving that the employee committed the offense for which he was discharged. To put it another way, did the company meet its burden of proof?

Case 10 is surely one of the strangest cases in the annals of arbitration. A comparatively small telephone company was privately owned by its president. For about one year, the employer paid an employee full wages and fringe benefits even though he did not require the employee to work! Then the company discharged the employee, alleging that his productivity was deficient and that he was psychologically unfit to work. Despite the odd character of the dispute, the arbitrator attempted to apply sound arbitration principles as the basis of his decision. As you read the case, try to determine the real reason why the employer paid the employee even though the latter was not required to work.

Employee Discipline: The Case of the Permission to Leave the Plant

C A S E

9

Cast of Characters

Mack	Grievant
Back	Manufacturing Manager
Moore	Plant Superintendent
Bloom	Employee
Diltz	Employee

*Y*ou are the arbitrator in this case. It involves an employee, Steve Mack, who was terminated when the company alleged that he left the plant without permission. Under Article VIII (Seniority) an employee loses his seniority and the employment relationship is terminated when he or she leaves the plant without permission. On its part, the union claims that the grievant was not discharged for just cause under Article VIII, Section 5(b). Therefore, he did not lose his seniority, and the employment relationship was not terminated.

Given the contradictions between the principals of this case, there exists the problem of credibility. Who is to be believed and why? Other matters warrant your attention—the grievant's claim of illness and the dangers of the job.

Probably the grievant would claim that the following statement that Moore made to him demonstrates that the plant superintendent in effect gave him permission to leave the plant. At the locker room door, said the grievant, Moore told him "Well, if you think you have to go home, go on home." Diltz said he heard Moore make the statement.* In your decision, you must confront the credibility problem and resolve it.

Consider also the union's statement that the grievant is a long-term employee with an impeccable record. Unions make such an argument to mitigate the employee's offense. They will tell the arbitrator something like this: "Not for a minute do we agree that the grievant committed the offense. The evidence shows he did not. But should you [the arbitrator] believe that he did so, you should consider that he has many years of service, and no prior discipline." In other words, even if the employee committed the offense, the arbitrator should keep in mind the mitigating factors and reduce the discharge to a less severe penalty.

So, in the case at hand, would you set aside the discharge and lower the penalty on the basis of mitigating factors? Arbitration precedent is that, unless a contract

---

*Diltz was terminated in November 1998, charged with a drug offense. He and the grievant drove to work together and jointly participated in social affairs.

says otherwise, the arbitrator has the authority to set aside a discharge and impose a lesser penalty.

GRIEVANCE

Protesting his termination, Steve Mack filed a grievance dated July 9, 1998, which stated:

> The Foreman asked Grievant (Steve) to help unload a trailer. Steve informed the Foreman the job was not safe. He then told Foreman he was sick and wished to go home. He told him if he wanted to go home to go on. Steve clocked out, and went home. The next morning he was fired for leaving. Remedy to this grievance, the Grievant must be reinstated to his job and made whole for all lost wages & benefits.

Failing to settle the dispute in the Grievance Procedure, the Parties convened this arbitration for its determination.

LABOR AGREEMENT

ARTICLE VIII—SENIORITY

Section 5. Loss of Seniority

Seniority and the employment relationship will be terminated when an employee:

A. Quits.
B. Is discharged for cause.

●●●

J. Leaves work without permission.

ISSUE

Under the circumstances of this case, did the Company properly terminate Grievant Mack's employment under Article VIII, Section 5 of the Labor Agreement? If not, what should the remedy be?

BACKGROUND

Events of July 8, 1998: Arrival of Truck

Starting operations in February 1994, Moline Manufacturing manufactures radiators for trucks and automobiles. By 1998, it had hired about fifteen (15) bargaining unit employees. Wayne Back served as Manufacturing Manager during the circumstances of this case, and Jack Moore was Plant Superintendent.

At about 9 A.M., July 8, 1998, a closed van truck arrived containing tubes used in the production of radiators. They were packed in wooden crates, each crate eleven feet long and six to eight inches high and wide. Each crate weighed between 100 and 200 pounds. Normally the crates are stacked waist high, but this time, because of a large back order, the crates were stacked to the ceiling. Mack was hired on June 6, 1997, and terminated July 9, 1998. He did not have any discipline before his discharge.

Assignment of Mack: First Conversation

When the truck arrived, Moore secured employees to unload the crates. No specific classification exists for the purpose of loading or unloading trucks, and Moore assigns employees who are available for the work. Moore approached the Grievant, who at that time was working with Kenneth Bloom testing cores. Their work area was about 120 feet from the loading dock. A conversation occurred between the Plant Superintendent and the Grievant. According to Moore, after he told Mack he was needed to unload the truck, the Grievant replied:

> No, I'm not going to unload that truck. It's hot in here. It's hernia material, and I'm not going to unload it.

After the interchange, Moore left to get other employees to unload the truck. Eventually it was unloaded by five employees.

As to this conversation, the Grievant testified:

> Jack walks back and asks me to unload the truck. And I said, "Jack, I'm not feeling good, and I don't want to unload the truck."

Second Conversation

Within five or ten minutes, Moore returned to Mack's work area, and a second conversation took place. According to Moore, it went this way:

> "I need your help unloading that truck." And at that point, Steve said, "I am not going to unload that truck." He said, "It's hernia material." And he said, "I am going home." And I said, "Now Steve, you do not want to leave without permission." He said, "I am going to go home," and he started walking off.

As to that interchange, the Grievant testified:

> About five or ten minutes later he comes back and he says, "Steve, you've got to unload the truck." And I said, "Jack, I'm not going to unload the truck because I don't feel good. Besides the truck is stacked too dangerously, and it looks like hernia material to me."

Mack also declared that Moore started to yell and scream, throwing his arms in the air. In turn, the Grievant testified, he also started to yell. After five or ten minutes, during which time the yelling and screaming continued, the Grievant testified:

> I started feeling sick, so I started walking up toward the front.

According to Mack, he had some kind of stomach flu and a real bad headache, made worse by the 90 degree temperature.

Moore testified that he did not raise his voice during the exchange between the Grievant and himself.

At the Locker Room Door

After the second conversation, Mack started to walk to the front of the plant, headed for the locker room. Moore followed him. While walking in that direction, Mack stopped where Kirk Diltz was working, asked for and received keys to his [Diltz's] truck in case, said the Grievant, he had to go home.

Diltz's work station was located about fifteen to twenty feet from the locker room door. He testified that he heard Moore tell Mack "If you believe you want to go home, go on home."

As the Grievant was walking, he said, Moore was behind him yelling and screaming about unloading the truck, and Mack kept yelling he felt bad. At the door to the locker room, the Grievant testified, he said:

"Now, Jack, I've got to go home." He said, "Well, if you think you have to go home, go on home."

Meeting between Back, Moore, and Mack

Moore followed Mack to the locker room, testifying that he had no recollection of a conversation between them at that location. At this time, he reported the incident to Back, Manufacturing Manager, who was in his office. Moore said he told Back that the Grievant had refused to unload the truck and was leaving the plant without his permission. They left the office to find the Grievant. Back testified that they encountered Mack at the time clock and Back assumed that he had just left the locker room.

According to Mack, he met Back and Moore when he returned to the plant after he previously had clocked out. He said that he returned to the plant to make sure Back knew why he was going home, testifying:

Q: If you felt that Mr. Moore had given you permission to go home and you were already outside, why did you come back into the plant?
A: Because we had a heated argument, and we was both pretty well mad at each other, and I just wanted to make sure the stories got straight.

After Back asked the Grievant "what are you doing," Back said Mack replied:

"I'm not going to unload that truck. It's hernia material and I am just not going to do it."

•••

"I'm not going to unload the truck. I'm going home sick."

At this point, Moore told the Grievant it was the first time "you ever said anything to me about being sick." According to Back, the Grievant then said: "Well, I'm telling you now, and I'm going home." Back also testified that Mack refused several requests to discuss the matter in his office.

Mack denied that Back invited him to discuss the incident in his office. He also testified that he had previously told Moore he was leaving the plant because he was sick. According to the Grievant, Back asked him why he refused to unload the truck, and Mack said he replied that it was too dangerous, he was not feeling well, and he was going home.

In any event, the Grievant clocked out at 9:29 A.M. He said he went home, lay down, and did not seek medical attention.

Events of July 9, 1998

When Mack reported to work on July 9, a meeting was held attended by Back, Moore, and the Grievant. At that time, the Grievant said, he had not unloaded the truck and had left the plant because he was sick, but he did not go to a doctor because he was feeling better later. He also told the two Management representatives that Moore had given him permission to leave the plant on July 8. Moore related that he had not given Mack permission to leave the plant. At the end of the session, Back told the Grievant that he was terminated.

POSITIONS OF THE PARTIES

According to the Union, the Grievant did not lose his seniority and job, because he had Moore's permission to leave the plant. Moore denied that he had given him permission, testifying: "I did not give him permission to leave the plant." One of the problems of this case will be to determine the credibility of the two principals. According to the Union, the Grievant's version should be accepted because "Steve Mack was a long-term employee with an unblemished record. He would not have left if his supervisor had not given him permission."

Directing attention to a statement allegedly made by Moore to the Grievant at the door of the locker room, the Grievant testified that Moore told him: "Well, if you think you have to go home, go on home."

On his behalf, the Union stresses that Mack was ill on July 8, and that this fact should be taken into account before the decision is made. In addition, the Union charges that the Employer did not warn the Grievant that he would be terminated if he left the plant without permission. It also claims that the Grievant believed the job was dangerous, pointing to his testimony:

> I was not going to unload it because it was too dangerous, and I was sick, and would not have my full strength. If I dropped one of those 100 to 200 pound boxes, I could hurt myself or hurt someone else.

In contrast, Moline Manufacturing argues that the grievance should be denied. It asserts:

> A fair evaluation of the evidence demonstrates that beyond a shadow of doubt, the Grievant did not receive permission to leave the plant on July 8. (Company Posthearing Brief, p. 15)

It stresses that it did not discharge the Grievant because he refused to unload the truck, faked illness to cover up his offense, or for any reason other than that he left the plant without permission. "So, even if he engaged in insubordination or lied to us," the Employer asserts, "we did not terminate him for those reasons. We stand or fall on our charge that Mack left the plant without permission on July 8." (Company Posthearing Brief, p. 12)

Commenting on the contradictory testimony, Moline Manufacturing claims that the Grievant's testimony should not be credited and instead that the testimony offered by its two officials should be accepted.

Employee Discipline: The Case of the Employee Who Was Paid and Not Required to Work

Cast of Characters

Hall	Discharged Employee
Jones	A Union Witness
Thomas	President of Company
Fells	Superintendent

GRIEVANCE AND LABOR AGREEMENT

*I*n protest against his discharge, effective October 1, 1985, Hall filed a grievance dated October 2, 1985. It states:

> In reference to letter received by aggrieved employee Sept. 30, 1985 from employer stating that his job would be terminated Oct. 1, 1985 for violation of Paragraph 2, Page 1, of Contract. Aggrieved employee has not violated Paragraph 2, Page 1, of Contract and has no knowledge of why he is accused of doing so or for what reasons the Company has for stating that his job would be terminated Oct. 1, 1985.
>
> He requests that he be reinstated to his regular and/or normal job with full seniority and made whole for any and all monies and benefits due him in accordance with terms and conditions of contract.
>
> The employer has not found proper cause to discharge aggrieved employee.

Having failed to settle the dispute in the Grievance Procedure, the Parties convened this arbitration for its final and binding determination. Material to the dispute are the following provisions of the Labor Agreement:

Paragraph 2

The Union agrees that its said members will individually and collectively, at all times perform loyal and efficient service, comply with the terms and working conditions of this Agreement, use their influence and best efforts to protect the property of the Company and all its employees to such ends.

Paragraph 3(b)

Subject to the provisions of this Agreement, the Company shall have the right to schedule and assign work, to hire, promote, recall, demote, suspend, transfer, lay off and for proper cause to discharge employees.

Paragraph 16

The arbitrator or arbitrators shall have no authority to add to, subtract from, or modify any provision of this Agreement, or to rule on any questions except the ones submitted for arbitration.

BASIC QUESTION

The basic question to be determined in this arbitration is framed as follows: Under the circumstances of this case, was Grievant Hall discharged for proper cause? If not, what should the remedy be?

BACKGROUND

Grievant Hall was hired by the Company on June 6, 1976. On August 4, 1984, he broke a leg while riding a horse. Though the Labor Agreement does not contain a sickness-accident program that pays employees for non-work-related accidents or sickness, employee Jones said that it was the policy of the Company to pay employees about six or seven weeks' pay when they were disabled as a result of such circumstances.

Some time in September 1984, Hall called Thomas, President of the Company. The Grievant testified that two weeks prior to the call he had received four days' pay, and a week before the call, he did not receive any pay. He testified that the purpose of the call was to discuss the problem with Thomas.

According to the testimony of Thomas, at one point in this phone conversation Hall said to him:

The only reason I work for a S.O.B. like you is because I have a wife and children to support.

As to this event, the Grievant denied that he had made the aforecited statement attributed to him by the Company President. Hall testified that he said to Thomas:

I have a wife and two children who depend on me and that is why I work.

Hall declared that Thomas replied:

If you don't like to work for me, why don't you work for a good guy?

On or about October 14, 1984, Hall reported to work though he still had a cast on his leg. Fells, Superintendent, assigned him to driving a truck. However, at times, Fells said, the Grievant buried cables, using a vibrator and a backhoe. On November 18, 1984, Hall buried cables for nine hours.

The next day, November 19, 1984, Fells called the Grievant and told him to bring his truck in for repairs. He did so and had a conversation with the Superintendent. Hall testified that he told Fells that work was falling behind, and asked for another truck. Fells refused. Instead, Fells told the Grievant to go home and wait until he was called back to work. In this regard, Hall testified:

Fells told me that my truck needed repairs. He told me to go home and wait until I was called.

Also, Fells told the Grievant that he would get full pay for all the time he did not work. As events turned out, the Company paid the Grievant his full pay and fringe benefits from November 19, 1984, until October 1, 1985, on which date he was discharged. In other words, for about one year, the Company paid the Grievant although he did not work. During this period of time, Hall periodically executed a Daily Time Report. On this report, he would write: "Waiting on truck." These reports were sent to Fells, who approved them, and the Company paid the Grievant although he did not actually perform work for his employer.

Thomas explained the reason for such a state of affairs. He testified:

> I heard for a long period of time many complaints from my customers. This indicated to me that Hall was not working. Also, after he called me in September 1984 and said "the only reason I would work for a S.O.B. like you is because I have a wife and children to support," I assumed that he did not want to work for me. I decided that we would be better off to leave him on the payroll and not have him work. I did not want any more customer complaints. He was impeding the progress of other employees. But the precipitating cause for this action (pay and no work) is that he simply did not want to work for me. It was in the best interest of the Company for us to take a $20,000 loss by paying him for not working than to assume the risk of having him work.

In addition, Thomas said the reason why the Grievant was not discharged on November 19, 1984, was that "I was not certain about the problems of terminating an employee."

Superintendent Fells also explained why the Company paid the Grievant though he did not perform any work. He said:

> We were unhappy with him because of his work performance. We did not think we were getting the job done. It was our judgment that he was not producing enough. He took too much time on a job.

During the period of time in which the Grievant was paid though he did not perform any work, there was no contact between the Grievant and the Company except the sending of his paychecks by the Company, the acceptance of them by the Grievant, and the filing of periodic Daily Time Reports. The Company did not call or write him, nor did Hall come to the Company, or write or phone.

In any event, effective October 20, 1985, the Grievant was discharged. Thomas wrote him:

> Mr. Hall:
>
> Paragraph 2 in the contracts [*sic*] reads:
>
> The Union agrees that its said members will individually and collectively, at all times perform loyal and efficient service, comply with the terms and working conditions of this Agreement, use their influence and best efforts to protect the property of the Company and all its employees to such ends.
>
> It is because you have violated these terms of this contractual agreement, you are hereby terminated effective October 1, 1985.

Thomas disclosed the circumstances that prompted him to discharge the Grievant. It so happened that an employee of the Company had a son with some degree of mental deficiency. The employee asked Thomas to hire his son. Thomas did not hire the young son because he feared that he might have an accident. In light of this event, Thomas said:

> I had a man [Grievant] who was not working and drawing full pay. The boy could probably have performed more work than Hall. After serious thought, I wrote the termination letter.

During the processing of the grievance, Thomas made two offers to settle the dispute. On October 15, 1985, he offered to pay the Grievant his full wages until July 1986, at which time Hall would qualify for early retirement. Under the applicable early retirement provisions of the Labor Agreement, the Grievant would then receive $210.00 per month for life. The offer was refused by the Grievant.

A second offer was made in the middle of December 1985. Thomas proposed that he would return the Grievant to his job provided that Hall visit a psychological social worker weekly. Such treatment, Thomas explained, would be at the Company expense. Hall refused this offer. In the Company brief, Thomas stated:

> If I could have come up with any other new and better ideas to help this man, I would have done so. As I explained at the hearing, we are operating with a Humanitarian philosophy of business management, and we care for the people who work for us.

ANALYSIS OF THE EVIDENCE

Strange Character of Case

To say the least, this is a very strange case. In the Arbitrator's long experience, he knows of no situation in which a company paid an employee and did not require that person to perform any work. The fact that this was done for about one year underscores its extraordinary nature. It was not a situation in which the Grievant was physically disabled and received accident benefits. For about five weeks before his discharge, Hall was working, though he had a cast on his leg. Also, in February 1985, Hall was released by his doctor, demonstrating that his leg was fully healed. Thus, during the year or so in question, Hall was physically qualified to work and received full pay and fringe benefits, but the Company did not require him to work.

In any event, the uniqueness of the dispute should not serve to mask its substantive issues. As the Company's termination letter demonstrates, Hall was discharged on the grounds that he violated Paragraph 2 of the Labor Agreement. Under this provision, the Union agreed that its members would perform loyal and efficient service for the Company. Should the evidence demonstrate that Hall violated his obligations under this provision, it would follow that his discharge was for "proper cause" under the terms of Paragraph 3. Of course, if Hall engaged in conduct that offended his obligations as an employee, he could be discharged for "proper cause" without reference to Paragraph 2.

Grievant's Work Performance

As Company testimony demonstrates, one charge against the Grievant was that he did not satisfactorily perform his job. Fells testified that Hall "was not producing enough," and that he "took too much time on a job." Thomas said that he received customer complaints about the Grievant. In other words, when the Grievant was actively working for the Company, he failed to produce satisfactorily. His productivity did not measure up to acceptable standards.

As a threshold observation, it may be stated that an employer may properly discharge an employee under such circumstances. An employer must produce satisfactorily or face the consequences. Indeed, the Arbitrator has sustained the discharges of employees who failed to meet reasonable production standards. Professional arbitrators have recognized that to keep a job, an employee must satisfactorily meet reasonable standards of productivity.

Thus, the first question to be determined is whether the evidence demonstrates that the Grievant produced satisfactorily. In this respect, the Company has the obligation to provide competent and convincing evidence to prove that Hall did not measure up to reasonable production standards. As countless arbitration decisions demonstrate, in a disciplinary case the employer bears the burden of proof. In short, the employer must supply convincing evidence that the employee committed the offense for which he was discharged. It is up to the employer to prove the employee "guilty," and not the employee who must prove himself "not guilty." This is a rock-bottom principle of arbitration and so familiar that no citation of arbitral precedent is necessary.

Quality of Company Evidence

When this principle is applied to the circumstances of the case, the conclusion is inescapable that the Company failed to prove that the Grievant did not produce satisfactorily. All that the Company supplies in this respect is the judgment of its two officials that the Grievant failed to produce adequately. With respect to the customer complaints against Hall, Thomas testified that he received two phone calls from the Company's customers complaining about the Grievant. He said:

> These two complaints were from women who complained that the Grievant was in the coffee shop. I probably got these calls in 1984.

Note that the Grievant was employed by the Company for about nine years. Even if the complaints were fully justified, the occurrence of two complaints of this nature in a nine-year period does not demonstrate that the Grievant was not a satisfactory employee. Beyond this, the Company apparently did not regard these two complaints to be of much consequence because it did not call them to the attention of the Grievant.

In addition, the judgment of the Company officials that the Grievant was taking too much time on his jobs and did not produce enough is not backed up by objective evidence. Note the testimony of Fells:

> It was our *judgment* that he was not producing enough. He took too much time on a job. (Emphasis added)

Though the judgment or opinions of supervision deserve consideration, they are not of much evidentiary value unless supported by objective evidence. Any supervisor can testify that in his opinion or judgment an employee is not doing his job. In this respect, the Company has not provided any evidence whatsoever to support the judgment or opinions of its officials. Daily time sheets are filled out by the employees, and these documents are inspected by the Superintendent. Such time sheets show the kinds of jobs performed by the Company's employees and disclose the time spent on such jobs. In other words, there exists objective evidence to demonstrate the productivity of the employees. However, before the Company discharged the Grievant, no reference was made to such documents. Fells testified: "I did not examine his time sheets before we discharged him."

Progressive Discipline

Added to these considerations, the record shows that at no time did the Company ever warn the Grievant that his production was not satisfactory. During his nine years of service, Hall did not receive any warnings, reprimands, or suspensions. In fact, Fells testified that his work was "average,"* and that "I never told him that his work was taking too long."

It is a matter of common sense that when an employee falls below par, the worker should be counseled, warned, reprimanded, and even suspended before discharge takes place. This is what is meant by progressive discipline, a system used by employers to rehabilitate an employee. In cases of this sort, where the allegation is made that an employee fails to meet reasonable standards of production, the employer first counsels the employee in the effort to improve his or her performance. If such counseling, fairly given, fails to correct the employee's deficiencies, the next step is to implement discipline. Normally, the employee is first warned orally or in writing or both. If this does not induce the employee to improve production, the next step is a suspension. When all this fails, the employer then discharges the employee on the grounds that all efforts to rehabilitate the employee have failed.

In this case, even if we assume that the Grievant did not meet production standards, the Company made no effort to rehabilitate him. As a matter of fact, at no time did the Company even tell the employee that he was not producing satisfactorily. Clearly, it is a matter of common sense that when an employee does not turn out a "fair day's work" the employer calls this to his attention. If the employer does not do this, how does the employee know that his work is not satisfactory? In the absence of counseling or warnings, the employee has reason to believe that his or her work meets production standards.

In any event, in this case, the evidence simply does not support the charge that the Grievant was not doing his job. All that we have in the way of evidence is the unsupported opinion of the two Company officials. Beyond this, the Company did not offer a scintilla of evidence to prove the charge. Indeed, the very fact that the Company never counseled or warned the Grievant discloses that his work was satisfactory. In short, in light of the available evidence, it would be absolutely improper to sustain the discharge of the Grievant. Such a decision would be totally unwarranted given the state of the evidence and would fly in the face of settled and recognized principles of the arbitration process.

Psychological Fitness of Grievant

In addition, the Company argues that Hall is psychologically unfit to return to work. With respect to this feature of the case, Thomas says:

> Offered early retirement of $210.00 per month, he refused. Offered his regular job provided he would see a psychological social worker on company time and at company expense, he refused this also.
>
> Still he persists he wants to come back to work for a man he intensely dislikes. This is not the behavior of a rational man; rather, it is the behavior of a very neurotic man. In the interest of the company and its customers, I can and will not gainfully employ anyone too sick to do an adequate job, whether it be physical or psychological.
>
> Hall has not always been willing to follow instructions from the company in the past. The only possible explanation for the fact that he could take

---

*In all fairness, in light of the general testimony of Fells, when he described the work of the Grievant as "average," he was apparently making the assessment in reference to the quality of the Grievant's work rather than its quantity.

full pay for doing absolutely no work for almost a year, and rather dutifully stay around Dover, because he was "waiting on truck" as ordered, and never in the entire time communicate with me is an indication of the seriousness of his neurosis.

What alternatives do I have where an employee is physically healthy, but is not at all well psychologically? We accept the responsibility of taking care of our employees from their time of employment to their death. However, when one is sick, should that man get full pay? I think not, in fairness to our other employees, the company owners, and the telephone customers.

Termination was my last alternative, only because I could not think of any other options to offer Hall.

Under proper circumstances, an employer may properly terminate an employee for reasons of psychological or mental unfitness to hold a job, or, under proper circumstances, an employer may require an employee to be treated for mental or psychological disorders as the prerequisite for holding a job. In this case, the Company relies upon these propositions to justify the discharge of the Grievant.

To support its position, the Company says that Hall demonstrated irrational and psychologically unsound behavior because he accepted pay for about one year without performing work. It argues that this state of affairs "is an indication of the seriousness of his neurosis."

Certainly, this feature of the case demonstrates its rare character. Here we had an employee receiving full pay and fringe benefits, and the Company did not require him to work. As noted earlier, the Arbitrator has never been confronted with such a situation, and it is probably unique in labor relations. To conclude on this basis, however, that the Grievant is psychologically unsound to work is unwarranted. The bottom line is that the Grievant did exactly what the Company told him to do. On November 19, 1984, the Company told the Grievant to "go home and wait until he was called back to work." He was told that while he waited for the call he would receive full pay and fringe benefits. If it is held that it was strange behavior on the part of the Grievant to accept such payments, it was just as strange for the Company to have permitted this state of affairs to occur.

At any time, the Company had the power to stop this unusual condition. At any time, it could have directed the Grievant to return to work or discharged him as it eventually did on October 1, 1985. True, the Grievant testified that he felt "uncomfortable" when he received pay without working. But what was Hall supposed to do? He did not have the authority to work without receiving such permission to work. It was the responsibility of the Company to direct him to work. In the absence of a call to work, should he have refused payment and thereby lose the source of income to support his family? Should he have quit his job, and thereby forfeit his contractual rights gained over nine years of service? Should he have quit his job and taken his chances on getting another job given the fact that jobs are scarce because of the current national problem of unemployment? Clearly, if the Company was willing to tolerate this strange state of affairs, it was to be expected that Hall would accept payment. Indeed, it would be an irrational act on his part to refuse payment or to quit his job. In short, the Arbitrator finds that the Grievant's acceptance of payment does not demonstrate irrational behavior or show that he was psychologically unfit to hold his job, or that he required psychological or psychiatric treatment.

In support of the Company's argument herein considered, the Company also argues that Hall

> still . . . persists he wants to come back to work for a man he intensely dislikes. This is not the behavior of a rational man; . . . it is the behavior of a very neurotic man.

Even if for the sake of argument we may assume that the Grievant does not like Thomas,* this does not make Hall a psychological cripple unable to hold his job. Many employees do not necessarily like their employers, but they still work for them given the realities of life. We do not have a society or an economy where employees are free to quit their jobs just because they do not like their employers. A man has to work, and he subordinates his resentment of his employer to the necessity of earning a living.

Apparently the Company regards the workplace as some sort of idyllic society wherein each member plays his or her role with contentment and where peace and harmony prevail. To the contrary, in the real world, frictions develop in the employer-employee relationship, and there does not exist a condition of love and contentment between employees and employers. Conditions develop in which employers resent employees, and employees resent employers, but still they tolerate each other. No one has as yet devised a system wherein the workplace would be converted into some sort of idealistic community in which love characterizes the employer-employee relationship. In any event, it would be a masterpiece of error to hold that the Grievant is psychologically unfit to hold his job even if it is true that he may not like Thomas.

Beyond these observations, the Arbitrator finds nothing in the record to demonstrate that the Grievant is psychologically unfit to hold his job. He testified in the arbitration in a rational manner, spoke clearly, and was in full control of his behavior. He was tuned into reality and did not demonstrate the behavior of a psychological cripple. He worked for the Company for nine years, and nothing in the record demonstrates irrational behavior while he was on the job. If it is true that the Grievant was psychologically unsound, there would have been evidence of irrational behavior while he was on the job. No such evidence was supplied by the Company.

For nine years, he had a spotless disciplinary record. At no time was he warned, reprimanded, or suspended for any employee offense. Indeed, the charge that he did not produce enough and took too much time to do his work was not proved by the evidence.

CONCLUSIONS

In arbitration, we base decisions on facts and evidence. We do not make decisions on the basis of suppositions or unsupported allegations. Indeed, the published and unpublished decisions of this Arbitrator demonstrate that he has frequently sus-

---

*Apparently the Company concludes that the Grievant "intensely dislikes" Thomas because of the nature of the phone conversation of September 1984. Without exploring in depth the character of this Company argument, the fact that the Grievant vented his anger about being denied sick pay (with or without justification) does not necessarily show that he "intensely dislikes" Thomas. It is not uncommon for employees to say things in anger about their supervisors. This does not necessarily prove that the employees harbor a deep-seated and irreversible hatred of their employers. Indeed, in the course of human events, we all say things in anger (even between husband and wife) that do not reflect a permanent dislike for one another. In fact, the venting of anger, some say, is a healthy psychological therapeutic device.

tained discharges of employees. In those cases, he found on the evidence that employees engaged in offensive conduct of a serious nature and that the employers proved that the employees had committed the offenses for which they were discharged.

In the case at hand, the Company did not prove that the Grievant was deficient in his obligations as an employee. The evidence does not support the charge that he did not perform his work satisfactorily. The evidence does not support the charge that he was psychologically unsound in the sense that he cannot hold his job. For these reasons, the Arbitrator shall grant the grievance. In the final analysis, the Company has failed to prove that it discharged the Grievant for proper cause within the meaning of the Labor Agreement.

Questions

1. Now that you have read the case, what do you believe to be the real reason why the employee was paid for not working?
2. What evidence did the arbitrator use to show that the employee was not a psychological cripple?
3. How did the arbitrator deal with the charge that the employee's productivity was not sufficient?
4. Why do you believe that the employee refused the two offers made by the company to settle the grievance?

Mock Negotiation

Problem

*T*he purpose of this problem is to familiarize students with the negotiation of a labor contract. The problem is strictly a hypothetical one and does not pertain to any actual management or union. It is designed to test in a practical way the student's understanding of the issues of collective bargaining studied during the semester and the strategy of the bargaining process. The strategy and techniques of negotiations are treated in Chapter 5, and the issues of collective bargaining are dealt with primarily in Chapters 7 through 10. Before the actual mock negotiation, the student should carefully reread those chapters.

PROCEDURE AND GROUND RULES

1. Class will be divided into labor and management negotiation teams. Each team will elect a chairperson at the first meeting of the team.
2. Teams will meet in a sufficient number of planning sessions to be ready for the negotiations. Each participant will be required to engage in necessary research for the negotiation.
3. In light of the following problem, each team will establish *not more* than eight items *nor fewer* than six that it will demand. *All demands must be based on the problem. No team will be permitted to make a demand that is not so based.* For purposes of this problem, a union wage demand and all fringe issues, if demanded, will be considered as only *one* demand. WAGES + BENEFITS.
4. Each team should strive to negotiate demands that it believes to be most important. This requires the weighing of the alternatives in light of respective needs of the group the team is representing.
5. Compromises, counterproposals, trading, and the dropping of demands to secure a contract will be permitted in light of the give and take of the actual negotiations.
6. Each team should strive sincerely and honestly in the role playing to do the best job possible for the group it represents. This is a *learning situation*, and to learn, one must have a sincere dedication to the job ahead.
7. *Absolutely no consultation with any of the other teams, regardless of whether management or union, will be permitted. Each team must depend entirely upon its own resources.*
8. Chairpersons should coordinate the planning of each team, decide on the time and place for planning sessions, and assign work to be done to members of the team. Chairpersons, however, are not to do all the talking in the actual negotiations. To maximize the learning situation, each member of the team should positively participate in the negotiations.

9. There must either be a settlement of all issues in the negotiation or a work stoppage. *No extension of the existing contract will be permitted.*

10. Someone on each team should keep track of the settlements. Do not write out the actual contractual clauses agreed to. It will suffice only to jot down the substance of agreements.

11. There will be a general discussion of the case after the negotiation. Each team chairperson will make a brief statement to the entire class as to the final outcome.

Herein follows the case on which the demands will be based and which provides the framework for the negotiations. *Read it very carefully to size up the situation. Base your demands only on the facts given here.*

Representatives of the Auto Products Corporation of Indianapolis, Indiana, and Local 5000, United Metal Workers of America, are in the process of negotiating their collective bargaining contract. The current contract expires at the close of today's negotiations. *(Instructor should set the date of the mock negotiation, and the exact clock time that the contract expires.)* The negotiations cover the Indianapolis plant.* Auto Products also owns a plant in Little Rock, Arkansas, but the southern plant is not organized and is not a part of the current negotiations. The current contract, which covers only the Indianapolis plant, was negotiated for a three-year period. *The time of the negotiation is the present, and, accordingly, the parties are conditioned by current economic trends, patterns of collective bargaining, and labor relations law.*

The Indianapolis plant has been in business for 61 years and has steadily expanded. At present, 3,800 production and maintenance employees are in the bargaining unit of the plant.

The financial structure of the firm has been relatively good. Here are some financial data from the Indianapolis plant for the fiscal year preceding these negotiations:

Net sales	$200,825,900
Material costs	79,250,000
Direct labor costs (includes fringe benefits and reflects layoffs in previous fiscal year)	72,635,000
Other variable costs	13,265,000
Fixed costs	5,500,000
Total expenses	170,650,000
Income before taxes	30,175,000
Net income after taxes (federal, state, county, municipal)	9,400,000

In the past, the practice has been to distribute about 65 percent of net profits in dividends and to hold 35 percent as retained earnings. Last year the company borrowed $6.3 million from the Hoosier National Bank. The rate of interest on the loan was 8.2 percent. The proceeds of the loan were used to expand the Little Rock plant. The loan is scheduled for liquidation in 10 years.

The company manufactures a variety of auto accessories. These include auto heaters, oil pumps, fan belts, rear-view mirrors, and piston rings, and in the last year the company has also started production of auto air conditioners. About 65 percent of its sales are to the basic auto companies (General Motors, Ford, and DaimlerChrysler), 25 percent to auto-repair facilities, and the rest to government

---

*The location of the plant may be shifted to your own area to provide more local relevance.

agencies. The plant operates on a two-shift basis. A $.15 per hour premium is paid to employees who work the second shift.

The employees of the company were unionized in 1946. In August of that year, the union was victorious in an NLRB election. As a result of the election, certification was awarded, on August 17, 1946, to Local 5000, since which time Local 5000 has represented the production and maintenance workers of the company. The first collective bargaining agreement between the company and Local 5000 was signed on November 14, 1946.

Only one contract strike has taken place since the union came into the picture. It occurred in 1959; the issues were the union's demands for a union shop, increased wages, and six paid holidays. The strike lasted six weeks. When it terminated, the union had obtained for its members a $.04 hourly wage increase (the union had demanded $.07) retroactive to the day of the strike, and four paid holidays. The union failed in its attempt to obtain any arrangement requiring membership in the union as a condition of employment. Also, the current contract does not include a checkoff. At the time of these negotiations, all except 400 workers in the bargaining unit are in the union.

The average hourly earnings for the production workers in the Indianapolis plant are $13.06. Of the 3,800 employees, there are 175 skilled maintenance employees (electricians, plumbers, carpenters, mechanics, and tool and die makers), and their average hourly earnings are $14.02. The existing contract contains an escalator (COLA) clause providing for the adjustment of wages in accordance with changes in the consumer price index. There is no "cap" on the amount of the increase. It provides for a $.01 increase in wages for each 0.4-point increase in the CPI. The escalator arrangement is reviewed on a semiannual basis. The current hourly rates include the increases generated from the escalator clause and the annual improvement factor. During the term of the three-year contract, workers received a $.50 increase in wages: $.20 from the operation of the escalator clause and $.30 from the operation of the annual improvement factor (a $.15 increase on the anniversary date of the contract in each of the past two years).

The Little Rock plant was built five years ago. It started with a modest-sized labor force, but during the past three years the southern plant has expanded sharply, and it now employs about 1,500 production and maintenance workers. Efforts to organize the southern plant have so far been unsuccessful. The union lost an NLRB election last year by 300 votes. Of the 1,500 employees, 1,300 cast ballots, with 800 voting against the union and 500 voting for it. The average wage in the Little Rock plant is $8.80 per hour. Currently, 450 employees in the Indianapolis plant are on layoff. It is no secret that one reason for this has been the increase of output in the Little Rock plant. Another reason was the decrease in sales at the Indianapolis plant. In Little Rock, essentially the same products are made as in Indianapolis. Of the 450 on layoff, reduction in sales caused by the state of the automobile industry accounts for 300, and the remainder is attributable to the southern situation. There is talk in the plant that some laid-off employees will never be recalled to work. Of the 450 laid-off employees, 75 have exhausted their benefits under the Indiana Unemployment Compensation Act. The present contract does not provide for a supplementary unemployment benefit program.

In general, the relations between the management and the union have been satisfactory. There have, of course, been the usual disagreements, but all in all, relations have been quite harmonious. However, last month there was a wildcat strike, the first one since the union came into the picture. It occurred in the Oil Pump

Department, and the alleged cause was the discharge of the steward of the department on the grounds that he shoved a supervisor while he was discussing a grievance with him. The union disclaimed all responsibility for the strike, and its officers stated that they did all they could to get the workers back to work. However, the employees in the Oil Pump Department picketed the plant, and the incident, which lasted two days, shut down all production in the plant for those two days. There is a no-strike clause in the contract that states:

> There will be no strikes, slowdowns, or other interruptions of production because of labor disputes during the contract period. Employees who engage in such prohibited activity are subject to discharge.

The company threatened to sue the union for damages under the Taft-Hartley law, but management finally decided not to go to court after the employees returned to work. No employee was disciplined because of the strike; however, at present, the steward remains discharged, and the union has demanded that he be returned to his job. Under the contract, the company has the right to discharge for "just cause." The steward is 64 years old and was one of the leading figures in earlier years of the union. He is known affectionately by his fellow workers as "Old Joe."

The existing contract contains a standard grievance procedure and provides for arbitration for all disputes arising under the contract, except production standards, which management has the unilateral right to establish. During the last contractual period (three years), 75 written grievances were filed by employees protesting "unreasonably" high production standards. As required by the contract, the company negotiated the production standard grievances, but the union did not have the right to appeal to arbitration or to strike over them. In three cases sparked by the production standard grievances, the company reduced the standards. In all other cases, the company denied the grievances. The management rights clause states in effect that the company retains all rights except as limited by express provisions of the labor agreement.

Provided in the contract are a series of benefits: eight paid holidays; a pension plan similar to the one negotiated in the basic automobile industry; and a paid vacation program wherein employees receive one week's vacation for one year of service, two weeks for five years, and three weeks for 20 or more years of service.

A medical insurance program covers the entire bargaining unit. However, the program does not cover employees laid off for more than 30 consecutive days. Of the 450 employees on layoff, 80 percent have been laid off for more than 30 consecutive days. This program does cover physician and hospital services, including emergency room treatment. It provides "first dollar coverage"—no deductions are assessed against the employee before insurance kicks in. Reflecting national trends, the costs of the medical insurance program have been mounting: $2,209 per employee in 1992 and $2,750 per employee at the present time. The company pays the entire cost of the plan.

It is well known that the company wants relief from the burden of the medical insurance program. Rumors are that the company intends to demand from the union that workers pay a stiff deductible before an insurance plan kicks in. Also, there is reason to believe that the company will demand that treatment in the hospital's emergency room be eliminated from the insurance program. Another rumor is that the company will demand that employees be enrolled in a health maintenance organization to save money. The union has indicated that it will not permit any change whatsoever in the medical insurance program.

Under the corporate pension program, employees with 20 or more years of service may retire at age 65 and receive full benefits, though retirement is not required of anyone. The average age of the employees in the plant is 39. About 8 percent are over 65 years of age and have more than 20 years of service. The average pension for the last fiscal year was $298 per month. The total cost of the pension program for the last fiscal year amounted to $4.81 per hour.

The current seniority clause provides for promotions based on length of service and ability. That is, seniority governs when the senior employee has qualifications reasonably equal to those of junior employees who bid on the job. During the contract period, 21 grievances were filed by employees who protested against the company's filling jobs with junior service employees. The company's position in these grievances was that the junior employees had far more ability than the senior employees. Five of these grievances went to arbitration, the company winning four and the union winning only one. Promotions are bid for on a departmental basis.

The seniority area of the existing contract provides for plantwide application of seniority credits for layoffs and recalls, provided that the senior employee has the necessary qualifications to perform the available work. During the recent period in which layoffs occurred, the company, as required by the contract, laid off many junior employees rather than senior employees because of the plantwide system. Supervisors have complained to management that, in many cases, the junior employees who had been laid off were more efficient than the senior employees who had to be retained because of the plantwide system.

Also, the current contract provides that an employee whose job goes down, or whose job is preempted by a more senior employee, may bump any junior employee in the plant, provided that the preempting employee has the qualifications to fill the job. During layoff periods, the company became aware that this situation caused a great deal of expense because of an unreasonable amount of job displacement. Also, the current contract does not contain a temporary layoff clause. This means that displaced employees may exercise their bumping rights on the basis of their plantwide seniority regardless of the length of the layoff. Supervisors have complained to the management that employees should be laid off without regard to seniority when the layoff is for a short period of time.

The existing contract provides for superseniority for stewards and other union officials. This provision protects the stewards and union officials only from layoffs. There are 60 stewards in the plant. Last year, stewards spent, on the average, about 10 hours each per week on grievance work, for which they were paid by the company. There are no limitations on stewards for grievance work. Supervisors have complained that some stewards are "goofing off," using "union business" as a pretext not to work. All the stewards deny this. In fact, the stewards claim that it is the unreasonable attitude of supervisors that provokes grievances and complaints. Also, the stewards claim that there cannot be a true measure of their time on the basis of the number of written grievances (a total of 450 grievances, including the production standard complaints, were filed during the last three years), since a good share of their time is spent discussing grievances with employees and supervisors before a written grievance is filed. There is no record to show how many of these oral discussions ended problems without written grievances being filed.

Last year, because of an unexpected order from the government, the plant worked Saturday and Sunday overtime for a period of two weekends. Under the existing contract, the company has the right to require overtime. About 200 employees did not want to work overtime but did so only because the company threatened to fire them if they refused. These 200 employees have been raising a lot of trouble in the union about this overtime affair. Also, the company has the right to select the employees to work overtime. Some employees have claimed that supervisors are not fair, giving their friends the opportunity to earn the extra money and discriminating against the other employees.

For many years, by custom, each skilled tradesperson has worked only within his or her trade. Five months ago, the company required a mechanic to do a job normally performed by a plumber. The employee and union filed a grievance, and the case went all the way to arbitration. The arbitrator sustained the position of the union on the basis of the "past practice" principle.

Some maintenance people have been affected by the current layoff, with 25 laid off. They charge that the company has been subcontracting out skilled work that could be done by them. Last year, for example, the company subcontracted out electrical work while three electricians were on layoff. The subcontract job lasted six days. Under the current contract, there is no restriction on the company's right to subcontract.

The present contract, as stated, was negotiated for a three-year period. Both sides have indicated that in the future they may want to move away from this long-term arrangement for a variety of reasons. However, there is no assurance of whether this attitude indicates the parties' sincere position or is merely an expression of a possible bargaining position.

Technological change has been a problem in the company for several years. About 250 workers have been permanently separated because of it. Union and management meetings to deal with the problem during the past several years have proved fruitless. Previous discussions have centered on the rate of change, the problem of income for the displaced employees, and the training of employees for the jobs created by the new technology. All indications are that the next wave of automation will cost about 390 bargaining unit jobs. The 250 employees who have been permanently separated are in addition to the 450 employees who are currently on layoff because of the southern situation and the drop in sales.

There has been considerable controversy over the problem of temporary transfers. Under the existing contract, the company may not transfer an employee to a job not in his or her job classification.

There are also problems regarding other working rules. These now include a 15-minute rest period every four hours; a stipulation that no supervisor may perform bargaining unit work regardless of circumstances; paid lunch periods of 20-minute duration; and paid "wash-up" time for 10 minutes before quitting time. The company contends that these "working rules" are costing it a lot of money. Whenever this issue has been brought up in the past, the union has refused any change.

Company records show that 60 percent of the workers have seniority up to 10 years; 30 percent, between 10 and 20 years; and 10 percent, more than 20 years. About 20 percent of the bargaining unit are women, and 15 percent are blacks. Some black employees have complained that they have not been given equal opportunity to get better jobs. Of the 175 employees in the skilled trades, only eight are black. They have threatened to file complaints against both the company and the union under Title VII of the Civil Rights Act and Taft-Hartley. They have retained an attorney for this purpose.

Two final issues appear to be involved in the current bargaining. First, a number of employees have told the union leadership that it is high time that at least one union representative was offered a seat on the nine-person company board of directors. These workers, who are particularly vocal ones as it happens, feel that this matter deserves considerable priority.

Second, the company's president tends to favor the imposition of a two-tier wage system, whereby all workers hired after the new labor agreement is signed would receive pay rates well below those of the current employees. He has publicly declared that "two-tiering could well be the salvation of this company."

Glossary

A

ability-to-pay criterion the ability of the employer (or industry, where negotiations are on an industrywide basis) to pay a wage increase. It is a leading criterion involved in wage determination under collective bargaining.

ad hoc method of arbitrator selection a method whereby an arbitrator is specifically chosen to decide a given arbitration case as it arises, as opposed to the permanent arbitration method, under which a preselected arbitrator (or a rotating panel of predetermined people) decides all disputes that are arbitrated.

agency shop a union security arrangement under which nonunion members of the bargaining unit must make a regular financial contribution—usually the equivalent of union dues—to the union, but no one is forced to become a union member.

American Arbitration Association (AAA) with the Federal Mediation and Conciliation Service, one of the two major providers of arbitrator names. Upon request by the parties to an arbitration, it will supply the management and union with a list of names from its national panel, and the parties will then select the arbitrator from the list. It also administers arbitration hearings in accordance with a number of formalized rules.

American Federation of Labor-Congress of Industrial Organizations (AFL-CIO) the major labor union federation in the United States, with some four-fifths of the nation's union members currently in unions that belong to it. It was formed by a merger of the AFL and CIO in 1955.

American Plan an extensive antiunion propaganda campaign conducted by American employers in the 1920s. It portrayed unions as alien to the nation's individualistic spirit and often dominated by radical elements who did not have America's best interests at heart.

Americans with Disabilities Act (ADA) enacted by Congress in 1990, this law provides that employers with more than 25 employees must make "reasonable accommodation" for those with physical or mental disabilities and bans discrimination against qualified employees and applicants with disabilities.

annual improvement factor a definite and guaranteed increase in wages for each year of a multiyear labor agreement.

arbitration the process whereby a union and management that have exhausted all bilateral steps in the grievance procedure and still are in disagreement over an issue arising under the contract's terms select an impartial outsider to decide the controversy. The latter's decision is invariably stipulated in the contract as being "final and binding" upon both parties.

attrition principle an agreement to reduce jobs solely by attrition—through, in other words, deaths, voluntary resignations, retirements, and similar events.

automation a system of automatic devices that integrate an entire productive process.

B

Bill of Rights a variety of provisions that are contained in the Laudrum-Griffin Act of 1959 and are collectively designed to ensure that union members are served by responsive, democratic unions.

blue-collar worker an employee whose job duties are primarily manual, as opposed to mental, in nature.

blue-skying the practice of making excessive and unrealistic demands, for strategic reasons, at the labor–management bargaining table.

Boulwarism General Electric's practice from the 1940s until the 1970s of making to its unions early in the bargaining a "final and best" offer and essentially not changing it in the course of the negotiations. The National Labor Relations Board ruled that this was an unfair labor practice in 1964 and five years later the U.S. Court of Appeals in New York upheld this ruling.

bumping the right of a senior employee in the event of a layoff to displace a junior worker and move into the latter's job.

C

cap a ceiling placed on contractually authorized cost-of-living wage increases. Only about 25 percent of labor agreements with cost-of-living increases currently have such a ceiling.

captive audience meeting a meeting held by an employer on the employer's property and time, during a union representation campaign. Such meetings, typically designed to dissuade employees from voting for the union in the upcoming election, cannot legally be held within 24 hours of the scheduled election.

card check a process whereby the National Labor Relations Board can dispense with a union certification election and simply certify the union as exclusive representative of all employees in the designated bargaining unit based on the board's having been shown cards signed by members of the potential unit that indicate that the union is backed by a majority of all of the workers. The employer must agree to this procedure for the certification to be granted.

certification election a government-conducted secret-ballot election to assess whether or not a union seeking to serve as exclusive representative of the employees in a specific bargaining unit has majority support. If the latter situation is the case, the governmental board then certifies the union as the exclusive bargaining representative.

Civil Rights Act of 1964 landmark legislation whose focal point, in the opinion of many, is Title VII. That section's language bans employment discrimination on grounds of race, color, religion, sex, and national origin.

Civil Rights Act of 1991 an extension of the 1964 Civil Rights Act, which among other tenets calls for punitive damages to victims of employment discrimination based on sex, race, or disability.

closed shop a union security labor agreement provision, illegal in most situations since 1947, under which workers must be union members before they can be hired.

codetermination the practice of workers directly playing a major role in corporate decision making by means of board of director membership.

collective bargaining the process whereby unions and managements negotiate and administer labor agreements.

Committee on Political Education (COPE) the political arm of the AFL-CIO. It operates at the national, state, and local levels, raising money on a voluntary basis from union members through political action committees and recruiting thousands of volunteers at election times.

comparative norm the concept that the employer's general wage level should neither fall substantially behind nor be greatly superior to that of any other comparable employment relationship.

contributory pension plans pension arrangements that are financed jointly by the employer and employee.

coordinated bargaining the banding together of unions for contract negotiation purposes. The concept not only involves a united union front but also, often, common union demands.

core time typically part of flextime arrangements (see later), such core time is a daily fixed schedule during which all employees are expected to work. This period may range between four and six hours per day.

counterproposals compromise proposals that both parties normally make in the course of contract negotiations. The use of such proposals is one element that the National Labor Relations Board considers in deciding whether or not the parties have bargained in good faith.

craft union a union whose membership is confined to workers in a specific craft—as, for example, the Plumbers, Electricians and Carpenters—as opposed to unions whose recruitment efforts extend to everyone in a specific industry whom they can win over.

D

decertification election a government conducted secret-ballot election to ascertain whether an incumbent union still has worker majority support. A majority vote in this election (for "no union") rescinds the union's bargaining agency.

defined benefit pension plans pension plans through which fixed, periodic payments (most often, so much per month per year of credited service) are made to retirees.

defined contribution pension plans pension plans in which employers make specified, usually percentage-of-pay, contributions to participant accounts, but there are no guaranteed fixed amounts and the investment risks are borne entirely by the workers.

dismissal pay also known as severance pay, this still uncommon collective bargaining product normally goes only to workers displaced by technological change, plant merger, permanent curtailment of operation, permanent disability, or retirement before the employee earns a pension. It rarely goes to workers discharged for cause, or to those who voluntarily quit.

dual unionism an effort on the part of a union member to take the local out of one national union and place it in another. Such an action normally results in the expulsion of the involved member from the original local.

dues checkoff a dues-collection method, whereby the employer deducts from the employee's pay the monthly union dues (and sometimes also initiation fees, fines, and special assessments) for transmittal to the union.

E

Employee Retirement Income Security Act (ERISA) passed by Congress in 1974, this first comprehensive pension protection legislation contains some hard-hitting vesting and funding provisions. ERISA also established the Pension Benefit Guaranty Corporation (PBGC), which guarantees pensions should an employer go out of business or otherwise terminate a plan.

Employee stock ownership plans (ESOPs) plans through which employees either get shares of stock without cost to them or are allowed to buy the shares at a discount. Employers can realize significant tax benefits from the mechanism, and ESOPs have also been shown, often if not always, to improve the level of corporate efficiency.

escalator clauses cost-of-living adjustment provisions in labor contracts that let wages rise and fall automatically with fluctuations in the cost of living.

exclusive jurisdiction the longstanding key concept of the AFL whereby only one national union would be chartered in each trade jurisdiction.

Executive Order 10988 issued by President John F. Kennedy in 1962, this order constituted the first recognition ever on the part of the federal government that its employees were entitled to join unions.

Executive Order 11491 President Richard Nixon's 1970 liberalization of Kennedy's treatment of unions, making it easier for federal government employees to gain collective bargaining representation.

F

Fair Labor Standards Act (FLSA) the legislation, originally enacted in 1938 and liberalized many times since then, that governs federal minimum wages and overtime requirements. It is also known as the Wages and Hours Act.

fast-track authority   the ability of U.S. presidents to negotiate foreign trade pacts with low-wage nations without congressional amendments or codicils. The AFL-CIO has tended to oppose such authority in recent years, with significant success.

featherbedding   the receipt of payment for unperformed work.

Federal Labor Relations Authority (FLRA)   the independent federal agency charged with enforcing the rights and duties of federal employees and agencies in the collective bargaining arena.

Federal Mediation and Conciliation Service (FMCS)   a governmental agency administered independently from the U.S. Department of Labor, the FMCS—not unlike the private American Arbitration Association—maintains a national roster of labor–management arbitrators from which the parties to arbitrations can select. The arbitrators on its roster are not FMCS employees, but the agency does itself have many mediators on its payroll. The latter try to persuade the parties, when bargaining impasses are reached, to come to a settlement.

federal preemption doctrine   the constitutional stricture that forbids states to pass laws that conflict with a federal statute.

flextime   a relatively recent innovation in the world of work whereby employees can, within limits, select their daily work schedules.

free riders   bargaining unit employees who choose not to join the union and, thus, gain the benefits of unionism without helping to pay for those benefits. Under the law, unions must represent *all* bargaining unit employees. Where everyone must join the union, free riders cannot by definition exist.

funded pension plans   plans in which the pension is paid from funds that are isolated from the general assets of the organization and earmarked specifically for retirees, hence ensuring that the benefits are in fact guaranteed.

G

grievance   an official complaint that the labor–management contract has been violated.

grievance mediation   the use of an impartial outsider who first tries to assist the parties, after the final step of the internal grievance procedure has been exhausted, in reaching a mutually satisfactory settlement. The neutral may, in these circumstances, issue an opinion that the parties are free to accept or reject. If they reject it, or otherwise cannot be persuaded to settle by the outsider, the grievance typically then proceeds to a regular arbitration.

grievance procedure   the process whereby the parties bilaterally attempt to resolve their grievances at successively higher levels of the union and management hierarchies.

I

industrial union   a union that tries to represent as many types of workers as it can—whether these are skilled, unskilled, or professional—in a given facility or industry. The Automobile Workers and Steelworkers are examples.

injunction   a judicial order calling for the cessation of certain actions deemed injurious.

J

job comparison   a relatively unsystematic method of determining wage rates so that jobs of greater worth to the management can be rewarded by greater pay. Generally some number of labor grades with accompanying wage rates or ranges is established and then each job is slotted into one of these labor grades on the basis of which already classified jobs it most closely resembles.

job evaluation   any *formalized* system that tries to determine the relative worth of different jobs in the organization for differential pay purposes. Through complete job descriptions and equally detailed analyses of these descriptions, an effort is made to rank jobs in terms of their (1) skill, (2) effort, (3) responsibility, and (4) working condition demands on the jobholder.

K

Knights of Labor   an ambitious and temporarily successful national labor organization that with few exceptions recruited all types of workers starting in 1869 and reached a zenith of 700,000 members following a major 1885 strike victory against the Wabash Railroad. It then rapidly dwindled away, a victim of its own membership diversity, its proneness to ill-advised strikes, and its impractical leadership.

L

labor union   a permanent employee association that has as its primary goal the preservation or improvement of employment conditions.

Landrum-Griffin Act   the fourth, chronologically, of the four major laws governing labor–management relations (after Norris–LaGuardia in 1932, Wagner in 1935, and Taft-Hartley in 1947). This 1959 legislation contains an ambitious and wide-sweeping "Bill of Rights" for union members and otherwise imposes regulations on unions in the interests of imposing union democracy. It also constrains such union self-help weapons as secondary boycotts and picketing more fully than they were prior to 1959.

M

maintenance of membership   a union security arrangement that lets workers elect whether or not to join the union but requires them, if they do join, to remain union members for the duration of the contract or else forfeit their jobs.

management rights clauses   contractual clauses that explicitly recognize certain stipulated types of decisions as being "vested exclusively in the management." They are also known as management prerogative and management security clauses.

mandatory subject of bargaining   a negotiation subject with which the parties must deal in good faith at the bargaining table. As determined by the NLRB and the courts, these now include wages, hours, and a variety of other terms and conditions of employment. Neither side is required to make concessions on these subjects or agree to the other side's proposals here. Each is, however, obligated to meet with the other at reasonable times and with the good-faith intention of reaching an agreement.

mediation   the process whereby an outside party makes suggestions or recommendations to labor or management, generally in a crisis situation in negotiations for a new contract. These suggestions or recommendations need not be accepted; unlike the arbitrator, the mediator has no conclusive powers in a dispute.

mini-arbitration   expedited arbitration, generally dealing only with relatively simple and routine cases and making use of comparatively inexperienced arbitrators. Typically transcripts and briefs are dispensed with, only short written awards are issued, and arbitrator decisions are forthcoming within a very few days after the close of the hearing.

multinationals   corporations that operate plants in various countries.

N

national emergency strikes   as delineated by the Taft-Hartley Act, threatened or actual strikes that, in the opinion of the president of the United States affect "an entire industry or a substantial part thereof" so as to "imperil the national health or safety." In such cases, the president may take certain carefully circumscribed action enjoining the strike for up to 80 days.

National Industrial Recovery Act (NIRA) 1933 New Deal legislation that paved the way for mass-production industry unionization by specifically guaranteeing employees "the right to organize and bargain collectively through representatives of their own choosing . . . free from the interference, restraint or coercion of employers." Declared unconstitutional by the U.S. Supreme Court in 1935, it was soon thereafter replaced by the even more prolabor Wagner Act.

National Labor Relations Board (NLRB)   the independent federal agency that since 1935 has supervised union certification and decertification elections and ruled on unfair labor practice charges brought by unions and managements.

national union   a union whose membership is nationwide. Such labor organizations are generally also known as international unions because they typically have locals in Canada as well as in the United States.

noncontributory pension plan   a pension plan in which employees make no financial contribution and the employer instead foots the entire bill.

nonmandatory subject of bargaining   a bargaining subject that has not been deemed to be mandatory by the NLRB and the courts. Either party is entirely free to refuse to bargain about such topics.

Norris–La Guardia Act   the first major federal legislation to be applied to collective bargaining. Enacted in 1932, it greatly restricted the power of federal courts to issue injunctions in labor disputes and made yellow-dog contracts (see later) unenforceable.

no-strike clauses   clauses in labor contracts that prohibit unions from striking during the life of the contract.

O

Occupational Safety and Health Act (OSHA) Congressional law enacted in 1970 to assure safe and healthy workplaces. Inspectors under OSHA have authority to inspect for violations of standards promulgated by the U.S. Secretary of Labor and to issue citations leading to possibly heavy fines and even jail sentences.

P

permanent arbitrator   a person appointed by a union and a management to decide all disputes that will be arbitrated.

permanent replacement workers   workers who replace those who have gone on strike. If the strike has been for economic reasons such as increased pay or benefits or for improved working conditions, the strikers cannot legally reclaim their jobs once the strike is over. They can do so only if the courts find that the employer has engaged in an unfair labor practice.

preferential shop   a union security arrangement under which union members receive preference in hiring but nonunionists can be employed.

Professional Air Traffic Controllers Organization (PATCO)   the national union of flight controllers, most of whose members illegally struck against the federal government in 1981. President Ronald Reagan fired all 11,500 strikers and set the wheels in motion for PATCO to be removed as the controllers' legally recognized bargaining representative. In 1987, a new union won the right to represent the controllers.

Public Review Board   the seven-member panel established by the United Automobile Workers in 1957 to investigate all credible complaints from union members that they have been unfairly disciplined for allegedly violating union rules.

pyramiding of overtime   receiving weekly overtime premiums for hours for which daily overtime premiums have already been paid. Most labor agreements prohibit such "double-dipping."

Q

quality of work life programs   employee activities that allow direct participation in day-to-day decision making on the job. Most often, workers get a voice in work scheduling, quality control, compensation, a determination of the job environment itself, and/or other significant working factors. Many QWL programs go by some other name—"employee involvement" or "worker participation," for example.

R

raiding the attempt on the part of one union to dislodge an established union that already represents workers within an organization and set itself up as the bargaining agent.

reporting pay contractually guaranteed minimum compensation for employees who are scheduled to work and who do not have instructions from the employer *not* to report to their jobs.

residual theory of management rights the concept that all rights reside in management except those that are limited by the labor agreement or conditioned by a past practice between the parties.

right-to-work legislation a state law that bans any form of compulsory union membership within the borders of the state. Twenty-one states currently have such laws.

S

sabbatical paid vacation a pioneering vacation experiment negotiated in 1962 between the Steelworkers and metal can manufacturers and extended to the basic steel industry the following year. Under it, workers with sufficient seniority (15 years in metals, and enough to place them in the senior half of the workforce in steel) got a 13-week paid vacation every five years. The arrangement is no longer available to workers, however. It was a victim of the union bargaining concessions of the 1980s.

salting the union practice of placing paid union organizers in nonunion firms for the purpose of organizing such firms. In late 1995, the U.S. Supreme Court ruled that employers couldn't discriminate against such unionists on the grounds of their union activity or affiliation.

secret-ballot election the process by which both certification and decertification elections are held, as under the law of the land they must be.

Section 14b of the Taft-Hartley Act the provision of the Taft-Hartley Act that permits states to enact right-to-work laws.

seniority the length of time that an employee has been with an organization or organizational sub-unit. Greater seniority normally gives the worker increased job security, improved working conditions, and greater entitlement to benefits.

sit-down strike protest work stoppages in the automobile, rubber, and glass industries during the 1930s in which the strikers remained at their places of work and were furnished with food by allies outside the plant. Highly effective in their day as a means of gaining representation rights for unions, they are now illegal as trespasses upon private property.

staff representative a full-time employee of a national union who provides services to the local unions, especially help in negotiating labor agreements and in the grievance arbitration process. Staff representatives are also at times called upon to organize new facilities, to help federal, state, and local political candidates favored by the union, to direct strikes, and to represent the union before federal and state agencies.

subcontracting an arrangement made by an employer—for reasons such as cost, quality, or speed of delivery—to have some portion of its work performed by employees of another organization.

superseniority preferred seniority status, beyond what one is entitled to by sheer length of service, in the event of layoff. Designated union officers often have such protection, as (under some labor agreements) do some nonunion-officer employees. The latter are typically designated as "exceptional," "specially skilled," "indispensable," "or meritorious" in collective bargaining contracts.

supplementary unemployment benefit (SUB) plans employer-financed plans that supplement the unemployment benefits of the various state unemployment insurance systems and allow further income to still unemployed workers after the state payments have been exhausted. SUBs, as they are known, originated in the mid-1950s, when both the nation's automobile manufacturers and its basic steel companies negotiated such plans with their unionized employees.

T

Taft-Hartley Act officially the Labor–Management Relations Act, this 1947 legislation reflected a gradual turn of public opinion against unionism in the mid-1940s. Among its other measures, the law (1) enumerated six unfair labor practices that unions could no longer engage in; (2) outlawed the closed shop and provided that should any state wish to outlaw the union shop in addition (through right-to-work legislation) it was free to do so; (3) explicitly gave employers certain collective bargaining rights; (4) provided for governmental intervention in the case of national emergency strikes; and (5) regulated certain internal affairs of unions.

tax-deferred retirement savings plans retirement plans through which employees can get tax breaks by contributing their own money to their own accounts. Almost 70 percent of all managements with such plans match at least some portion of the employee contributions.

Teamwork for Employees and Management (TEAM) Bill a 1996 business-supported bill that would have given employers greater leeway in establishing labor–management teams to address such issues as quality control, productivity, and health and safety. Announcing that a TEAM Act would effectively repeal that portion of the Wagner Act prohibiting company-dominated unions, President Clinton successfully vetoed the bill.

trading points a technique used in contract negotiations in which the party employing it evaluates the other side's demands not only along quantitative lines but also to assess which of these demands the other side is most anxious to realize. It then offers to agree to such demands but only if the other side makes significant concessions elsewhere (such as by dropping other of its demands).

trusteeship the prevailing situation when a national union takes control of the affairs of a subordinate body for alleged wrongdoing. Governmental bodies have also at times placed unions under trusteeship, although this is not as common a situation.

trusteeship theory of management rights the concept that management is the "trustee" of the interests of not only the employees, the society, the business, the stockholders, and the management hierarchy, but also of the union and, therefore, that any union demand should be discussed on its merits rather than being rejected out of hand because it would impose additional limitations on the organization. The goal of such discussion is to arrive at a mutually satisfactory solution.

24-hour rule the Taft-Hartley stricture that employers may not hold a meeting with employees on company time within 24 hours of a union representation election.

two-tier wage systems the employer practice of according workers who are hired after a labor agreement is signed lower pay rates than those whose dates of hire predate this date. Although the system has obvious economic advantages to employers, it tends to cause interworker tensions and sometimes employee retention and recruitment problems. Although it spread in the 1980s, it has diminished in more recent years and today only about 5 percent of newly bargained labor–management contacts provide for it.

U

unfair labor practice types of management or labor collective bargaining action that are specifically banned by the laws of the land. At the federal level, five types of management action are prohibited by the Wagner Act and six kinds of union action are illegal under the Taft-Hartley Act. Many states have counterparts to these prohibitions for intrastate labor relationships.

union security provisions provisions in the labor agreement that supply the institutional needs of the labor union. Until it was prohibited for interstate commerce in 1947 by Taft-Hartley, the closed shop was the most advantageous arrangement from labor's point of view, since under it only union members could be hired in the first place. Today, except in right-to-work states, where it is banned, the union shop (see later) is labor's most beneficial union security option.

Dues checkoff arrangements are also generally considered union security provisions.

union shop a union security arrangement under which workers need not belong to the union before obtaining other jobs but must join within a specified time period after being hired and maintain this union membership for the duration of the contract period as a condition of continuing employment.

United States Bureau of Labor Statistics (BLS) agency of the U.S. Department of Labor that is concerned principally with the compilation, analysis, and dissemination of statistics involving the nation's labor force. It regularly issues information on wages, prices, labor union membership, and strike incidences.

V

vesting the right of workers to take their credited pension entitlements with them should their employment terminate before they reach a previously stipulated retirement age or achieve a prestated amount of seniority.

W

wage reopeners contractual provisions that permit either the employer or the union to reopen the labor agreement prior to its expiration to renegotiate wage issues. Although such provisions are technically to be used *only* to negotiate a new wage structure, some employers and unions have used the opportunity to gain changes in other areas of the contract, using the wage issue as the pretext.

Wagner Act officially the National Labor Relations Act, this 1935 legislation greatly stimulated union growth in two major ways: (1) it specifically banned five types of management action as constituting unfair labor practices; and (2) it set forth the principle of majority rule for the selection of employee bargaining representa-

tives and provided that, should the employer question the union's majority status, a secret-ballot election of the employees would determine if the majority existed. It also created an independent, quasi-judicial agency—the National Labor Relations Board (NLRB)—to provide the machinery for enforcing both these provisions.

welfare capitalism the name given to a widespread effort on the part of managements in the 1920s to demonstrate to employees that unions were unnecessary. In this effort, companies featured the implementation of employee benefit programs and employee representation plans.

white-collar workers workers whose occupations are primarily mental, as opposed to manual, in nature.

wildcat strikes work stoppages that are not authorized by the union. Under many labor agreements, the employer has the right to discharge employees who participate in such stoppages or to otherwise penalize them for such activities.

Worker Adjustment and Retraining Notification Act (WARN) a law enacted by Congress in 1988 that requires employers with 100 or more full-time employees to give their workers and communities at least 60 days' notice of shutdowns and major layoffs in a variety of specified circumstances.

Workplace Fairness bill: a labor-backed congressional bill that would ban the permanent replacement of strikers. It passed the House of Representatives twice in the early 1990s, but on both occasions died in the Senate.

Y

yellow-dog contracts agreements extracted by employers whereby workers promised not to join or participate in a labor union as a condition of their employment. Such agreements were declared unenforceable by the Norris–LaGuardia Act of 1932.

Author Index

Italic *n* denotes note listing.

Subject Index

Italic *n* denotes note listing.